ICARUS

JOHN H. BENS
DOUGLAS R. BAUGH

ICARUS

AN ANTHOLOGY OF
LITERATURE

THE MACMILLAN COMPANY

THE MACMILLAN COMPANY
866 Third Avenue, New York, New York 10022

COLLIER-MACMILLAN CANADA, LTD., Toronto, Ontario

Library of Congress catalog card number: 70–85790

Second Printing, 1971

ACKNOWLEDGMENTS

W. H. AUDEN, "The Unknown Citizen" and "Musée des Beaux Arts" (*Another Time*) from *Collected Shorter Poems 1927–1957* by W. H. Auden. © Copyright 1966 by W. H. Auden. Reprinted by permission of Random House, Inc.

W. H. AUDEN, WILLIAM BARRETT, ROBERT GORHAM DAVIS, CLEMENT GREENBERG, IRVING HOWE, GEORGE ORWELL, KARL SHAPIRO, and ALLEN TATE, "The Question of the Pound Award" from *Partisan Review*, May 1949, Vol. 16, No. 5. © 1949 by *Partisan Review*. Reprinted by permission of *Partisan Review*, the authors, and Mrs. George Orwell.

WILLIAM BARRETT, "A Prize for Ezra Pound" from *Partisan Review*, April 1949, Vol. 16, No. 4. © 1949 by *Partisan Review*. Reprinted by permission of *Partisan Review* and William Barrett.

JOHN BETJEMAN, "In Westminster Abbey" from *Collected Poems* by John Betjeman. Reprinted by permission of John Murray Ltd.

GORDON E. BIGELOW, "A Primer of Existentialism" from *College English*, December 1961. Reprinted with the permission of The National Council of Teachers of English and Gordon E. Bigelow.

BERTOLT BRECHT, *Galileo*, translated by Charles Laughton, from *The Modern Repertoire*, Vol. II, by Eric Bentley. Reprinted by permission of Indiana University Press.

GREGORY CORSO, "Uccello" from *Gasoline* by Gregory Corso. Copyright © 1958 by Gregory Corso. Reprinted by permission of City Lights Books. "Marriage" from *The Happy Birthday of Death* by Gregory Corso. © by New Directions. Reprinted by permission of New Directions Publishing Corporation.

STEPHEN CRANE, "The Wayfarer" from *Collected Poems of Stephen Crane*, edited by Wilson Follett. Published 1926 by Alfred A. Knopf, Inc. Reprinted by permission.

E. E. CUMMINGS, "anyone lived in a pretty how town," copyright, 1940, by E. E. Cummings; "come, gaze with me upon this dome" and "my sweet old etcetera," copyright, 1926, by Horace Liveright; copyright, 1954, by E. E. Cummings; "i sing of Olaf," copyright, 1931, 1959, by E. E. Cummings. "pity this busy monster,manunkind" and "plato told," copyright, 1944, by E. E. Cummings. Reprinted from his volume *Poems 1923–1954* by permission of Harcourt, Brace & World, Inc.

JOHN DOS PASSOS, "The Body of an American" from *Nineteen Nineteen*, second volume of *USA* trilogy by John Dos Passos. Copyright by John Dos Passos 1932 and 1960. Published by Houghton Mifflin Company. Reprinted by permission of the author.

ALAN DUGAN, "Elegy," "On a Seven-Day Diary," "Romance of the Escaped Children," "To a Red-Headed Do-Good Waitress," and "Winter for an Untenable Situation" from *Poems 2* by Alan Dugan. Copyright © 1963 by Yale University. Reprinted by permission of Yale University Press.

RICHARD EBERHART, "The Fury of Aerial Bombardment" and "The Groundhog" from *Collected Poems 1930–1960* by Richard Eberhart. © 1960 by Richard Eberhart. Reprinted by permission of Oxford University Press, Inc., and Chatto & Windus Ltd.

T. S. ELIOT, "Macavity: The Mystery Cat" from *Old Possum's Book of Practical Cats;* "The Hollow Men," "Journey of the Magi," "The Love Song of J. Alfred Prufrock," "Sweeney Among the Nightingales," and "Whispers of Immortality" from *Collected Poems 1909–1962* by T. S. Eliot, copyright, 1936, by Harcourt, Brace & World, Inc.; copyright, ©, 1963, 1964, by T. S. Eliot. Reprinted by permission of Harcourt, Brace & World, Inc., and Faber and Faber Ltd.

WILLIAM FAULKNER, "That Evening Sun" (*These

Thirteen). Copyright 1931 and renewed 1958 by William Faulkner. Reprinted from *Collected Stories of William Faulkner* by permission of Random House, Inc.

ROBERT FROST, "The Road Not Taken," "The Subverted Flower," and "Two Tramps in Mud-Time" from *Complete Poems of Robert Frost*. Copyright 1916 by Holt, Rinehart and Winston, Inc. Copyright 1936, 1942, 1944 by Robert Frost. Copyright © 1964 by Lesley Frost Ballantine. Reprinted by permission of Holt, Rinehart and Winston, Inc.

CHRISTOPHER FRY, *A Phoenix Too Frequent.* © by Christopher Fry and reprinted by permission of Oxford University Press, Inc. No performance or reading of this play may be given unless a license has been obtained in advance from the author's agents, Dramatists Play Service for amateur performances and Leah Salisbury, Inc. for professional performances, and no copy of the play or any part thereof may be reproduced for any purposes whatsoever by any printing or duplicating or photographic or other method without written permission obtained in advance from Oxford University Press.

ANDRÉ GIDE, *Philoctetes* from *My Theatre* by André Gide. Copyright 1951 by Alfred A. Knopf, Inc. Reprinted by permission.

ALLEN GINSBERG, "Howl" Parts I and II and "A Supermarket in California" from *Howl and Other Poems* by Allen Ginsberg. Copyright © 1956, 1959 by Allen Ginsberg. Reprinted by permission of City Lights Books.

ROBERT GRAVES, "Down, Wanton, Down!," "The Philosopher," "Ulysses," and "Warning to Children" from *Collected Poems* by Robert Graves. Reprinted by permission of Collins-Knowlton-Wing, Inc. Copyright © 1955 by Robert Graves.

THOMAS HARDY, "Channel Firing" and "The Man He Killed" from *Collected Poems* by Thomas Hardy. Copyright 1925 by The Macmillan Company. Reprinted by permission of The Macmillan Company, the Trustees of the Hardy Estate, Macmillan & Co. Ltd., London, and The Macmillan Company of Canada Limited.

ERNEST HEMINGWAY, "The Killers" (Copyright 1927 Charles Scribner's Sons; renewal copyright © 1955) is reprinted with the permission of Charles Scribner's Sons from *Men Without Women* by Ernest Hemingway.

MITCH HOLT, "Icarus." Reprinted by permission of the author.

GERARD MANLEY HOPKINS, "No Worst, There Is None" from *Poems of Gerard Manley Hopkins*, Third Edition, edited by W. H. Gardner. Copyright 1948 by Oxford University Press, Inc. Reprinted by permission.

A. E. HOUSMAN, "Terence, this is stupid stuff" from "A Shropshire Lad"—Authorised Edition—from *The Collected Poems of A. E. Housman.* Copyright 1939, 1940, © 1959 by Holt, Rinehart and Winston, Inc. Copyright © 1967 by Robert E. Symons. Reprinted by permission of Holt, Rinehart and Winston, Inc., The Society of Authors as the literary

representative of the Estate of the late A. E. Housman, and Messrs. Jonathan Cape Ltd., publishers of A. E. Housman's *Collected Poems*.

TED HUGHES, "Pike" from *Lupercal* by Ted Hughes. Copyright © 1959 by Ted Hughes. Reprinted by permission of Harper & Row, Publishers, Incorporated, and Faber and Faber Ltd.

RANDALL JARRELL, "The Death of the Ball Turret Gunner," "8th Air Force," and "90 North" from *Complete Poems* by Randall Jarrell. Reprinted by permission of Mrs. Randall Jarrell.

ROBINSON JEFFERS, "Shine, Perishing Republic" (*Roan Stallion, Tamar and Other Poems*). Copyright 1925 and renewed 1953 by Robinson Jeffers. "Love the Wild Swan" (*Solstice and Other Poems*). Copyright 1935 and renewed 1962 by Donnan Jeffers and Garth Jeffers. Both reprinted from *Selected Poetry of Robinson Jeffers* by permission of Random House, Inc.

LEROI JONES, *Dutchman.* Copyright © 1964 by LeRoi Jones. Published by William Morrow and Company. Reprinted by permission of Sterling Lord Agency.

JAMES JOYCE, excerpt from *Ulysses,* by James Joyce. Copyright 1914, 1918 by Margaret Caroline Anderson and renewed 1942, 1946 by Nora Joseph Joyce. Reprinted by permission of Random House, Inc., and The Bodley Head Limited.

FRANZ KAFKA, "A Hunger Artist," reprinted by permission of Schocken Books Inc. from *The Penal Colony* by Franz Kafka. Copyright © 1948 by Schocken Books Inc.

VALDEMAR KARKLINS, "The Tunnel." Reprinted by permission from *The Hudson Review,* Vol. XII, No. 3 (Autumn, 1959). Copyright © 1959 by The Hudson Review, Inc.

JAN KOTT, "King Lear or Endgame" from *Shakespeare Our Contemporary* by Jan Kott, translated by Boleslaw Taborski. Copyright © 1964 by Panstwowe Wydawnictwo Naukowe. Reprinted by permission of Doubleday & Company, Inc.

JOSEPH LANGLAND, "Fall of Icarus: Breughel" (Copyright 1951 *Accent*) from *The Green Town: Poems* by Joseph Langland, *Poets of Today III*. Reprinted with the permission of Charles Scribner's Sons.

G. LEGMAN, "Institutionalized Lynch" from *Love and Death* by G. Legman. Copyright © 1949 by Gershon Legman. Reprinted by permission of the author.

C. DAY LEWIS, "Newsreel" copyright by C. Day Lewis. Reprinted by permission of Harold Matson Company, Inc.

ARCHIBALD MACLEISH, "Ars Poetica" and "Not Marble, Nor the Gilded Monuments." Reprinted by permission of Houghton Mifflin Company.

EDNA ST. VINCENT MILLAY, "Euclid alone has looked on Beauty bare" and "Sonnet to Gath" from *Collected Poems,* Harper & Row. Copyright 1923, 1928, 1931, 1951, 1955, 1958 by Edna St. Vincent Millay and Norma Millay Ellis.

HENRY MILLER, excerpt from Part II, *The*

Colossus of Maroussi. Copyright 1941 by Henry Miller. Reprinted by permission of New Directions Publishing Corporation.

VASSAR MILLER, "The New Icarus" from *Wage War on Silence* by Vassar Miller. Copyright © 1960 by Vassar Miller. Reprinted by permission of Wesleyan University Press.

MARIANNE MOORE, "The Hero," copyright 1951 by Marianne Moore; "Poetry," copyright 1935 by Marianne Moore, renewed 1963 by Marianne Moore and T. S. Eliot. Reprinted with permission of The Macmillan Company from *Collected Poems* by Marianne Moore.

HOWARD NEMEROV, "Life Cycle of Common Man." Reprinted by permission of the Margot Johnson Agency.

WILFRED OWEN, "Anthem for Doomed Youth," "Dulce et Decorum Est," "Insensibility," and "Greater Love" from *Collected Poems* by Wilfred Owen. Copyright © Chatto and Windus Ltd, 1946, 1963. Reprinted by permission of New Directions Publishing Corporation, Chatto and Windus Ltd, and Harold Owen.

EZRA POUND, "Epitaphs: Fu I, Li Po," "Song of the Bowmen of Shu," "Salutation," "The River-Merchant's Wife: A Letter," "In a Station of the Metro," "E. P. Ode pour l'Élection de son Sépulcre," I and II from *Hugh Selwyn Mauberley,* and "Mauberley" (IV) from *Personae.* Copyright 1926, 1954 by Ezra Pound. "Canto LXXXI" from *The Pisan Cantos.* Copyright 1948 by Ezra Pound. Reprinted by permission of New Directions Publishing Corporation.

HENRY REED, "Lessons of the War: Naming of Parts" from *A Map of Verona and Other Poems,* copyright, 1947, by Henry Reed. Reprinted by permission of Harcourt, Brace & World, Inc. and Jonathan Cape Ltd.

IRVING RIBNER, Revised Notes. Reprinted by permission of the publisher, from William Shakespeare, *The Tragedy of King Lear,* edited by George Lyman Kittredge, revised by Irving Ribner (Waltham, Mass.: Blaisdell Publishing Company, 1967).

EDWIN ARLINGTON ROBINSON, "Mr. Flood's Party." Copyright 1921 by Edwin Arlington Robinson, renewed 1949 by Ruth Nivison. "Ben Jonson Entertains a Man from Stratford" and "Flammonde." Copyright 1916 by Edwin Arlington Robinson, renewed 1944 by Ruth Nivison. Reprinted with permission of The Macmillan Company from *Collected Poems* by Edwin Arlington Robinson.

THEODORE ROETHKE, "I knew a woman," copyright 1954 by Theodore Roethke; "In a dark time," copyright © 1960 by Beatric Roethke as Administratrix of the Estate of Theodore Roethke; both from *The Collected Poems of Theodore Roethke.* Reprinted by permission of Doubleday & Company, Inc.

BERTRAND RUSSELL, "Galileo" reprinted from *The Scientific Outlook* by Bertrand Russell. By permission of W. W. Norton & Company, Inc. and George Allen & Unwin Ltd. Copyright 1931 by Bertrand Russell. Copyright renewed 1959 by Bertrand Russell.

CARL SANDBURG, "Red-Headed Restaurant Cashier" from *Smoke and Steel* by Carl Sandburg, copyright 1920, by Harcourt, Brace & World, Inc. and reprinted with their permission. "I Am the People—the Mob" from *Chicago Poems* by Carl Sandburg. Copyright 1916 by Holt, Rinehart and Winston, Inc. Copyright 1944 by Carl Sandburg. Reprinted by permission of Holt, Rinehart and Winston, Inc.

GEORGE SANTAYANA, "On the Death of a Metaphysician" from *Poems* by George Santayana. Reprinted with the permission of Charles Scribner's Sons.

SIEGFRIED SASSOON, "On Reading the War Diary of a Defunct Ambassador" from *Collected Poems* by Siegfried Sassoon. All Rights Reserved. Reprinted by permission of the Viking Press, Inc. and G. T. Sassoon.

JEAN-PAUL SARTRE, "The Wall." Copyright 1945 by Random House, Inc. Reprinted from *Bedside Book of Famous French Stories,* edited by B. Becker and R. N. Linscott, by permission of New Directions Publishing Corporation and Random House, Inc.

DELMORE SCHWARTZ, "In the naked bed, in Plato's cave" and "Socrates' ghost must haunt me now" from *Selected Poems: Summer Knowledge* by Delmore Schwartz. Copyright 1938 by New Directions, © 1966 by Delmore Schwartz. Reprinted by permission of New Directions Publishing Corporation.

KARL SHAPIRO, "Auto Wreck" (*Person, Place and Thing*). Copyright 1941 by Karl Shapiro. Reprinted from *Poems 1940–1953,* by Karl Shapiro, by permission of Random House, Inc.

JEFF SHURIN, "The Hillside Wanderers." Reprinted by permission of the author.

WALLACE STEVENS, "Domination of Black." Copyright 1923 and renewed 1951 by Wallace Stevens. Reprinted from *The Collected Poems of Wallace Stevens* by permission of Alfred A. Knopf, Inc.

ALLEN TATE, "Ode to the Confederate Dead" (Copyright 1932 Charles Scribner's Sons; renewal copyright © 1960 Allen Tate) from *Poems* by Allen Tate. Reprinted with the permission of Charles Scribner's Sons.

DYLAN THOMAS, "Fern Hill," "If I were tickled by the rub of love," and "In my craft or sullen art" from *Collected Poems* by Dylan Thomas. Copyright 1939 by New Directions, 1946 by Dylan Thomas. "A Story" from *Quite Early One Morning* by Dylan Thomas. Copyright 1954 by New Directions. Reprinted by permission of New Directions Publishing Corporation, J. M. Dent & Sons Ltd, and the Trustees for the copyrights of the late Dylan Thomas.

LEO TOLSTOY, "The Death of Ivan Ilych" reprinted from *The Death of Ivan Ilych* by Leo Tolstoy, translated by Louise and Aylmer Maude and published by Oxford University Press.

LIONEL TRILLING, "The Lesson and the Secret." Copyright 1945 by Lionel Trilling. Reprinted by permission of The Viking Press, Inc.

MARY WALKER, "Mrs. Confedrington" from *Mademoiselle,* February 1952. Copyright ©

1952 by Street and Smith. Reprinted by permission of Ann Elmo Agency, Inc.

NATHANIEL WEYL, "The Strange Case of Ezra Pound" from *Treason: The Story of Disloyalty and Betrayal in American History* (Washington, D.C.: Public Affairs Press, 1950). Reprinted by permission.

E. B. WHITE, "Song of the Queen Bee" from *The Second Tree from the Corner* by E. B. White. Copyright 1945 by E. B. White. Originally appeared in *The New Yorker,* and reprinted by permission of Harper & Row, Publishers, Incorporated.

RICHARD WILBUR, "Still, citizen sparrow" from *Ceremony and Other Poems,* copyright, 1948, 1949, 1950, by Richard Wilbur. Reprinted by permission of Harcourt, Brace & World, Inc.

WILLIAM CARLOS WILLIAMS, "Landscape with the Fall of Icarus" from *Pictures from Brueghel and Other Poems* by William Carlos Williams. Copyright 1959, 1962 by William Carlos Williams. Reprinted by permission of New Directions Publishing Corporation.

WILLIAM BUTLER YEATS, "An Irish Airman Foresees His Death," copyright 1919 by The Macmillan Company, renewed 1946 by Bertha Georgie Yeats; "Byzantium" and "Crazy Jane Talks with the Bishop," copyright 1933 by The Macmillan Company, renewed 1961 by Bertha Georgie Yeats; "Lapis Lazuli" and "Long-Legged Fly," copyright 1940 by Georgie Yeats, renewed 1968 by Bertha Georgie Yeats, Michael Butler Yeats and Anne Yeats; "The Lover Tells of the Rose in His Heart" and "The Song of Wandering Aengus," copyright 1906 by The Macmillan Company, renewed 1934 by William Butler Yeats; "No Second Troy," copyright 1912 by The Macmillan Company, renewed 1940 by Bertha Georgie Yeats; "Sailing to Byzantium," copyright 1928 by The Macmillan Company, renewed 1956 by Georgie Yeats; "The Second Coming," copyright 1924 by The Macmillan Company, renewed 1952 by Bertha Georgie Yeats. Reprinted from *Collected Poems* by William Butler Yeats with permission of The Macmillan Company, The Macmillan Company of Canada, Limited, and M. B. Yeats.

YEVGENY YEVTUSHENKO, "Babii Yar" from *The New Russian Poets 1953–1966,* Selected, Edited and Translated by George Reavey. Copyright © 1966 by George Reavey. Reprinted by permission of October House, Inc.

PREFACE

ICARUS was the son of Daedalus, artist and craftsman of archaic Greece. Daedalus devised wings so that he and his son could escape from the wrath of King Minos of Crete. The father flew safely to Sicily, but Icarus flew too close to the sun. The wax in his wings melted and he drowned in the Aegean. Like many myths, this one is as evocative for what it does not tell as it is for what it tells. Love of flying, the beauty of sunlight, the exultant liberation from earth and dazzle of freedom, a hatred of practical matters, defiance, thrill of speed, suicide—what explains why Icarus flew to such a height?

What one stresses in the myth will determine whether Icarus' story symbolizes man's aspirations or his foolhardiness, whether his fall expresses the cruelty of fate crushing the hopes of man or whether it brings to mind the relative position that man occupies in the greater framework of nature. Men have identified many feelings and thoughts with this myth. A youth, winging to the sun, is an image which suggests thoughts of daring and adventure, perhaps even pride that man can approach to the level of gods. But Icarus falling expresses imminent loss and the failure to gain wisdom until too late. Seen as admonition, however, this image is not necessarily defeatist.

All the selections in *Icarus: An Anthology of Literature* can be related to the myth. The illustration in Section I, Brueghel's "The Fall of Icarus," depicts one famous version of the story. The editors suggest the Icarus leitmotif for the English course in which the text is used, although there are other ways of unifying the same material.

Two tables of contents are provided. The first table of contents is for those who might want a thematic development. While all of the materials can be either directly or indirectly related to the Icarus theme, students will probably more readily see the relationship in Section I, "The Road Not Taken," where the selections present the heroic and exceptional in contrast to the unheroic and commonplace. To aid the student in his independent reading and to accommodate those instructors who do not care to use a theme or pattern of another's devising, the second table of contents is organized by literary types.

Section II, "In a Dark Time," presents a world in which chaotic forces, human or otherwise, dominate. Indirectly the question is posed: What is the importance of man's extraordinary capacities if they do not permit him either to control or to live with these forces? Why emulate Icarus? In such a world, "swept with confused alarms of struggle and flight," all values can be questioned, including questioning itself.

Section III presents a garden of delights large enough to include Brueghel's farmer, orderly but unaware, and Icarus, aware but in disorder. The garden is an unweeded one in which there is innocence and sin. Some instructors may wish to use "In a Dark Time" as the final selections. That we closed with "The Garden of Delights" indicates our own philosophical position.

J. H. B.

D. R. B.

TABLE OF CONTENTS
BY THEMES

SECTION I

THE ROAD NOT TAKEN
Page 7

[xi]

SECTION II

IN A DARK TIME
Page 195

SECTION III
THE GARDEN OF DELIGHTS
Page 447

TABLE OF CONTENTS
BY LITERARY TYPES

SECTION I

THE ROAD NOT TAKEN

W HAT an artist communicates in a work of art depends not only upon what is "there" to be communicated, but also upon the audience, viewer, or reader. Textbooks of literature and classes in literature should help create the ideal reader. He should be one who is favorably disposed toward literature, one who actively receives communication, and where necessary, one who will fight back. Most undergraduates are not favorably disposed toward literature, often not only because of a background that has not equipped them for the fullest understanding of a work or works, but also because many times they can see no relationship between their world and that of a work of literature which they are required to study. Like everyone else, artists who write literature have definite points of view. Works of literature do, too. And professors. Being favorably disposed to a work of literature does not mean that one accepts its point of view. Ideally, it does mean that one is sufficiently aware of that point of view either to accept it or to reject it, thus enlarging one's frame of reference. And this frame of reference, in the ideal reader, includes not only an awareness of what is, but also of what might have been and of what might be. There are many roads, those that are taken and not taken, by ourselves and by others.

We use three interpretations of Brueghel's painting "The Fall of Icarus" as a theme to return to as the student comes in contact with the literary

[1]

selections in this text. These interpretations are very broad, for within each one, numerous emphases are not only possible but unavoidable and desirable. Using Robert Frost's title "The Road Not Taken" as the title for the first section, we suggest one interpretation of Brueghel's Icarus. The speaker in that yellow wood of Frost's poem regards two diverging paths and chooses the less traveled one. For him, that choice has made all the difference, but he does not assign a value for others to either path. In the depiction of the farmer, the shepherd, the fisherman, the sailors, and of Icarus in his painting, Brueghel appears nonpartisan. He seems to be depicting the world as it is, without editorializing. People in their ordinary pursuits continue to be absorbed in their choices, while Icarus, traveling certainly the path less traveled, falls virtually unnoticed into the sea. W. H. Auden, Joseph Langland, and William Carlos Williams, to name some of those who look directly at the Brueghel painting for meaning, each communicates a different idea by emphasizing different aspects of the work. George Santayana and Vassar Miller may or may not have looked at the painting. They are certainly not in agreement about the value of an Icarus. Brecht's Galileo, Gide's Philoctetes, in addition to all else they do, should provoke the reader to question the paths or lack of paths available to men. The essays in the first section raise the question of the relevance of the arts as a map or aid. The poetry, in addition to all else it does, speaks of the obligations of society and of art to make and illuminate paths.

We hope the atmosphere of any classroom in which *Icarus: An Anthology of Literature* is used will be amenable to such questions as these: Aren't most artists biased in favor of their own paths? Is the common, unheroic life as wholesome and forthright as Sandburg depicts it? Or as mean and petty as Edna St. Vincent Millay and Robinson Jeffers depict it? What basic questions regarding the role of the artist (or of anyone who chooses a less traveled path are raised by a story such as Kafka's "A Hunger Artist"? Finally, what meanings *can* the myth of Icarus reveal?

Icarus was the son of Daedalus, artist and craftsman of archaic Greece. Daedalus devised wings so that he and his son could escape the wrath of King Minos of Crete. The father flew safely to Sicily, but Icarus flew too close to the sun. The wax in his wings melted and he drowned in the Aegean.

GALILEO

Bertolt Brecht

It is my opinion that the earth is very noble and admirable by reason of so many and so different alterations and generations which are incessantly made therein.

GALILEO GALILEI

~~~

CHARACTERS

Galileo Galilei
Andrea Sarti (*two actors: boy and man*)
Mrs. Sarti
Ludovico Marsili
Priuli, the Curator
Sagredo, *Galileo's friend*
Virginia Galilei
Two Senators
Matti, *an iron founder*
Philosopher (*later, Rector of the University*)
Elderly Lady
Young Lady
Federzoni, *assistant to Galileo*
Mathematician
Lord Chamberlain
Fat Prelate
Two Scholars
Two Monks
Infuriated Monk
Old Cardinal
Attendant Monk

Christopher Clavius
Fulganzio, the Little Monk
Two Secretaries
Cardinal Bellarmin
Cardinal Barberini (*later, Pope Urban VIII*)
Cardinal Inquisitor
Young Girl
Her Friend
Giuseppe
Ballad Singer
His Wife
Reveller
A Loud Voice
Informer
Town Crier
Official
Peasant
Customs Officer
Boy
Senators, Officials, Professors, Artisans, Ladies, Guests, Children

There are two wordless roles: The DOGE *in Scene 2 and* PRINCE COSIMO DE' MEDICI *in Scene 4. The ballad of Scene 9 is filled out by a pantomime: among the individuals in the pantomimic crowd are three extras (including the* "KING OF HUNGARY"), COBBLER'S BOY, THREE CHILDREN, PEASANT WOMAN, MONK, RICH COUPLE, DWARF, BEGGAR, *and* GIRL.

[3]

SCENE 1

In the year sixteen hundred and nine
Science' light began to shine.
At Padua City, in a modest house,
Galileo Galilei set out to prove
The sun is still, the earth is on the move.

Galileo's scantily furnished study. Morning. GALILEO *is washing himself. A barefooted boy,* ANDREA, *son of his housekeeper,* MRS. SARTI, *enters with a big astronomical model.*

GALILEO: Where did you get that thing?

ANDREA: The coachman brought it.

GALILEO: Who sent it?

ANDREA: It said "From the Court of Naples" on the box.

GALILEO: I don't want their stupid presents. Illuminated manuscripts, a statue of Hercules the size of an elephant—they never send money.

ANDREA: But isn't this an astronomical instrument, Mr. Galilei?

GALILEO: That is an antique too. An expensive toy.

ANDREA: What's it for?

GALILEO: It's a map of the sky according to the wise men of ancient Greece. Bosh! We'll try and sell it to the university. They still teach it there.

ANDREA: How does it work, Mr. Galilei?

GALILEO: It's complicated.

ANDREA: I think I could understand it.

GALILEO (*interested*): Maybe. Let's begin at the beginning. Description!

ANDREA: There are metal rings, a lot of them.

GALILEO: How many?

ANDREA: Eight.

GALILEO: Correct. And?

ANDREA: There are words painted on the bands.

GALILEO: What words?

ANDREA: The names of stars.

GALILEO: Such as?

ANDREA: Here is a band with the sun on it and on the inside band is the moon.

GALILEO: Those metal bands represent crystal globes, eight of them.

ANDREA: Crystal?

GALILEO: Like huge soap bubbles one inside the other and the stars are supposed to be tacked onto them. Spin the band with the sun on it. (ANDREA *does so.*) You see the fixed ball in the middle?

ANDREA: Yes.

GALILEO: That's the earth. For two thousand years man has chosen to believe that the sun and all the host of stars revolve about him.

Well. The Pope, the cardinals, the princes, the scholars, captains, merchants, housewives, have pictured themselves squatting in the middle of an affair like that.

ANDREA: Locked up inside?

GALILEO (*triumphant*): Ah!

ANDREA: It's like a cage.

GALILEO: So you sensed that. (*Standing near the model*): I like to think the ships began it.

ANDREA: Why?

GALILEO: They used to hug the coasts and then all of a sudden they left the coasts and spread over the oceans. A new age was coming. I was onto it years ago. I was a young man, in Siena. There was a group of masons arguing. They had to raise a block of granite. It was hot. To help matters, one of them wanted to try a new arrangement of ropes. After five minutes' discussion, out went a method which had been employed for a thousand years. The millennium of faith is ended, said I, this is the millennium of doubt. And we are pulling out of that contraption. The sayings of the wise men won't wash any more. Everybody, at last, is getting nosy. I predict that in our time astronomy will become the gossip of the market place and the sons of fishwives will pack the schools.

ANDREA: You're off again, Mr. Galilei. Give me the towel. (*He wipes some soap from* GALILEO's *back.*)

GALILEO: By that time, with any luck, they will be learning that the earth rolls round the sun, and that their mothers, the captains, the scholars, the princes, and the Pope are rolling with it.

ANDREA: That turning-around business is no good. I can see with my own eyes that the sun comes up one place in the morning and goes down in a different place in the evening. It doesn't stand still —I can see it move.

GALILEO: You see nothing, all you do is gawk. Gawking is not seeing. (*He puts the iron washstand in the middle of the room.*) Now— that's the sun. Sit down. (ANDREA *sits on a chair.* GALILEO *stands behind him.*) Where is the sun, on your right or on your left?

ANDREA: Left.

GALILEO: And how will it get to the right?

ANDREA: By your putting it there, of course.

GALILEO: Of course? (*He picks* ANDREA *up, chair and all, and carries him round to the other side of the washstand.*) Now where is the sun?

ANDREA: On the right.

GALILEO: And did it move?

ANDREA: I did.

GALILEO: Wrong. Stupid! The chair moved.

ANDREA: But I was on it.

GALILEO: Of course. The chair is the earth, and you're sitting on it.

    MRS. SARTI, *who has come in with a glass of milk and a roll, has been watching.*

MRS. SARTI: What are you doing with my son, Mr. Galilei?

ANDREA: Now, mother, you don't understand.

MRS. SARTI: You understand, don't you? Last night he tried to tell me that the earth goes round the sun. You'll soon have him saying that two times two is five.

GALILEO (*eating his breakfast*): Apparently we are on the threshold of a new era, Mrs. Sarti.

MRS. SARTI: Well, I hope we can pay the milkman in this new era. A young gentleman is here to take private lessons and he is well-dressed and don't you frighten him away like you did the others. Wasting your time with Andrea! (*To* ANDREA): How many times have I told you not to wheedle free lessons out of Mr. Galilei? (*She goes.*)

GALILEO: So you thought enough of the turning-around business to tell your mother about it.

ANDREA: Just to surprise her.

GALILEO: Andrea, I wouldn't talk about our ideas outside.

ANDREA: Why not?

GALILEO: Certain of the authorities won't like it.

ANDREA: Why not, if it's the truth?

GALILEO (*laughs*): Because we are like the worms who are little and have dim eyes and can hardly see the stars at all, and the new astronomy is a framework of guesses or very little more—yet.

MRS. SARTI *shows in* LUDOVICO MARSILI, *a presentable young man.*

GALILEO: This house is like a market place. (*Pointing to the model*): Move that out of the way! Put it down there!

LUDOVICO *does so.*

LUDOVICO: Good morning, sir. My name is Ludovico Marsili.

GALILEO (*reading a letter of recommendation he has brought*): You came by way of Holland and your family lives in the Campagna? Private lessons, thirty scudi a month.

LUDOVICO: That's all right, of course, sir.

GALILEO: What is your subject?

LUDOVICO: Horses.

GALILEO: Aha.

LUDOVICO: I don't understand science, sir.

GALILEO: Aha.

LUDOVICO: They showed me an instrument like that in Amsterdam. You'll pardon me, sir, but it didn't make sense to me at all.

GALILEO: It's out of date now.

ANDREA *goes.*

LUDOVICO: You'll have to be patient with me, sir. Nothing in science makes sense to me.

GALILEO: Aha.

LUDOVICO: I saw a brand-new instrument in Amsterdam. A tube affair. "See things five times as large as life!" It had two lenses, one at each end, one lens bulged and the other was like that. (*Gesture.*) Any normal person would think that different lenses cancel each other out. They didn't! I just stood and looked a fool.

GALILEO: I don't quite follow you. What does one see enlarged?

LUDOVICO: Church steeples, pigeons, boats. Anything at a distance.

GALILEO: Did you yourself—see things enlarged?

LUDOVICO: Yes, sir.

GALILEO: And the tube had two lenses? Was it like this?
> (*He has been making a sketch.*)
>> LUDOVICO *nods.*

GALILEO: A recent invention?

LUDOVICO: It must be. They only started peddling it on the streets a few days before I left Holland.

GALILEO (*starts to scribble calculations on the sketch; almost friendly*): Why do you bother your head with science? Why don't you just breed horses?
> *Enter* MRS. SARTI. GALILEO *doesn't see her. She listens to the following.*

LUDOVICO: My mother is set on the idea that science is necessary nowadays for conversation.

GALILEO: Aha. You'll find Latin or philosophy easier. (MRS. SARTI *catches his eye.*) I'll see you on Tuesday afternoon.

LUDOVICO: I shall look forward to it, sir.

GALILEO: Good morning. (*He goes to the window and shouts into the street:*) Andrea! Hey, Redhead, Redhead!

MRS. SARTI: The curator of the museum is here to see you.

GALILEO: Don't look at me like that. I took him, didn't I?

MRS. SARTI: I caught your eye in time.

GALILEO: Show the curator in.
> *She goes. He scribbles something on a new sheet of paper. The* CURATOR *comes in.*

CURATOR: Good morning, Mr. Galilei.

GALILEO: Lend me a scudo. (*He takes it and goes to the window, wrapping the coin in the paper on which he has been scribbling.*) Redhead, run to the spectacle-maker and bring me two lenses; here are the measurements. (*He throws the paper out the window. During the following scene* GALILEO *studies his sketch of the lenses.*)

CURATOR: Mr. Galilei, I have come to return your petition for an honorarium. Unfortunately I am unable to recommend your request.

GALILEO: My good sir, how can I make ends meet on five hundred scudi?

CURATOR: What about your private students?

GALILEO: If I spend all my time with students, when am I to study? My particular science is on the threshold of important discoveries. (*He throws a manuscript on the table.*) Here are my findings on the laws of falling bodies. That should be worth two hundred scudi

CURATOR: I am sure that any paper of yours is of infinite worth, Mr. Galilei. . . .

GALILEO: I was limiting it to two hundred scudi.

CURATOR (*cool*): Mr. Galilei, if you want money and leisure, go to

Florence. I have no doubt Prince Cosimo de' Medici will be glad to subsidize you, but eventually you will be forbidden to think—in the name of the Inquisition. (GALILEO *says nothing.*) Now let us not make a mountain out of a molehill. You are happy here in the Republic of Venice but you need money. Well, that's human, Mr. Galilei. May I suggest a simple solution? You remember that chart you made for the army to extract cube roots without any knowledge of mathematics? Now that was practical!

GALILEO: Bosh!

CURATOR: Don't say bosh about something that astounded the Chamber of Commerce. Our city elders are businessmen. Why don't you invent something useful that will bring them a little profit?

GALILEO (*playing with the sketch of the lenses; suddenly*): I see. Mr. Priuli, I may have something for you.

CURATOR: You don't say so.

GALILEO: It's not quite there yet, but . . .

CURATOR: You've never let me down yet, Galilei.

GALILEO: You are always an inspiration to me, Priuli.

CURATOR: You are a great man: a discontented man, but I've always said you are a great man.

GALILEO (*tartly*): My discontent, Priuli, is for the most part with myself. I am forty-six years of age and have achieved nothing which satisfies me.

CURATOR: I won't disturb you any further.

GALILEO: Thank you. Good morning.

CURATOR: Good morning. And thank you.

    He goes. GALILEO *sighs.* ANDREA *returns, bringing lenses.*

ANDREA: One scudo was not enough. I had to leave my cap with him before he'd let me take them away.

GALILEO: We'll get it back someday. Give them to me. (*He takes the lenses over to the window, holding them in the relation they would have in a telescope.*)

ANDREA: What are those for?

GALILEO: Something for the Senate. With any luck, they will rake in two hundred scudi. Take a look!

ANDREA: My, things look close! I can read the copper letters on the bell in the Campanile. And the washerwomen by the river, I can see their washboards!

GALILEO: Get out of the way. (*Looking through the lenses himself.*) Aha!

SCENE 2

No one's virtue is complete:
Great Galileo liked to eat.
You will not resent, we hope,
The truth about his telescope.

The Great Arsenal of Venice, overlooking the harbor full of ships. SENATORS *and* OFFICIALS *on one side,* GALILEO, *his daughter* VIRGINIA, *and his friend* SAGREDO, *on the other side. They are dressed in formal, festive clothes.* VIRGINIA *is fourteen and charming. She carries a velvet cushion on which lies a brand-new telescope. Behind* GALILEO *are some* ARTISANS *from the Arsenal. There are onlookers,* LUDOVICO *among them.*

CURATOR (*announcing*): Senators, Artisans of the Great Arsenal of Venice; Mr. Galileo Galilei, professor of mathematics at your University of Padua.

  GALILEO *steps forward and starts to speak.*

GALILEO: Members of the High Senate! Gentlemen: I have great pleasure, as director of this institute, in presenting for your approval and acceptance an entirely new instrument originating from this our Great Arsenal of the Republic of Venice. As professor of mathematics at your University of Padua, your obedient servant has always counted it his privilege to offer you such discoveries and inventions as might prove lucrative to the manufacturers and merchants of our Venetian Republic. Thus, in all humility, I tender you this, my optical tube, or telescope, constructed, I assure you, on the most scientific and Christian principles, the product of seventeen years' patient research at your University of Padua.

  GALILEO *steps back. The* SENATORS *applaud.*

SAGREDO (*aside to* GALILEO): Now you will be able to pay your bills.

GALILEO: Yes. It will make money for them. But you realize that it is more than a money-making gadget? I turned it on the moon last night . . .

CURATOR (*in his best chamber-of-commerce manner*): Gentlemen: Our Republic is to be congratulated not only because this new acquisition will be one more feather in the cap of Venetian culture —(*polite applause*)—not only because our own Mr. Galilei has generously handed this fresh product of his teeming brain entirely over to you, allowing you to manufacture as many of these highly salable articles as you please—(*considerable applause*)—but, Gentlemen of the Senate, has it occurred to you that—with the help of this remarkable new instrument—the battle fleet of the enemy will be visible to us a full two hours before we are visible to him? (*Tremendous applause.*)

GALILEO (*aside to* SAGREDO): We have been held up three generations for lack of a thing like this. I want to go home.

SAGREDO: What about the moon?

GALILEO: Well, for one thing, it doesn't give off its own light.

CURATOR (*continuing his oration*): And now, Your Excellency, and Members of the Senate, Mr. Galilei entreats you to accept the instrument from the hands of his charming daughter Virginia.

  Polite applause. He beckons to Virginia, who steps forward and presents the telescope to the DOGE.

CURATOR (*during this*): Mr. Galilei gives his invention entirely into your hands, Gentlemen, enjoining you to construct as many of these instruments as you may please.

> *More applause. The* SENATORS *gather round the telescope, examining it, and looking through it.*

GALILEO (*aside to* SAGREDO): Do you know what the Milky Way is made of?

SAGREDO: No.

GALILEO: I do.

CURATOR (*interrupting*): Congratulations, Mr. Galilei. Your extra five hundred scudi a year are safe.

GALILEO: Pardon? What? Of course, the *five hundred* scudi! Yes!

> *A prosperous man is standing beside the* CURATOR.

CURATOR: Mr. Galilei, Mr. Matti of Florence.

MATTI: You're opening new fields, Mr. Galilei. We could do with you at Florence.

CURATOR: Now, Mr. Matti, leave something to us poor Venetians.

MATTI: It is a pity that a great republic has to seek an excuse to pay its great men their right and proper dues.

CURATOR: Even a great man has to have an incentive. (*He joins the* SENATORS *at the telescope.*)

MATTI: I am an iron founder.

GALILEO: Iron founder!

MATTI: With factories at Pisa and Florence. I wanted to talk to you about a machine you designed for a friend of mine in Padua.

GALILEO: I'll put you onto someone to copy it for you, I am not going to have the time. How are things in Florence?

> *They wander away.*

FIRST SENATOR (*peering*): Extraordinary! They're having their lunch on that frigate. Lobsters! I'm hungry!

> *Laughter.*

SECOND SENATOR: Oh, good heavens, look at her! I must tell my wife to stop bathing on the roof. When can I buy one of these things?

> *Laughter.* VIRGINIA *has spotted* LUDOVICO *among the onlookers and drags him to* GALILEO.

VIRGINIA (*to* LUDOVICO): Did I do it nicely?

LUDOVICO: I thought so.

VIRGINIA: Here's Ludovico to congratulate you, father.

LUDOVICO (*embarrassed*): Congratulations, sir.

GALILEO: I improved it.

LUDOVICO: Yes, sir. I am beginning to understand science.

> GALILEO *is surrounded.*

VIRGINIA: Isn't father a great man?

LUDOVICO: Yes.

VIRGINIA: Isn't that new thing father made pretty?

LUDOVICO: Yes, a pretty red. Where I saw it first it was covered in green.

VIRGINIA: What was?

LUDOVICO: Never mind. (*A short pause.*) Have you ever been to Holland?

> *They go. All Venice is congratulating* GALILEO, *who wants to go home.*

SCENE 3

January ten, sixteen ten:
Galileo Galilei abolishes heaven.

> *Galileo's study at Padua. It is night.* GALILEO *and* SAGREDO *at a telescope.*

SAGREDO (*softly*): The edge of the crescent is jagged. All along the dark part, near the shiny crescent, bright particles of light keep coming up, one after the other, and growing larger and merging with the bright crescent.

GALILEO: How do you explain those spots of light?

SAGREDO: It can't be true . . .

GALILEO: It *is* true: they are high mountains.

SAGREDO: On a star?

GALILEO: Yes. The shining particles are mountain peaks catching the first rays of the rising sun while the slopes of the mountains are still dark, and what you see is the sunlight moving down from the peaks into the valleys.

SAGREDO: But this gives the lie to all the astronomy that's been taught for the last two thousand years.

GALILEO: Yes. What you are seeing now has been seen by no other man besides myself.

SAGREDO: But the moon can't be an earth with mountains and valleys like our own any more than the earth can be a star.

GALILEO: The moon *is* an earth with mountains and valleys, and the earth *is* a star. As the moon appears to us, so we appear to the moon. From the moon, the earth looks something like a crescent, sometimes like a half globe, sometimes a full globe, and sometimes it is not visible at all.

SAGREDO: Galileo, this is frightening.

> *An urgent knocking on the door.*

GALILEO: I've discovered something else, something even more astonishing.

> *More knocking.* GALILEO *opens the door and the* CURATOR *comes in.*

CURATOR: There it is—your "miraculous optical tube." Do you know that this invention he so picturesquely termed "the fruit of seventeen years' research" will be on sale tomorrow for two scudi apiece at every street corner in Venice? A shipload of them has just arrived from Holland.

SAGREDO: Oh, dear!

GALILEO *turns his back and adjusts the telescope.*

CURATOR: When I think of the poor gentlemen of the Senate who believed they were getting an invention they could monopolize for their own profit. . . . Why, when they took their first look through the glass, it was only by the merest chance that they didn't see a peddler, seven times enlarged, selling tubes exactly like it at the corner of the street.

SAGREDO: Mr. Priuli, with the help of this instrument, Mr. Galilei has made discoveries that will revolutionize our concept of the universe.

CURATOR: Mr. Galilei provided the city with a first-rate water pump and the irrigation works he designed function splendidly. How was I to expect this?

GALILEO (*still at the telescope*): Not so fast, Priuli. I may be on the track of a very large gadget. Certain of the stars appear to have regular movements. If there were a clock in the sky, it could be seen from anywhere. That might be useful for your shipowners.

CURATOR: I won't listen to you. I listened to you before, and as a reward for my friendship you have made me the laughingstock of the town. You can laugh—you got your money. But let me tell you this: you've destroyed my faith in a lot of things, Mr. Galilei. I'm disgusted with the world. That's all I have to say. (*He storms out.*)

GALILEO (*embarrassed*): Businessmen bore me, they suffer so. Did you see the frightened look in his eyes when he caught sight of a world not created solely for the purpose of doing business?

SAGREDO: Did you know that telescopes had been made in Holland?

GALILEO: I'd heard about it. But the one I made for the Senators was twice as good as any Dutchman's. Besides, I needed the money. How can I work, with the tax collector on the doorstep? And my poor daughter will never acquire a husband unless she has a dowry, she's not too bright. And I like to buy books—all kinds of books. Why not? And what about my appetite? I don't think well unless I eat well. Can I help it if I get my best ideas over a good meal and a bottle of wine? They don't pay me as much as they pay the butcher's boy. If only I could have five years to do nothing but research! Come on. I am going to show you something else.

SAGREDO: I don't know that I want to look again.

GALILEO: This is one of the brighter nebulae of the Milky Way. What do you see?

SAGREDO: But it's made up of stars—countless stars.

GALILEO: Countless worlds.

SAGREDO (*hesitating*): What about the theory that the earth revolves round the sun? Have you run across anything about that?

GALILEO: No. But I noticed something on Tuesday that might prove a step towards even that. Where's Jupiter? There are four lesser stars near Jupiter. I happened on them on Monday but didn't take any particular note of their position. On Tuesday I looked again. I could have sworn they had moved. They have changed again. Tell me what you see.

SAGREDO: I only see three.

GALILEO: Where's the fourth? Let's get the charts and settle down to work.

> *They work and the lights dim. The lights go up again. It is near dawn.*

GALILEO: The only place the fourth can be is round at the back of the larger star where we cannot see it. This means there are small stars revolving around a big star. Where are the crystal shells now, that the stars are supposed to be fixed to?

SAGREDO: Jupiter can't be attached to anything: there are other stars revolving round it.

GALILEO: There is no support in the heavens. (SAGREDO *laughs awkwardly*.) Don't stand there looking at me as if it weren't true.

SAGREDO: I suppose it is true. I'm afraid.

GALILEO: Why?

SAGREDO: What do you think is going to happen to you for saying that there is another sun around which other earths revolve? And that there are only stars and no difference between earth and heaven? Where is God then?

GALILEO: What do you mean?

SAGREDO: God? Where is God?

GALILEO (*angrily*): Not there! Any more than He'd be here—if creatures from the moon came down to look for Him!

SAGREDO: Then where is He?

GALILEO: I'm not a theologian: I'm a mathematician.

SAGREDO: You are a human being! (*Almost shouting*): Where is God in your system of the universe?

GALILEO: Within ourselves. Or—nowhere.

SAGREDO: Ten years ago a man was burned at the stake for saying that.

GALILEO: Giordano Bruno was an idiot: he spoke too soon. He would never have been condemned if he could have backed up what he said with proof.

SAGREDO (*incredulously*): Do you really believe proof will make any difference?

GALILEO: I believe in the human race. The only people that can't be reasoned with are the dead. Human beings are intelligent.

SAGREDO: Intelligent—or merely shrewd?

GALILEO: I know they call a donkey a horse when they want to sell it, and a horse a donkey when they want to buy it. But is that the whole story? Aren't they susceptible to truth as well? (*He fishes a small pebble out of his pocket.*) If anybody were to drop a stone— (*drops the pebble*)—and tell them that it didn't fall, do you think they would keep quiet? The evidence of your own eyes is a very seductive thing. Sooner or later everybody must succumb to it.

SAGREDO: Galileo, I am helpless when you talk.

A church bell has been ringing for some time, calling people to mass. Enter VIRGINIA, *muffled up for mass, carrying a candle, protected from the wind by a globe.*

VIRGINIA: Oh, father, you promised to go to bed tonight, and it's five o'clock again.

GALILEO: Why are you up at this hour?

VIRGINIA: I'm going to mass with Mrs. Sarti. Ludovico is going too. How was the night, father?

GALILEO: Bright.

VIRGINIA: What did you find through the tube?

GALILEO: Only some little specks by the side of a star. I must draw attention to them somehow. I think I'll name them after the Prince of Florence. Why not call them the Medicean planets? By the way, we may move to Florence. I've written to His Highness, asking if he can use me as Court Mathematician.

VIRGINIA: Oh, father, we'll be at the court!

SAGREDO (*amazed*): Galileo!

GALILEO: My dear Sagredo, I must have leisure. My only worry is that His Highness after all may not take me. I'm not accustomed to writing formal letters to great personages. Here, do you think this is the right sort of thing?

SAGREDO (*reads*): "Whose sole desire is to reside in Your Highness' presence—the rising sun of our great age." Cosimo de' Medici is a boy of nine.

GALILEO: The only way a man like me can land a good job is by crawling on his stomach. Your father, my dear, is going to take his share of the pleasures of life in exchange for all his hard work, and about time too. I have no patience, Sagredo, with a man who doesn't use his brains to fill his belly. Run along to mass now.

VIRGINIA *goes.*

SAGREDO: Galileo, do not go to Florence.

GALILEO: Why not?

SAGREDO: The monks are in power there.

GALILEO: Going to mass is a small price to pay for a full belly. And there are many famous scholars at the court of Florence.

SAGREDO: Court monkeys.

GALILEO: I shall enjoy taking them by the scruff of the neck and making them look through the telescope.

SAGREDO: Galileo, you are traveling the road to disaster. You are suspicious and skeptical in science, but in politics you are as naïve as your daughter! How can people in power leave a man at large who tells the truth, even if it be the truth about the distant stars? Can you see the Pope scribbling a note in his diary: "Tenth of January, 1610, Heaven abolished"? A moment ago, when you were at the telescope, I saw you tied to the stake, and when you said you believed in proof, I smelt burning flesh!

GALILEO: I am going to Florence.

Before the next scene, a curtain with the following legend on it is lowered:

> By setting the name of Medici in the sky, I
> am bestowing immortality upon the stars. I
> commend myself to you as your most faith-
> ful and devoted servant, whose sole desire
> is to reside in Your Highness' presence, the
> rising sun of our great age.
>
> —Galileo Galilei

SCENE 4

Galileo's house at Florence. Well-appointed. galileo *is demonstrating his telescope to* prince cosimo de' medici, *a boy of nine, accompanied by his* lord chamberlain, ladies *and* gentlemen *of the court, and an assortment of university* professors. *With* galileo *are* andrea *and* federzoni, *the new assistant (an old man).* mrs. sarti *stands by. Before the scene opens, the voice of the* philosopher *can be heard.*

voice of the philosopher: Quaedam miracula universi. Orbes mystice canorae, arcus crystallini, circulatio corporum coelestium. Cyclorum epicyclorumque intoxicatio, integritas tabulae chordarum et architectura elata globorum coelestium.[1]

galileo: Shall we speak in everyday language? My colleague Mr. Federzoni does not understand Latin.

philosopher: Is it necessary that he should?

galileo: Yes.

philosopher: Forgive me. I thought he was your mechanic.

andrea: Mr. Federzoni is a mechanic and a scholar.

philosopher: Thank you, young man. If Mr. Federzoni insists . . .

galileo: I insist.

philosopher: It will not be as clear, but it's your house. Your Highness . . . (*The* prince *is ineffectually trying to establish contact with* andrea.) I was about to recall to Mr. Galilei some of the wonders of the universe as they are set down for us in the Divine Classics. (*The* ladies *"ah."*) Remind him of the "mystically musical spheres, the crystal arches, the circulation of the heavenly bodies—"

elderly lady: Perfect poise!

philosopher: "—the intoxication of the cycles and epicycles, the integrity of the tables of chords, and the enraptured architecture of the celestial globes."

---

[1] *Quaedam*   Certain wonders of the universe. The mystically melodious spheres, the crystal arches, the revolution of the celestial bodies. The intoxicating fascination of the eccentric circles and the epicycles, the integrity of the table of chords, and the exalted architecture of the celestial globes.

ELDERLY LADY: What diction!

PHILOSOPHER: May I pose the question: Why should we go out of our way to look for things that can only strike a discord in the ineffable harmony?

The LADIES *applaud.*

FEDERZONI: Take a look through here—you'll be interested.

ANDREA: Sit down here, please.

The PROFESSORS *laugh.*

MATHEMATICIAN: Mr. Galilei, nobody doubts that your brain child —or is it your adopted brain child?—is brilliantly contrived.

GALILEO: Your Highness, one can see the four stars as large as life, you know.

The PRINCE *looks to the* ELDERLY LADY *for guidance.*

MATHEMATICIAN: Ah. But has it occurred to you that an eyeglass through which one sees such phenomena might not be a too reliable eyeglass?

GALILEO: How is that?

MATHEMATICIAN: If one could be sure you would keep your temper, Mr. Galilei, I could suggest that what one sees in the eyeglass and what is the heavens are two entirely different things.

GALILEO (*quietly*): You are suggesting fraud?

MATHEMATICIAN: No! How could I, in the presence of His Highness?

ELDERLY LADY: The gentlemen are just wondering if Your Highness' stars are really, really there!

Pause.

YOUNG LADY (*trying to be helpful*): Can one see the claws on the Great Bear?

GALILEO: And everything on Taurus the Bull.

FEDERZONI: Are you going to look through it or not?

MATHEMATICIAN: With the greatest of pleasure.

Pause. Nobody goes near the telescope. All of a sudden the boy ANDREA *turns and marches pale and erect past them through the whole length of the room. The* GUESTS *follow with their eyes.*

MRS. SARTI (*as he passes her*): What is the matter with you?

ANDREA (*shocked*): They are wicked.

PHILOSOPHER: Your Highness, it is a delicate matter and I had no intention of bringing it up, but Mr. Galilei was about to demonstrate the impossible. His new stars would have broken the outer crystal sphere—which we know of on the authority of Aristotle. I am sorry.

MATHEMATICIAN: The last word.

FEDERZONI: He had no telescope.

MATHEMATICIAN: Quite.

GALILEO (*keeping his temper*): "Truth is the daughter of Time, not of Authority." Gentlemen, the sum of our knowledge is pitiful. It has been my singular good fortune to find a new instrument which brings a small patch of the universe a little bit closer. It is at your disposal.

PHILOSOPHER: Where is all this leading?

GALILEO: Are we, as scholars, concerned with where the truth might lead us?

PHILOSOPHER: Mr. Galilei, the truth might lead us anywhere!

GALILEO: I can only beg you to look through my eyeglass.

MATHEMATICIAN (*wild*): If I understand Mr. Galilei correctly, he is asking us to discard the teachings of two thousand years.

GALILEO: For two thousand years we have been looking at the sky and didn't see the four moons of Jupiter, and there they were all the time. Why defend shaken teachings? You should be doing the shaking. (*The* PRINCE *is sleepy.*) Your Highness! My work in the Great Arsenal of Venice brought me in daily contact with sailors, carpenters, and so on. These men are unread. They depend on the evidence of their senses. But they taught me many new ways of doing things. The question is whether these gentlemen here want to be found out as fools by men who might not have had the advantages of a classical education but who are not afraid to use their eyes. I tell you that our dockyards are stirring with that same high curiosity which was the true glory of ancient Greece.
Pause.

PHILOSOPHER: I have no doubt Mr. Galilei's theories will arouse the enthusiasm of the dockyards.

CHAMBERLAIN: Your Highness, I find to my amazement that this highly informative discussion has exceeded the time we had allowed for it. May I remind Your Highness that the State Ball begins in three-quarters of an hour?
The COURT *bows low.*

ELDERLY LADY: We would really have liked to look through your eyeglass, Mr. Galilei, wouldn't we, Your Highness?
The PRINCE *bows politely and is led to the door.* GALILEO *follows the* PRINCE, CHAMBERLAIN, *and* LADIES *toward the exit. The* PROFESSORS *remain at the telescope.*

GALILEO (*almost servile*): All anybody has to do is look through the telescope, Your Highness.
MRS. SARTI *takes a plate with candies to the* PRINCE *as he is walking out.*

MRS. SARTI: A piece of homemade candy, Your Highness?

ELDERLY LADY: Not now. Thank you. It is too soon before His Highness' supper.

PHILOSOPHER: Wouldn't I like to take that thing to pieces.

MATHEMATICIAN: Ingenious contraption. It must be quite difficult to keep clean. (*He rubs the lens with his handkerchief and looks at the handkerchief.*)

FEDERZONI: We did not paint the Medicean stars on the lens.

ELDERLY LADY (*to the* PRINCE, *who has whispered something to her*): No, no, no, there is nothing the matter with your stars!

CHAMBERLAIN (*across the stage to* GALILEO): His Highness will of course seek the opinion of the greatest living authority: Christopher Clavius, Chief Astronomer to the Papal College in Rome.

SCENE 5

Things take indeed a wondrous turn
When learned men do stoop to learn.
Clavius, we are pleased to say,
Upheld Galileo Galilei.

A burst of laughter is heard and the curtains reveal a hall in the Collegium Romanum. HIGH CHURCHMEN, MONKS, *and* SCHOLARS *standing about talking and laughing.* GALILEO *by himself in a corner.*

FAT PRELATE (*shaking with laughter*): Hopeless! Hopeless! Hopeless! Will you tell me something people won't believe?

A SCHOLAR: Yes, that you don't love your stomach!

FAT PRELATE: They'd believe that. They only do not believe what's good for them. They doubt the devil, but fill them up with some fiddle-de-dee about the earth rolling like a marble in the gutter and they swallow it hook, line, and sinker. Sancta simplicitas!

He laughs until the tears run down his cheeks. The others laugh with him. A group has formed whose members boisterously begin to pretend they are standing on a rolling globe.

A MONK: It's rolling fast, I'm dizzy. May I hold onto you, Professor? (*He sways dizzily and clings to one of the scholars for support.*)

THE SCHOLAR: Old Mother Earth's been at the bottle again. Whoa!

MONK: Hey! Hey! We're slipping off! Help!

SECOND SCHOLAR: Look! There's Venus! Hold me, lads. Whee!

SECOND MONK: Don't, don't hurl us off onto the moon. There are nasty sharp mountain peaks on the moon, brethren!

VARIOUSLY: Hold tight! Hold tight! Don't look down! Hold tight! It'll make you giddy!

FAT PRELATE: And we cannot have giddy people in Holy Rome.

They rock with laughter. An INFURIATED MONK *comes out from a large door at the rear holding a Bible in his hand and pointing out a page with his finger.*

INFURIATED MONK: What does the Bible say—"Sun, stand thou still on Gideon and thou, moon, in the valley of Ajalon." Can the sun come to a standstill if it doesn't ever move? Does the Bible lie?

FAT PRELATE: How did Christopher Clavius, the greatest astronomer we have, get mixed up in an investigation of this kind?

INFURIATED MONK: He's in there with his eye glued to that diabolical instrument.

FAT PRELATE (*to* GALILEO, *who has been playing with his pebble and has dropped it*): Mr. Galilei, something dropped down.

GALILEO: Monsignor, are you sure it didn't drop up?

INFURIATED MONK: As astronomers we are aware that there are phenomena which are beyond us, but man can't expect to understand everything!

Enter a very old CARDINAL *leaning on a* MONK *for support. Others move aside.*

OLD CARDINAL: Aren't they out yet? Can't they reach a decision on that paltry matter? Christopher Clavius ought to know his astronomy after all these years. I am informed that Mr. Galilei transfers mankind from the center of the universe to somewhere on the outskirts. Mr. Galilei is therefore an enemy of mankind and must be dealt with as such. Is it conceivable that God would trust this most precious fruit of His labor to a minor, frolicking star? Would He have sent His Son to such a place? How can there be people with such twisted minds that they believe what they're told by the slave of a multiplication table?

FAT PRELATE (*quietly to* CARDINAL): The gentleman is over there.

OLD CARDINAL: So you are the man. You know my eyes are not what they were, but I can see you bear a striking resemblance to the man we burned. What was his name?

MONK: Your Eminence must avoid excitement the doctor said . . .

OLD CARDINAL (*disregarding him*): So you have degraded the earth despite the fact that you live by her and receive everything from her. I won't have it! I won't have it! I won't be a nobody on an inconsequential star briefly twirling hither and thither. I tread the earth, and the earth is firm beneath my feet, and there is no motion to the earth, and the earth is the center of all things, and I am the center of the earth, and the eye of the Creator is upon me. About me revolve, affixed to their crystal shells, the lesser lights of the stars and the great light of the sun, created to give light upon me that God might see me—Man, God's greatest effort, the center of creation. "In the image of God created He him." Immortal . . .

(*His strength fails him and he catches for the* MONK *for support.*)

MONK: You mustn't overtax your strength, Your Eminence.

At this moment the door at the rear opens and CHRISTOPHER CLAVIUS *enters followed by his* ASTRONOMERS. *He strides hastily across the hall, looking neither to right nor left. As he goes by we hear him say—*

CLAVIUS: He is right.

Deadly silence. All turn to GALILEO.

OLD CARDINAL: What is it? Have they reached a decision?

No one speaks.

MONK: It is time that Your Eminence went home.

The hall is emptying fast. One little MONK *who had entered with* CLAVIUS *speaks to* GALILEO.

LITTLE MONK: Mr. Galilei, I heard Father Clavius say: "Now it's for the theologians to set the heavens right again." You have won.

Before the next scene, a curtain with the following legend on it is lowered:

AS THESE NEW ASTRONOMICAL CHARTS ENABLE US
TO DETERMINE LONGITUDES AT SEA AND SO MAKE
IT POSSIBLE TO REACH THE NEW CONTINENTS BY
THE SHORTEST ROUTES, WE WOULD BESEECH YOUR

EXCELLENCY TO AID US IN REACHING MR. GALILEI,
MATHEMATICIAN TO THE COURT OF FLORENCE,
WHO IS NOW IN ROME . . .
—FROM A LETTER WRITTEN BY A MEMBER
OF THE GENOA CHAMBER OF COMMERCE
AND NAVIGATION TO THE PAPAL LEGATION.

SCENE 6

When Galileo was in Rome
A Cardinal asked him to his home.
He wined and dined him as his guest
And only made one small request.

Cardinal Bellarmin's house in Rome. Music is heard and the
chatter of many guests. Two SECRETARIES *are at the rear of the*
stage at a desk. GALILEO, *his daughter* VIRGINIA, *now twenty-one,*
and LUDOVICO MARSILI, *who has become her fiancé, are just*
arriving. A few GUESTS, *standing near the entrance with masks in*
their hands, nudge each other and are suddenly silent. GALILEO
looks at them. They applaud him politely and bow.

VIRGINIA: Oh, father! I'm so happy. I won't dance with anyone but
you, Ludovico.
GALILEO (*to a* SECRETARY): I was to wait here for His Eminence.
FIRST SECRETARY: His Eminence will be with you in a few minutes.
VIRGINIA: Do I look proper?
LUDOVICO: You are showing some lace.
GALILEO *puts his arms around their shoulders.*
GALILEO (*quoting mischievously*):
Fret not, daughter, if perchance
You attract a wanton glance.
The eyes that catch a trembling lace
Will guess the heartbeat's quickened pace.
Lovely woman still may be
Careless with felicity.
VIRGINIA (*to* GALILEO): Feel my heart.
GALILEO (*to* LUDOVICO): It's thumping.
VIRGINIA: I hope I always say the right thing.
LUDOVICO: She's afraid she's going to let us down.
VIRGINIA: Oh, I want to look beautiful.
GALILEO: You'd better. If you don't they'll start saying all over again
that the earth doesn't turn.
LUDOVICO (*laughing*): It *doesn't* turn, sir.
GALILEO *laughs.*
GALILEO: Go and enjoy yourselves. (*He speaks to one of the* SECRE-
TARIES): A large fete?
FIRST SECRETARY: Two hundred and fifty guests, Mr. Galilei. We have
represented here this evening most of the great families of Italy, the

Orsinis, the Villanis, the Nuccolis, the Soldanieris, the Canes, the Lecchis, the Estes, the Colombinis, the . . .

> VIRGINIA *comes running back.*

VIRGINIA: Oh, father, I didn't tell you: you're famous.

GALILEO: Why?

VIRGINIA: The hairdresser in the Via Vittorio kept four other ladies waiting and took me first. (*Exit.*)

GALILEO (*at the stairway, leaning over the well*): Rome!

> Enter CARDINAL BELLARMIN, *wearing the mask of a lamb, and* CARDINAL BARBERINI, *wearing the mask of a dove.*

SECRETARIES: Their Eminences, Cardinals Bellarmin and Barberini.

> *The* CARDINALS *lower their masks.*

GALILEO (*to* BELLARMIN): Your Eminence.

BELLARMIN: Mr. Galilei, Cardinal Barberini.

GALILEO: Your Eminence.

BARBERINI: So you are the father of that lovely child!

BELLARMIN: Who is inordinately proud of being her father's daughter.

> *They laugh.*

BARBERINI (*points his finger at* GALILEO): "The sun riseth and setteth and returneth to its place," saith the Bible. What saith Galilei?

GALILEO: Appearances are notoriously deceptive, Your Eminence. Once, when I was so high, I was standing on a ship that was pulling away from the shore and I shouted, "The shore is moving!" I know now that it was the ship which was moving.

BARBERINI (*laughs*): You can't catch that man. I tell you, Bellarmin, his moons around Jupiter are hard nuts to crack. Unfortunately for me I happened to glance at a few papers on astronomy once. It is harder to get rid of than the itch.

BELLARMIN: Let's move with the times. If it makes navigation easier for sailors to use new charts based on a new hypothesis, let them have them. We only have to scotch doctrines that contradict Holy Writ.

> *He leans over the balustrade of the well and acknowledges various* GUESTS.

BARBERINI: But Bellarmin, you haven't caught onto this fellow. The scriptures don't satisfy him. Copernicus does.

GALILEO: Copernicus? "He that withholdeth corn, the people shall curse him." Book of Proverbs.

BARBERINI: "A prudent man concealeth knowledge." Also Book of Proverbs.

GALILEO: "Where no oxen are, the crib is clean: but much increase is by the strength of the ox."

BARBERINI: "He that ruleth his spirit is better than he that taketh a city."

GALILEO: "But a broken spirit drieth the bones." (*Pause.*) "Doth not wisdom cry?"

BARBERINI: "Can one go upon hot coals and his feet not be burned?" Welcome to Rome, friend Galileo. You recall the legend of our city's origin? Two small boys found sustenance and refuge with a she-wolf and from that day we have paid the price for the she-wolf's milk. But the place is not bad. We have everything for your pleasure—from a scholarly dispute with Bellarmin to ladies of high degree. Look at that woman flaunting herself. No? He wants a weighty discussion! All right! (*To* GALILEO): You people speak in terms of circles and ellipses and regular velocities—simple movements that the human mind can grasp—very convenient—but suppose Almighty God had taken it into His head to make the stars move like that—(*he describes an irregular motion with his fingers through the air*)—then where would you be?

GALILEO: My good man—the Almighty would have endowed us with brains like that—(*repeats the movement*)—so that we could grasp the movements—(*repeats the movement*)—like that. I believe in the brain.

BARBERINI: I consider the brain inadequate. He doesn't answer. He is too polite to tell me he considers *my* brain inadequate. What is one to do with him? Butter wouldn't melt in his mouth. All he wants to do is to prove that God made a few boners in astronomy. God didn't study His astronomy hard enough before He composed Holy Writ. (*To the* SECRETARIES): Don't take anything down. This is a scientific discussion among friends.

BELLARMIN (*to* GALILEO): Does it not appear more probable—even to you—that the Creator knows more about His work than the created?

GALILEO: In his blindness man is liable to misread not only the sky but also the Bible.

BELLARMIN: The interpretation of the Bible is a matter for the ministers of God. (GALILEO *remains silent.*) At last you are quiet. (*He gestures to the* SECRETARIES. *They start writing.*) Tonight the Holy Office has decided that the theory according to which the earth goes around the sun is foolish, absurd, and a heresy. I am charged, Mr. Galilei, with cautioning you to abandon these teachings. (*To the* FIRST SECRETARY): Would you repeat that?

FIRST SECRETARY (*reading*): "His Eminence, Cardinal Bellarmin, to the aforesaid Galilei: 'The Holy Office has resolved that the theory according to which the earth goes around the sun is foolish, absurd, and a heresy. I am charged, Mr. Galilei, with cautioning you to abandon these teachings.' "

GALILEO (*rocking on his base*): But the facts!

BARBERINI (*consoling*): Your findings have been ratified by the Papal Observatory, Galilei. That should be most flattering to you . . .

BELLARMIN (*cutting in*): The Holy Office formulated the decree without going into details.

GALILEO (*to* BARBERINI): Do you realize, the future of all scientific research is—

BELLARMIN (*cutting in*): Completely assured, Mr. Galilei. It is not given to man to know the truth: it is granted to him to seek after the truth. Science is the legitimate and beloved daughter of the Church. She must have confidence in the Church.

GALILEO (*infuriated*): I would not try confidence by whistling her too often.

BARBERINI (*quickly*): Be careful what you're doing—you'll be throwing out the baby with the bath water, friend Galilei. (*Serious*): We need you more than you need us.

BELLARMIN: Well, it is time we introduced our distinguished friend to our guests. The whole country talks of him!

BARBERINI: Let us replace our masks, Bellarmin. Poor Galilei hasn't got one. (*He laughs.*)

    They take GALILEO *out.*

FIRST SECRETARY: Did you get his last sentence?

SECOND SECRETARY: Yes. Do you have what he said about believing in the brain?

    Another cardinal—the INQUISITOR—*enters.*

INQUISITOR: Did the conference take place?

    The FIRST SECRETARY *hands him the papers and the* INQUISITOR *dismisses the* SECRETARIES. *They go. The* INQUISITOR *sits down and starts to read the transcription. Two or three* YOUNG LADIES *skitter across the stage; they see the* INQUISITOR *and curtsy as they go.*

YOUNG GIRL: Who was that?

HER FRIEND: The Cardinal Inquisitor.

    They giggle and go. Enter VIRGINIA. *She curtsies as she goes. The* INQUISITOR *stops her.*

INQUISITOR: Good evening, my child. Beautiful night. May I congratulate you on your betrothal? Your young man comes from a fine family. Are you staying with us here in Rome?

VIRGINIA: Not now, Your Eminence. I must go home to prepare for the wedding.

INQUISITOR: Ah. You are accompanying your father to Florence. That should please him. Science must be cold comfort in a home. Your youth and warmth will keep him down to earth. It is easy to get lost up there. (*He gestures to the sky.*)

VIRGINIA: He doesn't talk to me about the stars, Your Eminence.

INQUISITOR: No. (*He laughs.*) They don't eat fish in the fisherman's house. I can tell you something about astronomy. My child, it seems that God has blessed our modern astronomers with imaginations. It is quite alarming! Do you know that the earth—which we old fogies supposed to be so large—has shrunk to something no bigger than a walnut, and the new universe has grown so vast that prelates —and even cardinals—look like ants. Why, God Almighty might lose sight of a Pope! I wonder if I know your Father Confessor.

VIRGINIA: Father Christopherus, from Saint Ursula's at Florence, Your Eminence.

INQUISITOR: My dear child, your father will need you. Not so much now perhaps, but one of these days. You are pure, and there is strength in purity. Greatness is sometimes, indeed often, too heavy a burden for those to whom God has granted it. What man is so great that he has no place in a prayer? But I am keeping you, my dear. Your fiancé will be jealous of me, and I am afraid your father will never forgive me for holding forth on astronomy. Go to your dancing and remember me to Father Christopherus.

VIRGINIA *kisses his ring and runs off. The* INQUISITOR *resumes his reading.*

SCENE 7

Galileo, feeling grim,
A young monk came to visit him.
The monk was born of common folk.
It was of science that they spoke.

Garden of the Florentine Ambassador in Rome. Distant hum of a great city. GALILEO *and the* LITTLE MONK *of Scene 5 are talking.*

GALILEO: Let's hear it. That robe you're wearing gives you the right to say whatever you want to say. Let's hear it.

LITTLE MONK: I have studied physics, Mr. Galilei.

GALILEO: That might help us if it enabled you to admit that two and two are four.

LITTLE MONK: Mr. Galilei, I have spent four sleepless nights trying to reconcile the decree that I have read with the moons of Jupiter that I have seen. This morning I decided to come to see you after I had said mass.

GALILEO: To tell me that Jupiter has no moons?

LITTLE MONK: No, I found out that I think the decree a wise decree. It has shocked me into realizing that free research has its dangers. I have had to decide to give up astronomy. However, I felt the impulse to confide in you some of the motives which have impelled even a passionate physicist to abandon his work.

GALILEO: Your motives are familiar to me.

LITTLE MONK: You mean, of course, the special powers invested in certain commissions of the Holy Office? But there is something else. I would like to talk to you about my family. I do not come from the great city. My parents are peasants in the Campagna, who know about the cultivation of the olive tree, and not much about anything else. Too often these days when I am trying to concentrate on tracking down the moons of Jupiter, I see my parents. I see them sitting by the fire with my sister, eating their curded cheese. I see the beams of the ceiling above them, which the smoke of centuries has blackened, and I can see the veins stand out on their toil-worn hands, and the little spoons in their hands. They scrape a living, and underlying their poverty there is a sort of order. There are routines. The routine of scrubbing the floors, the routine of the seasons in the olive orchard, the routine of paying taxes. The troubles that come to them are recurrent troubles. My father did not get his poor bent back all at once, but little by little, year by year, in the olive orchard; just as year after year, with unfailing regularity, childbirth has made my mother more and more sexless. They draw the strength they need to sweat with their loaded baskets up the stony paths, to bear children, even to eat, from the sight of the trees greening each year anew, from the reproachful face of the soil, which is never satisfied, and from the little church and Bible texts they hear there on Sunday. They have been told that God relies upon them and that the pageant of the world has been written around them that they may be tested in the important or unimportant parts handed out to them. How could they take it, were I to tell them that they are on a lump of stone ceaselessly spinning in empty space, circling around a second-rate star? What, then, would be the use of their patience, their acceptance of misery? What comfort, then, the Holy Scriptures, which have mercifully explained their crucifixion? The Holy Scriptures would then be proved full of mistakes. No, I see them begin to look frightened. I see them slowly put their spoons down on the table. They would feel cheated. "There is no eye watching over us, after all," they would say. "We have to start out on our own, at our time of life. Nobody has planned a part for us beyond this wretched one on a worthless star. There is no meaning in our misery. Hunger is just not having eaten. It is no test of strength. Effort is just stooping and carrying. It is not a virtue." Can you understand that I read into the decree of the Holy Office a noble, motherly pity and a great goodness of the soul?

GALILEO (*embarrassed*): Hm, well at least you have found out that it is not a question of the satellites of Jupiter, but of the peasants of the Campagna! And don't try to break me down by the halo of beauty that radiates from old age. How does a pearl develop in an oyster? A jagged grain of sand makes its way into the oyster's shell and makes its life unbearable. The oyster exudes slime to cover the grain of sand and the slime eventually hardens into a pearl. The oyster nearly dies in the process. To hell with the pearl, give me the healthy oyster! And virtues are not exclusive to misery. If your parents were prosperous and happy, they might develop the virtues of happiness and prosperity. Today the virtues of exhaustion are caused by the exhausted land. For that, my new water pumps could work more wonders than their ridiculous super-human efforts. Be fruitful and multiply: for war will cut down the population, and our fields are barren! (*A pause.*) Shall I lie to your people?

LITTLE MONK: We must be silent from the highest of motives: the inward peace of less fortunate souls.

GALILEO: My dear man, as a bonus for not meddling with your parents' peace, the authorities are tendering me, on a silver platter, persecution-free, my share of the fat sweated from your parents, who, as you know, were made in God's image. Should I condone this decree, my motives might not be disinterested: easy life, no persecution and so on.

LITTLE MONK: Mr. Galilei, I am a priest.

GALILEO: You are also a physicist. How can new machinery be evolved to domesticate the river water if we physicists are forbidden to study, discuss, and pool our findings about the greatest machinery of all, the machinery of the heavenly bodies? Can I reconcile my findings on the paths of falling bodies with the current belief in the tracks of witches on broomsticks? (*A pause.*) I am sorry—I shouldn't have said that.

LITTLE MONK: You don't think that the truth, if it is the truth, would make its way without us?

GALILEO: No! No! No! As much of the truth gets through as we push through. You talk about the Campagna peasants as if they were the moss on their huts. Naturally, if they don't get a move on and learn to think for themselves, the most efficient of irrigation systems cannot help them. I can see their divine patience, but where is their divine fury?

LITTLE MONK (*helpless*): They are old!

GALILEO *stands for a moment, beaten; he cannot meet the Little Monk's eyes. He takes a manuscript from the table and throws it violently on the ground.*

LITTLE MONK: What is that?

GALILEO: Here is writ what draws the ocean when it ebbs and flows. Let it lie there. Thou shalt not read. (*The* LITTLE MONK *has picked up the manuscript.*) Already! An apple of the tree of knowledge, he can't wait, he wolfs it down. He will rot in hell for all eternity. Look at him, where are his manners? Sometimes I think I would let them imprison me in a place a thousand feet beneath the earth, where no light could reach me, if in exchange I could find out what stuff that is: "Light." The bad thing is that, when I find something, I have to boast about it like a lover or a drunkard or a traitor. That is a hopeless vice and leads to the abyss. I wonder how long I shall be content to discuss it with my dog!

LITTLE MONK (*immersed in the manuscript*): I don't understand this sentence.

GALILEO: I'll explain it to you, I'll explain it to you.
They are sitting on the floor.

SCENE 8

Eight long years with tongue in cheek
Of what he knew he did not speak.
Then temptation grew too great
And Galileo challenged fate.

Galileo's house in Florence again. GALILEO *is supervising his assistants*—ANDREA, FEDERZONI, *and the* LITTLE MONK—*who are about to prepare an experiment.* MRS. SARTI *and* VIRGINIA *are at a long table sewing bridal linen. There is a new telescope, larger than the old one. At the moment it is covered with a cloth.*

ANDREA (*looking up a schedule*): Thursday. Afternoon. Floating bodies again. Ice, bowl of water, scales, and it says here an iron needle. Aristotle.

VIRGINIA: Ludovico likes to entertain. We must take care to be neat. His mother notices every stitch. She doesn't approve of father's books.

MRS. SARTI: That's all a thing of the past. He hasn't published a book for years.

VIRGINIA: That's true. Oh, Sarti, it's fun sewing a trousseau.

MRS. SARTI: Virginia, I want to talk to you. You are very young, and you have no mother, and your father is putting those pieces of ice in water, and marriage is too serious a business to go into blind. Now you should go to see a real astronomer from the university and have him cast your horoscope so you know where you stand. (VIRGINIA *giggles.*) What's the matter?

VIRGINIA: I've been already.

MRS. SARTI: Tell Sarti.

VIRGINIA: I have to be careful for three months now because the sun is in Capricorn, but after that I get a favorable ascendant, and I can undertake a journey if I am careful of Uranus, as I'm a Scorpion.

MRS. SARTI: What about Ludovico?

VIRGINIA: He's a Leo, the astronomer said. Leos are sensual. (*Giggles.*)

> There is a knock at the door, it opens. Enter the RECTOR OF THE UNIVERSITY, *the philosopher of Scene 4, bringing a book.*

RECTOR (*to* VIRGINIA): This is about the burning issue of the moment. He may want to glance over it. My faculty would appreciate his comments. No, don't disturb him now, my dear. Every minute one takes of your father's time is stolen from Italy. (*He goes.*)

VIRGINIA: Federzoni! The rector of the university brought this.

> FEDERZONI *takes it.*

GALILEO: What's it about?

FEDERZONI (*spelling*): D-e m-a-c-u-l-i-s i-n s-o-l-e.[2]

ANDREA: Oh, it's on the sun spots!

> ANDREA *comes to one side, and the* LITTLE MONK *the other, to look at the book.*

ANDREA: A new one!

> FEDERZONI *resentfully puts the book into their hands and continues with the preparation of the experiment.*

ANDREA: Listen to this dedication. (*Quotes*): "To the greatest living authority on physics, Galileo Galilei." I read Fabricius' paper the other day. Fabricius says the spots are clusters of planets between us and the sun.

LITTLE MONK: Doubtful.

GALILEO (*noncommittal*): Yes?

ANDREA: Paris and Prague hold that they are vapors from the sun. Federzoni doubts that.

---

[2] About spots on the sun.

FEDERZONI: Me? You leave me out. I said "hm," that was all. And don't discuss new things before me. I can't read the material, it's in Latin. (*He drops the scales and stands trembling with fury.*) Tell me, can I doubt anything?

> GALILEO *walks over and picks up the scales silently. Pause.*

LITTLE MONK: There is happiness in doubting, I wonder why.

ANDREA: Aren't we going to take this up?

GALILEO: At the moment we are investigating floating bodies.

ANDREA: Mother has baskets full of letters from all over Europe asking his opinion.

FEDERZONI: The question is whether you can afford to remain silent.

GALILEO: I cannot afford to be smoked on a wood fire like a ham.

ANDREA (*surprised*): Ah. You think the sun spots may have something to do with that again? (GALILEO *does not answer.*) Well, we stick to fiddling about with bits of ice in water. That can't hurt you.

GALILEO: Correct. Our thesis!

ANDREA: All things that are lighter than water float, and all things that are heavier sink.

GALILEO: Aristotle says—

LITTLE MONK (*reading out of a book, translating*): "A broad and flat disk of ice, although heavier than water, still floats, because it is unable to divide the water."

GALILEO: Well. Now I push the ice below the surface. I take away the pressure of my hands. What happens?

> *Pause.*

LITTLE MONK: It rises to the surface.

GALILEO: Correct. It seems to be able to divide the water as it's coming up, doesn't it?

LITTLE MONK: Could it be lighter than water after all?

GALILEO: Aha!

ANDREA: Then all things that are lighter than water float, and all things that are heavier sink. Q.E.D.

GALILEO: Not at all. Hand me that iron needle. Heavier than water? (*They all nod.*) A piece of paper. (*He places the needle on a piece of paper and floats it on the surface of the water. Pause.*) Do not be hasty with your conclusion. (*Pause.*) What happens?

FEDERZONI: The paper has sunk, the needle is floating. (*They laugh.*)

VIRGINIA: What's the matter?

MRS. SARTI: Every time I hear them laugh it send shivers down my spine.

> *There is a knocking at the outer door.*

MRS. SARTI: Who's that at the door?

> *Enter* LUDOVICO. VIRGINIA *runs to him. They embrace.* LUDOVICO *is followed by a* SERVANT *with baggage.*

MRS. SARTI: Well!

VIRGINIA: Oh! Why didn't you write that you were coming?

LUDOVICO: I decided on the spur of the moment. I was over inspecting our vineyards at Bucciole. I couldn't keep away.

GALILEO: Who's that?

LITTLE MONK: Miss Virginia's intended. What's the matter with your eyes?

GALILEO (*blinking*): Oh, yes, it's Ludovico, so it is. Well! Sarti, get a jug of that Sicilian wine, the old kind. We celebrate.

Everybody sits down. MRS. SARTI *has left, followed by* LUDOVICO'S SERVANT.

GALILEO: Well, Ludovico, old man. How are the horses?

LUDOVICO: The horses are fine.

GALILEO: Fine.

LUDOVICO: But those vineyards need a firm hand. (*To* VIRGINIA): You look pale. Country life will suit you. Mother's planning on September.

VIRGINIA: I suppose I oughtn't, but stay here, I've got something to show you.

LUDOVICO: What?

VIRGINIA: Never mind. I won't be ten minutes. (*She runs out.*)

LUDOVICO: How's life these days, sir?

GALILEO: Dull. How was the journey?

LUDOVICO: Dull. Before I forget, mother sends her congratulations on your admirable tact over the latest rumblings of science.

GALILEO: Thank her from me.

LUDOVICO: Christopher Clavius had all Rome on its ears. He said he was afraid that the turning-around business might crop up again on account of these spots on the sun.

ANDREA: Clavius is on the same track! (*To* LUDOVICO): My mother's baskets are full of letters from all over Europe asking Mr. Galilei's opinion.

GALILEO: I am engaged in investigating the habits of floating bodies. Any harm in that?

MRS. SARTI *re-enters, followed by the* SERVANT. *They bring wine and glasses on a tray.*

GALILEO (*hands out the wine*): What news from the Holy City, apart from the prospect of my sins?

LUDOVICO: The Holy Father is on his deathbed. Hadn't you heard?

LITTLE MONK: My goodness! What about the succession?

LUDOVICO: All the talk is of Barberini.

GALILEO: Barberini?

ANDREA: Mr. Galilei knows Barberini.

LITTLE MONK: Cardinal Barberini is a mathematician.

FEDERZONI: A scientist in the chair of Peter!

Pause.

GALILEO (*cheering up enormously*): This means change. We might live to see the day, Federzoni, when we don't have to whisper that two and two are four. (*To* LUDOVICO): I like this wine. Don't you, Ludovico?

LUDOVICO: I like it.

GALILEO: I know the hill where it is grown. The slope is steep and stony, the grape almost blue. I am fond of this wine.

LUDOVICO: Yes, sir.

GALILEO: There are shadows in this wine. It is almost sweet but just stops short. . . . Andrea, clear that stuff away, ice, bowl, and needle. . . . I cherish the consolations of the flesh. I have no patience with cowards who call them weaknesses. I say there is a certain achievement in enjoying things.

The PUPILS *get up and go to the experiment table.*

LITTLE MONK: What are we to do?

FEDERZONI: He is starting on the sun.

They begin with clearing up.

ANDREA (*singing in a low voice*):

> The Bible proves the earth stands still,
> The Pope, he swears with tears:
> The earth stands still. To prove it so
> He takes it by the ears.

LUDOVICO: What's the excitement?

MRS. SARTI: You're not going to start those hellish goings-on again, Mr. Galilei?

ANDREA:

> And gentlefolk, they say so too.
> Each learned doctor proves
> (If you grease his palm): The earth stands still.
> And yet—and yet it moves.

GALILEO: Barberini is in the ascendant, so your mother is uneasy, and you're sent to investigate me. Correct me if I am wrong, Ludovico. Clavius is right: these spots on the sun interest me.

ANDREA: We might find out that the sun also revolves. How would you like that, Ludovico?

GALILEO: Do you like my wine, Ludovico?

LUDOVICO: I told you I did, sir.

GALILEO: You really like it?

LUDOVICO: I like it.

GALILEO: Tell me, Ludovico, would you consider going so far as to accept a man's wine or his daughter without insisting that he drop his profession? I have no wish to intrude, but have the moons of Jupiter affected Virginia's bottom?

MRS. SARTI: That isn't funny, it's just vulgar. I am going for Virginia.

LUDOVICO (*keeps her back*): Marriages in families such as mine are not arranged on a basis of sexual attraction alone.

GALILEO: Did they keep you back from marrying my daughter for eight years because I was on probation?

LUDOVICO: My future wife must take her place in the family pew.

GALILEO: You mean, if the daughter of a bad man sat in your family pew, your peasants might stop paying the rent?

LUDOVICO: In a sort of way.

GALILEO: When I was your age, the only person I allowed to rap me on the knuckles was my girl.

LUDOVICO: My mother was assured that you had undertaken not to get mixed up in this turning-around business again, sir.

GALILEO: We had a conservative Pope then.

MRS. SARTI: Had! His Holiness is not dead yet!

GALILEO (*with relish*): Pretty nearly.

MRS. SARTI: That man will weigh a chip of ice fifty times, but when it comes to something that's convenient, he believes it blindly. "Is His Holiness dead?" "Pretty nearly!"

LUDOVICO: You will find, sir, if His Holiness passes away, the new Pope, whoever he turns out to be, will respect the convictions held by the solid families of the country.

GALILEO (*to* ANDREA): That remains to be seen. Andrea, get out the screen. We'll throw the image of the sun on our screen to save our eyes.

LITTLE MONK: I thought you'd been working at it. Do you know when I guessed it? When you didn't recognize Mr. Marsili.

MRS. SARTI: If my son has to go to hell for sticking to you, that's my affair, but you have no right to trample on your daughter's happiness.

LUDOVICO (*to his* SERVANT): Giuseppe, take my baggage back to the coach, will you?

MRS. SARTI: This will kill her. (*She runs out, still clutching the jug.*)

LUDOVICO (*politely*): Mr. Galilei, if we Marsilis were to countenance teachings frowned on by the church, it would unsettle our peasants. Bear in mind: these poor people in their brute state get everything upside down. They are nothing but animals. They will never comprehend the finer points of astronomy. Why, two months ago a rumor went around, an apple had been found on a pear tree, and they left their work in the fields to discuss it.

GALILEO (*interested*): Did they?

LUDOVICO: I have seen the day when my poor mother has had to have a dog whipped before their eyes to remind them to keep their place. Oh, you may have seen the waving corn from the window of your comfortable coach. You have, no doubt, nibbled our olives, and absentmindedly eaten our cheese, but you can have no idea how much responsibility that sort of thing entails.

GALILEO: Young man, I do not eat my cheese absentmindedly. (*To* ANDREA): Are we ready?

ANDREA: Yes, sir.

GALILEO (*leaves* LUDOVICO *and adjusts the mirror*): You would not confine your whippings to dogs to remind your peasants to keep their places, would you, Marsili?

LUDOVICO (*after a pause*): Mr. Galilei, you have a wonderful brain, it's a pity.

LITTLE MONK (*astonished*): He threatened you.

GALILEO: Yes. And he threatened you too. We might unsettle his peasants. Your sister, Fulganzio, who works the lever of the olive press, might laugh out loud if she heard the sun is not a gilded coat of arms but a lever too. The earth turns because the sun turns it.

ANDREA: That could interest his steward too and even his moneylender —and the seaport towns . . .

FEDERZONI: None of them speak Latin.

GALILEO: I might write in plain language. The work we do is exacting. Who would go through the strain for less than the population at large!

LUDOVICO: I see you have made your decision. It was inevitable. You will always be a slave of your passions. Excuse me to Virginia. I think it's as well I don't see her now.

GALILEO: The dowry is at your disposal at any time.

LUDOVICO: Good afternoon. (*He goes, followed by the* SERVANT.)

ANDREA: Exit Ludovico. To hell with all Marsilis, Villanis, Orsinis, Canes, Nuccolis, Soldanieris . . .

FEDERZONI: . . . who ordered the earth stand still because their castles might be shaken loose if it revolves . . .

LITTLE MONK: . . . and who only kiss the Pope's feet as long as he uses them to trample on the people. God made the physical world, God made the human brain. God will allow physics.

ANDREA: They will try to stop us.

GALILEO: Thus we enter the observation of these spots on the sun in which we are interested, at our own risk, not counting on protection from a problematical new Pope . . .

ANDREA: . . . but with great likelihood of dispelling Fabricius' vapors, and the shadows of Paris and Prague, and of establishing the rotation of the sun . . .

GALILEO: . . . and with *some* likelihood of establishing the rotation of the sun. My intention is not to prove that I was right but to find out *whether* I was right. "Abandon hope all ye who enter—an observation." Before assuming these phenomena are spots, which would suit us, let us first set about proving that they are not—fried fish. We crawl by inches. What we find today we will wipe from the blackboard tomorrow and reject it—unless it shows up again the day after tomorrow. And if we find anything which would suit us, that thing we will eye with particular distrust. In fact, we will approach this observing of the sun with the implacable determination to prove that the earth stands still, and only if hopelessly defeated in this pious undertaking can we allow ourselves to wonder if we may not have been right all the time: the earth revolves. Take the cloth off the telescope and turn it on the sun.

> *Quietly they start work. When the coruscating image of the sun is focused on the screen,* VIRGINIA *enters hurriedly, her wedding dress on, her hair disheveled,* MRS. SARTI *with her, carrying her wedding veil. The two women realize what has happened.* VIRGINIA *faints.* ANDREA, LITTLE MONK, *and* GALILEO *rush to her.* FEDERZONI *continues working.*

SCENE 9

On April Fools' Day, thirty two,
Of science there was much ado.

People had learned from Galilei:
They used his teaching in their way.

Around the corner from the market place a BALLAD SINGER *and*
his WIFE, *who is costumed to represent the earth in a skeleton*
globe made of thin bands of brass, are holding the attention of a
sprinkling of representative citizens, some in masquerade, who
were on their way to see the carnival procession. From the mar-
ket place the noise of an impatient crowd.

BALLAD SINGER (*accompanied by his* WIFE *on the guitar*):
　　When the Almighty made the universe
　　He made the earth and then he made the sun.
　　Then round the earth he bade the sun to turn—
　　That's in the Bible, Genesis, Chapter One.
　　And from that time all beings here below
　　Were in obedient circles meant to go:
　　　　Around the pope the cardinals
　　　　Around the cardinals the bishops
　　　　Around the bishops the secretaries
　　　　Around the secretaries the aldermen
　　　　Around the aldermen the craftsmen
　　　　Around the craftsmen the servants
　　　　Around the servants the dogs, the chickens, and the beggars.
A conspicuous reveller—henceforth called the SPINNER—*has*
slowly caught on and is exhibiting his idea of spinning around. He
does not lose dignity, he faints with mock grace.
BALLAD SINGER:
　　Up stood the learned Galileo
　　Glanced briefly at the sun
　　And said: "Almighty God was wrong
　　In Genesis, Chapter One!"
　　　　Now that was rash, my friends, it is no matter small:
　　　　For heresy will spread today like foul diseases.
　　　　Change Holy Writ, forsooth? What will be left at all?
　　　　Why: each of us would say and do just what he pleases!
Three wretched EXTRAS, *employed by the Chamber of Com-*
merce, enter. Two of them, in ragged costumes, moodily bear a
litter with a mock throne. The third sits on the throne. He
wears sacking, a false beard, a prop crown, he carries a prop
*orb and sceptre, and around his chest the inscription "*THE KING
OF HUNGARY." *The litter has a card with "No. 4" written on it.*
The litter bearers dump him down and listen to the BALLAD
SINGER.
BALLAD SINGER:
　　Good people, what will come to pass
　　If Galileo's teachings spread?
　　No altar boy will serve the mass

No servant girl will make the bed.

Now that is grave, my friends, it is no matter small:

For independent spirit spreads like foul diseases!

(Yet life is sweet and man is weak and after all—

How nice it is, for a little change, to do just as one pleases!)

The BALLAD SINGER *takes over the guitar. His* WIFE *dances around him, illustrating the motion of the earth. A* COBBLER'S BOY *with a pair of resplendent lacquered boots hung over his shoulder has been jumping up and down in mock excitement. There are three more children, dressed as grownups, among the spectators, two together and a single one with mother. The* COBBLER'S BOY *takes the three* CHILDREN *in hand, forms a chain and leads it, moving to the music, in and out among the spectators, "whipping" the chain so that the last child bumps into people. On the way past a* PEASANT WOMAN, *he steals an egg from her basket. She gestures to him to return it. As he passes her again he quietly breaks the egg over her head. The* KING OF HUNGARY *ceremoniously hands his orb to one of his bearers, marches down with mock dignity, and chastises the* COBBLER'S BOY. *The parents remove the three* CHILDREN. *The unseemliness subsides.*

BALLAD SINGER:

The carpenters take wood and build

Their houses—not the church's pews.

And members of the cobblers' guild

Now boldly walk the streets—in shoes.

The tenant kicks the noble lord

Quite off the land he owned—like that!

The milk his wife once gave the priest

Now makes (at last!) her children fat.

Ts, ts, ts, ts, my friends, this is no small matter:

For independent spirit spreads like foul diseases.

People must keep their place, some down and some on top!

(Though it is nice, for a little change, to do just as one pleases!)

The COBBLER'S BOY *has put on the lacquered boots he was carrying. He struts off. The* BALLAD SINGER *takes over the guitar again. His* WIFE *dances around him in increased tempo. A* MONK *has been standing near a* RICH COUPLE, *who are in subdued, costly clothes, without masks; shocked at the song, he now leaves. A* DWARF *in the costume of an astronomer turns his telescope on the departing* MONK, *thus drawing attention to the* RICH COUPLE. *In imitation of the* COBBLER'S BOY, *the* SPINNER *forms a chain of grownups. They move to the music, in and out, and between the* RICH COUPLE. *The* SPINNER *changes the gentleman's bonnet for the ragged hat of a beggar. The* GENTLEMAN *decides to take this in good part, and a* GIRL *is emboldened to take his dagger. The* GENTLEMAN *is miffed, throws the beggar's hat back. The* BEGGAR *discards the gentleman's bonnet and drops it on the ground. The* KING OF HUNGARY *has walked from his throne, taken an egg from the* PEASANT WOMAN, *and paid for it. He now ceremoniously breaks it over the gentleman's head as he is bending down to pick up his bonnet. The* GENTLEMAN *conducts the* LADY *away from the scene. The* KING OF HUNGARY, *about to resume his throne, finds one of the* CHILDREN *sitting on it. The* GENTLEMAN *returns to retrieve his dagger. Merriment. The* BALLAD SINGER *wanders off. This is part of his routine. His* WIFE *sings to the* SPINNER.

WIFE:

Now speaking for myself I feel
That I could also do with a change.
You know, for me—(*turning to a reveller*)—you have appeal
Maybe tonight we could arrange . . .

> *The* DWARF-ASTRONOMER *has been amusing the people by focusing his telescope on her legs. The* BALLAD SINGER *has returned.*

BALLAD SINGER:

No, no, no, no, no, stop, Galileo, stop!
For independent spirit spreads like foul diseases.
People must keep their place, some down and some on top!
(Though it is nice, for a little change, to do just as one pleases!)

> *The* SPECTATORS *stand embarrassed. A* GIRL *laughs loudly.*

BALLAD SINGER AND HIS WIFE:

Good people who have trouble here below
In serving cruel lords and gentle Jesus
Who bids you turn the other cheek just so . . . (*With mimicry.*)
While they prepare to strike the second blow:
Obedience will never cure your woe
So each of you wake up and do just as he pleases!

> *The* BALLAD SINGER *and his* WIFE *hurriedly start to try to sell pamphlets to the spectators.*

BALLAD SINGER: Read all about the earth going round the sun, two centesimi only. As proved by the great Galileo. Two centesimi only. Written by a local scholar. Understandable to one and all. Buy one for your friends, your children and your Aunty Rosa, two centesimi only. Abbreviated but complete. Fully illustrated with pictures of the planets, including Venus, two centesimi only.

> *During the speech of the* BALLAD SINGER *we hear the carnival procession approaching, followed by laughter. A* REVELLER *rushes in.*

REVELLER: The procession!

> *The litter bearers speedily joggle out the* KING OF HUNGARY. *The* SPECTATORS *turn and look at the first float of the procession, which now makes its appearance. It bears a gigantic figure of* GALILEO, *holding in one hand an open Bible with the pages crossed out. The other hand points to the Bible, and the head mechanically turns from side to side as if to say "No! No!"*

A LOUD VOICE: Galileo, the Bible-killer!

> *The laughter from the market place becomes uproarious. The* MONK *comes flying from the market place followed by delighted* CHILDREN.

SCENE 10

The depths are hot, the heights are chill,
The streets are loud, the court is still.

Antechamber and staircase in the Medicean palace in Florence.
GALILEO, *with a book under his arm, waits with his daughter*
VIRGINIA *to be admitted to the presence of the* PRINCE.

VIRGINIA: They are a long time.

GALILEO: Yes.

VIRGINIA: Who is that funny-looking man? (*She indicates the* IN-
FORMER, *who has entered casually and seated himself in the background, taking no apparent notice of* GALILEO.)

GALILEO: I don't know.

VIRGINIA: It's not the first time I have seen him around. He gives me
the creeps.

GALILEO: Nonsense. We're in Florence, not among robbers in the
mountains of Corsica.

VIRGINIA: Here comes the Rector.

The RECTOR *comes down the stairs.*

GALILEO: Gaffone is a bore. He attaches himself to you.

The RECTOR *passes, scarcely nodding.*

GALILEO: My eyes are bad today. Did he acknowledge us?

VIRGINIA: Barely. (*Pause.*) What's in your book? Will they say it's
heretical?

GALILEO: You hang around church too much. And getting up at dawn
and scurrying to mass is ruining your skin. You pray for me, don't
you?

A MAN *comes down the stairs.*

VIRGINIA: Here's Mr. Matti. You designed a machine for his iron
foundries.

MATTI: How were the squabs, Mr. Galilei? (*Low*): My brother and
I had a good laugh the other day. He picked up a racy pamphlet
against the Bible somewhere. It quoted you.

GALILEO: The squabs, Matti, were wonderful, thank you again.
Pamphlets I know nothing about. The Bible and Homer are my
favorite reading.

MATTI: No necessity to be cautious with me, Mr. Galilei. I am on
your side. I am not a man who knows about the motions of the
stars, but you have championed the freedom to teach new things.
Take that mechanical cultivator they have in Germany which you
described to me. I can tell you, it will never be used in this country.
The same circles that are hampering you now will forbid the
physicians at Bologna to cut up corpses for research. Do you know,
they have such things as money markets in Amsterdam and in London? Schools for business, too. Regular papers with news. Here we
are not even free to make money. I have a stake in your career.
They are against iron foundries because they say the gathering of

so many workers in one place fosters immorality! If they ever try anything, Mr. Galilei, remember you have friends in all walks of life, including an iron founder. Good luck to you. (*He goes.*)

GALILEO: Good man, but need he be so affectionate in public? His voice carries. They will always claim me as their spiritual leader, particularly in places where it doesn't help me at all. I have written a book about the mechanics of the firmament, that is all. What they do or don't do with it is not my concern.

VIRGINIA (*loud*): If people only knew how you disagreed with those goings-on all over the country last All Fools' day.

GALILEO: Yes. Offer honey to a bear, and lose your arm if the beast is hungry.

VIRGINIA (*low*): Did the Prince ask you to come here today?

GALILEO: I sent word I was coming. He will want the book, he has paid for it. My health hasn't been any too good lately. I may accept Sagredo's invitation to stay with him in Padua for a few weeks.

VIRGINIA: You couldn't manage without your books.

GALILEO: Sagredo has an excellent library.

VIRGINIA: We haven't had this month's salary yet—

GALILEO: Yes. (*The* CARDINAL INQUISITOR *passes down the staircase. He bows deeply in answer to Galileo's bow.*) What is he doing in Florence? If they try to do anything to me, the new Pope will meet them with an iron NO. And the Prince is my pupil, he would never have me extradited.

VIRGINIA: Psst. The Lord Chamberlain.

The LORD CHAMBERLAIN *comes down the stairs.*

LORD CHAMBERLAIN: His Highness had hoped to find time for you, Mr. Galilei. Unfortunately, he has to leave immediately to judge the parade at the Riding Academy. On what business did you wish to see His Highness?

GALILEO: I wanted to present my book to His Highness.

LORD CHAMBERLAIN: How are your eyes today?

GALILEO: So, so. With His Highness' permission, I am dedicating the book . . .

LORD CHAMBERLAIN: Your eyes are a matter of great concern to His Highness. Could it be that you have been looking too long and too often through your marvelous tube? (*He leaves without accepting the book.*)

VIRGINIA (*greatly agitated*): Father, I am afraid.

GALILEO: He didn't take the book, did he? (*Low and resolute*): Keep a straight face. We are not going home, but to the house of the lens-grinder. There is a coach and horses in his backyard. Keep your eyes to the front, don't look back at that man.

They start. The LORD CHAMBERLAIN *comes back.*

LORD CHAMBERLAIN: Oh, Mr. Galilei, His Highness has just charged me to inform you that the Florentine court is no longer in a position to oppose the request of the Holy Inquisition to interrogate you in Rome.

SCENE 11

The Pope

A chamber in the Vatican. The POPE, URBAN VIII—*formerly Cardinal Barberini—is giving audience to the* CARDINAL INQUISI-TOR. *The trampling and shuffling of many feet is heard throughout the scene from the adjoining corridors. During the scene the* POPE *is being robed for the conclave he is about to attend: at the beginning of the scene he is plainly Barberini, but as the scene proceeds he is more and more obscured by grandiose vestments.*

POPE: No! No! No!

INQUISITOR (*referring to the owners of the shuffling feet*): Doctors of all chairs from the universities, representatives of the special orders of the Church, representatives of the clergy as a whole, who have come believing with childlike faith in the word of God as set forth in the Scriptures, who have come to hear Your Holiness confirm their faith: and Your Holiness is really going to tell them that the Bible can no longer be regarded as the alphabet of truth?

POPE: I will not set myself up against the multiplication table. No!

INQUISITOR: Ah, that is what these people say, that it is the multiplication table. Their cry is, "The figures compel us," but where do these figures come from? Plainly they come from doubt. These men doubt everything. Can society stand on doubt and not on faith? "Thou are my master, but I doubt whether it is for the best." "This is my neighbor's house and my neighbor's wife, but why shouldn't they belong to me?" After the plague, after the new war, after the unparalleled disaster of the Reformation, your dwindling flock look to their shepherd, and now the mathematicians turn their tubes on the sky and announce to the world that you have not the best advice about the heavens either—up to now your only uncontested sphere of influence. This Galilei started meddling in machines at an early age. Now that men in ships are venturing on the great oceans —I am not against that of course—they are putting their faith in a brass bowl they call a compass and not in Almighty God.

POPE: This man is the greatest physicist of our time. He is the light of Italy, and not just any muddlehead.

INQUISITOR: Would we have had to arrest him otherwise? This bad man knows what he is doing, not writing his books in Latin, but in the jargon of the market place.

POPE (*occupied with the shuffling feet*): That was not in the best of taste. (*A pause.*) These shuffling feet are making me nervous.

INQUISITOR: May they be more telling than my words, Your Holiness. Shall all these go from you with doubt in their hearts?

POPE: This man has friends. What about Versailles? What about the Viennese court? They will call Holy Church a cesspool for defunct ideas. Keep your hands off him.

INQUISITOR: In practice it will never get far. He is a man of the flesh. He would soften at once.

POPE: He has more enjoyment in him than any man I ever saw. He loves eating and drinking and thinking. To excess. He indulges in thinking-bouts! He cannot say no to an old wine or a new thought. (*Furious*): I do not want a condemnation of physical facts. I do not want to hear battle cries: Church, Church, Church! Reason, Reason, Reason! (*Pause*.) These shuffling feet are intolerable. Has the whole world come to my door?

INQUISITOR: Not the whole world, Your Holiness. A select gathering of the faithful.

    Pause.

POPE (*exhausted*): It is clearly understood: he is not to be tortured. (*Pause*.) At the very most, he may be shown the instruments.

INQUISITOR: That will be adequate, Your Holiness. Mr. Galilei understands machinery.

    The eyes of BARBERINI *look helplessly at the* CARDINAL INQUISITOR *from under the completely assembled panoply of* POPE URBAN VIII.

SCENE 12

June twenty second, sixteen thirty three,
A momentous date for you and me.
Of all the days that was the one
An age of reason could have begun.

Again the garden of the Florentine AMBASSADOR *at Rome, where Galileo's assistants wait the news of the trial. The* LITTLE MONK *and* FEDERZONI *are attempting to concentrate on a game of chess.* VIRGINIA *kneels in a corner, praying and counting her beads.*

LITTLE MONK: The Pope didn't even grant him an audience.

FEDERZONI: No more scientific discussions.

ANDREA: The "Discorsi" will never be finished. The sum of his findings. They will kill him.

FEDERZONI (*stealing a glance at him*): Do you really think so?

ANDREA: He will never recant.

    Silence.

LITTLE MONK: You know when you lie awake at night how your mind fastens on to something irrelevant. Last night I kept thinking: if only they would let him take his little stone in with him, the appeal-to-reason-pebble that he always carries in his pocket.

FEDERZONI: In the room *they'll* take him to, he won't have a pocket.

ANDREA: But he will not recant.

LITTLE MONK: How can they beat the truth out of a man who gave his sight in order to see?

FEDERZONI: Maybe they can't.
> *Silence.*

ANDREA (*speaking about* VIRGINIA): She is praying that he will recant.

FEDERZONI: Leave her alone. She doesn't know whether she's on her head or on her heels since they got hold of her. They brought her Father Confessor from Florence.
> *The* INFORMER *of Scene 10 enters.*

INFORMER: Mr. Galilei will be here soon. He may need a bed.

FEDERZONI: Have they let him out?

INFORMER: Mr. Galilei is expected to recant at five o'clock. The big bell of Saint Marcus will be rung and the complete text of his recantation publicly announced.

ANDREA: I don't believe it.

INFORMER: Mr. Galilei will be brought to the garden gate at the back of the house, to avoid the crowds collecting in the streets. (*He goes.*)
> *Silence.*

ANDREA: The moon is an earth because the light of the moon is not her own. Jupiter is a fixed star, and four moons turn around Jupiter, therefore we are not shut in by crystal shells. The sun is the pivot of our world, therefore the earth is not the center. The earth moves, spinning about the sun. And he showed us. You can't make a man unsee what he has seen.
> *Silence.*

FEDERZONI: Five o'clock is one minute.
> VIRGINIA *prays louder.*

ANDREA: Listen all of you, they are murdering the truth.
> *He stops up his ears with his fingers. The two other pupils do the same.* FEDERZONI *goes over to the* LITTLE MONK, *and all of them stand absolutely still in cramped positions. Nothing happens. No bell sounds. After a silence, filled with the murmur of Virginia's prayers,* FEDERZONI *runs to the wall to look at the clock. He turns around, his expression changed. He shakes his head. They drop their hands.*

FEDERZONI: No. No bell. It is three minutes after.

LITTLE MONK: He hasn't.

ANDREA: He held true. It is all right, it is all right.

LITTLE MONK: He did not recant.

FEDERZONI: No.
> *They embrace each other, they are delirious with joy.*

ANDREA: So force cannot accomplish everything. What has been seen can't be unseen. Man is constant in the face of death.

FEDERZONI: June 22, 1633: dawn of the age of reason. I wouldn't have wanted to go on living if he had recanted.

LITTLE MONK: I didn't say anything, but I was in agony. O ye of little faith!

ANDREA: I was sure.

FEDERZONI: It would have turned our morning to night.

ANDREA: It would have been as if the mountain had turned to water.

LITTLE MONK (*kneeling down, crying*) : O God, I thank Thee.

ANDREA: Beaten humanity can lift its head. A man has stood up and said No.

> *At this moment the bell of Saint Marcus begins to toll. They stand like statues.* VIRGINIA *stands up.*

VIRGINIA: The bell of Saint Marcus. He is not damned.

> *From the street one hears the* TOWN CRIER *reading* GALILEO'S *recantation.*

TOWN CRIER: I, Galileo Galilei, Teacher of Mathematics and Physics, do hereby publicly renounce my teaching that the earth moves. I forswear this teaching with a sincere heart and unfeigned faith and detest and curse this and all other errors and heresies repugnant to the Holy Scriptures.

> *The lights dim; when they come up again the bell of Saint Marcus is petering out.* VIRGINIA *has gone but the* SCHOLARS *are still there waiting.*

ANDREA (*loud*) : The mountain did turn to water.

> GALILEO *has entered quietly and unnoticed. He is changed, almost unrecognizable. He has heard* ANDREA. *He waits some seconds by the door for somebody to greet him. Nobody does. They retreat from him. He goes slowly and, because of his bad sight, uncertainly, to the front of the stage, where he finds a chair and sits down.*

ANDREA: I can't look at him. Tell him to go away.

FEDERZONI: Steady.

ANDREA (*hysterically*) : He saved his big gut.

FEDERZONI: Get him a glass of water.

> *The* LITTLE MONK *fetches a glass of water for* ANDREA. *Nobody acknowledges the presence of* GALILEO, *who sits silently on his chair listening to the voice of the* TOWN CRIER, *now in another street.*

ANDREA: I can walk. Just help me a bit.

> *They help him to the door.*

ANDREA (*in the door*) : "Unhappy is the land that breeds no hero."

GALILEO: No, Andrea: "Unhappy is the land that needs a hero."

> *Before the next scene, a curtain with the following legend on it is lowered:*

> YOU CAN PLAINLY SEE THAT IF A HORSE WERE TO FALL FROM A HEIGHT OF THREE OR FOUR FEET, IT COULD BREAK ITS BONES, WHEREAS A DOG WOULD NOT SUFFER INJURY. THE SAME APPLIES TO A CAT FROM A HEIGHT OF AS MUCH AS EIGHT OR TEN FEET, TO A GRASSHOPPER FROM THE TOP OF A TOWER, AND TO AN ANT FALLING DOWN FROM THE MOON. NATURE COULD NOT ALLOW A HORSE TO BECOME AS BIG AS TWENTY HORSES NOR A GIANT AS BIG AS TEN MEN, UNLESS SHE WERE TO

CHANGE THE PROPORTIONS OF ALL ITS MEMBERS,
PARTICULARLY THE BONES. THUS THE COMMON
ASSUMPTION THAT GREAT AND SMALL STRUCTURES
ARE EQUALLY TOUGH IS OBVIOUSLY WRONG.
—FROM THE "DISCORSI"

SCENE 13

1633–1642
Galileo Galilei remains a prisoner
of the Inquisition until his death.

*A country house near Florence. A large room simply furnished.
There is a huge table, a leather chair, a globe of the world on a
stand, and a narrow bed. A portion of the adjoining anteroom
is visible, and the front door, which opens into it. An* OFFICIAL *of
the Inquisition sits on guard in the anteroom. In the large room,*
GALILEO *is quietly experimenting with a bent wooden rail and a
small ball of wood. He is still vigorous but almost blind. After a
while there is a knocking at the outside door. The* OFFICIAL
opens it to a PEASANT *who brings a plucked goose.* VIRGINIA
comes from the kitchen. She is past forty.

PEASANT (*handing the goose to* VIRGINIA): I was told to deliver this
here.

VIRGINIA: I didn't order a goose.

PEASANT: I was told to say it's from someone who was passing through.

VIRGINIA *takes the goose, surprised. The* OFFICIAL *takes it from
her and examines it suspiciously. Then, reassured, he hands it
back to her. The* PEASANT *goes.* VIRGINIA *brings the goose in to*
GALILEO.

VIRGINIA: Somebody who was passing through sent you something.

GALILEO: What is it?

VIRGINIA: Can't you see it?

GALILEO: No. (*He walks over.*) A goose. Any name?

VIRGINIA: No.

GALILEO (*weighing the goose*): Solid.

VIRGINIA (*cautiously*): Will you eat the liver, if I have it cooked with
a little apple?

GALILEO: I had my dinner. Are you under orders to finish me off with
food?

VIRGINIA: It's not rich. And what is wrong with your eyes again? You
should be able to see it.

GALILEO: You were standing in the light.

VIRGINIA: I was not. You haven't been writing again?

GALILEO (*sneering*): What do you think?

VIRGINIA *takes the goose out into the anteroom and speaks to the*
OFFICIAL.

VIRGINIA: You had better ask Monsignor Carpula to send the doctor. Father couldn't see this goose across the room. Don't look at me like that. He has not been writing. He dictates everything to me, as you know.

OFFICIAL: Yes?

VIRGINIA: He abides by the rules. My father's repentance is sincere. I keep an eye on him. (*She hands him the goose.*) Tell the cook to fry the liver with an apple and an onion. (*She goes back into the large room.*) And you have no business to be doing that with those eyes of yours, father.

GALILEO: You may read me some Horace.

VIRGINIA: We should go on with your weekly letter to the Archbishop. Monsignor Carpula, to whom we owe so much, was all smiles the other day because the Archbishop had expressed his pleasure at your collaboration.

GALILEO: Where were we?

VIRGINIA (*sits down to take his dictation*): Paragraph four.

GALILEO: Read what you have.

VIRGINIA: "The position of the Church in the matter of the unrest at Genoa. I agree with Cardinal Spoletti in the matter of the unrest among the Venetian ropemakers . . ."

GALILEO: Yes. (*Dictates*): I agree with Cardinal Spoletti in the matter of the unrest among the Venetian ropemakers: it is better to distribute good, nourishing food in the name of charity than to pay them more for their bell ropes. It being surely better to strengthen their faith than to encourage their acquisitiveness. St. Paul says: Charity never faileth. . . . How is that?

VIRGINIA: It's beautiful, father.

GALILEO: It couldn't be taken as irony?

VIRGINIA: No. The Archbishop will like it. It's so practical.

GALILEO: I trust your judgment. Read it over slowly.

VIRGINIA: "The position of the Church in the matter of the unrest—"
There is a knocking at the outside door. VIRGINIA *goes into the anteroom. The* OFFICIAL *opens the door. It is* ANDREA.

ANDREA: Good evening. I am sorry to call so late, I'm on my way to Holland. I was asked to look him up. Can I go in?

VIRGINIA: I don't know whether he will see you. You never came.

ANDREA: Ask him.
GALILEO *recognizes the voice. He sits motionless.* VIRGINIA *comes in to* GALILEO.

GALILEO: Is that Andrea?

VIRGINIA: Yes. (*Pause.*) I will send him away.

GALILEO: Show him in.
VIRGINIA *shows* ANDREA *in.* VIRGINIA *sits,* ANDREA *remains standing.*

ANDREA (*cool*): Have you been keeping well, Mr. Galilei?

GALILEO: Sit down. What are you doing these days? What are you working on? I heard it was something about hydraulics in Milan.

ANDREA: As he knew I was passing through, Fabricius of Amsterdam asked me to visit you and inquire about your health.
Pause.
GALILEO: I am very well.
ANDREA (*formally*): I am glad I can report you are in good health.
GALILEO: Fabricius will be glad to hear it. And you might inform him that, on account of the depth of my repentance, I live in comparative comfort.
ANDREA: Yes, we understand that the Church is more than pleased with you. Your complete acceptance has had its effect. Not one paper expounding a new thesis has made its appearance in Italy since your submission.
Pause.
GALILEO: Unfortunately there are countries not under the wing of the Church. Would you not say the erroneous, condemned theories are still taught—there?
ANDREA (*relentless*): Things are almost at a standstill.
GALILEO: Are they? (*Pause.*) Nothing from Descartes in Paris?
ANDREA: Yes. On receiving the news of your recantation, he shelved his treatise on the nature of light.
GALILEO: I sometimes worry about my assistants, whom I led into error. Have they benefited by my example?
ANDREA: In order to work I have to go to Holland.
GALILEO: Yes.
ANDREA: Federzoni is grinding lenses again, back in some shop.
GALILEO: He can't read the books.
ANDREA: Fulganzio, our little monk, has abandoned research and is resting in peace in the Church.
GALILEO: So. (*Pause.*) My superiors are looking forward to my spiritual recovery. I am progressing as well as can be expected.
VIRGINIA: You are doing well, father.
GALILEO: Virginia, leave the room.
VIRGINIA *rises uncertainly and goes out.*
VIRGINIA (*to the* OFFICIAL): He was his pupil, so now he is his enemy. Help me in the kitchen.
She leaves the anteroom with the OFFICIAL.
ANDREA: May I go now, sir?
GALILEO: I do not know why you came, Sarti. To unsettle me? I have to be prudent.
ANDREA: I'll be on my way.
GALILEO: As it is, I have relapses. I completed the "Discorsi."
ANDREA: You completed what?
GALILEO: My "Discorsi."
ANDREA: How?
GALILEO: I am allowed pen and paper. My superiors are intelligent men. They know the habits of a lifetime cannot be broken abruptly. But they protect me from any unpleasant consequences: they lock my pages away as I dictate them. And I should know better than to risk my comfort. I wrote the "Discorsi" out again during the

night. The manuscript is in the globe. My vanity has up to now prevented me from destroying it. If you consider taking it, you will shoulder the entire risk. You will say it was pirated from the original in the hands of the Holy Office.

> ANDREA, *as in a trance, has gone to the globe. He lifts the upper half and gets the book. He turns the pages as if wanting to devour them. In the background the opening sentences of the "Discorsi" appear:*

> MY PURPOSE IS TO SET FORTH A VERY NEW SCI-
> ENCE DEALING WITH A VERY ANCIENT SUBJECT—
> MOTION. . . . AND I HAVE DISCOVERED BY EXPERI-
> MENT SOME PROPERTIES OF IT WHICH ARE WORTH
> KNOWING. . . .

GALILEO: I had to employ my time somehow.
> *The text disappears.*

ANDREA: Two new sciences! This will be the foundation stone of a new physics.

GALILEO: Yes. Put it under your coat.

ANDREA: And we thought you had deserted. (*In a low voice*): Mr. Galilei, how can I begin to express my shame. Mine has been the loudest voice against you.

GALILEO: That would seem to have been proper. I taught you science and I decried the truth.

ANDREA: Did you? I think not. Everything is changed!

GALILEO: What is changed?

ANDREA: You shielded the truth from the oppressor. Now I see! In your dealings with the Inquisition you used the same superb common sense you brought to physics.

GALILEO: Oh!

ANDREA: We lost our heads. With the crowd at the street corners we said: "He will die, he will never surrender!" You came back: "I surrendered but I am alive." We cried: "Your hands are stained!" You say: "Better stained than empty."

GALILEO: "Better stained than empty." It sounds realistic. Sounds like me.

ANDREA: And I of all people should have known. I was twelve when you sold another man's telescope to the Venetian Senate, and saw you put it to immortal use. Your friends were baffled when you bowed to the Prince of Florence: science gained a wider audience. You always laughed at heroics. "People who suffer bore me," you said. "Misfortunes are due mainly to miscalculations." And: "If there are obstacles, the shortest line between two points may be the crooked line."

GALILEO: It makes a picture.

ANDREA: And when you stooped to recant in 1633, I should have understood that you were again about your business.

GALILEO: My business being?

ANDREA: Science. The study of the properties of motion, mother of the machines which will themselves change the ugly face of the earth.

GALILEO: Aha!

ANDREA: You gained time to write a book that only you could write. Had you burned at the stake in a blaze of glory they would have won.

GALILEO: They have won. And there is no such thing as a scientific work that only one man can write.

ANDREA: Then why did you recant, tell me that!

GALILEO: I recanted because I was afraid of physical pain.

ANDREA: No!

GALILEO: They showed me the instruments.

ANDREA: It was not a plan?

GALILEO: It was not.

Pause.

ANDREA: But you have contributed. Science has only one commandment: contribution. And you have contributed more than any man for a hundred years.

GALILEO: Have I? Then welcome to my gutter, dear colleague in science and brother in treason: I sold out, you are a buyer. The first sight of the book! His mouth watered and his scoldings were drowned. Blessed be our bargaining, whitewashing, death-fearing community!

ANDREA: The fear of death is human.

GALILEO: Even the Church will teach you that to be weak is not human. It is just evil.

ANDREA: The Church, yes! But science is not concerned with our weaknesses.

GALILEO: No? My dear Sarti, in spite of my present convictions, I may be able to give you a few pointers as to the concerns of your chosen profession. (*Enter* VIRGINIA *with a platter.*) In my spare time, I happen to have gone over this case. I have spare time. Even a man who sells wool, however good he is at buying wool cheap and selling it dear, must be concerned with the standing of the wool trade. The practice of science would seem to call for valor. She trades in knowledge, which is the product of doubt. And this new art of doubt has enchanted the public. The plight of the multitude is old as the rocks, and is believed to be basic as the rocks. But now they have learned to doubt. They snatched the telescopes out of our hands and had them trained on their tormentors: prince, official, public moralist. The mechanism of the heavens was clearer, the mechanism of their courts was still murky. The battle to measure the heavens is won by doubt; by credulity the Roman housewife's battle for milk will always be lost. Word is passed down that this is of no concern to the scientist, who is told he will only release such of his findings as do not disturb the peace, that is, the peace of mind of the well-to-do. Threats and bribes fill the air. Can the scientist hold out on the numbers? For what reason do you labor?

I take it that the intent of science is to ease human existence. If you give way to coercion, science can be crippled, and your new machines may simply suggest new drudgeries. Should you, then, in time, discover all there is to be discovered, your progress must become a progress away from the bulk of humanity. The gulf might even grow so wide that the sound of your cheering at some new achievement would be echoed by a universal howl of horror. As a scientist I had an almost unique opportunity. In my day astronomy emerged into the market place. At that particular time, had one man put up a fight, it could have had wide repercussions. I have come to believe that I was never in real danger; for some years I was as strong as the authorities, and I surrendered my knowledge to the powers that be, to use it, no, not *use* it, *abuse* it, as it suits their ends. I have betrayed my profession. Any man who does what I have done must not be tolerated in the ranks of science.

VIRGINIA, *who has stood motionless, puts the platter on the table.*

VIRGINIA: You are accepted in the ranks of the faithful, father.

GALILEO (*sees her*): Correct. (*He goes over to the table.*) I have to eat now.

VIRGINIA: We lock up at eight.

ANDREA: I am glad I came. (*He extends his hand.* GALILEO *ignores it and goes over to his meal.*)

GALILEO (*examining the plate; to* ANDREA): Somebody who knows me sent me a goose. I still enjoy eating.

ANDREA: And your opinion is now that the "new age" was an illusion?

GALILEO: Well. This age of ours turned out to be a whore, spattered with blood. Maybe, new ages look like blood-spattered whores. Take care of yourself.

ANDREA: Yes. (*Unable to go.*) With reference to your evaluation of the author in question—I do not know the answer. But I cannot think that your savage analysis is the last word.

GALILEO: Thank you, sir.

OFFICIAL *knocks at the door.*

VIRGINIA (*showing* ANDREA *out*): I don't like visitors from the past, they excite him.

She lets him out. The OFFICIAL *closes the iron door.* VIRGINIA *returns.*

GALILEO (*eating*): Did you try and think who sent the goose?

VIRGINIA: Not Andrea.

GALILEO: Maybe not. I gave Redhead his first lesson; when he held out his hand, I had to remind myself he is teaching now. How is the sky tonight?

VIRGINIA (*at the window*): Bright.

GALILEO *continues eating.*

SCENE 14

The great book o'er the border went
And, good folk, that was the end.

>*But we hope you'll keep in mind*
>*You and I were left behind.*

Before a little Italian customs house early in the morning. ANDREA
*sits upon one of his traveling trunks at the barrier and reads
Galileo's book. The window of a small house is still lit, and a big
grotesque shadow, like an old witch and her cauldron, falls upon
the house wall beyond. Barefoot* CHILDREN *in rags see it and
point to the little house.*

CHILDREN (*singing*):

>One, two, three, four, five, six,
>Old Marina is a witch.
>At night, on a broomstick she sits
>And on the church steeple she spits.

CUSTOMS OFFICER (*to* ANDREA): Why are you making this journey?

ANDREA: I am a scholar.

CUSTOMS OFFICER (*to his* CLERK): Put down under "Reason for
Leaving the Country": Scholar. (*He points to the baggage*): Books!
Anything dangerous in these books?

ANDREA: What is dangerous?

CUSTOMS OFFICER: Religion. Politics.

ANDREA: These are nothing but mathematical formulas.

CUSTOMS OFFICER: What's that?

ANDREA: Figures.

CUSTOMS OFFICER: Oh, figures. No harm in figures. Just wait a minute,
sir, we will soon have your papers stamped. (He exits with CLERK.)
Meanwhile, a little council of war among the CHILDREN *has taken
place.* ANDREA *quietly watches. One of the* BOYS, *pushed forward
by the others, creeps up to the little house from which the shadow
comes, and takes the jug of milk on the doorstep.*

ANDREA (*quietly*): What are you doing with that milk?

BOY (*stopping in mid-movement*): She is a witch.
The other CHILDREN *run away behind the customs house. One
of them shouts,* "Run, Paolo!"

ANDREA: Hmm! And because she is a witch she mustn't have milk.
Is that the idea?

BOY: Yes.

ANDREA: And how do you know she is a witch?

BOY (*points to shadow on house wall*): Look!

ANDREA: Oh! I see.

BOY: And she rides on a broomstick at night—and she bewitches the
coachman's horses. My cousin Luigi looked through the hole in the
stable roof, that the snow storm made, and heard the horses coughing something terrible.

ANDREA: Oh! How big was the hole in the stable roof?

BOY: Luigi didn't tell. Why?

ANDREA: I was asking because maybe the horses got sick because it
was cold in the stable. You had better ask Luigi how big that hole is.

BOY: You are not going to say Old Marina isn't a witch, because you can't.

ANDREA: No, I can't say she isn't a witch. I haven't looked into it. A man can't know about a thing he hasn't looked into, or can he?

BOY: No! But THAT! (*He points to the shadow.*) She is stirring hellbroth.

ANDREA: Let's see. Do you want to take a look? I can lift you up.

BOY: You lift me to the window, mister! (*He takes a slingshot out of his pocket.*) I can really bash her from there.

ANDREA: Hadn't we better make sure she is a witch before we shoot? I'll hold that.

> The BOY *puts the milk jug down and follows him reluctantly to the window.* ANDREA *lifts the boy up so that he can look in.*

ANDREA: What do you see?

BOY (*slowly*): Just an old girl cooking porridge.

ANDREA: Oh! Nothing to it then. Now look at her shadow, Paolo.

> The BOY *looks over his shoulder and back and compares the reality and the shadow.*

BOY: The big thing is a soup ladle.

ANDREA: Ah! A ladle! You see, I would have taken it for a broomstick, but I haven't looked into the matter as you have, Paolo. Here is your sling.

CUSTOMS OFFICER (*returning with the* CLERK *and handing* ANDREA *his papers*): All present and correct. Good luck, sir.

> ANDREA *goes, reading Galileo's book. The* CLERK *starts to bring his baggage after him. The barrier rises.* ANDREA *passes through, still reading the book. The* BOY *kicks over the milk jug.*

BOY (*shouting after* ANDREA): She *is* a witch! She *is* a witch!

ANDREA: You saw with your own eyes: think it over!

> The BOY *joins the others. They sing:*

> > One, two, three, four, five, six,
> > Old Marina is a witch.
> > At night, on a broomstick she sits
> > And on the church steeple she spits.

> The CUSTOMS OFFICERS *laugh.* ANDREA *goes.*

> > *May you now guard science' light,*
> > *Kindle it and use it right,*
> > *Lest it be a flame to fall*
> > *Downward to consume us all.*

PHILOCTETES

OR

THE TREATISE ON THREE ETHICS

André Gide

CHARACTERS

Neoptolemus   Ulysses   Philoctetes

ACT I

A level waste of snow and ice; a low gray sky.

SCENE I

(ULYSSES and NEOPTOLEMUS)

NEOPTOLEMUS: Everything is ready, Ulysses. The boat is moored. I left it in deep water, sheltered on the north, for fear the wind might freeze the sea around it. This island is so cold it seems to be inhabited by nothing but birds along the sea cliffs; but I took the precaution to tie up the boat in a spot where no one passing along the coast could see it.

My mind too is made up; it is ready for sacrifice. Speak now, Ulysses, and tell me; all is ready. For fourteen days, you have been leaning on the oars or the tiller, perfectly silent except for the sharp words of command needed to steer us out of danger of waves. Faced with your obstinate silence, I soon ceased to ask questions; I understood that a great sadness was oppressing your dear spirit, because you were taking me toward death. And I fell silent too, feeling that all our words were too quickly swept away by the wind over the immensity of the sea. I waited. I saw the beautiful shore of Skyros falling way behind us, beyond the horizon of the sea; then the islands of golden sand or stone, which I loved because I thought they were like Pylos; thirteen times I saw the sun go down in the sea; and each morning it rose from paler waves, mounted less high, more slowly, until at last, on the fourteenth morning, we waited for it in vain; and ever since then we have been living, as it were, beyond night and day. We have seen ice floating on the sea, and were unable to sleep because of the constant pale glimmer; the only words I heard from you then were those that signaled icebergs to be avoided by the stroke of an oar. But speak now, Ulysses! My spirit is prepared, not like the goats of Bacchus led to the sacrifice covered with festal ornaments, but like Iphigenia [1] advancing to the altar, simple, decent, and unadorned. To be sure, since, like her, I wish to die for my country without complaint, I should have preferred to die among the Greeks, in a land bright with sunshine, and to show, by accepting death, all my respect for the gods and all the beauty of my spirit; it is valiant and has not fought. It is hard to die without glory. Yet, O gods! I hold no bitterness; though reluctantly, I have left everything, men, sun-warmed shores . . . and now, coming to this inhospitable island, with no trees, no sunlight, where every green thing is covered with snow, where everything is frozen, and the sky so blank, so gray, it is like another plain of snow stretched above us, far away from everything . . . this seems like death already, here; every hour my mind has been growing so much colder, and purer, all passion gone, that now nothing is left but for the body to die.

Ulysses, at least tell me that Zeus, mysterious Zeus, will be appeased by my faithful death and will give victory to the Greeks; at least you will tell them, won't you, Ulysses! tell them that is why I died without fear . . . you will tell them . . .

ULYSSES: Child, you are not here to die. Don't smile. Now I can tell you. Listen to me and don't interrupt. Would that the gods might be satisfied simply by the sacrifice of one of us! What we have come here to do, Neoptolemus, is not so easy as dying. . . .

This island that looks deserted to you is not so at all. It is inhabited by a Greek; his name is Philoctetes, and your father loved him. Long ago he set sail with us in the fleet that left Greece for Asia, full of hope and pride; he was the friend of Hercules, and one of the noblemen among us; if you had lived in camp before now, you would already know his story. In those days everyone admired his courage; later on they all called it rashness. It was what moved him once when we rested our oars at an unknown island. The shore had a strange aspect; bad omens had undermined our courage. The gods had ordered us to make sacrifice on this island, so Calchas [2] told us, but each one of us was waiting for some other to make the first move; then Philoctetes volunteered, with a smile. On the shore of the island a treacherous snake bit him. Philoctetes was still smiling when he came back on board and first showed us his little wound, just above his foot. It grew worse. Philoctetes soon stopped smiling; his face turned pale, then his troubled eyes filled with an astonished anguish. After a few days his swollen foot stiffened; and he, who had never complained, began to groan pitifully. At first everyone gathered around, eager to console and amuse him; nothing could do so, except to cure him; and, when it was proved

---

[1] Daughter of Agamemnon. She was sacrificed to secure a wind so that the Greek fleet could sail for Troy.
[2] Greek priest and soothsayer.

that the art of Machaon had no power over his wound, since his cries were likely to weaken our courage, and since the ship was approaching another island, this one, we left him here, alone with his bow and arrows, which are our business today.

NEOPTOLEMUS: What, Ulysses! You left him? Alone?

ULYSSES: Of course, if he had been going to die, I think we might have kept him a little while longer. But no: his wound is not mortal.

NEOPTOLEMUS: But even so?

ULYSSES: Well, do you think the courage of a whole army should have been subjected to the suffering and wailing of a single man? It is easy to see that you never heard him!

NEOPTOLEMUS: Were his cries frightful?

ULYSSES: No, not frightful: plaintive, dampening our souls with pity.

NEOPTOLEMUS: Couldn't someone at least stay and take care of him? What can he do, sick and alone here?

ULYSSES: He has his bow.

NEOPTOLEMUS: His bow?

ULYSSES: Yes: the bow of Hercules. And then I must tell you, child: his rotting foot filled the whole ship with the most unbearable stench.

NEOPTOLEMUS: Ah?

ULYSSES: Yes, and he was obsessed with his illness, incapable ever again of any devotion to Greece. . . .

NEOPTOLEMUS: Too bad. And now we have come, Ulysses. . . .

ULYSSES: Listen, again, Neoptolemus: you know Troy has long been condemned; you know how much blood has been spilled, how much virtue, patience, and courage spent there, far from home and our dear land. . . . Well, none of all that has sufficed. Through the priest Calchas the gods have finally declared that the bow and arrows of Hercules alone, in one final test of virtue, could give the victory to Greece. That is why we two have come; blessed be the fate that chose us! And now it seems that on this distant island, all passion put behind us, our great destinies at last are to be resolved, and our hearts, here, more completely dedicated, are at last to achieve the most perfect virtue.

NEOPTOLEMUS: Is that all, Uslysses? And now, after such a fine speech, what do you plan to do? My mind still refuses to understand your words completely. . . . Tell me: why have we come here?

ULYSSES: To take the bow of Hercules; now do you understand?

NEOPTOLEMUS: Is that your idea, Ulysses?

ULYSSES: Not mine; it is one the gods put into me.

NEOPTOLEMUS: Philoctetes will not want to let us have it.

ULYSSES: Therefore we shall take it by trickery.

NEOPTOLEMUS: Ulysses, you are detestable. My father taught me never to use trickery.

ULYSSES: It is stronger than force; force doesn't know how to wait. Your father is dead, Neoptolemus; I am alive.

NEOPTOLEMUS: Weren't you saying that it is better to die?

ULYSSES: Not better; it is easier to die. Nothing is worse for Greece.

NEOPTOLEMUS: Ulysses! Why did you choose me? Why did you need me for this act? My whole soul disapproves it.

ULYSSES: Because I cannot do it myself; Philoctetes knows me too well. If he sees me alone, he will suspect some trick. Your innocence will protect us. You must be the one to do this act.

NEOPTOLEMUS: No, Ulysses; by Zeus, I will not do it.

ULYSSES: Child, do not speak of Zeus. You don't understand me. Listen. Do you think I am less sad than you because my tormented soul is masked, and accepts? You do not know Philoctetes; he is my friend. It is harder for me than for you to betray him. The gods' commands are cruel; they are the gods. I did not talk to you in the boat because my great saddened heart no longer even dreamed of words. . . . But you flare up as your father used to and no longer listen to reason.

NEOPTOLEMUS: My father is dead, Ulysses; do not speak of him; he died for Greece. Ah, to struggle, suffer, die for her! Ask whatever you will of me, but not to betray my father's friend!

ULYSSES: Child, listen and answer me: are you not the friend of all the Greeks rather than the friend of a single one? Or, rather, isn't our country greater than one man? And could you bear to save one man, if, to save him, Greece must be lost?

NEOPTOLEMUS: It is true, Ulysses, I could not bear it.

ULYSSES: And you agree that, though friendship is a very precious thing, our land is still more precious? . . . Tell me, Neoptolemus, what is virtue?

NEOPTOLEMUS: Teach me, wise son of Laertes.

ULYSSES: Calm your passion; put duty above everything. . . .

NEOPTOLEMUS: But what is duty, Ulysses?

ULYSSES: The voice of the gods, the order of the city, giving ourselves to Greece; just as we see lovers looking about them for the most precious flowers as gifts for their mistresses, and wanting to die for them, as if the unhappy things had nothing better to give than themselves, what is there too dear for you to give to your country if it is dear to you? And didn't you agree awhile ago that friendships came next after your country? What did Agamemnon [3] have dearer than his daughter, except his country? You must sacrifice, as on an altar . . . but now, in the same way, what does Philoctetes have, living all alone on this island, what does he have more precious than this bow to give to his country?

NEOPTOLEMUS: Well, in that case, Ulysses, ask him.

ULYSSES: He might refuse. I do not know what mood he is in, but I do know that his abandonment angered him against the leaders of the army. It may be he has angered the gods with his thoughts and, shockingly, no longer wishes us victory. And maybe the offended

---

[3] Greek king and general.

gods have decided to punish him again, through us. If we force
virtue upon him by obliging him to give up his weapons, the gods
will be less severe with him.

NEOPTOLEMUS: But, Ulysses, can deeds we do against our will be
praiseworthy?

ULYSSES: Don't you think, Neoptolemus, that what is most important
of all is that the gods' orders be carried out? Even if it must be
done without everybody's consent?

NEOPTOLEMUS: All you said before, I approve; but now I no longer
know what to say, and it even seems to me—

ULYSSES: Shsh! Listen. . . . Don't you hear something?

NEOPTOLEMUS: Yes: the sound of the sea.

ULYSSES: No. It's he! His frightful cries are just beginning to reach us.

NEOPTOLEMUS: Frightful? On the contrary, Ulysses, I hear singing.

ULYSSES [*listening closely*]: It's true, he is singing. He's a good one!
Now that he's alone, he sings! When he was with us, he screamed.

NEOPTOLEMUS: What is he singing?

ULYSSES: I can't yet make out the words. Listen: he's coming nearer.

NEOPTOLEMUS: He has stopped singing. He is standing still. He has
seen our tracks in the snow.

ULYSSES [*laughing*]: And now he is beginning to scream again. Ah,
Philoctetes!

NEOPTOLEMUS: It's true, his cries are horrible.

ULYSSES: Look, run put my sword on that rock, so he will recognize
a Greek weapon and know the tracks he has seen are those of a
man from his own country. —Hurry, he is getting near.—Good.—
Now come; let's post ourselves behind this mound of snow, so we
can see him without being seen. How he will curse us! "Beggars,"
he will say, "perish the Greeks who abandoned me here! Com-
manders of the army! You liar, Ulysses! You, Agamemnon, Mene-
laus! [4] May they all be devoured by my disease! Oh, death! Death,
I call on you every day, will you not hear my complaint? Will
you never come? O caves! Rocks! Promontories! Mute witnesses of
my suffering, will you never—"

[*Enter* PHILOCTETES; *he sees the helmet and weapons placed in
the center of the stage.*]

SCENE II

(PHILOCTETES, ULYSSES, NEOPTOLEMUS)

PHILOCTETES: [*He is silent.*]

---

[4] Greek king and general. Husband of Helen.

ACT II

SCENE I

(ULYSSES, PHILOCTETES, NEOPTOLEMUS)

[*All three are sitting.*]

PHILOCTETES: I tell you, Ulysses, only since I have lived apart from men do I understand what is called virtue. The man who lives among others is incapable, believe me, incapable of a pure and really disinterested action. You, for instance—came here—for what?

ULYSSES: Why to see you, my dear Philoctetes.

PHILOCTETES: I don't believe a word of it, but no matter; it is a great pleasure to see you again, and that is enough. I have lost the talent for seeking the motives of what people do, since my own are no longer secret. To whom would I need to appear what I am? My only care is to be. I have stopped groaning, because I knew there was no ear to hear me; I have stopped wishing because I knew that I could get nothing by it.

ULYSSES: Why didn't you stop groaning sooner, Philoctetes? We might have kept you with us.

PHILOCTETES: That is just what should not have happened, Ulysses. In the presence of others my silence would have been a lie.

ULYSSES: Whereas here?

PHILOCTETES: My suffering no longer needs words to make itself known, being known only to me.

ULYSSES: So, you have been silent ever since we left, Philoctetes?

PHILOCTETES: Not at all. But since I no longer use my complaint to manifest my suffering, it has become beautiful, so beautiful that it consoles me.

ULYSSES: Good, my poor Philoctetes.

PHILOCTETES: Above all, don't pity me! I stopped wishing, as I was telling you, because I knew that I could get nothing by it. . . . I could get nothing from others, it is true, but a great deal from myself; it was then that I began to desire virtue; my spirit is now wholly occupied with that, and I am at peace, despite my pain. At least I was at peace when you came. . . . Why do you smile?

ULYSSES: I see that you have been busy.

PHILOCTETES: You listen but do not understand me. Don't you love virtue?

ULYSSES: Yes: my own.

PHILOCTETES: What is it?

ULYSSES: You would listen but would not understand me. . . . Let's talk about the Greeks instead. Has your solitary virtue made you forget them?

PHILOCTETES: So as not to be angry with them, yes indeed.

ULYSSES: You hear, Neoptolemus! So our success in the battle which—

PHILOCTETES: —made you leave me here—what do you expect me to think of it, Ulysses? You left me here so as to conquer, didn't you? Then I hope for your sake that you are conquerors. . . .

ULYSSES: And if not?

PHILOCTETES: If not, then we have believed Hellas greater than she was. On this island, you know, I have become every day less Greek, every day more a man. . . . Yet when I see you, I feel— Is Achilles dead, Ulysses?

ULYSSES: Achilles is dead; my companion here is his son. Why, you are sobbing, Philoctetes? . . . Where is the calm you have been seeking? . . .

PHILOCTETES: Achilles! . . . Child, let me stroke your fine forehead. . . . It has been a long time, a long time since my hand touched a warm body; even the birds I kill fall in the water or the snow, and when my hands reach them, their bodies are as cold as those upper regions of the atmosphere where they fly. . . .

ULYSSES: You express yourself well for one who is in pain.

PHILOCTETES: Wherever I go, always, I am a son of Greece.

ULYSSES: But you have no one to talk to here.

PHILOCTETES: Didn't you understand me? I told you that I express myself better now that I no longer talk with men. Except for hunting and sleeping, my whole occupation is thinking. In this solitude nothing, not even pain, interferes with my ideas; and they have taken a course so subtle that I follow them sometimes myself only with difficulty. I have come to understand more of the secrets of life than all my teachers ever revealed to me. I tried telling myself of my suffering, and if the sentence were beautiful, I was comforted accordingly; sometimes I even forgot my troubles in telling them. I learned that words are more beautiful when they ask for nothing. With neither ears nor mouths around me, I used only the beauty of my words; I called them out to the whole island, along the beaches; and the island listened and seemed less solitary; nature seemed the image of my distress; it seemed that I was nature's voice and that the mute rocks were waiting for my voice to tell their illnesses; for I learned that everything around me is sick . . . and that this cold is not normal, for I remember Greece. . . . And I gradually got the habit of crying the distress of things, rather than my own; that seemed better, but how can I explain to you? Anyway, their distress and mine were the same and I was comforted. It was in speaking of the sea and the interminable wave that I made my finest phrases. Do you know, Ulysses—O Ulysses!—some were so beautiful that I sobbed with sadness because there was no man to hear them. It seemed to me his soul would have been changed by them. Listen, Ulysses! Listen. No one has heard me yet.

ULYSSES: I see you got the habit of talking without interruption. Come, recite for us.

PHILOCTETES [*declaiming*]: The numberless smiling waves of the sea—

ULYSSES [*laughing*]: Why, Philoctetes, that's from Aeschylus.[5]

PHILOCTETES: Perhaps. . . . Does that bother you?

[*Continuing*]

Numberless sobbing waves of the sea—

[*Silence*]

ULYSSES: And then—

PHILOCTETES: I don't know any more. . . . I am mixed up.

ULYSSES: Too bad! But you can go on another time.

NEOPTOLEMUS: Oh, please go on now, Philoctetes!

ULYSSES: Well! The child was listening to you! . . .

PHILOCTETES: I don't know how to talk, any longer.

ULYSSES [*rising*]: I will leave you for a moment to collect your thoughts. Good-by, Philoctetes. But tell me: no captivity is so hard that it doesn't allow some repose, some forgetfulness, some respite, is there?

PHILOCTETES: True, Ulysses; one day I shot a bird and it fell; my arrow had only wounded it, and I hoped to revive it. But how could it keep that airy emotion that made it fly, down here on this hardened earth where the cold fixes even upon water, when it freezes, the form of my logical thought. The bird died; I watched it die in a few hours; to warm it again, I smothered it with kisses and warm breath. It died of the need to fly. . . .

It even seems to me, dear Ulysses, that the stream of poetry, as soon as it leaves my lips, freezes and dies because it cannot be repeated, propagated, and that the intimate flame that animates it is steadily shrinking. I shall soon be, though still alive, quite abstract. Dear Ulysses, the cold is invading me, and I am frightened, for I find beauty in it, even in its rigor.

I walk securely over things, over frozen fluids. I never dream any more; I only think. I can no longer taste hope, and for that reason I am never elated. Here, where everything is hard stone, when I set anything whatever down—even a seed—I find it again long afterwards, just as it was; it has never sprouted. Here, Ulysses, nothing becomes: everything is, everything remains. In short, here one can speculate! I kept the dead bird; here it is; the freezing air keeps it ever from rotting. And my acts, Ulysses, and my words, as if they were frozen in permanence, surround me like rocks arranged in a circle. And because I find them there every day, all my passion is quieted, and I feel the Truth always firmer—and I should wish my actions likewise always sounder and more beautiful; true, pure, crystalline, and beautiful; as beautiful, Ulysses, as those crystals of clear frost through which the sun, if the sun ever appeared, could be seen whole. I do not wish to stop a single ray of Zeus; let him transpierce me, Ulysses, like a prism, and the refracted light make my acts lovable and beautiful. I should like to achieve the greatest transparency, the clarification of all my opacity; and I should like for you, watching me act, to feel the light yourself. . . .

[5] Greek playwright.

ULYSSES [*leaving*]: Well, good-by. [*Pointing to Neoptolemus*] Chat
with him, he's listening. [*Exit.*]

SCENE II

(PHILOCTETES *and* NEOPTOLEMUS)

NEOPTOLEMUS: Philoctetes! Teach me virtue. . . .

ACT III

SCENE I

(PHILOCTETES)

PHILOCTETES [*entering; overcome with surprise and grief*]: Blind
Philoctetes! Recognize your error, weep for your folly! That the
sight of Greeks should have stolen your heart. . . . Did I hear
rightly? To be sure: Ulysses was sitting there, and near by was
Neoptolemus; they didn't know I was there, they didn't even lower
their voices; Ulysses was advising Neoptolemus, teaching him to
betray me; telling him— You are cursed, Philoctetes! They came
only to steal your bow! How they must need it! . . . Precious
bow, my only possession, without it— [*Listening intently*] They
are coming! Defend yourself, Philoctetes! Your bow is good, your
arm is sure. Virtue! Virtue I cherished so much when I was alone!
My silent heart had grown calm before they came. Ah, now I know
what it's worth, the friendship they offer! Is Greece my country,
detestable Ulysses? And you, Neoptolemus. . . . And yet how he
listened to me! So gentle! Child—as fair, oh, fairer than your
father was fair. . . . How can so pure a forehead conceal such a
thought? "Virtue," he said, "Philoctetes, teach me virtue." What
did I tell him? I don't remember anything but him. . . . But what
does it matter now, whatever I told him! . . . [*Listening*] Footsteps! . . . Who is coming? Ulysses! [*Seizing his bow*] No, it's—
Neoptolemus.
    [*Enter* NEOPTOLEMUS.]

SCENE II

(PHILOCTETES *and* NEOPTOLEMUS)

NEOPTOLEMUS [*calling*]: . . . Philoctetes! [*Coming, nearly fainting*]
    Ah! I'm sick.
PHILOCTETES: Sick?
NEOPTOLEMUS: You are the cause of my trouble. Make me calm

again, Philoctetes. All you told me has taken root in my heart. While you were talking, I did not know what to answer. I listened, and my heart opened naively to your words. Ever since you stopped, I have kept on listening. But now I am troubled, and waiting. Speak! I have not heard enough. . . . What were you saying? A man must devote himself—

PHILOCTETES [*unresponsive*]: —devote himself.

NEOPTOLEMUS: But that is what Ulysses teaches me too. Devote himself to what, Philoctetes? He says, to one's country—

PHILOCTETES: —to one's country.

NEOPTOLEMUS: Ah, tell me, Philoctetes; you must go on now.

PHILOCTETES [*evasive*]: Child—do you know how to draw the bow?

NEOPTOLEMUS: Yes. Why?

PHILOCTETES: Could you string this one?

NEOPTOLEMUS: [*disconcerted*]: You mean— I don't know. [*Trying it*] Yes, perhaps. —You see!

PHILOCTETES [*aside*]: What ease! He is like—

NEOPTOLEMUS [*uncertain*]: And now—

PHILOCTETES: I have seen all I wanted to see. [*He takes the bow.*]

NEOPTOLEMUS: I don't understand you.

PHILOCTETES: No matter, alas! . . . [*Changing his mind*] Listen, child. Don't you believe the gods are above Greece, more important than Greece?

NEOPTOLEMUS: No, by Zeus, I don't believe it.

PHILOCTETES: But why not, Neoptolemus?

NEOPTOLEMUS: Because the gods I serve serve Greece.

PHILOCTETES: So! You mean they are subject?

NEOPTOLEMUS: Not subject—I don't know how to say it. . . . But look! You know they are unknown outside Greece; Greece is their country as well as ours; by serving her, I serve them; they are no different from my country.

PHILOCTETES: Yet, look, I have something to say, there; I no longer belong to Greece, yet—I serve them.

NEOPTOLEMUS: You think so? Ah, poor Philoctetes! Greece is not so easily shaken off . . . and even—

PHILOCTETES [*attentive*]: And even—?

NEOPTOLEMUS: Ah, if you knew. . . . Philoctetes—

PHILOCTETES: If I knew—what?

NEOPTOLEMUS [*recovering*]: No, you, you must talk; I came to listen, and now you question me. . . . I see plainly that Ulysses' virtue and yours are not the same. . . . You used to speak so well, but now when you have to speak, you hesitate. . . . Devote oneself to what, Philoctetes?

PHILOCTETES: I was going to say; to the gods. . . . But the truth is, Neoptolemus, there is something above the gods.

NEOPTOLEMUS: Above the gods!

PHILOCTETES: Yes. I will not act like Ulysses.

NEOPTOLEMUS: Devote oneself to what, Philoctetes? What is there, above the gods?

PHILOCTETES: There is— [*Taking his head in his hands, overcome*] I don't know. . . . Ah! Ah, oneself! . . . I don't know how to say it any longer, Neoptolemus. . . .

NEOPTOLEMUS: Devote oneself to what? Tell me, Philoctetes.

PHILOCTETES: Devote oneself—devote—

NEOPTOLEMUS: You are weeping!

PHILOCTETES: Child! Ah, if I could only *show* you virtue. . . . [*Standing up suddenly*] I hear Ulysses! Good-by. . . . [*Going*] Shall I ever see you again? [*Exit.*]

NEOPTOLEMUS: Farewell, Philoctetes.

[*Enter* ULYSSES.]

SCENE III

(ULYSSES *and* NEOPTOLEMUS)

ULYSSES: Did I come in time? What did he say? Did you talk well, my scholar?

NEOPTOLEMUS: Thanks to you, better than he. But what does it matter? Ulysses—he gave me his bow to string!

ULYSSES: His bow! What irony! Well, why didn't you keep it, son of Achilles?

NEOPTOLEMUS: What good is a bow without arrows? While I had the bow, he wisely kept the arrows.

ULYSSES: Our friend is clever! . . . Does he suspect, do you think? What did he say?

NEOPTOLEMUS: Oh, nothing, or almost.

ULYSSES: And did he recite his virtue to you again?

NEOPTOLEMUS: He talked so well awhile ago; but when I questioned him, he shut up.

ULYSSES: You see! . . .

NEOPTOLEMUS: And when I asked him what else there is to devote oneself to except Greece, he said—

ULYSSES: What?

NEOPTOLEMUS: He didn't know. And when I said that even the gods, as you taught me, are subject to Greece, he answered: then, above the gods, there is—

ULYSSES: What?

NEOPTOLEMUS: He said he didn't know.

ULYSSES: Well! Now you see, Neoptolemus! . . .

NEOPTOLEMUS: No, Ulysses, it seems to me now that I understand it.

ULYSSES: You understand what?

NEOPTOLEMUS: Something. Because, after all, on this solitary island, when we were not here, what was Philoctetes devoted to?

ULYSSES: Why, you have already said it: to nothing. What good is solitary virtue? Despite what he believes, it was dissipated, to no use. What good are all these phrases, however fine? . . . Did they convince you? Nor me either.

The reason he was left here, alone on this island, as I have already proved to you, was to rid the army of his groaning and his stench; that is his first devotion; that is his virtue, whatever he may say. His second virtue will be, if he is so virtuous, to be consoled when he loses his bow, by remembering that it was done for Greece. What other devotion, if not to one's country, is imaginable? He was waiting, you see, for us to come and give him the chance. . . . But since it is possible he might refuse, we'd better force his virtue, impose the sacrifice on him—and I think the wisest course is to put him to sleep. You see this bottle. . . .

NEOPTOLEMUS: Ah, don't talk so much, Ulysses. Philoctetes was silent.

ULYSSES: That was because he had nothing to say.

NEOPTOLEMUS: And that was why he was weeping?

ULYSSES: He was weeping because he was wrong.

NEOPTOLEMUS: No, he was weeping because of me.

ULYSSES [*smiling*]: You? . . . What begins as nonsense, we later call virtue, out of pride.

NEOPTOLEMUS [*bursting into sobs*]: Ulysses! You don't understand Philoctetes. . . .

ACT IV

SCENE I

(PHILOCTETES *and* NEOPTOLEMUS)

[PHILOCTETES *is sitting, alone; he seems overcome with grief, or in meditation.*]

NEOPTOLEMUS [*enters, running*]: I must find him in time! . . . Ah, it's you, Philoctetes. Quick, listen to me. What we came here for is shameful; but you must be greater than we are and forgive me. We came—oh, I am ashamed to say it—to steal your bow, Philoctetes!

PHILOCTETES: I knew.

NEOPTOLEMUS: You don't understand me—we came to steal your bow, I tell you. . . . Ah, defend yourself!

PHILOCTETES: Against whom? You, dear Neoptolemus?

NEOPTOLEMUS: Certainly not against me; I love you and am trying to warn you.

PHILOCTETES: And you are betraying Ulysses. . . .

NEOPTOLEMUS: And I am in despair. . . . It's to you I'm devoted. Do you love me? Say, Philoctetes, is that what virtue is?

PHILOCTETES: Child! . . .

NEOPTOLEMUS: Look what I bring you. This phial is meant to put you to sleep. But I give it to you. Here it is. Is that virtue?—Tell me.

PHILOCTETES: Child! Superior virtue is attained only step by step; you are trying to make it at a leap.

NEOPTOLEMUS: Then teach me, Philoctetes.

PHILOCTETES: This phial was to put me to sleep, you say? [*Taking it, looking at it*] Little phial—you, at least, do not miss your aim! Do you see what I am doing, Neoptolemus? [*Drinks.*]

NEOPTOLEMUS: What! This is awful, it is—

PHILOCTETES: Go and tell Ulysses. Tell him—he can come.

[*Exit* NEOPTOLEMUS, *terrified, running, shouting.*]

SCENE II

(PHILOCTETES, *then* ULYSSES *and* NEOPTOLEMUS)

PHILOCTETES [*alone*]: And you shall admire me, Ulysses; I want to compel you to admire me. My virtue rises above yours and you feel yourself diminished. Be exalted, my virtue! Be content with your own beauty! Neoptolemus, why did you not take my bow at once? The more you loved me, the more difficult that was for you: you were not devoted enough. Take them. . . . [*Looking about him*] He's gone. . . .

That drink had an awful taste; it turns my stomach to think of it; I wish it would put me to sleep faster. . . . Of all devotions the craziest is to be devoted to others, for then you become their superior. I am devoted, yes, but not to Greece. . . . I regret but one thing, and that is that my devotion serves Greece. . . . Yet, no, I don't even regret it. . . . But don't thank me: I am acting for myself, not for you. —You will admire me, won't you, Ulysses? Won't you admire me, Ulysses? Ulysses! Ulysses! Where are you? You must understand: I am devoted, but not to Greece—to something else, you understand, to something—what? I don't know. Will you understand? Ulysses! You will probably think I am devoted to Greece! Ah, this bow and these arrows will help you to think that! . . . Where can I throw them? The sea! [*He tries to run, but falls overcome by the philter.*] I am too weak. Ah, my head whirls. . . . He is coming. . . .

Virtue! Virtue! Let me find in your bitter name some exaltation. Could it be I have already drained it all? My sustaining pride totters and gives way; my life is leaking out on every side. "Don't leap; don't leap," I told him. Whatever we try beyond our strength, Neoptolemus, that is what we call virtue. Virtue—I don't believe in it any longer, Neoptolemus. Listen to me, Neoptolemus! Neoptolemus, there is no virtue. —Neoptolemus! . . . He can't hear me.

[*Overcome, he falls and sleeps. Enter* ULYSSES *and* NEOPTOLEMUS.]

ULYSSES [*seeing* PHILOCTETES]: And now leave me with him, alone.

[NEOPTOLEMUS *greatly moved, hesitates.*]

Yes! Go anywhere; run and get the boat ready, if you wish.

[*Exit* NEOPTOLEMUS. ULYSSES *approaches* PHILOCTETES, *bends down.*]

Philoctetes! . . . Can't you hear me, Philoctetes?—You will never hear me again?—What can I do? I wanted to tell you—you have convinced me, Philoctetes. I see virtue now; it is so beautiful that in your presence I no longer dare to act. To me, my duty seems crueler than yours, because it seems less dignified. Your bow—I can't, I no longer want to take it: you have given it.—Nepotolemus is a child: let him obey. Ah, here he is! [*In a tone of command*] And now, Neoptolemus, take the bow and the arrows and carry them to the boat.

[NEOPTOLEMUS *approaches* PHILOCTETES *in grief, falls to his knees, kisses his forehead.*]

I order you to do it. Isn't it enough to have betrayed me? Do you wish to betray your country as well? Look how he has devoted himself to his country.

[NEOPTOLEMUS *obediently takes the bow and arrows; exit.*]

And now farewell, harsh Philoctetes. Did you despise me very much? Ah, I should like to know. . . . I should like him to know, I think he is admirable—and that—thanks to him, we shall win.

NEOPTOLEMUS [*calling from a distance*]: Ulysses!

ULYSSES: I'm coming. [*Exit.*]

ACT V

PHILOCTETES *is alone, on a rock. The sun is rising in a perfectly clear sky. Over the sea, in the distance, a boat is moving away.* PHILOCTETES *looks at it, long.*

PHILOCTETES [*murmuring, very calmly*]: They will never come back; they have no more bows to seek. . . . I am happy.

[*His voice has become extraordinarily mild and beautiful; around him flowers are showing through the snow, and birds from heaven come down to feed him.*]

A HUNGER ARTIST

Franz Kafka

DURING these last decades the interest in professional fasting has markedly diminished. It used to pay very well to stage such great performances under one's own management, but today that is quite impossible. We live in a different world now. At one time the whole town took a lively interest in the hunger artist; from day to day of his fast the excitement mounted; everybody wanted to see him at least once a day; there were people who bought season tickets for the last few days and sat from morning till night in front of his small barred cage; even in the night-time there were visiting hours, when the whole effect was heightened by torch flares; on fine days the cage was set out in the open air, and then it was the children's special treat to see the hunger artist; for their elders he was often just a joke that happened to be in fashion, but the children stood open-mouthed, holding each other's hands for greater security, marveling at him as he sat there pallid in black tights, with his ribs sticking out so prominently, not even on a seat but down among straw on the ground, sometimes giving a courteous nod, answering questions with a constrained smile, or perhaps stretching an arm through the bars so that one might feel how thin it was, and then again withdrawing deep into himself, paying no attention to anyone or anything, not even to the all-important striking of the clock that was the only piece of furniture in his cage, but merely staring into vacancy with half-shut eyes, now and then taking a sip from a tiny glass of water to moisten his lips.

Besides casual onlookers there were also relays of permanent watchers selected by the public, usually butchers, strangely enough, and it was their task to watch the hunger artist day and night, three of them at a time, in case he should have some secret recourse to nourishment. This was nothing but a formality, instituted to reassure the masses, for the initiates knew well enough that during his fast the artist would never in any circumstances, not even under forcible compulsion, swallow the smallest morsel of food; the honor of his profession forbade it. Not every watcher, of course, was capable of understanding this, there were often groups of night watchers who were very lax in carrying out their duties and deliberately huddled together in a retired corner to play cards with great absorption, obviously intending to give the hunger artist the chance of a little refreshment, which they supposed he could draw from some private hoard. Nothing annoyed the artist more than such watchers; they made him miserable; they made his fast seem unendurable; sometimes he mastered his feebleness sufficiently to sing during their watch for as long as he could keep going, to show them how unjust their suspicions were. But that was of little use; they only wondered at his cleverness in being able to fill his mouth even while singing. Much more to his taste were the watchers who sat close up to the bars, who were not content with the dim night lighting of the hall but focused him in the full glare of the electric pocket torch given them by the impresario. The harsh light did not trouble him at all. In any case he could never sleep properly, and he could always drowse a little, whatever the light, at any hour, even when the hall was thronged with noisy onlookers. He was quite happy at the prospect of spending a sleepless night with such watchers; he was ready to exchange jokes with them, to tell them stories out of his nomadic life, anything at all to keep them awake and demonstrate to them again that he had no eatables in his cage and that he was fasting as not one of them could fast. But his happiest moment was when the morning came and an enormous breakfast was brought them, at his expense, on which they flung themselves with the keen appetite of healthy men after a weary night of wakefulness. Of course there were people who argued that this breakfast was an unfair attempt to bribe the watchers, but that was going rather too far, and when they were invited to take on a night's vigil without a breakfast, merely for the sake of the cause, they made themselves scarce, although they stuck stubbornly to their suspicions.

Such suspicions, anyhow, were a necessary accompaniment to the profession of fasting. No one could possibly watch the hunger artist continuously, day and night, and so no one could produce first-hand evidence that the fast had really been rigorous and continuous; only the artist himself could know that; he was therefore bound to be the sole completely satisfied spectator of his own fast. Yet for other reasons he was never satisfied; it was not perhaps mere fasting that had brought him to such skeleton thinness that many people had regretfully to keep away from his exhibitions, because the sight of him was too much for them, perhaps it was dissatisfaction with himself that had worn him down. For he alone knew, what no other initiate knew, how easy it was to fast. It was the easiest thing in the world. He made no secret of this, yet people did not believe him; at the best they set him down as modest, most of them, however, thought he was out for publicity or else was some kind of cheat who found it easy to fast because he had discovered a way of making it easy, and then had the impudence to admit the fact, more or less. He had to put up with all that, and in the course of time had got used to it, but his inner dissatisfaction always rankled, and never yet, after any term of fasting—this must be granted to his credit—had he left the cage of his own free will. The longest period of fasting was fixed by his impresario at forty days, beyond that term he was not allowed to go, not even in great cities, and there was good reason for it, too. Experience had proved that for about forty days the interest of the public could be stimulated by a steadily increasing pressure of advertisement, but after that the town began to lose interest, sympathetic support began notably to fall off; there were of course local variations as between one town and another or one country and another, but as a general rule forty days marked the limit. So on the fortieth day the flower-bedecked cage was opened, enthusiastic spectators filled the hall, a military band played, two doctors entered the cage to measure the results of the fast, which were announced through a megaphone, and finally two young ladies appeared, blissful at having been selected for the honor, to help the hunger artist down the few steps leading to a small table on which was spread a carefully chosen invalid repast. And at this very moment the artist always turned stubborn. True, he would entrust his bony arms to the outstretched helping hands of the ladies bending over him, but stand up he would not. Why stop fasting at this particular moment, after forty days of it? He had held out for a long time, an illimitably long time; why stop now, when he was in his best fasting form, or rather, not yet quite in his best fasting form? Why should he be cheated of the fame he would get for fasting longer, for being not only the record hunger artist of all time, which presumably he was already, but for beating his own record by a performance beyond human imagination, since he felt that there were no limits to his capacity for fasting? His public pretended to admire him so much, why should it have so little patience with him; if he could endure fasting longer, why shouldn't the public endure it? Besides, he was tired, he was comfortable sitting in the straw, and now he was supposed to lift himself to his full height and go down to a meal the very thought of which gave him a nausea that only the presence of the ladies kept him from betraying, and even that with an effort. And he looked up into the eyes of the ladies who were apparently so friendly and in reality so cruel, and shook his head, which felt too heavy on its strengthless neck. But then there happened yet again what always happened. The impresario came forward, without a word—for the band made speech impossible—lifted his arms in the air above the artist, as if inviting Heaven to look down upon its creature here in the straw, this suffering martyr, which indeed he was, although in quite another sense; grasped him round the emaciated waist, with exaggerated caution, so that the frail condition he was in might be appreciated; and committed him to the care of the blenching ladies, not without secretly giving him a shaking so that his legs and body tottered and swayed. The artist now submitted completely; his head lolled on his breast as if it had landed there by chance; his body was hollowed out; his legs in a spasm of self-preservation clung close to each other at the knees, yet scraped on the ground as if it were not really solid ground, as if they were only trying to find solid ground; and the whole weight of his body, a featherweight after all, relapsed onto one of the ladies, who, looking round for help and panting a little—this post of honor was not at all what she had expected it to be —first stretched her neck as far as she could to keep her face at least free from contact with the artist, then finding this impossible, and her more fortunate companion not coming to her aid but merely holding extended on her own trembling hand the little bunch of knucklebones that was the artist's, to the great delight of the spectators burst into tears and had to be replaced by an attendant who had long been stationed in readiness. Then came the food, a little of which the impresario managed to get between the artist's lips, while he sat in a kind of half-fainting trance, to the accompaniment of cheerful patter designed to distract the public's attention from the artist's condition; after that, a toast was drunk to the public, supposedly prompted by a whisper from the artist in the impresario's ear; the band confirmed it with a mighty flourish, the spectators melted away, and no one had any cause to be dissatisfied with the proceedings, no one except the hunger artist himself, he only, as always.

So he lived for many years, with small regular intervals of recuperation, in visible glory, honored by the world, yet in spite of that troubled in spirit, and all the more troubled because no one would take his trouble seriously. What comfort could he possibly need? What more could he possibly wish for? And if some good-natured person, feeling sorry for him, tried to console him by pointing out that his melancholy was probably caused by fasting, it could happen, especially when he had been fasting for some time, that he reacted with an outburst of fury and to the general alarm began to shake the bars of his cage like a wild animal. Yet the impresario had a way of punishing these outbreaks which he rather enjoyed putting into operation. He would apologize publicly for the artist's behavior, which was only to be excused, he admitted, because of the irritability caused by fasting; a condition hardly to be understood by well-fed people; then by natural transition he went on to mention the artist's equally incomprehensible boast that he could fast for much longer than he was doing; he praised the high ambition, the good will, the great self-denial undoubtedly implicit in such a statement; and then quite simply countered it by bringing out photographs, which were also on sale to the public, showing the artist on the fortieth day of a fast lying in bed almost dead from exhaustion. This perversion of the truth, familiar to the artist though it was, always unnerved him afresh and proved too much for him. What was a consequence of the premature ending of his fast was here presented as the cause of it! To fight against this lack of understanding, against a whole world of nonunderstanding, was impossible. Time and again in good faith he stood by the bars listening to the impresario, but as soon as the photographs appeared he always let go and sank with a groan back on to his straw, and the reassured public could once more come close and gaze at him.

A few years later when the witnesses of such scenes called them to mind, they often failed to understand themselves at all. For meanwhile the aforementioned change in public interest had set in; it seemed to happen almost overnight; there may have been profound causes for it, but who was going to bother about that; at any rate the pampered hunger artist suddenly found himself deserted one fine day by the amusement seekers, who went streaming past him to other more favored attractions. For the last time the impresario hurried him over half Europe to discover whether the old interest might still survive here and there; all in vain; everywhere, as if by secret agreement, a positive revulsion from professional fasting was in evidence. Of course it could not really have sprung up so suddenly as all that, and many premonitory symptoms which had not been sufficiently remarked or suppressed during the rush and glitter of success now came retrospectively to mind, but it was now too late to take any

countermeasures. Fasting would surely come into fashion again at some future date, yet that was no comfort for those living in the present. What, then, was the hunger artist to do? He had been applauded by thousands in his time and could hardly come down to showing himself in a street booth at village fairs, and as for adopting another profession, he was not only too old for that but too fanatically devoted to fasting. So he took leave of the impresario, his partner in an unparalleled career, and hired himself to a large circus; in order to spare his own feelings he avoided reading the conditions of his contract.

A large circus with its enormous traffic in replacing and recruiting men, animals and apparatus can always find a use for people at any time, even for a hunger artist, provided of course that he does not ask too much, and in this particular case anyhow it was not only the artist who was taken on but his famous and long-known name as well; indeed considering the peculiar nature of his performance, which was not impaired by advancing age, it could not be objected that here was an artist past his prime, no longer at the height of his professional skill, seeking a refuge in some quiet corner of a circus; on the contrary, the hunger artist averred that he could fast as well as ever, which was entirely credible; he even alleged that if he were allowed to fast as he liked, and this was at once promised him without more ado, he could astound the world by establishing a record never yet achieved, a statement which certainly provoked a smile among the other professionals, since it left out of account the change in public opinion, which the hunger artist in his zeal conveniently forgot.

He had not, however, actually lost his sense of the real situation and took it as a matter of course that he and his cage should be stationed, not in the middle of the ring as a main attraction, but outside, near the animal cages, on a site that was after all easily accessible. Large and gaily painted placards made a frame for the cage and announced what was to be seen inside it. When the public came thronging out in the intervals to see the animals, they could hardly avoid passing the hunger artist's cage and stopping there for a moment, perhaps they might even have stayed longer had not those pressing behind them in the narrow gangway, who did not understand why they should be held up on their way towards the excitements of the menagerie, made it impossible for anyone to stand gazing quietly for any length of time. And that was the reason why the hunger artist, who had of course been looking forward to these visiting hours as the main achievement of his life, began instead to shrink from them. At first he could hardly wait for the intervals; it was exhilarating to watch the crowds come streaming his way, until only too soon—not even the most obstinate self-deception, clung to almost consciously, could hold out against the fact— the conviction was borne in upon him that these people, most of them, to judge from their actions, again and again, without exception, were all on their way to the menagerie. And the first sight of him from the distance remained the best. For when they reached his cage he was at once deafened by the storm of shouting and abuse that arose from the two contending factions, which renewed themselves continuously, of those who wanted to stop and stare at him—he soon began to dislike them more than the others— not out of real interest but only out of obstinate self-assertiveness, and those who wanted to go straight on to the animals. When the first great rush was past, the stragglers came along, and these, whom nothing could have prevented from stopping to look at him as long as they had breath, raced past with long strides, hardly even glancing at him, in their haste to get to the menagerie in time. And all too rarely did it happen that he had a stroke of luck, when some father of a family fetched up before him with his children, pointed a finger at the hunger artist and explained at length what the phenomenon meant, telling stories of earlier years when he himself had watched similar but much more thrilling performances, and the children, still rather uncomprehending, since neither inside nor outside school had they been sufficiently prepared for this lesson—what did they care about fasting?—yet showed by the brightness of their intent eyes that new and better times might be coming. Perhaps, said the hunger artist to himself many a time, things would be a little better if his cage were set not quite so near the menagerie. That made it too easy for people to make their choice, to say nothing of what he suffered from the stench of the menagerie, the animals' restlessness by night, the carrying past of raw lumps of flesh for the beasts of prey, the roaring at feeding times, which depressed him continually. But he did not dare to lodge a complaint with the management; after all, he had the animals to thank for the troops of people who passed his cage, among whom there might always be one here and there to take an interest in him, and who could tell where they might seclude him if he called attention to his existence and thereby to the fact that, strictly speaking, he was only an impediment on the way to the menagerie.

A small impediment, to be sure, one that grew steadily less. People grew familiar with the strange idea that they could be expected, in times like these, to take an interest in a hunger artist, and with this familiarity the verdict went out against him. He might fast as much as he could, and he did so; but nothing could save him now, people passed him by. Just try to explain to anyone the art of fasting! Anyone who has no feeling for it cannot be made to understand it. The fine placards grew dirty and illegible, they were torn down; the little notice board telling the number of fast days achieved, which at first was changed carefully every day, had long stayed at the same figure, for after the first few weeks even this small task seemed pointless to the staff; and so the artist simply fasted on and on, as he had once dreamed of doing, and it was no trouble to him, just as he had always foretold, but no one counted the days, no one, not even the artist himself, knew what records he was already breaking, and his heart grew heavy. And when once in a time some leisurely passer-by stopped, made merry over the old figure on the board and spoke of swindling, that was in its way the stupidest lie ever invented by indifference and inborn malice, since it was not the hunger artist who was cheating; he was working honestly, but the world was cheating him of his reward.

Many more days went by, however, and that too came to an end. An overseer's eye fell on the cage one day and he asked the attendants why this perfectly good cage should be left standing there unused with dirty straw inside it; nobody knew, until one man, helped out by the notice board, remembered about the hunger artist. They poked into the straw with sticks and found him in it. "Are you still fasting?" asked the overseer. "When on earth do you mean to stop?" "Forgive me, everybody," whispered the hunger artist; only the overseer, who had his ear to the bars, understood him. "Of course," said the overseer, and tapped his forehead with a finger to let the attendants know what state the man was in, "we forgive you." "I always wanted you to admire my fasting," said the hunger artist. "We do admire it," said the overseer, "but why shouldn't we admire it?" "Because I have to fast, I can't help it," said the hunger artist, lifting his head a little and speaking, with his lips pursed, as if for a kiss, right into the overseer's ear, so that no syllable might be lost, "because I couldn't find the food I liked. If I had found it, believe me, I should have made no fuss and stuffed myself like you or anyone else." These were his last words, but in his dimming eyes remained the firm though no longer proud persuasion that he was still continuing to fast.

"Well, clear this out now!" said the overseer, and they buried the hunger artist, straw and all. Into the cage they put a young panther. Even the most insensitive felt it refreshing to see this wild creature leaping around the cage that had so long been dreary. The panther was all right. The food he liked was brought him without hesitation by the attendants; he seemed not even to miss his freedom; his noble body, furnished almost to the bursting point with all that it needed, seemed to carry freedom around with it too; somewhere in his jaws it seemed to lurk; and the joy of life streamed with such ardent passion from his throat that for the onlookers it was not easy to stand the shock of it. But they braced themselves, crowded round the cage, and did not want ever to move away.

THE DEATH OF IVAN ILYCH

Leo Tolstoy

I

DURING an interval in the Melvinski trial in the large building of the Law Courts the members and public prosecutor met in Ivan Egorobich Shebek's private room, where the conversation turned on the celebrated Krasovski case. Fëdor Vasilievich warmly maintained that it was not subject to their jurisdiction, Ivan Egorovich maintained the contrary, while Peter Ivanovich, not having entered into the discussion at the start, took no part in it but looked through the *Gazette* which had just been handed in.

"Gentlemen," he said, "Ivan Ilych has died!"

"You don't say so!"

"Here, read it yourself," replied Peter Ivanovich, handing Fëdor Vasilievich the paper still damp from the press. Surrounded by a black border were the words: "Praskovya Fëdorovna Golovina, with profound sorrow, informs relatives and friends of the demise of her beloved husband Ivan Ilych Golovin, Member of the Court of Justice, which occurred on February the 4th of this year 1882. The funeral will take place on Friday at one o'clock in the afternoon."

Ivan Ilych had been a colleague of the gentlemen present and was liked by them all. He had been ill for some weeks with an illness said to be incurable. His post had been kept open for him, but there had been conjectures that in case of his death Alexeev might receive his appointment, and that either Vinnikov or Shtabel would succeed Alexeev. So on receiving the news of Ivan Ilych's death the first thought of each of the gentlemen in that private room was of the changes and promotions it might occasion among themselves or their acquaintances.

"I shall be sure to get Shtabel's place or Vinnikov's," thought Fëdor Vasilievich. "I was promised that long ago, and the promotion means an extra eight hundred rubles a year for me besides the allowance."

"Now I must apply for my brother-in-law's transfer from Kaluga," thought Peter Ivanovich. "My wife will be very glad, and then she won't be able to say that I never do anything for her relations."

"I thought he would never leave his bed again," said Peter Ivanovich aloud. "It's very sad."

"But what really was the matter with him?"

"The doctors couldn't say—at least they could, but each of them said something different. When last I saw him I thought he was getting better."

"And I haven't been to see him since the holidays. I always meant to go."

"Had he any property?"

"I think his wife had a little—but something quite trifling."

"We shall have to go to see her, but they live so terribly far away."

"Far away from you, you mean. Everything's far away from your place."

"You see, he never can forgive my living on the other side of the river," said Peter Ivanovich, smiling at Shebek. Then, still talking of the distances between different parts of the city, they returned to the Court.

Besides considerations as to the possible

transfers and promotions likely to result from Ivan Ilych's death, the mere fact of the death of a near acquaintance aroused, as usual, in all who heard of it the complacent feeling that, "it is he who is dead and not I."

Each one thought or felt, "Well, he's dead but I'm alive!" But the more intimate of Ivan Ilych's acquaintances, his so-called friends, could not help thinking also that they would now have to fulfill the very tiresome demands of propriety by attending the funeral service and paying a visit of condolence to the widow.

Fëdor Vasilievich and Peter Ivanovich had been his nearest acquaintances. Peter Ivanovich had studied law with Ivan Ilych and had considered himself to be under obligations to him.

Having told his wife at dinner-time of Ivan Ilych's death, and of his conjecture that it might be possible to get her brother transferred to their circuit, Peter Ivanovich sacrificed his usual nap, put on his evening clothes, and drove to Ivan Ilych's house.

At the entrance stood a carriage and two cabs. Leaning against the wall in the hall downstairs near the cloak-stand was a coffin-lid covered with cloth of gold, ornamented with gold cord and tassels, that had been polished up with metal powder. Two ladies in black were taking off their fur cloaks. Peter Ivanovich recognized one of them as Ivan Ilych's sister, but the other was a stranger to him. His colleague Schwartz was just coming downstairs, but on seeing Peter Ivanovich enter he stopped and winked at him, as if to say: "Ivan Ilych has made a mess of things—not like you and me."

Schwartz's face with his Piccadilly whiskers, and his slim figure in evening dress, had as usual an air of elegant solemnity which contrasted with the playfulness of his character and had a special piquancy here, or so it seemed to Peter Ivanovich.

Peter Ivanovich allowed the ladies to precede him and slowly followed them upstairs. Schwartz did not come down but remained where he was, and Peter Ivanovich understood that he wanted to arrange where they should play bridge that evening. The ladies went upstairs to the widow's room, and Schwartz with seriously compressed lips but a playful look in his eyes, indicated by a twist of his eyebrows the room to the right where the body lay.

Peter Ivanovich, like everyone else on such occasions, entered feeling uncertain what he would have to do. All he knew was that at such times it is always safe to cross oneself. But he was not quite sure whether one should make obeisances while doing so. He therefore adopted a middle course. On entering the room he began crossing himself and made a slight movement resembling a bow. At the same time, as far as the motion of his head and arm allowed, he surveyed the room. Two young men—apparently nephews, one of whom was a high-school pupil—were leaving the room, crossing themselves as they did so. An old woman was standing motionless, and a lady with strangely arched eyebrows was saying something to her in a whisper. A vigorous, resolute Church Reader, in a frock-coat, was reading something in a loud voice with an expression that precluded any contradiction. The butler's assistant, Gerasim, stepping lightly in front of Peter Ivanovich, was strewing something on the floor. Noticing this, Peter Ivanovich was immediately aware of a faint odour of a decomposing body.

The last time he had called on Ivan Ilych, Peter Ivanovich had seen Gerasim in the study. Ivan Ilych had been particularly fond of him and he was performing the duty of a sick-nurse.

Peter Ivanovich continued to make the sign of the cross slightly inclining his head in an intermediate direction between the coffin, the Reader, and the icons on the table in a corner of the room. Afterwards, when it seemed to him that this movement of his arm in crossing himself had gone on too long, he stopped and began to look at the corpse.

The dead man lay, as dead men always lie, in a specially heavy way, his rigid limbs sunk in the soft cushions of the coffin, with the head forever bowed on the pillow. His yellow waxen brow with bald patches over his sunken temples was thrust up in the way peculiar to the dead, the protruding nose seeming to press on the upper lip. He was much changed and had grown even thinner since Peter Ivanovich had last seen him, but, as is always the case with the dead, his face was handsomer and above all more dignified than when he was alive. The expression on the face said that what was necessary had been accomplished, and accomplished rightly. Besides this there was in that expression a reproach and a warning to the living. This warning seemed to Peter Ivanovich out of place, or at least not applicable to him. He felt a certain discomfort and so he hurriedly crossed himself once more and turned and went out of the door—too hurriedly and too regardless of propriety, as he himself was aware.

Schwartz was waiting for him in the adjoining room with legs spread wide apart and both hands toying with his top-hat behind his back. The mere sight of that playful, well-groomed, and elegant figure refreshed Peter Ivanovich. He felt that Schwartz was above all these happenings and would not surrender to any depressing influences. His very look said that this incident of a church service for Ivan Ilych could not be a sufficient reason for infringing the order of the session—in other words, that it would certainly not prevent his unwrapping a new pack of cards and shuffling them that evening while a footman placed four fresh candles on the table: in fact, there was no reason for supposing that this incident would hinder their spending the evening

agreeably. Indeed he said this in a whisper as Peter Ivanovich passed him, proposing that they should meet for a game at Fëdor Vasilievich's. But apparently Peter Ivanovich was not destined to play bridge that evening. Praskovya Fëdorovna (a short, fat woman who despite all efforts to the contrary had continued to broaden steadily from her shoulders downwards and who had the same extraordinarily arched eyebrows as the lady who had been standing by the coffin), dressed all in black, her head covered with lace, came out of her own room with some other ladies, conducted them to the room where the dead body lay, and said: "The service will begin immediately. Please go in."

Schwartz, making an indefinite bow, stood still, evidently neither accepting nor declining this invitation. Praskovya Fëdorovna recognizing Peter Ivanovich, sighed, went close up to him, took his hand, and said: "I know you were a true friend to Ivan Ilych . . ." and looked at him awaiting some suitable response. And Peter Ivanovich knew that, just as it had been the right thing to cross himself in that room, so what he had to do here was to press her hand, sigh, and say, "Believe me . . . " So he did all this and as he did it felt that the desired result had been achieved: that both he and she were touched.

"Come with me. I want to speak to you before it begins," said the widow. "Give me your arm."

Peter Ivanovich gave her his arm and they went to the inner rooms, passing Schwartz who winked at Peter Ivanovich compassionately.

"That does for our bridge! Don't object if we find another player. Perhaps you can cut in when you do escape," said his playful look.

Peter Ivanovich sighed still more deeply and despondently, and Praskovya Fëdorovna pressed his arm gratefully. When they reached the drawing-room, upholstered in pink cretonne and lighted by a dim lamp, they sat down at the table —she on a sofa and Peter Ivanovich on a low pouffe, the springs of which yielded spasmodically under his weight. Praskovya Fëdorovna had been on the point of warning him to take another seat, but felt that such a warning was out of keeping with her present condition and so changed her mind. As he sat down on the pouffe Peter Ivanovich recalled how Ivan Ilych had arranged this room and had consulted him regarding this pink cretonne with green leaves. The whole room was full of furniture and knick-knacks, and on her way to the sofa the lace of the widow's black shawl caught on the carved edge of the table. Peter Ivanovich rose to detach it, and the springs of the pouffe, relieved of his weight, rose also and gave him a push. The widow began detaching her shawl herself, and Peter Ivanovich again sat down, suppressing the rebellious springs of the pouffe under him. But the widow had not quite freed herself and Peter Ivanovich got up again, and again the pouffe rebelled and even creaked. When this was all over she took out a clean cambric handkerchief and began to weep. The episode with the shawl and the struggle with the pouffe had cooled Peter Ivanovich's emotions and he sat there with a sullen look on his face. This awkward situation was interrupted by Sokolov, Ivan Ilych's butler, who came to report that the plot in the cemetery that Praskovya Fëdorovna had chosen would cost two hundred rubles. She stopped weeping and, looking at Peter Ivanovich with the air of a victim, remarked in French that it was very hard for her. Peter Ivanovich made a silent gesture signifying his full conviction that it must indeed be so.

"Please smoke," she said in a magnanimous yet crushed voice, and turned to discuss with Sokolov the price of the plot for the grave.

Peter Ivanovich while lighting his cigarette heard her inquiring very circumstantially into the price of different plots in the cemetery and finally decide which she would take. When that was done she gave instructions about engaging the choir. Sokolov then left the room.

"I look after everything myself," she told Peter Ivanovich, shifting the albums that lay on the table; and noticing that the table was endangered by his cigarette-ash, she immediately passed him an ashtray, saying as she did so: "I consider it an affectation to say that my grief prevents my attending to practical affairs. On the contrary, if anything can—I won't say console me, but—distract me, it is seeing to everything concerning him." She again took out her handkerchief as if preparing to cry, but suddenly, as if mastering her feeling, she shook herself and began to speak calmly. "But there is something I want to talk to you about."

Peter Ivanovich bowed, keeping control of the springs of the pouffe, which immediately began quivering under him.

"He suffered terribly the last few days."

"Did he?" said Peter Ivanovich.

"Oh, terribly! He screamed unceasingly, not for minutes but for hours. For the last three days he screamed incessantly. It was unendurable. I cannot understand how I bore it; you could hear him three rooms off. Oh, what I have suffered!"

"Is it possible that he was conscious all that time?" asked Peter Ivanovich.

"Yes," she whispered. "To the last moment. He took leave of us a quarter of an hour before he died, and asked us to take Volodya away."

The thought of the sufferings of this man he had known so intimately, first as a merry little boy, then as a school-mate, and later as a grown-up colleague, suddenly struck Peter Ivanovich with horror, despite an unpleasant consciousness of his own and this woman's dissimulation. He again saw that brow, and that nose pressing down on the lip, and felt afraid for himself.

"Three days of frightful suffering and

then death! Why, that might suddenly, at any time, happen to me," he thought, and for a moment felt terrified. But—he did not himself know how—the customary reflection at once occurred to him that this had happened to Ivan Ilych and not to him, and that it should not and could not happen to him, and that to think that it could would be yielding to depression which he ought not to do, as Schwartz's expression plainly showed. After which reflection Peter Ivanovich felt reassured, and began to ask with interest about the details of Ivan Ilych's death, as though death was an accident natural to Ivan Ilych but certainly not to himself.

After many details of the really dreadful physical sufferings Ivan Ilych had endured (which details he learnt only from the effect those sufferings had produced on Praskovya Fëdorovna's nerves) the widow apparently found it necessary to get to business.

"Oh, Peter Ivanovich, how hard it is! How terribly, terribly hard!" and she again began to weep.

Peter Ivanovich sighed and waited for her to finish blowing her nose. When she had done so he said, "Believe me . . ." and she again began talking and brought out what was evidently her chief concern with him—namely, to question him as to how she could obtain a grant of money from the government on the occasion of her husband's death. She made it appear that she was asking Peter Ivanovich's advice about her pension, but he soon saw that she already knew about that to the minutest detail, more even than he did himself. She knew how much could be got out of the government in consequence of her husband's death, but wanted to find out whether she could not possibly extract something more. Peter Ivanovich tried to think of some means of doing so, but after reflecting for a while and, out of propriety, condemning the government for its niggardliness, he said he thought that nothing more could be got. Then she sighed and evidently began to devise means of getting rid of her visitor. Noticing this, he put out his cigarette, rose, pressed her hand, and went out into the anteroom.

In the dining-room where the clock stood that Ivan Ilych had liked so much and had bought at an antique shop, Peter Ivanovich met a priest and a few acquaintances who had come to attend the service, and he recognized Ivan Ilych's daughter, a handsome young woman. She was in black and her slim figure appeared slimmer than ever. She had a gloomy, determined, almost angry expression, and bowed to Peter Ivanovich as though he were in some way to blame. Behind her, with the same offended look, stood a wealthy young man, an examining magistrate, whom Peter Ivanovich also knew and who was her fiancé, as he had heard. He bowed mournfully to them and was about to pass into the death-chamber, when from under the stairs appeared the figure of Ivan Ilych's schoolboy son, who was extremely like his father. He seemed a little Ivan Ilych, such as Peter Ivanovich remembered when they studied law together. His tear-stained eyes had in them the look that is seen in the eyes of boys of thirteen or fourteen who are not pure-minded. When he saw Peter Ivanovich he scowled morosely and shamefacedly. Peter Ivanovich nodded to him and entered the death-chamber. The service began: candles, groans, incense, tears, and sobs. Peter Ivanovich stood looking gloomily down at his feet. He did not look once at the dead man, did not yield to any depressing influence, and was one of the first to leave the room. There was no one in the anteroom, but Gerasim darted out of the dead man's room, rummaged with his strong hands among the fur coats to find Peter Ivanovich's and helped him on with it.

"Well, friend Gerasim," said Peter Ivanovich, so as to say something. "It's a sad affair, isn't it?"

"It's God's will. We shall all come to it some day," said Gerasim, displaying his teeth—the even, white teeth of a healthy peasant—and, like a man in the thick of urgent work, he briskly opened the front door, called the coachman, helped Peter Ivanovich into the sledge, and sprang back to the porch as if in readiness for what he had to do next.

Peter Ivanovich found the fresh air particularly pleasant after the smell of incense, the dead body, and carbolic acid.

"Where to, sir?" asked the coachman.

"It's not too late even now. . . . I'll call round on Fëdor Vasilievich.

He accordingly drove there and found them just finishing the first rubber, so that it was quite convenient for him to cut in.

II

Ivan Ilych's life had been most simple and most ordinary and therefore most terrible.

He had been a member of the Court of Justice, and died at the age of forty-five. His father had been an official who after serving in various ministries and departments in Petersburg had made the sort of career which brings men to positions from which by reason of their long service they cannot be dismissed, though they are obviously unfit to hold any responsible position, and for whom therefore posts are specially created, which though fictitious carry salaries of from six to ten thousand rubles that are not fictitious, and in receipt of which they live on to a great age.

Such was the Privy Councillor and superfluous member of various superfluous institutions, Ilya Epimovich Golovin.

He had three sons, of whom Ivan Ilych was the second. The eldest son was following in his father's footsteps only in another department, and was already approaching that stage in the service at which a similar sinecure would be reached. The third son was a failure. He had ruined his prospects in a number of positions and was now serving in the railway department. His father and brothers, and still more their wives, not merely disliked meeting him, but avoided remembering his existence unless compelled to do so. His sister had married Baron Greff, a Petersburg official of her father's type. Ivan Ilych was *le phénix de la famille* as people said. He was neither as cold and formal as his elder brother nor as wild as the younger, but was a happy mean between them—an intelligent, polished, lively and agreeable man. He had studied with his younger brother at the School of Law, but the latter had failed to complete the course and was expelled when he was in the fifth class. Ivan Ilych finished the course well. Even when he was at the School of Law he was just what he remained for the rest of his life: a capable, cheerful, good-natured, and sociable man, though strict in the fulfillment of what he considered to be his duty: and he considered his duty to be what was so considered by those in authority. Neither as a boy nor as a man was he a toady, but from early youth was by nature attracted to people of high station as a fly is drawn to the light, assimilating their ways and views of life and establishing friendly relations with them. All the enthusiasms of childhood and youth passed without leaving much trace on him; he succumbed to sensuality, to vanity, and latterly among the highest classes to liberalism, but always within limits which his instinct unfailingly indicated to him as correct.

At school he had done things which had formerly seemed to him very horrid and made him feel disgusted with himself when he did them; but when later on he saw that such actions were done by people of good position and that they did not regard them as wrong, he was able not exactly to regard them as right, but to forget about them entirely or not be at all troubled at remembering them.

Having graduated from the School of Law and qualified for the tenth rank of the civil service, and having received money from his father for his equipment, Ivan Ilych ordered himself clothes at Scharmer's, the fashionable tailor, hung a medallion inscribed *respice finem* on his watch-chain, took leave of his professor and the prince who was patron of the school, had a farewell dinner with his comrades at Donon's first-class restaurant, and with his new and fashionable portmanteau, linen, clothes, shaving and other toilet appliances, and a travelling rug, all purchased at the best shops, he set off for one of the provinces where, through his father's influence, he had been attached to the Governor as an official for special service.

In the province Ivan Ilych soon arranged as easy and agreeable a position for himself as he had had at the School of Law. He performed his official tasks, made his career, and at the same time amused himself pleasantly and decorously. Occasionally he paid official visits to country districts, where he behaved with dignity both to his superiors and inferiors, and performed the duties entrusted to him, which related chiefly to the sectarians, with an exactness and incorruptible honesty of which he could not but feel proud.

In official matters, despite his youth and taste for frivolous gaiety, he was exceedingly reserved, punctilious, and even severe; but in society he was often amusing and witty, and always good-natured, correct in his manner, and *bon enfant,* as the governor and his wife— with whom he was like one of the family —used to say of him.

In the provinces he had an affair with a lady who made advances to the elegant young lawyer, and there was also a milliner; and there were carousals with aides-de-camp who visited the district, and

after-supper visits to a certain outlying street of doubtful reputation; and there was too some obsequiousness to his chief and even to his chief's wife, but all this was done with such a tone of good breeding that no hard names could be applied to it. It all came under the heading of the French saying: *"Il faut que jeunesse se passe."* It was all done with clean hands, in clean linen, with French phrases, and above all among people of the best society and consequently with the approval of people of rank.

So Ivan Ilych served for five years and then came a change in his official life. The new and reformed judicial institutions were introduced, and new men were needed. Ivan Ilych became such a new man. He was offered the post of Examining Magistrate, and he accepted it though the post was in another province and obliged him to give up the connexions he had formed and to make new ones. His friends met to give him a send-off; they had a group-photograph taken and presented him with a silver cigarette-case, and he set off to his new post.

As examining magistrate Ivan Ilych was just as *comme il faut* and decorous a man, inspiring general respect and capable of separating his official duties from his private life, as he had been when acting as an official on special service. His duties now as examining magistrate were far more interesting and attractive than before. In his former position it had been pleasant to wear an undress uniform made by Scharmer, and to pass through the crowd of petitioners and officials who were timorously awaiting an audience with the governor, and who envied him as with free and easy gait he went straight into his chief's private room to have a cup of tea and a cigarette with him. But not many people had then been directly dependent on him—only police officials and the sectarians when he went on special missions—and he liked to treat them politely, almost as comrades, as if he were letting them feel that he who had the power to crush them was treating them in this simple, friendly way. There were then but few such people. But now, as an examining magistrate, Ivan Ilych felt that everyone without exception, even the most important and self-satisfied, was in his power, and that he need only write a few words on a sheet of paper with a certain heading, and this or that important, self-satisfied person would be brought before him in the role of an accused person or a witness, and if he did not choose to allow him to sit down, would have to stand before him and answer his questions. Ivan Ilych never abused his power; he tried on the contrary to soften its expression, but the consciousness of it and of the possibility of softening its effect, supplied the chief interest and attraction of his office. In his work itself, especially in his examinations, he very soon acquired a method of eliminating all considerations irrelevant to the legal aspect of the case, and reducing even the most complicated case to a form in which it would be presented on paper only in its externals, completely excluding his personal opinion of the matter, while above all observing every prescribed formality. The work was new and Ivan Ilych was one of the first men to apply the new Code of 1864.[1]

On taking up the post of examining magistrate in a new town, he made new acquaintances and connexions, placed himself on a new footing, and assumed a somewhat different tone. He took up an attitude of rather dignified aloofness towards the provincial authorities, but picked out the best circle of legal gentlemen and wealthy gentry living in the town and assumed a tone of slight dissatisfaction with the government, of moderate liberalism, and of enlightened citizenship. At the same time, without at all altering

the elegance of his toilet, he ceased shaving his chin and allowed his beard to grow as it pleased.

Ivan Ilych settled down very pleasantly in this new town. The society there, which inclined towards opposition to the Governor, was friendly, his salary was larger, and he began to play *vint* [a form of bridge], which he found added not a little to the pleasure of life, for he had a capacity for cards, played good-humouredly, and calculated rapidly and astutely, so that he usually won.

After living there for two years he met his future wife, Praskovya Fëdorovna Mikhel, who was the most attractive, clever, and brilliant girl of the set in which he moved, and among other amusements and relaxation from his labours as examining magistrate, Ivan Ilych established light and playful relations with her.

While he had been an official on special service he had been accustomed to dance, but now as an examining magistrate it was exceptional for him to do so. If he danced now, he did it as if to show that though he served under the reformed order of things, and had reached the fifth official rank, yet when it came to dancing he could do it better than most people. So at the end of an evening he sometimes danced with Praskovya Fëdorovna, and it was chiefly during these dances that he captivated her. She fell in love with him. Ivan Ilych had at first no definite intention of marrying, but when the girl fell in love with him he said to himself: "Really, why shouldn't I marry?"

Praskovya Fëdorovna came of a good family, was not bad looking, and had some little property. Ivan Ilych might have aspired to a more brilliant match, but even this was good. He had his salary, and she, he hoped, would have an equal income. She was well connected, and was a sweet, pretty, and thoroughly correct young woman. To say that Ivan Ilych married because he fell in love with Praskovya Fëdorovna and found that she

[1] The emancipation of the serfs in 1861 was followed by a thorough all-round reform of judicial proceedings.—Aylmer Maud [translator].

sympathized with his views of life would be as incorrect as to say that he married because his social circle approved of the match. He was swayed by both these considerations: the marriage gave him personal satisfaction, and at the same time it was considered the right thing by the most highly placed of his associates.

So Ivan Ilych got married.

The preparations for marriage and the beginning of married life, with its conjugal caresses, the new furniture, new crockery, and new linen, were very pleasant until his wife became pregnant—so that Ivan Ilych had begun to think that marriage would not impair the easy, agreeable, gay and always decorous character of his life, approved of by society and regarded by himself as natural, but would even improve it. But from the first months of his wife's pregnancy, something new, unpleasant, depressing, and unseemly, and from which there was no way of escape, unexpectedly showed itself.

His wife, without any reason—*de gaieté de coeur* as Ivan Ilych expressed it to himself—began to disturb the pleasure and propriety of their life. She began to be jealous without any cause, expected him to devote his whole attention to her, found fault with everything, and made coarse and ill-mannered scenes.

At first Ivan Ilych hoped to escape from the unpleasantness of this state of affairs by the same easy and decorous relation to life that had served him heretofore: he tried to ignore his wife's disagreeable moods, continued to live in his usual easy and pleasant way, invited friends to his house for a game of cards, and also tried going out to his club or spending his evenings with friends. But one day his wife began upbraiding him so vigorously, using such coarse words, and continued to abuse him every time he did not fulfil her demands, so resolutely and with such evident determination not to give way till he submitted—that is, till he stayed at home and was bored just as

she was—that he became alarmed. He now realized that matrimony—at any rate with Praskovya Fëdorovna—was not always conducive to the pleasures and amenities of life but on the contrary often infringed both comfort and propriety, and that he must therefore entrench himself against such infringement. And Ivan Ilych began to seek for means of doing so. His official duties were the one thing that imposed upon Praskovya Fëdorovna, and by means of his official work and the duties attached to it he began struggling with his wife to secure his own independence.

With the birth of their child, the attempts to feed it and the various failures in doing so, and with the real and imaginary illnesses of mother and child, in which Ivan Ilych's sympathy was demanded but about which he understood nothing, the need of securing for himself an existence outside his family life became still more imperative.

As his wife grew more irritable and exacting and Ivan Ilych transferred the centre of gravity of his life more and more to his official work, so did he grow to like his work better and became more ambitious than before.

Very soon, within a year of his wedding, Ivan Ilych had realized that marriage, though it may add some comforts to life, is in fact a very intricate and difficult affair towards which in order to perform one's duty, that is, to lead a decorous life approved of by society, one must adopt a definite attitude just as towards one's official duties.

And Ivan Ilych evolved such an attitude towards married life. He only required of it those conveniences—dinner at home, housewife, and bed—which it could give him, and above all that propriety of external forms required by public opinion. For the rest he looked for light-hearted pleasure and propriety, and was very thankful when he found them, but if he met with antagonism and querulousness he at once retired into his separate fenced-off world of official duties, where he found satisfaction.

Ivan Ilych was esteemed a good official, and after three years was made Assistant Public Prosecutor. His new duties, their importance, the possibility of indicting and imprisoning anyone he chose, the publicity his speeches received, and the success he had in all these things, made his work still more attractive.

More children came. His wife became more and more querulous and ill-tempered, but the attitude Ivan Ilych had adopted towards his home life rendered him almost impervious to her grumbling.

After seven years' service in that town he was transferred to another province as Public Prosecutor. They moved, but were short of money and his wife did not like the place they moved to. Though the salary was higher the cost of living was greater, besides which two of their children died and family life became still more unpleasant for him.

Praskovya Fëdorovna blamed her husband for every inconvenience they encountered in their new home. Most of the conversations between husband and wife, especially as to the children's education, led to topics which recalled former disputes, and those disputes were apt to flare up at any moment. There remained only those rare periods of amorousness which still came to them at times but did not last long. These were islets at which they anchored for a while and then again set out upon that ocean of veiled hostility which showed itself in their aloofness from one another. This aloofness might have grieved Ivan Ilych had he considered that it ought not to exist, but he now regarded the position as normal, and even made it the goal at which he aimed in family life. His aim was to free himself more and more from those unpleasantnesses and to give them a semblance of harmlessness and propriety. He attained

this by spending less and less time with his family, and when obliged to be at home he tried to safeguard his position by the presence of outsiders. The chief thing however was that he had his official duties. The whole interest of his life now centred in the official world and that interest absorbed him. The consciousness of his power, being able to ruin anybody he wished to ruin, the importance, even the external dignity of his entry into court, or meetings with his subordinates, his success with superiors and inferiors, and above all his masterly handling of cases, of which he was conscious—all this gave him pleasure and filled his life, together with chats with his colleagues, dinners, and bridge. So that on the whole Ivan Ilych's life continued to flow as he considered it should do—pleasantly and properly.

So things continued for another seven years. His eldest daughter was already sixteen, another child had died, and only one son was left, a schoolboy and a subject of dissension. Ivan Ilych wanted to put him in the School of Law, but to spite him Praskovya Fëdorovna entered him at the High School. The daughter had been educated at home and had turned out well: the boy did not learn badly either.

III

So Ivan Ilych lived for seventeen years after his marriage. He was already a Public Prosecutor of long standing, and had declined several proposed transfers while awaiting a more desirable post, when an unanticipated occurrence quite upset the peaceful course of his life. He was expecting to be offered the post of presiding judge in a University town, but Happe somehow came to the front and obtained the appointment instead. Ivan Ilych became irritable, reproached Happe, and quarrelled both with him and with his immediate superiors—who became colder to him and again passed him over when other appointments were made.

This was in 1880, the hardest year of Ivan Ilych's life. It was then that it became evident on the one hand that his salary was insufficient for them to live on, and on the other that he had been forgotten, and not only this, but that what was for him the greatest and most cruel injustice appeared to others a quite ordinary occurrence. Even his father did not consider it his duty to help him. Ivan Ilych felt himself abandoned by everyone, and that they regarded his position with a salary of 3,500 rubles [about $2,000] as quite normal and even fortunate. He alone knew that with the consciousness of the injustices done him, with his wife's incessant nagging, and with the debts he had contracted by living beyond his means, his position was far from normal.

In order to save money that summer he obtained leave of absence and went with his wife to live in the country at her brother's place.

In the country, without his work, he experienced *ennui* for the first time in his life, and not only *ennui* but intolerable depression, and he decided that it was impossible to go on living like that, and that it was necessary to take energetic measures.

Having passed a sleepless night pacing up and down the veranda, he decided to go to Petersburg and bestir himself, in order to punish those who had failed to appreciate him and to get transferred to another ministry.

Next day, despite many protests from his wife and her brother, he started for Petersburg with the sole object of obtaining a post with a salary of five thousand rubles a year. He was no longer bent on any particular department, or tendency, or kind of activity. All he now wanted was an appointment to another post with a salary of five thousand rubles, either in the administration, in the banks,

with the railways, in one of the Empress Marya's Institutions, or even in the customs—but it had to carry with it a salary of five thousand rubles and be in a ministry other than that in which they had failed to appreciate him.

And this quest of Ivan Ilych's was crowned with remarkable and unexpected success. At Kursk an acquaintance of his, F. I. Ilyin, got into the first-class carriage, sat down beside Ivan Ilych, and told him of a telegram just received by the Governor of Kursk announcing that a change was about to take place in the ministry: Peter Ivanovich was to be superseded by Ivan Semënovich.

The proposed change, apart from its significance for Russia, had a special significance for Ivan Ilych, because by bringing forward a new man, Peter Petrovich, and consequently his friend Zachar Ivanovich, it was highly favourable for Ivan Ilych, since Zachar Ivanovich was a friend and colleague of his.

In Moscow this news was confirmed, and on reaching Petersburg Ivan Ilych found Zachar Ivanovich and received a definite promise of an appointment in his former Department of Justice.

A week later he telegraphed to his wife: "Zachar in Miller's place. I shall receive appointment on presentation of report."

Thanks to this change of personnel, Ivan Ilych had unexpectedly obtained an appointment in his former ministry which placed him two stages above his former colleagues besides giving him five thousand rubles salary and three thousand five hundred rubles for expenses connected with his removal. All his ill humour towards his former enemies and the whole department vanished, and Ivan Ilych was completely happy.

He returned to the country more cheerful and contented than he had been for a long time. Praskovya Fëdorovna also cheered up and a truce was arranged between them. Ivan Ilych told of how he had been fêted by everybody in Petersburg, how all those who had been his enemies were put to shame and now fawned on him, how envious they were of his oppointment, and how much everybody in Petersburg had liked him.

Praskovya Fëdorovna listened to all this and appeared to believe it. She did not contradict anything, but only made plans for their life in the town to which they were going. Ivan Ilych saw with delight that these plans were his plans, that he and his wife agreed, and that, after a stumble, his life was regaining its due and natural character of pleasant lightheartedness and decorum.

Ivan Ilych had come back for a short time only, for he had to take up his new duties on the 10th of September. Moreover, he needed time to settle into the new place, to move all his belongings from the province, and to buy and order many additional things: in a word, to make such arrangements as he had resolved on, which were almost exactly what Praskovya Fëdorovna too had decided on.

Now that everything had happened so fortunately, and that he and his wife were at one in their aims and moreover saw so little of one another, they got on together better than they had done since the first years of marriage. Ivan Ilych had thought of taking his family away with him at once, but the insistence of his wife's brother and her sister-in-law, who had suddenly become particularly amiable and friendly to him and his family, induced him to depart alone.

So he departed, and the cheerful state of mind induced by his success and by the harmony between his wife and himself, the one intensifying the other, did not leave him. He found a delightful house, just the thing both he and his wife had dreamt of. Spacious, lofty reception rooms in the old style, a convenient and dignified study, rooms for his wife and daughter, a study for his son—it might have been specially built for them. Ivan

Ilych himself superintended the arrangements, chose the wall-papers, supplemented the furniture (preferably with antiques which he considered particularly *comme il faut*), and supervised the upholstering. Everything progressed and progressed and approached the ideal he had set himself: even when things were only half completed they exceeded his expectations. He saw what a refined and elegant character, free from vulgarity, it would all have when it was ready. On falling asleep he pictured to himself how the reception-room would look. Looking at the yet unfinished drawing-room he could see the fireplace, the screen, the what-not, the little chairs dotted here and there, the dishes and plates on the walls, and the bronzes, as they would be when everything was in place. He was pleased by the thought of how his wife and daughter, who shared his taste in this matter, would be impressed by it. They were certainly not expecting as much. He had been particularly successful in finding, and buying cheaply, antiques which gave a particularly aristocratic character to the whole place. But in his letters he intentionally understated everything in order to be able to surprise them. All this so absorbed him that his new duties—though he liked his official work—interested him less than he had expected. Sometimes he even had moments of absent-mindedness during the Court Sessions, and would consider whether he should have straight or curved cornices for his curtains. He was so interested in it all that he often did things himself, rearranging the furniture, or rehanging the curtains. Once when mounting a stepladder to show the upholsterer, who did not understand, how he wanted the hangings draped, he made a false step and slipped, but being a strong and agile man he clung on and only knocked his side against the knob of the window frame. The bruised place was painful but the pain soon passed, and he felt particularly bright and well just then. He wrote: "I feel fifteen years younger." He thought he would have everything ready by September, but it dragged on till mid-October. But the result was charming not only in his eyes but to everyone who saw it.

In reality it was just what is usually seen in the houses of people of moderate means who want to appear rich, and therefore succeed only in resembling others like themselves: there were damasks, dark wood, plants, rugs, and dull and polished bronzes—all the things people of a certain class have in order to resemble other people of that class. His house was so like the others that it would never have been noticed, but to him it all seemed to be quite exceptional. He was very happy when he met his family at the station and brought them to the newly furnished house all lit up, where a footman in a white tie opened the the door into the hall decorated with plants, and when they went on into the drawing-room and the study uttering exclamations of delight. He conducted them everywhere, drank in their praises eagerly, and beamed with pleasure. At tea that evening, when Praskovya Fëdorovna among other things asked him about his fall, he laughed, and showed them how he had gone flying and had frightened the upholsterer.

"It's a good thing I'm a bit of an athlete. Another man might have been killed, but I merely knocked myself, just here; it hurts when it's touched, but it's passing off already—it's only a bruise."

So they began living in their new home —in which, as always happens, when they got thoroughly settled in they found they were just one room short—and with the increased income, which as always was just a little (some five hundred rubles) too little, but it was all very nice.

Things went particularly well at first, before everything was finally arranged and while something had still to be done: this thing bought, that thing ordered, another thing moved, and something else adjusted. Though there were some disputes between husband and wife, they were both so well satisfied and had so much to do that it all passed off without any serious quarrels. When nothing was left to arrange it became rather dull and something seemed to be lacking, but they were then making acquaintances, forming habits, and life was growing fuller.

Ivan Ilych spent his mornings at the law court and came home to dinner, and at first he was generally in a good humour, though he occasionally became irritable just on account of his house. (Every spot on the tablecloth or the upholstery, and every broken window-blind string, irritated him. He had devoted so much trouble to arranging it all that every disturbance of it distressed him.) But on the whole his life ran its course as he believed life should do: easily, pleasantly, and decorously.

He got up at nine, drank his coffee, read the paper, and then put on his undress uniform and went to the law courts. There the harness in which he worked had already been stretched to fit him and he donned it without a hitch: petitioners, inquiries at the chancery, the chancery itself, and the sittings public and administrative. In all this the thing was to exclude everything fresh and vital, which always disturbs the regular course of official business, and to admit only official relations with people, and then only on official grounds. A man would come, for instance, wanting some information. Ivan Ilych, as one in whose sphere the matter did not lie, would have nothing to do with him: but if the man had some business with him in his official capacity, something that could be expressed on officially stamped paper, he would do everything, positively everything he could within the limits of such relations, and in doing so would maintain the semblance of friendly human relations, that is, would observe the courtesies of life. As soon as the official relations ended, so did everything else. Ivan Ilych possessed this capacity to separate his real life from the official side of affairs and not mix the two, in the highest degree, and by long practice and natural aptitude had brought it to such a pitch that sometimes, in the manner of a virtuoso, he would even allow himself to let the human and official relations mingle. He let himself do this just because he felt that he could at any time he chose resume the strictly official attitude again and drop the human relation. And he did it all easily, pleasantly, correctly, and even artistically. In the intervals between the sessions he smoked, drank tea, chatted a little about politics, a little about general topics, a little about cards, but most of all about official appointments. Tired, but with the feelings of a virtuoso—one of the first violins who has played his part in an orchestra with precision—he would return home to find that his wife and daughter had been out paying calls, or had a visitor, and that his son had been to school, had done his homework with his tutor, and was duly learning what is taught at High Schools. Everything was as it should be. After dinner, if they had no visitors, Ivan Ilych sometimes read a book that was being much discussed at the time, and in the evening settled down to work, that is, read official papers, compared the depositions of witnesses, and noted paragraphs of the Code applying to them. This was neither dull nor amusing. It was dull when he might have been playing bridge, but if no bridge was available it was at any rate better than doing nothing or sitting with his wife. Ivan Ilych's chief pleasure was giving little dinners to which he invited men and women of good social position, and just as his drawing-room resembled all other drawing-rooms so did his enjoyable little parties resemble all other such parties.

Once they even gave a dance. Ivan Ilych enjoyed it and everything went off well, except that it led to a violent quarrel with his wife about the cakes and sweets. Praskovya Fëdorovna had made her own plans, but Ivan Ilych insisted on getting everything from an expensive confectioner and ordered too many cakes, and the quarrel occurred because some of those cakes were left over and the confectioner's bill came to forty-five rubles. It was a great and disagreeable quarrel. Praskovya Fëdorovna called him "a fool and an imbecile," and he clutched at his head and made angry allusions to divorce.

But the dance itself had been enjoyable. The best people were there, and Ivan Ilych had danced with Princess Trufonova, a sister of the distinguished founder of the Society "Bear by Burden."

The pleasures connected with his work were pleasures of ambition; his social pleasures were those of vanity; but Ivan Ilych's greatest pleasure was playing bridge. He acknowledged that whatever disagreeable incident happened in his life, the pleasure that beamed like a ray of light above everything else was to sit down to bridge with good players, not noisy partners, and of course to four-handed bridge (with five players it was annoying to have to stand out, though one pretended not to mind), to play a clever and serious game (when the cards allowed it) and then to have supper and drink a glass of wine. After a game of bridge, especially if he had won a little (to win a large sum was unpleasant), Ivan Ilych went to bed in specially good humour.

So they lived. They formed a circle of acquaintances among the best people and were visited by people of importance and by young folk. In their views as to their acquaintances, husband, wife and daughter were entirely agreed, and tacitly and unanimously kept at arm's length and shook off the various shabby friends and relations who, with much show of affection, gushed into the drawing-room with its Japanese plates on the walls. Soon these shabby friends ceased to obtrude themselves and only the best people remained in the Golovins' set.

Young men made up to Lisa, and Petrishchev, an examining magistrate and Dmitri Ivanovich Petrishchev's son and sole heir, began to be so attentive to her that Ivan Ilych had already spoken to Praskovya Fëdorovna about it, and considered whether they should not arrange a party for them, or get up some private theatricals.

So they lived, and all went well, without change, and life flowed pleasantly.

IV

They were all in good health. It could not be called ill health if Ivan Ilych sometimes said that he had a queer taste in his mouth and felt some discomfort in his left side.

But this discomfort increased and, though not exactly painful, grew into a sense of pressure in his side accompanied by ill humour. And his irritability became worse and worse and began to mar the agreeable, easy, and correct life that had established itself in the Golovin family. Quarrels between husband and wife became more and more frequent, and soon the ease and amenity disappeared and even the decorum was rarely maintained. Scenes again became frequent, and very few of those islets remained on which husband and wife could meet without an explosion. Praskovya Fëdorovna now had good reason to say that her husband's temper was trying. With characteristic exaggeration she said he had always had a dreadful temper, and that it had needed all her good nature to put up with it for twenty years. It was true that now the quarrels were started by him. His bursts of temper always came just before dinner, often just as he began to eat his soup. Sometimes he noticed that a plate or dish was chipped, or the food was not right, or his son put his elbow on the table, or his daughter's hair was not done

as he liked it, and for all this he blamed Praskovya Fëdorovna. At first she retorted and said disagreeable things to him, but once or twice he fell into such a rage at the beginning of dinner that she realized it was due to some physical derangement brought on by taking food, and so she restrained herself and did not answer, but only hurried to get the dinner over. She regarded this self-restraint as highly praiseworthy. Having come to the conclusion that her husband had a dreadful temper and made her life miserable, she began to feel sorry for herself, and the more she pitied herself the more she hated her husband. She began to wish he would die; yet she did not want him to die because then his salary would cease. And this irritated her against him still more. She considered herself dreadfully unhappy just because not even his death could save her, and though she concealed her exasperation, that hidden exasperation of hers increased his irritation also.

After one scene in which Ivan Ilych had been particularly unfair and after which he had said in explanation that he certainly was irritable but that it was due to his not being well, she said that if he was ill it should be attended to, and insisted on his going to see a celebrated doctor.

He went. Everything took place as he had expected and as it always does. There was the usual waiting and the important air assumed by the doctor, with which he was so familiar (resembling that which he himself assumed in court), and the sounding and listening, and the questions which called for answers that were foregone conclusions and were evidently unnecessary, and the look of importance which implied that "if only you put yourself in our hands we will arrange everything—we know indubitably how it has to be done, always in the same way for everybody alike." It was all just as it was in the law courts. The doctor put on just the same air towards him as he himself put on to-wards an accused person.

The doctor said that so-and-so indicated that there was so-and-so inside the patient, but if the investigation of so-and-so did not confirm this, then he must assume that and that. If he assumed that and that, then . . . and so on. To Ivan Ilych only one question was important: was his case serious or not? But the doctor ignored that inappropriate question. From his point of view it was not the one under consideration, the real question was to decide between a floating kidney, chronic catarrh, or appendicitis. It was not a question of Ivan Ilych's life or death, but one between a floating kidney and appendicitis. And that question the doctor solved brilliantly, as it seemed to Ivan Ilych, in favour of the appendix, with the reservation that should an examination of the urine give fresh indications the matter would be reconsidered. All this was just what Ivan Ilych had himself brilliantly accomplished a thousand times in dealing with men on trial. The doctor summed up just as brilliantly, looking over his spectacles triumphantly and even gaily at the accused. From the doctor's summing up Ivan Ilych concluded that things were bad, but that for the doctor, and perhaps for everybody else, it was a matter of indifference, though for him it was bad. And this conclusion struck him painfully, arousing in him a great feeling of pity for himself and of bitterness towards the doctor's indifference to a matter of such importance.

He said nothing of this, but rose, placed the doctor's fee on the table, and remarked with a sigh: "We sick people probably often put inappropriate questions. But tell me, in general, is this complaint dangerous, or not? . . ."

The doctor looked at him sternly over his spectacles with one eye, as if to say: "Prisoner, if you will not keep to the questions put to you, I shall be obliged to have you removed from the court."

"I have already told you what I consider necessary and proper. The analysis may show something more." And the doctor bowed.

Ivan Ilych went out slowly, seated himself disconsolately in his sledge, and drove home. All the way home he was going over what the doctor had said, trying to translate those complicated, obscure, scientific phrases into plain language and find in them an answer to the question: "Is my condition bad? Is it very bad? Or is there as yet nothing much wrong?" and it seemed to him that the meaning of what the doctor had said was that it was very bad. Everything in the streets seemed depressing. The cabmen, the houses, the passers-by, and the shops, were dismal. His ache, this dull gnawing ache that never ceased for a moment, seemed to have acquired a new and more serious significance from the doctor's dubious remarks. Ivan Ilych now watched it with a new and oppressive feeling.

He reached home and began to tell his wife about it. She listened, but in the middle of his account his daughter came in with her hat on, ready to go out with her mother. She sat down reluctantly to listen to this tedious story, but could not stand it long, and her mother too did not hear him to the end.

"Well, I am very glad," she said. "Mind now to take your medicine regularly. Give me the prescription and I'll send Gerasim to the chemist's." And she went to get ready to go out.

While she was in the room Ivan Ilych had hardly taken time to breathe, but he sighed deeply when she left it.

"Well," he thought, "perhaps it isn't so bad after all."

He began taking his medicine and following the doctor's directions, which had been altered after the examination of the urine. But then it happened that there was a contradiction between the indications drawn from the examination of the urine and the symptoms that showed themselves. It turned out that what was happening differed from what the doctor had told him, and that he had either forgotten, or blundered, or hidden something from him. He could not, however, be blamed for that, and Ivan Ilych still obeyed his orders implicitly and at first derived some comfort from doing so.

From the time of his visit to the doctor, Ivan Ilych's chief occupation was the exact fulfilment of the doctor's instructions regarding hygiene and the taking of medicine, and the observation of his pain and his excretions. His chief interest came to be people's ailments and people's health. When sickness, deaths, or recoveries, were mentioned in his presence, especially when the illness resembled his own, he listened with agitation which he tried to hide, asked questions, and applied what he heard to his own case.

The pain did not grow less, but Ivan Ilych made efforts to force himself to think that he was better. And he could do this so long as nothing agitated him. But as soon as he had any unpleasantness with his wife, any lack of success in his official work, or held bad cards at bridge, he was at once acutely sensible of his disease. He had formerly borne such mischances, hoping soon to adjust what was wrong, to master it and attain success, or make a grand slam. But now every mischance upset him and plunged him into despair. He would say to himself: "There now, just as I was beginning to get better and the medicine had begun to take effect, comes this accursed misfortune, or unpleasantness. . . ." And he was furious with the mishap, or with the people who were causing the unpleasantness and killing him, for he felt that his fury was killing him but could not restrain it. One would have thought that it should have been clear to him that this exasperation with circumstances and people aggravated his illness, and that he ought therefore to ignore unpleasant occurrences. But he drew the very opposite

conclusion: he said that he needed peace, and he watched for everything that might disturb it and became irritable at the slightest infringement of it. His condition was rendered worse by the fact that he read medical books and consulted doctors. The progress of his disease was so gradual that he could deceive himself when comparing one day with another— the difference was so slight. But when he consulted the doctors it seemed to him that he was getting worse, and even very rapidly. Yet despite this he was continually consulting them.

That month he want to see another celebrity, who told him almost the same as the first had done but put his questions rather differently, and the interview with this celebrity only increased Ivan Ilych's doubts and fears. A friend of a friend of his, a very good doctor, diagnosed his illness again quite differently from the others, and though he predicted recovery, his questions and suppositions bewildered Ivan Ilych still more and increased his doubts. A homeopathist diagnosed the disease in yet another way, and prescribed medicine which Ivan Ilych took secretly for a week. But after a week, not feeling any improvement and having lost confidence both in the former doctor's treatment and in this one's, he became still more despondent. One day a lady acquaintance mentioned a cure effected by a wonder-working icon. Ivan Ilych caught himself listening attentively and beginning to believe that it had occurred. This incident alarmed him. "Has my mind really weakened to such an extent?" he asked himself. "Nonsense! It's all rubbish. I mustn't give way to nervous fears but having chosen a doctor must keep strictly to his treatment. That is what I will do. Now it's all settled. I won't think about it, but will follow the treatment seriously till summer, and then we shall see. From now there must be no more of this wavering!" This was easy to say but impossible to carry out. The pain

in his side oppressed him and seemed to
grow worse and more incessant, while the
taste in his mouth grew stranger and
stranger. It seemed to him that his breath
had a disgusting smell, and he was conscious of a loss of appetite and strength.
There was no deceiving himself: something terrible, new, and more important
than anything before in his life, was taking place within him of which he alone
was aware. Those about him did not
understand or would not understand it,
but thought everything in the world was
going on as usual. That tormented Ivan
Ilych more than anything. He saw that his
household, especially his wife and daughter who were in a perfect whirl of visiting,
did not understand anything of it and
were annoyed that he was so depressed
and so exacting, as if he were to blame
for it. Though they tried to disguise it he
saw that he was an obstacle in their path,
and that his wife had adopted a definite
line in regard to his illness and kept to it
regardless of anything he said or did. Her
attitude was this: "You know," she would
say to her friends, "Ivan Ilych can't do as
other people do, and keep to the treatment prescribed for him. One day he'll
take his drops and keep strictly to his
diet and go to bed in good time, but the
next day unless I watch him he'll suddenly forget his medicine, eat sturgeon—
which is forbidden—and sit up playing
cards till one o'clock in the morning."

"Oh, come, when was that?" Ivan Ilych
would ask in vexation. "Only once at
Peter Ivanovich's."

"And yesterday with Shebek."

"Well, even if I hadn't stayed up, this
pain would have kept me awake."

"Be that as it may you'll never get well
like that, but will always make us
wretched."

Praskovya Fëdorovna's attitude to Ivan
Ilych's illness, as she expressed it both to
others and to him, was that it was his
own fault and was another of the an-
noyances he caused her. Ivan Ilych felt

that this opinion escaped her involuntarily
—but that did not make it easier for
him.

At the law courts too, Ivan Ilych
noticed, or thought he noticed, a strange
attitude towards himself. It sometimes
seemed to him that people were watching
him inquisitively as a man whose place
might soon be vacant. Then again, his
friends would suddenly begin to chaff
him in a friendly way about his low
spirits, as if the awful, horrible, and unheard-of thing that was going on within
him, incessantly gnawing at him and irresistibly drawing him away, was a very
agreeable subject for jests. Schwartz in
particular irritated him by his jocularity,
vivacity, and *savoir-faire,* which reminded
him of what he himself had been ten years
ago.

Friends came to make up a set and
they sat down to cards. They dealt, bending the new cards to soften them, and he
sorted the diamonds in his hand and
found he had seven. His partner said
"No trumps" and supported him with two
diamonds. What more could be wished
for? It ought to be jolly and lively. They
would make a grand slam. But suddenly
Ivan Ilych was conscious of that gnawing
pain, that taste in his mouth, and it
seemed ridiculous that in such circumstances he should be pleased to make a
grand slam.

He looked at his partner Mikhail
Mikhaylovich, who rapped the table with
his strong hand and instead of snatching up the tricks pushed the cards
courteously and indulgently towards Ivan
Ilych that he might have the pleasure of
gathering them up without the trouble of
stretching out his hand for them. "Does
he think I am too weak to stretch out my
arm?" thought Ivan Ilych, and forgetting
what he was doing he over-trumped his
partner, missing the grand slam by three
tricks. And what was most awful of all
was that he saw how upset Mikhail
Mikhaylovich was about it but did not

himself care. And it was dreadful to realize why he did not care.

They all saw that he was suffering, and said: "We can stop if you are tired. Take a rest." Lie down? No, he was not at all tired, and he finished the rubber. All were gloomy and silent. Ivan Ilych felt that he had diffused this gloom over them and could not dispel it. They had supper and went away, and Ivan Ilych was left alone with the consciousness that his life was poisoned and was poisoning the lives of others, and that this poison did not weaken but penetrated more and more deeply into his whole being.

With this consciousness, and with physical pain besides the terror, he must go to bed, often to lie awake the greater part of the night. Next morning he had to get up again, dress, go to the law courts, speak, and write; or if he did not go out, spend at home those twenty-four hours a day each of which was a torture. And he had to live thus all alone on the brink of an abyss, with no one who understood or pitied him.

V

So one month passed and then another. Just before the New Year his brother-in-law came to town and stayed at their house. Ivan Ilych was at the law courts and Praskovya Fëdorovna had gone shopping. When Ivan Ilych came home and entered his study he found his brother-in-law there—a healthy, florid man—unpacking his portmanteau himself. He raised his head on hearing Ivan Ilych's footsteps and looked up at him for a moment without a word. That stare told Ivan Ilych everything. His brother-in-law opened his mouth to utter an exclamation of surprise but checked himself, and that action confirmed it all.

"I have changed, eh?"

"Yes, there is a change."

And after that, try as he would to get his brother-in-law to return to the subject of his looks, the latter would say nothing about it. Praskovya Fëdorovna came home and her brother went out to her. Ivan Ilych locked the door and began to examine himself in the glass, first full face, then in profile. He took up a portrait of himself taken with his wife, and compared it with what he saw in the glass. The change in him was immense. Then he bared his arms to the elbow, looked at them, drew the sleeves down again, sat down on an ottoman, and grew blacker than night.

"No, no, this won't do!" he said to himself, and jumped up, went to the table, took up some law papers and began to read them, but could not continue. He unlocked the door and went into the reception-room. The door leading to the drawing-room was shut. He approached it on tiptoe and listened.

"No, you are exaggerating!" Praskovya Fëdorovna was saying.

"Exaggerating! Don't you see it? Why, he's a dead man! Look at his eyes—there's no light in them. But what is it that is wrong with him?"

"No one knows. Nikolaevich [that was another doctor] said something, but I don't know what. And Leshchetitsky [this was the celebrated specialist] said quite the contrary. . . ."

Ivan Ilych walked away, went to his own room, lay down, and began musing: "The kidney, a floating kidney." He recalled all the doctors had told him of how it detached itself and swayed about. And by an effort of imagination he tried to catch that kidney and arrest it and support it. So little was needed for this, it seemed to him. "No, I'll go to see Peter Ivanovich again." [That was the friend whose friend was a doctor.] He rang, ordered the carriage, and got ready to go.

"Where are you going, Jean?" asked his wife, with a specially sad and exceptionally kind look.

This exceptionally kind look irritated him. He looked morosely at her.

"I must go to see Peter Ivanovich."

He went to see Peter Ivanovich, and together they went to see his friend, the doctor. He was in, and Ivan Ilych had a long talk with him.

Reviewing the anatomical and physiological details of what in the doctor's opinion was going on inside him, he understood it all.

There was something, a small thing, in the vermiform appendix. It might all come right. Only stimulate the energy of one organ and check the activity of another, then absorption would take place and everything would come right. He got home rather later for dinner, ate his dinner, and conversed cheerfully, but could not for a long time bring himself to go back to work in his room. At last, however, he went to his study and did what was necessary, but the consciousness that he had put something aside— an important, intimate matter which he would revert to when his work was done —never left him. When he had finished his work he remembered that this intimate matter was the thought of his vermiform appendix. But he did not give himself up to it, and went to the drawing-room for tea. There were callers there, including the examining magistrate who was a desirable match for his daughter, and they were conversing, playing the piano and singing. Ivan Ilych, as Praskovya Fëdorovna remarked, spent that evening more cheerfully than usual, but he never for a moment forgot that he had postponed the important matter of the appendix. At eleven o'clock he said good-night and went to his bedroom. Since his illness he had slept alone in a small room next to his study. He undressed and took up a novel by Zola, but instead of reading it he fell into thought, and in his imagination that desired improvement in the vermiform appendix occurred. There was the absorption and evacuation and the reestablishment of normal activity. "Yes, that's it," he said to himself. "One need

only assist nature, that's all." He remembered his medicine, rose, took it, and lay down on his back watching for the beneficent action of the medicine and for it to lessen the pain. "I need only take it regularly and avoid all injurious influences. I am already feeling better, much better." He began touching his side: it was not painful to the touch. "There, I really don't feel it. It's much better already." He put out the light and turned on his side . . . "The appendix is getting better, absorption is occurring." Suddenly he felt the old, familiar, dull, gnawing pain, stubborn and serious. There was the same familiar loathsome taste in his mouth. His heart sank and he felt dazed. "My God! My God!" he muttered. "Again, again! And it will never cease." And suddenly the matter presented itself in a quite different aspect. "Vermiform appendix! Kidney!" he said to himself. "It's not a question of appendix or kidney, but of life . . . and death. Yes, life was there and now it is going, going and I cannot stop it. Yes. Why deceive myself? Isn't it obvious to everyone but me that I'm dying, and that it's only a question of weeks, days . . . It may happen this moment. There was light and now there is darkness. I was here and now I'm going there! Where?" A chill came over him, his breathing ceased, and he felt only the throbbing of his heart.

"When I am not, what will there be? There will be nothing. Then where shall I be when I am no more? Can this be dying? No, I don't want to!" He jumped up and tried to light the candle, felt for it with trembling hands, dropped candle and candlestick on the floor, and fell back on his pillow.

"What's the use? It makes no difference," he said to himself, staring with wide-open eyes into the darkness. "Death. Yes, death. And none of them know or wish to know it, and they have no pity for me. Now they are playing." (He heard through the door the distant sound of a song and its accompaniment.) "It's all the same to them, but they will die too! Fools! I first, and they later, but it will be the same for them. And now they are merry . . . the beasts!"

Anger choked him and he was agonizingly, unbearably miserable. "It is impossible that all men have been doomed to suffer this awful horror!" He raised himself.

"Something must be wrong. I must calm myself—must think it all over from the beginning." And he again began thinking. "Yes, the beginning of my illness: I knocked my side, but I was still quite well that day and the next. It hurt a little, then rather more. I saw the doctors, then followed despondency and anguish, more doctors, and I drew nearer to the abyss. My strength grew less and I kept coming nearer and nearer, and now I have wasted away and there is no light in my eyes. I think of the appendix—but this is death! I think of mending the appendix, and all the while here is death! Can it really be death?" Again terror seized him and he gasped for breath. He leant down and began feeling for the matches, pressing with his elbow on the stand beside the bed. It was in his way and hurt him, he grew furious with it, pressed on it still harder, and upset it. Breathless and in despair he fell on his back, expecting death to come immediately.

Meanwhile the visitors were leaving. Praskovya Fëdorovna was seeing them off. She heard something fall and came in.

"What has happened?"

"Nothing. I knocked it over accidentally."

She went out and returned with a candle. He lay there panting heavily, like a man who has run a thousand yards, and stared upwards at her with a fixed look.

"What is it, Jean?"

"No . . . o . . . thing. I upset it." ("Why speak of it? She won't understand," he thought.)

And in truth she did not understand.

She picked up the stand, lit his candle, and hurried away to see another visitor off. When she came back he still lay on his back, looking upwards.

"What is it? Do you feel worse?"

"Yes."

She shook her head and sat down.

"Do you know, Jean, I think we must ask Leshchetitsky to come and see you here."

This meant calling in the famous specialist, regardless of expense. He smiled malignantly and said "No." She remained a little longer and then went up to him and kissed his forehead.

While she was kissing him he hated her from the bottom of his soul and with difficulty refrained from pushing her away.

"Good-night. Please God you'll sleep."

"Yes."

VI

Ivan Ilych saw that he was dying, and he was in continual despair.

In the depth of his heart he knew he was dying, but not only was he not accustomed to the thought, he simply did not and could not grasp it.

The syllogism he had learnt from Kiezewetter's Logic: "Caius is a man, men are mortal, therefore Caius is mortal," had always seemed to him correct as applied to Cauis, but certainly not as applied to himself. That Caius—man in the abstract—was mortal, was perfectly correct, but he was not Caius, not an abstract man, but a creature quite, quite separate from all others. He had been little Vanya, with a mamma and a papa, with Mitya and Volodya, with the toys, a coachman and a nurse, afterwards with Katenka and with all the joys, griefs, and delights of childhood, boyhood, and youth. What did Caius know of the smell of that striped leather ball Vanya had been so fond of? Had Caius kissed his mother's hand like that, and did the silk of her dress rustle so for Caius? Had he rioted like that at school when the pastry was bad? Had Caius been in love like that? Could Caius preside at a session as he did? "Caius really was mortal, and it was right for him to die; but for me, little Vanya, Ivan Ilych, with all my thoughts and emotions, it's altogether a different matter. It cannot be that I ought to die. That would be too terrible."

Such was his feeling.

"If I had to die like Caius I should have known it was so. An inner voice would have told me so, but there was nothing of the sort in me and I and all my friends felt that our case was quite different from that of Caius. And now here it is!" he said to himself. "It can't be. It's impossible! But here it is. How is this? How is one to understand it?"

He could not understand it, and tried to drive this false, incorrect, morbid thought away and to replace it by other proper and healthy thoughts. But that thought, and not the thought only but the reality itself, seemed to come and confront him.

And to replace that thought he called up a succession of others, hoping to find in them some support. He tried to get back into the former current of thoughts that had once screened the thought of death from him. But strange to say, all that had formerly shut off, hidden, and destroyed, his consciousness of death, no longer had that effect. Ivan Ilych now spent most of his time in attempting to reestablish that old current. He would say to himself: "I will take up my duties again—after all I used to live by them." And banishing all doubts he would go to the law courts, enter into conversation with his colleagues, and sit carelessly as was his wont, scanning the crowd with a thoughtful look and leaning both his emaciated arms on the arms of his oak chair; bending over as usual to a colleague and drawing his papers nearer he would interchange whispers with him, and then

suddenly raising his eyes and sitting erect would pronounce certain words and open the proceedings. But suddenly in the midst of those proceedings the pain in his side, regardless of the stage the proceedings had reached, would begin its own gnawing work. Ivan Ilych would turn his attention to it and try to drive the thought of it away, but without success. *It* would come and stand before him and look at him, and he would be petrified and the light would die out of his eyes, and he would again begin asking himself whether *It* alone was true. And his colleagues and subordinates would see with surprise and distress that he, the brilliant and subtle judge, was becoming confused and making mistakes. He would shake himself, try to pull himself together, manage somehow to bring the sitting to a close, and return home with the sorrowful consciousness that his judicial labours could not as formerly hide from him what he wanted them to hide, and could not deliver him from *It*. And what was worst of all was that *It* drew his attention to itself not in order to make him take some action but only that he should look at *It*, look it straight in the face: look at it and without doing anything, suffer inexpressibly.

And to save himself from this condition Ivan Ilych looked for consolations—new screens—and new screens were found and for a while seemed to save him, but then they immediately fell to pieces or rather became transparent, as if *It* penetrated them and nothing could veil *It*.

In these latter days he would go into the drawing-room he had arranged—that drawing-room where he had fallen and for the sake of which (how bitterly ridiculous it seemed) he had sacrificed his life —for he knew that his illness originated with that knock. He would enter and see that something had scratched the polished table. He would look for the cause of this and find that it was the bronze ornamentation of an album, that had got bent. He would take up the expensive album which he had lovingly arranged, and feel vexed with his daughter and her friends for their untidiness—for the album was torn here and there and some of the photographs turned upside down. He would put it carefully in order and bend the ornamentation back into position. Then it would occur to him to place all those things in another corner of the room, near the plants. He would call the footman, but his daughter or wife would come to help him. They would not agree, and his wife would contradict him, and he would dispute and grow angry. But that was all right, for then he did not think about *It*. *It* was invisible.

But then, when he was moving something himself, his wife would say: "Let the servants do it. You will hurt yourself again." And suddenly *It* would flash through the screen and he would see it. *It* was just a flash, and he hoped it would disappear, but he would involuntarily pay attention to his side. "It sits there as before, gnawing just the same!" And he could no longer forget *It*, but could distinctly see it looking at him from behind the flowers. "What is it all for?"

"It really is so! I lost my life over that curtain as I might have done when storming a fort. Is that possible? How terrible and how stupid. It can't be true! It can't, but it is."

He would go to his study, lie down, and again be alone with *It*: face to face with *It*. And nothing could be done with *It* except to look at it and shudder.

VII

How it happened it is impossible to say because it came about step by step, unnoticed, but in the third month of Ivan Ilych's illness, his wife, his daughter, his son, his acquaintances, the doctors, the servants, and above all he himself, were aware that the whole interest he had for other people was whether he would soon vacate his place, and at last release the living from the discomfort caused by his presence and he himself released from his sufferings.

He slept less and less. He was given opium and hypodermic injections of morphine, but this did not relieve him. The dull depression he experienced in a somnolent condition at first gave him a little relief, but only as something new, afterwards it became as distressing as the pain itself or even more so.

Special foods were prepared for him by the doctors' orders, but all those foods became increasingly distasteful and disgusting to him.

For his excretions also special arrangements had to be made, and this was a torment to him every time—a torment from the uncleanliness, the unseemliness, and the smell, and from knowing that another person had to take part in it.

But just through this most unpleasant matter Ivan Ilych obtained comfort. Gerasim, the butler's young assistant, always came in to carry the things out. Gerasim was a clean, fresh peasant lad, grown stout on town food and always cheerful and bright. At first the sight of him, in his clean Russian peasant costume, engaged on that disgusting task embarrassed Ivan Ilych.

Once when he got up from the commode too weak to draw up his trousers, he dropped into a soft armchair and looked with horror at his bare, enfeebled thighs with the muscles so sharply marked on them.

Gerasim with a firm light tread, his heavy boots emitting a pleasant smell of tar and fresh winter air, came in wearing a clean Hessian apron, the sleeves of his print shirt tucked up over his strong bare young arms; and refraining from looking at his sick master out of consideration for his feelings, and restraining the joy of life that beamed from his face, went up to the commode.

"Gerasim!" said Ivan Ilych in a weak voice.

Gerasim started, evidently afraid he might have committed some blunder, and with a rapid movement turned his fresh, kind, simple young face which just showed the first downy signs of a beard.

"Yes, sir?"

"That must be very unpleasant for you. You must forgive me. I am helpless."

"Oh, why, sir," and Gerasim's eyes beamed and he showed his glistening white teeth, "what's a little trouble? It's a case of illness with you, sir."

And his deft strong hands did their accustomed task, and he went out of the room stepping lightly. Five minutes later he as lightly returned.

Ivan Ilych was still sitting in the same position in the armchair.

"Gerasim," he said when the latter had replaced the freshly-washed utensil. "Please come here and help me." Gerasim went up to him. "Lift me up. It is hard for me to get up, and I have sent Dmitri away."

Gerasim went up to him, grasped his master with his strong arms deftly but gently, in the same way that he stepped— lifted him, supported him with one hand, and with the other drew up his trousers and would have set him down again, but Ivan Ilych asked to be led to the sofa. Gerasim, without an effort and without apparent pressure, led him, almost lifting him, to the sofa and placed him on it.

"Thank you. How easily and well you do it all!"

Gerasim smiled again and turned to leave the room. But Ivan Ilych felt his presence such a comfort that he did not want to let him go.

"One thing more, please move up that chair. No, the other one—under my feet. It is easier for me when my feet are raised."

Gerasim brought the chair, set it down gently in place, and raised Ivan Ilych's legs on to it. It seemed to Ivan Ilych that he felt better while Gerasim was holding up his legs.

"It's better when my legs are higher," he said. "Place that cushion under them."

Gerasim did so. He again lifted the legs and placed them, and again Ivan Ilych felt better while Gerasim held his legs. When he set them down Ivan Ilych fancied he felt worse.

"Gerasim," he said. "Are you busy now?"

"Not at all, sir," said Gerasin, who had learnt from the townsfolk how to speak to gentlefolk.

"What have you still to do?"

"What have I to do? I've done everything except chopping the logs for to-morrow."

"Then hold my legs up a bit higher, can you?"

"Of course I can. Why not?" And Gerasim raised his master's legs higher and Ivan Ilych thought that in that position he did not feel any pain at all.

"And how about the logs?"

"Don't trouble about that, sir. There's plenty of time."

Ivan Ilych told Gerasim to sit down and hold his legs, and began to talk to him. And strange to say it seemed to him that he felt better while Gerasim held his legs up.

After that Ivan Ilych would sometimes call Gerasim and get him to hold his legs on his shoulders, and he liked talking to him. Gerasim did it all easily, willingly, simply, and with a good nature that touched Ivan Ilych. Health, strength, and vitality in other people were offensive to him, but Gerasim's strength and vitality did not mortify but soothed him.

What tormented Ivan Ilych most was the deception, the lie, which for some reason they all accepted, that he was not dying but was simply ill, and that he only need keep quiet and undergo a treatment and then something very good would result. He however knew that do what they would nothing would come of it, only still more agonizing suffering and death. This deception tortured him—their not wishing to admit what they all knew and what he knew, but wanting to lie to him concerning his terrible condition, and wishing and forcing him to participate in that lie. Those lies—lies enacted over him on the eve of his death and destined to degrade this awful, solemn act to the level of their visitings, their curtains, their sturgeon for dinner—were a terrible agony for Ivan Ilych. And strangely enough, many times when they were going through their antics over him he had been within a hair-breadth of calling out to them: "Stop lying! You know and I know that I am dying. Then at least stop lying about it!" But he had never had the spirit to do it. The awful, terrible act of his dying was, he could see, reduced by those about him to the level of a casual, unpleasant, and almost indecorous incident (as if someone entered a drawing-room diffusing an unpleasant odour) and this was done by that very decorum which he had served all his life long. He saw that no one felt for him, because no one even wished to grasp his position. Only Gerasim recognized it and pitied him. And so Ivan Ilych felt at ease only with him. He felt comforted when Gerasim supported his legs (sometimes all night long) and refused to go to bed, saying: "Don't you worry, Ivan Ilych. I'll get sleep enough later on," or when he suddenly became familiar and exclaimed: "If you weren't sick it would be another matter, but as it is, why should I grudge a little trouble?" Gerasim alone did not lie; everything showed that he alone understood the facts of the case and did not consider it necessary to disguise them, but simply felt sorry for his emaciated and enfeebled master. Once when Ivan Ilych was sending him away he even said straight out: "We shall all of us die, so why should I grudge a little trouble?"—expressing the fact that he did not think his work burdensome, because he was doing it for a dying man and hoped someone would do the same for him when his time came.

Apart from this lying, or because of it, what most tormented Ivan Ilych was that no one pitied him as he wished to be pitied. At certain moments after prolonged suffering he wished most of all (though he would have been ashamed to confess it) for someone to pity him as a sick child is pitied. He longed to be petted and comforted. He knew he was an important functionary, that he had a beard turning grey, and that therefore what he longed for was impossible, but still he longed for it. And in Gerasim's attitude towards him there was something akin to what he wished for, and so that attitude comforted him. Ivan Ilych wanted to weep, wanted to be petted and cried over, and then his colleague Shebek would come, and instead of weeping and being petted, Ivan Ilych would assume a serious, severe, and profound air, and by force of habit would express his opinion on a decision of the Court of Cassation and would stubbornly insist on that view. This falsity around him and within him did more than anything else to poison his last days.

VIII

It was morning. He knew it was morning because Gerasim had gone, and Peter the footman had come and put out the candles, drawn back one of the curtains, and begun quietly to tidy up. Whether it was morning or evening, Friday or Sunday, made no difference, it was all just the same: the gnawing, unmitigated, agonizing pain, never ceasing for an instant, the consciousness of life inexorably waning but not yet extinguished, that approach of that ever dreaded and hateful Death which was the only reality, and always the same falsity. What were days, weeks, hours, in such a case?

"Will you have some tea, sir?"

"He wants things to be regular, and

wishes the gentlefolk to drink tea in the morning," thought Ivan Ilych, and only said "No."

"Wouldn't you like to move onto the sofa, sir?"

"He wants to tidy up the room, and I'm in the way. I am uncleanliness and disorder," he thought, and said only:

"No, leave me alone."

The man went on bustling about. Ivan Ilych stretched out his hand. Peter came up, ready to help.

"What is it, sir?"

"My watch."

Peter took the watch which was close at hand and gave it to his master.

"Half-past eight. Are they up?"

"No sir, except Vladimir Ivanich" (the son) "who has gone to school. Praskovya Fëdorovna ordered me to wake her if you asked for her. Shall I do so?"

"No, there's no need to." "Perhaps I'd better have some tea," he thought, and added aloud: "Yes, bring me some tea."

Peter went to the door but Ivan Ilych dreaded being left alone. "How can I keep him here? Oh yes, my medicine." "Peter, give me my medicine." "Why not? Perhaps it may still do me some good." He took a spoonful and swallowed it. "No, it won't help. It's all tomfoolery, all deception," he decided as soon as he became aware of the familiar, sickly, hopeless taste. "No, I can't believe in it any longer. But the pain, why this pain? If it would only cease just for a moment!" And he moaned. Peter turned towards him. "It's all right. Go and fetch me some tea."

Peter went out. Left alone Ivan Ilych groaned not so much with pain, terrible though that was, as from mental anguish. Always and for ever the same, always these endless days and nights. If only it would come quicker! If only *what* would come quicker? Death, darkness? . . . No, no! Anything rather than death!

When Peter returned with the tea on a tray, Ivan Ilych stared at him for a time in perplexity, not realizing who and what he was. Peter was disconcerted by that look and his embarrassment brought Ivan Ilych to himself.

"Oh, tea! All right, put it down. Only help me to wash and put on a clean shirt."

And Ivan Ilych began to wash. With pauses for rest, he washed his hands and then his face, cleaned his teeth, brushed his hair, and looked in the glass. He was terrified by what he saw, especially by the limp way in which his hair clung to his pallid forehead.

While his shirt was being changed he knew that he would be still more frightened at the sight of his body, so he avoided looking at it. Finally he was ready. He drew on a dressing-gown, wrapped himself in a plaid, and sat down in the armchair to take his tea. For a moment he felt refreshed, but as soon as he began to drink the tea he was again aware of the same taste, and the pain also returned. He finished it with an effort, and then lay down stretching out his legs, and dismissed Peter.

Always the same. Now a spark of hope flashes up, then a sea of despair rages, and always pain; always pain, always despair, and always the same. When alone he had a dreadful and distressing desire to call someone, but he knew beforehand that with others present it would be still worse. "Another dose of morphine—to lose consciousness. I will tell him, the doctor, that he must think of something else. It's impossible, impossible, to go on like this."

An hour and another pass like that. But now there is a ring at the door bell. Perhaps it's the doctor? It is. He comes in fresh, hearty, plump, and cheerful, with that look on his face that seems to say: "There now, you're in a panic about something, but we'll arrange it all for you directly!" The doctor knows this expression is out of place here, but he has put it on once for all and can't take it off—like a man who has put on a frock-coat in the morning to pay a round of calls.

The doctor rubs his hands vigorously and reassuringly.

"Brr! How cold it is! There's such a sharp frost; just let me warm myself!" he says, as if it were only a matter of waiting till he was warm, and then he would put everything right.

"Well now, how are you?"

Ivan Ilych feels that the doctor would like to say: "Well, how are our affairs?" but that even he feels that this would not do, and says instead: "What sort of a night have you had?"

Ivan Ilych looks at him as much as to say: "Are you really never ashamed of lying?" But the doctor does not wish to understand this question, and Ivan Ilych says: "Just as terrible as ever. The pain never leaves me and never subsides. If only something. . . ."

"Yes, you sick people are always like that. . . . There, now I think I am warm enough. Even Praskovya Fëdorovna, who is so particular, could find no fault with my temperature. Well, now I can say good morning," and the doctor presses his patient's hand.

Then, dropping his former playfulness, he begins with a most serious face to examine the patient, feeling his pulse and taking his temperature, and then begins the sounding and auscultation.

Ivan Ilych knows quite well and definitely that all this is nonsense and pure deception, but when the doctor, getting down on his knee, leans over him, putting his ear first higher then lower, and performs various gymnastic movements over him with a significant expression on his face, Ivan Ilych submits to it all as he used to submit to the speeches of the lawyers, though he knew very well that they were all lying and why they were lying.

The doctor, kneeling on the sofa, is still sounding him when Praskovya Fëdorovna's silk dress rustles at the door and she is heard scolding Peter for not having let her know of the doctor's arrival.

She comes in, kisses her husband, and at once proceeds to prove that she has been up a long time already, and only owing to a misunderstanding failed to be there when the doctor arrived.

Ivan Ilych looks at her, scans her all over, sets against her the whiteness and plumpness and cleanness of her hands and neck, the gloss of her hair, and the sparkle of her vivacious eyes. He hates her with his whole soul. And the thrill of hatred he feels for her makes him suffer from her touch.

Her attitude towards him and his disease is still the same. Just as the doctor had adopted a certain relation to his patient which he could not abandon, so had she formed one towards him—that he was not doing something he ought to do and was himself to blame, and that she reproached him lovingly for this— and she could not now change that attitude.

"You see he doesn't listen to me and doesn't take his medicine at the proper time. And above all he lies in a position that is no doubt bad for him—with his legs up."

She described how he made Gerasim hold his legs up.

The doctor smiled with a contemptuous affability that said: "What's to be done? These sick people do have foolish fancies of that kind, but we must forgive them."

When the examination was over the doctor looked at his watch, and then Praskovya Fëdorovna announced to Ivan Ilych that it was of course as he pleased, but she had sent to-day for a celebrated specialist who would examine him and have a consultation with Michael Danilovich (their regular doctor).

"Please don't raise any objections. I am doing this for my own sake," she said ironically, letting it be felt that she was doing it all for his sake and only said this to leave him no right to refuse. He remained silent, knitting his brows. He felt that he was so surrounded and involved in a mesh of falsity that it was hard to unravel anything.

Everything she did for him was entirely for her own sake, and she told him she was doing for herself what she actually was doing for herself, as if that was so incredible that he must understand the opposite.

At half-past eleven the celebrated specialist arrived. Again the sounding began and the significant conversations in his presence and in another room, about the kidneys and the appendix, and the questions and answers, with such an air of importance that again, instead of the real question of life and death which now alone confronted him, the question arose of the kidney and appendix which were not behaving as they ought to and would now be attacked by Michael Danilovich and the specialist and forced to amend their ways.

The celebrated specialist took leave of him with a serious though not hopeless look, and in reply to the timid question Ivan Ilych, with eyes glistening with fear and hope, put to him as to whether there was a chance of recovery, said that he could not vouch for it but there was a possibility. The look of hope with which Ivan Ilych watched the doctor out was so pathetic that Praskovya Fëdorovna, seeing it, even wept as she left the room to hand the doctor his fee.

The gleam of hope kindled by the doctor's encouragement did not last long. The same room, the same pictures, curtains, wall-paper, medicine bottles, were all there, and the same aching suffering body, and Ivan Ilych began to moan. They gave him a subcutaneous injection and he sank into oblivion.

It was twilight when he came to. They brought him his dinner and he swallowed some beef tea with difficulty, and then everything was the same again and night was coming on.

After dinner, at seven o'clock, Praskovya Fëdorovna came into the room in evening dress, her full bosom pushed up by her corset, and with traces of powder on her face. She had reminded him in the morning that they were going to the theatre. Sarah Bernhardt was visiting the town and they had a box, which he had insisted on their taking. Now he had forgotten about it and her toilet offended him, but he concealed his vexation when he remembered that he had himself insisted on their securing a box and going because it would be an instructive and aesthetic pleasure for the children.

Praskovya Fëdorovna came in, self-satisfied but yet with a rather guilty air. She sat down and asked how he was but, as he saw, only for the sake of asking and not in order to learn about it, knowing that there was nothing to learn—and then went on to what she really wanted to say: that she would not on any account have gone but that the box had been taken and Helen and their daughter were going, as well as Petrishchev (the examining magistrate, their daughter's fiancé) and that it was out of the question to let them go alone; but that she would have much preferred to sit with him for a while; and he must be sure to follow the doctor's orders while she was away.

"Oh, and Fëdor Petrovich" (the fiancé) "would like to come in. May he? And Lisa?"

"All right."

Their daughter came in in full evening dress, her fresh young flesh exposed (making a show of that very flesh which in his own case caused so much suffering), strong, healthy, evidently in love, and impatient with illness, suffering, and death, because they interfered with her happiness.

Fëdor Petrovich came in too, in evening dress, his hair curled *à la Capoul*, a tight stiff collar round his long sinewy neck, an enormous white shirt-front and narrow black trousers tightly stretched over his strong thighs. He had one white glove tightly drawn on, and was holding his opera hat in his hand.

Following him the schoolboy crept in unnoticed, in a new uniform, poor little fellow, and wearing gloves. Terribly dark shadows showed under his eyes, the meaning of which Ivan Ilych knew well.

His son had always seemed pathetic to him, and now it was dreadful to see the boy's frightened look of pity. It seemed to Ivan Ilych that Vasya was the only one besides Gerasim who understood and pitied him.

They all sat down and again asked how he was. A silence followed. Lisa asked her mother about the opera-glasses, and there was an altercation between mother and daughter as to who had taken them and where they had been put. This occasioned some unpleasantness.

Fëdor Petrovich inquired of Ivan Ilych whether he had ever seen Sarah Bernhardt. Ivan Ilych did not at first catch the question, but then replied: "No, have you seen her before?"

"Yes, in *Adrienne Lecouvreur*."

Praskovya Fëdorovna mentioned some rôles in which Sarah Bernhardt was particularly good. Her daughter disagreed. Conversation sprang up as to the elegance and realism of her acting—the sort of conversation that is always repeated and is always the same.

In the midst of the conversation Fëdor Petrovich glanced at Ivan Ilych and became silent. The others also looked at him and grew silent. Ivan Ilych was staring with glittering eyes straight before him, evidently indignant with them. This had to be rectified, but it was impossible to do so. The silence had to be broken, but for a time no one dared to break it and they all became afraid that the conventional deception would suddenly become obvious and the truth become plain to all. Lisa was the first to pluck up courage and break that silence, but by trying to hide what everybody was feeling, she betrayed it.

"Well, if we are going it's time to start," she said, looking at her watch, a present from her father, and with a faint and significant smile at Fëdor Petrovich relating to something known only to them. She got up with a rustle of her dress.

They all rose, said good-night, and went away.

When they had gone it seemed to Ivan Ilych that he felt better; the falsity had gone with them. But the pain remained —that same pain and that same fear that made everything monotonously alike, nothing harder and nothing easier. Everything was worse.

Again minute followed minute and hour followed hour. Everything remained the same and there was no cessation. And the inevitable end of it all became more and more terrible.

"Yes, send Gerasim here," he replied to a question Peter asked.

IX

His wife returned late at night. She came in on tiptoe, but he heard her, opened his eyes, and made haste to close them again. She wished to send Gerasim away and to sit with him herself, but he opened his eyes and said: "No, go away."

"Are you in great pain?"

"Always the same."

"Take some opium."

He agreed and took some. She went away.

Till about three in the morning he was in a state of stupefied misery. It seemed to him that he and his pain were being thrust into a narrow, deep black sack, but though they were pushed further and further in they could not be pushed to the bottom. And this, terrible enough in itself, was accompanied by suffering. He was frightened yet wanted to fall through the sack, he struggled but yet co-operated. And suddenly he broke through, fell, and regained consciousness. Gerasim was sitting at the foot of the bed dozing quietly and patiently, while he himself lay with his emaciated stockinged legs resting on Gerasim's shoulders; the same shaded candle was there and the same unceasing pain.

"Go away, Gerasim," he whispered.

"It's all right, sir. I'll stay a while."

"No. Go away."

He removed his legs from Gerasim's shoulders, turned sideways into his arm, and felt sorry for himself. He only waited till Gerasim had gone into the next room and then restrained himself no longer but wept like a child. He wept on account of his helplessness, his terrible loneliness, the cruelty of man, the cruelty of God, and the absence of God.

"Why hast Thou done all this? Why hast Thou brought me here? Why, why dost Thou torment me so terribly?"

He did not expect an answer and yet wept because there was no answer and could be none. The pain again grew more acute, but he did not stir and did not call. He said to himself: "Go on! Strike me! But what is it for? What have I done to Thee? What is it for?"

Then he grew quiet and not only ceased weeping but even held his breath and became all attention. It was as though he were listening not to an audible voice but to the voice of his soul, to the current of thoughts arising within him.

"What is it you want?" was the first clear conception capable of expression in words, that he heard.

"What do you want? What do you want?" he repeated to himself.

"What do I want? To live and not to suffer," he answered.

And again he listened with such concentrated attention that even his pain did not distract him.

"To live? How?" asked his inner voice.

"Why, to live as I used to—well and pleasantly."

"As you lived before, well and pleasantly?" the voice repeated.

And in imagination he began to recall the best moments of his pleasant life. But strange to say none of these best moments of his pleasant life now seemed at all what they had then seemed—none of them except the first recollections of childhood. There, in childhood, there had been something really pleasant with which it would be possible to live if it could return. But the child who had experienced that happiness existed no longer, it was like a reminiscence of somebody else.

As soon as the period began which had produced the present Ivan Ilych, all that had then seemed joys now melted before his sight and turned into something trivial and often nasty.

And the further he departed from childhood and the nearer he came to the present the more worthless and doubtful were the joys. This began with the School of Law. A little that was really good was still found there—there was light-heartedness, friendship, and hope. But in the upper classes there had already been fewer of such good moments. Then during the first years of his official career, when he was in the service of the Governor, some pleasant moments again occurred: they were the memories of love for a woman. Then all became confused and there was still less of what was good; later on again there was still less that was good, and the further he went the less there was. His marriage, a mere accident, then the disenchantment that followed it, his wife's bad breath and the sensuality and hypocrisy: then that deadly official life and those preoccupations about money, a year of it, and two, and ten, and twenty, and always the same thing. And the longer it lasted the more deadly it became. "It is as if I had been going downhill while I imagined I was going up. And that is really what it was. I was going up in public opinion, but to the same extent life was ebbing away from me. And now it is all done and there is only death."

"Then what does it mean? Why? It can't be that life is so senseless and horrible. But if it really has been so horrible and senseless, why must I die in agony? There is something wrong!"

"Maybe I did not live as I ought to have done," it suddenly occurred to him. "But how could that be, when I did everything properly?" he replied, and immediately dismissed from his mind this, the sole solution of all the riddles of life and death, as something quite impossible.

"Then what do you want now? To live: Live how? Live as you lived in the law courts when the usher proclaimed "The judge is coming!" "The judge is coming, the judge!" he repeated to himself. "Here he is, the judge. But I am not guilty!" he exclaimed angrily. "What is it for?" And he ceased crying, but turning his face to the wall continued to ponder on the same question: Why, and for what purpose, is there all this horror? But however much he pondered he found no answer. And whenever the thought occurred to him, as it often did, that it all resulted from his not having lived as he ought to have done, he at once recalled the correctness of his whole life and dismissed so strange an idea.

X

Another fortnight passed. Ivan Ilych now no longer left his sofa. He would not lie in bed but lay on the sofa, facing the wall nearly all the time. He suffered ever the same unceasing agonies and in his loneliness pondered always on the same insoluble question: "What is this? Can it be that it is Death?" And the inner voice answered: "Yes, it is Death."

"Why these sufferings?" And the voice answered, "For no reason—they just are so." Beyond and besides this there was nothing.

From the very beginning of his illness, ever since he had first been to see the doctor, Ivan Ilych's life had been divided between two contrary and alternating moods: now it was despair and the expectation of this uncomprehended and terrible death, and now hope and an intently interested observation of the functioning of his organs. Now before his eyes there was only a kidney or an intestine that temporarily evaded its duty, and now only that incomprehensible and dreadful death from which it was impossible to escape.

These two states of mind had alternated from the very beginning of his illness, but the further it progressed the more doubtful and fantastic became the conception of the kidney, and the more real the sense of impending death.

He had but to call to mind what he had been three months before and what he was now, to call to mind with what regularity he had been going downhill, for every possibility of hope to be shattered.

Latterly during that loneliness in which he found himself as he lay facing the back of the sofa, a loneliness in the midst of a populous town and surrounded by numerous acquaintances and relations but that yet could not have been more complete anywhere—either at the bottom of the sea or under the earth—during that terrible loneliness Ivan Ilych had lived only in memories of the past. Pictures of his past rose before him one after another. They always began with what was nearest in time and then went back to what was most remote—to his childhood—and rested there. If he thought of the stewed prunes that had been offered him that day, his mind went back to the raw shrivelled French plums of his childhood, their peculiar flavour and the flow of saliva when he sucked their stones, and along with the memory of that taste came a whole series of memories of those days: his nurse, his brother, and their toys. "No, I mustn't think of that. . . . It is too painful," Ivan Ilych said to himself, and brought himself back to the present—to the button on the back of the sofa and the creases in its morocco. "Morocco is expensive, but it does not wear well: there had been a quarrel about it. It was a different kind of quarrel and a different kind of morocco that time when we tore father's portfolio and were punished, and mamma brought us some tarts. . . ." And again his thoughts dwelt on his childhood, and again it was painful and he tried to banish them and fix his mind on something else.

Then again together with that chain of memories another series passed through his mind—of how his illness had progressed and grown worse. There also the further back he looked the more life there had been. There had been more of what was good in life and more of life itself. The two merged together. "Just as the pain went on getting worse and worse so my life grew worse and worse," he thought. "There is one bright spot there at the back, at the beginning of life, and afterwards all becomes blacker and blacker and proceeds more and more rapidly—in inverse ratio to the square of the distance from death," thought Ivan Ilych. And the example of a stone falling downwards with increasing velocity entered his mind. Life, a series of increasing sufferings, flies further and further towards its end—the most terrible suffering. "I am flying. . . ." He shuddered, shifted himself, and tried to resist, but was already aware that resistance was impossible, and again with eyes weary of gazing but unable to cease seeing what was before them, he stared at the back of the sofa and waited—awaiting that dreadful fall and shock and destruction.

"Resistance is impossible!" he said to himself. "If I could only understand what it is all for! But that too is impossible. An explanation would be possible if it could be said that I have not lived as I ought to. But it is impossible to say that," and he remembered all the legality, correctitude, and propriety of his life. "That at any rate can certainly not be admitted," he thought, and his lips smiled ironically as if someone could see that smile and be taken in by it. "There is no explanation! Agony, death. . . . What for?"

XI

Another two weeks went by in this way and during that fortnight an event occurred that Ivan Ilych and his wife had desired. Petrischev formally proposed. It happened in the evening. The next day Praskovya Fëdorovna came into her husband's room considering how best to inform him of it, but that very night there had been a fresh change for the worse in his condition. She found him still lying on the sofa but in a different position. He lay on his back, groaning and staring fixedly straight in front of him.

She began to remind him of his medicines, but he turned his eyes towards her with such a look that she did not finish what she was saying; so great an animosity, to her in particular, did that look express.

"For Christ's sake, let me die in peace!" he said.

She would have gone away, but just then their daughter came in and went up to say good morning. He looked at her as he had done at his wife, and in reply to her inquiry about his health said dryly that he would soon free them all of himself. They were both silent and after sitting with him for a while went away.

"Is it our fault?" Lisa said to her mother. "It's as if we were to blame! I am sorry for papa, but why should we be tortured?"

The doctor came at his usual time. Ivan Ilych answered "Yes" and "No," never taking his angry eyes from him, and at last said: "You know you can do nothing for me, so leave me alone."

"We can ease your sufferings."

"You can't even do that. Let me be."

The doctor went into the drawing-room

and told Praskovya Fëdorovna that the case was very serious and that the only resource left was opium to allay her husband's sufferings, which must be terrible.

It was true, as the doctor said, that Ivan Ilych's physical sufferings were terrible, but worse than the physical sufferings were his mental sufferings which were his chief torture.

His mental sufferings were due to the fact that that night, as he looked at Gerasim's sleepy, good-natured face with its prominent cheek-bones, the question suddenly occurred to him: "What if my whole life has really been wrong?"

It occurred to him that what had appeared perfectly impossible before, namely that he had not spent his life as he should have done, might after all be true. It occurred to him that his scarcely perceptible attempts to struggle against what was considered good by the most highly placed people, those scarcely noticeable impulses which he had immediately suppressed, might have been the real thing, and all the rest false. And his professional duties and the whole arrangement of his life and of his family, and all his social and official interests, might all have been false. He tried to defend all those things to himself and suddenly felt the weakness of what he was defending. There was nothing to defend.

"But if that is so," he said to himself, "and I am leaving this life with the consciousness that I have lost all that was given me and it is impossible to rectify it —what then?"

He lay on his back and began to pass his life in review in quite a new way. In the morning when he saw first his footman, then his wife, then his daughter, and then the doctor, their every word and movement confirmed to him the awful truth that had been revealed to him during the night. In them he saw himself— all that for which he had lived—and saw clearly that it was not real at all, but a terrible and huge deception which had hidden both life and death. This consciousness intensified his physical suffering tenfold. He groaned and tossed about, and pulled at his clothing which choked and stifled him. And he hated them on that account.

He was given a large dose of opium and became unconscious, but at noon his sufferings began again. He drove everybody away and tossed from side to side.

His wife came to him and said:

"Jean, my dear, do this for me. It can't do any harm and often helps. Healthy people often do it."

He opened his eyes wide.

"What? Take communion? Why? It's unnecessary! However. . . ." She began to cry.

"Yes, do, my dear. I'll send for our priest. He is such a nice man."

"All right. Very well," he muttered.

When the priest came and heard his confession, Ivan Ilych was softened and seemed to feel a relief from his doubts and consequently from his sufferings, and for a moment there came a ray of hope. He again began to think of the vermiform appendix and the possibility of correcting it. He received the sacrament with tears in his eyes.

When they laid him down again afterwards he felt a moment's ease, and the hope that he might live awoke in him again. He began to think of the operation that had been suggested to him. "To live! I want to live!" he said to himself.

His wife came in to congratulate him after his communion, and when uttering the usual conventional words she added:

"You feel better, don't you?"

Without looking at her he said "Yes."

Her dress, her figure, the expression of her face, the tone of her voice, all revealed the same thing. "This is wrong, it is not as it should be. All you have lived for and still live for is falsehood and deception, hiding life and death from you." And as soon as he admitted that thought, his hatred and his agonizing physical suffering again sprang up, and with that suffering a consciousness of the unavoidable, approaching end. And to this was added a new sensation of grinding shooting pain and a feeling of suffocation.

The expression of his face when he uttered that "yes" was dreadful. Having uttered it, he looked her straight in the eyes, turned on his face with a rapidity extraordinary in his weak state and shouted:

"Go away! Go away and leave me alone!"

XII

From that moment the screaming began that continued for three days, and was so terrible that one could not hear it through two closed doors without horror. At the moment he answered his wife he realized that he was lost, that there was no return, that the end had come, the very end, and his doubts were still unsolved and remained doubts.

"Oh! Oh! Oh!" he cried in various intonations. He had begun by screaming "I won't!" and continued screaming on the letter "o."

For three whole days, during which time did not exist for him, he struggled in that black sack into which he was being thrust by an invisible, resistless force. He struggled as a man condemned to death struggles in the hands of the executioner, knowing that he cannot save himself. And every moment he felt that despite all his efforts he was drawing nearer and nearer to what terrified him. He felt that his agony was due to his being thrust into that black hole and still more to his not being able to get right into it. He was hindered from getting into it by his conviction that his life had been a good one. That very justification of his life held him fast and prevented his moving forward, and it caused him most torment of all.

Suddenly some force struck him in the chest and side, making it still harder to breathe, and he fell through the hole and there at the bottom was a light. What had happened to him was like the sensation one sometimes experiences in a railway carriage when one thinks one is going backwards while one is really going forwards and suddenly becomes aware of the real direction.

"Yes, it was all not the right thing," he said to himself, "but that's no matter. It can be done. But what *is* the right thing?" he asked himself, and suddenly grew quiet.

This occurred at the end of the third day, two hours before his death. Just then his schoolboy son had crept softly in and gone up to the bedside. The dying man was still screaming desperately and waving his arms. His hand fell on the boy's head, and the boy caught it, pressed it to his lips, and began to cry.

At that very moment Ivan Ilych fell through and caught sight of the light, and it was revealed to him that though his life had not been what it should have been, this could still be rectified. He asked himself, "What *is* the right thing?" and grew still, listening. Then he felt that someone was kissing his hand. He opened his eyes, looked at his son, and felt sorry for him. His wife came up to him and he glanced at her. She was gazing at him openmouthed, with undried tears on her nose and cheek and a despairing look on her face. He felt sorry for her too.

"Yes, I am making them wretched," he thought. "They are sorry, but it will be better for them when I die." He wished to say this but had not the strength to utter it. "Besides, why speak? I must act," he thought. With a look at his wife he indicated his son and said: "Take him away . . . sorry for him . . . sorry for you too. . . ." He tried to add, "forgive me," but said "forego" and waved his hand, knowing that He whose understanding mattered would understand.

And suddenly it grew clear to him that

what had been oppressing him and would not leave him was all dropping away at once from two sides, from ten sides, and from all sides. He was sorry for them, he must act so as not to hurt them: release them and free himself from these sufferings. "How good and how simple!" he thought. "And the pain?" he asked himself. "What has become of it? Where are you, pain?"

He turned his attention to it.

"Yes, here it is. Well, what of it? Let the pain be."

"And death . . . where is it?"

He sought his former accustomed fear of death and did not find it. "Where is it? What death?" There was no fear because there was no death.

In place of death there was light.

"So that's what it is!" he suddenly exclaimed aloud. "What joy!"

To him all this happened in a single instant, and the meaning of that instant did not change. For those present his agony continued for another two hours. Something rattled in his throat, his emaciated body twitched, then the gasping and rattle became less and less frequent.

"It is finished!" said someone near him.

He heard these words and repeated them in his soul.

"Death is finished," he said to himself. "It is no more!"

He drew in a breath, stopped in the midst of a sigh, stretched out, and died.

THE LESSON AND THE SECRET

Lionel Trilling

THE nine women of the Techniques of Creative Writing Group sat awaiting the arrival of their instructor, Vincent Hammell. He was not late but they were early and some of them were impatient. The room they sat in was beautiful and bright; its broad windows looked out on the little lake around which the buildings of the city's new cultural center were grouped. The women were disposed about a table of plate glass and their nine handbags lay in an archipelago upon its great lucid surface.

Mrs. Stocker said, "Mr. Hammell isn't here, it seems." There was the intention of irony in her voice—she put a querulous emphasis on the "seems."

Miss Anderson said, "Oh, but it's that we are early—because of our being at the luncheon." She glanced for confirmation at the watch on her wrist.

"Perhaps so," Mrs. Stocker said, "But you know, Constance—speaking metaphorically, Hammell is *not here,* he—is—just—not—here."

At this remark there were nods of considered agreement. Mrs. Territt said, "I think so too. I agree," and brought the palm of her hand down upon her thigh in a sharp slap of decision.

Mrs. Stocker ignored this undesirable ally. She went on, "Not really *here* at all. Oh, I grant you that he is brilliant in a theoretical sense. But those of us who come here"—she spoke tenderly, as if referring to a sacrifice in a public cause— "those of us who come here, come for practice, not for theory. You can test the matter very easily—you can test it by results. And you know as well as I do,

Constance, that—there—are—just—no—results—at—all."

Miss Anderson had gone through uprisings like this every spring and she knew that there was no standing against Mrs. Stocker. Mrs. Stocker would have her own way, especially since the group that opposed her was so small and uncourageous, consisting, in addition to Miss Anderson herself, only of Mrs. Knight and Miss Wilson. Young Mrs. Knight was extremely faithful and quite successful in carrying out the class assignments and this naturally put her under suspicion of being prejudiced in favor of the instructor. Her opinion was bound to be discounted. As for Miss Wilson, her presence in the group was generally supposed to have merely the therapeutic purpose of occupying her unhappy mind. It was not a frequent presence, for she shrank from society, and now she looked miserably away from the insupportable spectacle of anyone's being blamed for anything whatsoever.

Miss Anderson said, "But surely we can't blame that all on Mr. Hammell."

"No, not all," Mrs. Stocker conceded handsomely because it was so little to concede. "I grant you it isn't *all* his fault. But I think we have the right to expect—. It isn't as if we weren't paying. And generously, too, I might add. And there's nothing to show. Not one of us has sold herself."

Mrs. Territt gave vent to an explosive snicker. At once Mrs. Stocker traced the reason for the outburst to Mrs. Territt's primitive sexual imagination and said sharply, "Not one of us has sold herself

[105]

to a single magazine. Not one of us has put herself across."

Of the nine women, all were very wealthy. They made Vincent Hammell's first experience of wealth, and nothing he had learned from books had prepared him for what he found. It seemed to Vincent that only in the case of Miss Anderson had wealth been a true condition of life, shaping and marking her as nothing else could have done. She alone bore something of the imagined appearance of wealth, the serenity and disinterestedness to which wealth is supposed ideally to aspire.

Vincent supposed that either the size or the age or the nature of Miss Anderson's fortune had led her—as fortunes of a kind sometimes do—into a historical lapse, an aberration of her sense of time. For Miss Anderson, although not "old-fashioned" nor long past her youth, seemed not to inhabit quite the same present in which her friends lived. She seemed, indeed, to live in reference to certain delicate points of honor such as Edith Wharton, but few after her, would have been concerned with. Vincent assumed, for example, that some high moral decision, its meaning now obscured, accounted for the unmarried state of a woman so pleasant as Miss Anderson. It was surely to be laid to some sacrifice of herself, some service of an idea. The idea which she served would not have to be very complex or important, but still it was an idea. Perhaps this explained the historical impression she made, for to many people the present consists of things, while the past consists of ideas. Like the past, Miss Anderson was a failure. Yet in some way she continued to exist with a gentle unsought authority which perhaps came from her friends' dim response to the power of the idea and their recognition of the magical, if limited, potency of the past; she was not aggressive or competitive and it was felt that she shed a justification upon whatever groups she joined.

Now and then Miss Anderson submitted to Vincent's criticism the stories she wrote. They were elaborate and literate—well written, the class called them—but they had no relation to any reality Vincent could identify. In the world of Miss Anderson's stories, servants were old and loyal; wives hid nameless diseases from their husbands or silently bore the most torturing infidelities, or found themselves hideously in the power of depraved lovers; memories played a great part, the memories of single passionate nights or of single significant phrases, and it sometimes happened that flowers or white gloves were forever cherished. When Vincent discussed these stories with Miss Anderson, he was always surprised at the small conviction with which he spoke about their lack of reality—he almost believed, as he spoke to her, that there might actually be such a world beyond his strict modern knowledge.

The distinction which Miss Anderson had was perhaps but a weak one, yet it gave Vincent Hammell a standard by which he could fairly measure the inadequacy of her colleagues. If she did not carry the power of her position, she at least carried its tragic consciousness. Wealth and position, Vincent felt, should appear in their proper forms and add to the variety of life. He was sure that there were proper forms both of refinement and vulgarity. But these women made but a commonplace spectacle. Thus, the meager taste in dress of Mrs. Stocker quite matched the meagerness of her face, which showed the irritable energy of a person whose social self-esteem is not matched by cash in the bank. Or Mrs. Territt was so very coarse in complexion, so drab in dress and so brutally dull in manner that it was inevitable to suppose that what gentility she had was hanging only by a thread of income. Mrs. Knight was ruddy and healthy from an expensive outdoor life, but in other respects she appeared no more than merely well off. Poor Miss Wilson's truly painful nervousness and her evasive eye quite transcended the bounds of class.

Yet on the other hand, it was even more difficult to believe in the actual status of Mrs. Broughton, Mrs. Forrester and old Mrs. Pomeroy, for wealth had marked them only in the way of parody and they were all so "typical" that one had to suppose that they had been produced not so much by nature and circumstance as by certain artistic imaginations of rather limited range. Vincent felt that in the east, in cities of complex culture, wealth would surely make a better show, would impart a more firmly bottomed assurance, a truer arrogance. Then too he could suppose that these women were the failures and misfits of their class, else they would not have to meet weekly to devote themselves to literature.

"I have nothing against Hammell personally, nothing whatsoever," Mrs. Stocker said. "What I think is that we need a different *kind* of person. Hammell is very modern, but we need somebody more practical. It seems to me that if we could have a literary agent who could give us the straight dope, tell us about contacts and the right approach . . ."

Mrs. Stocker had no need to complete her conditional clause. The straight dope, the contacts and the right approach went directly to the hearts of Mrs. Territt, Mrs. Broughton, and Mrs. Forrester. They murmured a surprised approval of the firm originality of the suggestion. Even old Mrs. Pomeroy raised her eyebrows to indicate that although human nature did not change, it sometimes appeared in interesting new aspects. To all the ladies, indeed, it came as a relief that Mrs. Stocker should suggest that there was another secret than that of creation. There was a power possibly more efficacious, the secret of selling, of contacts and the right approach.

Miss Anderson said, "But aren't all the literary agents in New York?" She said it tentatively, for she was without worldly knowledge, but what she said was so sensibly true that the general enthusiasm was dampened.

"But surely," Mrs. Stocker said, and her voice was almost desperate, "but surely there must be somebody?"

Mrs. Broughton, who was staring out of the window, said, "Here he comes," whispering it like a guilty conspiratorial schoolgirl. Mrs. Forrester closed her dark expressive eyes to the group to signal "mum" and the ladies composed their faces.

Could Vincent Hammell have heard the conversation of which he was the subject, he would have been surprised by only one element in it—the lack of any response to him personally. He knew he was not succeeding with the group, but he knew, too, that none of the instructors who had come before him had succeeded any better. The university had sent its best men, professors first, then young assistants, likely to be more modern. Each autumn the new man had been received with taut feminine expectancy; each spring he had been discarded, for he had not conveyed the precious, the inconceivable secret which the women had come in hopes to receive. Yet though Hammell might understand that he was not successful, he always supposed that he was a little forgiven by reason of his sex and age. He was wrong to count on this feminine extenuation—his masculinity and youth made his case, if anything, even worse.

His failure had no doubt begun when, upon being invited to instruct the group, he had conjured up a vision of gently bred ladies, all pretty and all precisely thirty years old, gracefully filling empty days and hearts with the delicate practice of a craft humbly loved. He had not been prepared for the urgent women who were actually his pupils, nor for their grim dark worship of the potency that print conferred, nor for their belief—more intense than any coterie in metropolitan garrets could have—that they were held in bondage by a great conspiracy of editors.

Vincent Hammell was carrying his briefcase, an elegant piece of luggage of excellent leather and the best bronze hardware. It had been a gift from his parents who with such gifts, useful but very fine and extravagant, kept for themselves and their son the memory and hope of better days. Vincent was glad of the briefcase, for it helped to arm his youth and poverty against the wealth and years of his pupils. He laid it on the plate-glass table beneath which his own legs and the legs of the women were visible. He opened it and took out a thin folder of manuscript. Miss Anderson cleared her throat, caught the eye of member after member and brought the meeting to order. Hammell looked up and took over the class. It was only his entrance into the room that gave him trouble and now he spoke briskly and with authority.

"Two weeks ago," he said, "I asked you to write an account of some simple outdoor experience. You were to concentrate on the physical details. You remember we discussed as models a passage from *Huckleberry Finn* and a story of Ernest Hemingway's." He picked up the folder of manuscript and examined its thinness. "Some of you," he said drily, "carried out the assignment."

Mrs. Stocker moved in her seat to signalize a protest which Vincent understood—all this was elementary. "I'd like to read one example," he said.

He took a manuscript from the folder. Only three of the women had attempted the assignment, two of them dully. But he was rather proud of Mrs. Knight's little story. It was quite unpretentious, about a young wife who is left by her husband in their hunting lodge in the Canadian woods. She wakes in the night to hear a howling that can be only that of wild animals and then the creaking hinge of an unlatched door opening and closing. She is not alone, but of the two guests one is another woman and the man is incompetent. She lies still and miserable, bearing all the sad isolation of responsibility; the conflict of her emotions is not between fear of the beasts and the impulse to protect herself, but rather between fear of the beasts and fear of her husband's contempt for her lack of courage. But at last she becomes bold—and finds that though indeed the door is unlatched, the howling is only that of a high wind. It was perhaps not entirely convincing that she should have deceived herself, but something in the matter of the story was indeed convincing, her desire to seem manly to her husband and the whole impulse of the story itself to discover safety where danger had been imagined.

Vincent began to read this story aloud. Just then the door opened and two women came in. They made little gestures of greeting to their friends and politely indicated, by exhibiting how they were out of breath, that their lateness had been unavoidable. Vincent waited for them to settle and then again began to read. When he came to the end, he paused for a while and looked around the table.

"What do you think of it?" he asked.

"Very nice," Mrs. Broughton said. "Very nice indeed." Mrs. Broughton, it always seemed to Vincent, had been imagined by a radical caricaturist of rather conventional fancy. Careless of verisimilitude, concerned only with the political passions he would arouse, the artist had drawn her short and pudgy, with a face of gross and foolish pride and a bridling neck which gave an air of condescension to her remarks, many of which were in their intention really quite good-natured. Mrs. Knight was not gratified by Mrs. Broughton's praise.

"Yes, it is very nice," Mrs. Stocker said, suppressing as much as she could the condescension she felt. "Of course, it has no plot, no complication, no conflict really, but it has a kind of twist at the end, it is true to life and it has touches of realism."

"Oh, very realistic," said Mrs. Broughton.

"Well, I don't think it *is* very realistic," said Mrs. Forrester with sudden authority. As compared with the inventor of Mrs. Broughton, the imagination that had conceived Mrs. Forrester was of greater complexity—some social satirist, gifted but not profound, had projected this elegant woman, not young but still beautiful, and had endowed her with an intensity of self-regard and a sense of noblesse so petulant and shoulder-shrugging, yet so easily snubbed, that poor Mrs. Forrester lived in a constant alternation of blind attack and bewildered retreat, with the result that since her beautiful girlhood scarcely anyone had felt toward her any emotion save the various degrees of contempt. "Not at all—to me it doesn't seem at all realistic." She held her pretty head high to front the refutation which her judgments inevitably and bewilderingly provoked. "It isn't *convincing*," she said. "Now take the central problem— yes, take the central *problem*. That definitely is *not* convincing. She lies there worrying about what she should do. *Why? What for?*"—her appeal was vehement. All she had to do was ring for the guides, and that would be *that!*" Her beautiful dark eyes flashed finality.

There was a gasp from Mrs. Knight. Her cheeks flamed. She almost rose from her chair. Her voice was choked. "It just so happens," she said with terrible scorn, "it just so happens that she couldn't ring for the guides because in our lodge—there—are—no—guides—to —ring for."

The group was wholly with Mrs. Knight in the matter. As usual, Mrs. Forrester was silenced.

Mrs. Stocker said, "Mr. Hammell, I gather that you like that story of Mrs. Knight's. And I like it too. It has a very fresh quality, definitely fresh. But the question I want to ask is whether in your opinion a story like that has a marketable value."

There were little nods around the table as the spirit of the junta asserted itself once more, but there was a constraining sense of guilt now that Vincent Hammell was here. Mrs. Knight looked very conscious. She was humble about her writing and near enough to her college days to submit to the discipline of an assigned exercise, but she was naturally not averse to knowing whether or not she had produced a commodity.

"Now you take Constance's stories— Miss Anderson's stories, Mr. Hammell. You yourself admit that they have something. They're well thought out and they're well written, they have suspense and a twist at the end. But the editors just never take them."

Miss Anderson looked up in surprise and unhappiness. Although now and then she sent her stories to market, she seemed to feel no chagrin at their refusal.

"Now why do you think that is, Mr. Hammell?" Mrs. Stocker said. There was a silence, a degree of attention that Hammell saw the significance in. He considered how to answer. Miss Anderson looked withdrawn from the inquisition.

Mrs. Broughton broke the silence. "It's because they are refined and charming and what they want nowadays is coarse —and middle class. About miners. There was a story I read about two children who could hear each other practicing the piano through the walls of their apartment." She tossed her head in resentment. "Who cares?"

Mrs. Territt broke in and her coarse voice was injured and defensive. She said, "You all talk about selling stories. What I want to know is how to write them. That's what I came here to find out." She looked hostilely at Vincent. "All this talk about what's been done already! I came here to learn *how to do it at all!*"

Three or four women were swayed by this utterance to confess among themselves what they had never before realized. "Yes, yes," they murmured and nodded to each other. The group was now divided between those who believed that the secret lay in learning to sell and those who believed that it lay in learning to write.

"Personally," Mrs. Terrett said, and her glance at Hammell was now malevolent, "personally, that is what I give up my time to come here for. And I haven't got it—*nothing.*" The murmur of agreement she had won had gone to her head and she was breathing hard.

Vincent said, "Mrs. Territt, one can only learn to write by writing." For the fact was that Mrs. Territt had never yet submitted a manuscript.

She bridled. "I suppose that's very smart." She used the word *smart* not in the English sense of something clean and precise or fashionable and elegant but in the old American sense of something clever and impertinent. In the eyes of all present this declassed her.

Vincent said, "How long do you spend at your desk every day, Mrs. Territt?"

She did not answer but looked sullenly at the table before her.

"Four hours a day?" Vincent said inexorably. He could feel the solidifying interest of the group. The many handsomely shod feet seen through the top of the table looked like aquarial creatures as they shifted a little with interest.

"Three hours? Two? One solid hour every day?"

Mrs. Territt was sulking like a scolded chambermaid with an inexpressible grievance. Suddenly she flashed out, "No, why should I? When I never get any ideas?"

It was a direct accusation against Hammell.

Someone snickered and no doubt the fight was won, but Hammell went on: "How long do you spend every day trying to get ideas?"

She looked at him blankly from her raging sulks.

It was necessary to bring the matter to an end. Vincent took a book from his briefcase. It was a volume of stories by a writer he much admired, Garda Thorne. "Shall we continue the class?" he said. The women nodded.

Vincent began to read aloud the story he had selected. It was about two young American girls who were visiting friends in an Austrian village. They were Catholics and they were sent by their hostess to pay a call of ceremony on the priest of the village. The priest had received them charmingly, he was very polite. He was in an especially good humor because the new wine from the grapes of his own little arbor was just ready. It stood in his tin bathtub on the floor. Just as the visit began, the priest was urgently sent for. He begged his young guests to remain until his return. They could not but agree, yet as his absence continued they sat there bored and impatient and wondering how to amuse themselves until first one and then the other took off her shoes and stockings, held her skirts high and stepped into the tub. If you stopped to think of it, it was not quite probable, but it was a wonderfully funny and charming picture, the first girl standing in the wine, then the second, then both together, elegantly dressed and with their wide straw hats on, the drops of red wine splashing up to their thighs, their white feet and ankles scarcely visible to themselves as they looked down into the roiled wine.

Then there was the scramble to get themselves decent before the priest should come home, the scrubbing with inadequate handkerchiefs, the sanding of the soapstone floor to clean off the prints of their feet. When the priest returned they had to sit there demure, with their legs still sticky under their stockings. The priest served them the wine they had bathed in and their manners were perfect as they heard him say that never had he known the wine to be so good.

As the story went on to its end, Vincent was sorry he had chosen it to read. The silence was becoming unusually intense. He had especially wanted Miss Anderson to hear the story, for he thought it might suggest to her, with its simplicity, gaiety and elegance, that there were better subjects than the unreal complexities she so feelingly conceived. But, as he read, he felt that it had been a cruel mistake to read this story to these women. As it went on through its narration of the flash of skirts and underskirts, of white stained thighs, the grave silence of the girls and then their giggles and the beautiful prints of their naked feet on the stone floor, it seemed to him that his own youth had been thoughtless to have chosen the story. He felt, too, like an intruder into feminine mysteries and the sweat came to his forehead. He dreaded the return of the priest and the end of the story when he would have to take his eyes from the book and look around. At last he finished. He did not look up but moodily sifted through the pages of the book. This had the histrionic effect of letting the story hang for a while in the air.

For a moment the silence continued. Then it was broken by Miss Anderson, crying, "Oh that was lovely, Mr. Hammell," and "lovely," "lovely," "lovely," echoed the women around the glass table, beneath whose surface there was a shifting of legs and a pulling down of skirts over knees.

Vincent Hammell now ventured to look at their faces, which were relaxed and benign. There were little half-smiles on their mouths, directed tangentially at him. It was as if he himself had been the author of the story and as if the story had celebrated the things that were their peculiar possessions, their youth, their beauty, their femininity.

In the sunlit room, in the soft spring air, there was a moment of musing silence as the quest for the precious secret was abandoned. Despite himself, Vincent Hammell experienced a sense of power, in all his months of teaching the class the first he had felt. Yet in the entrancement of the women, in their moment of brooding relaxation, there was something archaic and mythological, something latently dangerous. It was thus that the women of Thrace must have sat around Orpheus before they had had occasion to be enraged with him. He would have liked to remind them, but it was not possible, that he had merely read aloud to them the story which a woman, Garda Thorne, had written.

It was old Mrs. Pomeroy who memorialized the moment. Mrs. Pomeroy was by far a gayer creation than either Mrs. Broughton or Mrs. Forrester. Perhaps she was aware of her role, perhaps she had even had the charming wit to invent it herself—she was the old lady of widest experience and profoundest wisdom and it was impossible not to see her lengthy past of drawing rooms (at home and abroad) in which the brilliant and the famous were received. Silence and a twinkle were the evidences of Mrs. Pomeroy's breadth of culture. At certain literary names she would smile, as at the memory of old, intimate and special delights. But only once had she made vocal her feeling for the great past. On that occasion the name of Proust had been mentioned by Vincent Hammell and what Mrs. Pomeroy had said was, "And also Paul Bourget." [1]

[1] Proust and Bourget were French writers. Proust, today, is better known.

She had added a knowledgeable whisper of explanation, "Psychology!" And now, as her way was, she smiled sadly and wisely as she spoke. She closed her eyes and said, "Such a story makes one truly glad there is literature. We should be grateful."

She spoke so seldom and perhaps she was really wise—at her benediction upon literature and her admonition to gratitude everyone looked solemn, as if, in the moving picture, they were listening to Anatole France delivering the panegyric at Zola's funeral.

"Very excellent," said Mrs. Broughton. "Very."

And now Mrs. Stocker spoke. "What I like about the story," she said, "is that it is neither one thing nor another. I mean it isn't high-brow *or* commercial."

It was not that she wanted to bring the discussion back again to the matter which so much interested her. No doubt she as much as anyone else had been caught in the moment of contemplation, but in uttering her feeling about it she used the only language she knew. And having used that language, it was now natural for her to say, "Tell me, Mr. Hammell, does this writer sell well?"

At the question there was a noisy little murmur of agreement to its relevance as the eyes turned to Vincent Hammell to demand his answer.

THE QUESTION OF THE POUND AWARD

W. H. Auden
and others

Comments on William Barrett's editorial, "A Prize for Ezra Pound," which appeared in the April 1949 issue of the *Partisan Review*. See page 121.

W. H. AUDEN:

I fully share Mr. Barrett's concern over the excessive preoccupation of contemporary criticism with Form and its neglect of Content. I am not sure however that this is the precise problem which his comment raises. In stating my own views, I should like to emphasize that I am speaking purely for myself and am not to be construed as representing any other colleague with whom at any time I may have been associated.

1) According to one theory, art, both in intention and effect, is a means by which emotions are aroused in the spectator or reader, either in order that, by re-living them imaginatively, he may get rid of them, or because he needs to be roused to feel in a certain way. If this theory is adopted, then it seems to me that Plato and Tolstoy are irrefutable. No works of art may be permitted which do not purge men of their bad feelings and stimulate good ones. The criterion of value may vary—Plato thought the supreme value was love of justice and loyalty to the Good State, Tolstoy thought it was love of one's neighbor—but the principle is the same. Applied to the present issue, the conclusion would be obvious—no prize; suppression.

2) One may, on the other hand, hold another theory of art, that, in intention, at least, it is a mirror in which the spectator sees reflected himself and the world, and becomes conscious of his feelings good and bad, and of what their relations to each other are in fact. This theory presupposes, I believe, certain other beliefs into which there is no time to go now, beyond baldly stating them:

a) All created existence is a good.

b) Evil is a negative perversion of created good.

c) Man has free will to choose between good and evil.

d) But all men are sinners with a perverted will.

An art which did not accurately reflect evil would not be good art.

3) This does not dispose, however, of the question of censorship. Whatever its intention, a work of art cannot compel the reader to look at it with detachment, and prevent him from using it as a stimulus to and excuse for feelings which he should condemn. Everyone, I am sure, has had the experience of reading a book which he was aware, at the time or later, was bad for him personally, whatever its artistic merit, or however harmless it might be for others, because, in this case, he was not capable of exercising free will, and was therefore not reading it as a work of art. For instance, Baudelaire's poem *La Charogne* [1] would not be healthy reading for a necrophilist. Antisemitism is, unfortunately, not only a feeling which all gentiles at times feel, but also, and this is what matters, a feeling of which the majority of them are not

[1] Carrion.

[113]

ashamed. Until they are, they must be regarded as children who have not yet reached the age of consent in this matter and from whom, therefore, all books, whether works of art or not, which reflect feeling about Jews—and it doesn't make the slightest difference whether they are pro or anti, the *New York Post* can be as dangerous as *Der Stürmer*—must be withheld.

If it were to seem likely that the *Pisan Cantos* would be read by people of this kind, I would be in favor of censoring it (as in the case of the movie *Oliver Twist*). That would not however prevent me awarding the *Pisan Cantos* a prize before withholding it from the public. But I do not believe that the likelihood exists in this case.

ROBERT GORHAM DAVIS:

The Pound award, it seems to me, is not most profitably taken as a problem in aesthetics. When form and content or free will and determinism or nominalism and realism are allowed to fall into this kind of abstract polarity, they can be argued about fruitlessly until doomsday. What confronts us in the Pound case is a complex of ideas dominant in American criticism during the forties, and made so largely by the talents and critical activities of some of the judges, of Eliot, Auden, Tate and Warren. The judges were judging themselves along with Pound, their master. But nearly everyone in America who is serious about literature is involved in one way or another.

The complex of ideas I speak of has been promoted with tactical skill, group movements, concerted attacks and extremes of mutual laudation. Snobbery and prestige have counted heavily. But it is not a conspiracy. There are truths in it, and much immediate support from the particular history of our time. It asserts that living language, literary sensibility and poetic values are supported by the traditional, the Catholic, the regional, the mythic, the aristocratic, and by a sense of the tragic, of transcendental absolutes, of sin and grace. Language and sensibility and values are destroyed by rationalism, liberalism, positivism, progressivism, equalitarianism, Shelleyanism, sociology, and the ideology of the Enlightenment. This has been made explicit by Eliot in *After Strange Gods* and *The Idea of a Christian Society;* by the Southern Regionalists, including Tate and Warren in much that they have written since their first manifesto, *I'll Take My Stand;* and by Auden in the Herod-as-liberal speech in *A Christmas Oratorio* and in the various reviews urging liberals and reformers to go jump in the lake.

In this complex of ideas the antisemitism with which William Barrett is principally concerned has a vital part. For these ideas did not originate with Eliot or Pound or Hulme, but with the French reactionary critics at the end of the nineteenth century, and were made into a program of action by Charles Maurras of whom Eliot used to speak with favor in *Criterion* days. Under the influence of Maurras, the virulently antisemitic students of the *Action Française* stormed the Sorbonne, beat up liberal professors, and howled down plays by Jewish writers, as untroubled as their Fascist and Nazi successors by problems of form and content. This mob antisemitism was the antisemitism of Pound's broadcasts when he, like Maurras, became a traitor both to his country and humane culture. (John Berryman's extenuating all this in PARTISAN REVIEW by comparing Pound to Roger Casement is one of the more fantastic examples of the way we are all involved.)

Eliot's antisemitism is different in kind but just as essential in his poetry and social ideas. Awed by his great achievements, fearful of showing insensibility, of introducing irrelevant "liberalism," most critics have accepted this in Eliot's terms. As homeless cosmopolitans and usurers, the Bleisteins and Sir Ferdinand Kleins represent the debasements of modern commercialism. As intellectuals, the Jews are the foremost carriers of disintegrative rationalism, earthly messianism. For the Southern Regionalists, Negroes are less interesting ideologically, but equally outside the tradition, and not to be made part of it by any liberal rhetoric.

Here we have not a question of form and content, of purity in art, but of the requirement of certain social attitudes, particularly ethical and communal ones, for literature, and rejection of certain others. These are programmatic demands, which are quite separable from the real achievements and values which they rationalize or exploit. Such demands can be refuted even by the example of many of the masters these critics claim as their own, and they are inapplicable to whole areas of literary experience which these critics undervalue or ignore. If Ezra Pound's *Cantos* are read with a wider literary and historical sense than the "new criticism" permits, they gain in meaning. As poetry they fail, despite Pound's sensibility. Their incoherence is real incoherence; it is not "achieved form." But against the author's intention they are highly revealing. They are a test case for a whole set of values, and stand self-condemned. They are important documents; they should be available, they should be read. But they deserve no prize.

CLEMENT GREENBERG:

I agree with Mr. Barrett. The Fellows in American Letters should have said more—that is, if they had more to say, and they should have had. As a Jew, I myself cannot help being offended by the matter of Pound's latest poetry; and since 1943 things like that make me feel *physically* afraid too.

I do not quarrel here with the Fellows' aesthetic verdict, but I question its primacy in the affair at hand, a primacy that hints at an absolute acceptance of the autonomy not only of art but of every separate field of human activity. Does no hierarchy of value obtain among them? Would Mr. Eliot, for instance, approve of this for his "Christian society?"

Life includes and is more important than art, and it judges things by their consequences. I am not against the publication of *The Pisan Cantos,* even though they offend me; my perhaps irrational sensitivity as a Jew cedes to my fear of censorship in general, and to the anticipation of the pleasure to be gotten from reading poetry, and I have to swallow that consequence. But I wish the Fellows had been, or shown themselves, more aware of the additional consequence when they awarded their Bollingen Prize. They could have taken greater trouble to explain their decision and thereby spared me, and a good many Jews like me, additional offense. (This does not mean, necessarily, that I am against the award itself.)

In any case, I am sick of the art-adoration that prevails among cultured people, more in our time than in any other: that art silliness which condones almost any moral or intellectual failing on the artist's part as long as he is or seems a successful artist. It is still justifiable to demand that he be a successful human being before anything else, even if at the cost of his art. As it is, psychopathy has become endemic among artists and writers, in whose company the moral idiot is tolerated as perhaps nowhere else in society.

Although it is irrelevant to the discussion, I must not let fall the opportunity to say at this point, that long before I heard of Pound's fascist sympathies, I was struck by his chronic failure to apprehend the substance, the concrete reality, of the things he talked about or did. I feel this failure in his poetry just as much as in what he wrote about painting and music. As a poet he seems to me to have always been more virtuoso than artist and to have seldom grasped the reality of the poem as a whole, as something with a beginning, middle, and ending. Thus, usually, any line or group of lines of a poem by Pound impresses me as superior to the whole of which it is part. (I would, however, except the "Mauberley" poems and several others of the same period from this stricture.)

IRVING HOWE:

That "a poet's technical accomplishments can transform material that is ugly and vicious into beautful poetry" is at least possible; but *how far* (as Mr. Barret asks) he can do so I hardly know. One thing seems certain: Pound hasn't done it. There is nothing very beautiful in "the yidd is a stimulant," though there is in "pull down thy vanity." Pound the crank is only rarely Pound the poet.

Doesn't this split in Pound make possible a justification of the Bollingen award? I think not. I would move beyond Mr. Barrett's question and assume that the *Pisan Cantos did* contain the best poetry of 1948. That does not yet settle the question of whether Pound should have been given the award. For while believing in the autonomy of aesthetic judgment, I believe in it so deeply that I also think there are some situations when it must be disregarded.

I am against any attempt to curtail Pound's rights to publish, and I don't want to see him prosecuted. (I don't like police measures; and cops aren't qualified to handle poets, not even mad or fascist poets.) I am, however, also against any campaign to condemn the Bollingen judges. What is involved in the Pound case is not a matter for public action but for a dialogue of conscience. But while defending Pound's rights, I could not in good conscience acquiesce to *honor* him with a literary award—which, if you please, must also mean to honor him as a man.

To give Pound a literary prize is, willy-nilly, a moral act within the frame of our social world. To honor him is to regard him as a man with whom one can have decent, normal, even affectionately respectful human and intellectual relations; it means to extend a hand of public fraternity to Ezra Pound. Now a hand to help him when he is down, yes. A hand to defend him from censors, fools and blood-seekers, yes. But a hand of honor and congratulations, no. For Pound, by virtue of his public record and utterances, is beyond the bounds of our intellectual life. If the judges felt that he had written the best poetry of 1948, I think they should have publicly said so—but not awarded any prize for the year. That might, by the way, have been an appropriate symbol of our cultural situation.

My position has, I know, grave difficulties and can easily lead to abuse. Once you consider extra-literary matters in a literary judgment, where do you stop? You stop at the point where intelligence and sensibility tell you to—that is what they are for. But it would be absurd to deny that there are occasions when aesthetic standards and our central human values clash, and when the latter must seem more important. On such painful occasions one can only say: not that I love literature less, but that I love life more. Is there any other way of taking literature seriously?

GEORGE ORWELL:

I think the Bollingen Foundation were quite right to award Pound the prize, if they believed his poems to be the best of the year, but I think also that one ought to keep Pound's career in memory and not feel that his ideas are made respectable by the mere fact of winning a literary prize.

Because of the general revulsion against Allied war propaganda, there has been—indeed, there was, even before the war was over—a tendency to claim that Pound was "not really" a fascist and an anti-semite, that he opposed the war on pacifist grounds and that in any case his political activities only belonged to the war years. Some time ago I saw it stated in an American periodical that Pound‧ only broadcast on the Rome radio when "the balance of his mind was upset," and later (I think in the same periodical) that the Italian government had blackmailed him into broadcasting by threats to relatives. All this is plain falsehood. Pound was an ardent follower of Mussolini as far back as the nineteen-twenties, and never concealed it. He was a contributor to Mosley's review, the *British Union Quarterly,* and accepted a professorship from the Rome government before the war started. I should say that his enthusiasm was essentially for the Italian form of fascism. He did not seem to be very strongly pro-Nazi or anti-Russian, his real underlying motive being hatred of Britain, America and "the Jews." His broadcasts were disgusting. I remember at least one in which he approved the massacre of the East European Jews and "warned" the American Jews that their turn was coming presently. These broadcasts—I did not hear them, but only read them in the BBC monitoring report—did not give me the impression of being the work of a lunatic. Incidentally I am told that in delivering them Pound used to put on a pronounced American accent which he did not normally have, no doubt with the idea of appealing to the isolationists and playing on anti-British sentiment.

None of this is a reason for giving Pound the Bollingen Prize. There are times when such a thing might be undesirable—it would have been undesirable when the Jews were actually being killed in the gas vans, for instance—but I do not think this is one of them. But since the judges have taken what amounts to the "art for art's sake" position, that is, the position that aesthetic integrity and common decency are two separate things, then at least let us keep them separate and not excuse Pound's politcal career on the ground that he is a good writer. He *may* be a good writer (I must admit that I personally have always regarded him as an entirely spurious writer), but the opinions that he has tried to disseminate by means of his works are evil ones, and I think that the judges should have said so more firmly when awarding him the prize.

KARL SHAPIRO:

Mr. Barrett's analysis of the Pound award seems to be on the safe side, but his extension of the official statement of the Fellows makes it clear that we are dealing with the *pons asinorum* [2] of modern criticism.

I voted against Pound in the balloting for the Bollingen Prize. My first and more crucial reason was that I am a Jew and cannot honor antisemites. My second reason I stated in a report which was circulated among the Fellows: "I voted against Pound in the belief that the poet's political and moral philosophy ultimately vitiates his poetry and lowers its standards as literary work." This statement of principle I would place against the official statement of the Fellows, which seems to me evasive, historically untrue, and illogical. That it was a successful device in placating opinion you know. The newspaper editorials I saw all rejoiced in "the objective perception of value on which any civilized society must rest" and I heard one radio commentator remark benignly that "this could never happen in Russia."

What appeased the journalists must

[2] The bridge of asses. Any problem that is hard for beginners.

have been their belief that Pound, despite his unintelligibility to them, is on the side of beauty or "technical excellence." The Fellows and the newsmen meet at the point where an unspecified technical excellence is accepted by the lay reader as successful (i.e., "beautiful") poetry. What the journalists think would not matter very much, but Mr. Barrett follows the same line of reasoning. "How far is it possible, in a lyric poem," he asks, "for technical embellishments to transform vicious and ugly matter into beautiful poetry?" Shouldn't the question rather be: Through his experience with vicious and ugly ideas, what poetic insights into our world has this poet given us? Pound's worth as a poet rests upon some answer to such a question.

Another question is well worth asking, namely, how objective could the Fellows be in a decision of this kind? If we consider a work for literary merit alone (whatever that may mean) we imply a personal decision to disregard the mythopoeic and moral function of the artist. If Pound had sufficient intellectual honesty, he would be the first to oppose such a criterion of selection.

The jury that elected Pound was made up partly of Pound's contemporaries, those who had come under his influence as impresario and teacher, those who had at some time made declarations of political reaction, and those who had engaged in the literary struggle to dissociate art from social injunction. The presence of Mr. Eliot at the meetings gave these facts a reality which perhaps inhibited open discussion. For reasons of personal loyalty, which one must respect, and for reasons of sectarian literary loyalty, which one may or may not respect, few poets anywhere are in a position to say what they think of Pound's work. But eventually what the serious well-intentioned critic admires in Pound is his aesthetic integrity. It is curious to see the flower of this integrity grafted onto criminality, but this should not lead us to the conclusion that artists can be criminals without incriminating their art.

The technical charge of treason against Pound is not our concern, but all artists should stand against this poet for his greater crime against civilization. Let the same charge be laid against Stalinist artists. But even if we claim to be objective perceptionists about it, let us at least ask ourselves whether fascism is or is not one of the "myths" of *The Cantos*. Who will deny that it is?

ALLEN TATE:

I do not propose to express any extensive views on Mr. Barrett's article, but rather to set down a brief statement of my own position on the only serious question that it raises.

A few weeks before the Bollingen Prize was awarded some persons of antisemitic feelings expressed to me their alarm lest it be given to Mr. Pound.

Mr. Barrett, it seems to me, goes a long way round, through a good deal of cant and vulgarity (to say nothing of the effrontery with which he invents the "difficulties" of the Fellows in coming to their decision), in order to arrive at the following insinuation: The decision of the Fellows in American Letters of the Library of Congress was dominated by antisemitic prejudice.

I consider any special attitude toward Jews, in so far as they may be identified as individuals or as a group, a historical calamity; and it is not less calamitous when the attitude is their own. I consider antisemitism to be both cowardly and dishonorable; I consider it cowardly and dishonorable to insinuate, as Mr. Barrett does, without candor, a charge of antisemitism against the group of writers of which I am a member.

I hope that persons who wish to accuse me of cowardice and dishonor will do so henceforth personally, in my presence, so that I may dispose of the charge at some other level than that of public discussion. Courage and honor are not subjects of literary controversy, but occasions of action.

FURTHER COMMENT
BY WILLIAM BARRETT:

I am not a Jew, but surely it must be clear to everyone by this time that antisemitism is a problem for gentiles as much as for Jews. When Jews whom I know and respect feel uneasy, as Mr. Clement Greenberg does, about a public award to Pound, I am bound to feel uneasy myself and to question the judgment of the Bollingen jury. Some of these questions I tried to raise in my brief comment. Mr. Tate's explosion in reply seems to us astonishing, to say the least. Neither Mr. Auden nor Mr. Shapiro, who were his colleagues on the Bollingen jury, have responded in his fashion; and the fact that among all the foregoing comments Mr. Tate's alone sticks out like a very sore and angry thumb is sufficient evidence that his reply was a complete and unwarranted misconstruction of my editorial, which contained absolutely no allegation whatever of antisemitism on the part of the judges. The question was, and is, the public wisdom of an award to Pound, and not the private psychology of the judges. It is Mr. Tate who has injected the personal issues. Surely Mr. Tate must recognize that he has a public responsibility to answer, not me personally, but all those people who have not forgotten what happened in Germany during this last War and who, like Mr. Greenberg, feel threatened by an award to Pound. Mr. Tate still has the opportunity open to him to offer a reasoned justification of the award, and we hope that he will do so. In the meantime, his challenge to a personal duel is strictly extra-curricular sport—having nothing to do with the public issue.

The comments explain themselves sufficiently so that it is unnecessary for me to linger in detailed examination of all of them. I should like to confine the rest of my remarks to the statements by Mr. Davis and Mr. Auden.

I agree with Mr. Davis that the context in which this question is raised has to be extended to include the historical circumstances that now condition literary judgment in the United States. What the present controversy demonstrates is that the category of the aesthetic is not the primary one for human life, and that the attitude which holds aesthetic considerations to be primary is far from primary itself, but produced by very many historical, social, and moral conditions. It would be hard to define just what the reigning climate of opinion has become in literary America since the collapse of the 'thirties; but perhaps it is high time we sought to establish a new climate, beginning with a re-examination of some of these "non-aesthetic" bases of literary judgment.

Mr. Auden's letter is the kind of rational, impersonal, and calm justification of the prize that we had hoped to have from Mr. Tate. I respect Mr. Auden's position, but I am not altogether convinced by his arguments. I would agree with everything that he says if the question had been one of censorship. But the question I raised was not one of suppressing Pound's book but of publicly honoring it with a prize. Mr. Auden's jump—"no prize; suppression"—is his own inference and not mine.

This point must be stressed since, as Mr. Shapiro remarks in his comment, some people are glad to celebrate the awards for Pound just *because* it seems a triumph of liberalism. Such is the line taken by Mr. Dwight Macdonald, who in an editorial in his magazine *Politics* finds the award "the brightest political act in a dark period." One can be in favor of the prize for Pound and still find Mr. Macdonald's enthusiasm here just a little extreme. I am against censorship in principle even though in particular cases it might be publicly beneficial, because censorship, once invoked, is difficult to control and therefore dangerous. I think this is as far as liberalism need go. To push it further is to indulge in a bohemian attitude of liberalism for liberalism's sake, which can become as unbalanced as the traditional attitude of art-for-art's sake, or of any part of life for that part's sake as abstracted from the whole. Liberalism is urged here to countenance things that deny its own right to exist— and for no other purpose but to show off. There is a kind of childishly competitive bravado in this need to show that one can out-liberal all other liberals. One step further, and Mr. Macdonald will be seeking out for a prize a *bad* poet who expresses antisemitism just in order to show how liberal he (Macdonald) can be.

Mr. Auden makes his most significant point, I think, when he argues that because evil is a part of life we have often to place great value upon works of art that do express evil attitudes. I agree with him in this, and I also agree that in his example of Baudelaire's *La Charogne* much of the power of this poem does derive from the fact that the poet participates, up to a point, in the emotions of necrophilia. For the aesthetic exploration of his subject matter the poet identifies himself with the emotions he expresses. But I doubt very much that one

can call Baudelaire a necrophilist in the same public sense in which one can call Pound an antisemite. Moreover, it seems to me to make a difference that necrophilia (so far as I know) has not been connected in our time with any large political movements, necrophiliac speeches have not been broadcast over the radio, and there are not large numbers of decent people who feel that their lives are threatened by necrophilists. Thus Mr. Orwell's remarks about Pound's broadcasts do not seem irrelevant to the present problem: the antisemitic lines I quoted from *The Pisan Cantos* simply versify statements made by Pound in his broadcasts to the effect that the War was brought about by the Jews, for whose interests American soldiers were being killed like cattle. In comparison, necrophilia still remains a private evil.

Since the discussion has unfortunately brought out some acrimony, I am glad to resign my part in it on at least one note of unqualified admiration—and that is for Mr. Karl Shapiro's comment, which is the kind of courageous and outspoken statement that has become a rare thing on our literary scene. I would agree with Mr. Shapiro that he has made a much better statement of the question of form and content in a literary work than I did in my comment. I also think with him that fascism is part of the "myth" of the *Cantos* generally—and that it can be found in *The Pisan Cantos* too.

A PRIZE FOR EZRA POUND

William Barrett

THE awarding of a prize is a public act usually surrounded with many difficulties. When the prize is literary, there are not only all the difficulties that attend literary judgment, but the further complications from the fact that the judges, because of the public nature of the award, act both as citizens and literary critics.

The Bollingen Foundation has recently announced that the Bollingen Prize for Poetry, the first of an annual series, has been awarded to Ezra Pound for *The Pisan Cantos* as the best book of poetry published during 1948. The judges were the Fellows in American Letters of the Library of Congress, among whom are T. S. Eliot, W. H. Auden, Allen Tate, Robert Penn Warren, Katherine Anne Porter, and Robert Lowell. In the public statement accompanying the award the judges tell us that they were aware that the choice of Pound was likely to provoke objections, and their brief statement implies that they have given these objections careful consideration, ending with something like an affirmation of a general principle:

To permit other considerations than that of poetic achievement to sway the decision would destroy the significance of the award and would in principle deny the validity of that objective perception of value on which any civilized society must rest.

The sentiments behind this declaration seem to us admirable. Our only interest here is to insist on the application of this principle. Civilization is a difficult task for all of us, requiring that we live in many different domains of human life at once, in each of which we are called on to affirm the principle of the "objective perception of value." It would be a pity if in the enthusiasm of affirming an "objective perception of value" in one direction we ceased to affirm it in another; if in the aesthetic recognition of Pound's poetry as valuable we chose to forget all about the humanly ugly attitudes of which he has been a spokesman both in his writing and in his brief and lamentable career as a broadcaster.

In this number of *Partisan Review* we print a long essay on Pound's poetry by John Berryman. Our printing of this essay is an affirmation of our belief that independent aesthetic judgment must be the continuing task of criticism, and in this belief we are clearly in agreement with the attitude enunciated by the Bollingen judges. It is not likely that Mr. Berryman has said the last word in the criticism of Pound (in these matters there is never a last word), but it is likely that he has made out the strongest possible case for Pound's having a subject matter as a poet. Mr. Berryman deals chiefly with the earlier and middle phases of Pound's career, and does not touch upon what Pound's subject matter became in recent years. This is perhaps incomplete, since our understanding of the whole career of a writer must surely take into view what his subject matter was capable of degenerating into under the pressures of personal and social disintegration. But whatever the critical truth here may be, it seems to us that Mr. Berryman's essay is in a different boat from the statement by the Bollingen judges, who were making a public award and were therefore more directly involved in public responsibilities.

Two things have to be, and are here distinguished: the case of Pound the man, and the value of the particular book, *The Pisan Cantos*. Pound the man has passed beyond the court of literary criticism into the jurisdiction of psychiatry and public justice, and it would be gratuitously vindictive for anyone to heap new tribulation on his wretched figure. Therefore our concern is, like that of the Bollingen judges, directly with the single book.

The statement by the judges shows an admirable frankness, but it is a pity that having gone so far in being frank, they did not go all the way, and actually name and face the specific objections they foresaw. The possible statement, which they might have made and the details of which each judge may have traced mentally, might then run something like this (considerations of style omitted):

"We are aware of the objections that may be raised concerning Pound's career as a fascist and anti-semite. However, under the terms of this award, we have confined our judgment to his poetry, and specifically the poetry found in the particular book under consideration, *The Pisan Cantos*. Of course, we have not missed the fact that this book itself expresses some of those unfortunate attitudes that led to Pound's downfall:

> Pétain defended Verdun while Blum
> was defending a bidet.

These lines express a vicious anti-semitic lie that was a part of the official Vichy propaganda during the War. Nevertheless, under the terms of the award, our judgment is of the poetry as poetry, and therefore we cannot reject it because of political considerations.

"To be sure, we know that the matter of these lines is not a political belief (with which we might disagree), but a deep human attitude, an emotion of hatred that is hideous, ugly and vicious and is expressed even more painfully in other lines in the book:

> the yidd is a stimulant, and the goyim are
>   cattle
> in gt/proportion and go to saleable slaughter
> with the maximum of docility

and again:

> and the goyim are undoubtedly in great
>   numbers cattle
> whereas a jew will receive information.

But if the reader considers these verses carefully for their rhythm and diction, their effective use of a living colloquial language, he will be led to overlook, we think, the vicious and ugly emotion expressed.

"Our problem would be much easier if this were a dramatic poem, in which this odious human attitude was expressed by one of the characters with whom the author need not be in agreement. But *The Pisan Cantos* is a lyrical poem, or group of lyrical poems, in which Pound is expressing Pound, and this ugly human attitude expressed in the lines above is one that the poet seeks to convey as his own to the reader. This has been another difficulty we have had to surmount in making our award.

"Nor do we feel that the difficulty is overcome by saying, in excuse of Pound, that this hideous attitude is the expression of a pathological mind. We know that, however privately pathological this mind may be, the attitudes it expresses are historically connected with certain objective facts like six million Jews dead in Europe, in crematory ovens or battles of extermination; and historical facts like these make it immensely more difficult to perform that necessary aesthetic judgment that separates matter from form in a poem.

"All these difficulties might have been shirked if we had chosen not to make the award at all for the year 1948. Nobody compelled us to grant this prize. Under the terms of the award, the prize need not be given in a year when no book is deemed to meet critical standards. But it seemed to us more important that all the foregoing difficulties be met, and that in the interests of civilization the aesthetic principles be affirmed that a poet's technical accomplishments can transform material that is ugly and vicious into beautiful poetry."

Naturally, it would be foolish to expect any jury of selection ever to make a statement like this. Nobody is compelled to wear his complete honesty in public; it would be tedious to assemble such a costume, and tedious to have to observe it. The brief statement accompanying the award seems to show that the judges may have traversed these details involved in their choice. We hope that they did. We hope even more that all those persons interested in literature and "civilized society" who have read the news of the award and its accompanying statement will be moved to follow through the details of the judges' difficulties outlined above.

Every particular literary judgment brings us in the end to some question of principle, and we should not like to leave the Pound case without bringing out this general question to which it has led us. During the 'thirties literature was subjected uncritically to all kinds of aesthetically distorting or irrelevant political attitudes. These political attitudes have by his time collapsed, leaving behind them a deposit of vague sentimentalities which, while obstructing any current of new political thought, still makes it impossible for many people to separate aesthetic from other considerations. When a historical movement collapses, it seems, it does not leave even the virtues of its vices. The statement by the Bollingen judges shows a laudable intention to reaffirm the validity of aesthetic principles. Our history, however, would be incomplete if we did not notice that within American literary criticism over the past decade or more there has developed another attitude which is so obsessed with formal and technical questions that it has time for only a hasty glimpse at content. Given these two conflicting tendencies, the perennial question of form and matter in a literary work seems to be still with us and is perhaps not altogether solved by the brief statement of the Bollingen judges. The Pound case enables us to put it to aestheticians in this definite way:

How far is it possible, in a lyric poem, for technical embellishments to transform vicious and ugly matter into beautiful poetry?

GALILEO

Bertrand Russell

SCIENTIFIC method, although in its more refined forms it may seem complicated, is in essence remarkably simple. It consists in observing such facts as will enable the observer to discover general laws governing facts of the kind in question. The two stages, first of observation, and second of inference to a law, are both essential, and each is susceptible of almost indefinite refinement; but in essence the first man who said "fire burns" was employing scientific method, at any rate if he had allowed himself to be burnt several times. This man had already passed through the two stages of observation and generalization. He had not, however, what scientific technique demands—a careful choice of significant facts on the one hand, and, on the other hand, various means of arriving at laws otherwise than by mere generalization. The man who says "unsupported bodies in air fall" has merely generalized, and is liable to be refuted by balloons, butterflies, and aeroplanes; whereas the man who understands the theory of falling bodies knows also why certain exceptional bodies do not fall.

Scientific method, simple as it is in essence, has been acquired only with great difficulty, and is still employed only by a minority, who themselves confine its employment to a minority of the questions upon which they have opinions. If you number among your acquaintances some eminent man of science, accustomed to the minutest quantitative precision in his experiments and the most abstruse skill in his inference from them, you will be able to make him the subject of a little experiment which is likely to be by no means unilluminating. If you tackle him on party politics, theology, income tax, house-agents, the bumptiousness of the working-classes and other topics of a like nature, you are pretty sure, before long, to provoke an explosion, and to hear him expressing wholly untested opinions with a dogmatism which he would never display in regard to the well-founded results of his laboratory experiments.

As this illustration shows, the scientific attitude is in some degree unnatural to man; the majority of our opinions are wish-fulfilments like dreams in the Freudian theory. The mind of the most rational among us may be compared to a stormy ocean of passionate convictions based upon desire, upon which float perilously a few tiny boats carrying a cargo of scientifically tested beliefs. Nor is this to be altogether deplored: life has to be lived, and there is no time to test rationally all the beliefs by which our conduct is regulated. Without a certain wholesome rashness, no one could long survive. Scientific method, therefore, must, in its very nature, be confined to the more solemn and official of our opinions. A medical man who gives advice on diet should give it after full consideration of all that science has to say on the matter, but the man who follows his advice cannot stop to verify it, and is obliged to rely, therefore, not upon science, but upon his belief that his medical adviser is scientific. A community impregnated with science is one in which the recognized experts have arrived at their opinions by scientific methods, but it is impossible for the ordinary citizen to repeat the work of the experts for himself. There is, in the modern world, a great body of well-attested knowledge on all kinds of subjects which the ordinary man accepts on authority without any need for hesitation; but as soon as any strong passion intervenes to warp the expert's judgment he becomes unreliable, whatever scientific equipment he may possess. The views of medical men on pregnancy, child-birth, and lactation were until fairly recently impregnated with sadism. It required, for example, more evidence to persuade them that anaesthetics may be used in child-birth than it would have required to persuade them of the opposite. Anyone who desires an hour's amusement may be advised to look up the tergiversations of eminent craniologists in their attempts to prove from brain measurements that women are stupider than men.[1]

It is not, however, the lapses of scientific men that concern us when we are trying to describe scientific method. A scientific opinion is one which there is some reason to believe true; an unscientific opinion is one which is held for some reason other than its probable truth. Our age is distinguished from all ages before the seventeenth century by the fact that some of our opinions are scientific in the above sense. I except bare matters of fact, since generality in a greater or less degree is an essential characteristic of science, and since men (with the exception of a few mystics) have never been able wholly to deny the obvious facts of their everyday existence.

The Greeks, eminent as they were in almost every department of human activity, did surprisingly little for the creation of science. The great intellectual achievement of the Greeks was geometry, which they believed to be an *a priori* study proceeding from self-evident premises, and not requiring experimental verification. The Greek genius was deductive rather than inductive, and was therefore at home in mathematics. In the ages that followed, Greek mathematics

[1] See Havelock Ellis, *Man and Woman*, 6th edition, p. 119 ff.

was nearly forgotten, while other products of the Greek passion for deduction survived and flourished, notably theology and law. The Greeks observed the world as poets rather than as men of science, partly, I think, because all manual activity was ungentlemanly, so that any study which required experiment seemed a little vulgar. Perhaps it would be fanciful to connect with this prejudice the fact that the department in which the Greeks were most scientific was astronomy, which deals with bodies that only can be seen and not touched.

However that may be, it is certainly remarkable how much the Greeks discovered in astronomy. They early decided that the earth is round, and some of them arrived at the Copernican theory that it is the earth's rotation, and not the revolution of the heavens, that causes the apparent diurnal motion of the sun and stars. Archimedes, writing to King Gelon of Syracuse, says: "Aristarchus of Samos brought out a book consisting of some hypotheses of which the premises lead to the conclusion that the universe is many times greater than that now so called. His hypotheses are that the fixed stars and the sun remain unmoved, that the earth revolves about the sun in the circumference of a circle, the sun lying in the centre of the orbit." Thus the Greeks discovered not only the diurnal rotation of the earth, but also its annual revolution about the sun. It was the discovery that a Greek had held this opinion which gave Copernicus courage to revive it. In the days of the Renaissance, when Copernicus lived, it was held that any opinion which had been entertained by an ancient might be true, but an opinion which no ancient had entertained could not deserve respect. I doubt whether Copernicus would ever have become a Copernican but for Aristarchus, whose opinion had been forgotten until the revival of classical learning.

The Greeks also discovered perfectly

valid methods of measuring the circumference of the earth. Eratosthenes the Geographer estimated it at 250,000 stadia (about 24,662 miles), which is by no means far from the truth.

The most scientific of the Greeks was Archimedes (287–212 B.C.). Like Leonardo da Vinci in a later period, he recommended himself to a prince on the ground of his skill in the arts of war, and like Leonardo he was granted permission to add to human knowledge on condition that he subtracted from human life. His activities in this respect were, however, more distinguished than those of Leonardo, since he invented the most amazing mechanical contrivances for defending the city of Syracuse against the Romans, and was finally killed by a Roman soldier when that city was captured. He is said to have been so absorbed in a mathematical problem that he did not notice the Romans coming. Plutarch is very apologetic on the subject of the mechanical inventions of Archimedes, which he feels to have been hardly worthy of a gentleman; but he considers him excusable on the ground that he was helping his cousin the king at a time of dire peril.

Archimedes showed great genius in mathematics and extraordinary skill in the invention of mechanical contrivances, but his contributions to science, remarkable as they are, still display the deductive attitude of the Greeks, which made the experimental method scarcely possible for them. His work on Statics is famous, and justly so, but it proceeds from axioms like Euclid's geometry, and the axioms are supposed to be self-evident, not the result of experiment. His book *On Floating Bodies* is the one which according to tradition resulted from the problem of King Hiero's crown, which was suspected of being not made of pure gold. This problem, as everyone knows, Archimedes is supposed to have solved while in his bath. At any rate, the method which he pro-

poses in his book for such cases is a perfectly valid one, and although the book proceeds from postulates by a method of deduction, one cannot but suppose that he arrived at the postulates experimentally. This is, perhaps, the most nearly scientific (in the modern sense) of the works of Archimedes. Soon after his time, however, such feeling as the Greeks had had for the scientific investigation of natural phenomena decayed, and though pure mathematics continued to flourish down to the capture of Alexandria by the Mohammedans, there were hardly any further advances in natural science, and the best that had been done, such as the theory of Aristarchus, was forgotten.

The Arabs were more experimental than the Greeks, especially in chemistry. They hoped to transmute base metals into gold, to discover the philosopher's stone, and to concoct the elixir of life. Partly on this account chemical investigations were viewed with favour. Throughout the Dark Ages it was mainly by the Arabs that the tradition of civilization was carried on, and it was largely from them that Christians such as Roger Bacon acquired whatever scientific knowledge the later Middle Ages possessed. The Arabs, however, had a defect which was the opposite of that of the Greeks: they sought detached facts rather than general principles, and had not the power of inferring general laws from the facts which they discovered.

In Europe, when the scholastic system first began to give way before the Renaissance, there came to be, for a time, a dislike of all generalizations and all systems. Montaigne illustrates this tendency. He likes queer facts particularly if they disprove something. He has no desire to make his opinions systematic and coherent. Rabelais also, with his motto: "Fais ce que voudras," * is as averse from intellectual as from other fetters. The Renaissance rejoiced in the recovered

* Do as you would like.—Ed.

liberty of speculation, and was not anxious to lose this liberty even in the interests of truth. Of the typical figures of the Renaissance by far the most scientific was Leonardo, whose note-books are fascinating and contain many brilliant anticipations of later discoveries, but he brought almost nothing to fruition, and remained without effect upon his scientific successors.

Scientific method, as we understand it, comes into the world full-fledged with Galileo (1564–1642), and, to a somewhat lesser degree, in his contemporary, Kepler (1571–1630). Kepler is known to fame through his three laws: he first discovered that the planets move round the sun in ellipses, not in circles. To the modern mind there is nothing astonishing in the fact that the earth's orbit is an ellipse, but to minds trained on antiquity anything except a circle, or some complication of circles, seemed almost incredible for a heavenly body. To the Greeks the planets were divine, and must therefore move in perfect curves. Circles and epicycles did not offend their aesthetic susceptibilities, but a crooked, skew orbit such as the earth's actually is would have shocked them deeply. Unprejudiced observation without regard to aesthetic prejudices required therefore, at that time, a rare intensity of scientific ardour. It was Kepler and Galileo who established the fact that the earth and the other planets go round the sun. This had been asserted by Copernicus, and, as we have seen, by certain Greeks, but they had not succeeded in giving proofs. Copernicus, indeed, had no serious arguments to advance in favour of his view. It would be doing Kepler more than justice to suggest that in adopting the Copernican hypothesis he was acting on purely scientific motives. It appears that, at any rate in youth, he was addicted to sun-worship, and thought the centre of the universe the only place worthy of so great a deity. None but scientific motives, however,

could have led him to the discovery that the planetary orbits are ellipses and not circles.

He, and still more Galileo, possessed the scientific method in its completeness. While much more is known than was known in their day, nothing essential has been added to method. They proceeded from observation of particular facts to the establishment of exact quantitative laws, by means of which future particular facts could be predicted. They shocked their contemporaries profoundly, partly because their conclusions were inherently shocking to the beliefs of that age, but partly also because the belief in authority had enabled learned men to confine their researches to libraries, and the professors were pained at the suggestion that it might be necessary to look at the world in order to know what it is like.

Galileo, it must be confessed, was something of a *gamin*. When still very young he became Professor of Mathematics at Pisa, but as the salary was only fifteen cents a day, he does not seem to have thought that a very dignified bearing could be expected of him. He began by writing a treatise against the wearing of cap and gown in the University, which may perhaps have been popular with undergraduates, but was viewed with grave disfavour by his fellow-professors. He would amuse himself by arranging occasions which would make his colleagues look silly. They asserted, for example, on the basis of Aristotle's *Physics,* that a body weighing ten pounds would fall through a given distance in one-tenth of the time that would be taken by a body weighing one pound. So he went up to the top of the Leaning Tower of Pisa one morning with a ten-pound shot, and just as the professors were proceeding with leisurely dignity to their respective lecture-rooms in the presence of their pupils, he attracted their attention and dropped the two weights from the top of the tower to their feet. The two weights arrived practically simultaneously. The professors, however, maintained that their eyes must have deceived them, since it was impossible that Aristotle could be in error.

On another occasion he was even more rash. Giovanni de' Medici, who was the Governor of Leghorn, invented a dredging machine of which he was very proud. Galileo pointed out that whatever else it might do it would not dredge, which proved to be a fact. This caused Giovanni to become an ardent Aristotelian.

Galileo became unpopular and was hissed at his lectures—a fate which has at times also befallen Einstein in Berlin. Then he made a telescope and invited the professors to look through it at Jupiter's moons. They refused on the ground that Aristotle had not mentioned these satellites, and therefore anybody who thought he saw them must be mistaken.

The experiment from the Leaning Tower of Pisa illustrated Galileo's first important piece of work, namely, the establishment of the Law of Falling Bodies, according to which all bodies fall at the same rate in a vacuum and at the end of a given time have a velocity proportional to the time in which they have been falling, and have traversed a distance proportional to the square of that time. Aristotle had maintained otherwise, but neither he nor any of his successors throughout nearly two thousand years had taken the trouble to find out whether what he said was true. The idea of doing so was a novelty, and Galileo's disrespect for authority was considered abominable. He had, of course, many friends, men to whom the spectacle of intelligence was delightful in itself. Few such men, however, held academic posts, and university opinion was bitterly hostile to his discoveries.

As everyone knows, he came in conflict with the Inquisition at the end of his life for maintaining that the earth goes round the sun. He had had a previous minor encounter from which he had emerged without great damage, but in the year of 1632 he published a book of dialogues on the Copernican and Ptolemaic systems, in which he had the temerity to place some remarks that had been made by the Pope into the mouth of a character named Simplicius. The Pope had hitherto been friendly to him, but at this point became furious. Galileo was living at Florence on terms of friendship with the Grand Duke, but the Inquisition sent for him to come to Rome to be tried, and threatened the Grand Duke with pains and penalties if he continued to shelter Galileo. Galileo was at this time seventy years old, very ill, and going blind; he sent a medical certificate to the effect that he was not fit to travel, so the Inquisition sent a doctor of their own with orders that as soon as he was well enough he should be brought in chains. Upon hearing that this order was on its way, he set out voluntarily. By means of threats he was induced to make submission. . . .

The formula of abjuration, which, as a consequence of this sentence, Galileo was compelled to pronounce, was as follows:—

I, Galileo Galilei, son of the late Vincenzio Galilei of Florence, aged seventy years, being brought personally to judgment, and kneeling before you, Most Eminent and Most Reverend Lords Cardinals, General Inquisitors of the Universal Christian Republic against heretical depravity, having before my eyes the Holy Gospels which I touch with my own hands, swear that I have always believed, and, with the help of God, will in future believe, every article which the Holy Catholic and Apostolic Church of Rome holds, teaches, and preaches. But because I have been enjoined, by this Holy Office, altogether to abandon the false opinion which maintains that the sun is the centre and immovable, and forbidden to hold, defend, or teach, the said false doctrine in any manner; and because, after it had been signified to me that the said doctrine is repugnant to the Holy Scripture, I have written and printed a book, in which I treat of the same condemned doctrine, and adduce reasons with great force in support of the same, without giving any solution, and therefore have been judged grievously suspected of heresy; that is to say, that I held and believed that the sun is the centre of the world and immovable, and that the earth is not the centre and movable, I am willing to remove from the minds of your Eminences, and of every Catholic Christian, this vehement suspicion rightly entertained towards me, therefore, with a sincere heart and unfeigned faith, I abjure, cure, and detest the said errors and heresies, and generally every other error and sect contrary to the said Holy Church; and I swear that I will never more in future say, or assert anything, verbally or in writing, which may give rise to a similar suspicion of me; but that if I shall know any heretic, or anyone suspected of heresy, I will denounce him to this Holy Office, or to the Inquisitor and Ordinary of the place in which I may be. I swear, moreover, and promise that I will fulfil and observe fully all the penances which have been or shall be laid on me by this Holy Office. But if it shall happen that I violate any of my said promises, oaths, and protestations (which God avert!), I subject myself to all the pains and punishments which have been decreed and promulgated by the sacred canons and other general and particular constitutions against delinquents of this description. So, may God help me, and His Holy Gospels, which I touch with my own hands, I, the above-named Galileo Galilei, have abjured, sworn, promised, and bound myself as above; and, in witness thereof, with my own hand have subscribed this present writing of my abjuration, which I have recited word for word.

At Rome, in the Convent of Minerva, June 22, 1633, I Galileo Galilei, have abjured as above with my own hand.

It is not true that after reciting this abjuration, he muttered: *"Eppur si muove."* *
It was the world that said this—not Galileo.

.   .   .   .

The conflict between Galileo and the Inquisition is not merely the conflict be-

* And yet it does move.—Ed.

tween free thought and bigotry or between science and religion; it is a conflict between the spirit of induction and the spirit of deduction. Those who believe in deduction as the method of arriving at knowledge are compelled to find their premises somewhere, usually in a sacred book. Deduction from inspired books is the method of arriving at truth employed by jurists, Christians, Mohammedans, and Communists. Since deduction as a means of obtaining knowledge collapses when doubt is thrown upon its premises, those who believe in deduction must necessarily be bitter against men who question the authority of the sacred books. Galileo questioned both Aristotle and the Scriptures, and thereby destroyed the whole edifice of mediaeval knowledge. His predecessors had known how the world was created, what was man's destiny, the deepest mysteries of metaphysics, and the hidden principles governing the behaviour of bodies. Throughout the moral and material universe nothing was mysterious to them, nothing hidden, nothing incapable of exposition in orderly syllogisms. Compared with all this wealth, what was left to the followers of Galileo? —a law of falling bodies, the theory of the pendulum, and Kepler's ellipses. Can it be wondered at that the learned cried out at such a destruction of their hard-won wealth? As the rising sun scatters the multitude of stars, so Galileo's few proved truths banished the scintillating firmament of mediaeval certainties.

Socrates had said that he was wiser than his contemporaries because he alone knew that he knew nothing. This was a rhetorical device. Galileo could have said with truth that he knew something, but knew he knew little, while his Aristotelian contemporaries knew nothing, but thought they knew much. Knowledge, as opposed to fantasies of wish-fulfilment, is difficult to come by. A little contact with real knowledge makes fantasies less acceptable. As a matter of fact, knowledge is even harder to come by than Galileo supposed, and much that he believed was only approximate; but in the process of acquiring knowledge at once secure and general, Galileo took the first great step. He is, therefore, the father of modern times. Whatever we may like or dislike about the age in which we live, its increase of population, its improvement in health, its trains, motor-cars, radio, politics, and advertisements of soap—all emanate from Galileo. If the Inquisition could have caught him young, we might not now be enjoying the blessings of air-warfare and poisoned gas, nor, on the other hand, the diminution of poverty and disease which is characteristic of our age.

It is customary amongst a certain school of sociologists to minimize the importance of intelligence, and to attribute all great events to large impersonal causes. I believe this to be an entire delusion. I believe that if a hundred of the men of the seventeenth century had been killed in infancy, the modern world would not exist. And of these hundred, Galileo is the chief.

THE STRANGE CASE OF EZRA POUND

Nathaniel Weyl

> I could never take him as a steady diet. Never. He was often brilliant, but an ass. But I never . . . ceased to love him.
>
> —William Carlos Williams on Ezra Pound.

> He is abnormally grandiose, is expansive and exuberant in manner, exhibiting pressure of speech, discursiveness and distractibility. . . . He is, in other words, insane. . . .
>
> —Report of four alienists to Justice Bolitha J. Laws concerning Ezra Pound.

ON November 18, 1945, a man of sixty with unruly, graying hair and a stubble beard (which had once come to a fine Mandarin point) was removed from an Army plane and taken to the District of Columbia jail. The passenger was Ezra Loomis Pound, born in a pioneer's cabin in Hailey, Idaho. A distinguished critic, a revolutionist in poetry, a man of sprawling scholarship and subtle cadences, of lucid images and maundering hallucinations, he had at last come home to his native land. He had come home to stand trial for having betrayed it.

When he was arrested near Genoa in the springtime of 1945, Ezra Pound made a statement that was characteristic:

"If I ain't worth more alive than dead, that's that. If a man isn't willing to take some risk for his opinions, either his opinions are no good or he's no good."

A man going on trial for his life on a political charge should be buoyed by the belief that he stands for some general idea of principle. Here was Pound, the putative wizard of words and cadences, striving to hit a colloquial note and sounding as off-key as a high-school band grappling with a Beethoven symphony. To grasp the difference, compare Pound's political testament with almost anything John Brown had to say when on trial for his life.

Ezra Pound was the only American radio traitor who formed more than a ripple in the tidal stream of Western culture. His creative and critical work has constituted a contribution of undeniable consequence to that stream. He understood and had once spoken the common tongue of civilized man—and yet he had betrayed his birthright and deliberately merged with forces of nihilism. Pound's fellow workers in the field of radio treason had been the pygmies, the simians, the mercenaries and the frustrates found by the fascists in the backwash of Western culture. Surely, there must have been moments when Ezra Pound realized that he was keeping incongruous company.

To the intellectuals, Pound's betrayal seemed infinitely more heinous than that of the others. One expects little from an animal, but much from a man. The intellectuals were not emotionally interested in the fate of a street ruffian, such as Joe McWilliams, the Yorkville storm trooper. They could follow the trial of Mildred Gillars with a diluted sense of compassion. The psychoneurotic failures like Best and Chandler aroused no strong reactions of either pity or revulsion.

[131]

But precisely because he retained some of his standards of intelligent speech, Pound was the most guarded, unemotional and ineffective of all of America's radio traitors. To those who recall the almost unbearable tension of the blood-soaked Italian front, it will seem incredible that any of Pound's queries or metaphors could have induced American soldiers to throw down their rifles and surrender.

The Fugitive

Pound's entire life was a flight from the soil that had nurtured him. In college, he read world literature omnivorously and issued himself a party card in the American aristocracy of intellect. He was both shy and domineering. William Carlos Williams recollects how he would read his poetry—his voice trailing off into inaudibility. Pound was so unsure of himself that he once asked for male reinforcement in a tactical operation which, by its very nature, must be done alone— that of picking up a girl, *one* girl, Williams emphasizes. And even so, he botched it.

Shortly after Ehrlich discovered the "magic bullet"—606—Pound wanted to take Williams with him to the North Coast of Africa. He thought there were enough syphilitic chieftains there so that they could both make a fortune and retire within a year to write poetry. Nothing came of the scheme.

Shortly after being given a position on the faculty of Wabash College, he was discharged for being "the Latin Quarter type"; thereafter, all academic doors in the United States slammed in his face. At twenty-three, he was in London and had published *Personae*—a work described by Edward Thomas as replete with "the beauty of passion, sincerity and intensity, not of beautiful words and images and suggestions."

Pound was a constructive iconoclast. His "great contribution to the work of other poets," T. S. Eliot once said, ". . .

is his insistence upon the immensity of the amount of *conscious* labor to be performed by the poet; and his invaluable suggestions for the kind of training the poet should give himself—study of form, metric and vocabulary in the poetry of divers literature, and study of good prose."

Preoccupied with the language as music and with the subtlest tonal patterns which could be constructed with it, Pound advised the young poet to "fill his mind with the finest cadences he can discover, preferably in a foreign language so that the meaning of the words may be less likely to divert his attention from the movement; e.g. Saxon charms, Hebridean folk songs, the verse of Dante, and the lyrics of Shakespeare—if he can dissociate the vocabulary from the cadence."

His emphasis on poetry as cadence and pure music induced him to write verse which was a mélange of snatches from living and dead tongues, incomprehensible to all but an eclectic minority. A dilettante student of the Chinese written language, Pound was entranced with the ideogram and experimented with the instantaneous presentation of complex thought in an ultimate of compactness. This resulted often enough in "intellectualized chop suey," or, more accurately, in the reduction of poetry to cryptograms,—the deciphering of which was an arduous mental process wherein the emotional reactions of the reader were inevitably deadened.

Needless to say, Pound was an esoteric and a starving one at that. The young Pound of London and the Latin Quarter was the very model of a Bohemian. His beard was bright red and stiletto pointed. His hair was a lion's mane, his collars Byronic and his cape long and flowing. He was a rootless tumbleweed on the earth's surface.

About 1915, T. S. Eliot writes,

[Pound] was living in a small dark flat in Kensington. In the largest room he cooked, by artificial light; in the lightest but smallest room, which was inconveniently triangular, he did his work and received his visitors. There he lived until he moved, in 1922, I think, to Paris; but he seemed always to be only a temporary squatter. This appearance was due, not only to his restless energy—in which it was difficult to distinguish the energy from the restlessness and fidgets, so that every room, even a big one, seemed too small for him—but to a kind of resistance against growing into any environment. In America, he would no doubt have always seemed on the point of going abroad; in London, he always seemed on the point of crossing the Channel. I have never known a man, of any nationality, to live so long out of his native country without seeming to settle anywhere else.

His most salient characteristic was an Olympian arrogance and an urge to master others. Even the loyal T. S. Eliot describes him as "a dominating director," adding:

No one could have been kinder to younger men, or to writers who, whether younger or not, seemed to him worthy and unrecognized . . . He liked to be the impresario for younger men, as well as the animator of artistic activity in any milieu in which he found himself. In this role he would go to any lengths of generosity and kindness; from inviting constantly to dinner a struggling author whom he suspected of being underfed, of giving away clothing (though his shoes and underwear were almost the only garments which resembled those of other men sufficiently to be worn by them), to trying to find jobs, collect subsidies, get work published and then get it criticized and praised.

Pound "always had a passion to teach." A perfectionist, he regarded his protégés impersonally "as art or literature machines to be carefully tended and oiled, for the sake of their potential output." The obvious corollary which Eliot drew was: "Pound was always a masterly judge of poetry; a more fallible judge, I think, of men." He was also a perfectionist and unwilling to brook anything which he

thought smacked of mediocrity. He had a compelling desire to be the Dalai Lama of all poets.

This not unsympathetic portrayal is the work of a colleague and disciple, who shared Pound's strong antipathy toward American democracy. It was written at a time when Pound faced possible death as a traitor. Another poet, William Carlos Williams, sketched Pound's countenance with harsher lines.

"Ezra always insisted in the loudest terms," Williams writes, "on the brilliance and profundity of his mind. He doesn't have a great mind and never did but that doesn't make him any the less a good poet. His stupidities coupled with his overweening self esteem have brought him down. . . ." Pound had "the most acute ear for metrical sequences, to the point of genius, that we have ever known," but he was also—Williams said forthrightly—"the biggest damn fool and faker in the business."

Where T. S. Eliot speaks of Pound's incredible self-discipline and vast capacity for work (he had turned out twenty books by the time he was forty) Williams calls him "a lazy animal in many ways."

Although a close friend of his at the time, Williams was irritated at the way Ezra Pound would always walk one pace ahead of his companions. He commented: "I remember my brother once in the same situation turned and walked off in the opposite direction."

Wanderings of an Expatriate

Ezra Pound was for a long time one of the awe-inspiring figures of the Left Bank. Ernest Hemingway, James Joyce, Gertrude Stein and Ezra Pound were the four towering leaders of the Paris expatriate band of literary iconoclasts. Pound turned out massive works of criticism, creation and translation: the *Propertius*, the *Cantos*, renditions of Chinese literature, appraisals of the troubadours and of Japanese drama. "Thus, year after year, since the appearance of the *Personae*," Charles Norman writes, "Pound has brought forth a body of literature without parallel in our time, a mass of work which has inspired other writers and helped to shape their styles; and he did this without much encouragement from critics in the United States and on an income which few would have been content to struggle with."

Unfortunately, there is no place in our economic system for a writers' writer, particularly if he happens to be a pathbreaker in poetry. The successful writers are conformists who have no reason to subsidize literary revolutions; the others find it hard enough to support themselves.

Pound was never too busy or too poor to take up the battleaxe in defense of any powerful writing which fell dead from the presses. He championed Rabindranath Tagore and Richard Aldington. When a Paris crowd howled down the unconventional *Ballet Mecanique* of George Antheil, Pound wrote a book in defense of the composer. Though intellectually an anti-semite, Ezra Pound sang the praises of Heinrich Heine and dedicated his *Culture* to the poet, Louis Zukofsky. And when he was on trial for treason, the Jewish poet whom he had befriended wrote:

I never felt the least trace of anti-semitism in his presence. Nothing he ever said to me made me feel the embarrassment I always have for the "Goy" in whom a residue of antagonism to "Jew" remains. If we had occasion to use the word "Jew" and "Goy" they were no more or less ethnological in their sense than "Chinese" and "Italian."

At first, Ezra Pound was an expatriate only in the physical sense. When Harriet Monroe founded the important magazine, *Poetry,* Pound wrote her a long letter:

"Are you for American poetry or for poetry? The latter is more important, but it is important that America should boost the former, provided it don't mean a blindness to the art. The glory of any nation is to produce art that can be exported without disgrace to its origin." He appendaged this note, written in the summer of 1912:

P.S. Any agonizing that tends to hurry what I believe in the end to be inevitable, our American Risorgimento, is dear to me. That awakening will make the Italian Renaissance look like a tempest in a teapot! The force we have, and the impulse, but the guiding sense, the discrimination in applying the force, we must wait and strive for.

Miss Monroe appointed Pound as an unpaid foreign editor of her magazine. The relationship was reminiscent of that Greek philosopher, captured in war and sold into bondage, who auctioned himself off on the slave market with the dry: "Is there any man here who wants to buy a master?"

As Miss Monroe recalls their collaboration:

Thus began the rather violent, but on the whole salutary, discipline under the lash of which the editor of the new magazine felt herself being rapidly educated, while all incrustations of habit and prejudice were ruthlessly swept away. Ezra Pound was born to be a great teacher. The American universities, which, at this time of his developing strength, failed, one and all, to install him as the head of an English department, missed a dynamic influence which would have been felt wherever English writing is taught. It is not entirely his fault if he has become somewhat embittered . . .

In the middle twenties, Pound went to Rapallo, Italy, withdrawing from the world of the cafés. He read medieval manuscripts, and, when the depression came, began to pore over economic theories. The reasons for this decisive flight into solitude remain obscure and debatable. Among them surely were his poverty and rejection by his native land. Was he, as William Carlos Williams suggests, a giant in the creation of aesthetic form, lacking a content, or unifying force, with which to fill it? In plainer language was "the thing that finally ruined Ezra" nothing less than "plain emptiness"? J. V. Healy puts the same idea somewhat more tactfully when he remarks: ". . . Eliot's success and Pound's failure lay mostly in Eliot's possession of a synthesizing imagination and Pound's lack of one."

Under more favorable circumstances, Pound might have become a comparatively prosperous poet who resided in America, but he could never have become a poet of America in the sense that Walt Whitman was. He scorned the values of democracy, the discipline of science, the faith in technology and blunt tool of pragmatism. He had removed himself progressively from the American scene to the outmost limits of time and space. Other eminent Americans ultimately rejected American values—notably Henry James and Henry Adams— but none of them became traitors.

"Ezra is one of a well recognized group of Americans who can't take the democratic virus and stand up under it," Williams comments.

Monetary Economist

Pound was soon dating his letters to American friends from Rapallo according to the calendar of the fascist revolution. He published a book on economics with a postscript signed: *E. P., Feb. 12, anno XII dell' era Fascista*.[1] He had apparently been abroad long enough to forget that February 12th was Lincoln's birthday.

The Great Depression had come and Pound, along with many others, pondered over the fact that millions were idle and hungry while the machines that could clothe them and the farms that could feed them gathered dust and grew weeds.

In search for a solution, he turned his

[1] In the twelfth year of the Fascist era.

mind to the discipline of economics, and shortly found his economic Koran in the writings of one Silvio Gesell (1862–1930). To all respectable economists, Gesell seemed a crackpot and a denizen of an irrational scientific underworld. A German, he had retired from a successful career as a merchant to devote himself to experimental farming and the writing of polemics. When the Communists took power briefly in Bavaria in 1919, the 57-year-old Gesell joined the Soviet Republic as its Finance Minister. When it collapsed, he was court-martialed, but avoided execution.

Gesell was, however, by no means a Marxist. He believed in a highly competitive economic system kept on an even keel by an ingenious type of monetary manipulation coupled with the nationalization of land.

His starting point was the discovery that throughout history the interest rate had remained comparatively constant, whereas the earning power of capital had not. He inferred that the stickiness of interest rates forced fluctuations in investment levels which caused alternating periods of boom and crisis. His proposed remedy was to impose a stamp tax on money. In order to avoid paying the tax, people would spend more rapidly, money velocities would increase, interest rates would decline and rising investment would pull the world out of depression. This program would have been beneficial during depression. The late Lord Keynes rescued Gesell's reputation from the limbo of the little groups of monetary maniacs.

It was too bad that Ezra Pound had to dabble in these matters, since he did not have the type of mind which readily grasps them. But he had now found the central, unifying theme which he believed would impart significance to his life work of poetic creation. The motif was usury, or *usuria*, as he put it. Inflexible interest rates, he thought, produced economic disaster. And who, after all, were the usurers? They were Jews.

He then combined Gesell's theories, economic anti-semitism and an adulation of Mussolini as a symbol of ORDER. The product was a nonsensical book called *Jefferson and/or Mussolini,* which mirrored the rapid disintegration of his once powerful mind: "The fascist revolution was for the preservation of certain liberties and FOR the maintenance of a certain level of culture, certain standards of living, it was NOT a refusal to come down to a level of riches or poverty, but a refusal to surrender certain immaterial prerogatives, a refusal to surrender a great slice of the cultural heritage."

Toward the Abyss

Pound's last decade was one of swift demoralization and loss of creative power. The sensitive ear remained, but not the mind. Having become a camp-follower of the armies of terror, Ezra Pound marched into the mire of nihilism.

In 1939, he returned to the United States to spread anti-semitism and laud the nation of order and discipline where all trains ran on time. Some of his literary contemporaries took the charitable view that Pound was insane; others ostracized him. He lectured bankers on economics for hours at end—at least, those who would listen. He showed no desire to learn anything himself, but clung smugly to his obsolescent view of economic Truth.

He returned to Italy disappointed. When war came, he broadcast over the fascist radio. After Pearl Harbor, there was a brief month of silence from Ezra Pound. Then, in January 1942, he resumed his radio addresses and at once crossed the borderline between disloyalty and treason.

The Italian radio announced that Ezra Pound "will not be asked to say anything whatsoever that goes against his con-science, or anything incompatible with his duties as a citizen of the U.S.A." Whatever Pound's conscience, his duties as an American citizen did not include attempting to undermine the morale of the armed forces of his country.

In addition to being an economist and one of the few sane men in a mad world, it seems that Pound was also an expert on international law. On January 29, 1942, he announced:

"The United States has been for months illegally at war through what I consider to be the criminal acts of a President whose mental condition was not, so far as I could see, all that could or should be desired. . . .." It is difficult to see how America could be "illegally at war" when Mussolini and Hitler had first declared it. The only outlaws produced by this reasoning were the Fascist and Nazi leaders. But even this simple point escaped Pound.

A few months later, he broadcast some incoherent jargon that may have been calculated to impress the men on American warships: "I ask whether the spirit of '76 is helped by a-floodin' the lower ranks of the navy with bridge-sweepin's. . . ."

On May 26th, he told the American people: "Every reform, every lurch toward the just price, toward the control of a market is an act of homage to Mussolini and Hitler. They are your leaders. . . ." These four words were, in all probability, enough to entitle Pound to the electric chair had he been sane enough to stand trial for them.

His other broadcast ideas were also shoddy things clad in an incoherent vocabulary—hardly worth risking a life to express. For instance, the poet had ideas on the peace. It "will not be based on international lending. Get that for one . . . England certainly will have nothing whatever to say about what its terms are. Neither, I think, will simple-hearted Joe

Stalin, not wholly trusted by the kikery, which is his master."

He wrote former American friends in less cautious terms—the broadcasts were perhaps both a mirror of cerebral decomposition and of a squirming sort of cowardice. These letters laid bare an ugly streak of sadism and insensitivity. The civil war in Spain, he told Williams, was of "no more importance than the draining of some mosquito swamp in deepest Africa." He exulted over Gestapo butcheries on the Eastern Front, referring to "fresh meat on the Russian steppes." He spoke of "Hitler the martyr."

America, Ezra Pound declared, "never had a chance in this war." In reply, when Mussolini's papier-maché war machine collapsed the American military placed Pound in a prison camp near Pisa. His new leisure time went into writing the *Pisan Cantos,* to which none of his captors bothered to object.

The Verdict

Eventually, he was flown to Washington to stand trial for treason. Four alienists, after examining him and his writings, concluded:

At the present time he exhibits extremely poor judgment as to his situation, its seriousness and the manner in which the charges are to be met. He insists that his broadcasts were not treasonable, but that all of his radio activities have stemmed from his self appointed mission to "save the Constitution." He is abnormally grandiose, is expansive and exuberant in manner, exhibiting pressure of speech, discursiveness, and distractibility. In our opinion, with advancing years his personality, for so many years abnormal, has undergone further distortion to the extent that he is now suffering from a paranoid state which renders him mentally unfit to advise properly with counsel or to participate intelligently and reasonably in his own defense. He is, in other words, insane and mentally unfit for trial, and is in need of care in a mental hospital.

On the basis of this report, a jury in the District of Columbia decided on February 13, 1946, that Ezra Pound was of "unsound mind."

Poetic Justice

Pound now sits in a comfortable room in St. Elizabeth's Hospital on the outskirts of Washington. Friends and admirers supply him with books. He is writing more verse and studying Chinese.

This last fact apparently infuriated the poet, Robert Hillyer, who composed an article for the *Saturday Review of Literature* (June 18, 1949) in which he implied that a man sane enough to learn Chinese was also sane enough for hanging. But the asylums are, as a matter of fact, sprinkled with linguists and mathematical wizards. Hillyer was on more solid ground when he objected that the comfort of the poet's surroundings "may with just indignation be contrasted to the crowded wards in which are herded the soldiers who lost their minds, defending America, which Pound hated and betrayed."

There is at least poetic justice in the conclusion to the Pound affair, which is far more instructive than the crude alternative of penitentiary or execution. If the alienists were right in their unanimous judgment, the one American representative of Western culture who betrayed democracy to the fascists was a lunatic.

Thus adjudged, Ezra Pound cannot afford to be cured. Once he steps out of St. Elizabeth's he must stand trial for treason. The alienists decided that he was too unbalanced to stand trial, but they did not conclude that he had been mad when he took traitor's pay from Mussolini's government.

The Communist publication *New Masses* issued a symposium on Ezra Pound "in which all the contributors declared he should be executed forthwith, some favoring hanging, some shooting."

This was before Pound had been brought to trial and at a time when no jury had found him guilty, but Communist notions of democracy, justice and civil rights are, of course, more than slightly different from our own. In the People's Democracies, the judicial process frequently begins after officials have already returned the *Alice in Wonderland* decision, "Off with their heads!"

But even from the standpoint of political expediency, the Communists were short-sighted. Hanging an eminent American poet would have given fascism an aura of martyrdom which it did not deserve. The jury's restraint in taking nothing from Ezra Pound except his dignity and stature as a man is to be commended.

The Bollingen Award

Ezra Pound's betrayal stirred a tempest in the world of American verse. The literary world was further agitated when, in early 1949, a Library of Congress committee of eminent American poets granted him the Bollingen Award for *The Pisan Cantos*—the poems he had written as a military prisoner in Italy.

When the irrelevancies were stripped off, the intellectuals' attack on Pound boiled down to the belief that the rottenness of Pound's philosophy and the anti-human role which he had played in the world struggle of the thirties had also corrupted his poetry. This is very different from saying that because a man is a traitor he cannot be a great writer. It involves judging his work in terms of its content as well as its form, insisting that the meaning of poetry is as important as its cadence.

Unfortunately, Pound's assailants were not always clear as to the importance of this distinction, although it is the very knife edge separating literary criticism in the totalitarian states from that in a democratic society.

The fact that an artist holds ideas which we believe are not only wrong but pernicious obviously does not disqualify his work. If Pound hated the Jews, Dostoevsky had similar feelings about the Germans. If Pound wanted Western science and democracy ground into the *kulturkampf* of Hitler and Mussolini, Dostoevsky held not dissimilar views about Imperial Russia vis-a-vis the West. We cannot praise Dostoevsky merely because Czarism is a distant memory and castigate Pound because the enormity of fascism is of recent date.

The issue then is the work itself. The critics are most relevant when they assert that Pound's influence over poetry has been, on the whole, degenerative; that he has helped alienate poetry from life; that he has distorted song into acrostics for the pseudo-learned; and that, wherever he has plagiarized, he has also polluted. If all this is true—and the present writer feels incompetent to express any personal judgment—then the parallel between Pound's poetry and Pound's politics is so close that one must inevitably shed light on the other.

The Bollingen Award was a triumph for Ezra Pound, but, in a sense, also a culminating defeat. He may have been amused at the official verdict that America's greatest poetry was being written by a madman under indictment for treason. But a more significant consideration was that such an award, whether substantively right or wrong, could have been made at all. In judging Pound's poems without reference to his treason, the Bollingen committee revealed the immense vitality of the American tradition of liberalism which Pound had sought so vainly to destroy.

Peter Brueghel, "Landscape with the Fall of Icarus" [Musée Royaux des Beaux-Arts, Brussels].

MUSÉE DES BEAUX ARTS [1]

About suffering they were never wrong,
The Old Masters: how well they understood
Its human position; how it takes place
While someone else is eating or opening a window or just walking dully along;
How, when the aged are reverently, passionately waiting   5
For the miraculous birth, there always must be
Children who did not specially want it to happen, skating
On a pond at the edge of the wood:
They never forgot
That even the dreadful martyrdom must run its course   10
Anyhow in a corner, some untidy spot
Where the dogs go on with their doggy life and the torturer's horse
Scratches its innocent behind on a tree.

In Brueghel's *Icarus* for instance: how everything turns away
Quite leisurely from the disaster; the ploughman may   15
Have heard the splash, the forsaken cry,
But for him it was not an important failure; the sun shone
As it had to on the white legs disappearing into the green
Water; and the expensive delicate ship that must have seen
Something amazing, a boy falling out of the sky,   20
Had somewhere to get to and sailed calmly on.

W. H. AUDEN

THE UNKNOWN CITIZEN

(To JS/07/M/378
This Marble Monument
Is Erected by the State)

He was found by the Bureau of Statistics to be
One against whom there was no official complaint,
And all the reports on his conduct agree
That, in all the modern sense of an old-fashioned word, he was a saint,
For in everything he did he served the Greater Community.   5
Except for the War till the day he retired
He worked in a factory and never got fired,
But satisfied his employers, Fudge Motors Inc.
Yet he wasn't a scab or odd in his views,
For his Union reports that he paid his dues,   10
(Our report on his Union shows it was sound)
And our Social Psychology workers found

[1] Museum of Fine Arts, Brussels, Belgium.

That he was popular with his mates and liked a drink.
The Press are convinced that he bought a paper every day
And that his reactions to advertisements were normal in every way.   15
Policies taken out in his name proved that he was fully insured,
And his Health-card shows he was once in hospital but left it cured.
Both Producers Research and High-Grade Living declare
He was fully sensible to the advantages of the Instalment Plan
And had everything necessary to the Modern Man,   20
A phonograph, a radio, a car and a frigidaire.
Our researchers in Public Opinion are content
That he held the proper opinions for the time of year;
When there was peace, he was for peace; when there was war, he went.
He was married and added five children to the population,   25
Which our Eugenist says was the right number for a parent of his generation,
And our teachers report that he never interfered with their education.
Was he free? Was he happy? The question is absurd:
Had anything been wrong, we should certainly have heard.

W. H. AUDEN

FRA LIPPO LIPPI [1]

I am poor brother Lippo, by your leave!
You need not clap your torches to my face.
Zooks, what's to blame? you think you see a monk!
What, 'tis past midnight, and you go the rounds,
And here you catch me at an alley's end   5
Where sportive ladies leave their doors ajar?
The Carmine's my cloister: hunt it up,
Do—harry out, if you must show your zeal,
Whatever rat, there, haps on his wrong hole,
And nip each softling of a wee white mouse,   10
Weke, weke, that's crept to keep him company!
Aha, you know your betters! Then, you'll take
Your hand away that's fiddling on my throat,
And please to know me likewise. Who am I?
Why, one, sir, who is lodging with a friend   15
Three streets off—he's a certain . . . how d'ye call?
Master—a . . . Cosimo of the Medici,
I' the house that caps the corner. Boh! you were best!
Remember and tell me, the day you're hanged,
How you affected such a gullet's gripe!   20
But you, sir, it concerns you that your knaves
Pick up a manner nor discredit you:
Zooks, are we pilchards, that they sweep the streets

---

[1] Filippo Lippi, Italian painter, 1457?–1504.

And count fair prize what comes into their net?
He's Judas to a tittle, that man is! 25
Just such a face! Why, sir, you make amends.
Lord, I'm not angry! Bid your hangdogs go
Drink out this quarter-florin to the health
Of the munificent House that harbours me
(And many more beside, lads! more beside!) 30
And all's come square again. I'd like his face—
His, elbowing on his comrade in the door
With the pike and lantern—for the slave that holds
John Baptist's head a-dangle by the hair
With one hand ("look you, now," as who should say) 35
And his weapon in the other, yet unwiped!
It's not your chance to have a bit of chalk,
A wood-coal or the like? or you should see!
Yes, I'm the painter, since you style me so.
What, brother Lippo's doings, up and down, 40
You know them and they take you? like enough!
I saw the proper twinkle in your eye—
'Tell you, I liked your looks at very first.
Let's sit and set things straight now, hip to haunch.
Here's spring come, and the nights one makes up bands 45
To roam the town and sing out carnival,
And I've been three weeks shut within my mew,
A-painting for the great man, saints and saints
And saints again. I could not paint all night—
Ouf! I leaned out of window for fresh air. 50
There came a hurry of feet and little feet,
A sweep of lute-strings, laughs, and whifts of song—
Flower o' the broom,
Take away love, and our earth is a tomb!
Flower o' the quince, 55
I let Lisa go, and what good in life since?
Flower o' the thyme—and so on. Round they went.
Scarce had they turned the corner when a titter
Like the skipping of rabbits by moonlight—three slim shapes,
And a face that looked up . . . zooks, sir, flesh and blood, 60
That's all I'm made of! Into shreds it went,
Curtain and counterpane and coverlet,
All the bed-furniture—a dozen knots,
There was a ladder! Down I let myself,
Hands and feet, scrambling somehow, and so dropped, 65
And after them. I came up with the fun
Hard by Saint Laurence, hail fellow, well met—
Flower o' the rose,
If I've been merry, what matter who knows?
And so as I was stealing back again 70
To get to bed and have a bit of sleep
Ere I rise up tomorrow and go work

On Jerome knocking at his poor old breast
With his great round of stone to subdue the flesh,
You snap me of the sudden. Ah, I see!   75
Though your eye twinkles still, you shake your head—
Mine's shaved—a monk, you say—the sting's in that!
If Master Cosimo announced himself,
Mum's the word naturally; but a monk!
Come, what am I a beast for? tell us, now!   80
I was a baby when my mother died
And father died and left me in the street.
I starved there, God knows how, a year or two
On fig skins, melon parings, rinds and shucks,
Refuse and rubbish. One fine frosty day,   85
My stomach being empty as your hat,
The wind doubled me up and down I went.
Old Aunt Lapaccia trussed me with one hand
(Its fellow was a stinger as I knew),
And so along the wall, over the bridge,   90
By the straight cut to the convent. Six words, there,
While I stood munching my first bread that month:
"So, boy, you're minded," quoth the good fat father
Wiping his own mouth, 'twas refection time—
"To quit this very miserable world?   95
Will you renounce" . . . "The mouthful of bread?" thought I;
By no means! Brief, they made a monk of me;
I did renounce the world, its pride and greed,
Palace, farm, villa, shop and banking house,
Trash, such as these poor devils of Medici   100
Have given their hearts to—all at eight years old.
Well, sir, I found in time, you may be sure,
'Twas not for nothing—the good bellyful,
The warm serge and the rope that goes all round,
And day-long blessed idleness beside!   105
"Let's see what the urchin's fit for"—that came next.
Not overmuch their way, I must confess.
Such a to-do! They tried me with their books:
Lord, they'd have taught me Latin in pure waste!
Flower o' the clove,   110
All the Latin I construe is, "amo," I love!
But, mind you, when a boy starves in the streets
Eight years together, as my fortune was,
Watching folk's faces to know who will fling
The bit of half-stripped grape bunch he desires,   115
And who will curse or kick him for his pains—
Which gentleman processional and fine,
Holding a candle to the Sacrament,
Will wink and let him lift a plate and catch
The droppings of the wax to sell again,   120
Or holla for the Eight and have him whipped—

How say I?—nay, which dog bites, which lets drop
His bone from the heap of offal in the street—
Why, soul and sense of him grow sharp alike,
He learns the look of things, and none the less   125
For admonition from the hunger-pinch.
I had a store of such remarks, be sure,
Which, after I found leisure, turned to use.
I drew men's faces on my copybooks,
Scrawled them within the antiphonary's marge,   130
Joined legs and arms to the long music-notes,
Found eyes and nose and chin for A's and B's,
And made a string of pictures of the world
Betwixt the ins and outs of verb and noun,
On the wall, the bench, the door. The monks looked black.   135
"Nay," quoth the Prior, "turn him out, d'ye say?
In no wise. Lose a crow and catch a lark.
What if at last we get our man of parts,
We Carmelites, like those Camaldolese
And Preaching Friars, to do our church up fine   140
And put the front on it that ought to be!"
And hereupon they bade me daub away.
Thank you! my head being crammed, the walls a blank,
Never was such prompt disemburdening.
First, every sort of monk, the black and white,   145
I drew them, fat and lean: then, folk at church,
From good old gossips waiting to confess
Their cribs of barrel droppings, candle ends—
To the breathless fellow at the altar-foot,
Fresh from his murder, safe and sitting there   150
With the little children round him in a row
Of admiration, half for his beard and half
For that white anger of his victim's son
Shaking a fist at him with one fierce arm,
Signing himself with the other because of Christ   155
(Whose sad face on the cross sees only this
After the passion of a thousand years)
Till some poor girl, her apron o'er her head
(Which the intense eyes looked through), came at eve
On tiptoe, said a word, dropped in a loaf,   160
Her pair of earrings and a bunch of flowers
(The brute took growling), prayed, and so was gone.
I painted all, then cried " 'Tis ask and have—
Choose, for more's ready!"—laid the ladder flat,
And showed my covered bit of cloister wall.   165
The monks closed in a circle and praised loud
Till checked, taught what to see and not to see,
Being simple bodies—"That's the very man!
Look at the boy who stoops to pat the dog!
That woman's like the Prior's niece who comes   170

To care about his asthma: it's the life!"
But there my triumph's straw-fire flared and funked;
Their betters took their turn to see and say:
The Prior and the learned pulled a face
And stopped all that in no time. "How? what's here?   175
Quite from the mark of painting, bless us all!
Faces, arms, legs and bodies like the true
As much as pea and pea! it's devil's game!
Your business is not to catch men with show,
With homage to the perishable clay,   180
But lift them over it, ignore it all,
Make them forget there's such a thing as flesh.
Your business is to paint the souls of men—
Man's soul, and it's a fire, smoke . . . no, it's not . . .
It's vapor done up like a newborn babe—   185
(In that shape when you die it leaves your mouth)
It's . . . well, what matters talking, it's the soul!
Give us no more of body than shows soul!
Here's Giotto, with his Saint a-praising God,
That sets us praising—why not stop with him?   190
Why put all thoughts of praise out of our head
With wonder at lines, colours, and what not?
Paint the soul, never mind the legs and arms!
Rub all out, try at it a second time.
Oh, that white smallish female with the breasts,   195
She's just my niece . . . Herodias, I would say—
Who went and danced and got men's heads cut off!
Have it all out!" Now, is this sense, I ask?
A fine way to paint soul, by painting body
So ill, the eye can't stop there, must go further   200
And can't fare worse! Thus, yellow does for white
When what you put for yellow's simply black,
And any sort of meaning looks intense
When all beside itself means and looks nought.
Why can't a painter lift each foot in turn,   205
Left foot and right foot, go a double step,
Make his flesh liker and his soul more like,
Both in their order? Take the prettiest face,
The Prior's niece . . . patron-saint—is it so pretty
You can't discover if it means hope, fear,   210
Sorrow or joy? won't beauty go with these?
Suppose I've made her eyes all right and blue,
Can't I take breath and try to add life's flash,
And then add soul and heighten them threefold?
Or say there's beauty with no soul at all—   215
(I never saw it—put the case the same—)
If you get simple beauty and nought else,
You get about the best thing God invents:

That's somewhat: and you'll find the soul you have missed,
Within yourself, when you return him thanks.   220
"Rub all out!" Well, well, there's my life, in short,
And so the thing has gone on ever since.
I'm grown a man no doubt, I've broken bounds:
You should not take a fellow eight years old
And make him swear to never kiss the girls.   225
I'm my own master, paint now as I please—
Having a friend, you see, in the Corner-house!
Lord, it's fast holding by the rings in front—
Those great rings serve more purposes than just
To plant a flag in, or tie up a horse!   230
And yet the old schooling sticks, the old grave eyes
Are peeping o'er my shoulder as I work,
The heads shake still—"It's art's decline, my son!
You're not of the true painters, great and old;
Brother Angelico's the man, you'll find;   235
Brother Lorenzo stands his single peer:
Fag on at flesh, you'll never make the third!"
Flower o' the pine,
You keep your mistr . . . manners, and I'll stick to mine!
I'm not the third, then: bless us, they must know!   240
Don't you think they're the likeliest to know,
They with their Latin? So, I swallow my rage,
Clench my teeth, suck my lips in tight, and paint
To please them—sometimes do, and sometimes don't;
For, doing most, there's pretty sure to come   245
A turn, some warm eve finds me at my saints—
A laugh, a cry, the business of the world—
(*Flower o' the peach,*
Death for us all, and his own life for each!)
And my whole soul revolves, the cup runs over,   250
The world and life's too big to pass for a dream,
And I do these wild things in sheer despite,
And play the fooleries you catch me at,
In pure rage! The old mill-horse, out at grass
After hard years, throws up his stiff heels so,   255
Although the miller does not preach to him
The only good of grass is to make chaff.
What would men have? Do they like grass or no—
May they or mayn't they? all I want's the thing
Settled forever one way: as it is,   260
You tell too many lies and hurt yourself:
You don't like what you only like too much,
You do like what, if given you at your word,
You find abundantly detestable.
For me, I think I speak as I was taught;   265
I always see the Garden and God there

A-making man's wife: and, my lesson learned,
The value and significance of flesh,
I can't unlearn ten minutes afterwards.

You understand me: I'm a beast, I know.   270
But see, now—why, I see as certainly
As that the morning star's about to shine,
What will hap some day. We've a youngster here
Comes to our convent, studies what I do,
Slouches and stares and lets no atom drop: 275
His name is Guidi—he'll not mind the monks—
They call him Hulking Tom, he lets them talk—
He picks my practice up—he'll paint apace,
I hope so—though I never live so long,
I know what's sure to follow. You be judge!   280
You speak no Latin more than I, belike;
However, you're my man, you've seen the world
—The beauty and the wonder and the power,
The shapes of things, their colours, lights and shades,
Changes, surprises—and God made it all!   285
—For what? do you feel thankful, aye or no,
For this fair town's face, yonder river's line,
The mountain round it and the sky above,
Much more the figures of man, woman, child,
These are the frame to? What's it all about?   290
To be passed over, despised? or dwelt upon,
Wondered at? oh, this last of course!—you say.
But why not do as well as say—paint these
Just as they are, careless what comes of it?
God's works—paint anyone, and count it crime   295
To let a truth slip. Don't object, "His works
Are here already; nature is complete:
Suppose you reproduce her—(which you can't)
There's no advantage! you must beat her, then."
For, don't you mark? we're made so that we love   300
First when we see them painted, things we have passed
Perhaps a hundred times nor cared to see;
And so they are better, painted—better to us,
Which is the same thing. Art was given for that;
God uses us to help each other so,   305
Lending our minds out. Have you noticed, now,
Your cullion's hanging face? A bit of chalk,
And trust me but you should, though! How much more,
If I drew higher things with the same truth!
That were to take the Prior's pulpit-place,   310
Interpret God to all of you! Oh, oh,
It makes me mad to see what men shall do
And we in our graves! This world's no blot for us,
Nor blank; it means intensely, and means good:

To find its meaning is my meat and drink.   315
"Aye, but you don't so instigate to prayer!"
Strikes in the Prior: "when your meaning's plain
It does not say to folks—remember matins,
Or, mind you fast next Friday." Why, for this
What need of art at all? A skull and bones,   320
Two bits of stick nailed crosswise, or, what's best,
A bell to chime the hour with, does as well.
I painted a Saint Laurence six months since
At Prato, spashed the fresco in fine style:
"How looks my painting, now the scaffold's down?"   325
I ask a brother: "Hugely," he returns—
"Already not one phiz of your three slaves
Who turn the Deacon off his toasted side,
But's scratched and prodded to our heart's content,
The pious people have so eased their own   330
When coming to say prayers there in a rage:
We get on fast to see the bricks beneath.
Expect another job this time next year,
For pity and religion grow i' the crowd—
Your painting serves its purpose!" Hang the fools!   335

    —That is—you'll not mistake an idle word
Spoke in a huff by a poor monk, God wot,
Tasting the air this spicy night which turns
The unaccustomed head like Chianti wine!
Oh, the church knows! don't misreport me, now!   340
It's natural a poor monk out of bounds
Should have his apt word to excuse himself:
And hearken how I plot to make amends.
I have bethought me: I shall paint a piece
. . . There's for you! Give me six months, then go, see   345
Something in Sant' Ambrogio's! Bless the nuns!
They want a cast o' my office. I shall paint
God in the midst, Madonna and her babe,
Ringed by a bowery, flowery angel brood,
Lilies and vestments and white faces, sweet   350
As puff on puff of grated orris-root
When ladies crowd to church at midsummer.
And then i' the front, of course a saint or two—
Saint John, because he saves the Florentines,
Saint Ambrose, who puts down in black and white   355
The convent's friends and gives them a long day,
And Job, I must have him there past mistake,
The man of Uz, (and Us without the z,
Painters who need his patience). Well, all these
Secured at their devotions, up shall come   360
Out of a corner when you least expect,
As one by a dark stair into a great light,

Music and talking, who but Lippo! I!—
Mazed, motionless and moonstruck—I'm the man!
Back I shrink—what is this I see and hear?   365
I, caught up with my monk's things by mistake,
My old serge gown and rope that goes all round,
I, in this presence, this pure company!
Where's a hole, where's a corner for escape?
Then steps a sweet angelic slip of a thing   370
Forward, puts out a soft palm—"Not so fast!"
—Addresses the celestial presence, "nay—
He made you and devised you, after all,
Though he's none of you! Could Saint John there draw—
His camel-hair make up a painting-brush?   375
We come to brother Lippo for all that,
Iste perfecit opus!" [2] So, all smile—
I shuffle sideways with my blushing face
Under the cover of a hundred wings
Thrown like a spread of kirtles when you're gay   380
And play hot cockles, all the doors being shut,
Till, wholly unexpected, in there pops
The hothead husband! Thus I scuttle off
To some safe bench behind, not letting go
The palm of her, the little lily thing   385
That spoke the good word for me in the nick,
Like the Prior's niece . . . Saint Lucy, I would say.
And so all's saved for me, and for the church
A pretty picture gained. Go, six months hence!
Your hand, sir, and good-bye: no lights, no lights!   390
The street's hushed, and I know my own way back,
Don't fear me! There's the grey beginning. Zooks!

ROBERT BROWNING

THE WAYFARER

The wayfarer,
Perceiving the pathway to truth,
Was struck with astonishment.
It was thickly grown with weeds.
"Ha," he said,   5
"I see that no one has passed here
In a long time."
Later he saw that each weed
Was a singular knife.
"Well," he mumbled at last,   10
"Doubtless there are other roads."

STEPHEN CRANE

[2] "*He* (literally, "that one") carried out the work!"

[ANYONE LIVED IN A PRETTY HOW TOWN]

anyone lived in a pretty how town
(with up so floating many bells down)
spring summer autumn winter
he sang his didn't he danced his did.

Women and men(both little and small)   5
cared for anyone not at all
they sowed their isn't they reaped their same
sun moon stars rain

children guessed(but only a few
and down they forgot as up they grew   10
autumn winter spring summer)
that noone loved him more by more

when by now and tree by leaf
she laughed his joy she cried his grief
bird by snow and stir by still   15
anyone's any was all to her

someones married their everyones
laughed their cryings and did their dance
(sleep wake hope and then) they
said their nevers they slept their dream   20

stars rain sun moon
(and only the snow can begin to explain
how children are apt to forget to remember
with up so floating many bells down)

one day anyone died i guess   25
(and noone stooped to kiss his face)
busy folk buried them side by side
little by little and was by was

all by all and deep by deep
and more by more they dream their sleep   30
noone and anyone earth by april
wish by spirit and if by yes.

Women and men(both dong and ding)
summer autumn winter spring
reaped their sowing and went their came   35
sun moon stars rain

E. E. CUMMINGS

[PLATO TOLD]

plato told

him:he couldn't
believe it(jesus

told him;he
wouldn't believe 5
it)lao

tsze
certainly told
him,and general
(yes 10

mam)
sherman;
and even

(believe it
or 15

not)you
told him:i told
him;we told him
(he didn't believe it,no

sir)it took 20
a nipponized bit of
the old sixth

avenue
el;in the top of his head:to tell

him 25

E. E. CUMMINGS

[PITY THIS BUSY MONSTER, MANUNKIND]

pity this busy monster,manunkind,

not. Progress is a comfortable disease:
your victim(death and life safely beyond)

plays with the bigness of his littleness
—electrons deify one razor blade 5
into a mountainrange;lenses extend

unwish through curving wherewhen till unwish
returns on its unself.
                    A world of made
is not a world of born—pity poor flesh 10

and trees,poor stars and stones, but never this
fine specimen of hypermagical

ultraomnipotence. We doctors know

a hopeless case if—listen:there's a hell
of a good universe next door;let's go 15

E. E. CUMMINGS

ALEXANDER'S FEAST
OR, THE POWER OF MUSIC;

An Ode in Honour of St. Cecilia's Day: 1697

I

'T was at the royal feast, for Persia won
    By Philip's warlike son: [1]
Aloft in awful state
The godlike hero sate
    On his imperial throne;   5
His valiant peers were plac'd around;
Their brows with roses and with myrtles bound:
    (So should desert in arms be crown'd.)
The lovely Thaïs,[2] by his side,
Sate like a blooming Eastern bride   10
In flow'r of youth and beauty's pride.
    Happy, happy, happy pair!
        None but the brave,
        None but the brave,
        None but the brave deserves the fair.   15

CHORUS

Happy, happy, happy pair!
None but the brave,
None but the brave,
None but the brave deserves the fair.

II

Timotheus,[3] plac'd on high   20
    Amid the tuneful choir,
    With flying fingers touch'd the lyre:
    The trembling notes ascend the sky,
        And heav'nly joys inspire.
The song began from Jove,   25
Who left his blissful seats above
(Such is the pow'r of mighty love).
A dragon's fiery form belied the god:
Sublime on radiant spires he rode,
    When he to fair Olympia press'd;   30
    And while he sought her snowy breast:

[1] Alexander the Great, 356–323 B.C.
[2] Athenian courtesan.
[3] Greek musician and poet.

Then, round her slender waist he curl'd,
And stamp'd an image of himself, a sov'reign of the world.
The list'ning crowd admire the lofty sound:
"A present deity," they shout around;   35
"A present deity," the vaulted roofs rebound.
   With ravish'd ears
   The monarch hears,
   Assumes the god,
   Affects to nod,   40
And seems to shake the spheres.

CHORUS

*   With ravish'd ears*
*   The monarch hears,*
*   Assumes the god,*
*   Affects to nod,*   45
And seems to shake the spheres.

III

The praise of Bacchus [4] then the sweet musician sung,
  Of Bacchus ever fair and ever young:
    The jolly god in triumph comes;
    Sound the trumpets; beat the drums;   50
     Flush'd with a purple grace
     He shows his honest face:
Now give the hautboys breath; he comes, he comes!
  Bacchus, ever fair and young
   Drinking joys did first ordain;   55
  Bacchus' blessings are a treasure,
Drinking is a soldier's pleasure;
    Rich the treasure,
    Sweet the pleasure,
    Sweet is pleasure after pain.   60

CHORUS

* Bacchus' blessings are a treasure,*
* Drinking is the soldier's pleasure;*
*   Rich the treasure,*
*   Sweet the pleasure,*
*   Sweet is pleasure after pain.*   65

IV

Sooth'd with the sound, the king grew vain;
  Fought all his battles o'er again;

---

[4] Greek god of wine.

And thrice he routed all his foes, and thrice he slew the slain.
The master saw the madness rise,
His glowing cheeks, his ardent eyes;   70
And, while he heav'n and earth defied,
Chang'd his hand, and check'd his pride.
    He chose a mournful Muse,
       Soft pity to infuse:
He sung Darius [5] great and good,   75
       By too severe a fate
Fallen, fallen, fallen, fallen,
       Fallen from his high estate,
          And welt'ring in his blood;
Deserted at his utmost need   80
By those his former bounty fed;
On the bare earth expos'd he lies,
With not a friend to close his eyes.
With downcast looks the joyless victor sate,
    Revolving in his alter'd soul   85
       The various turns of chance below;
    And, now and then, a sigh he stole,
       And tears began to flow.

CHORUS

Revolving in his alter'd soul
    The various turns of chance below;   90
And, now and then, a sigh he stole,
    And tears began to flow.

V

The mighty master smil'd to see
That love was in the next degree;
'T was but a kindred sound to move,   95
For pity melts the mind to love.
    Softly sweet, in Lydian measures,
    Soon he sooth'd his soul to pleasures.
    "War," he sung, "is toil and trouble;
    Honor, but an empty bubble.   100
       Never ending, still beginning,
    Fighting still, and still destroying:
       If the world be worth thy winning,
    Think, O think it worth enjoying.
       Lovely Thaïs sits beside thee,   105
       Take the good the gods provide thee."
The many rend the skies with loud applause;
So Love was crown'd, but Music won the cause

[5] Persian king.

The prince, unable to conceal his pain,
    Gaz'd on the fair   110
    Who caus'd his care,
  And sigh'd and look'd, sigh'd and look'd,
Sigh'd and look'd, and sigh'd again:
At length, with love and wine at once oppress'd,
The vanquish'd victor sunk upon her breast.   115

CHORUS

The prince, unable to conceal his pain,
    Gaz'd on the fair
    Who caus'd his care,
  And sigh'd and look'd, sigh'd and look'd,
Sigh'd and look'd, and sigh'd again: 120
At length, with love and wine at once oppress'd,
The vanquish'd victor sunk upon her breast.

VI

Now strike the golden lyre again:
A louder yet, and yet a louder strain.
Break his bands of sleep asunder,   125
And rouse him, like a rattling peal of thunder.
    Hark, hark, the horrid sound
  Has rais'd up his head:
  As wak'd from the dead,
    And amaz'd, he stares around.   130
"Revenge, revenge!" Timotheus cries,
  "See the Furies arise!
  See the snakes that they rear,
  How they hiss in their hair,
  And the sparkles that flash from their eyes!   135
  Behold a ghastly band,
  Each a torch in his hand!
Those are Grecian ghosts, that in battle were slain,
    And unburied remain
    Inglorious on the plain: 140
    Give the vengeance due
    To the valiant crew.
Behold how they toss their torches on high,
  How they point to the Persian abodes,
And glitt'ring temples of their hostile gods!"   145
The princes applaud, with a furious joy;
And the king seiz'd a flambeau with zeal to destroy;
    Thaïs led the way,
    To light him to his prey,
And, like another Helen, fir'd another Troy.   150

CHORUS

And the king seiz'd a flambeau with zeal to destroy;
  Thaïs led the way,
  To light him to his prey,
And, like another Helen, fir'd another Troy.

VII

  Thus long ago,   155
  Ere heaving bellows learn'd to blow,
    While organs yet were mute;
  Timotheus, to his breathing flute,
    And sounding lyre,
Could swell the soul to rage, or kindle soft desire.   160
  At last, divine Cecilia [6] came,
  Inventress of the vocal frame;
The sweet enthusiast, from her sacred store,
  Enlarg'd the former narrow bounds,
  And added length to solemn sounds,   165
With nature's mother wit, and arts unknown before.
  Let old Timotheus yield the prize,
  Or both divide the crown:
  He rais'd a mortal to the skies;
  She drew an angel down.   170

GRAND CHORUS

  At last divine Cecilia came,
  Inventress of the vocal frame;
The sweet enthusiast, from her sacred store,
  Enlarg'd the former narrow bounds,
  And added length to solemn sounds,   175
With nature's mother wit, and arts unknown before.
  Let old Timotheus yield the prize,
  Or both divide the crown:
  He rais'd a mortal to the skies;
  She drew an angel down.   180

JOHN DRYDEN

TO A RED-HEADED DO-GOOD WAITRESS

  Every morning I went to her charity and learned
  to face the music of her white smile so well
  that it infected by black teeth as I escaped,

[6] Patron saint of musicians and sacred music.

and those who saw me smiled too and went in
the White Castle, where she is the inviolable lady.   5

There cripples must be bright, and starvers noble:
no tears, no stomach-cries, but pain made art
to move her powerful red pity toward philanthropy.
So I must wear my objectively stinking poverty
like a millionaire clown's rags and sing, "Oh I   10

got plenty o' nuttin'," as if I made
a hundred grand a year like Gershwin, while
I get a breakfast every day from her for two
weeks and nothing else but truth: she has
a policeman and a wrong sonnet in fifteen lines.   15

ALAN DUGAN

ROMANCE OF THE ESCAPED CHILDREN

Goodbye, children: the bad Good Knight
is through. The rescued girl is asleep,
dreaming of ransom and astrologers
in the highest room of the family Keep.

On the second floor the Him Himself   5
is sound asleep among his pudding wife
and in the great Ground Hall below
retainers denounce the family wine

and pick at the bones of a cold dwarf.
Down in the cellars you shivered about,   10
continuous shrieks applaud the rack: he is,
from top to bottom, a good to bad scout,

domestic in the middle. You are fortunate
to have escaped from this on muffled oars.

ALAN DUGAN

ON A SEVEN-DAY DIARY

Oh I got up and went to work
and worked and came back home
and ate and talked and went to sleep.

Then I got up and went to work
and worked and came back home   5
from work and ate and slept.
Then I got up and went to work
and worked and came back home
and ate and watched a show and slept.
Then I got up and went to work   10
and worked and came back home
and ate steak and went to sleep.
Then I got up and went to work
and worked and came back home
and ate and fucked and went to sleep.   15
Then it was Saturday, Saturday, Saturday!
Love must be the reason for the week!
We went shopping! I saw clouds!
The children explained everything!
I could talk about the main thing!   20
What did I drink on Saturday night
that lost the first, best half of Sunday?
The last half wasn't worth this "word."
Then I got up and went to work
and worked and came back home   25
From work and ate and went to sleep,
refreshed but tired by the week-end.

ALAN DUGAN

THE GROUNDHOG

In June, amid the golden fields,
I saw a groundhog lying dead.
Dead lay he; my senses shook,
And mind outshot our naked frailty.
There lowly in the vigorous summer   5
His form began its senseless change,
And made my senses waver dim
Seeing nature ferocious in him.
Inspecting close his maggots' might
And seething cauldron of his being,   10
Half with loathing, half with a strange love,
I poked him with an angry stick.
The fever arose, became a flame
And Vigour circumscribed the skies,
Immense energy in the sun,   15
And through my frame a sunless trembling.

My stick had done nor good nor harm.
Then stood I silent in the day
Watching the object, as before;
And kept my reverence for knowledge   20
Trying for control, to be still,
To quell the passion of the blood;
Until I had bent down on my knees
Praying for joy in the sight of decay.
And so I left: and I returned   25
In Autumn strict of eye, to see
The sap gone out of the groundhog,
But the bony sodden hulk remained.
But the year had lost its meaning,
And in intellectual chains   30
I lost both love and loathing,
Mured up in the wall of wisdom.
Another summer took the fields again
Massive and burning, full of life,
But when I chanced upon the spot   35
There was only a little hair left,
And bones bleaching in the sunlight
Beautiful as architecture;
I watched them like a geometer,
And cut a walking stick from a birch.   40
It has been three years, now.
There is no sign of the groundhog.
I stood there in the whirling summer,
My hand capped a withered heart,
And thought of China and of Greece,   45
Of Alexander in his tent;
Of Montaigne [1] in his tower,
Of Saint Theresa [2] in her wild lament.

RICHARD EBERHART

THE LOVE SONG
OF J. ALFRED PRUFROCK

S'io credesse che mia risposta fosse
A persona che mai tornasse al mondo,
Questa fiamma staria senza piu scosse.
Ma perciocche giammai di questo fondo

---

[1] French essayist.
[2] Martyred by the Saracens.

Non torno vivo alcun, s'i'odo il vero,
Senza tema d'infamia ti rispondo.[1]

Let us go then, you and I,
When the evening is spread out against the sky
Like a patient etherised upon a table;
Let us go, through certain half-deserted streets,
The muttering retreats   5
Of restless nights in one-night cheap hotels
And sawdust restaurants with oyster-shells:
Streets that follow like a tedious argument
Of insidious intent
To lead you to an overwhelming question . . .   10
Oh, do not ask, "What is it?"
Let us go and make our visit.

   In the room the women come and go
Talking of Michelangelo.

   The yellow fog that rubs its back upon the window-panes,   15
The yellow smoke that rubs its muzzle on the window-panes
Licked its tongue into the corners of the evening,
Lingered upon the pools that stand in drains,
Let fall upon its back the soot that falls from chimneys,
Slipped by the terrace, made a sudden leap,   20
And seeing that it was a soft October night,
Curled once about the house, and fell asleep.

   And indeed there will be time
For the yellow smoke that slides along the street,
Rubbing its back upon the window-panes;   25
There will be time, there will be time
To prepare a face to meet the faces that you meet;
There will be time to murder and create,
And time for all the works and days of hands
That lift and drop a question on your plate;   30
Time for you and time for me,
And time yet for a hundred indecisions,
And for a hundred visions and revisions,
Before the taking of a toast and tea.

   In the room the women come and go   35
Talking of Michelangelo.

---

[1] From Dante's *Inferno*, Book XXVII, Guido da Montefeltro, famed Ghibelline war counselor,
to Dante: If I thought my answer were to someone who could ever return to the world, this flame
would never shake again, but since no one ever returns alive from this depth, if I hear correctly,
then I answer you without fear of infamy.

And indeed there will be time
To wonder, "Do I dare?" and, "Do I dare?"
Time to turn back and descend the stair,
With a bald spot in the middle of my hair—   40
[They will say: "How his hair is growing thin!"]
My morning coat, my collar mounting firmly to the chin,
My necktie rich and modest, but asserted by a simple pin—
[They will say: "But how his arms and legs are thin!"]
Do I dare   45
Disturb the universe?
In a minute there is time
For decisions and revisions which a minute will reverse.

For I have known them all already, known them all:—
Have known the evenings, mornings, afternoons,   50
I have measured out my life with coffee spoons;
I know the voices dying with a dying fall
Beneath the music from a farther room.
    So how should I presume?

And I have known the eyes already, known them all—   55
The eyes that fix you in a formulated phrase,
And when I am formulated, sprawling on a pin,
When I am pinned and wriggling on the wall,
Then how should I begin
To spit out all the butt-ends of my days and ways?   60
    And how should I presume?

And I have known the arms already, known them all—
Arms that are braceleted and white and bare
[But in the lamplight, downed with light brown hair!]
Is it perfume from a dress   65
That makes me so digress?
Arms that lie along a table, or wrap about a shawl.
    And should I then presume?
    And how should I begin?
                              .   .   .

Shall I say, I have gone at dusk through narrow streets   70
And watched the smoke that rises from the pipes
Of lonely men in shirt-sleeves, leaning out of windows? . . .

    I should have been a pair of ragged claws
Scuttling across the floors of silent seas.
                              .   .   .

And the afternoon, the evening, sleeps so peacefully!   75
Smoothed by long fingers,
Asleep . . . tired . . . or it malingers,
Stretched on the floor, here beside you and me.
Should I, after tea and cakes and ices,

Have the strength to force the moment to its crisis?   80
But though I have wept and fasted, wept and prayed,
Though I have seen my head [grown slightly bald] brought in upon a platter,
I am no prophet—and here's no great matter;
I have seen the moment of my greatness flicker,
And I have seen the eternal Footman hold my coat, and snicker,   85
And in short, I was afraid.

   And would it have been worth it, after all,
After the cups, the marmalade, the tea,
Among the porcelain, among some talk of you and me,
Would it have been worth while,   90
To have bitten off the matter with a smile,
To have squeezed the universe into a ball
To roll it toward some overwhelming question,
To say: "I am Lazarus, come from the dead,
Come back to tell you all, I shall tell you all"—   95
If one, settling a pillow by her head,
   Should say: "That is not what I meant at all.
   That is not it, at all."

   And would it have been worth it, after all,
Would it have been worth while,   100
After the sunsets and the dooryards and the sprinkled streets,
After the novels, after the teacups, after the skirts that trail along the floor—
And this, and so much more?—
It is impossible to say just what I mean!
But as if a magic lantern threw the nerves in patterns on a screen: 105
Would it have been worth while
If one, settling a pillow or throwing off a shawl,
And turning toward the window, should say:
   "That is not it at all,
   That is not what I meant, at all."   110

       .   .   .

No! I am not Prince Hamlet, nor was meant to be;
Am an attendant lord, one that will do
To swell a progress, start a scene or two,
Advise the prince; no doubt, an easy tool,
Deferential, glad to be of use,   115
Politic, cautious, and meticulous;
Full of high sentence, but a bit obtuse;
At times, indeed, almost ridiculous—
Almost, at times, the Fool.

   I grow old . . . I grow old . . .   120
I shall wear the bottoms of my trousers rolled.

   Shall I part my hair behind? Do I dare to eat a peach?
I shall wear white flannel trousers, and walk upon the beach.

I have heard the mermaids singing, each to each.

I do not think that they will sing to me.   125

I have seen them riding seaward on the waves
Combing the white hair of the waves blown back
When the wind blows the water white and black.

We have lingered in the chambers of the sea
By sea-girls wreathed with seaweed red and brown   130
Till human voices wake us, and we drown.

T. S. ELIOT

THE ROAD NOT TAKEN

Two roads diverged in a yellow wood,
And sorry I could not travel both
And be one traveler, long I stood
And looked down one as far as I could
To where it bent in the undergrowth;   5

Then took the other, as just as fair,
And having perhaps the better claim,
Because it was grassy and wanted wear;
Though as for that the passing there
Had worn them really about the same,   10

And both that morning equally lay
In leaves no step had trodden black.
Oh, I kept the first for another day!
Yet knowing how way leads on to way,
I doubted if I should ever come back.   15

I shall be telling this with a sigh
Somewhere ages and ages hence:
Two roads diverged in a wood, and I—
I took the one less traveled by,
And that has made all the difference.   20

ROBERT FROST

A SUPERMARKET IN CALIFORNIA

What thoughts I have of you tonight, Walt Whitman, for I walked down the sidestreets under the trees with a headache self-conscious looking at the full moon.

In my hungry fatigue, and shopping for images, I went into the neon fruit supermarket, dreaming of your enumerations!

What peaches and what penumbras! Whole families shopping at night! Aisles full of husbands! Wives in the avocados, babies in the tomatoes!—and you, Garcia Lorca, what were you doing down by the watermelons?

I saw you, Walt Whitman, childless, lonely old grubber, poking among the meats in the refrigerator and eyeing the grocery boys.

I heard you asking questions of each: Who killed the pork chops? What price bananas? Are you my Angel?   5

I wandered in and out of the brilliant stacks of cans following you, and followed in my imagination by the store detective.

We strode down the open corridors together in our solitary fancy tasting artichokes, possessing every frozen delicacy, and never passing the cashier.

Where are we going, Walt Whitman? The doors close in an hour. Which way does your beard point tonight?

(I touch your book and dream of our odyssey in the supermarket and feel absurd.)

Will we walk all night through solitary streets? The trees add shade to shade, lights out in the houses, we'll both be lonely.   10

Will we stroll dreaming of the lost America of love past blue automobiles in driveways, home to our silent cottage?

Ah, dear father, graybeard, lonely old courage-teacher, what America did you have when Charon [1] quit poling his ferry and you got out on a smoking bank and stood watching the boat disappear on the black waters of Lethe? [2]

ALLEN GINSBERG

THE PHILOSOPHER

Three blank walls, a barred window with no view,
A ceiling within reach of the raised hands,
A floor blank as the walls.

And, ruling out distractions of the body   5
Growth of the hair and nails, a prison diet,
Thoughts of escape—

[1] Boatman of Hades.
[2] The river of forgetfulness in Hades.

Ruling out memory and fantasy,
The distant tramping of a gaoler's boots,
Visiting mice and such,

What solace here for a laborious mind!　　　　　　　　10
What a redoubtable and single task
One might attempt here:

Threading a logic between wall and wall,
Ceiling and floor, more accurate by far
Than the cob-spider's.　　　　　　　　　　　　　　15

Truth captured without increment of flies—
Spinning and knotting till the cell became
A spacious other head

In which the emancipated reason might
Learn in due time to walk at greater length　　　　20
And more unanswerably.

ROBERT GRAVES

ULYSSES

To the much-tossed Ulysses,[1] never done
　　With woman whether gowned as wife or whore,
Penelope [2] and Circe [3] seemed as one:
She like a whore made his lewed fancies run,
　　And wifely she a hero to him bore.　　　　　　　5

Their counter-changings terrified his way:
　　They were the clashing rocks, Symplegades,[4]
Scylla [5] and Charybdis [6] too were they;
Now they were storms frosting the sea with spray
　　And now the lotus island's drunken ease.[7]　　　10

They multiplied into the Sirens' throng,[8]
　　Forewarned by fear of whom he stood bound fast
Hand and foot helpless to the vessel's mast,

[1] His return after the Trojan war to Ithaca in Greece is chronicled in *The Odyssey*.
[2] His faithful wife.
[3] A sorceress.
[4] Two rocks at the entrance to the Black Sea.
[5] A rock on the Italian coast.
[6] A whirlpool off the Sicilian coast.
[7] A paradise.
[8] Beautiful women whose music lured sailors to destruction.

Yet would not stop his ears: daring their song
    He groaned and sweated till that shore was past.   15

One, two and many: flesh had made him blind,
    Flesh had one pleasure only in the act,
Flesh set one purpose only in the mind—
Triumph of flesh and afterwards to find
    Still those same terrors wherewith flesh was racked.   20

His wiles were witty and his fame far known,
Every king's daughter sought him for her own,
    Yet he was nothing to be won or lost.
    All lands to him were Ithaca: love-tossed
He loathed the fraud, yet would not bed alone.   25

ROBERT GRAVES

WARNING TO CHILDREN

Children, if you dare to think
Of the greatness, rareness, muchness,
Fewness of this precious only
Endless world in which you say
You live, you think of things like this: 5
Blocks of slate enclosing dappled
Red and green, enclosing tawny
Yellow nets, enclosing white
And black acres of dominoes,
Where a neat brown paper parcel   10
Tempts you to untie the string.
In the parcel a small island,
On the island a large tree,
On the tree a husky fruit.
Strip the husk and pare the rind off: 15
In the kernel you will see
Blocks of slate enclosed by dappled
Red and green, enclosed by tawny
Yellow nets, enclosed by white

And black acres of dominoes,   20
Where the same brown paper parcel—
Children, leave the string alone!
For who dares undo the parcel
Finds himself at once inside it,
On the island, in the fruit,   25
Blocks of slate about his head,
Finds himself enclosed by dappled
Green and red, enclosed by yellow
Tawny nets, enclosed by black
And white acres of dominoes,   30
With the same brown paper parcel
Still untied upon his knee.
And, if he then should dare to think
Of the fewness, muchness, rareness,
Greatness of this endless only   35
Precious world in which he says
He lives—he then unties the string.

ROBERT GRAVES

ICARUS

Icarus, in airy arcs,
Takes the smallness of the islands
for applause.

"To hold breath, this taut sky
must hold me!" He laughs,   5
and leaps chasms of light.

Icarus, turning
on the curve of his great wings,

meets for a moment the charioteer's
lidless and innocent eye.   10
The sea glitters attentively,
then,
Unfolds too quickly and is true.

Though the sun receded,
and the water was a stone slab—   15
Never did man fly higher.

MITCH HOLT

[TERENCE, THIS IS STUPID STUFF]

"Terence,[1] this is stupid stuff:
You eat your victuals fast enough;
There can't be much amiss, 'tis clear,
To see the rate you drink your beer.
But oh, good Lord, the verse you make,   5
It gives a chap the bellyache.
The cow, the old cow, she is dead;
It sleeps well, the hornéd head:
We poor lads, 'tis our turn now
To hear such tunes as killed the cow.   10
Pretty friendship 'tis to rhyme
Your friends to death before their time
Moping melancholy mad:
Come, pipe a tune to dance to, lad."

Why, if 'tis dancing you would be,   15
There's brisker pipes than poetry.
Say, for what were hopyards meant,
Or why was Burton built on Trent?
Oh many a peer of England brews
Livelier liquor than the Muse,   20
And malt does more than Milton can
To justify God's ways to man.
Ale, man, ale's the stuff to drink
For fellows whom it hurts to think:

[1] In the first stanza a friend complains of the poet's writing. In the remainder of the poem, the poet (Housman?) replies to his friend.

Look into the pewter pot   25
To see the world as the world's not.
And faith, 'tis pleasant till 'tis past:
The mischief is that 'twill not last.
Oh I have been to Ludlow fair
And left my necktie God knows where,   30
And carried halfway home, or near,
Pints and quarts of Ludlow beer:
Then the world seemed none so bad,
And I myself a sterling lad;
And down in lovely muck I've lain,   35
Happy till I woke again.
Then I saw the morning sky.
Heigho, the tale was all a lie;
The world, it was the old world yet,
I was I, my things were wet,   40
And nothing now remained to do
But begin the game anew.

　　Therefore, since the world has still
Much good, but much less good than ill,
And while the sun and moon endure   45
Luck's a chance, but trouble's sure,
I'd face it as a wise man would,
And train for ill and not for good.
'Tis true the stuff I bring for sale
Is not so brisk a brew as ale: 50
Out of a stem that scored the hand
I wrung it in a weary land.
But take it: if the smack is sour,
The better for the embittered hour;
It should do good to heart and head   55
When your soul is in my soul's stead;
And I will friend you, if I may,
In the dark and cloudy day.

　　There was a king reigned in the East:
There, when kings will sit to feast,   60
They get their fill before they think
With poisoned meat and poisoned drink.
He gathered all that springs to birth
From the many-venomed earth;
First a little, thence to more,   65
He sampled all her killing store;
And easy, smiling, seasoned sound,
Sate the king when healths went round.
They put arsenic in his meat
And stared aghast to watch him eat;   70
They poured strychnine in his cup

And shook to see him drink it up:
They shook, they stared as white's their shirt:
Them it was their poison hurt.
—I tell the tale that I heard told. 75
Mithridates,[2] he died old.

A. E. HOUSMAN

LOVE THE WILD SWAN

"I hate my verses, every line, every word,
Oh pale and brittle pencils ever to try
One grass-blade's curve, or the throat of one bird
That clings to twig, ruffled against white sky.
Oh cracked and twilight mirrors ever to catch 5
One color, one glinting flash, of the splendor of things.
Unlucky hunter, Oh bullets of wax,
The lion beauty, the wild-swan wings, the storm of the wings."
—This wild swan of a world is no hunter's game.
Better bullets than yours would miss the white breast, 10
Better mirrors than yours would crack in the flame.
Does it matter whether you hate your . . . self? At least
Love your eyes that can see, your mind that can
Hear the music, the thunder of the wings. Love the wild swan.

ROBINSON JEFFERS

SHINE, PERISHING REPUBLIC

While this America settles in the mould of its vulgarity, heavily thickening to
empire,
And protest, only a bubble in the molten mass, pops and sighs out, and the
mass hardens,

I sadly smiling remember that the flower fades to make the fruit, the fruit rots to
make earth.
Out of the mother; and through the spring exultances, ripeness and decadence;
and home to the mother.

You make haste on decay: not blameworthy; life is good, be it stubbornly long or
suddenly 5

[2] A king in ancient times who made himself immune to poison by taking small doses over a
long period.

A mortal splendor: meteors are not needed less than mountains: shine, perishing
  republic.

But for my children, I would have them keep their distance from the thickening
  center; corruption
Never has been compulsory, when the cities lie at the monster's feet there are
  left the mountains.

And boys, be in nothing so moderate as in love of man, a clever servant, insufferable master.
There is the trap that catches noblest spirits, that caught—they say—God, when
  he walked on earth.   10

ROBINSON JEFFERS

ON FIRST LOOKING INTO CHAPMAN'S HOMER [1]

Much have I travell'd in the realms of gold,
  And many goodly states and kingdoms seen;
  Round many western islands have I been
Which bards in fealty to Apollo hold.
Oft of one wide expanse had I been told   5
  That deep-brow'd Homer ruled as his demesne;
  Yet did I never breathe its pure serene
Till I heard Chapman speak out loud and bold:
Then felt I like some watcher of the skies
  When a new planet swims into his ken;   10
Or like stout Cortez [2] when with eagle eyes
  He star'd at the Pacific—and all his men
Look'd at each other with a wild surmise—
  Silent, upon a peak in Darien.

JOHN KEATS

ODE ON A GRECIAN URN

Thou still unravished bride of quietness,
  Thou foster child of silence and slow time,
Sylvan historian, who canst thus express
  A flowery tale more sweetly than our rhyme:

[1] George Chapman: English dramatic poet and translator of Homer (1559?–1634).
[2] For what it's worth: it was Balboa who stood silent on that peak in Darien (Panama).

What leaf-fringed legend haunts about thy shape   5
    Of deities or mortals, or of both,
        In Tempe or the dales of Arcady?
    What men or gods are these? What maidens loth?
What mad pursuit? What struggle to escape?
    What pipes and timbrels? What wild ecstasy?   10

Heard melodies are sweet, but those unheard
    Are sweeter; therefore, ye soft pipes, play on;
Not to the sensual ear, but, more endeared,
    Pipe to the spirit ditties of no tone:
Fair youth, beneath the trees, thou canst not leave   15
    Thy song, nor ever can those trees be bare;
        Bold Lover, never, never canst thou kiss,
Though winning near the goal—yet, do not grieve;
    She cannot fade, though thou hast not thy bliss,
        Forever wilt thou love, and she be fair!   20

Ah, happy, happy boughs! that cannot shed
    Your leaves, nor ever bid the Spring adieu;
And, happy melodist, unweariéd,
    Forever piping songs forever new;
More happy love! more happy, happy love!   25
    Forever warm and still to be enjoyed,
        Forever panting, and forever young;
All breathing human passion far above,
    That leaves a heart high-sorrowful and cloyed,
        A burning forehead, and a parching tongue.   30

Who are these coming to the sacrifice?
    To what green altar, O mysterious priest,
Lead'st thou that heifer lowing at the skies,
    And all her silken flanks with garlands dressed?
What little town by river or sea shore,   35
    Or mountain-built with peaceful citadel,
        Is emptied of this folk, this pious morn?
And, little town, thy streets for evermore
    Will silent be; and not a soul to tell
        Why thou art desolate, can e'er return.   40

O Attic shape! Fair attitude! with brede
    Of marble men and maidens overwrought,
With forest branches and the trodden weed;
    Thou, silent form, dost tease us out of thought
As doth eternity: Cold Pastoral!   45
    When old age shall this generation waste,
        Thou shalt remain, in midst of other woe

Than ours, a friend to man, to whom thou say'st,
　"Beauty is truth, truth beauty,"—that is all
　　Ye know on earth, and all ye need to know.　　　50

JOHN KEATS

ON SEEING THE ELGIN MARBLES [1]
FOR THE FIRST TIME

My spirit is too weak—mortality
Weighs heavily on me like unwilling sleep,
And each imagin'd pinnacle and steep
Of godlike hardship tells me I must die
Like a sick eagle looking at the sky.　　　5
Yet 'tis a gentle luxury to weep
That I have not the cloudy winds to keep,
Fresh for the opening of the morning's eye.
Such dim-conceivéd glories of the brain
Bring round the heart an undescribable feud;　　　10
So do these wonders a most dizzy pain,
That mingles Grecian grandeur with the rude
Wasting of old Time—with a billowy main—
A sun—a shadow of a magnitude.

JOHN KEATS

FALL OF ICARUS: BRUEGHEL

Flashing through falling sunlight
A frantic leg late plunging from its strange
Communicating moment
Flutters in shadowy waves.

Close by those shattered waters—　　　5
The spray, no doubt, struck shore—
One dreamless shepherd and his old sheep dog
Define outrageous patience
Propped on staff and haunches,
Intent on nothing, backs bowed against the sea,　　　10
While the slow flocks of sheep gnaw on the grass-thin coast.

[1] Sculptures removed from the Parthenon to England by Lord Elgin in the early nineteenth century.

Crouched in crimson homespun an indifferent peasant
Guides his blunt plow through gravelled ground,
Cutting flat furrows hugging this hump of land.
One partridge sits immobile on its bough   15
Watching a Flemish fisherman pursue
Fish in the darkening bay;
Their stillness mocks rude ripples rising and circling in.

Yet that was a stunning greeting
For any old angler, peasant, or the grand ship's captain,   20
Though sent by a mere boy
Bewildered in the gravitational air,
Flashing his wild white arms at the impassive sea-drowned sun.
Now only coastal winds
Ruffle the partridge feathers,·   25
Muting the soft ripping of sheep cropping,
The heavy whisper
Of furrows falling, ship cleaving,
Water lapping.

Lulled in the loose furl and hum of infamous folly,   30
Darkly, how silently, the cold sea suckles him.

JOSEPH LANGLAND

ARS POETICA [1]

A poem should be palpable and mute
As a globed fruit,

Dumb
As old medallions to the thumb,

Silent as the sleeve-worn stone   5
Of casement ledges where the moss has grown—

A poem should be wordless
As the flight of birds.

*

A poem should be motionless in time
As the moon climbs,   10

[1] The Art of Poetry.

Leaving, as the moon releases
Twig by twig the night-entangled trees,

Leaving, as the moon behind the winter leaves,
Memory by memory the mind—

A poem should be motionless in time   15
As the moon climbs.

*

A poem should be equal to:
Not true.

For all the history of grief
An empty doorway and a maple leaf.   20

For love
The leaning grasses and two lights above the sea—

A poem should not mean
But be.

ARCHIBALD MACLEISH

LUCIFER IN STARLIGHT

On a starred night Prince Lucifer uprose.
Tired of his dark dominion, swung the fiend
Above the rolling ball, in cloud part screened,
Where sinners hugged their spectre of repose.
Poor prey to his hot fit of pride were those.   5
And now upon his western wing he leaned,
Now his huge bulk o'er Afric's sands careened,
Now the black planet shadowed Arctic snows.
Soaring through wider zones that pricked his scars
With memory of the old revolt from Awe,   10
He reached a middle height, and at the stars,
Which are the brain of heaven, he looked, and sank.
Around the ancient track marched, rank on rank,
The army of unalterable law.

GEORGE MEREDITH

[EUCLID ALONE HAS LOOKED ON BEAUTY BARE]

Euclid [1] alone has looked on Beauty bare.
Let all who prate of Beauty hold their peace,
And lay them prone upon the earth and cease
To ponder on themselves, the while they stare
At nothing, intricately drawn nowhere   5
In shapes of shifting lineage; let geese
Gabble and hiss, but heroes seek release
From dusty bondage into luminous air.
O blinding hour, O holy, terrible day,
When first the shaft into his vision shone   10
Of light anatomized! Euclid alone
Has looked on Beauty bare. Fortunate they
Who, though once only and then but far away,
Have heard her massive sandal set on stone.

EDNA ST. VINCENT MILLAY

SONNET TO GATH [2]

Country of hunchhbacks!—where the strong, straight spine
Jeered at by crooked children, makes his way
Through by-streets at the kindest hour of day,
Till he deplore his stature, and incline
To measure manhood with a gibbous line;   5
Till out of loneliness, being flawed with clay,
He stoop into his neighbour's house and say,
"Your roof is low for me—the fault is mine."
Dust in an urn long since, dispersed and dead
Is great Apollo; and the happier he;   10
Since who amongst you all would lift a head
At a god's radiance on the mean door-tree,
Saving to run and hide your dates and bread,
And cluck your children in about your knee?

EDNA ST. VINCENT MILLAY

[1] Greek geometrician (300 B.C.).
[2] A city of the Philistines.

THE NEW ICARUS

Slip off the husk of gravity to lie
Bedded with wind; float on a whimsy, lift
Upon a wish: your bow's own arrow, rift
Newton's decorum—only when you fly.
But naked. No false-feathered fool, you try 5
Dalliance with heights, nor, plumed with metal, shift
And shear the clouds, imperiling lark and swift
And all birds bridal-bowered in the sky.

Your wreck of bone, barred their delight's dominions,
Lacking their formula for flight, holds imaged 10
Those alps of air no eagle's wing can quell.
With arms flung crosswise, pinioned to wooden pinions,
You, in one motion plucked and crimson-plumaged,
Outsoar all Heaven, plummeting all Hell.

VASSAR MILLER

THE HERO

Where there is personal liking we go.
   Where the ground is sour; where there are
   weeds of beanstalk height,
   snakes' hypodermic teeth, or
   the wind brings the "scarebabe voice" 5
   from the neglected yew set with
   the semi-precious cat's eyes of the owl—
awake, asleep, "raised ears extended to fine points," and so
on—love won't grow.

We do not like some things, and the hero 10
   doesn't; deviating head-stones
   and uncertainty;
   going where one does not wish
   to go; suffering and not
   saying so; standing and listening where something 15
   is hiding. The hero shrinks
as what it is flies out on muffled wings, with twin yellow
eyes—to and fro—

with quavering water-whistle note, low,
   high, in basso-falsetto chirps 20
   until the skin creeps.

Jacob [1] when a-dying, asked
Joseph: [2] Who are these? and blessed
both sons, the younger most, vexing Joseph. And
Joseph was vexing to some.
Cincinnatus [3] was; Regulus; [4] and some of our fellow
men have been, though   25

devout, like Pilgrim [5] having to go slow
   to find his roll; tired but hopeful—
   hope not being hope   30
   until all ground for hope has
   vanished; and lenient, looking
   upon a fellow creature's error with the
   feelings of a mother—a
woman or a cat. The decorous frock-coated Negro   35
by the grotto

answers the fearless sightseeing hobo
   who asks the man she's with, what's this,
   what's that, where's Martha
   buried, "Gen-ral Washington   40
   there; his lady, here"; speaking
   as if in a play—not seeing her; with a
   sense of human dignity
and reverence for mystery, standing like the shadow
of the willow.   45

Moses would not be grandson to Pharaoh.
   It is not what I eat that is
   my natural meat,
   the hero says. He's not out
   seeing a sight but the rock   50
   crystal thing to see—the startling El Greco [6]
   brimming with inner light—that
covets nothing that it has let go. This then you may know
as the hero.

MARIANNE MOORE

[1] See Genesis 27.
[2] *Ibid.,* 37.
[3] Roman dictator.
[4] Roman general.
[5] Hero of Bunyan's allegory *Pilgrim's Progress.*
[6] Painter in Venice and Spain (1548?–1625).

POETRY

I, too, dislike it: there are things that are important beyond all this fiddle.
  Reading it, however, with a perfect contempt for it, one discovers
  in it after all, a place for the genuine.
     Hands that can grasp, eyes
      that can dilate, hair that can rise   5
        if it must, these things are important not because a

high-sounding interpretation can be put upon them but because they are
  useful. When they become so derivative as to become unintelligible,
  the same thing may be said for all of us, that we
     do not admire what   10
     we cannot understand: the bat
        holding on upside down or in quest of something to

eat, elephants pushing, a wild horse taking a roll, a tireless wolf under
  a tree, the immovable critic twitching his skin like a horse that feels a flea,
        the base-   15
  ball fan, the statistician—
     nor is it valid
        to discriminate against "business documents and

school-books"; all these phenomena are important. One must make a distinction
  however: when dragged into prominence by half poets, the result is not poetry, 20
  nor till the poets among us can be
     "literalists of
     the imagination"—above
        insolence and triviality and can present

for inspection, "imaginary gardens with real toads in them" shall   25
  we have it. In the meantime, if you demand on the one hand,
  the raw material of poetry in
     all its rawness and
     that which is on the other hand
        genuine, you are interested in poetry.   30

MARIANNE MOORE

LIFE CYCLE OF COMMON MAN

Roughly figured, this man of moderate habits,
This average consumer of the middle class,
Consumed in the course of his average life span
Just under half a million cigarettes,

Four thousand fifths of gin and about   5
A quarter as much vermouth; he drank
Maybe a hundred thousand cups of coffee,
And counting his parents' share it cost
Something like half a million dollars
To put him through life. How many beasts   10
Died to provide him with meat, belt and shoes
Cannot be certainly said.
                                But anyhow,
It is in this way that a man travels through time,
Leaving behind him a lengthening trail   15
Of empty bottles and bones, of broken shoes,
Frayed collars and worn out or outgrown
Diapers and dinnerjackets, silk ties and slickers.

Given the energy and security thus achieved,
He did . . . ? What? The usual things, of course,   20
The eating, dreaming, drinking and begetting,
And he worked for the money which was to pay
For the eating, et cetera, which were necessary
If he were to go on working for the money, et cetera,
But chiefly he talked. As the bottles and bones   25
Accumulated behind him, the words proceeded
Steadily from the front of his face as he
Advanced into the silence and made it verbal.
Who can tally the tale of his words? A lifetime
Would barely suffice for their repetition;   30
If you merely printed all his commas the result
Would be a very large volume, and the number of times
He said "thank you" or "very little sugar, please,"
Would stagger the imagination. There were also
Witticisms, platitudes, and statements beginning   35
"It seems to me" or "As I always say."

Consider the courage in all that, and behold the man
Walking into deep silence, with the ectoplastic
Cartoon's balloon of speech proceeding
Steadily out of the front of his face, the words   40
Borne along on the breath which is his spirit
Telling the numberless tale of his untold Word
Which makes the world his apple, and forces him to eat.

                    HOWARD NEMEROV

EPITAPHS

Fu I

Fu I loved the high cloud and the hill,
Alas, he died of alcohol.

Li Po

And Li Po also died drunk.
He tried to embrace a moon
In the Yellow River.

EZRA POUND

FROM

HUGH SELWYN MAUBERLEY

E. P. Ode pour l'Élection de son Sépulcre [1]

I

For three years, out of key with his time,
He strove to resuscitate the dead art
Of poetry; to maintain "the sublime"
In the old sense. Wrong from the start—

No, hardly, but seeing he had been born   5
In a half savage country, out of date;
Bent resolutely on wringing lilies from the acorn;
Capaneus; trout for factitious bait;

Ἴδμεν γάρ τοι πάνθ', ὅσ' ἐνὶ Τροίη [2]
Caught in the unstopped ear;   10
Giving the rocks small lee-way
The chopped seas held him, therefore, that year.

His true Penelope was Flaubert,
He fished by obstinate isles;
Observed the elegance of Circe's hair   15
Rather than the mottoes on sun-dials.

Unaffected by "the march of events,"
He passed from men's memory in *l'an trentiesme*
De son eage; [3] the case presents
No adjunct to the Muses' diadem.   20

[1] Ode for the selection of his tomb.
[2] For indeed we know all that [occurred?] in Troy.
[3] The thirtieth year of his age.

II

The age demanded an image
Of its accelerated grimace,
Something for the modern stage,
Not, at any rate, an Attic grace;

Not, not certainly, the obscure reveries   25
Of the inward gaze;
Better mendacities
Than the classics in paraphrase!

The "age demanded" chiefly a mould in plaster,
Made with no loss of time,   30
A prose kinema, not, not assuredly, alabaster
Or the "sculpture" of rhyme.

EZRA POUND

FROM
MAUBERLEY
IV

Scattered Moluccas
Not knowing, day to day,
The first day's end, in the next noon;
The placid water
Unbroken by the Simoon;   5

Thick foliage
Placid beneath warm suns,
Tawn fore-shores
Washed in the cobalt of oblivions;

Or through dawn-mist   10
The grey and rose
Of the juridical
Flamingoes;

A consciousness disjunct,
Being but this overblotted   15
Series
Of intermittences;

Coracle of Pacific voyages,
The unforecasted beach;
Then on an oar   20
Read this:

"I was
And I no more exist;
Here drifted
An hedonist."   25

EZRA POUND

IN A STATION OF THE METRO

The apparition of these faces in the crowd;
Petals on a wet, black bough.

EZRA POUND

FROM
THE PISAN CANTOS
Canto LXXXI

Zeus lies in Ceres' bosom
Taishan is attended of loves
           under Cythera, before sunrise
and he said: Hay aquí mucho catolicismo—(sounded catoli*th*ismo)
  y muy poco reliHion"   5
and he said: Yo creo que los reyes desparecen" [1]
That was Padre José Elizondo
                in 1906 and in 1917
or about 1917
         and Dolores said: Come pan, niño," eat bread, me lad   10
Sargent had painted her
               before he descended
(i.e. if he descended)
            but in those days he did thumb sketches,
impressions of the Velasquez in the Museo del Prado   15
and books cost a peseta,
           brass candlesticks in proportion,
hot wind came from the marshes
      and death-chill from the mountains.
And later Bowers wrote: "but such hatred,   20
  I had never conceived such"
and the London reds wouldn't show up his friends
             (i.e. friends of Franco
working in London) and in Alcazar
forty years gone, they said: go back to the station to eat   25
you can sleep here for a peseta"
         goat bells tinkled all night
         and the hostess grinned: Eso es luto, *haw*!
mi marido es muerto [2]
         (it is mourning, my husband is dead)   30
when she gave me paper to write on
with a black border half an inch or more deep,
     say ⅝ths, of the locanda
"We call *all* foreigners frenchies"
and the egg broke in Cabranez' pocket,   35
         thus making history. Basil says
they beat drums for three days
till all the drumheads were busted
         (simple village fiesta)

---

[1] There is much Catholicism here—and very little religion . . . I believe that the kings are disappearing.

[2] That is mourning, *haw*! My husband is dead.

and as for his life in the Canaries . . .   40
Possum observed that the local   folk dance
was danced by the same dancers in divers localities
          in political welcome . . .
the technique of demonstration
          Cole studied that (not G.D.H., Horace)   45
"You will find" said old André Spire,
that every man on that board (Crédit Agricole)
has a brother-in-law
                    "You the one, I the few"
                    said John Adams   50
speaking of fears in the abstract
      to his volatile friend Mr Jefferson
(to break the pentameter, that was the first heave)
or as Jo Bard says: they never speak to each other,
if it is baker and concierge visibly   55
          it is La Rouchefoucauld and de Maintenon audibly.
"Te cavero lebudelle"
                    "La corata a te"
In less than a geological epoch
                    said Henry Mencken   60
"Some cook, some do not cook
   some things cannot be altered"
Ἰυγξ . . . ’εμὸν ποτί δῶματὸν ἄνδρα ³
What counts is the cultural level,
      thank Benin for this table ex packing box   65
   "doan yu tell no one I made it"
          from a mask fine as any in Frankfurt
"It'll get you offn th' groun"
                    Light as the branch of Kuanon
And at first disappointed with shoddy   70
the bare ram-shackle quais, but then saw the
high buggy wheels
                and was reconciled,
George Santayana arriving in the port of Boston
and kept to the end of his life that faint *thethear*   75
of the Spaniard
                as a grace quasi imperceptible
as did Muss the *v* for *u* of Romangna
and said the grief was a full act
          repeated for each new condoleress   80
working up to a climax.
and George Horace said he wd/ "get Beveridge" (Senator)
Beveridge wouldn't talk and he wouldn't write for the papers
but George got him by campin' in his hotel
and assailin' him at lunch breakfast an' dinner   85
                three articles

---

³ "The wryneck . . . the man to my home." The original appears to be Theocritus (writer of
pastoral poetry, 3rd cent. B.C.) "The wryneck attracts one to his home."

and my ole man went on hoein' corn
　　while George was a-tellin' him,
come across a vacant lot
　　　　where you'd occasionally see a wild rabbit　　　　90
or mebbe only a loose one
　　　AOI!
　　a leaf in the current
　　　　　　　　at my grates no Althea

　　Yet　　　　　　　　　　　　　　　　　　　95
Ere the season died a-cold
Borne upon a zephyr's shoulder
I rose through the aureate sky
　　　　　Lawes and Jenkyns guard thy rest
　　　　　Dolmetsch ever be thy guest,　　　　100
Has he tempered the viol's wood
To enforce　both the grave　and the acute?
Has he curved us the bowl of the lute?
　　　　　Lawes and Jenkyns guard thy rest
　　　　　Dolmetsch ever be thy guest　　　　105
Hast 'ou fashioned so airy a mood
　　To draw up leaf from the root?
Hast 'ou found　a cloud　so light
　　As seemed neither mist nor shade?
　　　　　Then resolve me, tell me aright　　　　110
　　　　　If Waller sang or Dowland played.
　　　Your eyen two wol sleye me sodenly
　　　I may the beauté of hem nat susteyne
And for 180 years almost nothing.
Ed ascoltando al leggier mormorio [4]　　　　115
　　　there came new subtlety of eyes into my tent,
whether of spirit or hypostasis,
　　　but what the blindfold hides
or at carneval
　　　　　　nor any pair showed anger　　　　120
　　Saw but the eyes and stance between the eyes,
colour, diastasis,
　　　careless or unaware it had not the
　　whole tent's room
nor was place for the full Εἰδῶς [5]　　　　125
interpass, penetrate
　　　casting but shade beyond the other lights
　　　　sky's clear
　　　　night's sea
　　　　green of the mountain pool　　　　130
　　　　shone from the unmasked eyes in half-mask's space.
What thou lovest well remains,
　　　　　　　　　the rest is dross

---

[4] And listening to the light murmur.　[5] Knowing (participle).

What thou lov'st well shall not be reft from thee
What thou lov'st well is thy true heritage   135
Whose world, or mine or theirs
                              or is it of none?
First came the seen, then thus the palpable
        Elysium, though it were in the halls of hell,
What thou lovest well is thy true heritage   140

The ant's a centaur in his dragon world.
Pull down thy vanity, it is not man
Made courage, or made order, or made grace,
        Pull down thy vanity, I say pull down.
Learn of the green world what can be thy place   145
In scaled invention or true artistry,
Pull down thy vanity,
                        Paquin pull down!
The green casque has outdone your elegance.

"Master thyself, then others shall thee beare"   150
        Pull down thy vanity
Thou art a beaten dog beneath the hail,
A swollen magpie in a fitful sun,
Half black half white
Nor knowst'ou wing from tail   155
Pull down thy vanity
                How mean thy hates
Fostered in Falsity,
                Pull down thy vanity,
Rathe to destroy, niggard in charity,   160
Pull down thy vanity,
                I say pull down.

But to have done instead of not doing
                this is not vanity
To have, with decency, knocked   165
That a Blunt should open
        To have gathered from the air a live tradition
or from a fine old eye the unconquered flame
This is not vanity.
        Here error is all in the not done,   170
all in the diffidence that faltered.

EZRA POUND

[I AM THE PEOPLE—THE MOB]

I am the people—the mob—the crowd—the mass.
Do you know that all the great work of the world is done through me?
I am the workingman, the inventor, the maker of the world's food and clothes.
I am the audience that witnesses history. The Napoleons come from me and the
    Lincolns. They die. And then I send forth more Napoleons and Lincolns.   5
I am the seed ground. I am a prairie that will stand for much plowing. Terrible
    storms pass over me. I forget. The best of me is sucked out and wasted. I forget.
    Everything but Death comes to me and makes me work and give up what I
    have. And I forget.
Sometimes I growl, shake myself and spatter a few red drops for history to re-   10
    member. Then—I forget.
When I, the People, learn to remember, when I, the People, use the lessons of
    yesterday and no longer forget who robbed me last year, who played me for a
    fool—then there will be no speaker in all the world say the name: "The Peo-
    ple," with any fleck of a sneer in his voice or any far-off smile of derision.   15
The mob—the crowd—the mass—will arrive then.

CARL SANDBURG

RED-HEADED RESTAURANT CASHIER

Shake back your hair, O red-headed girl.
Let go your laughter and keep your two proud freckles on your
           chin.
Somewhere is a man looking for a red-headed girl and some day
           maybe   5
      he will look into your eyes for a restaurant cashier
           and find a lover, maybe.
Around and around go ten thousand men hunting a red-headed
           girl
    with two freckles on her chin.   10
I have seen them hunting, hunting.
      Shake back your hair; let go your laughter.

CARL SANDBURG

ON THE DEATH OF A METAPHYSICIAN

Unhappy dreamer, who outwinged in flight
The pleasant region of the things I love,
And soared beyond the sunshine, and above

The golden cornfields and the dear and bright
Warmth of the hearth—blasphemer of delight,   5
Was your proud bosom not at peace with Jove,
That you sought, thankless for his guarded grove
The empty horror of abysmal night?

Ah, the thin air is cold above the moon!
I stood and saw you fall, befooled in death,   10
As, in your numbèd spirit's fatal swoon,
You cried you were a god, or were to be;
I heard with feeble moan your boastful breath
Bubble from depths of the Icarian sea.

GEORGE SANTAYANA

ON READING THE WAR DIARY
OF A DEFUNCT AMBASSADOR

So that's your Diary—that's your private mind
Translated into shirt-sleeved History. That
Is what diplomacy has left behind
For after-ages to peruse, and find
What passed beneath your elegant silk-hat.   5

You were a fine old gentleman; compact
Of shrewdness, charm, refinement and finesse.
Impeccable in breeding, taste and dress,
No diplomatic quality you lacked—
No tittle of ambassadorial tact.   10

I can imagine you among "the guns,"
Urbanely peppering partridge, grouse, or pheasant—
Guest of those infinitely privileged ones
Whose lives are padded, petrified, and pleasant.
I visualize you feeding off gold plate   15
And gossiping on grave affairs of State.

Now you're defunct; your gossip's gravely printed;
The world discovers where you lunched and dined
On such and such a day; and what was hinted
By ministers and generals far behind   20
The all-important conflict, carnage-tinted.

The world can read the rumours that you gleaned
From various Fronts; the well-known Names you met;

Each conference you attended and convened;
And (at appropriate moments) what you ate.   25
Thus (if the world's acute) it can derive
Your self, exact, uncensored and alive.

The world will find no pity in your pages;
No exercise of spirit worthy of mention;
Only a public-funeral grief-convention;   30
And all the circumspection of the ages.
But I, for one, am grateful, overjoyed,
And unindignant that your punctual pen
Should have been so constructively employed
In manifesting to unprivileged men   35
The visionless officialized fatuity
That once kept Europe safe for Perpetuity.

SIEGFRIED SASSOON

[IN THE NAKED BED, IN PLATO'S CAVE] [1]

In the naked bed, in Plato's cave,
Reflected headlights slowly slid the wall,
Carpenters hammered under the shaded window,
Wind troubled the window curtains all night long,
A fleet of trucks strained uphill, grinding,   5
Their freights covered, as usual.
The ceiling lightened again, the slanting diagram
Slid slowly forth.
     Hearing the milkman's chop,
His striving up the stair, the bottle's chink,   10
I rose from bed, lit a cigarette,
And walked to the window. The stony street
Displayed the stillness in which buildings stand,
The street-lamp's vigil and the horse's patience.
The winter sky's pure capital   15
Turned me back to bed with exhausted eyes.

Strangeness grew in the motionless air. The loose
Film grayed. Shaking wagons, hooves' waterfalls,
Sounded far off, increasing, louder and nearer.
A car coughed, starting. Morning, softly   20
Melting the air, lifted the half-covered chair
From underseas, kindled the looking-glass,

---

[1] See the sixth book of the *Republic*. Empirically minded people are prisoners chained in a cave. What they think is reality is not reality. The allegory explains(?) who is released or escapes from the chains and what happens to him.

Distinguished the dresser and the white wall.
The bird called tentatively, whistled, called,
Bubbled and whistled, so! Perplexed, still wet   25
With sleep, affectionate, hungry and cold. So, so,
O son of man, the ignorant night, the travail
Of early morning, the mystery of beginning
Again and again,
           While Time is unforgiven.   30

DELMORE SCHWARTZ

[SOCRATES' GHOST MUST HAUNT ME NOW]

Socrates' ghost must haunt me now,
Notorious death has let him go,
He comes to me with a clumsy bow,
Saying in his disuséd voice,
That I do not know I do not know,   5
The mechanical whims of appetite
Are all that I have of conscious choice,
The butterfly caged in electric light
Is my only day in the world's great night,
Love is not love, it is a child   10
Sucking his thumb and biting his lip,
But grasp it all, there may be more!
From the topless sky to the bottomless floor
With the heavy head and the finger tip:
All is not blind, obscene, and poor.   15
Socrates stands by me stockstill,
Teaching hope to my flickering will,
Pointing to the sky's inexorable blue
—Old Noumenon,[1] come true, come true!

DELMORE SCHWARTZ

OZYMANDIAS

I met a traveller from an antique land
Who said: Two vast and trunkless legs of stone
Stand in the desert . . . Near them, on the sand,
Half sunk, a shattered visage lies, whose frown,
And wrinkled lip, and sneer of cold command,   5

---

[1] A ground of phenomena that is unknowable by the senses but is conceivable by reason.

Tell that its sculptor well those passions read
Which yet survive, stamped on these lifeless things,
The hand that mocked them, and the heart that fed:
And on the pedestal these words appear:
"My name is Ozymandias, king of kings: 10
Look on my works, ye Mighty, and despair!"
Nothing beside remains. Round the decay
Of that colossal wreck, boundless and bare
The lone and level sands stretch far away.

PERCY BYSSHE SHELLEY

THE HILLSIDE WANDERERS

In overview, a statement on their ways

I

HOW HERS IS LOST

In ancient cave,
In robe of Theban rouge and dust,
In innocent gold morning,
With head blown free of codes and collars,
Hangs clay Antigone.   5
Heat, gone dry and deadly.

Her forceless feet
Drip down beneath pale ankles,
Rose clay waxed a soft white ash

Antigone,   10
Who sailed on Haemon's wavy grain,
A bright and reckless fishing boat,
Boating, fishing out simple love,
Would slip into forgetfulness

Except a knot, that holds her by the throat   15
And takes her tautly up from fishing days.

II

THE MUSE CAUTIONS THE WANDERER ON HIS

Hillside wanderer, homeward bent
Regard what costly show appease the Gods
Behold! A terminated woman therein.

Thus dies love   20
Betrayed by noble cause
Itself a prey to Creon's rotted pride.

Thus fades flower
Frailed by single bloom
To flourish under miracles of sky,   25
Then straight away to tighten at the dusk.
Antigone! Poor morning glory of a girl!
By family, blinded to all other ways.

Waste! Beauty.
Sing the mortal song   30
And, fireside again, think well
On safely having crossed immortal day!

III
THE WAY HE LIVES

The father king in halls of silver stalks,
Pale blue the mantle
Hanging from his back,   35
Attended by the babbling of the court,
In throne, in bed, in bearing thought, alone.

Creon paces the lengthy courtyard gardens.
Oppressing stars illumine all his moves
And outline shadows   40
Of a heavy man,
Until a marble bench
Is all the rest he has.
And there, in cold confusion, sits,
Undoes the mantle's ties,   45
And lets it slip,
And fall around his body on the stone.

IV
NOT KNOWING HIS WAY

A whittled Thebe
In skins of red and brown
Is sowing wheat,   50
He labors agelessly.

One dip inside his satchel,
One deep bend,
He pushes, with bronzed fingers,
In the earth,   55
Then drags across his forehead
An old arm.
Hot rays of sun stand, throbbing
On the soil.
He views the castle,   60
Waving in the pulse
Behind an afternoon of amber forests,

Regards the boiling landscape as he turns,
And moves again to plant another seed.

JEFF SHURIN

[IN MY CRAFT OR SULLEN ART]

In my craft or sullen art
Exercised in the still night
When only the moon rages
And the lovers lie abed
With all their griefs in their arms,   5
I labour by singing light
Not for ambition or bread
Or the strut and trade of charms
On the ivory stages
But for the common wages   10
Of their most secret heart.

Not for the proud man apart
From the raging moon I write
On these spindrift pages
Nor for the towering dead   15
With their nightingales and psalms
But for the lovers, their arms
Round the griefs of the ages,
Who pay no praise or wages
Nor heed my craft or art.   20

DYLAN THOMAS

[WHEN I HEARD THE LEARN'D ASTRONOMER]

When I heard the learn'd astronomer,
When the proofs, the figures, were ranged in columns before me,
When I was shown the charts and the diagrams, to add, divide, and measure them,
When I sitting heard the astronomer, where he lectured with much applause in the
   lecture-room,   5
How soon unaccountable I became tired and sick,
Till rising and gliding out, I wander'd off by myself,
In the mystical moist night-air, and from time to time,
Look'd up in perfect silence at the stars.

WALT WHITMAN

A NOISELESS PATIENT SPIDER

A noiseless patient spider,
I mark'd where on a little promontory it stood isolated,
Mark'd how to explore the vacant vast surrounding,
It launch'd forth filament, filament, filament, out of itself.
Ever unreeling them, ever tirelessly speeding them.   5

And you O my soul where you stand,
Surrounded, detached, in measureless oceans of space,
Ceaselessly musing, venturing, throwing, seeking the spheres to connect them.
Till the bridge you will need be form'd, till the ductile anchor hold,
Till the gossamer thread you fling catch somewhere, O my soul.   10

WALT WHITMAN

[STILL, CITIZEN SPARROW]

Still, citizen sparrow, this vulture which you call
Unnatural, let him but lumber again to air
Over the rotten office, let him bear
The carrion ballast up, and at the tall

Tip of the sky lie cruising. Then you'll see   5
That no more beautiful bird is in heaven's height,
No wider more placid wings, no watchfuller flight;
He shoulders nature there, the frightfully free,

The naked-headed one. Pardon him, you
Who dart in the orchard aisles, for it is he   10
Devours death, mocks mutability,
Has heart to make an end, keeps nature new.

Thinking of Noah, childheart, try to forget
How for so many bedlam hours his saw
Soured the song of birds with its wheezy gnaw,   15
And the slam of his hammer all the day beset

The people's ears. Forget that he could bear
To see the towns like coral under the keel,
And the fields so dismal deep. Try rather to feel
How high and weary it was, on the waters where   20

He rocked his only world, and everyone's.
Forgive the hero, you who would have died
Gladly with all you knew; he rode that tide
To Ararat; [1] all men are Noah's sons.

RICHARD WILBUR

[1] The mountain where Noah's ark came to rest.

LANDSCAPE WITH THE FALL OF ICARUS

According to Brueghel
when Icarus fell
it was spring

a farmer was ploughing
his field   5
the whole pageantry

of the year was
awake tingling
near

the edge of the sea   10
concerned

with itself

sweating in the sun
that melted
the wings' wax   15

unsignificantly
off the coast
there was

a splash quite unnoticed
this was   20
Icarus drowning

WILLIAM CARLOS WILLIAMS

LONG-LEGGED FLY

That civilisation may not sink,
Its great battle lost,
Quiet the dog, tether the pony
To a distant post;
Our master Caesar is in the tent   5
Where the maps are spread,
His eyes fixed upon nothing,
A hand under his head.
Like a long-legged fly upon the stream
His mind moves upon silence.   10

That the topless towers be burnt
And men recall that face,
Move most gently if move you must
In this lonely place.
She thinks, part woman, three parts a child,   15
That nobody looks; her feet
Practise a tinker shuffle
Picked up on a street.
Like a long-legged fly upon the stream
Her mind moves upon silence.   20

That girls at puberty may find
The first Adam in their thought,

Shut the door of the Pope's chapel,
Keep those children out.
There on that scaffolding reclines   25
Michael Angelo.
With no more sound than the mice make
His hand moves to and fro.
Like a long-legged fly upon the stream
His mind moves upon silence.   30

W. B. YEATS

THE SONG OF WANDERING AENGUS [1]

I went out to the hazel wood,
Because a fire was in my head,
And cut and peeled a hazel wand,
And hooked a berry to a thread;
And when white moths were on the wing,   5
And moth-like stars were flickering out,
I dropped the berry in a stream
And caught a little silver trout.

When I had laid it on the floor
I went to blow the fire aflame,   10
But something rustled on the floor,
And some one called me by my name:
It had become a glimmering girl
With apple blossom in her hair
Who called me by my name and ran   15
And faded through the brightening air.

Though I am old with wandering
Through hollow lands and hilly lands,
I will find out where she has gone,
And kiss her lips and take her hands;   20
And walk among long dappled grass,
And pluck till time and times are done
The silver apples of the moon,
The golden apples of the sun.

W. B. YEATS

[1] Irish god of love, youth, and beauty.

IN A DARK TIME

WHEN asked to describe a painting to be called "The Fall of Icarus" (and before they have seen the Brueghel painting), some students describe a beautiful, golden, winged figure twisting and falling and centered against a blue sky. They want the viewer to feel positively about their Icarus, to think that what he attempted was important and that his death was tragic (they've centered him on the canvas). The Brueghel painting almost invariably provokes the question: But where is Icarus? When his legs are located and identified, students often interpret the painting to mean that Icarus is not to be thought of positively, that what he attempted was unimportant, and that his death wasn't tragic; perhaps it was even comic.

But seeing the legs of Icarus doesn't apparently "explain" the painting. Like those poets who refer to the painting in their poems on Icarus, many fail or neglect to note that Icarus in this painting is not alone in his dying. One can see in the lower left-hand corner, where the horse leads the farmer, the head of a corpse, white as it rots in the sun. This corpse, maybe of an old man, and the corpse of Icarus are obscure. Their deaths seem equally unimportant. Flying to the sun or going about the normal business of the world—neither path makes a difference, and the ends are the same, unnoticed and inconsequential. In this second interpretation, the emphasis is on the fact that choosing a path of any kind makes no difference; in the end, death obliterates all distinctions.

In Ben Shahn's "The Red Stairway" the red stairs are built upon ruin and desolation. The beginning and the end of the stairs present the same world to the crippled man. Sisyphus-like, his task is meaningless, his way endless. Like Lear, he is bound upon a wheel of fire. The peace that Brecht's Galileo or Gide's Philoctetes achieve is an illusion. Not all of the selections in this second section present so bleak a point of view about man and the world, but the writers are concerned with man's mortality and with the problems of meaning in the face of it, with the irony of loss as a condition for insight, with the presence of pain and suffering and of their negative power. *King Lear* orchestrates these ideas, and Jan Kott's brilliant essay reveals Shakespeare's sensibility to the contemporary mind. Theodore Roethke's "In a Dark Time," LeRoi Jones in *Dutchman,* and G. Legman in "Institutionalized Lynch" indicate directly or indirectly that paths vary and that the endings need not be unnoticed or inconsequential.

DUTCHMAN

LeRoi Jones

CHARACTERS

Clay, twenty-year-old Negro   Young Negro
Lula, thirty-year-old white woman   Conductor
Riders of Coach, white and black

In the flying underbelly of the city. Steaming hot, and summer on top, outside. Underground. The subway heaped in modern myth.

Opening scene is a man sitting in a subway seat, holding a magazine but looking vacantly just above its wilting pages. Occasionally he looks blankly toward the window on his right. Dim lights and darkness whistling by against the glass. (Or paste the lights, as admitted props, right on the subway windows. Have them move, even dim and flicker. But give the sense of speed. Also stations, whether the train is stopped or the glitter and activity of these stations merely flashes by the windows.)

The man is sitting alone. That is, only his seat is visible, though the rest of the car is outfitted as a complete subway car. But only his seat is shown. There might be, for a time, as the play begins, a loud scream of the actual train. And it can recur throughout the play, or continue on a lower key once the dialogue starts.

The train slows after a time, pulling to a brief stop at one of the stations. The man looks idly up, until he sees a woman's face staring at him through the window; when it realizes that the man has noticed the face, it begins very premeditatedly to smile. The man smiles too, for a moment, without a trace of self-consciousness. Almost an instinctive though undesirable response. Then a kind of awkwardness or embarrassment sets in, and the man makes to look away, is further embarrassed, so he brings back his eyes to where the face was, but by now the train is moving again, and the face would seem to be left behind by the way the man turns his head to look back through the other windows at the slowly fading platform. He smiles then; more comfortably confident, hoping perhaps that his memory of this brief encounter will be pleasant. And then he is idle again.

SCENE I

Train roars. Lights flash outside the windows.

LULA *enters from the rear of the car in bright, skimpy summer clothes and sandals. She carries a net bag full of paper books, fruit, and other anonymous articles. She is wearing sunglasses, which she pushes up on her forehead from time to time.* LULA *is a tall, slender, beautiful woman with long red hair hanging straight down her back, wearing only loud lipstick in some-body's good taste. She is eating an apple, very daintily. Coming down the car toward* CLAY.

She stops beside CLAY'S *seat and hangs languidly from the strap, still managing to eat the apple. It is apparent that she is going to sit in the seat next to* CLAY, *and that she is only waiting for him to notice her before she sits.*

CLAY *sits as before, looking just beyond his magazine, now and again pulling the magazine slowly back and forth in front of his face in a hopeless effort to fan himself. Then he sees the woman hanging there beside him and he looks up into her face, smiling quizzically.*

LULA. Hello.
CLAY. Uh, hi're you?
LULA. I'm going to sit down. . . . O.K.?
CLAY. Sure.
LULA.
   [*Swings down onto the seat, pushing her legs straight out as if she is very weary*]
   Oooof! Too much weight.
CLAY. Ha, doesn't look like much to me.
   [*Leaning back against the window, a little surprised and maybe stiff*]
LULA. It's so anyway.
   [*And she moves her toes in the sandals, then pulls her right leg up on the left knee, better to inspect the bottoms of the sandals and the back of her heel. She appears for a second not to notice that* CLAY *is sitting next to her or that she has spoken to him just a second before.* CLAY *looks at the magazine, then out the black window. As he does this, she turns very quickly toward him*]
   Weren't you staring at me through the window?
CLAY.
   [*Wheeling around and very much stiffened*]
   What?

LULA. Weren't you staring at me through the window? At the last stop?

CLAY. Staring at you? What do you mean?

LULA. Don't you know what staring means?

CLAY. I saw you through the window . . . if that's what it means. I don't know if I was staring. Seems to me you were staring through the window at me.

LULA. I was. But only after I'd turned around and saw you staring through that window down in the vicinity of my ass and legs.

CLAY. Really?

LULA. Really. I guess you were just taking those idle potshots. Nothing else to do. Run your mind over people's flesh.

CLAY. Oh boy. Wow, now I admit I was looking in your direction. But the rest of that weight is yours.

LULA. I suppose.

CLAY. Staring through train windows is weird business. Much weirder than staring very sedately at abstract asses.

LULA. That's why I came looking through the window . . . so you'd have more than that to go on. I even smiled at you.

CLAY. That's right.

LULA. I even got into this train, going some other way than mine. Walked down the aisle . . . searching you out.

CLAY. Really? That's pretty funny.

LULA. That's pretty funny. . . . God, you're dull.

CLAY. Well, I'm sorry, lady, but I really wasn't prepared for party talk.

LULA. No, you're not. What are you prepared for?

[*Wrapping the apple core in a Kleenex and dropping it on the floor*]

CLAY.

[*Takes her conversation as pure sex talk. He turns to confront her squarely with this ideal*]

I'm prepared for anything. How about you?

LULA.

[*Laughing loudly and cutting it off abruptly*]

What do you think you're doing?

CLAY. What?

LULA. You think I want to pick you up, get you to take me somewhere and screw me, huh?

CLAY. Is that the way I look?

LULA. You look like you been trying to grow a beard. That's exactly what you look like. You look like you live in New Jersey with your parents and are trying to grow a beard. That's what. You look like you've been reading Chinese poetry and drinking lukewarm sugarless tea.

[*Laughs, uncrossing and recrossing her legs*]

You look like death eating a soda cracker.

CLAY.

[*Cocking his head from one side to the other, embarrassed and trying to make some comeback, but also intrigued by what the*

*woman is saying . . . even the sharp city coarseness of her
voice, which is still a kind of gentle sidewalk throb]*
Really? I look like all that?

LULA. Not all of it.
[She feints a seriousness to cover an actual somber tone]
I lie a lot.
[Smiling]
It helps me control the world.

CLAY.
[Relieved and laughing louder than the humor]
Yeah, I bet.

LULA. But it's true, most of it, right? Jersey? Your bumpy neck?

CLAY. How'd you know all that? Huh? Really, I mean about Jersey
. . . and even the beard. I met you before? You know Warren
Enright?

LULA. You tried to make it with your sister when you were ten.
*[CLAY leans back hard against the back of the seat, his eyes
opening now, still trying to look amused]*
But I succeeded a few weeks ago.
[She starts to laugh again]

CLAY. What're you talking about? Warren tell you that? You're a
friend of Georgia's?

LULA. I told you I lie. I don't know your sister. I don't know Warren
Enright.

CLAY. You mean you're just picking these things out of the air?

LULA. Is Warren Enright a tall skinny black black boy with a phony
English accent?

CLAY. I figured you knew him.

LULA. But I don't. I just figured you would know somebody like that.
[Laughs]

CLAY. Yeah, yeah.

LULA. You're probably on your way to his house now.

CLAY. That's right.

LULA.
*[Putting her hand on Clay's closest knee, drawing it from the
knee up to the thigh's hinge, then removing it, watching his
face very closely, and continuing to laugh, perhaps more gently
than before]*
Dull, dull, dull. I bet you think I'm exciting.

CLAY. You're O.K.

LULA. Am I exciting you now?

CLAY. Right. That's not what's supposed to happen?

LULA. How do I know?
*[She returns her hand, without moving it, then takes it away and
plunges it in her bag to draw out an apple]*
You want this?

CLAY. Sure.

LULA.
[She gets one out of the bag for herself]

Eating apples together is always the first step. Or walking up un-
inhabited Seventh Avenue in the twenties on weekends.

> [*Bites and giggles, glancing at* CLAY *and speaking in loose sing-
> song*]

Can get you involved . . . boy! Get us involved. Um-huh.

> [*Mock seriousness*]

Would you like to get involved with me, Mister Man?

CLAY.

> [*Trying to be as flippant as* LULA, *whacking happily at the apple*]
> Sure. Why not? A beautiful woman like you. Huh, I'd be a fool not
> to.

LULA. And I bet you're sure you know what you're talking about.

> [*Taking him a little roughly by the wrist, so he cannot eat the
> apple, then shaking the wrist*]
> I bet you're sure of almost everything anybody ever asked you about
> . . . right?

> [*Shakes his wrist harder*]
> Right?

CLAY. Yeah, right. . . . Wow, you're pretty strong, you know? Whatta
you, a lady wrestler or something?

LULA. What's wrong with lady wrestlers? And don't answer because
you never knew any. Huh.

> [*Cynically*]
> That's for sure. They don't have any lady wrestlers in that part of
> Jersey. That's for sure.

CLAY. Hey, you still haven't told me how you know so much about
me.

LULA. I told you I didn't know anything about *you* . . . you're a
well-known type.

CLAY. Really?

LULA. Or at least I know the type very well. And your skinny English
friend too.

CLAY. Anonymously?

LULA.

> [*Settles back in seat, single-mindedly finishing her apple and
> humming snatches of rhythm and blues song*]
> What?

CLAY. Without knowing us specifically?

LULA. Oh boy.

> [*Looking quickly at* CLAY]
> What a face. You know, you could be a handsome man.

CLAY. I can't argue with you.

LULA.

> [*Vague, off-center response*]
> What?

CLAY.

> [*Raising his voice, thinking the train noise has drowned part of
> his sentence*]
> I can't argue with you.

LULA. My hair is turning gray. A gray hair for each year and type I've
come through.

CLAY. Why do you want to sound so old?

LULA. But it's always gentle when it starts.

[*Attention drifting*]

Hugged against tenements, day or night.

CLAY. What?

LULA.

[*Refocusing*]

Hey, why don't you take me to that party you're going to?

CLAY. You must be a friend of Warren's to know about the party.

LULA. Wouldn't you like to take me to the party?

[*Imitates clinging vine*]

Oh, come on, ask me to your party.

CLAY. Of course I'll ask you to come with me to the party. And I'll
bet you're a friend of Warren's.

LULA. Why not be a friend of Warren's? Why not?

[*Taking his arm*]

Have you asked me yet?

CLAY. How can I ask you when I don't know your name?

LULA. Are you talking to my name?

CLAY. What is it, a secret?

LULA. I'm Lena the Hyena.

CLAY. The famous woman poet?

LULA. Poetess! The same!

CLAY. Well, you know so much about me . . . what's my name?

LULA. Morris the Hyena.

CLAY. The famous woman poet?

LULA. The same.

[*Laughing and going into her bag*]

You want another apple?

CLAY. Can't make it, lady. I only have to keep one doctor away a day.

LULA. I bet your name is . . . something like . . . uh, Gerald or
Walter. Huh?

CLAY. God, no.

LULA. Lloyd, Norman? One of those hopeless colored names creeping
out of New Jersey. Leonard? Gag. . . .

CLAY. Like Warren?

LULA. Definitely. Just exactly like Warren. Or Everett.

CLAY. Gag. . . .

LULA. Well, for sure, it's not Willie.

CLAY. It's Clay.

LULA. Clay? Really? Clay what?

CLAY. Take your pick. Jackson, Johnson, or Williams.

LULA. Oh, really? Good for you. But it's got to be Williams. You're
too pretentious to be a Jackson or Johnson.

CLAY. Thass right.

LULA. But Clay's O.K.

CLAY. So's Lena.

LULA. It's Lula.

CLAY. Oh?

LULA. Lula the Hyena.

CLAY. Very good.

LULA.

> [*Starts laughing again*]

Now you say to me, "Lula, Lula, why don't you go to this party with me tonight?" It's your turn, and let those be your lines.

CLAY. Lula, why don't you go to this party with me tonight, Huh?

LULA. Say my name twice before you ask, and no huh's.

CLAY. Lula, Lula, why don't you go to this party with me tonight?

LULA. I'd like to go, Clay, but how can you ask me to go when you barely know me?

CLAY. That is strange, isn't it?

LULA. What kind of reaction is that? You're supposed to say, "Aw, come on, we'll get to know each other better at the party."

CLAY. That's pretty corny.

LULA. What are you into anyway?

> [*Looking at him half sullenly but still amused*]

What thing are you playing at, Mister? Mister Clay Williams?

> [*Grabs his thigh, up near the crotch*]

What are *you* thinking about?

CLAY. Watch it now, you're gonna excite me for real.

LULA.

> [*Taking her hand away and throwing her apple core through the window*]

I bet.

> [*She slumps in the seat and is heavily silent*]

CLAY. I thought you knew everything about me? What happened?

> [LULA *looks at him, then looks slowly away, then over where the other aisle would be. Noise of the train. She reaches in her bag and pulls out one of the paper books. She puts it on her leg and thumbs the pages listlessly.* CLAY *cocks his head to see the title of the book. Noise of the train.* LULA *flips pages and her eyes drift. Both remain silent*]

Are you going to the party with me, Lula?

LULA.

> [*Bored and not even looking*]

I don't even know you.

CLAY. You said you know my type.

LULA.

> [*Strangely irritated*]

Don't get smart with me, Buster. I know you like the palm of my hand.

CLAY. The one you eat the apples with?

LULA. Yeh. And the one I open doors late Saturday evening with. That's my door. Up at the top of the stairs. Five flights. Above a lot of Italians and lying Americans. And scrape carrots with. Also . . .

> [*Looks at him*]

the same hand I unbutton my dress with, or let my skirt fall down. Same hand. Lover.

CLAY. Are you angry about anything? Did I say something wrong?

LULA. Everything you say is wrong.

[*Mock smile*]

That's what makes you so attractive. Ha. In that funnybook jacket with all the buttons.

[*More animate, taking hold of his jacket*]

What've you got that jacket and tie on in all this heat for? And why're you wearing a jacket and tie like that? Did your people ever burn witches or start revolutions over the price of tea? Boy, those narrow-shoulder clothes come from a tradition you ought to feel oppressed by. A three-button suit. What right do you have to be wearing a three-button suit and striped tie? Your grandfather was a slave, he didn't go to Harvard.

CLAY. My grandfather was a night watchman.

LULA. And you went to a colored college where everybody thought they were Averell Harriman.

CLAY. All except me.

LULA. And who did you think you were? Who do you think you are now?

CLAY.

[*Laughs as if to make light of the whole trend of the conversation*]

Well, in college I thought I was Baudelaire. But I've slowed down since.

LULA. I bet you never once thought you were a black nigger.

[*Mock serious, then she howls with laughter.* CLAY *is stunned but after initial reaction, he quickly tries to appreciate the humor.* LULA *almost shrieks*]

A black Baudelaire.

CLAY. That's right.

LULA. Boy, are you corny. I take back what I said before. Everything you say is not wrong. It's perfect. You should be on television.

CLAY. You act like you're on television already.

LULA. That's because I'm an actress.

CLAY. I thought so.

LULA. Well, you're wrong. I'm no actress. I told you I always lie. I'm nothing, honey, and don't you ever forget it.

[*Lighter*]

Although my mother was a Communist. The only person in my family ever to amount to anything.

CLAY. My mother was a Republican.

LULA. And your father voted for the man rather than the party.

CLAY. Right!

LULA. Yea for him. Yea, yea for him.

CLAY. Yea!

LULA. And yea for America where he is free to vote for the mediocrity of his choice! Yea!

CLAY. Yea!

LULA. And yea for both your parents who even though they differ about so crucial a matter as the body politic still forged a union of love and sacrifice that was destined to flower at the birth of the noble Clay . . . what's your middle name?

CLAY. Clay.

LULA. A union of love and sacrifice that was destined to flower at the birth of the noble Clay Clay Williams. Yea! And most of all yea yea for you, Clay Clay. The Black Baudelaire! Yes!

[*And with knifelike cynicism*]

My Christ. My Christ.

CLAY. Thank you, ma'am.

LULA. May the people accept you as a ghost of the future. And love you, that you might not kill them when you can.

CLAY. What?

LULA. You're a murderer, Clay, and you know it.

[*Her voice darkening with significance*]

You know goddamn well what I mean.

CLAY. I do?

LULA. So we'll pretend the air is light and full of perfume.

CLAY.

[*Sniffing at her blouse*]

It is.

LULA. And we'll pretend the people cannot see you. That is, the citizens. And that you are free of your own history. And I am free of my history. We'll pretend that we are both anonymous beauties smashing along through the city's entrails.

[*She yells as loud as she can*]

GROOVE!

SCENE II

Scene is the same as before, though now there are other seats visible in the car. And throughout the scene other people get on the subway. There are maybe one or two seated in the car as the scene opens, though neither CLAY nor LULA notices them. CLAY's tie is open. LULA is hugging his arm.

CLAY. The party!

LULA. I know it'll be something good. You can come in with me, looking casual and significant. I'll be strange, haughty, and silent, and walk with long slow strides.

CLAY. Right.

LULA. When you get drunk, pat me once, very lovingly on the flanks, and I'll look at you cryptically, licking my lips.

CLAY. It sounds like something we can do.

LULA. You'll go around talking to young men about your mind, and to old men about your plans. If you meet a very close friend who is also with someone like me, we can stand together, sipping our drinks and exchanging codes of lust. The atmosphere will be slithering in love and half-love and very open moral decision.

CLAY. Great. Great.

LULA. And everyone will pretend they don't know your name, and then . . .

[*She pauses heavily*]

later, when they have to, they'll claim a friendship that denies your sterling character.

CLAY.

[*Kissing her neck and fingers*]

And then what?

LULA. Then? Well, then we'll go down the street, late night, eating apples and winding very deliberately toward my house.

CLAY. Deliberately?

LULA. I mean, we'll look in all the shopwindows, and make fun of the queers. Maybe we'll meet a Jewish Buddhist and flatten his conceits over some very pretentious coffee.

CLAY. In honor of whose God?

LULA. Mine.

CLAY. Who is . . . ?

LULA. Me . . . and you?

CLAY. A corporate Godhead.

LULA. Exactly. Exactly.

[*Notices one of the other people entering*]

CLAY. Go on with the chronicle. Then what happens to us?

LULA.

[*A mild depression, but she still makes her description triumphant and increasingly direct*]

To my house, of course.

CLAY. Of course.

LULA. And up the narrow steps of the tenement.

CLAY. You live in a tenement?

LULA. Wouldn't live anywhere else. Reminds me specifically of my novel form of insanity.

CLAY. Up the tenement stairs.

LULA. And with my apple-eating hand I push open the door and lead you, my tender big-eyed prey, into my . . . God, what can I call it . . . into my hovel.

CLAY. Then what happens?

LULA. After the dancing and games, after the long drinks and long walks, the real fun begins.

CLAY. Ah, the real fun.

[*Embarrassed, in spite of himself*]

Which is . . . ?

LULA.

[*Laughs at him*]

Real fun in the dark house. Hah! Real fun in the dark house, high up above the street and the ignorant cowboys. I lead you in, holding your wet hand gently in my hand . . .

CLAY. Which is not wet?

LULA. Which is dry as ashes.

CLAY. And cold?

LULA. Don't think you'll get out of your responsibility that way. It's not cold at all. You Fascist! Into my dark living room. Where we'll sit and talk endlessly, endlessly.

CLAY. About what?

LULA. About what? About your manhood, what do you think? What do you think we've been talking about all this time?

CLAY. Well, I didn't know it was that. That's for sure. Every other thing in the world but that.

[*Notices another person entering, looks quickly, almost involuntarily up and down the car, seeing the other people in the car*]

Hey, I didn't even notice when those people got on.

LULA. Yeah, I know.

CLAY. Man, this subway is slow.

LULA. Yeah, I know.

CLAY. Well, go on. We were talking about my manhood.

LULA. We still are. All the time.

CLAY. We were in your living room.

LULA. My dark living room. Talking endlessly.

CLAY. About my manhood.

LULA. I'll make you a map of it. Just as soon as we get to my house.

CLAY. Well, that's great.

LULA. One of the things we do while we talk. And screw.

CLAY.

[*Trying to make his smile broader and less shaky*]

We finally got there.

LULA. And you'll call my rooms black as a grave. You'll say, "This place is like Juliet's tomb."

CLAY.

[*Laughs*]

I might.

LULA. I know. You've probably said it before.

CLAY. And is that all? The whole grand tour?

LULA. Not all. You'll say to me very close to my face, many, many times, you'll say, even whisper, that you love me.

CLAY. Maybe I will.

LULA. And you'll be lying.

CLAY. I wouldn't lie about something like that.

LULA. Hah. It's the only kind of thing you will lie about. Especially if you think it'll keep me alive.

CLAY. Keep you alive? I don't understand.

LULA.

[*Bursting out laughing, but too shrilly*]

Don't understand? Well, don't look at me. It's the path I take, that's all. Where both feet take me when I set them down. One in front of the other.

CLAY. Morbid. Morbid. You sure you're not an actress? All that self-aggrandizement.

LULA. Well, I told you I wasn't an actress . . . but I also told you I lie all the time. Draw your own conclusions.

CLAY. Morbid. Morbid. You sure you're not an actress? All scribed? There's no more?

LULA. I've told you all I know. Or almost all.

CLAY. There's no funny parts?

LULA. I thought it was all funny.

CLAY. But you mean peculiar, not ha-ha.

LULA. You don't know what I mean.

CLAY. Well, tell me the almost part then. You said almost all. What else? I want the whole story.

LULA.

> [*Searching aimlessly through her bag. She begins to talk breathlessly, with a light and silly tone*]

All stories are whole stories. All of 'em. Our whole story . . . nothing but change. How could things go on like that forever? Huh?

> [*Slaps him on the shoulder, begins finding things in her bag, taking them out and throwing them over her shoulder into the aisle*]

Except I do go on as I do. Apples and long walks with deathless intelligent lovers. But you mix it up. Look out the window, all the time. Turning pages. Change change change. Till, shit, I don't know you. Wouldn't, for that matter. You're too serious. I bet you're even too serious to be psychoanalyzed. Like all those Jewish poets from Yonkers, who leave their mothers looking for other mothers, or others' mothers, on whose baggy tits they lay their fumbling heads. Their poems are always funny, and all about sex.

CLAY. They sound great. Like movies.

LULA. But you change.

> [*Blankly*]

And things work on you till you hate them.

> [*More people come into the train. They come closer to the couple, some of them not sitting, but swinging drearily on the straps, staring at the two with uncertain interest*]

CLAY. Wow. All these people, so suddenly. They must all come from the same place.

LULA. Right. That they do.

CLAY. Oh? You know about them too?

LULA. Oh yeah. About them more than I know about you. Do they frighten you?

CLAY. Frighten me? Why should they frighten me?

LULA. 'Cause you're an escaped nigger.

CLAY. Yeah?

LULA. 'Cause you crawled through the wire and made tracks to my side.

CLAY. Wire?

LULA. Don't they have wire around plantations?

CLAY. You must be Jewish. All you can think about is wire. Plantations didn't have any wire. Plantations were big open whitewashed places like heaven, and everybody on 'em was grooved to be there. Just strummin' and hummin' all day.

LULA. Yes, yes.

CLAY. And that's how the blues was born.

LULA. Yes, yes. And that's how the blues was born.

[*Begins to make up a song that becomes quickly hysterical. As she sings she rises from her seat, still throwing things out of her bag into the aisle, beginning a rhythmical shudder and twistlike wiggle, which she continues up and down the aisle, bumping into many of the standing people and tripping over the feet of those sitting. Each time she runs into a person she lets out a very vicious piece of profanity, wiggling and stepping all the time*]

And that's how the blues was born. Yes. Yes. Son of a bitch, get out of the way. Yes. Quack. Yes. Yes. And that's how the blues was born. Ten little niggers sitting on a limb, but none of them ever looked like him.

[*Points to* CLAY, *returns toward the seat, with her hands extended for him to rise and dance with her*]

And that's how blues was born. Yes. Come on, Clay. Let's do the nasty. Rub bellies. Rub bellies.

CLAY.

[*Waves his hands to refuse. He is embarrassed, but determined to get a kick out of the proceedings*]

Hey, what was in those apples? Mirror, mirror on the wall, who's the fairest one of all? Snow White, baby, and don't you forget it.

LULA.

[*Grabbing for his hands, which he draws away*]

Come on, Clay. Let's rub bellies on the train. The nasty. The nasty. Do the gritty grind, like your ol' rag-head mammy. Grind till you lose your mind. Shake it, shake it, shake it, shake it! OOOOweeee! Come on, Clay. Let's do the choo-choo train shuffle, the navel scratcher.

CLAY. Hey, you coming on like the lady who smoked up her grass skirt.

LULA.

[*Becoming annoyed that he will not dance, and becoming more animated as if to embarrass him still further*]

Come on, Clay . . . let's do the thing. Uhh! Uhh! Clay! Clay! You middle-class black bastard. Forget your social-working mother for a few seconds and let's knock stomachs. Clay, you liver-lipped white man. You would-be Christian. You ain't no nigger, you're just a dirty white man. Get up, Clay. Dance with me, Clay.

CLAY. Lula! Sit down, now. Be cool.

LULA.

[*Mocking him, in wild dance*]

Be cool. Be cool. That's all you know . . . shaking that wildroot cream-oil on your knotty head, jackets buttoning up to your chin, so full of white man's words. Christ. God. Get up and scream at these people. Like scream meaningless shit in these hopeless faces.

[*She screams at people in train, still dancing*]

Red trains cough Jewish underwear for keeps! Expanding smells of silence. Gravy snot whistling like sea birds. Clay. Clay, you got to break out. Don't sit there dying the way they want you to die. Get up.

CLAY. Oh, sit the fuck down.

[*He moves to restrain her*]

Sit down, goddamn it.

LULA.

[*Twisting out of his reach*]

Screw yourself, Uncle Tom. Thomas Woolly-Head.

[*Begins to dance a kind of jig, mocking CLAY with loud forced humor*]

There is Uncle Tom . . . I mean, Uncle Thomas Woolly-Head. With old white matted mane. He hobbles on his wooden cane. Old Tom. Old Tom. Let the white man hump his ol' mama, and he jes' shuffle off in the woods and hide his gentle gray head. Ol' Thomas Woolly-Head.

[*Some of the other riders are laughing now. A drunk gets up and joins LULA in her dance, singing, as best he can, her "song." CLAY gets out of his seat and visibly scans the faces of the other riders*]

CLAY. Lula! Lula!

[*She is dancing and turning, still shouting as loud as she can. The drunk too is shouting, and waving his hands wildly*]

Lula . . . you dumb bitch. Why don't you stop it?

[*He rushes half stumbling from his seat, and grabs one of her flailing arms*]

LULA. Let me go! You black son of a bitch.

[*She struggles against him*]

Let me go! Help!

[*CLAY is dragging her towards her seat, and the drunk seeks to interfere. He grabs CLAY around the shoulders and begins wrestling with him. CLAY clubs the drunk to the floor without releasing LULA, who is still screaming. CLAY finally gets her to the seat and throws her into it*]

CLAY. Now you shut the hell up.

[*Grabbing her shoulders*]

Just shut up. You don't know what you're talking about. You don't know anything. So just keep your stupid mouth closed.

LULA. You're afraid of white people. And your father was. Uncle Tom Big Lip!

CLAY.

[*Slaps her as hard as he can, across the mouth. LULA's head bangs against the back of the seat. When she raises it again, CLAY slaps her again*]

Now shut up and let me talk.

[*He turns toward the other riders, some of whom are sitting on*]

*the edge of their seats. The drunk is on one knee, rubbing his
head, and singing softly the same song. He shuts up too when
he sees* CLAY *watching him. The others go back to newspapers
or stare out the windows*]

Shit, you don't have any sense, Lula, nor feelings either. I could
murder you now. Such a tiny ugly throat. I could squeeze it flat,
and watch you turn blue, on a humble. For dull kicks. And all these
weak-faced ofays squatting around here, staring over their papers
at me. Murder them too. Even if they expected it. That man
there . . .

[*Points to well-dressed man*]

I could rip that *Times* right out of his hand, as skinny and middle-
classed as I am, I could rip that paper out of his hand and just as
easily rip out his throat. It takes no great effort. For what? To kill
you soft idiots? You don't understand anything but luxury.

LULA. You fool!

CLAY.

[*Pushing her against the seat*]

I'm not telling you again, Tallulah Bankhead! Luxury. In your
face and your fingers. You telling me what I ought to do.

[*Sudden scream frightening the whole coach*]

Well, don't! Don't you tell me anything! If I'm a middle-class fake
white man . . . let me be. And let me be in the way I want.

[*Through his teeth*]

I'll rip your lousy breasts off! Let me be who I feel like being.
Uncle Tom. Thomas. Whoever. It's none of your business. You
don't know anything except what's there for you to see. An act.
Lies. Device. Not the pure heart, the pumping black heart. You
don't ever know that. And I sit here, in this buttoned-up suit, to keep
myself from cutting all your throats. I mean wantonly. You great
liberated whore! You fuck some black man, and right away you're
an expert on black people. What a lotta shit that is. The only thing
you know is that you come if he bangs you hard enough. And
that's all. The belly rub? You wanted to do the belly rub? Shit,
you don't even know how. You don't know how. That ol' dipty-dip
shit you do, rolling your ass like an elephant. That's not my kind of
belly rub. Belly rub is not Queens. Belly rub is dark places, with
big hats and overcoats held up with one arm. Belly rub hates you.
Old bald-headed four-eyed ofays popping their fingers . . . and
don't know yet what they're doing. They say, "I love Bessie Smith."
And don't even understand that Bessie Smith is saying, "Kiss my
ass, my black unruly ass." Before love, suffering, desire, anything
you can explain, she's saying, and very plainly, "Kiss my black
ass." And if you don't know that, it's you that's doing the kissing.

Charlie Parker? Charlie Parker. All the hip white boys scream for
Bird. And Bird saying, "Up your ass, feeble-minded ofay! Up your
ass." And they sit there talking about the tortured genius of Charlie Parker. Bird would've played not a note of music if he just

walked up to East Sixty-seventh Street and killed the first ten white people he saw. Not a note! And I'm the great would-be poet. Yes. That's right! Poet. Some kind of bastard literature . . . all it needs is a simple knife thrust. Just let me bleed you, you loud whore, and one poem vanished. A whole people of neurotics, struggling to keep from being sane. And the only thing that would cure the neurosis would be your murder. Simple as that. I mean if I murdered you, then other white people would begin to understand me. You understand? No. I guess not. If Bessie Smith had killed some white people she wouldn't have needed that music. She could have talked very straight and plain about the world. No metaphors. No grunts. No wiggles in the dark of her soul. Just straight two and two are four. Money. Power. Luxury. Like that. All of them. Crazy niggers turning their backs on sanity. When all it needs is that simple act. Murder. Just murder! Would make us all sane.

[*Suddenly weary*]

Ahhh. Shit. But who needs it? I'd rather be a fool. Insane. Safe with my words, and no deaths, and clean, hard thoughts, urging me to new conquests. My people's madness. Hah! That's a laugh. My people. They don't need me to claim them. They got legs and arms of their own. Personal insanities. Mirrors. They don't need all those words. They don't need any defense. But listen, though, one more thing. And you tell this to your father, who's probably the kind of man who needs to know at once. So he can plan ahead. Tell him not to preach so much rationalism and cold logic to these niggers. Let them alone. Let them sing curses at you in code and see your filth as simple lack of style. Don't make the mistake, through some irresponsible surge of Christian charity, of talking too much about the advantages of Western rationalism, or the great intellectual legacy of the white man, or maybe they'll begin to listen. An then, maybe one day, you'll find they actually do understand exactly what you are talking about, all these fantasy people. All these blues people. And on that day, as sure as shit, when you really believe you can "accept" them into your fold, as half-white trusties late of the subject peoples. With no more blues, except the very old ones, and not a watermelon in sight, the great missionary heart will have triumphed, and all of those ex-coons will be stand-up Western men, with eyes for clean hard useful lives, sober, pious and sane, and they'll murder you. They'll murder you, and have very rational explanations. Very much like your own. They'll cut your throats, and drag you out to the edge of your cities so the flesh can fall away from your bones, in sanitary isolation.

LULA.

[*Her voice takes on a different, more businesslike quality*]

I've heard enough.

CLAY.

[*Reaching for his books*]

I bet you have. I guess I better collect my stuff and get off this train. Looks like we won't be acting out that little pageant you outlined before.

LULA. No. We won't. You're right about that, at least.

[*She turns to look quickly around the rest of the car*]

All right!

[*The others respond*]

CLAY.

[*Bending across the girl to retrieve his belongings*]

Sorry, baby, I don't think we could make it.

[*As he is bending over her, the girl brings up a small knife and plunges it into* CLAY's *chest. Twice. He slumps across her knees, his mouth working stupidly*]

LULA. Sorry is right.

[*Turning to the others in the car who have already gotten up from their seats*]

Sorry is the rightest thing you've said. Get this man off me! Hurry, now!

[*The others come and drag* CLAY's *body down the aisle*]

Open the door and throw his body out.

[*They throw him off*]

And all of you get off at the next stop.

[LULA *busies herself straightening her things. Getting everything in order. She takes out a notebook and makes a quick scribbling note. Drops it in her bag. The train apparently stops and all the others get off, leaving her alone in the coach.*

Very soon a young Negro of about twenty comes into the coach, with a couple of books under his arm. He sits a few seats in back of LULA. *When he is seated she turns and gives him a long slow look. He looks up from his book and drops the book on his lap. Then an old Negro conductor comes into the car, doing a sort of restrained soft shoe, and half mumbling the words of some song. He looks at the young man, briefly, with a quick greeting*]

CONDUCTOR. Hey, brother!

YOUNG MAN. Hey.

[*The conductor continues down the aisle with his little dance and the mumbled song.* LULA *turns to stare at him and follows his movements down the aisle. The conductor tips his hat when he reaches her seat, and continues out the car*]

THE TRAGEDY OF KING LEAR

William Shakespeare

ACT ONE

SCENE 1

[KING LEAR'S *Palace.*]
Enter KENT, GLOUCESTER, *and* EDMUND. [KENT *and* GLOUCESTER
converse. EDMUND *stands back.*]

KENT. I thought the King had more affected the Duke of Albany than
    Cornwall.

GLOU. It did always seem so to us; but now, in the division of the
    kingdom, it appears not which of the Dukes he values most, for
    equalities are so weigh'd that curiosity in neither can make choice   5
    of either's moiety.

KENT. Is not this your son, my lord?

GLOU. His breeding, sir, hath been at my charge. I have so often
    blush'd to acknowledge him that now I am braz'd to't.

KENT. I cannot conceive you.   10

I.1. 1 *more affected* been more inclined to favour [K]. 5–6 *equalities . . .
moiety* the equality of their shares is so well balanced (so exact) that careful
scrutiny on the part of neither can choose the other's share as better than his
own [K]. *equalities* Q¹; F¹: "qualities." 8 *breeding* rearing, education. 9. *braz'd*
hardened—literally, plated with brass [K]. 10 *conceive* understand. Gloucester
puns on the word.

[214]

GLOU. Sir, this young fellow's mother could; whereupon she grew
round-womb'd, and had indeed, sir, a son for her cradle ere she
had a husband for her bed. Do you smell a fault?

KENT. I cannot wish the fault undone, the issue of it being so proper.

GLOU. But I have, sir, a son by order of law, some year elder than 15
this, who yet is no dearer in my account. Though this knave came
something saucily into the world before he was sent for, yet was
his mother fair, there was good sport at his making, and the
whoreson must be acknowledged.—Do you know this noble gentleman, Edmund? 20

EDM. [*comes forward*] No, my lord.

GLOU. My Lord of Kent. Remember him hereafter as my honourable
friend.

EDM. My services to your lordship.

KENT. I must love you, and sue to know you better. 25

EDM. Sir, I shall study deserving.

GLOU. He hath been out nine years, and away he shall again.
      Sound a sennet.
      The King is coming.
      Enter one bearing a coronet; then LEAR; *then the* DUKES OF
      ALBANY *and* CORNWALL; *next,* GONERIL, REGAN, CORDELIA, *with*
      FOLLOWERS.

LEAR. Attend the lords of France and Burgundy, Gloucester.

GLOU. I shall, my liege. 30
      Exeunt [GLOUCESTER *and* EDMUND].

LEAR. Meantime we shall express our darker purpose.
      Give me the map there. Know we have divided
      In three our kingdom; and 'tis our fast intent
      To shake all cares and business from our age,
      Conferring them on younger strengths while we 35
      Unburden'd crawl toward death. Our son of Cornwall,
      And you, our no less loving son of Albany,
      We have this hour a constant will to publish
      Our daughters' several dowers, that future strife

14 *proper* handsome. 15 *some year* about a year. 16 *account* estimation. *knave*
boy, fellow (not used in any pejorative sense, but as a term of affection). 17
saucily (a) with impertinence (b) in a bawdy manner. 19 *whoreson* Although
the word does mean "bastard" and is perfectly applicable to Edmund in that
sense, Gloucester seems to be using it in the general sense of "rogue," a term
of affectionate abuse. There is some irony here. 24 *services* duty. 26 *study
deserving* make every effort to be worthy of your favour [K]. 27 *out* away
from home. s.d. *sennet* a series of notes on a trumpet. 31 *darker purpose*
more secret intentions. He has not yet revealed exactly how he will divide
his kingdom—giving the largest share to the daughter who loves him most.
33 *three* three parts—not necessarily equal ones. *fast intent* fixed purpose.
35–40 *while we . . . prevented now* F¹; not in Q¹. 36 *crawl* That Lear's old
age is not feeble (however he may express himself) is clear from the whole of
Act I. He still goes a-hunting (I.3.7) [K]. 38 *constant will* fixed purpose.
publish announce publicly. 39 *dowers* Apparently Goneril and Regan have
married only recently and their dowries have not yet been determined.

May be prevented now. The princes, France and Burgundy,   40
Great rivals in our youngest daughter's love,
Long in our court have made their amorous sojourn,
And here are to be answer'd. Tell me, my daughters
(Since now we will divest us both of rule,
Interest of territory, cares of state),   45
Which of you shall we say doth love us most?
That we our largest bounty may extend
Where nature doth with merit challenge. Goneril,
Our eldest-born, speak first.
GON. Sir, I love you more than word can wield the matter;   50
Dearer than eyesight, space, and liberty;
Beyond what can be valued, rich or rare;
No less than life, with grace, health, beauty, honour;
As much as child e'er lov'd, or father found;
A love that makes breath poor, and speech unable.   55
Beyond all manner of so much I love you.
COR. [aside] What shall Cordelia speak? Love, and be silent.
LEAR. Of all these bounds, even from this line to this,
With shadowy forests and with champains rich'd,
With plenteous rivers and wide-skirted meads,   60
We make thee lady. To thine and Albany's issue
Be this perpetual.—What says our second daughter,
Our dearest Regan, wife to Cornwall? Speak.
REG. Sir, I am made of that self metal as my sister,
And prize me at her worth. In my true heart   65
I find she names my very deed of love;
Only she comes too short, that I profess
Myself an enemy to all other joys
Which the most precious square of sense possesses,
And find I am alone felicitate   70

40 *prevented* forestalled; hindered in advance [K]. 44–5 *Since now . . . of state* F^1; not in Q^1. 48 *Where nature . . . challenge* to her whose merit, added to my natural affection, constitutes a claim to the most generous gift [K] *with merit* in addition to merit. 50 *word* F^1; Q^1, K: "words." *wield the matter* serve to express the fact [K]. 51 *space, and liberty* "Space" expresses the idea of "freedom from confinement"; "liberty" adds the idea of "personal freedom in action" [K]. 52 *what* whatever, anything that [K]. 53 *grace* favour. 54 *found* discovered in his child. 56 *Beyond . . . so much* beyond every kind of comparison that can be imagined; not—beyond the comparisons that I have just expressed. "Manner" is the emphatic word [K]. 58 *these bounds* Lear indicates the boundaries in the map. Though he seems to give Goneril and Regan a chance to obtain the largest of the three shares, he has already determined their portions (as we learn from lines 1–6), and he is reserving the "largest bounty" for Cordelia, since he is confident that she loves him most [K]. 59–60 *and . . . rivers* F^1; not in Q^1. 59 *champains* fertile plains. *rich'd* enriched. 60 *wide-skirted* extensive. 64 *of that . . . sister* F^1; Q^1, K: "Of the selfe same metall that my sister is." *self* same. 65 *prize me* value myself. 66 *my very deed of love* my love as it actually is in fact [K]. 69 *Which . . . possesses* which the most delicate test of one's sensibility can claim as joys [K]. *square* criterion (from the carpenter's "square" used for exact measurements). *possesses* Q^1; F^1: "professes." 70 *felicitate* made happy.

In your dear Highness' love.

COR.   [*aside*]   Then poor Cordelia!
  And yet not so; since I am sure my love 's
  More ponderous than my tongue.

LEAR. To thee and thine hereditary ever   75
  Remain this ample third of our fair kingdom,
  No less in space, validity, and pleasure
  Than that conferr'd on Goneril.—Now, our joy,
  Although our last and least; to whose young love
  The vines of France and milk of Burgundy   80
  Strive to be interess'd; what can you say to draw
  A third more opulent than your sisters? Speak.

COR. Nothing, my lord.

LEAR. Nothing?

COR. Nothing.   85

LEAR. Nothing will come of nothing. Speak again.

COR. Unhappy that I am, I cannot heave
  My heart into my mouth. I love your Majesty
  According to my bond; no more nor less.

LEAR. How, how, Cordelia? Mend your speech a little,   90
  Lest it may mar your fortunes.

COR.   Good my lord,
  You have begot me, bred me, lov'd me; I
  Return those duties back as are right fit,
  Obey you, love you, and most honour you.   95
  Why have my sisters husbands, if they say
  They love you all? Haply, when I shall wed,
  That lord whose hand must take my plight shall carry
  Half my love with him, half my care and duty.
  Sure I shall never marry like my sisters,   100
  To love my father all.

LEAR. But goes thy heart with this?

COR.   Ay, good my lord.

LEAR. So young, and so untender?

COR. So young, my lord, and true.   105

LEAR. Let it be so! thy truth then be thy dower!
  For, by the sacred radiance of the sun,

74 *ponderous* weighty. Her love is of heavier and thus more precious metal
than that of her sisters (F¹; Q¹, K: "richer"). 77 *validity* value. 79 *our last
and least* youngest and smallest in stature (F¹; Q¹, K: "the last, not least").
81 *interess'd* interested, closely connected (F¹, K: "interest," a variant spelling).
86 *Nothing will* F¹; Q¹: "How, nothing can"; THEOBALD, K: "Nothing can."
89 *my bond* my bounden duty; as a daughter ought to love a father [K]. In
larger terms it may be conceived of as the "bond of nature," that which links
child to father as it links mankind to God, all being part of a great and
harmonious cosmic order. 94–5 *Return . . . honour you* in return I give you
those duties that are most fitting—obedience, love, and the highest honour.
Thus Cordelia explains what she means by "my bond." "Duties" are "things
that are due to one, whether in act or feeling" [K]. 98 *plight* pledge of faith
in marriage. 101 *To love . . . all* Q¹; not in F¹.

The mysteries of Hecate and the night;
By all the operation of the orbs
From whom we do exist and cease to be; 110
Here I disclaim all my paternal care,
Propinquity and property of blood,
And as a stranger to my heart and me
Hold thee from this for ever. The barbarous Scythian,
Or he that makes his generation messes 115
To gorge his appetite, shall to my bosom
Be as well neighbour'd, pitied, and reliev'd,
As thou my sometime daughter.

KENT.   Good my liege—

LEAR. Peace, Kent! 120
Come not between the dragon and his wrath.
I lov'd her most, and thought to set my rest
On her kind nursery.—Hence and avoid my sight!—
So be my grave my peace as here I give
Her father's heart from her! Call France! Who stirs? 125
Call Burgundy! Cornwall and Albany,
With my two daughters' dowers digest this third;
Let pride, which she calls plainness, marry her.
I do invest you jointly in my power,
Preëminence, and all the large effects 130
That troop with majesty. Ourself, by monthly course,
With reservation of an hundred knights,
By you to be sustain'd, shall our abode
Make with you by due turns. Only we still retain
The name, and all th' additions to a king. The sway, 135
Revenue, execution of the rest,
Beloved sons, be yours; which to confirm,
This coronet part betwixt you.

KENT.   Royal Lear,
Whom I have ever honour'd as my king, 140

108 *mysteries* secret rites (F²; F¹: "miseries"; Q¹: "mistresse"). *Hecate* goddess of the lower world, patroness of witches and magic. 109 *operation* astrological influence (upon man's character and fortunes). *orbs* stars. 112 *Propinquity* near relationship. *property* identity. Lear disclaims all kinship whatsoever [K]. 114 *barbarous Scythian* By literary tradition from classical times the Scythians were regarded as the acme of all barbarians [K]. 115 *makes . . . messes* eats his own children. *generation* children. *messes* portions of food. 116–17 *to my . . . neighbour'd* as closely hugged to my breast; so dearly loved [K]. 118 *sometime* former. 121 *the dragon* A dragon was the traditional crest of the ancient British kings [K]. *wrath* object of anger. 122 *to set my rest* to rely with confidence and to the full. An idiom derived from the game of primero, meaning literally, to "make one's bet in reliance upon the cards in one's hand" [K]. 123 *nursery* nursing, tender care [K]. *avoid* leave. 127 *digest* combine, incorporate. The word implies such perfect assimilation that no distinction shall hereafter be possible [K]. 128 *Let pride . . . marry her* let her self-confidence be her dowry and (if it can) win a husband for her [K]. *plainness* frankness. 130 *large effects* splendid outward tokens [K]. 135 *additions* titles and honours [K]. *sway* power of rule. 136 *the rest* everything else that pertains to royalty [K].

Lov'd as my father, as my master follow'd,
As my great patron thought on in my prayers—
LEAR. The bow is bent and drawn; make from the shaft.
KENT. Let it fall rather, though the fork invade
    The region of my heart! Be Kent unmannerly   145
    When Lear is mad. What wouldst thou do, old man?
    Think'st thou that duty shall have dread to speak
    When power to flattery bows? To plainness honour's bound
    When majesty falls to folly. Reserve thy state;
    And in thy best consideration check   150
    This hideous rashness. Answer my life my judgment,
    Thy youngest daughter does not love thee least,
    Nor are those empty-hearted whose low sound
    Reverbs no hollowness.
LEAR.   Kent, on thy life, no more!   155
KENT. My life I never held but as a pawn
    To wage against thine enemies; nor fear to lose it,
    Thy safety being the motive.
LEAR.   Out of my sight!
KENT. See better, Lear, and let me still remain   160
    The true blank of thine eye.
LEAR. Now by Apollo—
KENT.   Now by Apollo, King,
    Thou swear'st thy gods in vain.
LEAR.   O vassal! miscreant!   165
      [*Lays his hand on his sword.*]
ALB., CORN. Dear sir, forbear!
KENT. Do!
    Kill thy physician, and the fee bestow
    Upon the foul disease. Revoke thy gift,
    Or, whilst I can vent clamour from my throat,   170
    I'll tell thee thou dost evil.
LEAR.   Hear me, recreant!
    On thine allegiance, hear me!
    Since thou hast sought to make us break our vow—
    Which we durst never yet—and with strain'd pride   175
    To come between our sentence and our power,—

143 *make from* avoid. 144 *the fork* an arrowhead that, instead of a barb, has two points like a pitchfork [K]. 149 *Reserve thy state* retain thy kingly authority (F¹; Q¹, K: "Reuerse thy doome"). 151 *rashness* unthinking haste. *Answer my life* let my life be answerable for. 154 *Reverbs* reverberates. An old proverb says that empty vessels have the loudest sounds. 156 *pawn* pledge (as the stake in a wager). 157 *wage* wager, risk. 158 *motive* moving cause. 160 *still* always, forever. 161 *The true blank of thine eye* the mark at which thine eye directs itself in accurate sight; the counsellor to whom thou dost look for sound advice. The "blank" is the white circle at the centre of the target [K]. 165 *vassal* A term of contempt. *miscreant* man without faith. 166 *Dear sir, forbear* F¹; not in Q¹. 170 *vent clamour* utter outcries. 172 *recreant* traitor—one who proves false to his allegiance [K]. 175 *strain'd* over-strained, excessive, unnatural. 176 *To come . . . our power* to interfere with my power to impose a sentence.

Which nor our nature nor our place can bear,—
Our potency made good, take thy reward.
Five days we do allot thee for provision
To shield thee from disasters of the world,   180
And on the sixth to turn thy hated back
Upon our kingdom. If, on the tenth day following,
Thy banish'd trunk be found in our dominions,
The moment is thy death. Away! By Jupiter,
This shall not be revok'd.   185
KENT. Fare thee well, King. Since thus thou wilt appear,
  Freedom lives hence, and banishment is here.
    [*To* CORDELIA]
  The gods to their dear shelter take thee, maid,
  That justly think'st and hast most rightly said!
  [*To* REGAN *and* GONERIL] And your large speeches may your deeds   190
    approve,
  That good effects may spring from words of love.
  Thus Kent, O princes, bids you all adieu;
  He'll shape his old course in a country new.
    Exit.
    Flourish. Enter GLOUCESTER, *with* FRANCE *and* BURGUNDY; AT-
    TENDANTS.
GLOU. Here's France and Burgundy, my noble lord.   195
LEAR. My Lord of Burgundy,
  We first address toward you, who with this king
  Hath rivall'd for our daughter. What in the least
  Will you require in present dower with her,
  Or cease your quest of love?   200
BUR.   Most royal Majesty,
  I crave no more than hath your Highness offer'd,
  Nor will you tender less.
LEAR.   Right noble Burgundy,
  When she was dear to us, we did hold her so;   205
  But now her price is fall'n. Sir, there she stands.
  If aught within that little seeming substance,
  Or all of it, with our displeasure piec'd,
  And nothing more, may fitly like your Grace,

178 *Our potency made good* my royal power being in this edict asserted and carried into effect [K]. 179 *for provision* to enable thee to provide means [K]. 180 *disasters* misfortunes (F¹; Q¹, K: "diseases"). 186 *thus* as a tyrant. 191 *approve* prove true, confirm. 192 *effects* deeds, consequences. 194 *his old course* as a faithful and plain-spoken subject [K]. 195 *Here's* A singular verb is common with two subjects, especially when the verb precedes [K]. 199 *require* ask. Not so imperative as in modern usage [K]. *present* immediate. 205 *hold her so* place such a value upon her. 207 *that little seeming substance* that little creature, who seems to be something real, but is in fact a mere vain semblance of reality [K]. "Substance" is commonly used to indicate reality as opposed to mere show or pretense. Lear is implying that since the love she had always shown him was mere pretense, she is entirely a creature without substance. 208 *piec'd* attached, joined to it. 209 *fitly like* properly please.

She's there, and she is yours. 210
BUR.   I know no answer.
LEAR. Will you, with those infirmities she owes,
    Unfriended, new adopted to our hate,
    Dow'r'd with our curse, and stranger'd with our oath,
    Take her, or leave her? 215
BUR.   Pardon me, royal sir.
    Election makes not up on such conditions.
LEAR. Then leave her, sir; for, by the pow'r that made me,
    I tell you all her wealth. [*To* FRANCE] For you, great King,
    I would not from your love make such a stray 220
    To match you where I hate; therefore beseech you
    T' avert your liking a more worthier way
    Than on a wretch whom nature is asham'd
    Almost t' acknowledge hers.
FRANCE.   This is most strange, 225
    That she that even but now was your best object,
    The argument of your praise, balm of your age,
    Most best, most dearest, should in this trice of time
    Commit a thing so monstrous to dismantle
    So many folds of favour. Sure her offence 230
    Must be of such unnatural degree
    That monsters it, or your fore-vouch'd affection
    Fall'n into taint; which to believe of her
    Must be a faith that reason without miracle
    Should never plant in me. 235
COR.   I yet beseech your Majesty,
    If for I want that glib and oily art
    To speak and purpose not, since what I well intend,
    I'll do't before I speak—that you make known
    It is no vicious blot, murder, or foulness, 240
    No unchaste action or dishonoured step,
    That hath depriv'd me of your grace and favour;
    But even for want of that for which I am richer—

212 *infirmities* defects of fortune, disabilities (not "physical weaknesses"). *owes* possesses. 214 *Dow'r'd . . . oath* with my curse as her sole dowry, and disowned by my oath of rejection [K]. 217 *Election . . . conditions* to choose is impossible when the conditions of the choice are so unfavourable. 219 *For* as for. 220 *make such a stray* stray so far as. 222 *avert your liking* turn your preference. 226 *your best object* the main object of your love and favour [K]. 227 *argument* theme, constant subject. 228 *trice* moment. 229 *dismantle* strip off. "Favour" is conceived of in terms of clothing which had protected Cordelia but has now been stripped off. 232 *monsters it* makes it a monster. *fore-vouch'd* heretofore attested. 233 *Fall'n into taint* suffered decay. *her* emphatic. Of the two alternatives France chooses the second, for the first is to him incredible [K]. 238 *purpose not* have no intention of abiding by what I have spoken. 240 *no vicious blot* no fault that leaves a stain on my moral character [K]. *murder, or foulness* Cordelia is thinking of such "offences" as would be "unnatural" and "monstrous"; and, of these, murder and unchastity ("foulness") are the worst that she can imagine [K]. 241 *dishonoured* dishonourable. 243 *for which* for want of which.

> A still-soliciting eye, and such a tongue
> As I am glad I have not, though not to have it
> Hath lost me in your liking.
> LEAR.   Better thou
> Hadst not been born than not t' have pleas'd me better.
> FRANCE. Is it but this—a tardiness in nature
> Which often leaves the history unspoke
> That it intends to do? My Lord of Burgundy,
> What say you to the lady? Love 's not love
> When it is mingled with regards that stands
> Aloof from th' entire point. Will you have her?
> She is herself a dowry.
> BUR.   Royal Lear,
> Give but that portion which yourself propos'd,
> And here I take Cordelia by the hand,
> Duchess of Burgundy.
> LEAR. Nothing! I have sworn; I am firm.
> BUR. I am sorry then you have so lost a father
> That you must lose a husband.
> COR.   Peace be with Burgundy!
> Since that respect and fortunes are his love,
> I shall not be his wife.
> FRANCE. Fairest Cordelia, that art most rich, being poor;
> Most choice, forsaken; and most lov'd, despis'd!
> Thee and thy virtues here I seize upon.
> Be it lawful I take up what's cast away.
> Gods, gods! 'tis strange that from their cold'st neglect
> My love should kindle to inflam'd respect.
> Thy dow'rless daughter, King, thrown to my chance,
> Is queen of us, of ours, and our fair France.
> Not all the dukes in wat'rish Burgundy
> Can buy this unpriz'd precious maid of me.
> Bid them farewell, Cordelia, though unkind.
> Thou losest here, a better where to find.
> LEAR. Thou hast her, France; let her be thine; for we
> Have no such daughter, nor shall ever see
> That face of hers again. Therefore be gone
> Without our grace, our love, our benison.
> Come, noble Burgundy.

244 *still-soliciting* always begging favours [K]. 246 *lost me in your liking* ruined me in your regard [K]. 249 *tardiness in nature* natural reticence or slowness of speech [K]. 253–4 *When it . . . entire point* when it involves considerations that have nothing to do with the complete and unqualified gist of the matter—i.e. with love that is purely and simply love [K]. 264 *respect and fortunes* considerations of social status and of money (F¹; Q¹, K: "respects of fortune"). 271 *inflam'd respect* passionate regard. 271 *wat'rish* (a) full of streams (b) diluted, weak. 275 *unpriz'd* unvalued by others. 276 *unkind* devoid of natural feeling. 277 *Thou losest . . . find* you lose this place in order to find a better place (France). "Here" and "where" are used as nouns. 281 *benison* blessing.

Flourish. Exeunt LEAR, BURGUNDY, [CORNWALL, ALBANY, GLOUCESTER, *and* ATTENDANTS].

FRANCE. Bid farewell to your sisters.

COR. The jewels of our father, with wash'd eyes
   Cordelia leaves you. I know you what you are;   285
   And, like a sister, am most loath to call
   Your faults as they are nam'd. Love well our father.
   To your professed bosoms I commit him;
   But yet, alas, stood I within his grace,
   I would prefer him to a better place!   290
   So farewell to you both.

GON. Prescribe not us our duties.

REG.   Let your study
   Be to content your lord who hath receiv'd you
   At fortune's alms. You have obedience scanted,   295
   And well are worth the want that you have wanted.

COR. Time shall unfold what plighted cunning hides.
   Who covers faults, at last shame them derides.
   Well may you prosper!

FRANCE.   Come, my fair Cordelia.   300

   Exeunt FRANCE *and* CORDELIA.

GON. Sister, it is not little I have to say of what most nearly appertains to us both. I think our father will hence to-night.

REG. That's most certain, and with you; next month with us.

GON. You see how full of changes his age is. The observation we have made of it hath not been little. He always lov'd our sister most, and   305 with what poor judgment he hath now cast her off appears too grossly.

REG. 'Tis the infirmity of his age; yet he hath ever but slenderly known himself.

GON. The best and soundest of his time hath been but rash; then   310 must we look to receive from his age, not alone the imperfections of long-ingraffed condition, but therewithal the unruly waywardness that infirm and choleric years bring with them.

284 *jewels* objects held precious. *wash'd* by tears. 287 *as they are nam'd* by their right names. *Love* F¹; Q¹, K: "Use." 288 *professed* stored with mere professions of love [K]. 290 *prefer* recommend. 293 *study* most zealous endeavour [K]. 294 *content* please. Much stronger than in modern usage [K]. 295 *At fortune's alms* when fortune was doling out petty charities, not bestowing bounteous awards [K]. 296 *the want that you have wanted* the same lack of affection that you have shown. Your own lack of affection for your father deserves a similar lack of affection from your husband [K]. 297 *plighted* enfolded. Their true feelings are covered by many folds of cunning hypocrisy [K]. 298 *Who covers . . . derides* time, who at first conceals misdoings, at last exposes them to shame. *covers* F¹; JENNINS, K: "cover." 302 *will hence* will go hence. Such ellipsis of a verb of motion is very common [K]. 306 *hath now* Q¹; F¹: "hath." 306-7 *with what poor judgment . . . grossly* With cynical frankness Goneril admits that she and Regan have spoken hypocritically and that Lear's love for Cordelia has been well deserved [K]. *grossly* crudely obvious. 310 *The best . . . but rash* even in the prime of his life (time) he has been hasty (rash) in his actions. 312 *long-ingraffed condition* a temperament that has been for a long time firmly imbedded in his nature. "Graff" is an old form of "graft" [K]. *therewithal* therewith; together with them. 313 *choleric* irritable.

REG. Such unconstant starts are we like to have from him as this of
    Kent's banishment.   315

GON. There is further compliment of leave-taking between France
    and him. Pray you let's hit together. If our father carry anthority
    with such disposition as he bears, this last surrender of his will
    but offend us.

REG. We shall further think on't.   320

GON. We must do something, and i' th' heat.

    Exeunt.

314 *unconstant starts* sudden whims (a metaphor from horsemanship). *like*
likely. 316 *compliment* ceremony, formality. 317 *hit together* agree in our conduct toward him [K]. 317–18 *carry authority . . . bears* shows such a mood in
wielding his power as he now manifests [K]. *disposition* F¹; Q¹, K: "dispositions." 319 *offend us* cause us trouble. 321 *i' th' heat* while the iron is hot
(an old proverb).

SCENE 2

    [*The* EARL OF GLOUCESTER'S *Castle.*]
    Enter [EDMUND *the*] BASTARD *solus,* [*with a letter*].

EDM. Thou, Nature, art my goddess; to thy law
    My services are bound. Wherefore should I
    Stand in the plague of custom, and permit
    The curiosity of nations to deprive me,
    For that I am some twelve or fourteen moon-shines   5
    Lag of a brother? Why bastard? wherefore base?
    When my dimensions are as well compact,
    My mind as generous, and my shape as true,
    As honest madam's issue? Why brand they us
    With base? with baseness? bastardy? base, base?   10
    Who, in the lusty stealth of nature, take
    More composition and fierce quality
    Than doth, within a dull, stale, tired bed,
    Go to th' creating a whole tribe of fops
    Got 'tween asleep and wake? Well then,   15

I.2. 1 *Nature* The "Nature" which Edmund worships is conceived of as a
force independent of supernatural authority, governed only by its own mechanical laws. These laws make no distinction between the legitimate child and the
illegitimate, and thus he feels that he need not respect the merely human law
(custom) which because of his bastardy would deprive him of rights to his
father's estate. 3 *Stand in . . . custom* occupy a position that exposes me to
the grievous disabilities that mere "custom" inflicts [K]. 4 *curiosity of nations*
nice distinctions which the laws of nations make in defiance of nature and common sense [K]. *deprive me* deprive me of the right to be my father's heir; dis-
inherit me. Edmund is a younger son, so that even if he were legitimate, he could
not inherit his father's lands [K]. 6 *Lag of* behind (in age). 7 *my dimensions
. . . compact* my bodily frame is as well constructed [K]. 8 *generous* befitting
a nobleman. *true* symmetrical [K]. 9 *honest* chaste. *issue* child. 11 *lusty*
vigorous. 12 *composition . . . quality* strength of constitution and more energetic quality of body and mind [K]. 14 *fops* fools, weaklings. 15 *Got* begotten, conceived.

Legitimate Edgar, I must have your land.
Our father's love is to the bastard Edmund
As to th' legitimate. Fine word—"legitimate"!
Well, my legitimate, if this letter speed,
And my invention thrive, Edmund the base   20
Shall top th' legitimate. I grow; I prosper.
Now, gods, stand up for bastards!
     Enter GLOUCESTER.
GLOU. Kent banish'd thus? and France in choler parted?
And the King gone to-night? prescrib'd his pow'r?
Confin'd to exhibition? All this done   25
Upon the gad? Edmund, how now? What news?
EDM. So please your lordship, none.
     [*Puts up the letter.*]
GLOU. Why so earnestly seek you to put up that letter?
EDM. I know no news, my lord.
GLOU. What paper were you reading?   30
EDM. Nothing, my lord.
GLOU. No? What needed then that terrible dispatch of it into your
    pocket? The quality of nothing hath not such need to hide itself.
    Let's see. Come, if it be nothing, I shall not need spectacles.
EDM. I beseech you, sir, pardon me. It is a letter from my brother   35
    that I have not all o'erread; and for so much as I have perus'd, I
    find it not fit for your o'erlooking.
GLOU. Give me the letter, sir.
EDM. I shall offend, either to detain or give it. The contents, as
    in part I understand them, are to blame.   40
GLOU. Let's see, let's see!
EDM. I hope, for my brother's justification, he wrote this but as an
    essay or taste of my virtue.
GLOU. (*reads*) "This policy and reverence of age makes the world
    bitter to the best of our times; keeps our fortunes from us till our   45
    oldness cannot relish them. I begin to find an idle and fond bond-
    age in the oppression of aged tyranny, who sways, not as it hath
    power, but as it is suffer'd. Come to me, that of this I may speak
    more. If our father would sleep till I wak'd him, you should

19 *speed* prosper, succeed in its purpose. 21 *top th'* CAPELL; F¹: "to' th'";
Q¹: "tooth." 23 *choler* anger. *parted* departed. 24 *prescrib'd* limited, restricted
(F¹; Q¹, K: "subscribed"). 25 *exhibition* an allowance or pension (from his
daughters). 26 *Upon the gad* on the spur of the moment [K]. 28 *put up*
pocket, conceal. 32 *terrible dispatch* fearful haste in disposing. 33 *quality* nature. 35 *pardon me* excuse me (from showing the letter). 37 *o'erlooking* inspection. 39 *to detain* by withholding. 40 *to blame* blameworthy, objectionable.
43 *essay* trial. *taste* test. 44–5 *This policy . . . times* the established order of
society that forces the young to stand in awe of the aged deprives us of the
enjoyment of life when life is at its best. "Policy" (which often means "cunning"
or "strategic art") suggests that this order of society is a clever trick on the
part of the aged [K]. 46–7 *an idle and fond bondage* a servitude to which it is
foolish to submit [K]. *idle* foolish. *fond* foolish. 47–8 *not as it . . . suffer'd*
not by virtue of any power that it has but merely as the result of our submission [K]. *suffer'd* submitted to.

enjoy half his revenue for ever, and live the beloved of your   50
brother,

"EDGAR."

Hum! Conspiracy? "Sleep till I wak'd him, you should enjoy half
his revenue." My son Edgar! Had he a hand to write this? a heart
and brain to breed it in? When came this to you? Who brought it?   55

EDM. It was not brought me, my lord: there's the cunning of it. I
found it thrown in at the casement of my closet.

GLOU. You know the character to be your brother's?

EDM. If the matter were good, my lord, I durst swear it were his; but
in respect of that, I would fain think it were not.   60

GLOU. It is his.

EDM. It is his hand, my lord; but I hope his heart is not in the contents.

GLOU. Hath he never before sounded you in this business?

EDM. Never, my lord. But I have heard him oft maintain it to be fit
that, sons at perfect age, and fathers declining, the father should   65
be as ward to the son, and the son manage his revenue.

GLOU. O villain, villain! His very opinion in the letter! Abhorred
villain! Unnatural, detested, brutish villain! worse than brutish! Go,
sirrah, seek him. I'll apprehend him. Abominable villain! Where is
he?   70

EDM. I do not well know, my lord. If it shall please you to suspend
your indignation against my brother till you can derive from him
better testimony of his intent, you should run a certain course;
where, if you violently proceed against him, mistaking his purpose,
it would make a great gap in your own honour and shake in pieces   75
the heart of his obedience. I dare pawn down my life for him that
he hath writ this to feel my affection to your honour, and to no
other pretence of danger.

GLOU. Think you so?

EDM. If your honour judge it meet, I will place you where you shall   80
hear us confer of this and by an auricular assurance have your
satisfaction, and that without any further delay than this very
evening.

GLOU. He cannot be such a monster.

EDM. Nor is not, sure.   85

GLOU. To his father, that so tenderly and entirely loves him. Heaven
and earth! Edmund, seek him out; wind me into him, I pray you;

---

50 *revenue* income.   53 *wak'd* Q1; F1: "wake."   57 *casement* window opening on
hinges.   *closet* private room.   58 *character* handwriting.   59 *matter* subject
matter.   60 *in respect of that* considering what that subject matter is.   *fain*
rather.   63 *sounded* probed (a nautical metaphor).   65 *perfect age* prime of
life.   69 *Abominable* unnatural, unfit for human society.   73 *run a certain
course* be sure to proceed without the risk of making a mistake [K].   74 *where*
whereas.   75 *gap* breach.   77 *feel my affection* test my sentiments [K].   78 *pretence of danger* dangerous purpose.   80 *meet* fitting, proper.   81 *an auricular
assurance* the evidence of actually hearing the facts.   82 *satisfaction* full information, confirmation.   85-7 *Nor is . . . and earth* Q1; not in F1.   87 *wind me
into him* worm your way into his confidence for me [K].

frame the business after your own wisdom. I would unstate myself
to be in a due resolution.

EDM. I will seek him, sir, presently; convey the business as I shall find   90
  means, and acquaint you withal.

GLOU. These late eclipses in the sun and moon portend no good to us.
  Though the wisdom of nature can reason it thus and thus, yet
  nature finds itself scourg'd by the sequent effects. Love cools, friendship falls off, brothers divide. In cities, mutinies; in countries, dis-   95
  cord; in palaces, treason; and the bond crack'd 'twixt son and father.
  This villain of mine comes under the prediction; there's son against
  father: the King falls from bias of nature; there's father against
  child. We have seen the best of our time. Machinations, hollowness,
  treachery, and all ruinous disorders follow us disquietly to our   100
  graves. Find out this villain, Edmund; it shall lose thee nothing;
  do it carefully. And the noble and true-hearted Kent banish'd!
  his offence, honesty! 'Tis strange.   *Exit.*

EDM. This is the excellent foppery of the world, that, when we are
  sick in fortune, often the surfeit of our own behaviour, we make   105
  guilty of our disasters the sun, the moon, and the stars; as if we
  were villains on necessity; fools by heavenly compulsion; knaves,
  thieves, and treachers by spherical predominance; drunkards, liars,
  and adulterers by an enforc'd obedience of planetary influence; and
  all that we are evil in, by a divine thrusting on. An admirable eva-   110
  sion of whoremaster man, to lay his goatish disposition to the
  charge of a star! My father compounded with my mother under
  the Dragon's Tail, and my nativity was under Ursa Major, so that

88–9 *I would . . . resolution* I would abandon my rank and fortune to have my
doubts cleared up one way or the other [K]. 90 *presently* at once. *convey*
manage. 91 *withal* with it; with the facts in the case [K]. 92 *late eclipses*
Actual eclipses occurred in September and October of 1605, a fact often used
to date the play. Disturbances in physical nature in Shakespeare's plays often
accompany or foreshadow disturbances in the state. *late* recent. 93 *wisdom
of nature* scientific reasoning, learning. 93 *reason it thus and thus* explain it (the
eclipses) in one way or another. 94 *nature* the natural world of man. *sequent
effects* results which follow (the eclipses). 95 *mutinies* insurrections, riots.
96 *the bond . . . father* This should be compared to the "bond" which Cordelia
invokes at I.1.89. 97–101 *This villain . . . graves* F¹; not in Q¹. 98 *bias of
nature* natural course or tendency. A figure from bowling. The "bias" is the
curve that the bowl makes in its course [K]. 99 *Machinations* plottings.
hollowness insincerity. 101 *lose thee nothing* cause thee no loss. A backhanded
promise to reward his detective work [K]. 104 *foppery* foolishness. 105 *surfeit
. . . behaviour* the sickness being the result of the excesses of our own behaviour.
"Surfeit" means "overeating"; fortune has had more of us than she can stand
and thus must grow sick. 107 *on* by. 108 *treachers* traitors. *by spherical
predominance* as the result of the predominance of some planet; i.e. of its being
the most powerful of all the planets at the moment of our birth [K]. 109
influence An astrological term for the effect of a planet on one's nature and
fortunes. It means literally "on-flowing," as if a mysterious force came streaming down on us [K]. 111 *goatish* lustful; the goat is a traditional symbol for
lechery. 112 *compounded* (a) created (b) came to agreement. 113 *Dragon's
Tail* the constellation Draco, between Ursa Major (the Big Bear) and Cepheus.
nativity birth.

it follows I am rough and lecherous. Fut! I should have been that
I am, had the maidenliest star in the firmament twinkled on my 115
bastardizing. Edgar—

Enter EDGAR.

and pat! he comes, like the catastrophe of the old comedy. My cue
is villainous melancholy, with a sigh like Tom o' Bedlam. O, these
eclipses do portend these divisions! Fa, sol, la, mi.

EDG. How now, brother Edmund? What serious contemplation are 120
you in?

EDM. I am thinking, brother, of a prediction I read this other day,
what should follow these eclipses.

EDG. Do you busy yourself with that?

EDM. I promise you, the effects he writes of succeed unhappily: as of 125
unnaturalness between the child and the parent; death, dearth, dis-
solutions of ancient amities; divisions in state, menaces and
maledictions against king and nobles; needless diffidences, banishment of friends, dissipation of cohorts, nuptial breaches, and I
know not what. 130

EDG. How long have you been a sectary astronomical?

EDM. Come, come! When saw you my father last?

EDG. The night gone by.

EDM. Spake you with him?

EDG. Ay, two hours together. 135

EDM. Parted you in good terms? Found you no displeasure in him by
word or countenance?

EDG. None at all.

EDM. Bethink yourself wherein you may have offended him; and at
my entreaty forbear his presence until some little time hath quali- 140
fied the heat of his displeasure, which at this instant so rageth in
him that with the mischief of your person it would scarcely allay.

EDG. Some villain hath done me wrong.

EDM. That's my fear. I pray you have a continent forbearance till the
speed of his rage goes slower; and, as I say, retire with me to my 145

114 *Fut* Q¹; not in F¹. 116 *Edgar* Q¹; not in F¹. 117 *and pat* and just exactly
when he is needed (STEEVENS; F¹: "Pat"; Q¹: "and out"). *catastrophe* event
which brings the plot to an end [K]. 118 *villainous* miserable. 118 *Tom o'
Bedlam* A common phrase for a vagabond maniac [K], or one who pretended to
be mad. "Bedlam" was Bethlehem Hospital, the London madhouse. 119 *Fa . . .
mi* Edmund sings to himself in order to seem to be in a brown study and
unaware of his brother's approach [K] (F¹; not in Q¹). 125 *effects* several
fulfillments of the prediction [K]. *succeed* follow. 125–32 *as of . . . come* Q¹;
not in F¹. 126 *dearth* famine. 128 *diffidences* cases of mutual distrust [K].
129 *dissipation of cohorts* the breaking up of armed troops [K]. 131 *sectary
astronomical* devotee of the astrological sect; a believer in astrology. We may
note that both Edmund and Edgar have no respect for astrology [K]. 132 *Come,
come* A smiling protest against being regarded as "a sectary astronomical."
Then Edmund becomes serious, as his question shows [K]. 137 *countenance*
behaviour, manner [K]. 140 *forbear* avoid. 140–1 *qualified* modified, lessened.
142 *with the mischief . . . allay* his doing you bodily harm would not even be
enough to satisfy his anger. 144–8 *I pray you . . . brother* F¹; not in Q¹.
144 *have a continent forbearance* restrain yourself and keep out of his presence [K].

lodging, from whence I will fitly bring you to hear my lord speak.
Pray ye, go! There's my key. If you do stir abroad, go arm'd.

EDG. Arm'd, brother?

EDM. Brother, I advise you to the best. Go arm'd. I am no honest man
　　if there be any good meaning toward you. I have told you what I   150
　　have seen and heard; but faintly, nothing like the image and horror
　　of it. Pray you, away!

EDG. Shall I hear from you anon?

EDM. I do serve you in this business.

　　　Exit EDGAR.

　　A credulous father! and a brother noble,   155
　　Whose nature is so far from doing harms
　　That he suspects none; on whose foolish honesty
　　My practices ride easy! I see the business.
　　Let me, if not by birth, have lands by wit;
　　All with me's meet that I can fashion fit.   160

　　　Exit.

146 *fitly* opportunely, at the proper time. 151 *the image and horror* the horrible reality [K]. 158 *practices* plots. 159 *wit* intelligence. 160. *All with . . .
fit* everything, in my opinion, is proper for me that I can shape to fit my de-
signs [K]. *fashion fit* literally, make fitting by manipulation [K].

SCENE 3

[*The* DUKE OF ALBANY'S *Palace.*]
Enter GONERIL *and* [*her*] STEWARD [OSWALD].

GON. Did my father strike my gentleman for chiding of his fool?

OSW. Ay, madam.

GON. By day and night, he wrongs me! Every hour
　　He flashes into one gross crime or other
　　That sets us all at odds. I'll not endure it.   5
　　His knights grow riotous, and himself upbraids us
　　On every trifle. When he returns from hunting,
　　I will not speak with him. Say I am sick.
　　If you come slack of former services,
　　You shall do well; the fault of it I'll answer.   10
　　　[*Horns within.*]

OSW. He's coming, madam; I hear him.

GON. Put on what weary negligence you please,
　　You and your fellows. I'd have it come to question.
　　If he distaste it, let him to our sister,
　　Whose mind and mine I know in that are one,   15
　　Not to be overrul'd. Idle old man,
　　That still would manage those authorities
　　That he hath given away! Now, by my life,

I.3. 3 *By day and night* A mild oath. 4 *crime* offence. The word was less
specialized than in modern usage [K]. 7 *On* for. 10 *answer* be answerable for.
13 *to question* to be discussed—an issue for argument. 14 *distaste* dislike.
16–20 *Not to . . . abus'd* Q¹; not in F¹. 16 *Idle* foolish.

Old fools are babes again, and must be us'd
With checks as flatteries, when they are seen abus'd.   20
Remember what I have said.

osw.   Very well, madam.

GON. And let his knights have colder looks among you.
What grows of it, no matter. Advise your fellows so.
I would breed from hence occasions, and I shall,   25
That I may speak. I'll write straight to my sister
To hold my very course. Prepare for dinner.

    Exeunt.

19 *us'd* treated. 20 *With checks . . . abus'd* not merely with soothing words,
but, when they are seen to be deluded as to their position in life, with rebukes
as well. Children are sometimes coaxed, sometimes scolded; the same treatment
must be applied to childish old men [K]. *they* The antecedent is "old fools"
[K]. 24 *Advise . . . so* give similar instructions to your fellow servants. 25–6
I would . . . speak Q¹; not in F¹. 25 *breed . . . occasions* cause opportunities
to grow out of this; make an issue of it. 26 *straight* immediately.

SCENE 4

    [*The* DUKE OF ALBANY'S *Palace.*]
    Enter KENT, [*disguised*].

KENT. If but as well I other accents borrow,
That can my speech defuse, my good intent
May carry through itself to that full issue
For which I raz'd my likeness. Now, banish'd Kent,
If thou canst serve where thou dost stand condemn'd,   5
So may it come, thy master, whom thou lov'st,
Shall find thee full of labours.

    Horns within. Enter Lear, [KNIGHTS,] *and* ATTENDANTS.

LEAR. Let me not stay a jot for dinner; go get it ready. [*Exit an* AT-
TENDANT.] How now? What art thou?

KENT. A man, sir.   10

LEAR. What dost thou profess? What wouldst thou with us?

KENT. I do profess to be no less than I seem, to serve him truly that
will put me in trust, to love him that is honest, to converse with him
that is wise and says little, to fear judgment, to fight when I cannot
choose, and to eat no fish.   15

LEAR. What art thou?

KENT. A very honest-hearted fellow, and as poor as the King.

LEAR. If thou be'st as poor for a subject as he's for a king, thou art
poor enough. What wouldst thou?

I.4. 2 *defuse* disguise—literally, disorder [K]. 3 *full issue* perfect result. 4
raz'd my likeness erased my true appearance (by assuming a disguise). 5 *canst
serve* canst manage to be engaged as a servant. Thus Kent explains why he has
"raz'd" his "likeness" [K]. 8 *stay* wait. 11 *dost thou profess* is your profession
or calling. 12 *do profess* do claim. 13 *honest* honourable. 13 *converse* associate. 14 *judgment* God's judgment. *cannot choose* cannot help it. 15 *eat
no fish* i.e. be a good Protestant and thus a defender of the church and state in
Elizabethan times (an obvious anachronism).

KENT. Service.

LEAR. Who wouldst thou serve?

KENT. You.   20

LEAR. Dost thou know me, fellow?

KENT. No, sir; but you have that in your countenance which I would
    fain call master.

LEAR. What's that?   25

KENT. Authority.

LEAR. What services canst thou do?

KENT. I can keep honest counsel, ride, run, mar a curious tale in telling
    it and deliver a plain message bluntly. That which ordinary men
    are fit for, I am qualified in, and the best of me is diligence.   30

LEAR. How old art thou?

KENT. Not so young, sir, to love a woman for singing, nor so old to
    dote on her for anything. I have years on my back forty-eight.

LEAR. Follow me; thou shalt serve me. If I like thee no worse after
    dinner, I will not part from thee yet. Dinner, ho, dinner! Where's   35
    my knave? my fool? Go you and call my fool hither.

    [*Exit an* ATTENDANT.]

    Enter [OSWALD *the*] STEWARD.

    You, you, sirrah, where's my daughter?

OSW. So please you—

    Exit.

LEAR. What says the fellow there? Call the clotpoll back.

    [*Exit a Knight.*]   40

    Where's my fool, ho? I think the world's asleep.

    [*Enter* KNIGHT.]

    How now? Where's that mongrel?

KNIGHT. He says, my lord, your daughter is not well.

LEAR. Why came not the slave back to me when I call'd him?

KNIGHT. Sir, he answered me in the roundest manner, he would not.

LEAR. He would not?   45

KNIGHT. My lord, I know not what the matter is; but to my judgment
    your Highness is not entertain'd with that ceremonious affection as
    you were wont. There's a great abatement of kindness appears as
    well in the general dependants as in the Duke himself also and your
    daughter.   50

LEAR. Ha! say'st thou so?

KNIGHT. I beseech you pardon me, my lord, if I be mistaken; for my
    duty cannot be silent when I think your Highness wrong'd.

24 *countenance* bearing—not *merely* "face" [K].   25 *fain* be glad to.   29 *keep
honest counsel* keep a secret when it is an honourable one [K].   *curious* elaborate, complicated. Kent implies that he is too outspoken to be a skillful
talker [K].   33 *to love* as to love.   37 *knave* boy. Often used as a term of familiarity—sometimes in affection, sometimes in contempt [K].   39 *So please you*
if you please—literally, may it be pleasing to you. Oswald obeys Goneril and
"puts on weary negligence" in his treatment of the King [K].   40 *clotpoll*
stupid person—literally, one who has a clod of earth for a head.   45 *roundest*
plainest, most outspoken.   48 *entertain'd* treated.   49 *wont* accustomed to be.
appears that appears. The ellipsis of a relative pronoun in the nominative
was formerly very common and still occurs in colloquial speech [K].

LEAR. Thou but rememb'rest me of mine own conception. I have per-   55
ceived a most faint neglect of late, which I have rather blamed as
mine own jealous curiosity than as a very pretence and purpose of
unkindness. I will look further into't. But where's my fool? I have
not seen him this two days.

KNIGHT. Since my young lady's going into France, sir, the fool hath   60
much pined away.

LEAR. No more of that; I have noted it well. Go you and tell my
daughter I would speak with her. [*Exit* KNIGHT.] Go you, call hither
my fool.
        [*Exit an* ATTENDANT.]
        Enter [OSWALD *the*] STEWARD.
O, you, sir, you! Come you hither, sir. Who am I, sir?   65

OSW. My lady's father.

LEAR. "My lady's father"? My lord's knave! You whoreson dog! you
slave! you cur!

OSW. I am none of these, my lord; I beseech your pardon.

LEAR. Do you bandy looks with me, you rascal?   70
        [*Strikes him.*]

OSW. I'll not be strucken, my lord.

KENT. Nor tripp'd neither, you base football player?
        [*Trips up his heels.*]

LEAR. I thank thee, fellow. Thou serv'st me, and I'll love thee.

KENT. Come, sir, arise, away! I'll teach you differences. Away, away!
If you will measure your lubber's length again, tarry; but away! Go   75
to! Have you wisdom? So.
        [*Pushes him out.*]

LEAR. Now, my friendly knave, I thank thee. There's earnest of thy
service.
        [*Gives money.*]
        Enter FOOL.

FOOL. Let me hire him too. Here's my coxcomb.
        [*Offers* KENT *his cap.*]

LEAR. How now, my pretty knave? How dost thou?   80

FOOL. Sirrah, you were best take my coxcomb.

KENT. Why, fool?

FOOL. Why? For taking one's part that's out of favour. Nay, an thou

---

55 *rememb'rest* remindest. *conception* idea—that which has already occurred
to me.   56 *a most faint neglect* a very languid and neglectful manner [K].
57 *jealous curiosity* suspicious watchfulness about trifles [K].   57 *very pretence*
true intention.   70 *bandy* literally, to "bat to and fro," as a ball in tennis [K].
71 *strucken* struck.   72 *football* an impromptu game, played both in the fields
and the streets of towns, which was held in very low repute in Shakespeare's
time.   74 *teach you differences* teach you to observe the proper distinctions of
rank [K].   76 *wisdom* sanity. 77 *earnest* a small sum paid in advance to bind a
bargain [K].   79 *coxcomb* The professional fool (the jester), whether in real life
or on the stage, wore a hood or cap crested with a piece of red flannel, pat-
terned after the comb of a cock [K].   81 *were best* had better.   82 *fool* Q¹; F¹
"my boy," and gives the line to Lear.

canst not smile as the wind sits, thou'lt catch cold shortly. There, take my coxcomb! Why, this fellow hath banish'd two on's daugh- 85
ters, and did the third a blessing against his will. If thou follow him, thou must needs wear my coxcomb.—How now, nuncle? Would I had two coxcombs and two daughters!

LEAR. Why, my boy?

FOOL. If I gave them all my living, I'ld keep my coxcombs myself. 90
There's mine! beg another of thy daughters.

LEAR. Take heed, sirrah—the whip.

FOOL. Truth's a dog must to kennel; he must be whipp'd out, when the Lady Brach may stand by th' fire and stink.

LEAR. A pestilent gall to me! 95

FOOL. Sirrah, I'll teach thee a speech.

LEAR. Do.

FOOL. Mark it, nuncle.

> Have more than thou showest,
> Speak less than thou knowest, 100
> Lend less than thou owest,
> Ride more than thou goest,
> Learn more than thou trowest,
> Set less than thou throwest;
> Leave thy drink and thy whore, 105
> And keep in-a-door,
> And thou shalt have more
> Than two tens to a score.

KENT. This is nothing, fool.

FOOL. Then 'tis like the breath of an unfeed lawyer—you gave me 110
nothing for't. Can you make no use of nothing, nuncle?

LEAR. Why, no boy. Nothing can be made out of nothing.

FOOL. [*to* KENT] Prithee tell him, so much the rent of his land comes to. He will not believe a fool.

LEAR. A bitter fool! 115

FOOL. Dost thou know the difference, my boy, between a bitter fool and a sweet fool?

LEAR. No, lad; teach me.

84 *smile as the wind sits* take sides with the party that's in power [K]. 85 *banish'd* By dividing his kingdom between Goneril and Regan, Lear has made his daughters independent, and so he has lost them [K]. *on's* of his. 86 *did the third a blessing* His banishment of Cordelia has made her Queen of France [K]. 87 *nuncle* mine uncle. 90 *living* property. 92 *the whip* Whipping was the punishment for fools who took too great liberties, as it was for naughty children [K]. 93–4 *Truth's a dog . . . and stink* Truth is whipped out of the hall; but Flattery is allowed to keep a comfortable place by the fire, no matter how ill she behaves [K]. 93–4 *the Lady Brach* A contemptuous expression for a female dog, like "Madam Bitch." Shakespeare often associates dogs with flattery (F¹; Q¹: "Ladie oth'e brach"; STEEVENS, K: "Lady the Brach"). 95 *pestilent gall* plaguy irritation. 101 *owest* ownest, dost possess. 102 *goest* walkest. An old proverb holds that he is a fool who walks while his horse stands still. 103 *Learn . . . trowest* don't believe everything you hear. 104 *Set . . . throwest* don't stake all your money on a single throw of the dice. 106 *in-a-door* indoors. 110 *breath* speech.

FOOL.

That lord that counsell'd thee
To give away thy land,   120
Come place him here by me—
Do thou for him stand.
The sweet and bitter fool
Will presently appear;
The one in motley here,   125
The other found out there.

LEAR. Dost thou call me fool, boy?

FOOL. All thy other titles thou hast given away; that thou wast born
with.

KENT. This is not altogether fool, my lord.   130

FOOL. No, faith; lords and great men will not let me. If I had a monopoly out, they would have part on't. And ladies too, they will not
let me have all the fool to myself; they'll be snatching. Give me an
egg, nuncle, and I'll give thee two crowns.

LEAR. What two crowns shall they be?   135

FOOL. Why, after I have cut the egg i' th' middle and eat up the meat,
the two crowns of the egg. When thou clovest thy crown i' th'
middle and gav'st away both parts, thou bor'st thine ass on thy back
o'er the dirt. Thou hadst little wit in thy bald crown when thou
gav'st thy golden one away. If I speak like myself in this, let him   140
be whipp'd that first finds it so.

[Sings]

Fools had ne'er less grace in a year,
For wise men are grown foppish;
They know not how their wits to wear,
Their manners are so apish.   145

119–33 *That lord . . . snatching* Q¹; not in F¹. As he speaks these verses the Fool
places himself opposite Lear and at some little distance. He accompanies the
recitation with gestures [K]. 119–20 *That lord . . . land* The fool implies that
nobody gave Lear such idiotic advice; Lear was his own foolish counsellor [K].
125 *The one* the sweet fool. He points at himself. "Motley" is the regular word
for the fool's ludicrously variegated costume [K]. 126 *The other* yourself, "the
bitter fool." He points at Lear [K]. 131–2 *monopoly* royal patent entitling me to
be the sole dealer in foolishness [K]. 132–3 *they would have . . . snatching*
the courtiers who had helped me to secure the monopoly would insist on having
their share—and so would the court ladies. Monopolies, and the bribery or cor-
rupt influence by means of which they were often obtained, were constant subjects of satire in Shakespeare's time [K]. 135 *What two . . . be* The answer to
the Fool's conundrum is obvious, since "crowns" was a common term for the two
parts of the eggshell; but Lear wishes to let him make his joke. Conundrums are
not meant to be guessed [K]. 138–9 *thou bor'st . . . the dirt* you acted as
foolishly as a man who carries his ass instead of letting it carry him. The Fool
remembers a well-known fable [K]. 140 *like myself* like a fool—if it is foolish
for me to be so outspoken. 141 *that first finds it so* who first discovers that I
have told you the truth. "So" is emphatic. The implication is that Lear has already made this discovery and that he, if anybody, should be whipped for folly
[K]. 142 *Fools . . . year* fools are now in less favour than at any other time.
143 *foppish* foolish—thus supplying the place of fools. 144 *their wits to wear* to
use their intelligence. 145 *apish* ridiculous, grotesque [K].

LEAR. When were you wont to be so full of songs, sirrah?

FOOL. I have us'd it, nuncle, ever since thou mad'st thy daughters thy
mothers; for when thou gav'st them the rod, and put'st down thine
own breeches,

> [*Sings*]
>> Then they for sudden joy did weep,   150
>>> And I for sorrow sung,
>> That such a king should play bo-peep
>>> And go the fools among.

Prithee, nuncle, keep a schoolmaster that can teach thy fool to lie.
I would fain learn to lie.   155

LEAR. An you lie, sirrah, we'll have you whipp'd.

FOOL. I marvel what kin thou and thy daughters are. They'll have me
whipp'd for speaking true; thou'lt have me whipp'd for lying; and
sometimes I am whipp'd for holding my peace. I had rather be any
kind o' thing than a fool! And yet I would not be thee, nuncle.   160
Thou hast pared thy wit o' both sides and left nothing i' th' middle.
Here comes one o' the parings.

> *Enter* GONERIL.

LEAR. How now, daughter? What makes that frontlet on? Methinks
you are too much o' late i' th' frown.

FOOL. Thou wast a pretty fellow when thou hadst no need to care for   165
her frowning. Now thou art an O without a figure. I am better than
thou art now: I am a fool, thou art nothing. [*To* GONERIL] Yes,
forsooth, I will hold my tongue. So your face bids me, though you
say nothing. Mum, mum!

>> He that keeps nor crust nor crum,   170
>> Weary of all, shall want some.—

[*Points at* LEAR] That's a sheal'd peascod.

GON. Not only, sir, this your all-licens'd fool,
But other of your insolent retinue
Do hourly carp and quarrel, breaking forth   175
In rank and not-to-be-endured riots. Sir,
I had thought, by making this well known unto you,
To have found a safe redress, but now grow fearful,
By what yourself, too, late have spoke and done,
That you protect this course, and put it on   180
By your allowance; which if you should, the fault
Would not scape censure, nor the redresses sleep,

---

146 *wont* accustomed.   147 *us'd* practiced.   148 *mothers* F[1]; Q[1], K: "mother."
152 *play bo-peep* be so childish as to hide himself—i.e. renounce his royalty [K].
162 *one o' the parings* Goneril, he argues, must have half of the King's wits,
since he parted with all his wits when he gave away his kingdom [K]. 163 *frontlet* a cloth worn across the forehead by ladies—hence, a frown. 166 *an O* a
zero, without a digit to give it value.   170 *nor* Q[1]; F[1]; "not," *crum* the soft
part of the loaf of bread. 172 *sheal'd peascod* empty (shelled) peapod. 173
all-licens'd privileged to say and do anything and everything [K]. 175 *carp* complain, find fault. 176 *rank* excessive. 178 *safe* sure. 180 *put it on* encourage
it. 181 *allowance* approval.

Which, in the tender of a wholesome weal,
Might in their working do you that offence
Which else were shame, that then necessity   185
Must call discreet proceeding.

FOOL. For you know, nuncle,

      The hedge-sparrow fed the cuckoo so long
      That it had it head bit off by it young.

So out went the candle, and we were left darkling.   190

LEAR. Are you our daughter?

GON. Come, sir,
I would you would make use of your good wisdom
Whereof I know you are fraught, and put away
These dispositions which of late transport you   195
From what you rightly are.

FOOL. May not an ass know when the cart draws the horse?
Whoop, Jug, I love thee!

LEAR. Doth any here know me? This is not Lear.
Doth Lear walk thus? speak thus? Where are his eyes?   200
Either his notion weakens, his discernings
Are lethargied—Ha! waking? 'Tis not so!
Who is it that can tell me who I am?

FOOL. Lear's shadow.

LEAR. I would learn that; for, by the marks of sovereignty, Knowledge,   205
and reason, I should be false persuaded I had daughters.

FOOL. Which they will make an obedient father.

LEAR. Your name, fair gentlewoman?

GON. This admiration, sir, is much o' th' savour
Of other your new pranks. I do beseech you   210
To understand my purposes aright.
As you are old and reverend, should be wise.
Here do you keep a hundred knights and squires;
Men so disorder'd, so debosh'd, and bold
That this our court, infected with their manners,   215

183–6 *Which . . . proceeding* and the acts of redress that we should find necessary in our care for a sound condition of the state might, in their operation,
annoy you to an extent which, under other circumstances, would be shameful,
but which the necessities of the case would at this juncture force one to style
discreet procedure on our part [K]. 188–9 *hedge-sparrow . . . young* The
cuckoo lays its eggs in the nests of other birds. 190 *darkling* in the dark (like
the dead hedge sparrow; Lear is being destroyed by his daughters as the bird
is destroyed by the cuckoo it has nourished). 193 *of your* F¹; Q¹, K: "of that."
194 *fraught* well furnished—literally, freighted [K]. 195 *dispositions* states of
mind; fits of capricious temper [K]. *which of late transport* F¹; Q¹, K: "that of
late transforme." 198 *Jug* A nickname for "Joan" [K]. 201 *notion* understanding. 205–7 *I would . . . father* Q¹; not in F¹. 205–6 *the marks . . .
daughters* the outward signs of sovereignty, my knowledge, and my reason would
all falsely convince me that I have daughters (which I see by your present action
that I do not really have). 209 *admiration* pretending to wonder who you
are [K]. 212 *should* F¹, Q¹; Q², K: "you should." 213 *keep* support, maintain.
214 *disorder'd* disorderly. *debosh'd* debauched. 215 *manners* conduct and
character.

Shows like a riotous inn. Epicurism and lust
Makes it more like a tavern or a brothel
Than a grac'd palace. The shame itself doth speak
For instant remedy. Be then desir'd
By her that else will take the thing she begs   220
A little to disquantity your train,
And the remainder that shall still depend
To be such men as may besort your age,
Which know themselves, and you.
LEAR.   Darkness and devils!   225
Saddle my horses! Call my train together!
Degenerate bastard, I'll not trouble thee;
Yet have I left a daughter.
GON. You strike my people, and your disorder'd rabble
Make servants of their betters.   230
        Enter ALBANY.
LEAR. Woe that too late repents!—O, sir, are you come?
Is it your will? Speak, sir!—Prepare my horses.
Ingratitude, thou marble-hearted fiend,
More hideous when thou show'st thee in a child
Than the sea-monster!   235
ALB.   Pray, sir, be patient.
LEAR. [*to* GONERIL] Detested kite, thou liest!
My train are men of choice and rarest parts,
That all particulars of duty know
And in the most exact regard support   240
The worships of their name.—O most small fault,
How ugly didst thou in Cordelia show!
Which, like an engine, wrench'd my frame of nature
From the fix'd place; drew from my heart all love
And added to the gall. O Lear, Lear, Lear!   245
Beat at this gate that let thy folly in
    [*Strikes his head.*]
And thy dear judgment out! Go, go, my people.

---

216 *Shows* appears. *Epicurism* gluttony and riotous living. Shakespeare shows
nothing in the conduct of Lear's knights to warrant these accusations by Goneril.
217 *Makes* F¹; ROWE, K: "Make." 218 *grac'd* honourable. *speak* call. 219
desir'd requested. 221 *disquantity* reduce in number. *train* retinue, followers.
222 *depend* attend you as dependents; remain in your service [K]. 223 *besort*
befit. 231 *that* to him that. *O, sir . . . come* Q¹; not in F¹. 235 *Than the
sea-monster* than any monster of the deep [K]; he is not referring to any specific
monster. 238 *parts* qualities. Those critics who regard Goneril's complaints
about the behaviour of Lear's attendants as more or less justified fail to note
the manifest purpose of Lear's words here. That his Knights were well behaved
is indicated also by the moderation of speech and manner shown by one of
them in line 43ff [K]. 241 *worships* honour. Abstract nouns are often pluralized
when they refer to more than one person [K]. 242 *show* appear. 243 *frame
of nature* the whole structure of my nature. The figure is that of a building that
is thrown off its foundation ("the fix'd place") by a powerful mechanical contrivance [K]. 24E *gall* bitterness. 247 *dear,* precious.

ALB. My lord, I am guiltless, as I am ignorant
  Of what hath mov'd you.
LEAR.   It may be so, my lord.   250
  Hear, Nature, hear! dear goddess, hear!
  Suspend thy purpose, if thou didst intend
  To make this creature fruitful.
  Into her womb convey sterility;
  Dry up in her the organs of increase;   255
  And from her derogate body never spring
  A babe to honour her! If she must teem,
  Create her child of spleen, that it may live
  And be a thwart disnatur'd torment to her.
  Let it stamp wrinkles in her brow of youth,   260
  With cadent tears fret channels in her cheeks.
  Turn all her mother's pains and benefits
  To laughter and contempt, that she may feel
  How sharper than a serpent's tooth it is
  To have a thankless child! Away, away!   265
    Exit.
ALB. Now, gods that we adore, whereof comes this?
GON. Never afflict yourself to know more of it;
  But let his disposition have that scope
  That dotage gives it.
    Enter LEAR.
LEAR. What, fifty of my followers at a clap?   270
  Within a fortnight?
ALB.   What's the matter, sir?
LEAR. I'll tell thee. [*To* GONERIL] Life and death! I am asham'd
  That thou hast power to shake my manhood thus;
  That these hot tears, which break from me perforce,   275
  Should make thee worth them. Blasts and fogs upon thee!
  Th' untented woundings of a father's curse
  Pierce every sense about thee!—Old fond eyes,
  Beweep this cause again, I'll pluck ye out,
  And cast you, with the waters that you lose,   280
  To temper clay. Yea, is it come to this?
  Ha! Let it be so. I have another daughter,

249 *Of . . . you* F¹; not in Q¹. 255 *increase* reproduction. 256 *derogate* blighted (by barrenness)—literally, deteriorated [K]. 257 *teem* have offspring (a term usually applied to the reproduction of the lower forms of life, such as insects and fish). 258 *spleen* malice and perversity. The spleen was regarded as the source of these passions. 259 *thwart* perverse. *disnatur'd* unnatural. 261 *cadent* falling. *fret* wear. 262 *pains* care. 267 *more of it* F¹; Q¹, K: "the cause." 268 *disposition* mood. 275 *perforce* against my will. 276 *Blasts . . . thee* Fog and mist were thought to contain the seeds of pestilence [K]. *Blasts* lightning strokes of pestilence [K]. 277 *untented* that are too deep to be probed; or, more exactly, to be searched with a "tent"—a slender roll of lint with which wounds are cleaned [K]. 278 *fond* foolish. 280 *lose waste*—since these tears are of no avail [K]. 281 *temper* moisten, soften. *Yea . . . this* Q¹, not in F¹. 282 *Ha* F¹; not in Q¹, K. *I have another* F¹; Q¹, K: "Yet haue I left a."

Who I am sure is kind and comfortable.
When she shall hear this of thee, with her nails
She'll flay thy wolvish visage. Thou shalt find   285
That I'll resume the shape which thou dost think
I have cast off for ever; thou shalt, I warrant thee.
     Exeunt [LEAR, KENT *and* ATTENDANTS.]
GON. Do you mark that, my lord?
ALB. I cannot be so partial, Goneril,
  To the great love I bear you—   290
GON. Pray you, content.—What, Oswald, ho!
    [*To the* FOOL]
  You, sir, more knave than fool, after your master!
FOOL. Nuncle Lear, nuncle Lear, tarry! Take the fool with thee.
          A fox, when one has caught her,
          And such a daughter,   295
          Should sure to the slaughter,
          If my cap would buy a halter.
          So the fool follows after.

    Exit.
GON. This man hath had good counsel! A hundred knights?
  'Tis politic and safe to let him keep   300
  At point a hundred knights; yes, that on every dream,
  Each buzz, each fancy, each complaint, dislike,
  He may enguard his dotage with their pow'rs
  And hold our lives in mercy.—Oswald, I say!
ALB. Well, you may fear too far.   305
GON.   Safer than trust too far.
  Let me still take away the harms I fear,
  Not fear still to be taken. I know his heart.
  What he hath utter'd I have writ my sister.
  If she sustain him and his hundred knights,   310
  When I have show'd th' unfitness—
    Enter [OSWALD *the*] STEWARD.
               How now, Oswald?
  What, have you writ that letter to my sister?
OSW. Yes, madam.
GON. Take you some company, and away to horse!   315
  Inform her full of my particular fear,
  And thereto add such reasons of your own
  As may compact it more. Get you gone,

283 *comfortable* ready to comfort. 285–7 *Thou shalt . . . thee* Q¹; not in F¹.
293 *Take the fool with thee* An absolutely perfect pun. The literal sense is
obvious, but the phrase was a regular farewell gibe: "Take the epithet 'fool'
with you as you go!" [K]. 296 *sure to* certainly be sent to. 297 *halter* hang-
man's rope. Pronounced "haiter" to rhyme with "after," pronounced "auter."
299–311 *This man . . . th' unfitness* F¹; not in Q¹. 301 *At point* fully armed.
302 *buzz* whisper, idle rumour. 303 *enguard* protect. 304 *in mercy* at his
mercy. 307 *still* always. 308 *Not . . . taken* rather than always live in fear
to be attacked by some harm [K]. 315 *company* escort. 316 *particular* own,
personal. 318 *compact it more* make what I fear seem more solid, more sub-
stantial [K].

And hasten your return. [*Exit* OSWALD.] No, no, my lord!
This milky gentleness and course of yours,   320
Though I condemn not, yet, under pardon,
You are much more at task for want of wisdom
Than prais'd for harmful mildness.
ALB. How far your eyes may pierce I cannot tell.
Striving to better, oft we mar what's well.   325
GON. Nay then—
ALB. Well, well; th' event.
   Exeunt.

320 *milky . . . course* mild and gentle way that you prefer. 321 *condemn not* F[1]; Q[1]: "dislike not"; POPE, K: "condemn it not." *under pardon* if you will pardon me for saying so [K]. 322 *at task* taken to task, blameworthy [K]. 323 *harmful mildness* lenity that may prove injurious [K]. 325 *Striving . . . well* An old proverb, equivalent to "let well enough alone."

SCENE 5

[*Court before the* DUKE OF ALBANY'S *Palace.*]
Enter LEAR, KENT, and FOOL.

LEAR. Go you before to Gloucester with these letters. Acquaint my daughter no further with anything you know than comes from her demand out of the letter. If your diligence be not speedy, I shall be there afore you.
KENT. I will not sleep, my lord, till I have delivered your letter.   5
   Exit.
FOOL. If a man's brains were in's heels, were't not in danger of kibes?
LEAR. Ay, boy.
FOOL. Then I prithee be merry. Thy wit shall ne'er go slipshod.
LEAR. Ha, ha, ha!
FOOL. Shalt see thy other daughter will use thee kindly; for though   10
she's as like this as a crab 's like an apple, yet I can tell what I can tell.
LEAR. What canst tell, boy?
FOOL. Sh'll taste as like this as a crab does to a crab. Thou can'st tell why one's nose stands i' th' middle on's face?   15
LEAR. No.
FOOL. Why, to keep one's eyes of either side's nose, that what a man cannot smell out, 'a may spy into.
LEAR. I did her wrong.
FOOL. Canst tell how an oyster makes his shell?   20
LEAR. No.

I.5. 1 *these letters* this letter (from the Latin "litterae"). 3 *demand . . . letter* questioning as a result of her reading the letter.   6 *kibes* chilblains.   8 *wit . . . slipshod* intelligence will never have to wear slippers (because of the kibes)—because you have no intelligence.   10 *Shalt* thou shalt. *kindly* The Fool puns on "kindly" in the ordinary sense and in the sense of "according to her nature" [K].   14 *a crab* a wild apple, very sour.   15 *on's* of his.   19 *her* Cordelia.

FOOL. Nor I neither; but I can tell why a snail has a house.

LEAR. Why?

FOOL. Why, to put 's head in; not to give it away to his daughters, and
leave his horns without a case.   25

LEAR. I will forget my nature. So kind a father!—Be my horses ready?

FOOL. Thy asses are gone about 'em. The reason why the seven stars
are no moe than seven is a pretty reason.

LEAR. Because they are not eight?

FOOL. Yes indeed. Thou wouldst make a good fool.   30

LEAR. To take't again perforce! Monster ingratitude!

FOOL. If thou wert my fool, nuncle, I'ld have thee beaten for being old
before thy time.

LEAR. How's that?

FOOL. Thou shouldst not have been old till thou hadst been wise.   35

LEAR. O, let me not be mad, not mad, sweet heaven!
  Keep me in temper; I would not be mad!
    [*Enter a* GENTLEMAN.]
  How now? Are the horses ready?

GENT. Ready, my lord.

LEAR. Come, boy.   40

FOOL. She that's a maid now, and laughs at my departure,
  Shall not be a maid long, unless things be cut shorter.
    Exeunt.

25 *horns* Shakespeare's audience were at liberty to recognize the everlasting
"horns" joke, for which they were on the alert. The Fool does not mean to call
Lear a cuckold; he simply accepts horns as the inevitable adornment of married
men [K]. *case* covering.   26 *forget my nature* cease to be a natural (kind and
loving) father.   27 *seven stars* the Pleiades.   28 *moe* more. Not a contraction
of "more," but an independent formation from the same root [K].   29 *not eight*
The Fool has intentionally prepared a conundrum so obvious that the answer is
inevitable. Then he can make the point that he wishes: "Thou wouldst make a
good fool"; "You're good at this kind of foolery" [K].   31 *To take't again* to
take back my royal powers.   *perforce* by force.   37 *in temper* in a normal condition of mind [K].   41–2 *She that's . . . shorter* This bit of buffoonery is addressed to the audience. The Fool holds the stage for a moment before he follows his master [K]. "Departure" and "shorter" would rhyme in Elizabethan
pronunciation.

ACT TWO

SCENE 1

[*A court within the Castle of the* EARL OF GLOUCESTER.]
Enter [EDMUND *the*] BASTARD *and* CURAN, *meeting.*

EDM. Save thee, Curan.

CUR. And you, sir. I have been with your father, and given him notice
that the Duke of Cornwall and Regan his Duchess will be here with
him this night.

II.1.   1 *Save thee* God save thee.

EDM. How comes that?   5

CUR. Nay, I know not. You have heard of the news abroad—I mean
the whisper'd ones, for they are yet but ear-kissing arguments?

EDM. Not I. Pray you, what are they?

CUR. Have you heard of no likely wars toward 'twixt the Dukes of
Cornwall and Albany?   10

EDM. Not a word.

CUR. You may do, then, in time. Fare you well, sir.
        Exit.

EDM. The Duke be here to-night? The better! best!
This weaves itself perforce into my business.
My father hath set guard to take my brother;   15
And I have one thing, of a queasy question,
Which I must act. Briefness and fortune, work!
Brother, a word! Descend! Brother, I say!
        Enter EDGAR.
My father watches. O sir, fly this place!
Intelligence is given where you are hid.   20
You have now the good advantage of the night.
Have you not spoken 'gainst the Duke of Cornwall?
He's coming hither; now, i' th' night, i' th' haste,
And Regan with him. Have you nothing said
Upon his party 'gainst the Duke of Albany?   25
Advise yourself.

EDG.   I am sure on't, not a word.

EDM. I hear my father coming. Pardon me!
In cunning I must draw my sword upon you.
Draw, seem to defend yourself; now quit you well.—   30
Yield! Come before my father. Light, ho, here!
Fly, brother.—Torches, torches!—So farewell.
        Exit EDGAR.
Some blood drawn on me would beget opinion
Of my more fierce endeavour. [*Stabs his arm.*] I have seen drunkards
Do more than this in sport.—Father, father!—   35
Stop, stop! No help?
        Enter GLOUCESTER, *and* SERVANTS *with torches.*

GLOU. Now, Edmund, where's the villain?

EDM. Here stood he in the dark, his sharp sword out,

---

7 *ones* "News" was originally a plural—"new things" [K]. *ear-kissing* whispered. *arguments* subjects of conversation. 9 *toward* impending. *the Dukes*
F¹; Q¹, K: "the two Dukes." 13 *The better* so much the better. 14 *perforce*
of its own accord. 15 *take* capture, arrest. 16 *of a queasy question* requiring delicate management [K]. 17 *Briefness* decisive speed, prompt action.
18 *Descend* Edgar is hiding in Edmund's chamber. See. **I.2.** 145 [K]. 22 *spoken*
'gainst committed yourself against the cause of (in the quarrel between the two
dukes). 25 *Upon his party* in support of his cause. 26 *Advise* bethink. 21
In cunning as a trick—in order that I may not seem to be in collusion with
you [K]. 30 *quit you well* put up a vigorous defence [K]. 34–5 *I have seen
. . . sport* A wild gallant would sometimes stab his arm and mix the blood with
the wine when he drank his lady's health [K].

Mumbling of wicked charms, conjuring the moon
To stand's auspicious mistress.   40
GLOU.   But where is he?
EDM. Look, sir, I bleed.
GLOU.   Where is the villain, Edmund?
EDM. Fled this way, sir. When by no means he could—
GLOU. Pursue him, ho! Go after. [*Exeunt some* SERVANTS.] By no   45
    means what?
EDM. Persuade me to the murder of your lordship;
    But that I told him the revenging gods
    'Gainst parricides did all the thunder bend;
    Spoke with how manifold and strong a bond   50
    The child was bound to the' father—sir, in fine,
    Seeing how loathly opposite I stood
    To his unnatural purpose, in fell motion
    With his prepared sword he charges home
    My unprovided body, lanch'd mine arm;   55
    But when he saw my best alarum'd spirits,
    Bold in the quarrel's right, rous'd to th' encounter,
    Or whether gasted by the noise I made,
    Full suddenly he fled.
GLOU.   Let him fly far.   60
    Not in this land shall he remain uncaught;
    And found—dispatch. The noble Duke my master,
    My worthy arch and patron, comes to-night.
    By his authority I will proclaim it,
    That he which finds him shall deserve our thanks,   65
    Bringing the murderous coward to the stake;
    He that conceals him, death.
EDM. When I dissuaded him from his intent
    And found him pight to do it, with curst speech
    I threaten'd to discover him. He replied,   70
    "Thou unpossessing bastard, dost thou think,
    If I would stand against thee, would the reposal
    Of any trust, virtue, or worth in thee
    Make thy words faith'd? No. What I should deny
    (As this I would; ay, though thou didst produce   75

39 *Mumbling of . . . the moon* Edmund adapts his story to his father's super-
stition [K]. 40 *stand's* serve as his Q¹; F¹: "stand"). 49 *the thunder* F¹; Q¹,
K: "their thunders." *bend* direct. 51 *in fine* finally. 52 *loathly opposite* bitterly opposed [K]. 53 *fell* fierce. 54 *charges home* makes a home thrust at.
55 *unprovided* undefended. *lanch'd* pierced, wounded (Q¹; F¹: "latch'd"). 56
my best alarum'd spirits all my best powers (energies) called to arms [K].
58 *gasted* struck aghast, panic-stricken. 62 *found—dispatch* when he is found
let him be killed at once. 63 *worthy* honourable *arch* patron, supporter,
66 *coward* F¹; Q¹, K: "caytife." *to the stake* to the place of execution; to his
death. A figure derived from the stake to which one was fastened for execution
by fire. Not to be taken literally [K]. 69 *pight* determined. *curst* angry. 70
discover him reveal his purpose. 71 *unpossessing* beggarly, incapable of holding
title to property. 72 *reposal* placing. 74 *faith'd* believed.

My very character), I'ld turn it all
To thy suggestion, plot, and damned practice;
And thou must make a dullard of the world,
If they not thought the profits of my death
Were very pregnant and potential spurs   80
To make thee seek it."

GLOU.   O strange and fast'ned villain!
Would he deny his letter? I never got him.
      Tucket within.
Hark, the Duke's trumpets! I know not why he comes.
All ports I'll bar; the villain shall not scape;   85
The Duke must grant me that. Besides, his picture
I will send far and near, that all the kingdom
May have due note of him, and of my land,
Loyal and natural boy, I'll work the means
To make thee capable.   90
      Enter CORNWALL, REGAN, *and* ATTENDANTS.
CORN. How now, my noble friend? Since I came hither
      (Which I can call but now) I have heard strange news.
REG. If it be true, all vengeance comes too short
      Which can pursue th' offender. How dost, my lord?
GLOU. O madam, my old heart is crack'd, it's crack'd!   95
REG. What, did my father's godson seek your life?
      He whom my father nam'd? your Edgar?
GLOU. O lady, lady, shame would have it hid!
REG. Was he not companion with the riotous knights
      That tended upon my father?   100
GLOU. I know not, madam. 'Tis too bad, too bad!
EDM. Yes, madam, he was of that consort.
REG. No marvel then though he were ill affected.
      'Tis they have put him on the old man's death,
      To have th' expense and waste of his revenues.   105
      I have this present evening from my sister
      Been well inform'd of them, and with such cautions
      That, if they come to sojourn at my house,
      I'll not be there.
CORN.   Nor I, assure thee, Regan.   110

76 *character* handwriting. 77 *suggestion* evil suggestion. *practice* Synonymous
with "plot." 78 *make . . . world* consider everyone to be stupid. 80 *pregnant
and potential* ready and powerful. *spurs* Q¹; F¹: "spirits." 82 *O strange* O unnatural (F¹; Q¹, K: "Strong"). *fast'ned* confirmed (in his villainy) [K]. 83 *got
him* begot him (Q¹; F¹: "got him. Said he?") 84 *why* Q¹; F¹: "wher." 85
ports seaports. 89 *natural* Gloucester has both senses of the word in mind.
Edmund is his "natural son" and (he thinks) feels for him the "natural affection" of a son for a father [K]. 90 *capable* legally capable of inheriting. Gloucester promises to legitimize the bastard by due process of law [K]. 92 *strange
news* Q¹; F¹: "strangenesse." 100 *tended* attended (F¹; Q¹: "tends"; THEOBALD,
K: "tend"). 102 *consort* company, gang (often used with contempt). 103
though if. *were ill affected* had disloyal sentiments toward you [K]. 104 *put him
on* incited him to. 105 *expense* privilege of spending. 110 *assure thee* be
assured.

Edmund, I hear that you have shown your father
  A childlike office.
EDM.   'Twas my duty, sir.
GLOU. He did bewray his practice, and receiv'd
  This hurt you see, striving to apprehend him.   115
CORN. Is he pursued?
GLOU.   Ay, my good lord.
CORN. If he be taken, he shall never more
  Be fear'd of doing harm. Make your own purpose,
  How in my strength you please. For you, Edmund,   120
  Whose virtue and obedience doth this instant
  So much commend itself, you shall be ours.
  Natures of such deep trust we shall much need;
  You we first seize on.
EDM.   I shall serve you, sir,   125
  Truly, however else.
GLOU.   For him I thank your Grace.
CORN. You know not why we came to visit you—
REG. Thus out of season, threading dark-ey'd night.
  Occasions, noble Glouscester, of some prize,   130
  Wherein we must have use of your advice.
  Our father he hath writ, so hath our sister,
  Of differences, which I best thought it fit
  To answer from our home. The several messengers
  From hence attend dispatch. Our good old friend,   135
  Lay comforts to your bosom, and bestow
  Your needful counsel to our businesses,
  Which craves the instant use.
GLOU.   I serve you, madam.
  Your Graces are right welcome.   140
    Exeunt. Flourish.

112 *childlike office* dutiful service befitting a son [K]. 114 *bewray* reveal. *practice* plot. 119 *of doing* lest he do. 119–20 *Make your . . . you please* form your own plan for his capture and punishment, using my authority in any way that may seem good to you [K]. 122 *ours* in our service. 124 *seize on* take possession of (a legal term). 129 *threading* making our way through [K]. 130 *prize* importance (F¹; Q¹, K: "poyse"). 133 *differences* disputes. *which* which letters 134 *from* when away from. 135 *attend dispatch* are waiting to be sent. 136 *Lay . . . bosom* be comforted (in your own troubles). 137 *businesses* F¹; Q¹, K: "busines." 138 *craves . . . use* requires to be carried out without delay [K].

SCENE 2

  [*Before* GLOUCESTER's *Castle.*]
  Enter KENT *and* [OSWALD *the*] STEWARD, *severally.*
OSW. Good dawning to thee, friend. Art of this house?
KENT. Ay.

II.2. 1 *Art . . . house* are you a servant here?

osw. Where may we set our horses?

KENT. I' th' mire.

osw. Prithee, if thou lov'st me, tell me. 5

KENT. I love thee not.

osw. Why then, I care not for thee.

KENT. If I had thee in Lipsbury Pinfold, I would make thee care for
me.

osw. Why dost thou use me thus? I know thee not. 10

KENT. Fellow, I know thee.

osw. What dost thou know me for?

KENT. A knave; a rascal; an eater of broken meats; a base, proud,
shallow, beggarly, three-suited, hundred-pound, filthy, worsted-
stocking knave; a lily-liver'd, action-taking, whoreson, glass-gazing, 15
superserviceable, finical rogue; one-trunk-inheriting slave; one that
wouldst be a bawd in way of good service, and art nothing but the
composition of a knave, beggar, coward, pander, and the son and
heir of a mongrel bitch; one whom I will beat into clamorous whin-
ing, if thou deny the least syllable of thy addition. 20

osw. Why, what a monstrous fellow art thou, thus to rail on one that's
neither known of thee nor knows thee!

KENT. What a brazen-fac'd varlet art thou, to deny thou knowest me!
Is it two days ago since I tripp'd up thy heels and beat thee before
the King? [*Draws his sword.*] Draw, you rogue! for, though it be 25
night, yet the moon shines. I'll make a sop o' th' moonshine o' you.
Draw, you whoreson cullionly barbermonger! draw!

osw. Away! I have nothing to do with thee.

KENT. Draw, you rascal! You come with letters against the King, and
take Vanity the puppet's part against the royalty of her father. 30

---

8 *in Lipsbury Pinfold* between my teeth. A "pinfold" is a pen for stray animals.
There is no such town as "Lipsbury," which literally translated means "the region around the lips." 13–20 *A knave . . . addition* Kent upbraids Oswald as
a cowardly menial who parades as a gentleman [K]. 13 *broken meats* leftover
table scraps. 14 *three-suited* This seems to have been the regular allowance for
a manservant [K]. *hundred-pound* the minimum property qualification for one
who aspired to be called a gentleman. 14–15 *worsted-stocking* Gentlemen wore
silk stockings [K]. 15 *lily-liver'd* white-livered; i.e. having no blood in your liver,
and therefore cowardly [K]. *action-taking* going to law instead of meeting
one's enemy in combat [K]. *glass-gazing* always preening himself in a mirror [K]. 16 *superserviceable* ready to serve one's master in ways that are beyond
the limits of honourable service—even to the extent, Kent adds, of acting as a
bawd [K]. *finical* fussy about trifles [K]. *one-trunk-inheriting* all of whose
possessions are contained in a single box or trunk. To "inherit" means to "possess" [K]. 17 *in way of good service* if it comes in your day's work as a devoted
servant [K]. 18 *composition* composite, compound. 18–19 *and heir* A fine
touch!—not merely the "son," but the "heir," inheriting all the mongrel's qualities [K]. 20 *thy addition* the titles I have just given thee [K]. 24 *tripp'd . . .
beat thee* F[1]; Q[1], K: "beat thee, and tript up thy heeles." 26 *I'll make . . . o'
you* I'll drill you full of holes so that the moonlight can soak into you until you
are a mere sop—steeped in moonshine [K]. 27 *cullionly barbermonger* vile fop,
always dealing with barbers for the care of your hair and beard. 30 *Vanity the
puppet* Vanity was a stock figure in the older morality plays, and it survived in
Elizabethan puppet shows. Kent equates the figure with Goneril.

Draw, you rogue, or I'll so carbonado your shanks! Draw, you
rascal! Come your ways!

osw. Help, ho! murder! help!

KENT. Strike, you slave! Stand, rogue! Stand, you neat slave! Strike!
[*Beats him.*]

osw. Help, ho! murder! murder!   35

    Enter EDMUND, *with his rapier drawn,* GLOUCESTER, CORNWALL,
    REGAN, SERVANTS.

EDM. How now? What's the matter? Part!

KENT. With you, goodman boy, an you please! Come, I'll flesh ye!
Come on, young master!

GLOU. Weapons? arms? What's the matter here?

CORN. Keep peace, upon your lives!   40
    He dies that strikes again. What is the matter?

REG. The messengers from our sister and the King.

CORN. What is your difference? Speak.

osw. I am scarce in breath, my lord.

KENT. No marvel, you have so bestirr'd your valour. You cowardly   45
rascal, nature disclaims in thee; a tailor made thee.

CORN. Thou art a strange fellow. A tailor make a man?

KENT. Ay, a tailor, sir. A stonecutter or a painter could not have made
him so ill, though he had been but two years o' th' trade.

CORN. Speak yet, how grew your quarrel?   50

osw. This ancient ruffian, sir, whose life I have spar'd
    At suit of his grey beard—

KENT. Thou whoreson zed! thou unnecessary letter! My lord, if you'll
give me leave, I will tread this unbolted villain into mortar and
daub the walls of a jakes with him. "Spare my grey beard," you   55
wagtail?

CORN. Peace, sirrah!
    You beastly knave, know you no reverence?

KENT. Yes, sir, but anger hath a privilege.

CORN. Why art thou angry?   60

KENT. That such a slave as this should wear a sword,
    Who wears no honesty. Such smiling rogues as these,
    Like rats, oft bite the holy cords atwain
    Which are too intrinse t' unloose; smooth every passion
    That in the natures of their lords rebel,   65

---

31 *carbonado* slice a piece of meat from. 34 *neat* foppish. 36 *Part* F¹; not in
Q¹, K; K adds s.d.: "Parts them." 37 *goodman boy* A form of address to a pre-
sumptuous youngster [K]. 37 *flesh ye* give you your first taste of fighting. 43
difference dispute. 46 *disclaims in thee* renounces all claim to have produced
thee [K]. 49 *years o' th'* F¹; Q¹, K: "houres at the." 53 *zed . . . letter* The
letter "z" is unnecessary because its sound is usually expressed by "s" [K].
54 *unbolted villain* unsifted rascal; this fellow who is rascal through and
through [K]. 55 *daub* plaster. *jakes* privy. 56 *wagtail* a comically uneasy bird,
so called from the spasmodic up-and-down jerking of its tail. Oswald is too
scared to stand still [K]. 62 *honesty* honourable character [K]. 63 *holy cords*
sacred bonds of family affection [K]. 64 *too intrinse* tied in too close and intricate a knot (like the "Gordian knot") [K]. *smooth* flatter.

Bring oil to fire, snow to their colder moods;
Renege, affirm, and turn their halcyon beaks
With every gale and vary of their masters,
Knowing naught (like dogs) but following.
A plague upon your epileptic visage!   70
Smile you my speeches, as I were a fool?
Goose, an I had you upon Sarum Plain,
I'ld drive ye cackling home to Camelot.
CORN. What, art thou mad, old fellow?
GLOU. How fell you out? Say that.   75
KENT. No contraries hold more antipathy
    Than I and such a knave.
CORN. Why dost thou call him knave? What is his fault?
KENT. His countenance likes me not.
CORN. No more perchance does mine, or his, or hers.   80
KENT. Sir, 'tis my occupation to be plain.
    I have seen better faces in my time
    Than stands on any shoulder that I see
    Before me at this instant.
CORN.   This is some fellow   85
    Who, having been prais'd for bluntness, doth affect
    A saucy roughness, and constrains the garb
    Quite from his nature. He cannot flatter, he!
    An honest mind and plain—he must speak truth!
    An they will take it, so; if not, he's plain.   90
    These kind of knaves I know which in this plainness
    Harbour more craft and more corrupter ends
    Than twenty silly-ducking observants
    That stretch their duties nicely.
KENT. Sir, in good faith, in sincere verity,   95
    Under th' allowance of your great aspect,

---

66 *Bring* Q¹; F¹: "Being." *Renege* deny. *halcyon beaks* It was believed that
the halcyon (kingfisher), if hung up, would serve as a weathervane, turning
about so that its beak would always point in the direction from which the wind
comes [K]. 68 *gale and vary* varying wind. 70 *epileptic* Oswald is trying to
smile, but he is so frightened that his face looks as if he were in a fit [K].
72 *Sarum* Salisbury. 73 *Camelot* the site of King Arthur's court. Tradition
identified it with an anciently fortified hill near Cadbury. In the moors in that
vicinity there were flocks of geese [K]. 76 *antipathy* The phenomena which more
recent science has explained by the doctrine of "attraction and repulsion" were
ascribed to "sympathy and antipathy" in the nature of objects [K]. 79 *likes*
pleases. 87–8 *constrains the garb . . . nature* puts on by force the style of
blunt sauciness in speech, quite contrary to his real nature [K]. 91 *plainness*
outspoken manner of speech. 92 *ends* purposes. 93 *silly-ducking observants*
obsequious parasites, who are always making low bows after their ridiculous
fashion [K]. 94 *stretch . . . nicely* exert themselves to be as precise and accurate as possible in performing their duties [K]. *nicely* punctiliously. 95 *sincere
verity* good faith (an affected manner of speech). 96 *Under th' allowance*
with the approval. *aspect* (a) appearance (b) great power and authority. The
"aspect" of a planet, in astrological terms, is its position in the heavens and the
consequent influence, for good or evil, which it exerts upon mankind.

Whose influence, like the wreath of radiant fire
On flickering Phoebus' front—
CORN.   What mean'st by this?
KENT. To go out of my dialect, which you discommend so much. I   100
    know, sir, I am no flatterer. He that beguil'd you in a plain accent
    was a plain knave, which, for my part, I will not be, though I
    should win your displeasure to entreat me to't.
CORN. What was th' offence you gave him?
OSW. I never gave him any.   105
    It pleas'd the King his master very late
    To strike at me, upon his misconstruction;
    When he, compact, and flattering his displeasure,
    Tripp'd me behind; being down, insulted, rail'd
    And put upon him such a deal of man   110
    That worthied him, got praises of the King
    For him attempting who was self-subdu'd;
    And, in the fleshment of this dread exploit,
    Drew on me here again.
KENT.   None of these rogues and cowards   115
    But Ajax is their fool.
CORN.   Fetch forth the stocks!
    You stubborn ancient knave, you reverent braggart,
    We'll teach you—
KENT.   Sir, I am too old to learn.   120
    Call not your stocks for me. I serve the King;
    On whose employment I was sent to you.
    You shall do small respect, show too bold malice
    Against the grace and person of my master,
    Stocking his messenger.   125
CORN. Fetch forth the stocks! As I have life and honour,
    There shall he sit till noon.
REG. Till noon? Till night, my lord, and all night too!
KENT. Why, madam, if I were your father's dog,
    You should not use me so.   130

97 *influence* force exerted by the planet (another astrological term). 98 *Phoe-bus' front* the forehead of the sun. Kent in this speech is parodying the style of a "silly-ducking observant." 101–3 *He that beguil'd you . . . to't* I infer from what you have said that in the past some such rascal as you describe has de-ceived you. If so, he was an out-and-out knave—and that I will never be, even if I could induce you to lay aside your displeasure so far as to beg me to be one [K]. 106 *late* recently. 107 *misconstruction* misunderstanding. 108 *com-pact* joined in a pact, in collusion (F¹; Q¹, K: "conjunct"). 111 *That worthied him* as won honour for himself [K]. 112 *For him . . . self-subdu'd* for attack-ing one who submitted without a struggle [K]. 113 *fleshment* of bloodthirsty mood induced by. 116 *Ajax is their fool* the great hero Ajax is (by their own account) a fool in comparison with them—i.e. vastly their inferior [K]. 118 *stubborn* fierce. 123 *malice* ill will. Not here used in the limited modern sense [K]. 124 *grace and person* As the King's messenger, Kent is to be treated with respect. Such a punishment would be not only an outrage on the King's "grace" (i.e. his royal honour) but a "personal" insult to him [K]. 130 *should* would certainly.

REG.   Sir, being his knave, I will.

CORN. This is a fellow of the selfsame colour
 Our sister speaks of. Come, bring away the stocks!
  Stocks brought out.

GLOU. Let me beseech your Grace not to do so.
 His fault is much, and the good King his master   135
 Will check him for't. Your purpos'd low correction
 Is such as basest and contemn'dest wretches
 For pilf'rings and most common trespasses
 Are punish'd with. The King must take it ill
 That he, so slightly valued in his messenger,   140
 Should have him thus restrain'd.

CORN.   I'll answer that.

REG. My sister may receive it much more worse,
 To have her gentleman abus'd, assaulted,
 For following her affairs. Put in his legs.—   145
  [KENT *is put in the stocks.*]
 Come, my good lord, away.
  Exeunt [all but GLOUCESTER *and* KENT].

GLOU. I am sorry for thee, friend. 'Tis the Duke's pleasure,
 Whose disposition, all the world well knows,
 Will not be rubb'd nor stopp'd. I'll entreat for thee.

KENT. Pray do not, sir. I have watch'd and travell'd hard. 150
 Some time I shall sleep out, the rest I'll whistle.
 A good man's fortune may grow out at heels.
 Give you good morrow!

GLOU. The Duke's to blame in this; 'twill be ill taken.
  Exit.

KENT. Good King, that must approve the common saw, 155
 Thou out of heaven's benediction com'st
 To the warm sun!
 Approach, thou beacon to this under globe,
 That by thy comfortable beams I may·
 Peruse this letter. Nothing almost sees miracles   160
 But misery. I know 'tis from Cordelia,
 Who hath most fortunately been inform'd
 Of my obscured course—and [*reads*] "shall find time

---

133 *bring away* bring along: bring hither. 135–9 *His fault . . . with* Q¹; not in
F¹. 136 *check* rebuke. 137 *contemn'dest* held in greatest contempt. 138 *pil-
f'rings* petty thefts. 139 *King must* Q¹; F¹: "King his Master needs must." 142
answer be answerable for. 145 *For . . . legs* Q¹; not in F¹. 149 *rubb'd* impeded,
interfered with. This sense comes from bowling. A "rub" is anything that hinders
or deflects the course of the bowl [K]. 150 *watch'd* gone without sleep. 152 *A
good . . . heels* A proverb meaning that it is no disgrace to decline in fortune.
154 *to blame* blameworthy. 155 *must approve . . . saw* art fated, it seems to
exemplify the familiar saying [K]. 156–7 *Thou out . . . sun* The proverb describes bad judgment by the figure of one who, on a hot day, leaves a comfortable seat in the shade for a place in the sun [K]. 159 *comfortable* comforting,
helpful. 160–1 *Nothing . . . misery* for, when we are in despair, any relief
seems miraculous [K]. 163 *obscured course* course of action in this disguise [K].

From this enormous state, seeking to give
Losses their remedies"—All weary and o'erwatch'd,   165
Take vantage, heavy eyes, not to behold
This shameful lodging.
Fortune, good night; smile once more, turn thy wheel.
   Sleeps.

164 *this enormous state* the present anomalous condition of the realm [K]. 165
o'erwatch'd worn out by lack of sleep. 166 *vantage* advantage. *heavy* drowsy.
167 *lodging* sleeping quarters for the night. He will take advantage of sleep so
as to avoid seeing the stocks. 168 *wheel* the proverbial wheel of fortune.

SCENE 3

  [The open country.]
  Enter EDGAR.

EDG. I heard myself proclaim'd,
  And by the happy hollow of a tree
  Escap'd the hunt. No port is free, no place
  That guard and most unusual vigilance
  Does not attend my taking. Whiles I may scape,   5
  I will preserve myself; and am bethought
  To take the basest and most poorest shape
  That ever penury, in contempt of man,
  Brought near to beast. My face I'll grime with filth,
  Blanket my loins, elf all my hairs in knots,   10
  And with presented nakedness outface
  The winds and persecutions of the sky.
  The country gives me proof and precedent
  Of Bedlam beggars, who, with roaring voices,
  Strike in their numb'd and mortified bare arms   15
  Pins, wooden pricks, nails, sprigs of rosemary;
  And with this horrible object, from low farms,
  Poor pelting villages, sheepcotes, and mills,
  Sometime with lunatic bans, sometime with prayers,
  Enforce their charity. "Poor Turlygod! poor Tom!"   20
  That's something yet! Edgar I nothing am.
    Exit.

II.3. 2 *happy* fortunate (as a hiding place). 5 *attend my taking* wait to capture me. 6 *am bethought* have thought of the idea. 8 *in contempt of man*
as if to show how contemptible a creature a man may be [K]. 10 *elf . . . in
knots* Matted and tangled locks of hair—due to neglect and filthy habits—were
ascribed to the action of mischievous elves and hence called "elflocks" [K].
hairs F[1]; Q[1], K: "hair." 11 *presented* fully exposed. *outface* defy. 13 *proof*
example. 15 *mortified* deadened by hardship and exposure [K]. 17 *object*
spectacle. *low* lowly, humble. 18 *pelting* paltry, insignificant. *sheepcotes,
and mills* both of which were often distant from any village [K]. 19 *bans* curses.
20 *Poor . . . Tom* Edgar practises the Bedlam beggar's whine. "Turlygod" seems
to have been a name by which such a beggar sometimes called himself, but it
occurs nowhere else [K]. 21 *That's something . . . nothing am* as Poor Tom
there is, after all, some hope for me. In my real character as Edgar, I am as good
as dead—i.e. I have no chance of preserving my life [K].

SCENE 4

[*Before* GLOUCESTER'S *Castle;* KENT *in the stocks.*]
Enter LEAR, FOOL, *and* GENTLEMAN.

LEAR. 'Tis strange that they should so depart from home,
And not send back my messenger.

GENT.   As I learn'd,
The night before there was no purpose in them
Of this remove.   5

KENT.   Hail to thee, noble master!

LEAR. Ha!
Mak'st thou this shame thy pastime?

KENT.   No, my lord.

FOOL. Ha, ha! look! he wears cruel garters. Horses are tied by the 10
heads, dogs and bears by th' neck, monkeys by th' loins, and men
by th' legs. When a man's over-lusty at legs, then he wears wooden
nether-stocks.

LEAR. What's he that hath so much thy place mistook
To set thee here?   15

KENT.   It is both he and she—
Your son and daughter.

LEAR. No.

KENT. Yes.

LEAR. No, I say.   20

KENT. I say yea.

LEAR. No, no, they would not!

KENT. Yes, they have.

LEAR. By Jupiter, I swear no!

KENT. By Juno, I swear ay!   25

LEAR.   They durst not do't;
They would not, could not do't. 'Tis worse than murder
To do upon respect such violent outrage.
Resolve me with all modest haste which way
Thou mightst deserve or they impose this usage,   30
Coming from us.

KENT.   My lord, when at their home
I did commend your Highness' letters to them,
Ere I was risen from the place that show'd
My duty kneeling, came there a reeking post,   35
Stew'd in his haste, half breathless, panting forth

II.4. 5 *remove* change of residence. 10 *cruel* with a pun on "crewel," a kind of worsted yarn used for garters. 11 *heads* F¹; Q¹: "heeles"; K: "head." 12 *over-lusty at legs* too vigorous in using his legs; too much of a vagabond [K]. 13 *nether-stocks* stockings. Overstocks (upper stocks) were breeches [K]. 14 *place* position (as in the King's messenger). 22–3 *No, no . . . have* Q¹; not in F¹. 25 *By . . . ay* F¹; not in Q¹. 28 *upon respect* against the respect due to the King [K]. 29 *Resolve me* explain to me. *modest* moderate. 31 *from us* from me, the King. 33 *commend* deliver. 36 *Stew'd* steaming. *panting* Q¹; F¹: "painting."

From Goneril his mistress salutations;
Deliver'd letters, spite of intermission,
Which presently they read; on whose contents,
They summon'd up their meiny, straight took horse,   40
Commanded me to follow and attend
The leisure of their answer, gave me cold looks,
And meeting here the other messenger,
Whose welcome I perceiv'd had poison'd mine—
Being the very fellow which of late   45
Display'd so saucily against your Highness—
Having more man than wit about me, drew.
He rais'd the house with loud and coward cries.
Your son and daughter found this trespass worth
The shame which here it suffers.   50
FOOL. Winter's not gone yet, if the wild geese fly that way.
    Fathers that wear rags
     Do make their children blind;
    But fathers that bear bags
     Shall see their children kind.   55
    Fortune, that arrant whore,
     Ne'er turns the key to th' poor.
But for all this, thou shalt have as many dolours for thy daughters
 as thou canst tell in a year.
LEAR. O, how this mother swells up toward my heart!   60
 Hysterica passio! Down, thou climbing sorrow!
 Thy element's below! Where is this daughter?
KENT. With the Earl, sir, here within.
LEAR.   Follow me not;
 Stay here.   65
  Exit.
GENT. Made you no more offence but what you speak of?
KENT. None.
 How chance the King comes with so small a number?
FOOL. An thou hadst been set i' th' stocks for that question, thou'dst
 well deserv'd it.   70
KENT. Why, fool?

---

38 *spite of intermission* in spite of the fact that it interrupted the audience they had granted me [K]. 40 *meiny* household servants. *straight* immediately. 46 *Display'd so saucily* made such an impudent exhibition of himself [K]. 47 *more man than wit* more courage than common sense [K]. *drew* my sword. 48 *rais'd* aroused. 51–9 *Winter's . . . a year* F¹; not in Q¹. 54 *bags* moneybags. 56 *Fortune . . . whore* Fortune is often called a harlot because she shows favour to every man and is constant to none [K]. 57 *turns the key* opens the door. 58 *dolours* sorrows (with a pun on "dollars"). 59 *tell* (a) recount (b) count up. 60 *this mother* The "mother" was the popular name for "hysterica passio"—"hysterical suffering," hysteria. Lear describes the symptoms—a feeling of distress rising from below toward the heart. Thence it often ascends into the throat with the sensation of choking—called "the hysteric ball" [K]. 62 *element* proper place. 69–70 *thou'dst well deserv'd it* because it's a foolish question, since the answer is so obvious [K].

FOOL. We'll set thee to school to an ant, to teach thee there's no
   labouring i' th' winter. All that follow their noses are led by their
   eyes but blind men, and there's not a nose among twenty but can
   smell him that's stinking. Let go thy hold when a great wheel runs   75
   down a hill, lest it break thy neck with following it; but the great
   one that goes upward, let him draw thee after. When a wise man
   gives thee better counsel, give me mine again. I would have none
   but knaves follow it, since a fool gives it.
                    That sir which serves and seeks for gain,   80
                       And follows but for form,
                    Will pack when it begins to rain
                       And leave thee in the storm.
                    But I will tarry; the fool will stay,
                       And let the wise man fly.   85
                    The knave turns fool that runs away;
                       The fool no knave, perdy.
KENT. Where learn'd you this, fool?
FOOL. Not i' th' stocks, fool.
        Enter LEAR *and* GLOUCESTER.
LEAR. Deny to speak with me? They are sick? they are weary?   90
   They have travell'd all the night? Mere fetches—
   The images of revolt and flying off!
   Fetch me a better answer.
GLOU.   My dear lord,
   You know the fiery quality of the Duke,   95
   How unremovable and fix'd he is
   In his own course.
LEAR. Vengeance! plague! death! confusion!
   Fiery? What quality? Why, Gloucester, Gloucester,
   I'ld speak with the Duke of Cornwall and his wife.   100
GLOU. Well, my good lord, I have inform'd them so.
LEAR. Inform'd them? Dost thou understand me, man?
GLOU. Ay, my good lord.

72–9 *We'll set . . . gives it* In a series of brief parables the Fool explains that
Lear's fortunes are in a bad way, and that it is therefore not strange that he
comes with so small a retinue [K].   73 *All that follow their noses* To "follow
one's nose" is an old jocose idiom (still in use) for "to go straight ahead in the
direction in which one's nose points." "All persons who follow a straight course
of judgment accept the evidence of their eyes, if they have any eyes. And even
the blind can follow their noses—can use the sense of smell as a guide. In the
present instance, then, even a blind man can discover the facts of the case (the
desperate condition of the King's fortunes), for among a score of noses there's
surely not one that is "not good enough to recognize a stench" [K].   81 *form*
show.   82 *pack* run away.   86–7 *The knave . . . no knave* the fellow that for-
sakes his master is (from the point of view of the higher wisdom) a fool, since
true wisdom implies fidelity; and the fool who, like me, remains faithful is, at all
events, no knave [K].   87 *perdy* assuredly.   90 *Deny* refuse.   91 *fetches* pretexts, excuses.   92 *images* plainest possible signs [K].   *revolt and flying off* To
explain or emphasize a word by adding a synonym is one of the commonest of
rhetorical devices [K].   95 *quality* nature, character.   101–2 *Well . . . man* F[1];
not in Q[1].

LEAR. The King would speak with Cornwall; the dear father
    Would with his daughter speak, commands her service.   105
    Are they inform'd of this? My breath and blood!
    Fiery? the fiery Duke? Tell the hot Duke that—
    No, but not yet! May be he is not well.
    Infirmity doth still neglect all office
    Whereto our health is bound. We are not ourselves   110
    When nature, being oppress'd, commands the mind
    To suffer with the body. I'll forbear;
    And am fallen out with my more headier will,
    To take the indispos'd and sickly fit
    For the sound man.—Death on my state! Wherefore   115
    Should he sit here? This act persuades me
    That this remotion of the Duke and her
    Is practice only. Give me my servant forth.
    Go tell the Duke and 's wife I'ld speak with them—
    Now, presently. Bid them come forth and hear me,   120
    Or at their chamber door I'll beat the drum
    Till it cry sleep to death.
GLOU. I would have all well betwixt you.
    Exit.
LEAR. O me, my heart, my rising heart! But down!
FOOL. Cry to it, nuncle, as the cockney did to the eels when she put   125
    'em i' th' paste alive. She knapp'd 'em o' th' coxcombs with a stick
    and cried "Down, wantons, down!" 'Twas her brother that, in pure
    kindness to his horse, buttered his hay.
    Enter CORNWALL, REGAN, GLOUCESTER, SERVANTS.
LEAR. Good morrow to you both.
CORN.   Hail to your grace!   130
    KENT *here set at liberty.*
REG. I am glad to see your Highness.
LEAR. Regan, I think you are; I know what reason
    I have to think so. If thou shouldst not be glad,
    I would divorce me from thy mother's tomb,
    Sepulchring an adultress. [*To* KENT] O, are you free?   135
    Some other time for that.—Beloved Regan,
    Thy sister's naught. O Regan, she hath tied
    Sharp-tooth'd unkindness, like a vulture, here!

105 *commands her service* Q¹; F¹: "commands, tends, service." 106 *My breath
and blood* Another oath, used merely as a passionate exclamation [K] (F¹; not
in Q¹). 109 *neglect* omit, leave undone. *office* service, duty. 113 *fallen out*
angry. *more headier* too impulsive. *will* impulse. 115 *state* royal power.
116 *he* Kent. 117 *remotion* keeping away from me; avoidance of an interview [K]. 118 *practice* trickery. *forth* release (from the stocks). 120 *presently*
at once. 122 *cry sleep to death* make sleep impossible by its din [K]. 125
cockney city-dweller (unfamiliar with the preparation of eels). The word also
may mean "spoiled child," "pampered darling," "cook," or "Londoner." 126
paste pastry, pie shell. *knapp'd* beat (F¹; Q¹: "rapt"). 126 *coxcombs* heads.
127 *wantons* naughty, frisky things. *brother* a member of the same family
of fools; another fool of the same breed [K]. 135 *Sepulchring* as being the
tomb of. 137 *naught* wicked. 138 *like a vulture* Such allusions to the torment of

[*Lays his hand on his heart.*]

I can scarce speak to thee. Thou'lt not believe
With how deprav'd a quality—O Regan! 140

REG. I pray you, sir, take patience. I have hope
You less know how to value her desert
Than she to scant her duty.

LEAR. Say, how is that?

REG. I cannot think my sister in the least 145
Would fail her obligation. If, sir, perchance
She have restrain'd the riots of your followers,
'Tis on such ground, and to such wholesome end,
As clears her from all blame.

LEAR. My curses on her! 150

REG. O, sir, you are old!
Nature in you stands on the very verge
Of her confine. You should be rul'd, and led
By some discretion that discerns your state
Better than you yourself. Therefore I pray you 155
That to our sister you do make return;
Say you have wrong'd her, sir.

LEAR. Ask her forgiveness?
Do you but mark how this becomes the house:
"Dear daughter, I confess that I am old. 160
[*Kneels.*]
Age is unnecessary. On my knees I beg
That you'll vouchsafe me raiment, bed, and food."

REG. Good sir, no more! These are unsightly tricks.
Return you to my sister.

LEAR. [*rises*] Never, Regan! 165
She hath abated me of half my train;
Look'd black upon me; struck me with her tongue,
Most serpent-like, upon the very heart.
All the stor'd vengeances of heaven fall
On her ingrateful top! Strike her young bones, 170

Prometheus are common [K]. 140 *quality* character, disposition. 142–3 *You less
. . . duty* she does not come short in doing her duty to you. The trouble is,
that you cannot appreciate her merits [K]. 143 *scant* This repeats the negative
idea, but the double negative does not make an affirmative. In modern English we
should say "to do her duty" [K]. 144–9 *Say . . . all blame* F¹; not in Q¹. 152–3
Nature . . . her confine your life is at the very end of its assigned period; you
are old and ready for death. 154 *some discretion . . . state* some understanding
person who understands your condition of mind. 156 *make return* go back again.
159 *becomes the house* befits family relations. Spoken with bitter irony; fathers
would not kneel to their children in any normal family [K]. 161 *Age is
unnecessary* old folk are of no use in the world [K]. 166 *abated* deprived,
curtailed. 170 *ingrateful top* ungrateful head. *her young bones* The context
makes it certain that this applies to Goneril's own youthful frame. "To breed
young bones" is, to be sure, an old phrase for "to be with child," but that
does not justify the strange interpretation ("Strike her unborn child") which
has found favour with some critics [K].

You taking airs, with lameness!
CORN.   Fie, sir, fie!
LEAR. You nimble lightnings, dart your blinding flames
  Into her scornful eyes! Infect her beauty,
  You fen-suck'd fogs, drawn by the pow'rful sun,   175
  To fall and blast her pride!
REG. O the blest gods! so will you wish on me
  When the rash mood is on.
LEAR. No, Regan, thou shalt never have my curse.
  Thy tender-hefted nature shall not give   180
  Thee o'er to harshness. Her eyes are fierce; but thine
  Do comfort, and not burn. 'Tis not in thee
  To grudge my pleasures, to cut off my train,
  To bandy hasty words, to scant my sizes,
  And, in conclusion, to oppose the bolt   185
  Against my coming in. Thou better know'st
  The offices of nature, bond of childhood,
  Effects of courtesy, dues of gratitude.
  Thy half o' th' kingdom hast thou not forgot,
  Wherein I thee endow'd.   190
REG.   Good sir, to th' purpose.
    Tucket within.
LEAR. Who put my man i' th' stocks?
CORN.   What trumpet 's that?
REG. I know't—my sister's. This approves her letter,
  That she would soon be here.   195
    Enter [OSWALD *the*] STEWARD.
                 Is your lady come?
LEAR. This is a slave, whose easy-borrowed pride
  Dwells in the fickle grace of her he follows.
  Out, varlet, from my sight!
CORN.   What means your Grace?   200
    Enter GONERIL.
LEAR. Who stock'd my servant? Regan, I have good hope
  Thou didst not know on't.—Who comes here? O heavens!
  If you do love old men, if your sweet sway
  Allow obedience—if yourselves are old,
  Make it your cause! Send down, and take my part!   205
  [*To* GONERIL] Art not asham'd to look upon this beard?—

171 *taking* infectious.   175 *fen-suck'd* drawn up from the swamps.   176 *blast
her* pride Q¹; F¹: "blister." Some editors read "blister her."   178 *rash* hasty.
180 *tender-hefted* swayed (heaved) by tender emotions. Some editors read
"tender-hearted."   184 *bandy* volley back and forth. *sizes* allowances.   185–6
oppose . . . coming in lock your doors against me.   187 *offices* duties. *bond of
childhood* obligations of a child toward a parent.   188 *Effects* actions   191 *purpose* point (of your speech). s.d. *Tucket* series of trumpet notes. *within* behind the
scenes.   194 *approves* confirms.   197 *easy-borrowed pride* easily borrowed because it does not take much to make him proud [K].   199 *varlet* fellow. A
common term of contempt [K].   203 *sweet sway* beneficent rule   204 *Allow*
approve of.

O Regan, wilt thou take her by the hand?
GON. Why not by th' hand, sir? How have I offended?
All's not offence that indiscretion finds
And dotage terms so.   210
LEAR.   O sides, you are too tough!
Will you yet hold? How came my man i' th' stocks?
CORN. I set him there, sir; but his own disorders
Deserv'd much less advancement.
LEAR.   You? Did you?   215
REG. I pray you, father, being weak, seem so.
If, till the expiration of your month,
You will return and sojourn with my sister,
Dismissing half your train, come then to me.
I am now from home, and out of that provision   220
Which shall be needful for your entertainment.
LEAR. Return to her, and fifty men dismiss'd?
No, rather I abjure all roofs, and choose
To wage against the enmity o' th' air,
To be a comrade with the wolf and owl—   225
Necessity's sharp pinch! Return with her?
Why, the hot-blooded France, that dowerless took
Our youngest born, I could as well be brought
To knee his throne, and, squire-like, pension beg
To keep base life afoot. Return with her?   230
Persuade me rather to be slave and sumpter
To this detested groom.
    [Points at OSWALD.]
GON.   At your choice, sir.
LEAR. I prithee, daughter, do not make me mad.
I will not trouble thee, my child; farewell.   235
We'll no more meet, no more see one another.
But yet thou art my flesh, my blood, my daughter;
Or rather a disease that's in my flesh,
Which I must needs call mine. Thou art a boil,
A plague sore, an embossed carbuncle   240
In my corrupted blood. But I'll not chide thee;
Let shame come when it will, I do not call it;
I do not bid the Thunder-bearer shoot,

209 *indiscretion finds* poor judgment considers. 213 *disorders* misconduct.
214 *much less advancement* far less honour than that [K]. 216 *seems so* i.e.
be content to speak and act like a feeble old man, and submit without protest
to those who have you in charge [K]. 221 *entertainment* proper maintenance;
care and attention [K]. 224 *To wage against* to wage war with; to meet in a
contest of strength [K]. 226 *Necessity's sharp pinch* This sums up (as an
appositive) what precedes (lines 223–5). It is the hard lot of poverty to be
homeless and exposed to cold and storm [K]. 227 *hot-blooded* choleric. 229
knee kneel before. *squire-like* as if I were one of his attendants [K]. 231
sumpter packhorse. 232 *detested groom* detestable underling. 240 *embossed*
headed; rising in a round knob (like the boss of a shield) [K]. 243 *the
Thunder-bearer* Jupiter. *shoot* dart his thunderbolts at thee [K].

Nor tell tales of thee to high-judging Jove.
Mend when thou canst; be better at thy leisure;   245
I can be patient, I can stay with Regan,
I and my hundred knights.
REG.   Not altogether so.
I look'd not for you yet, nor am provided
For your fit welcome. Give ear, sir, to my sister;   250
For those that mingle reason with your passion
Must be content to think you old, and so—
But she knows what she does.
LEAR.   Is this well spoken?
REG. I dare avouch it, sir. What, fifty followers?   255
Is it not well? What should you need of more?
Yea, or so many, sith that both charge and danger
Speak 'gainst so great a number? How in one house
Should many people, under two commands,
Hold amity? 'Tis hard; almost impossible.   260
GON. Why might not you, my lord, receive attendance
From those that she calls servants, or from mine?
REG. Why not, my lord? If then they chanc'd to slack ye,
We could control them. If you will come to me
(For now I spy a danger), I entreat you   265
To bring but five-and-twenty. To no more
Will I give place or notice.
LEAR. I gave you all—
REG.   And in good time you gave it!
LEAR. Made you my guardians, my depositaries;   270
But kept a reservation to be followed
With such a number. What, must I come to you
With five-and-twenty, Regan? Said you so?
REG. And speak't again, my lord. No more with me.
LEAR. Those wicked creatures yet do look well-favour'd   275
When others are more wicked; not being the worst
Stands in some rank of praise. [*To* GONERIL] I'll go with thee.
Thy fifty yet doth double five-and-twenty,
And thou art twice her love.
GON.   Hear me, my lord.   280

244 *high-judging Jove* Jove, who judges mankind from his high place in heaven.
245 *Mend* improve.   251 *mingle reason with your passion* consider your violent
words and actions in the light of reason and can tell you what such conduct
means [K].   252 *old* She breaks off abruptly, with a gesture: "You are old—
and no further explanation is necessary" [K].   255 *avouch* swear by.   257 *sith
that* since.   *charge* expense.   263 *slack* neglect.   264 *control* regulate.   267
notice recognition.   269 *And in . . . gave it* A characteristic interruption by the
soft-spoken but venomous Regan [K].   270 *Made you my guardians* entrusted all
my possessions to your care [K].   *depositaries* synonymous with "guardians" [K].
275 *Those wicked creatures* The demonstrative "those" has no personal application. Lear's remark is a general truth: "Such creatures as are wicked always have
a good appearance in contrast with others that are more wicked" [K].   *well-
favour'd* fair, handsome.

What need you five-and-twenty, ten, or five,
To follow in a house where twice so many
Have a command to tend you?
REG.   What need one?
LEAR. O, reason not the need! Our basest beggars   285
Are in the poorest thing superfluous.
Allow not nature more than nature needs,
Man's life is cheap as beast's. Thou art a lady:
If only to go warm were gorgeous,
Why, nature needs not what thou gorgeous wear'st,   290
Which scarcely keeps thee warm. But, for true need—
You heavens, give me that patience, patience I need!
You see me here, you gods, a poor old man,
As full of grief as age; wretched in both.
If it be you that stirs these daughters' hearts   295
Against their father, fool me not so much
To bear it tamely; touch me with noble anger,
And let not women's weapons, water drops,
Stain my man's cheeks! No, you unnatural hags!
I will have such revenges on you both   300
That all the world shall—I will do such things—
What they are yet, I know not; but they shall be
The terrors of the earth! You think I'll weep.
No, I'll not weep.
I have full cause of weeping, but this heart   305
Shall break into a hundred thousand flaws
Or ere I'll weep. O fool, I shall go mad!
        Exeunt LEAR, GLOUCESTER, KENT, *and* FOOL.
        Storm and tempest.
CORN. Let us withdraw; 'twill be a storm.
REG. This house is little; the old man and 's people
Cannot be well bestow'd.   310
GON. 'Tis his own blame; hath put himself from rest
And must needs taste his folly.

282 *To follow* to be your followers. 285–92 *O, reason not . . . I need* Lear
distinguishes between absolute necessity (in which sense his daughters have
used the word "need") and that which may be properly regarded as necessary for
comfort and dignity. But he breaks off abruptly when about to define "true
need" (line 291); for the thought forces itself upon him that the one thing
he really "needs" is the gift of "patience" (i.e. fortitude), which may keep
him from the shame of tears [K]. 285–6 *Our basest . . . superfluous* the most
miserable beggars have some things among their poorest possessions that they
do not actually need—that they could get along without [K]. 289–90 *If only
. . . gorgeous wear'st* if mere warmth were all the gorgeousness that a lady
required of her apparel, then the gorgeousness of your attire would not be
needed, for gorgeousness is certainly not—like warmth—a natural necessity [K].
292 *that patience . . . need* that degree of fortitude (strength to endure suffering) that my case requires—it is fortitude that I need [K]. 296 *fool me not so
much* do not make me so much of a weakling [K]. 303 *terrors of the earth*
things so terrible as to affright the whole world [K]. 306 *flaws* fragments.
307 *Or ere* before. 310 *bestow'd* accommodated. 312 *taste his folly* suffer the
consequences of his folly [K].

REG. For his particular, I'll receive him gladly,
But not one follower.
GON.   So am I purpos'd.   315
Where is my Lord of Gloucester?
CORN. Followed the old man forth.
    Enter GLOUCESTER.
                            He is return'd.
GLOU. The King is in high rage.
CORN.   Whither is he going?   320
GLOU. He calls to horse, but will I know not whither.
CORN. 'Tis best to give him way; he leads himself.
GON. My lord, entreat him by no means to stay.
GLOU. Alack, the night comes on, and the bleak winds
Do sorely ruffle. For many miles about   325
There's scarce a bush.
REG.   O, sir, to wilful men
The injuries that they themselves procure
Must be their schoolmasters. Shut up your doors.
He is attended with a desperate train,   330
And what they may incense him to, being apt
To have his ear abus'd, wisdom bids fear.
CORN. Shut up your doors, my lord; 'tis a wild night.
My Regan counsels well. Come out o' th' storm.
    Exeunt.

313 *For his particular* in so far as he personally is concerned—excluding his
followers. 315 *purpos'd* determined. 320–21 *Whither . . . horse* F¹; not in Q¹.
322 *to give him way* not to hinder his departure [K]. *he leads himself* he submits to no guidance; he insists on having his own way [K]. 324 *bleak* Q¹; F¹:
"high." 325 *ruffle* rage. A strong word. A "ruffler" is a brawling ruffian [K].
330 *a desperate train* Regan, like Goneril, shamelessly misrepresents the character
of Lear's knights [K]. 331 *incense* instigate. *apt* ready. Much more active than
in modern usage [K]. 332 *abus'd* deceived.

＊＊＊＊＊＊＊＊

ACT THREE

SCENE 1

[*A heath.*]
Storm still. Enter KENT *and a* GENTLEMAN *at several doors.*
KENT. Who's there, besides foul weather?
GENT. One minded like the weather, most unquietly.
KENT. I know you. Where's the King?
GENT. Contending with the fretful elements;
Bids the wind blow the earth into the sea,   5
Or swell the curled waters 'bove the main,

III.1. 2 *minded . . . unquietly* in a disturbed state of mind. 6 *curled waters*
waves. *main* land.

That things might change or cease; tears his white hair,
Which the impetuous blasts, with eyeless rage,
Catch in their fury and make nothing of;
Strives in his little world of man to outscorn   10
The to-and-fro-conflicting wind and rain.
This night, wherein the cub-drawn bear would couch,
The lion and the belly-pinched wolf
Keep their fur dry, unbonneted he runs,
And bids what will take all.   15

KENT.   But who is with him?

GENT. None but the fool, who labours to outjest
His heart-struck injuries.

KENT.   Sir, I do know you,
And dare upon the warrant of my note   20
Commend a dear thing to you. There is division
(Although as yet the face of it be cover'd
With mutual cunning) 'twixt Albany and Cornwall;
Who have (as who have not, that their great stars
Thron'd and set high?) servants, who seem no less,   25
Which are to France the spies and speculations
Intelligent of our state. What hath been seen,
Either in snuffs and packings of the Dukes,
Or the hard rein which both of them have borne
Against the old kind King, or something deeper,   30
Whereof, perchance, these are but furnishings—
But, true it is, from France there comes a power
Into this scattered kingdom, who already,
Wise in our negligence, have secret feet
In some of our best ports and are at point   35

7–15 *tears his . . . take all* Q¹; not in F¹.   8 *eyeless* blind—since they rage at
everything without discrimination or definite object [K].   9 *make nothing of*
show no respect for [K].   10 *his little world of man* A man is a microcosm
("a little cosmos," "a universe in miniature") in comparison with the macrocosm,
"the great cosmos" [K]. The analogy of the human body to the physical
earth, each being composed of the four elements of earth, air, fire, and water,
is a Renaissance commonplace.   11 *to-and-fro conflicting* moving in all directions
in angry conflict.   12 *cub-drawn* sucked dry by her cubs, and thus ravenous and
fierce.   *couch* lie hidden from the storm [K].   13 *belly-pinched* starved.   15
bids . . . take all "Take all!" is the cry of the gambler when he stakes, at a
final cast of the dice, all the money that he has left. Hence it is used figuratively
as a cry of despair or desperate defiance [K].   17 *to outjest* to relieve by his
jests. It is the Fool's tragedy that his efforts to cheer up his master serve only
to emphasize Lear's folly and its dreadful results; for the Fool's mind instinctively concentrates on that one idea and he calls Lear "fool" over and over
again [K].   20 *warrant of my note* assurance of my knowledge of you.   21
Commend entrust.   *dear thing* important matter.   24–31 *Who have . . . furnishings* F¹; not in Q¹.   25 *no less* nothing more or less than servants.   26 *speculations* spies.   27 *What hath been seen* what has been already discernible [K].
28 *snuffs* cases in which they have openly taken offence at each other's actions
[K].   *packings* intrigues, secret plots.   31 *furnishings* pretexts that conceal the
real purpose of the French invasion [K].   32–44 *But, true . . . to you* Q¹; not
in F¹.   32 *power* army.   33 *scattered* divided.   34 *Wise in* taking advantage of.
have secret feet have secretly set foot.   35 *at point* fully prepared.

To show their open banner. Now to you:
If on my credit you dare build so far
To make your speed to Dover, you shall find
Some that will thank you, making just report
Of how unnatural and bemadding sorrow   40
The King hath cause to plain.
I am a gentleman of blood and breeding,
And from some knowledge and assurance offer
This office to you.
GENT. I will talk further with you.   45
KENT.   No, do not.
For confirmation that I am much more
Than my out-wall, open this purse and take
What it contains. If you shall see Cordelia
(As fear not but you shall), show her this ring,   50
And she will tell you who your fellow is
That yet you do not know. Fie on this storm!
I will go seek the King.
GENT. Give me your hand. Have you no more to say?
KENT. Few words, but, to effect, more than all yet: 55
That, when we have found the King (in which your pain
That way, I'll this), he that first lights on him
Holla the other.
      Exeunt [severally].

37 *my credit* your trust in me.   39 *making* if you make.   *just* true and accurate.
41 *plain* complain.   43 *assurance* trustworthy information.   44 *office* duty.   48
out-wall exterior appearance (Kent is wearing a servant's clothes). 51 *your
fellow* your companion; your associate in the King's service. Thus Kent confirms
the suggestion that he is a more important person than his present position
would indicate [K].   55 *to effect* in importance.   56–7 *in which . . . this* in
which task (pain) you go that way while I go this way.

SCENE 2

[*Another part of the heath.*]
Storm still. Enter LEAR *and* FOOL.
LEAR. Blow, winds, and crack your cheeks! rage! blow!
You cataracts and hurricanoes, spout
Till you have drench'd our steeples, drown'd the cocks!
You sulph'rous and thought-executing fires,
Vaunt-couriers to oak-cleaving thunderbolts,   5
Singe my white head! And thou, all-shaking thunder,
Strike flat the thick rotundity o' th' world,

III.2.   2 *cataracts* the floodgates of heaven.   *hurricanoes* water-spouts. Lear is
calling for another Deluge to destroy the earth.   3 *drown'd* submerged.   *cocks*
weathercocks.   4 *thought-executing fires* lightning flashes as swift as thought.
5 *Vaunt-couriers* forerunners, heralds.   *thunderbolts* Fiery bolts, or stone missiles,
were supposed to be discharged from the clouds by the thunder [K].

Crack Nature's moulds, all germens spill at once.
That make ingrateful man!

FOOL. O nuncle, court holy water in a dry house is better than this   10
rain water out o' door. Good nuncle, in, and ask thy daughters
blessing! Here's a night pities neither wise men nor fools.

LEAR. Rumble thy bellyful! Spit, fire! spout, rain!
Nor rain, wind, thunder, fire are my daughters.
I tax not you, you elements, with unkindness.   15
I never gave you kingdom, call'd you children,
You owe me no subscription. Then let fall
Your horrible pleasure. Here I stand your slave,
A poor, infirm, weak, and despis'd old man.
But yet I call you servile ministers,   20
That will with two pernicious daughters join
Your high-engender'd battles 'gainst a head
So old and white as this! O! O! 'tis foul!

FOOL. He that has a house to put 's head in has a good headpiece.
      The codpiece that will house   25
         Before the head has any,
      The head and he shall louse:
         So beggars marry many.
      The man that makes his toe
         What he his heart should make   30
      Shall of a corn cry woe,
         And turn his sleep to wake.
For there was never yet fair woman but she made mouths in a
glass.
      Enter KENT.

LEAR. No, I will be the pattern of all patience; I will say nothing.   35

KENT. Who's there?

FOOL. Marry, here's grace and a codpiece; that's a wise man and a
fool.

KENT. Alas, sir, are you here? Things that love night
Love not such nights as these. The wrathful skies   40
Gallow the very wanderers of the dark

8 *Nature's moulds* the moulds that Nature uses in forming men [K]. *germens*
the seeds from which all matter springs. Lear is calling for the end of human
reproduction. *spill* destroy. 10 *court holy water* A slang expression for "flattering speech." 15 *tax not you* do not accuse you. 17 *subscription* deference,
obedience. 20 *ministers* agents. 22 *high-engender'd* engendered high in the
heavens. There is also a suggestion of the meaning "sublime" [K]. *battles*
battalions, armies. 24 *good headpiece* The Fool puns on two senses of the
phrase: (a) a good helmet, covering for the head, and (b) a good head—i.e.
a wise brain [K]. 25–8 *The codpiece . . . marry many* the man who begets
children before he has a house will surely become a lousy vagabond. Thus it
is that many beggars get married [K]. 29–32 *The man . . . wake* the man
who exchanges the places of his toe and his heart will get a corn on his
heart instead of on his foot, and that will give him a heartache as will keep
him awake nights. The Fool alludes to Lear's folly in showing favour to Goneril
and Regan and disowning Cordelia [K]. 33–4 *made . . . glass* practised making
pretty faces in a mirror [K]. 41 *Gallow* terrify. A very strong word. Whalemen
still used "gallied" to describe a whale that is panic-stricken [K]. *wanderers
of the dark* night-prowling wild beasts.

And make them keep their caves. Since I was man,
Such sheets of fire, such bursts of horrid thunder,
Such groans of roaring wind and rain, I never
Remember to have heard. Man's nature cannot carry   45
Th' affliction nor the fear.
LEAR.   Let the great gods,
That keep this dreadful pother o'er our heads,
Find out their enemies now. Tremble, thou wretch,
That hast within thee undivulged crimes   50
Unwhipp'd of justice. Hide thee, thou bloody hand;
Thou perjur'd, and thou simular man of virtue
That art incestuous. Caitiff, in pieces shake
That under covert and convenient seeming
Hast practis'd on man's life. Close pent-up guilts,   55
Rive your concealing continents, and cry
These dreadful summoners grace. I am a man
More sinn'd against than sinning.
KENT.   Alack, bareheaded?
Gracious my lord, hard by here is a hovel;   60
Some friendship will it lend you 'gainst the tempest.
Repose you there, whilst I to this hard house
(More harder than the stones whereof 'tis rais'd,
Which even but now, demanding after you,
Denied me to come in) return, and force   65
Their scanted courtesy.
LEAR.   My wits begin to turn.
Come on, my boy. How dost, my boy? Art cold?
I am cold myself. Where is this straw, my fellow?
The art of our necessities is strange,   70
That can make vile things precious. Come, your hovel.
Poor fool and knave, I have one part in my heart
That's sorry yet for thee.
FOOL. [*sings*]
              He that has and a little tiny wit—
                  With hey, ho, the wind and the rain—   75

45–6 *cannot carry . . . fear* cannot bear up under the actual bodily affliction
(the buffeting by the storm) and the terror that accompanies it [K]. 48 *pother*
hubbub, turmoil. The same word as "pudder" [K]. 49 *Find out* i.e. by the
terror which such offenders must show [K]. 51 *Unwhipp'd of* unpunished by.
52 *simular man* simulator, counterfeiter (Q¹, K; F¹: "simular"). 53 *Caitiff*
wretch. 54 *under covert . . . seeming* under such an appearance of conventional virtue as masked thy purpose [K]. 55 *practis'd on* plotted against.
56–7 *Rive . . . grace* break open the concealments that hide you, and
appeal to these dreadful summoners for mercy. A "summoner" is an officer who
summons offenders to an ecclesiastical court [K]. 57 *I* Emphatic. Thus Lear
points out his reason for not fearing the storm [K]. 61 *lend* afford. 62 *hard*
cruel. *house* household (the occupants as well as the building). 64 *demanding
after* asking for. 65 *Denied* forbade. 66 *scanted courtesy* niggardly hospitality.
67 *My wits begin to turn* The first intimation of Lear's delirium [K]. 70 *art* The
figure alludes to alchemy, which professed to turn base metals into gold and silver
[K]. 72–3 *Poor fool . . . for thee* Here for the first time Lear expresses real
concern and kindness for his fellow man.

> Must make content with his fortunes fit,
> Though the rain it raineth every day.

LEAR. True, my good boy. Come, bring us to this hovel.

Exeunt [LEAR *and* KENT].

FOOL. This is a brave night to cool a courtesan. I'll speak a prophecy
ere I go: 80

> When priests are more in word than matter;
> When brewers mar their malt with water;
> When nobles are their tailors' tutors,
> No heretics burn'd, but wenches' suitors;
> When every case in law is right,   85
> No squire in debt nor no poor knight;
> When slanders do not live in tongues,
> Nor cutpurses come not to throngs;
> When usurers tell their gold i' th' field,
> And bawds and whores do churches build: 90
> Then shall the realm of Albion
> Come to great confusion.
> Then comes the time, who lives to see't,
> That going shall be us'd with feet.

This prophecy Merlin shall make, for I live before his time.   95

Exit.

76 *Must . . . fit* must make his happiness fit his fortunes; must be contented
and happy, even when his fortunes are bad [K].   77 *Though the* F¹; Q¹, K:
"For the."   78 *True* Lear accepts the Fool's saying as applicable to himself [K].
my good Q¹; not in F¹.   79–95 *This is . . . his time* F¹; not in Q¹. Most critics
regard the passage as an interpolation. The verses are a parody of an old
epigram entitled "Merlin's Prophecy." The original (well known in Shakespeare's
time) was commonly, though absurdly, ascribed to Chaucer [K].   79 *brave*
fine.   81 *more in word than matter* better in talk than in substance; or better
in preaching than in practice [K].   83 *their tailors' tutors* even greater experts
in clothing than the tailors they employ [K].   88 *cutpurses* literally, thieves
who slash purses (worn as a pouch at the girdle) and steal the contents;
then, in general, pickpockets [K].   89 *tell* count.   92 *confusion* a ruinous condition [K].   93 *who* if anybody.   94 *That going . . . feet* when feet shall be
used for walking. An intentionally absurd truism—such as fools frequently
pronounced with a solemn air as a burlesque on the philosophers' profound
adages. The audience is at liberty to make it mean: "The world shall once
more be in a normal condition" [K].   95 *This . . . time* This line makes the
Fool a real prophet, for Merlin's date was centuries later than Lear's. He is the
seer of Arthurian legend [K].

SCENE 3

[GLOUCESTER'S *Castle.*]

Enter GLOUCESTER *and* EDMUND.

GLOU. Alack, alack, Edmund, I like not this unnatural dealing! When
I desir'd their leave that I might pity him, they took from me
the use of mine own house, charg'd me on pain of perpetual displeasure neither to speak of him, entreat for him, nor any way
sustain him.   5

EDM. Most savage and unnatural!

III.3.   4–5 *nor any way sustain him* nor do anything whatever to relieve him [K].

GLOU. Go to; say you nothing. There is division betwixt the Dukes,
and a worse matter than that. I have received a letter this night—
'tis dangerous to be spoken—I have lock'd the letter in my closet.
These injuries the King now bears will be revenged home; there's
part of a power already footed; we must incline to the King. I will   10
seek him and privily relieve him. Go you and maintain talk with
the Duke, that my charity be not of him perceived. If he ask for
me, I am ill and gone to bed. Though I die for't, as no less is
threat'ned me, the King my old master must be relieved. There is
some strange thing toward, Edmund. Pray you be careful.   15
　　　Exit.
EDM. This courtesy, forbid thee, shall the Duke
　　Instantly know, and of that letter too.
　　This seems a fair deserving, and must draw me
　　That which my father loses—no less than all.
　　The younger rises when the old doth fall.   20
　　Exit.

7 *division* strife, contention.　8 *worse* more serious.　9 *closet* private room.
10 *home* to the utmost.　11 *power* army.　*footed* landed.　*incline to* take the
part of.　12 *seek* Q¹; F¹: "look."　*privily* secretly.　16 *toward* in preparation,
coming.　17 *forbid* forbidden.　19 *This seems . . . deserving* my giving the
Duke this information will seem to him a good piece of service [K].

SCENE 4

　[*The heath. Before a hovel.*]
　Storm still. Enter LEAR, KENT, *and* FOOL.
KENT. Here is the place, my lord. Good my lord, enter.
　　The tyranny of the open night 's too rough
　　For nature to endure.
LEAR.　　　　　　　　Let me alone.
KENT. Good my lord, enter here.   5
LEAR.　　　　　　　　　　Wilt break my heart?
KENT. I had rather break mine own. Good my lord, enter.
LEAR. Thou think'st 'tis much that this contentious storm
　　Invades us to the skin. So 'tis to thee;
　　But where the greater malady is fix'd,   10
　　The lesser is scarce felt. Thou'dst shun a bear;
　　But if thy flight lay toward the roaring sea,
　　Thou'dst meet the bear i' th' mouth. When the mind 's free,
　　The body 's delicate. The tempest in my mind
　　Doth from my senses take all feeling else   15
　　Save what beats there. Filial ingratitude!
　　Is it not as this mouth should tear this hand
　　For lifting food to't? But I will punish home!

III.4. 2 *tyranny of the open night* boisterous roughness of such a night in the
open air [K].　3 *nature* a man's natural strength [K].　12 *roaring* F¹; Q¹, K: "raging."　13 *free* untroubled, at peace.　14 *delicate* sensitive to pain.　16 *beats
there* throbs in my mind and heart. "There" is emphatic [K].　17 *as* as if.　18
home to the utmost.

No, I will weep no more. In such a night
To shut me out! Pour on; I will endure.   20
In such a night as this! O Regan, Goneril!
Your old kind father, whose frank heart gave all!
O, that way madness lies; let me shun that!
No more of that.

KENT.   Good my lord, enter here.   25

LEAR. Prithee go in thyself; seek thine own ease.
This tempest will not give me leave to ponder
On things would hurt me more. But I'll go in.
[*To the* FOOL] In, boy; go first.—You houseless poverty—
Nay, get thee in. I'll pray, and then I'll sleep.   30
        Exit [FOOL].
Poor naked wretches, wheresoe'er you are,
That bide the pelting of this pitiless storm,
How shall your houseless heads and unfed sides,
Your loop'd and window'd raggedness, defend you
From seasons such as these? O, I have ta'en   35
Too little care of this! Take physic, pomp;
Expose thyself to feel what wretches feel,
That thou mayst shake the superflux to them
And show the heavens more just.

EDG. [*within*] Fathom and half, fathom and half! Poor Tom!   40
        Enter FOOL [*from the hovel*].

FOOL. Come not in here, nuncle, here's a spirit. Help me, help me!

KENT. Give me thy hand. Who's there?

FOOL. A spirit, a spirit! He says his name's poor Tom.

KENT. What art thou that dost grumble there i' th' straw? Come forth.
        Enter EDGAR [*disguised as a madman*].

EDG. Away! the foul fiend follows me! Through the sharp hawthorn   45
  blows the cold wind. Humh! go to thy bed, and warm thee.

LEAR. Didst thou give all to thy daughters, and art thou come to this?

EDG. Who gives anything to poor Tom? whom the foul fiend hath led
  through fire and through flame, through ford and whirlpool, o'er

19–20 *In such . . . endure* F¹; not in Q¹. 22 *frank* generous. 29–30 *In . . .
sleep* F¹; not in Q¹. 29 *houseless poverty* unsheltered pauper (the abstract
used for the concrete). 32 *bide* suffer, endure. 34 *loop'd and window'd*
Synonymous: "full of holes." A "loop" is, literally, a "loophole" [K]. 36 *Take
physic, pomp* O ye great and mighty ones of the earth, take this remedy to
cure your unfeeling hearts [K]. 38–9 *That thou . . . more just* that you may
cast off what you do not need ("the superflux," superfluity) and bestow it on
them, and so may make God's treatment of humanity more impartial than it
now seems to be. Precisely the same lesson is expressed by Gloucester in
IV.173–9 [K]. 40 *Fathom . . . Poor Tom* Edgar speaks as if he were a sailor
sounding the depth of the water in the hold of a leaking ship. He is almost
"swamped" by the storm [K] (F¹; not in Q¹). 45–6 *Through . . . cold wind*
A line from a popular ballad of the time (Q¹; F¹: "blow the winds"). 46
thy bed F¹; Q¹, K: "thy cold bed." 47 *Didst thou give* F¹; Q¹, K: "Hast thou
giuen." *daughters* F¹; Q¹, K: "two daughters." 48 *Who gives* Edgar, taking his
cue from Lear's word "give," repeats the kind of petition expected of Bedlam
beggars, who "enforce charity" with "prayers" as well as "with lunatic bans"
(II.3.19–20) [K].

bog and quagmire; that hath laid knives under his pillow and   50
halters in his pew, set ratsbane by his porridge, made him proud
of heart, to ride on a bay trotting horse over four-inch'd bridges, to
course his own shadow for a traitor. Bless thy five wits! Tom's
acold. O, do de, do de, do de. Bless thee from whirlwinds, star-
blasting, and taking! Do poor Tom some charity, whom the foul   55
fiend vexes. There could I have him now—and there—and there
again—and there!

    Storm still.

LEAR. What, have his daughters brought him to this pass?
  Couldst thou save nothing? Would'st thou give 'em all?
FOOL. Nay, he reserv'd a blanket, else we had been all sham'd.   60
LEAR. Now all the plagues that in the pendulous air
  Hang fated o'er men's faults light on thy daughters!
KENT. He hath no daughters, sir.
LEAR. Death, traitor! nothing could have subdu'd nature
  To such a lowness but his unkind daughters.   65
  Is it the fashion that discarded fathers
  Should have thus little mercy on their flesh?
  Judicious punishment! 'Twas this flesh begot
  Those pelican daughters.
EDG. Pillicock sat on Pillicock's Hill. 'Allow, 'allow, loo, loo!   70
FOOL. This cold night will turn us all to fools and madmen.
EDG. Take heed o' th' foul fiend; obey thy parents; keep thy word
  justly; swear not; commit not with man's sworn spouse; set not
  thy sweet heart on proud array. Tom 's acold.
LEAR. What hast thou been?   75
EDG. A servingman, proud in heart and mind; that curl'd my hair,
  wore gloves in my cap; serv'd the lust of my mistress' heart and
  did the act of darkness with her; swore as many oaths as I spake
  words, and broke them in the sweet face of heaven; one that slept

---

50–1 *laid knives . . . porridge* That demons might tempt a man to commit
suicide was a common idea of the time. 51 *pew* a gallery in a house or outside
a chamber window—not, a pew in church [K]. 53 *course* chase. *five wits*
These were common wit, imagination, fantasy, estimation, and memory—the
five mental powers of man. 54 *O, do . . . do de* He is shuddering with cold
[K]. 54–5 *star-blasting* being destroyed by the power of malignant stars. 55 *taking* infection; the stroke of disease [K]. 56–7 *There could . . . and there* Edgar
makes grabs at different parts of his body as if to catch vermin—or devils [K].
58 *What, have his* THEOBALD; F¹: "Ha's his"; Q¹: "What, his." 59 *Would'st*
F¹; Q¹, K: "Didst." 61 *pendulous* overhanging. 64 *subdu'd* reduced. *nature* a
man's natural powers. 67 *thus little . . . flesh* Edgar has gone so far in his
impersonation of a Bedlam beggar as to pierce his arms with splinters or thorns
[K]. 68 *Judicious* well judged, just and fitting, condign [K]. 69 *pelican* The
young of the pelican were believed to feed upon the blood of their mother.
70 *Pillicock* Edgar in pretended madness, echoes Lear's word "pelican," distorting it to "Pillicock" (a term of comic endearment) and reciting part of a
nursery rhyme [K]. *'Allow . . . loo* a wild "halloo," as if he were calling a
hawk [K]. 72 *obey thy parents* Edgar speaks solemnly as if he were trying to
recite the Ten Commandments [K]. 72–3 *word justly* POPE; F¹: "words Iustice";
Q¹: "words iustly." 77 *wore gloves in my cap* To wear a lady's glove in the
cap was a common attention on the part of a gallant [K].

in the contriving of lust, and wak'd to do it. Wine lov'd I deeply, 80
dice dearly; and in woman out-paramour'd the Turk. False of
heart, light of ear, bloody of hand; hog in sloth, fox in stealth,
wolf in greediness, dog in madness, lion in prey. Let not the creaking of shoes nor the rustling of silks betray thy poor heart to
woman. Keep thy foot out of brothel, thy hand out of placket, thy 85
pen from lender's book, and defy the foul fiend. Still through the
hawthorn blows the cold wind; says suum, mun, hey, no, nonny.
Dolphin my boy, boy, sessa! let him trot by.
　Storm still.

LEAR. Thou wert better in a grave than to answer with thy uncover'd
body this extremity of the skies. Is man no more than this? Con- 90
sider him well. Thou ow'st the worm no silk, the beast no hide, the
sheep no wool, the cat no perfume. Ha! Here's three on's are
sophisticated! Thou art the thing itself; unaccommodated man is
no more but such a poor, bare, forked animal as thou art. Off,
off, you lendings! Come, unbutton here. 95
　[Tears at his clothes.]

FOOL. Prithee, nuncle, be contented! 'Tis a naughty night to swim in.
Now a little fire in a wild field were like an old lecher's heart—a
small spark, all the rest on's body cold. Look, here comes a walking fire.
　Enter GLOUCESTER *with a torch.*

EDG. This is the foul Flibbertigibbet. He begins at curfew, and walks 100
till the first cock. He gives the web and the pin, squints the eye, and
makes the harelip; mildews the white wheat, and hurts the poor
creature of earth.
　　　Saint Withold footed thrice the 'old;

80 *deeply* Q¹; F¹: "deerely." 81 *out-paramour'd* surpassed in the number of
my mistresses [K]. *the Turk* the Great Turk, the Sultan. 82 *light of ear* ready
to listen to evil reports, slander, flattery. 82–3 *hog in sloth . . . lion in prey*
The Seven Deadly Sins were figured in the shape of seven animals [K]. 83–5
Let not . . . woman do not give your heart to a woman as soon as you hear
her shoes creak and her silk gown rustle. Shoes that creaked were fashionable
[K]. 85 *placket* the slit in a petticoat. 86 *lender's book* The borrower was expected to sign an acknowledgment of receipt in the moneylender's book of
record [K]. 87 *suum . . . nonny* He imitates the whistling of the wind [K].
hey, no, nonny K; F¹: "nonny"; Q¹: "hay no on ny." 88 *my boy, boy* F¹; Q¹, K:
"my boy, my boy." 89 *Thou wert* F¹; Q¹, K: "Why, thou wert." *a grave* F¹; Q¹,
K: "thy grave." 92 *the cat* civet cat. 93 *unaccommodated man* man pure and
simple—the thing itself—without any of the artificial furnishings to which he is
accustomed [K]. 94 *forked* two-legged. 94–5 *Off, off* To tear off one's clothes
is a common symptom of delirium [K]. 95 *lendings* Clothes are not given to man
by nature: they are "lent" him by art [K]. *unbutton* Lear instinctively uses the
imperative, for he has never before taken off his clothes without a valet's services [K]. 96 *naughty* very bad, wicked; not a trivial or childish word, as in
modern usage [K]. 100 *foul* F¹; Q¹, K: "foul fiend." *Flibbertigibbet* a dancing devil. *curfew* nine P.M. 101 *till the* Q¹; F¹: "at." *first cock* midnight.
the web and the pin An old name for the disease of the eye known as "cataract"
[K]. 102 *harelip* cleft upper lip. 104 *Saint Withold* a famous English exorcist
of evil spirits. Edgar is reciting a charm. To tell how St. Withold encountered
and subdued the demon and her offspring served as a charm against her power
(F¹: "Swithold," a popular corruption). *footed* traversed. *the 'old* the wold—
an upland plain.

He met the nightmare, and her nine fold; 105
    Bid her alight
    And her troth plight,
And aroint thee, witch, aroint thee!

KENT. How fares your Grace?

LEAR. What's he? 110

KENT. Who's there? What is't you seek?

GLOU. What are you there? Your names?

EDG. Poor Tom, that eats the swimming frog, the toad, the todpole,
    the wall-newt and the water; that in the fury of his heart, when
    the foul fiend rages, eats cow-dung for sallets, swallows the old rat 115
    and the ditch-dog, drinks the green mantle of the standing pool;
    who is whipp'd from tithing to tithing, and stock-punish'd and
    imprison'd; who hath had three suits to his back, six shirts to his
    body, horse to ride, and weapon to wear;
            But mice and rats, and such small deer, 120
            Have been Tom's food for seven long year.
    Beware my follower. Peace, Smulkin! peace, thou fiend!

GLOU. What, hath your Grace no better company?

EDG. The prince of darkness is a gentleman!
    Modo he's call'd, and Mahu. 125

GLOU. Our flesh and blood is grown so vile, my lord,
    That it doth hate what gets it.

EDG. Poor Tom 's acold.

GLOU. Go in with me. My duty cannot suffer
    T' obey in all your daughters' hard commands. 130
    Though their injunction be to bar my doors
    And let this tyrannous night take hold upon you,
    Yet have I ventur'd to come seek you out
    And bring you where both fire and food is ready.

LEAR. First let me talk with this philosopher. 135
    What is the cause of thunder?

KENT. Good my lord, take this offer; go into th' house.

107 *her troth plight* pledge her solemn word (not to do any harm [K]. 108
And aroint thee Addressed by the reciter directly to the demon: "Away with
thee"; "be gone" [K]. 113 *todpole* tadpole. 114 *wall-newt* wall-lizard. *water*
water-newt. 115 *sallets* salads. 116 *ditch-dog* dead dog thrown into a ditch.
mantle scum. *standing* stagnant. 117 *tithing* district within a parish; it contained
ten families. A statute of 1597 provided for the whipping of vagabonds from
parish to parish until they reached their own, if it could be determined. *stock-
punish'd* Q¹; F¹: "stockt, punish'd." 118 *hath had* Q¹; F¹: "hath." *three suits*
the regular wardrobe of a male servant. 120 *deer* game. 122 *Smulkin* one of
the devils described in Harsnet's DECLARATION, as creeping out of a man's ear in
the form of a mouse. 124 *The prince . . . gentleman* and therefore good enough
company even for a king [K]. 125 *Modo* a devil described by Harsnet as a
great general in hell. *Mahu* another devil described by Harsnet as "generall
Dictator of hell." 127 *gets* begets. 129 *suffer* permit. 135 *philosopher* man
of science. "Philosophy" was the regular word for what we call "science" [K].
Edgar's naked appearance might have recalled that of the philosopher Diogenes
in John Lyly's play CAMPASPE. Lear in what follows appears to be taking Edgar
for the traditional court philosopher and asking him such questions as these
court functionaries were called upon to answer. 136 *What . . . thunder* A
much-discussed scientific problem in old times [K].

LEAR. I'll talk a word with this same learned Theban.
  What is your study?
EDG. How to prevent the fiend and to kill vermin.   140
LEAR. Let me ask you one word in private.
KENT. Importune him once more to go, my lord.
  His wits begin t' unsettle.
GLOU.   Canst thou blame him?
    Storm still.
  His daughters seek his death. Ah, that good Kent!   145
  He said it would be thus—poor banish'd man!
  Thou say'st the King grows mad: I'll tell thee, friend,
  I am almost mad myself. I had a son,
  Now outlaw'd from my blood. He sought my life
  But lately, very late. I lov'd him, friend—   150
  No father his son dearer. True to tell thee,
  The grief hath craz'd my wits. What a night 's this!
  I do beseech your Grace—
LEAR.   O, cry you mercy, sir.
  Noble philosopher, your company.   155
EDG. Tom's acold.
GLOU. In, fellow, there, into th' hovel; keep thee warm.
LEAR. Come, let's in all.
KENT.   This way, my lord.
LEAR.   With him!   160
  I will keep still with my philosopher.
KENT. Good my lord, soothe him; let him take the fellow.
GLOU. Take him you on.
KENT. Sirrah, come on; go along with us.
LEAR. Come, good Athenian.   165
GLOU. No words, no words! hush.
EDG. Child Rowland to the dark tower came;
  His word was still

138 *Theban* Why Lear should associate Thebes with science has never been
explained. 139 *What is your study* what is your special department of scientific
research? Edgar picks up the word "study" and applies it in another sense:
"That to which I give all my attention is—how to forestall the assaults of the
fiend and kill the vermin that torment me" [K]. 141 *in private* Lear speaks
as if the learned philosopher had answered him sensibly, and as if, therefore, a
private conference with him might be useful in the present crisis [K]. 149
outlaw'd from my blood deprived of his position as my child. 152 *craz'd* The
literal meaning is "cracked" [K]. 154 *cry you mercy* I beg your pardon for
not attending to you. Lear is a little impatient at being interrupted in his
conference with the "noble philosopher" [K]. 162 *soothe him* indulge him;
let him have his own way. To "soothe" is literally to "reply 'Sooth'" (i.e.
"True!") to whatever a person says [K]. 165 *Athenian* Since Athenians were
considered more learned and civilized than Thebans, Lear's estimate of his
"philosopher" seems to be improving. 167 *Child Rowland . . . came* This may
or may not be a line from some ballad—now lost beyond recovery. "Child" was
the old title for a candidate for knighthood, not yet dubbed "Sir Knight" [K].
Rowland Roland, Charlemagne's nephew and the chief Knight in the Charlemagne epic cycle [K]. 168 *His word was still* his motto or watchword always
was.

Fie, foh, and fum!
I smell the blood of a British man. 170

Exeunt.

SCENE 5

[GLOUCESTER'S *Castle.*]
Enter CORNWALL *and* EDMUND.

CORN. I will have my revenge ere I depart his house.

EDM. How, my lord, I may be censured, that nature thus gives way to
loyalty, something fears me to think of.

CORN. I now perceive it was not altogether your brother's evil disposi- 5
tion made him seek his death; but a provoking merit, set awork by
a reproveable badness in himself.

EDM. How malicious is my fortune that I must repent to be just! This
is the letter he spoke of, which approves him an intelligent party
to the advantages of France. O heavens! that this treason were not
—or not I the detector! 10

CORN. Go with me to the Duchess.

EDM. If the matter of this paper be certain, you have mighty business
in hand.

CORN. True or false, it hath made thee Earl of Gloucester. Seek out
where thy father is, that he may be ready for our apprehension. 15

EDM. [*aside*] If I find him comforting the King, it will stuff his suspicion more fully.— I will persever in my course of loyalty, though
the conflict be sore between that and my blood.

CORN. I will lay trust upon thee, and thou shalt find a dearer father in
my love. 20

Exeunt.

III.5. 1 *I will have my revenge* Edmund has informed Cornwall of Gloucester's
intention to relieve Lear and to join the invading party in the King's interest
(III.3.7ff) [K]. 2 *censured* judged—not blamed [K]. 3 *something fears me*
frightens me somewhat. 4–6 *I now perceive . . . in himself* I had supposed that
it was merely your brother's evil disposition that made him seek your father's
death. I now perceive that there was something else that impelled him—
namely the fact that your father deserved to die. That fact, however, needed
your brother's evil nature to make it operate as a cause for his murderous plot
[K]. 5 *a provoking merit* i.e. on Gloucester's part. "Merit" means "deserts"
—a deserving (of death). Cornwall regards Gloucester as a traitor, and therefore
as a complete villain. His character, he suggests, might tempt anyone to kill
him. "Provoking" means "inciting" [K]. 6 *in himself* in Edgar. 7 *just* righteous,
upright. Loyalty, Edmund implies, has forced him to reveal his father's treason.
8 *approves* proves. 8–9 *an intelligent . . . France* a person engaged in giving information that will aid the invading King of France. "Intelligent" has the
active sense: "giving information" [K]. 15 *apprehension* arrest. 16 *comforting*
aiding. 18 *my blood* my natural feelings toward my kindred [K].

SCENE 6

[*A farmhouse near* GLOUCESTER'S *Castle.*]

Enter GLOUCESTER, LEAR, KENT, FOOL, *and* EDGAR.

GLOU. Here is better than the open air; take it thankfully. I will piece out the comfort with what addition I can. I will not be long from you.

KENT. All the power of his wits have given way to his impatience. The gods reward your kindness!   5

Exit [GLOUCESTER].

EDG. Frateretto calls me, and tells me Nero is an angler in the lake of darkness. Pray, innocent, and beware the foul fiend.

FOOL. Prithee, nuncle, tell me whether a madman be a gentleman or a yeoman.

LEAR. A king, a king!   10

FOOL. No, he's a yeoman that has a gentleman to his son; for he's a mad yeoman that sees his son a gentleman before him.

LEAR. To have a thousand with red burning spits
 Come hizzing in upon 'em—

EDG. The foul fiend bites my back.   15

FOOL. He's mad that trusts in the tameness of a wolf, a horse's health, a boy's love, or a whore's oath.

LEAR. It shall be done; I will arraign them straight.
 [*To* EDGAR] Come, sit thou here, most learned justicer.
 [*To the* FOOL] Thou, sapient sir, sit here. Now, you she-foxes! 20

EDG. Look, where he stands and glares!
 Want'st thou eyes at trial, madam?
     Come o'er the bourn, Bessy, to me.

FOOL.   Her boat hath a leak,
    And she must not speak   25
  Why she dares not come over to thee.

III.6. 4 *have* Attracted into the plural by the intervening "wits" [K]. *impatience* passion, lack of self-control. 6 *Frateretto* a devil mentioned in Harsnet's DECLARATION. *Nero* In Rabelais it is the Emperor Trajan who is doomed to fish (for frogs) in hell forever, whereas Nero is doomed to play his fiddle there, as he supposedly had done while Rome burned. 7 *innocent* fool. 8–9 *Prithee . . . yeoman* The Fool expects no answer to his conundrum and of course rejects Lear's passionate solution and furnishes the "correct" answer, which involves a wittily illogical inference from a bit of more or less proverbial worldly wisdom. Then he continues his discourse on madmen with a further definition: "He's mad that trusts," etc. [K]. *yeoman* one who holds property but is not a gentleman in rank [K]. 11–12 *No . . . him* F¹; not in Q¹. 14 *hizzing* A form of "hissing." It suggests the whizzing sound of the red-hot weapons as they are to be brandished by the thousand assailants [K]. 15–51 *The foul fiend . . . her scape* Q¹; not in F¹. 18 *arraign them* In his delirium Lear abandons the idea of attacking his daughters with an armed force and decides to bring them to trial [K]. 19 *justicer* judge. 22 *Want'st . . . madam* Edgar addresses the imaginary Goneril or Regan whom Lear is arraigning: "Do you wish for spectators at your trial, madam? If so, there's a fiend to glare at you" [K]. 23 *Come . . . to me* Edgar, with a beckoning gesture, addresses the imaginary Goneril or Regan in the words of an old song in which a lover calls upon his sweetheart to come to him "across the brook" [K]. *bourn* brook (CAPELL; Q¹: "broome").

EDG. The foul fiend haunts poor Tom in the voice of a nightingale.
Hoppedance cries in Tom's belly for two white herring. Croak not,
black angel; I have no food for thee.

KENT. How do you, sir? Stand you not so amaz'd.   30
Will you lie down and rest upon the cushions?

LEAR. I'll see their trial first. Bring in their evidence.
[*To* EDGAR] Thou, robed man of justice, take thy place.
[*To the* FOOL] And thou, his yokefellow of equity,
Bench by his side. [*To* KENT] You are o' th' commission,   35
Sit you too.

EDG. Let us deal justly.
Sleepest or wakest thou, jolly shepherd?
Thy sheep be in the corn;
And for one blast of thy minikin mouth   40
Thy sheep shall take no harm.
Purr! the cat is gray.

LEAR. Arraign her first. 'Tis Goneril. I here take my oath before this
honourable assembly, she kick'd the poor King her father.

FOOL. Come hither, mistress. Is your name Goneril?   45

LEAR. She cannot deny it.

FOOL. Cry you mercy, I took you for a joint-stool.

LEAR. And here's another, whose warp'd looks proclaim
What store her heart is made on. Stop her there!
Arms, arms! sword! fire! Corruption in the place!   50
False justicer, why hast thou let her scape?

EDG. Bless thy five wits!

KENT. O pity! Sir, where is the patience now
That you so oft have boasted to retain?

EDG. [*aside*] My tears begin to take his part so much   55
They'll mar my counterfeiting.

LEAR. The little dogs and all,
Tray, Blanch, and Sweetheart, see, they bark at me.

EDG. Tom will throw his head at them. Avaunt, you curs!
Be thy mouth or black or white,   60

27 *voice of a nightingale* The Fool has sung the three lines that precede, which
are his improvisation, not a part of the old song [K]. 28 *Hoppedance* a devil
in Harsnet's DECLARATION. *cries in Tom's belly* He refers to the rumbling
sound that indicates an empty stomach [K]. *white* unsmoked (as opposed to
the "black angel"—smoked devil). 30 *amaz'd* in a maze. A very strong word
indicating a state of utter confusion [K]. 32 *their evidence* the witnesses who
are to testify against them [K]. 33 *robed* Edgar wears a blanket which Lear
takes for a justice's robe of office [K] (POPE; Q¹: "robbed"). 35 *Bench* take
thy seat on the bench as a judge [K]. *o' th' commission* commissioned a judge.
39 *corn* wheatfield. 40 *one blast* the time it takes to play one strain on your
shepherd's pipe [K]. *minikin* delicate, little. 42 *cat is gray* Devils often took
the form of gray cats. 47 *Cry . . . stool* A conventional jocose apology for
overlooking a person. The Fool takes professional delight in this opportunity
to give the worn-out phrase a point; for, in this case, the stool is there and
Goneril is not. A "joint-stool" is a stool fitted together by a joiner (a furniture
maker) in distinction from one of ruder manufacture [K]. 48 *warp'd* perverse,
unnatural. 49 *store* material. *Stop her there* In his delirium Lear sees Regan
escaping from the courtroom [K]. 50 *Corruption in the place* bribery in the
seat of justice [K]. 53 *patience* self-control.

        Tooth that poisons if it bite;
        Mastiff, greyhound, mongrel grim,
        Hound or spaniel, brach or lym,
        Bobtail tyke or trundle-tail—
        Tom will make him weep and wail;   65
        For, with throwing thus my head,
        Dogs leap the hatch, and all are fled.
Do de, de, de. Sessa! Come, march to wakes and fairs and market
towns. Poor Tom, thy horn is dry.

LEAR. Then let them anatomize Regan. See what breeds about her   70
    heart. Is there any cause in nature that makes these hard hearts?
    [*To* EDGAR] You, sir—I entertain you for one of my hundred; only
    I do not like the fashion of your garments. You'll say they are
    Persian; but let them be chang'd.

KENT. Now, good my lord, lie here and rest awhile.   75

LEAR. Make no noise, make no noise; draw the curtains. So, so, so.
    We'll go to supper i' th' morning.

FOOL. And I'll go to bed at noon.

     Enter GLOUCESTER.

GLOU. Come hither, friend. Where is the King my master?

KENT. Here, sir; but trouble him not; his wits are gone.   80

GLOU. Good friend, I prithee take him in thy arms.
    I have o'erheard a plot of death upon him.
    There is a litter ready; lay him in't
    And drive towards Dover, friend, where thou shalt meet
    Both welcome and protection. Take up thy master.   85
    If thou shouldst dally half an hour, his life,
    With thine, and all that offer to defend him,
    Stand in assured loss. Take up, take up!
    And follow me, that will to some provision
    Give thee quick conduct.   90

KENT.   Oppressed nature sleeps.
    This rest might yet have balm'd thy broken sinews.
    Which, if convenience will not allow,
    Stand in hard cure. [*To the* FOOL] Come, help to bear thy master.

---

63 *lym* lymner, a kind of bloodhound (HANMER; F¹: "Hym"; Q¹: "him"). 64
tyke cur (Q¹; F¹: "tight"). *trundle-tail* a dog with a long drooping tail which
he seems to "trundle" or drag along after him [K]. 65 *him* F¹; Q¹, K: "them."
67 *leap* Q¹; F¹: "leapt." *hatch* lower half of a two-part or "Dutch" door. 68
wakes parish feasts 68–9 *fairs . . . towns* In such places a beggar is likely
to fare well. 69 *Poor Tom . . . dry* A Poor Tom formula in begging for drink
[K]. Tom o'Bedlams wore large horns about their necks for this purpose.
Edgar is suggesting also that he is too exhausted to maintain his role as Poor
Tom. 70 *anatomize* dissect. 72 *entertain* engage. 74 *Persian* Persian costumes
were proverbially gorgeous (F¹; Q¹, K: "Persian attire"). 76 *curtains* of an
imaginary bed. 77 *morning* F¹; Q¹, K: "morning, so, so, so." 78 *And I'll . . .
at noon* The Fool adds his logic to Lear's remark: if supper is in the morning,
bedtime must be at noon. These are the last words that the Fool speaks in the
play (F¹; not in Q¹). 88 *Stand in assured loss* are in a condition in which are
sure to be lost [K]. 89 *provision* means of providing for safety [K]. 91–4
Oppressed nature . . . thy master Q¹; not in F¹. 92 *sinews* nerves (F¹; THEO-
BALD, K: "senses"). 93 *convenience* propitious circumstances. 94 *Stand in hard
cure* are in a condition in which cure is difficult [K].

Thou must not stay behind.   95
GLOU.   Come, come, away!
   Exeunt [all but EDGAR].
EDG. When we our betters see bearing our woes,
     We scarcely think our miseries our foes.
     Who alone suffers suffers mos ti' th' mind,
     Leaving free things and happy shows behind;   100
     But then the mind much sufferance doth o'erskip
     When grief hath mates, and bearing fellowship.
     How light and portable my pain seems now,
     When that which makes me bend makes the King bow,
     He childed as I fathered! Tom, away!   105
     Mark the high noises, and thyself bewray
     When false opinion, whose wrong thoughts defile thee,
     In thy just proof repeals and reconciles thee.
     What will hap more to-night, safe scape the King!
     Lurk, lurk.   110
   [*Exit.*]

99 *When we . . . lurk* Q¹; not in F¹. *Who alone . . . mind* suffers in his mind
more than one who has companions in his misery. "Alone" and "most" are the
emphatic words. Edgar's reflections are merely an elaboration of the familiar
proverb: "Misery loves company" [K]. 100 *free* care-free. *happy shows* happy
looks; all appearances of happiness [K]. 101 *sufferance* suffering. *o'erskip* escape,
avoid. 102 *bearing* endurance. 103 *portable* endurable. 106 *Mark the high
noises* give careful attention to the discord among the great and high [K]. 106–8
thyself bewray . . . reconciles thee reveal thyself—throw off thy disguise—when
the false opinion that now mistakenly regards thee as a villain, shall, on proof
that thou art guiltless, correct itself, and so shall recall thee to favour and make
peace between thee and thy father [K]. 107 *thoughts defile* Q¹; THEOBALD, K:
"thought defiles." 109 *What* whatsoever. 110 *Lurk* remain in hiding.

～〜⌇✦⌇〜～

SCENE 7

[GLOUCESTER'S *Castle.*]
   Enter CORNWALL, REGAN, GONERIL, [EDMUND *the*] BASTARD, *and*
   SERVANTS.
CORN. [*to* GONERIL] Post speedily to my lord your husband, show him
    this letter. The army of France is landed.—Seek out the traitor
    Gloucester.
   [*Exeunt some of the* SERVANTS.]
REG. Hang him instantly.
GON. Pluck out his eyes.   5
CORN. Leave him to my displeasure. Edmund, keep you our sister
    company. The revenges we are bound to take upon your traitorous
    father are not fit for your beholding. Advise the Duke where you
    are going, to a most festinate preparation. We are bound to the like.

III.7. 7 *are bound* have sworn, are obliged. 8 *Duke* Albany. *where* to whose
palace. 9 *festinate* speedy (F²; Q¹: "festuant"; F¹: "festiuate"). *bound to
the like* on our way to the same speedy preparation [K].

> Our posts shall be swift and intelligent betwixt us. Farewell, dear   10
> sister; farewell, my Lord of Gloucester.
> > *Enter* [OSWALD *the*] STEWARD.
> How now? Where's the King?

OSW. My Lord of Gloucester hath convey'd him hence.
> Some five or six and thirty of his knights,
> Hot questrists after him, met him at gate;   15
> Who, with some other of the lord's dependants,
> Are gone with him towards Dover, where they boast
> To have well-armed friends.

CORN.   Get horses for your mistress.

GON. Farewell, sweet lord, and sister.   20

CORN. Edmund, farewell.
> > *Exeunt* GONERIL, [EDMUND, *and* OSWALD].
> > > Go seek the traitor Gloucester,
> Pinion him like a thief, bring him before us.
> > [*Exeunt other* SERVANTS.]
> Though well we may not pass upon his life
> Without the form of justice, yet our power   25
> Shall do a court'sy to our wrath, which men
> May blame, but not control.
> > *Enter* GLOUCESTER, *brought in by two or three.*
> > > Who's there? the traitor?

REG. Ingrateful fox! 'tis he.

CORN. Bind fast his corky arms.   30

GLOU. What means your Graces? Good my friends, consider
> You are my guests. Do me no foul play, friends.

CORN. Bind him, I say.
> [SERVANTS *bind him.*]

REG.   Hard, hard. O filthy traitor!

GLOU. Unmerciful lady as you are, I am none.   35

CORN. To this chair bind him. Villain, thou shalt find—
> [REGAN *plucks his beard.*]

GLOU. By the kind gods, 'tis most ignobly done
> To pluck me by the beard.

REG. So white, and such a traitor!

GLOU   Naughty lady,   40
> These hairs which thou dost ravish from my chin

---

10 *Our posts* the couriers between us and the Duke of Albany [K]. *intelligent* giving information; furnished with all necessary news of our warlike movements [K]. 11 *Lord of Gloucester* Edmund has now been endowed with his father's estates and his title. 15 *Hot questrists after him* who had been rapid and eager in their search for him [K]. 24 *pass upon* pass judgment upon. 25 *form* outward appearance. 25-7 *yet our . . . control* yet our power shall act in accordance with the wrath we feel; and nobody can hinder that action, though some may perhaps find it blameworthy [K]. 30 *corky* withered (by old age) [K]. 31 *means* F¹, Q¹; F⁴, K: "mean." 32 *foul play* This phrase was not, as in modern usage, confined to the sense of "murder." It is, in origin, the antithesis to "fair play," and suggests something that is out of accord with law and justice [K]. 40 *Naughty* wicked. A strong adjective in Elizabethan English [K].

Will quicken, and accuse thee. I am your host.
With robber's hands my hospitable favours
You should not ruffle thus. What will you do?

CORN. Come, sir, what letters had you late from France? 45

REG. Be simple-answer'd, for we know the truth.

CORN. And what confederacy have you with the traitors
Late footed in the kingdom?

REG.   To whose hands
You have sent the lunatic king: speak. 50

GLOU. I have a letter guessingly set down,
Which came from one that's of a neutral heart,
And not from one oppos'd.

CORN.   Cunning.

REG.   And false. 55

CORN. Where hast thou sent the King?

GLOU. To Dover.

REG. Wherefore to Dover? Wast thou not charg'd at peril—

CORN. Wherefore to Dover? Let him answer that.

GLOU. I am tied to th' stake, and I must stand the course. 60

REG. Wherefore to Dover?

GLOU. Because I would not see thy cruel nails
Pluck out his poor old eyes; nor thy fierce sister
In his anointed flesh stick boarish fangs.
The sea, with such a storm as his bare head 65
In hell-black night endur'd, would have buoy'd up
And quench'd the stelled fires.
Yet, poor old heart, he holp the heavens to rain.
If wolves had at thy gate howl'd that stern time,
Thou shouldst have said, "Good porter, turn the key." 70
All cruels else subscribe. But I shall see
The winged vengeance overtake such children.

CORN. See't shalt thou never. Fellows, hold the chair.
Upon these eyes of thine I'll set my foot.

GLOU. He that will think to live till he be old, 75
Give me some help!—O cruel! O ye gods!

42 *quicken* come to life. 43 *hospitable favours* features of your host. 44 *ruffle
thus* treat with such violence. 46 *Be simple-answer'd* give plain, straightfor-
ward answers. 48 *Late footed* recently landed. 50 *You have* F¹, Q¹; Q², K:
"Haue you." 51 *guessingly set down* written without certain knowledge. 58
at peril under penalty (of death). 59 *him answer* F¹; Q¹, K: "him first answer."
60 *tied . . . course* A figure from bear-baiting. The bear was tied to a post
and dogs were set on to attack him. A "course" (literally, a "running") was
one such attack, lasting until the dogs were called off [K]. 61 *Dover* F¹; Q¹, K:
"Dover, sir." 64 *anointed* Anointing with holy oil was a part of the ceremony
of coronation. Thus a king was a consecrated person, whom it was sacrilege to
attack [K]. 66 *buoy'd* surged. 67 *stelled fires* fires of the stars. 68 *holp*
helped. 69 *howl'd* come howling for shelter [K]. 70 *turn the key* to let them
enter. 71 *All cruels else* all other cruel creatures. *subscribe* relent, agree to
give up their cruelty (F¹; Q¹, K: "subscrib'd"). 72 *The winged vengeance* the
vengeance of the gods, sweeping down upon them like a bird of prey [K].

REG. One side will mock another. Th' other too!

CORN. If you see vengeance—

1. SERV.   Hold your hand, my lord!
  I have serv'd you ever since I was a child;   80
  But better service have I never done you
  Than now to bid you hold.

REG.   How now, you dog?

1. SERV. If you did wear a beard upon your chin,
  I'ld shake it on this quarrel.   85

REG.   What do you mean?

CORN. My villain!
      Draw and fight.

1. SERV. Nay, then, come on, and take the chance of anger.

REG. Give me thy sword. A peasant stand up thus?
      She takes a sword and runs at him behind.

1. SERV. O, I am slain! My lord, you have one eye left   90
  To see some mischief on him. O!
      He dies.

CORN. Lest it see more, prevent it. Out, vile jelly!
  Where is thy lustre now?

GLOU. All dark and comfortless! Where's my son Edmund?
  Edmund, enkindle all the sparks of nature   95
  To quit this horrid act.

REG.   Out, treacherous villain!
  Thou call'st on him that hates thee. It was he
  That made the overture of thy treasons to us;
  Who is too good to pity thee.   100

GLOU. O my follies! Then Edgar was abus'd.
  Kind gods, forgive me that, and prosper him!

REG. Go thrust him out at gates, and let him smell
  His way to Dover.
      Exit [one] with GLOUCESTER.
                    How is't, my lord? How look you?   105

CORN. I have receiv'd a hurt. Follow me, lady.
  Turn out that eyeless villain. Throw this slave
  Upon the dunghill. Regan, I bleed apace.
  Untimely comes this hurt. Give me your arm.
      *Exit [*CORNWALL, *led by* REGAN].

2. SERV. I'll never care what wickedness I do,   110
  If this man come to good.

---

85 *this quarrel* this cause—i.e. the cause for which I contend in this case; my
defence of the old man [K].   86 *What do you mean* K; F¹, Q¹ give the line to First
Servant. Some editors give it to Cornwall.   87 *villain* serf. Used rather as a
term of abuse than in the literal sense [K].   88 *chance of anger* risk of fighting
with an angry man.   91 *mischief* harm, injury   92 *prevent it* forestall it; prevent it by anticipatory action [K].   95 *nature* natural feeling.   96 *quit* repay.
97 *Out* out upon thee! An interjection of cursing [K].   99 *overture* disclosure.
101 *abus'd* deceived, wronged.   105 *How look you* how does it look with you;
how are you?   109 *Untimely* since it disables me when I should be leading my
army against the invaders [K].   110–19 *I'll never . . . help him* Q¹; not in F¹.

3. SERV.   If she live long,
    And in the end meet the old course of death,
    Women will all turn monsters.
2. SERV. Let's follow the old Earl, and get the bedlam   115
    To lead him where he would. His roguish madness
    Allows itself to anything.
3. SERV. Go thou. I'll fetch some flax and whites of eggs
    To apply to his bleeding face. Now heaven help him!
        Exeunt.

114 *Women will all turn monsters* because they will lose all fear of vengeance
from the gods for any misdeed, however flagrant [K].   115 *the bedlam* the mad
beggar—Edgar.   116–17 *His roguish . . . anything* the fact that he is a vagabond (a rogue) and a madman makes it possible for him to do anything without being called to account [K].

ACT FOUR

SCENE 1

[*The heath.*]
    Enter EDGAR.
EDG. Yet better thus, and known to be contemn'd,
    Than still contemn'd and flatter'd. To be worst,
    The lowest and most dejected thing of fortune,
    Stands still in esperance, lives not in fear.
    The lamentable change is from the best;   5
    The worst returns to laughter. Welcome then,
    Thou unsubstantial air that I embrace!
    The wretch that thou hast blown unto the worst
    Owes nothing to thy blasts.
        Enter GLOUCESTER, *led by an* OLD MAN.
                        But who comes here?   10
    My father, poorly led? World, world, O world!
    But that thy strange mutations make us hate thee,
    Life would not yield to age.
OLD MAN.   O my good lord,
    I have been your tenant, and your father's tenant,   15

IV.1.   1 *thus* in this beggarly condition [K].   *contemn'd* despised, held in contempt.   3 *most dejected* most cast down—synonymous with "lowest." Edgar
comforts himself with the commonplace reflection that any change from the
worst must be for the better [K].   *of* by, at the hands of.   4 *Stands still in
esperance* is in a condition that always admits of hope [K].   6 *returns to
laughter* marks a change for the better—to a state of happiness.   6–10 *Welcome
. . . But* F[1]; not in Q[1].   9 *Owes nothing to thy blasts* and therefore need have
no fear of what they can do to him. The figure is from the relation of creditor
and debtor; when a man's debts are paid, he fears no creditor [K].   11 *poorly
led* led by a poor man—a beggar.   12–13 *But that . . . to age* the only thing
that makes us grow old and die is our hatred of life in this world, and that
hatred is caused by the strange vicissitudes of fortune [K].

These fourscore years.

GLOU. Away, get thee away! Good friend, be gone.
  Thy comforts can do me no good at all;
  Thee they may hurt.

OLD MAN.   You cannot see your way.   20

GLOU. I have no way, and therefore want no eyes;
  I stumbled when I saw. Full oft 'tis seen
  Our means secure us, and our mere defects
  Prove our commodities. Ah dear son Edgar,
  The food of thy abused father's wrath!   25
  Might I but live to see thee in my touch,
  I'ld say I had eyes again!

OLD MAN.   How now? Who's there?

EDG. [aside] O gods! Who is't can say "I am at the worst"?
  I am worse than e'er I was.   30

OLD MAN.   'Tis poor mad Tom.

EDG. [aside] And worse I may be yet. The worst is not
  So long as we can say "This is the worst."

OLD MAN. Fellow, where goest?

GLOU.   Is it a beggarman?   35

OLD MAN. Madman and beggar too.

GLOU. He has some reason, else he could not beg.
  I' th' last night's storm I such a fellow saw,
  Which made me think a man a worm. My son
  Came then into my mind, and yet my mind   40
  Was then scarce friends with him. I have heard more since.
  As flies to wanton boys are we to th' gods.
  They kill us for their sport.

EDG.   [aside] How should this be?
  Bad is the trade that must play fool to sorrow,   45

18 *Thy comforts* thy attempts to aid me in my misery [K]. 22 *I stumbled when I saw* when I had my eyes, I walked recklessly and lost my footing. Gloucester refers to the terrible blunder he had made in believing Edmund's lies about Edgar, which, he thinks, ought to have been obvious to any clear-sighted judgment [K]. 22–4 *Full oft . . . commodities* Thus Gloucester interprets, "I stumbled when I saw," and applies it as a general truth of common experience: "Prosperity makes us careless, and adversity ("our mere defects") proves to be an advantage, for it forces us to recognize the facts of life." Now, in his blindness, he sees the truth [K]. 23 *secure* makes rash or careless, overconfident. *defects* lacks, deprivations. 24 *commodities* advantages, benefits. 25 *The food . . . wrath* that on which his anger fed; the object of his anger [K]. *abused* deceived, betrayed. 26–7 *Might I . . . again* to hold thee in my embrace once more would be as great a blessing as the restoration of eyesight [K]. 32–3 *The worst is not . . . worst* for so long as we can take comfort in assuring ourselves that we are at the worst, that comforting reflection shows that we are not hopeless and so not actually at the worst [K]. 39 *a worm* A portable echo of JOB, xxv, 6: "How much less man, that is a worm? and the son of man, which is a worm?" 40 *Came then into my mind* because I thought that my son was doubtless a homeless wanderer like that poor beggar [K]. 41 *friends* friendly, kindly disposed. 42 *wanton* playful, irresponsible. 45 *play fool to sorrow* act the fool (as I must do) to one who is in sorrow (as my father is) [K].

Ang'ring itself and others.—Bless thee, master!

GLOU. Is that the naked fellow?

OLD MAN.   Ay, my lord.

GLOU. Then prithee get thee gone. If for my sake

  Thou wilt o'ertake us hence a mile or twain   50

  I' th' way toward Dover, do it for ancient love;

  And bring some covering for this naked soul,

  Who I'll entreat to lead me.

OLD MAN.   Alack, sir, he is mad!

GLOU. 'Tis the time's plague when madmen lead the blind.   55

  Do as I bid thee, or rather do thy pleasure.

  Above the rest, be gone.

OLD MAN. I'll bring him the best 'parel that I have,

  Come on't what will.

        Exit.

GLOU. Sirrah naked fellow—   60

EDG. Poor Tom's a-cold. [*Aside*] I cannot daub it further.

GLOU. Come hither, fellow.

EDG. [*aside*] And yet I must.—Bless thy sweet eyes, they bleed.

GLOU. Know'st thou the way to Dover?

EDG. Both stile and gate, horseway and footpath. Poor Tom hath been   65

  scar'd out of his good wits. Bless thee, good man's son, from the

  foul fiend! Five fiends have been in poor Tom at once: of lust, as

  Obidicut; Hobbididence, prince of dumbness; Mahu, of stealing;

  Modo, of murder; Flibbertigibbet, of mopping and mowing, who

  since possesses chambermaids and waiting women. So, bless thee,   70

  master!

GLOU. Here, take this purse, thou whom the heavens' plagues

  Have humbled to all strokes. That I am wretched

  Makes thee the happier. Heavens, deal so still!

  Let the superfluous and lust-dieted man,   75

46 *Ang'ring* offending.   49 *Then . . . gone* Q¹; F¹: "Get thee away."   51 *ancient love* old-fashioned love, such as formerly bound the servant to his master. Gloucester in his despair sees such love as banished from the world.   55 *'Tis . . . blind* Gloucester makes a kind of parable out of his own situation: "So it is in the world. When the leaders of the people are mad and the people themselves are blind—that is a sad time for humanity" [K].   56 *do thy pleasure* do what you please. Gloucester remembers that he is in no condition to give an order to anybody [K].   61 *daub it further* continue my counterfeiting.   63 *And yet I must* F¹; not in Q¹.   67–71 *Five fiends . . . master* Q¹; not in F¹.   67 *Five fiends* All are described in Harsnet's DECLARATION.   69 *Flibbertigibbet* POPE; Q¹: "Stiberdigebit."   *mopping and mowing* grimacing and making faces (THEO-BALD; Q¹: "Mobing and Making").   69–70 *who since . . . waiting women* since Flibbertigibbet left me, he has possessed chambermaids and waiting women, who are for ever twisting their faces into strange shapes in the attempt to put on elegant airs. Cf. III.2.33–4 A "flibbertigibbet" is a "flirt," a "frivolous crea-ture." Hence this is a good name for the demon that prompts affected airs and graces [K].   73 *humbled to all strokes* brought so low that thou sufferest every kind of misery [K].   74 *happier* less wretched.   *deal so still* Gloucester calls upon the gods to make his sufferings a common experience of the great and high when—as in his own case—they have abused their prosperity [K].   75–9 *Let . . . enough* let the man who has far more than he needs and is able to gratify every

That slaves your ordinance, that will not see
Because he does not feel, feel your pow'r quickly;
So distribution should undo excess,
And each man have enough. Dost thou know Dover?
EDG. Ay, master.   80
GLOU. There is a cliff, whose high and bending head
Looks fearfully in the confined deep.
Bring me but to the very brim of it,
And I'll repair the misery thou dost bear
With something rich about me. From that place   85
I shall no leading need.
EDG.   Give me thy arm.
Poor Tom shall lead thee.
    Exeunt.

desire feel your power quickly (as I have been made to feel it). In this way such
men will learn to distribute their superfluous wealth among the needy, and no one
will be in want. Compare Lear's expression of the same idea in III.4.36–9 [K].   75
lust-dieted whose desires are fed to the full.   76 *slaves your ordinance* subordinates
and treats with contempt your injunction (the decree of the gods that man share
his wealth).   81 *bending* beetling, overhanging.   82 *fearfully* so as to inspire
terror in one who looks over the edge [K].   *in* down into.   *confined deep* the
Straits of Dover, hemmed in by land on both sides.

SCENE 2

[*Before the* DUKE OF ALBANY'S *Palace.*]
    Enter GONERIL *and* [EDMUND *the*] BASTARD.
GON. Welcome, my lord. I marvel our mild husband
Not met us on the way.
    Enter [OSWALD *the*] STEWARD.
                            Now, where's your master?
OSW. Madam, within, but never man so chang'd.
I told him of the army that was landed: 5
He smil'd at it. I told him you were coming:
His answer was, "The worse." Of Gloucester's treachery
And of the loyal service of his son
When I inform'd him, then he call'd me sot
And told me I had turn'd the wrong side out.   10
What most he should dislike seems pleasant to him;
What like, offensive.
GON. [*to* EDMUND] Then shall you go no further.
It is the cowish terror of his spirit,
That dares not undertake. He'll not feel wrongs   15
Which tie him to an answer. Our wishes on the way

IV.2.   9 *sot* fool.   10 *had turn'd the wrong side out* because I should have said
"Edmund's treachery" and "the loyal service of Gloucester" [K].   12 *What like*
what he should like.   14 *cowish* cowardly.   15 *undertake* show activity or enter-
prise in anything [K].   16 *tie* oblige.   *wishes on the way* hopes we discussed as
we travelled (that Albany might die).

May prove effects. Back, Edmund, to my brother.
Hasten his musters and conduct his pow'rs.
I must change arms at home and give the distaff
Into my husband's hands. This trusty servant   20
Shall pass between us. Ere long you are like to hear
(If you dare venture in your own behalf)
A mistress's command. Wear this.
    [*Gives a favour.*]
                         Spare speech.
Decline your head. This kiss, if it durst speak,   25
Would stretch thy spirits up into the air.
Conceive, and fare thee well.
EDM. Yours in the ranks of death!
    Exit.
GON.   My most dear Gloucester!
O, the difference of man and man!   30
To thee a woman's services are due;
My fool usurps my body.
OSW.   Madame, here comes my lord.
    Exit.
    Enter ALBANY.
GON. I have been worth the whistle.
ALB.   O Goneril,   35
You are not worth the dust which the rude wind
Blows in your face! I fear your disposition.
That nature which contemns its origin
Cannot be bordered certain in itself.
She that herself will sliver and disbranch   40
From her material sap, perforce must wither
And come to deadly use.
GON. No more! The text is foolish.
ALB. Wisdom and goodness to the vile seem vile;
Filths savour but themselves. What have you done?   45

17 *prove effects* be fulfilled. 18 *pow'rs* troops. 19 *change* exchange; for I must take the sword and give my husband the distaff. The distaff was a staff used in spinning. It was the regular emblem of wifely industry, and also (like the broom-stick in modern times) a woman's weapon [K]. *arms* Q¹; F¹: "names." 23 *A mistress's command* a command from one who is not only your mistress in rank but your lady-love as well [K]. 27 *Conceive* (a) understand (b) let the seed I have planted in your mind come to life. 30 *O . . . man* F¹; not in Q¹. 32 *My fool* one who should rather be the court fool than my husband [K]. *usurps* wrongfully possesses (since Edmund possesses her heart). 34 *worth the whistle* Goneril implies that her husband has been slow in meeting her: "There has been a time when I was worth whistling for" [K]. 37–56 *I fear . . . the deep* Q¹; not in F¹. 37 *fear* am worried about. 39 *Cannot be . . . in itself* can have no sure boundaries of conduct in its own character, There is no enormity that it may not perpetuate [K]. 40 *sliver and disbranch* cut off. The words are synony-mous. 41 *material sap* the tree whence she draws the vital element that con-stitutes and nourishes her frame [K]. 42 *to deadly use* to destruction—as the dead branches of a tree are of use only as fuel and so come to naught [K]. 45 *Filths . . . themselves* to the filthy all things taste filthy.

Tigers, not daughters, what have you perform'd?
A father, and a gracious aged man,
Whose reverence even the head-lugg'd bear would lick,
Most barbarous, most degenerate, have you madded.
Could my good brother suffer you to do it?   50
A man, a prince, by him so benefited!
If that the heavens do not their visible spirits
Send quickly down to tame these vile offences,
It will come,
Humanity must perforce prey on itself,   55
Like monsters of the deep.

GON.   Milk-liver'd man!
That bear'st a cheek for blows, a head for wrongs;
Who hast not in thy brows an eye discerning
Thine honour from thy suffering; that not know'st   60
Fools do those villains pity who are punish'd
Ere they have done their mischief. Where's thy drum?
France spreads his banners in our noiseless land,
With plumed helm thy state begins to threat,
Whiles thou, a moral fool, sits still, and cries   65
"Alack, why does he so?"

ALB.   See thyself, devil!
Proper deformity seems not in the fiend
So horrid as in woman.

GON.   O vain fool!   70

ALB. Thou changed and self-cover'd thing, for shame!
Bemonster not thy feature! Were't my fitness
To let these hands obey my blood,

---

48 *Whose reverence . . . lick* to whom even a sulky bear will do homage by licking his hand [K]. *head-lugg'd* tugged along by the head. The slow lumbering gait of a bear gives one the impression of surly reluctance [K]. 50 *suffer* permit. 52 *visible* Emphatic: "in visible form" [K]. 53 *tame* subdue, put down. *these vile* JENNENS; Q¹: "this vild." 54–5 *It will come . . . itself* the inevitable result will follow—all men will become ferocious animals and devour each other [K]. 57 *Milk-liver'd* white-livered. Cowardice was thought to be caused by lack of blood in the liver [K]. 59–60 *an eye discerning . . . suffering* an eye that can discriminate between what one may honourably endure and what should spur one to noble resentment [K]. 60–6 *that not . . . he so* Q¹; not in F¹. 62 *Ere . . . mischief* before they have committed the crime for which they are being punished. She is referring probably to the punishment inflicted upon Lear before he has had an opportunity to commit the crime of joining the French invaders. Her exact meaning has been much debated. 63 *noiseless* quiet—i.e. passive and unresisting [K]. 64 *state* government. *to threat* JENNENS; Q¹: thereat." 65 *moral* moralizing; i.e. arguing about the rights and wrongs of the matter instead of opposing the invader [K]. *sits* Q¹; K: "sit'st." *cries* Q¹; K: "criest." 68 *Proper* to a fiend, and therefore not so horrible as it is in a woman. 70 *vain* silly. 71–7 *Thou changed . . . mew* Q¹; not in F¹. 71 *self-cover'd* Various meanings are possible (a) your real fiendish self covered by the outward form of a woman (b) your natural womanly self covered by evil (c) your true self hidden from yourself. 72 *Bemonster . . . feature* do not allow thy form and features to be thus transformed into those of a monster [K]. *my fitness* fit for me. 73 *blood* passionate impulse.

They are apt enough to dislocate and tear
Thy flesh and bones. Howe'er thou art a fiend,   75
A woman's shape doth shield thee.
GON. Marry, your manhood mew!
       Enter a GENTLEMAN.
ALB. What news?
GENT. O, my good lord, the Duke of Cornwall's dead,
Slain by his servant, going to put out   80
The other eye of Gloucester.
ALB.   Gloucester's eyes?
GENT. A servant that he bred, thrill'd with remorse,
Oppos'd against the act, bending his sword
To his great master; who, thereat enrag'd,   85
Flew on him, and amongst them fell'd him dead;
But not without that harmful stroke which since
Hath pluck'd him after.
ALB.   This shows you are above,
You justicers, that these our nether crimes   90
So speedily can venge! But O poor Gloucester!
Lost he his other eye?
GENT.   Both, both, my lord.
This letter, madam, craves a speedy answer.
'Tis from your sister.   95
GON.   [*aside*] One way I like this well;
But being widow, and my Gloucester with her,
May all the building in my fancy pluck
Upon my hateful life. Another way
The news is not so tart.—I'll read, and answer.   100
       Exit.
ALB. Where was his son when they did take his eyes?
GENT. Come with my lady hither.
ALB.   He is not here.
GENT. No, my good lord; I met him back again.
ALB. Knows he the wickedness?   105
GENT. Ay, my good lord. 'Twas he informed'd against him,
And quit the house on purpose, that their punishment
Might have the freer course.

---

74 *apt* ready.   75–6 *Howe'er . . . shield thee* however much of a fiend thou art,
I see that thy shape is that of a woman; and so thou art safe from my attack
[K].   77 *mew* lock up. The mews were cages in which falcons were kept. Her
precise meaning is not clear, although it is obvious that she is being contemptuous.   83 *thrill'd* excited, moved. *remorse* pity.   85 *thereat enrag'd* F²; F¹:
"threat-enrag'd."   88 *pluck'd* pulled.   90 *justicers* judges (Q¹; F¹: "Iustices").
nether crimes crimes committed on earth.   96 *One way I like this well* In one
respect Cornwall's death is good news, since it has removed an obstacle to
Goneril's plans. Her hope was to get rid of her husband, marry Edmund, and
seize Regan's half of the kingdom, thus becoming sole Queen of Britain. See
IV.6.278ff; V.1.68–74; V.3.94ff [K].   98–9 *May . . . life* may pull down the
whole structure that I have raised in my imagination and bury the rest of my
life in its ruins—so that my life will be hateful to me [K].   100 *tart* disagreeable.   104 *back again* as he was on his way back to Gloucester's castle [K].

ALB.   Gloucester, I live
To thank thee for the love thou show'dst the King,   110
And to revenge thine eyes. Come hither, friend.
Tell me what more thou know'st.
    Exeunt.

SCENE 3

[The French camp near Dover.]
Enter KENT *and a* GENTLEMAN.

KENT. Why the King of France is so suddenly gone back know you no
    reason?

GENT. Something he left imperfect in the state, which since his coming
    forth is thought of, which imports to the kingdom so much fear and
    danger that his personal return was most required and necessary.   5

KENT. Who hath he left behind him general?

GENT. The Marshal of France, Monsieur La Far.

KENT. Did your letters pierce the Queen to any demonstration of grief?

GENT. Ay, sir. She took them, read them in my presence,
And now and then an ample tear trill'd down   10
Her delicate cheek. It seem'd she was a queen
Over her passion, who, most rebel-like,
Sought to be king o'er her.

KENT.   O, then it mov'd her?

GENT. Not to a rage. Patience and sorrow strove   15
Who should express her goodliest. You have seen
Sunshine and rain at once: her smiles and tears
Were like, a better way. Those happy smilets
That play'd on her ripe lip seem'd not to know
What guests were in her eyes, which parted thence   20
As pearls from diamonds dropp'd. In brief,
Sorrow would be a rarity most belov'd,
If all could so become it.

KENT.   Made she no verbal question?

GENT. Faith, once or twice she heav'd the name of father   25

IV.3 Q¹. The entire scene is omitted from F¹. 1–2 *no reason* Q¹; K: "the
reason." 3 *state* administration of the government. 4–5 *which imports . . .
danger* which, unless it is attended to, will bring upon the French kingdom so
much panic and danger [K]. 8 *pierce* excite, provoke. 9 *sir* THEOBALD; Q¹:
"say." 10 *trill'd* trickled. 12 *passion* emotion, sorrow. *rebel-like* Impulse and
passion or emotion are often figured as rebelling against one's reason or self-
control [K]. 15 *rage* a violent outburst of grief—not wrath [K]. *Patience* self-
control. *strove* POPE; Q¹: "streme." 16 *express her goodliest* give her the most
beautiful expression [K]. 18 *Were like, a better way* were like sunshine and
rain at once, but after a better fashion—i.e. the comparison does her smiles and
tears injustice; they were more beautiful than mingled sunshine and rain [K].
smilets little smiles. 19 *seem'd* POPE; Q¹; "seeme." 20 *which* who—i.e. the
guests in her eyes, the tears [K]. 21 *pearls from diamonds dropp'd* We should
remember that it is a courtly gentleman who is speaking, and that elegant lan-
gauge was expected of courtiers. Shakespeare often calls tears "pearls" [K]. 23
If all . . . it if it could be so becoming to all sorrowful people as it is to her.
25 *heav'd* uttered with difficulty.

Pantingly forth, as if it press'd her heart;
Cried "Sisters, sisters! Shame of ladies! Sisters!
Kent! father! sisters! What, i' th' storm? i' th' night?
Let pity not be believ'd!" There she shook
The holy water from her heavenly eyes,   30
And clamour moisten'd. Then away she started
To deal with grief alone.
KENT.   It is the stars,
The stars above us, govern our conditions;
Else one self mate and make could not beget   35
Such different issues. You spoke not with her since?
GENT. No.
KENT. Was this before the King return'd?
GENT.   No, since.
KENT. Well, sir, the poor distressed Lear's i' th' town;   40
Who sometime, in his better tune, remembers
What we are come about, and by no means
Will yield to see his daughter.
GENT.   Why, good sir?
KENT. A sovereign shame so elbows him; his own unkindness,   45
That stripp'd her from his benediction, turn'd her
To foreign casualties, gave her dear rights
To his dog-hearted daughters—these things sting
His mind so venomously that burning shame
Detains him from Cordelia.   50
GENT.   Alack, poor gentleman!
KENT. Of Albany's and Cornwall's powers you heard not?
GENT. 'Tis so; they are afoot.
KENT. Well, sir, I'll bring you to our master Lear
And leave you to attend him. Some dear cause   55
Will in concealment wrap me up awhile.
When I am known aright, you shall not grieve
Lending me this acquaintance. I pray you go
Along with me.
     Exeunt.

29 *believ'd* believed in (as existent in a world that sees such deeds) [K]. 31
And clamour moisten'd and thus she moistened her lamentation—i.e. followed
her cries of sorrow with tears. The gentleman outdoes himself in this phrase,
but the meaning is clear enough [K]. *moisten'd* CAPELL; Q¹: "moystened her."
34 *govern our conditions* determine our characters. 35 *one self* one and the
same. *and make* and mate, partner (Q¹; Q², K: "and mate). 41 *in his better
tune* in a comparatively lucid interval [K]. 45 *sovereign* overpowering. *elbows
him* stands by his side like a constant attendant [K]. 46 *stripp'd her from his
benediction* deprived her of his blessing when they parted [K]. *turn'd her*
turned her out. 47 *casualties* chances. 52 *powers* troops. 53 *afoot* on the
march. 55 *dear* important. 57 *grieve* regret.

SCENE 4

[*The French camp.*]

Enter, with Drum and Colours, CORDELIA, DOCTOR, *and* SOLDIERS.

COR. Alack, 'tis he! Why, he was met even now
As mad as the vex'd sea, singing aloud,
Crown'd with rank fumiter and furrow weeds,
With hardocks, hemlock, nettles, cuckoo flow'rs,
Darnel, and all the idle weeds that grow   5
In our sustaining corn. A century send forth.
Search every acre in the high-grown field
And bring him to our eye. [*Exit an* OFFICER.] What can man's
    wisdom
In the restoring his bereaved sense?   10
He that helps him take all my outward worth.
DOCT. There is means, madam.
Our foster nurse of nature is repose,
The which he lacks. That to provoke in him
Are many simples operative, whose power   15
Will close the eye of anguish.
COR.   All blest secrets,
All you unpublish'd virtues of the earth,
Spring with my tears! be aidant and remediate
In the good man's distress! Seek, seek for him!   20
Lest his ungovern'd rage dissolve the life
That wants the means to lead it.
    Enter MESSENGER.
MESS.   News, madam.
The British pow'rs are marching hitherward.
COR. 'Tis known before. Our preparation stands   25
In expectation of them. O dear father,
It is thy business that I go about.
Therefore great France
My mourning and importun'd tears hath pitied.

IV.4.   3 *fumiter* fumitory—an herb (THEOBALD; F¹: "Fenitar"; Q¹: "femiter").
furrow weeds weeds that appear after plowing. 4 *hardocks* Variously explained as "hardbacks," "burdocks," or "harlocks," various weeds. *cuckoo
flow'rs* flowers which bloom in the early spring, when the cuckoo builds its nest.
5 *Darnel* tares. 6 *sustaining corn* life-supporting wheat. *century* troop of a
hundred soldiers. 8–9 *man's wisdom* science. 11 *worth* property, possessions.
13 *Our . . . nature* the foster nurse of our nature; that which fosters and sus-
tains our life [K]. 14 *provoke* induce. 15 *simples* medicinal plants—so called
in contradistinction to "compounds" [K]. 17 *secrets* In old times every distinguished physician claimed the knowledge of "secrets"—special remedies, unknown
to the majority. The next line repeats the sense with elaboration of phrase [K].
18 *unpublish'd* unknown. *virtues* efficacious medicinal plants [K]. *of the earth*
that grow in the earth. Medicine in Shakespeare's day was, for the most part,
botanical medicine [K]. 19 *be aidant and remediate* act as aids and remedies
[K]. 20 *distress* Q¹; F¹: "desires." 21 *rage* frenzy. 22 *means to lead it* the
power of reason. 25–6 *Our preparation . . . them* our troops stand ready to
meet them [K]. 29 *importun'd* importunate (F¹; Q¹, K: "important").

No blown ambition doth our arms incite,   30
But love, dear love, and our ag'd father's right.
Soon may I hear and see him!
    Exeunt.

30 *blown* puffed up, swollen.

─────⌠⌡─────

SCENE 5

[GLOUCESTER'S *Castle.*]
    Enter REGAN *and* [OSWALD *the*] STEWARD.
REG. But are my brother's pow'rs set forth?
OSW.   Ay, madam.
REG. Himself in person there?
OSW.   Madam, with much ado
    Your sister is the better soldier.   5
REG. Lord Edmund spake not with your lord at home?
OSW. No, madam.
REG. What might import my sister's letter to him?
OSW. I know not, lady.
REG. Faith, he is posted hence on serious matter.   10
    It was great ignorance, Gloucester's eyes being out,
    To let him live. Where he arrives he moves
    All hearts against us. Edmund, I think, is gone,
    In pity of his misery, to dispatch
    His nighted life; moreover, to descry   15
    The strength o' th' enemy.
OSW. I must needs after him, madam, with my letter.
REG. Our troops set forth to-morrow. Stay with us.
    The ways are dangerous.
OSW.   I may not, madam.   20
    My lady charg'd my duty in this business.
REG. Why should she write to Edmund? Might not you
    Transport her purposes by word? Belike,
    Something—I know not what—I'll love thee much—
    Let me unseal the letter.   25
OSW.   Madam, I had rather—
REG. I know your lady does not love her husband;
    I am sure of that; and at her late being here
    She gave strange eliads and most speaking looks
    To noble Edmund. I know you are of her bosom.   30
OSW. I, madam?
REG. I speak in understanding. Y'are! I know't.

IV.5. 4 *much ado* great effort. Albany has been reluctant to join in the battle.
8 *might import* could signify. *my sister's letter* the letter with which Oswald
was entrusted by Goneril. Regan is justly suspicious as to its contents. See
IV.6.278ff [K]. 10 *serious matter* important business. 11 *ignorance* folly, error.
15 *nighted* blinded. 19 *ways* roads. 23 *Belike* probably. 29 *eliads* œillades,
languishing looks [K]. 30 *of her bosom* in her confidence.

Therefore I do advise you take this note.
My lord is dead; Edmund and I have talk'd,
And more convenient is he for my hand   35
Than for your lady's. You may gather more.
If you do find him, pray you give him this;
And when your mistress hears thus much from you,
I pray desire her call her wisdom to her.
So farewell.   40
If you do chance to hear of that blind traitor,
Preferment falls on him that cuts him off.
osw. Would I could meet him, madam! I should show
   What party I do follow.
REG.   Fare thee well.   45
      Exeunt.

33 *take this note* take note of this.   34 *talk'd* come to an understanding.   34
convenient fitting.   36 *gather more* draw a further inference from the hints that
I have given you [K].   37 *this* some love token—not a letter, for when Oswald
is searched by Edgar, only the letter from Goneril is found (IV.6.272*ff*) [K].
She may mean "this message" or "this information."   38 *thus much* what I have
told you.   42 *Preferment* promotion, advancement.

~~~~~~~~~~~~~~~

SCENE 6

[*The country near Dover.*]
   Enter GLOUCESTER, *and* EDGAR [*like a* PEASANT].
GLOU. When shall I come to th' top of that same hill?
EDG. You do climb up it now. Look how we labour.
GLOU. Methinks the ground is even.
EDG.   Horrible steep.
   Hark, do you hear the sea?   5
GLOU.   No, truly.
EDG. Why then, your other senses grow imperfect
   By your eyes' anguish.
GLOU.   So may it be indeed.
   Methinks thy voice is alter'd, and thou speak'st   10
   In better phrase and matter than thou didst.
EDG. Y'are much deceiv'd. In nothing am I chang'd
   But in my garments.
GLOU.   Methinks y'are better spoken.
EDG. Come on, sir; here's the place. Stand still. How fearful   15
   And dizzy 'tis to cast one's eyes so low!
   The crows and choughs that wing the midway air
   Show scarce so gross as beetles. Halfway down
   Hangs one that gathers sampire—dreadful trade!

IV.6.   8 *anguish* physical pain (not "grief").   11 *In better phrase and matter*
Shakespeare marks the change in Edgar's speech by having him speak in blank
verse.   17 *choughs* jackdaws.   18 *gross* large.   19 *sampire* samphire, an aro-
matic herb which was used in meat relishes after pickling in vinegar. It grew
on cliffs overlooking the sea and was gathered by men lowered by ropes for
the purpose.

Methincks he seems no bigger than his head.   20
The fishermen that walk upon the beach
Appear like mice; and yond tall anchoring bark,
Diminish'd to her cock; her cock, a buoy
Almost too small for sight. The murmuring surge
That on th' unnumb'red idle pebble chafes   25
Cannot be heard so high. I'll look no more,
Lest my brain turn, and the deficient sight
Topple down headlong.
GLOU.   Set me where you stand.
EDG. Give me your hand. You are now within a foot   30
Of th' extreme verge. For all beneath the moon
Would I not leap upright.
GLOU.   Let go my hand.
Here, friend, 's another purse; in it a jewel
Well worth a poor man's taking. Fairies and gods   35
Prosper it with thee! Go thou further off;
Bid me farewell, and let me hear thee going.
EDG. Now fare ye well, good sir.
GLOU.   With all my heart.
EDG. [*aside*]. Why I do trifle thus with his despair   40
Is done to cure it.
GLOU.   O you mighty gods!
   He kneels.
This world I do renounce, and, in your sights
Shake patiently my great affliction off.
If I could bear it longer and not fall   45
To quarrel with your great opposeless wills,
My snuff and loathed part of nature should
Burn itself out. If Edgar live, O, bless him!
Now, fellow, fare thee well.
   He falls [forward and swoons].
EDG.   Gone, sir, farewell.—   50

---

21 *walk* Q¹; F¹: "walk'd." 23 *Diminish'd . . . cock* reduced to the size of her cockboat—a small ship's boat. 25 *unnumb'red* innumerable. *idle* useless. *pebble* Common as a plural [K]. 27–8 *and the deficient . . . headlong* and I, my sight failing me, fall headlong [K]. 32 *leap upright* Being so near the edge of the cliff to leap upright—let alone forward—would land him in the gulf below. 35 *Fairies* There are two superstitious notions about "fairy gold." One is that it merely seems to be gold, and resumes its real nature as rubbish when the finder has stored it away. The other is that hidden treasure is guarded by fairies and that they make it multiply miraculously in the possession of the discoverer [K]. 40–1 *Why I . . . cure it* A very necessary "aside" for the enlightenment of the audience. Edgar is trying a dangerous experiment, for the agitation may be too great for Gloucester's strength; but the experiment succeeds [K]. 45–6 *fall To quarrel with* come to a state of rebellion against. Gloucester implies that such rebellion would be a greater sin than suicide [K]. 46 *opposeless* irresistible. 47 *My snuff* The snuff is the burnt piece of wick which dims the light of a lamp or candle and causes a disagreeable smoke. The meaning here is explained by the phrase that follows [K]. *loathed part of nature* the remnant of my natural life, which is hateful to me [K].

And yet I know not how conceit may rob
The treasury of life when life itself
Yields to the theft. Had he been where he thought,
By this had thought been past.—Alive or dead?
Ho you, sir! friend! Hear you, sir? Speak!—   55
Thus might he pass indeed. Yet he revives.
What are you, sir?
GLOU.   Away, and let me die.
EDG. Hadst thou been aught but gossamer, feathers, air,
   So many fathom down precipitating,   60
   Thou'dst shiver'd like an egg; but thou dost breathe;
   Hast heavy substance; bleed'st not; speak'st; art sound.
   Ten masts at each make not the altitude
   Which thou hast perpendicularly fell.
   Thy life's a miracle. Speak yet again.   65
GLOU. But have I fall'n, or no?
EDG. From the dread summit of this chalky bourn.
   Look up a-height. The shrill-gorg'd lark so far
   Cannot be seen or heard. Do but look up.
GLOU. Alack, I have no eyes!   70
   Is wretchedness depriv'd that benefit
   To end itself by death? 'Twas yet some comfort
   When misery could beguile the tyrant's rage
   And frustrate his proud will.
EDG.   Give me your arm.   75
   Up—so. How is't? Feel you your legs? You stand.
GLOU. Too well, too well.
EDG.   This is above all strangeness.
   Upon the crown o' th' cliff what thing was that
   Which parted from you?   80
GLOU.   A poor unfortunate beggar.
EDG. As I stood here below, methought his eyes
   Were two full moons; he had a thousand noses,
   Horns whelk'd and wav'd like the enridged sea.
   It was some fiend. Therefore, thou happy father,   85
   Think that the clearest gods, who make them honours
   Of men's impossibilities, have preserv'd thee.

51-3 *how conceit . . . theft* how powerful imagination may be in rifling life's treasury of all its stores (i.e. of vitality) when life itself does not resist such robbery [K]. 55 *Ho you, sir* Edgar now plays the part of a man who, walking on the beach below, has seen Gloucester fall from the cliff [K]. 56 *pass* pass away, die. 59 *gossamer* a floating thread of a spider's web. 60 *precipitating* falling headlong. 63 *at each* one on top of another. 64 *fell* fallen. 67 *summit* ROWE; F¹: "Somnet"; Q¹: "sommons". *bourn* boundary. 68 *a-height* on high. *shrill-gorg'd* shrill-throated, shrill-voiced. 73 *beguile* deceive, cheat, elude —i.e. by suicide [K]. 84 *whelk'd and wav'd* rising on the surface into wavelike ridges [K]. *enridged* Q¹; F¹: "enraged." Edgar is not thinking of huge billows but of the normal appearance of the surface of the ocean [K]. 85 *happy father* fortunate old man. Edgar is not revealing his identity. 86 *clearest* most glorious, most pure. 86-7 *who make . . . impossibilities* who win honour by helping men who cannot help themselves [K].

GLOU. I do remember now. Henceforth I'll bear
Affliction till it do cry out itself
"Enough, enough," and die. That thing you speak of, 90
I took it for a man. Often 'twould say
"The fiend, the fiend"—he led me to that place.

EDG. Bear free and patient thoughts.

Enter LEAR, *mad, [fantastically dressed with weeds].*

But who comes here?
The safer sense will ne'er accommodate 95
His master thus.

LEAR. No, they cannot touch me for coining; I am the King himself.

EDG. O thou side-piercing sight!

LEAR. Nature's above art in that respect. There's your press money.
That fellow handles his bow like a crow-keeper. Draw me a clothier's 100
yard. Look, look, a mouse! Peace, peace; this piece of toasted cheese
will do't. There's my gauntlet; I'll prove it on a giant. Bring up the
brown bills. O, well flown, bird! i' th' clout, i' th' clout! Hewgh!
Give the word.

EDG. Sweet marjoram. 105

LEAR. Pass.

GLOU. I know that voice.

LEAR. Ha! Goneril with a white beard? They flatter'd me like a dog,
and told me I had the white hairs in my beard ere the black ones
were there. To say "ay" and "no" to everything I said! "Ay" and 110
"no" too was no good divinity. When the rain came to wet me once,
and the wind to make me chatter; when the thunder would not
peace at my bidding; there I found 'em, there I smelt 'em out. Go

89–90 *till it . . . and die* until it has had enough of the struggle, gives up, and dies—i.e. affliction itself will die before Gloucester does. 93 *free* free from sorrow, cheerful [K]. 95–6 *The safer sense . . . thus* a sound mind would never let its possessor dress himself up in this fashion [K]. 97–104 *No, they cannot . . . the word* Lear has wandered away from Dover (IV.3.40). In his delirium he sees constables who try to arrest him as a coiner of counterfeit money. The next moment he is a captain engaged in the enlistment of drafted men and in testing the recruits. Suddenly he catches sight of an imaginary mouse. (Compare his delirium about barking dogs in III.6.57–8.) Then he is a champion defying all opponents; then a captain once more; then a spectator at an archery contest; then, catching sight of Edgar, he becomes a sentry and challenges him: "Give the word" [K]. 97 *coining* Q¹; F¹: "crying." 99 *Nature's . . . respect* A mildly philosophical reflection: "Art is said to improve nature; but that does not hold true in the case of kingship, for a king's authority comes by nature and nothing can abrogate it" [K]. *press money* money paid to a man being recruited. 100 *like a crow-keeper* in a clumsy manner, like a farmboy used to ward off crows. 100–1 *clothier's yard* The standard English arrow was a cloth-yard in length [K]. 102 *prove it* put my cause (signified by the gauntlet) to the test of combat [K]. 103 *brown bills* halberds or pikes varnished to prevent rust. *bird* The arrow is compared to a falcon. *clout* bull's eye. 104 *word* password. 108 *Goneril . . . beard* He takes Gloucester for Goneril in disguise. *like a dog* fawningly. 109–10 *told me . . . there* when I was a beardless boy they told me that I was as wise as an old man [K]. 109 *the white* F¹; Q¹, K: "white." 111 *no good divinity* bad theology. The right doctrine is to let your "ay" mean "ay" and your "no" mean "no" (MATTHEW, V, 37; JAMES, V, 12) [K].

to, they are not men o' their words! They told me I was everything.
'Tis a lie—I am not ague proof.   115
GLOU. The trick of that voice I do well remember.
Is't not the King?
LEAR.   Ay, every inch a king!
When I do stare, see how the subject quakes.
I pardon that man's life. What was thy cause?   120
Adultery?
Thou shalt not die. Die for adultery? No.
The wren goes to't, and the small gilded fly
Does lecher in my sight.
Let copulation thrive; for Gloucester's bastard son   125
Was kinder to his father than my daughters
Got 'tween the lawful sheets.
To't, luxury, pell-mell! for I lack soldiers.
Behold yond simp'ring dame,
Whose face between her forks presageth snow,   130
That minces virtue, and does shake the head
To hear of pleasure's name.
The fitchew nor the soiled horse goes to't
With a more riotous appetite.
Down from the waist they are Centaurs,   135
Though women all above.
But to the girdle do the gods inherit,
Beneath is all the fiend's.
There's hell, there's darkness, there's the sulphurous pit; burning,
scalding, stench, consumption. Fie, fie, fie! pah, pah! Give me an   140
ounce of civet, good apothecary, to sweeten my imagination. There's
money for thee.
GLOU. O, let me kiss that hand!
LEAR. Let me wipe it first; it smells of mortality.
GLOU. O ruin'd piece of nature! This great world   145
Shall so wear out to naught. Dost thou know me?
LEAR. I remember thine eyes well enough. Dost thou squiny at me? No,
do thy worst, blind Cupid! I'll not love. Read thou this challenge;
mark but the penning of it.
GLOU. Were all thy letters suns, I could not see.   150
EDG. [aside] I would not take this from report. It is,
And my heart breaks at it.

116 *trick* peculiarity.   117 *Is't not the King* Gloucester's question recalls Lear to
the subject with which he began, that of sovereignty [K].   120 *cause* offence.
128 *luxury* lechery.   131 *minces virtue* counterfeits virtue by her mincing airs—
her pretence of delicate prudery [K].   133 *fitchew* polecat. *soiled* full-fed with
grass in the spring [K].   135 *Centaurs* wildly lustful creatures of Greek mythology, half man and half horse.   137 *inherit* possess, hold sway.   141 *to sweeten*
Q¹; F¹: "sweaten."   145 *piece of nature* masterpiece of Nature's workmanship
[K].   145–6 *This great . . . to naught* the universe (the macrocosm) will decay,
just as this individual man (the microcosm) decays.   147 *squiny* squint.   150
all thy F¹; Q¹, K: "all the." *see* F¹; Q¹, K: "see one."   151 *take* believe. *this* the
scene he is witnessing.

LEAR. Read. 155

GLOU. What, with the case of eyes?

LEAR. O, ho, are you there with me? No eyes in your head, nor no money in your purse? Your eyes are in a heavy case, your purse in a light. Yet you see how this world goes.

GLOU. I see it feelingly.

LEAR. What, art mad? A man may see how this world goes with no eyes. Look with thine ears. See how yond justice rails upon yond 160 simple thief. Hark in thine ear. Change places and, handy-dandy, which is the justice, which is the thief? Thou hast seen a farmer's dog bark at a beggar?

GLOU. Ay, sir.

LEAR. And the creature run from the cur? There thou mightst behold 165
the great image of authority: a dog's obey'd in office.
Thou rascal beadle, hold thy bloody hand!
Why dost thou lash that whore? Strip thine own back.
Thou hotly lusts to use her in that kind
For which thou whip'st her. The usurer hangs the cozener. 170
Through tatter'd clothes small vices do appear;
Robes and furr'd gowns hide all. Plate sin with gold,
And the strong lance of justice hurtless breaks;
Arm it in rags, a pygmy's straw does pierce it.
None does offend, none—I say none! I'll able 'em. 175
Take that of me, my friend, who have the power
To seal th' accuser's lips. Get thee glass eyes
And, like a scurvy politician, seem
To see the things thou dost not. Now, now, now, now!
Pull off my boots. Harder, harder! So. 180

EDG. O, matter and impertinency mix'd!
Reason in madness!

LEAR. If thou wilt weep my fortunes, take my eyes.
I know thee well enough; thy name is Gloucester.
Thou must be patient. We came crying hither; 185
Thou know'st, the first time that we smell the air

154 *the case* the mere sockets. 155 *are you there with me* is that what you are trying to tell me? 156 *in a heavy case* in a sad condition (with a pun on "case" and "heavy") [K]. 158 *feelingly* (a) keenly (b) with my sense of feeling—since I have no eyes. 159 *this world* F¹; Q¹, K: "the world." 161 *simple* ordinary, mere. *handy-dandy* take your choice. A formula used in a children's game; the child must choose which hand contains the candy or toy. 166 *image* likeness, figure. 167 *beadle* parish officer whose duty it was to whip vagabonds and whores. 169 *kind* manner. 170 *The usurer hangs the cozener* Lear implies that justices are often guilty of usury, and thus far greater criminals than the cozeners (sharpers, petty cheats) whom they sentence to be hanged [K]. 171 *small* Q¹; F¹: "great." *appear* show clearly. 172-7 *Plate . . . lips* F¹; not in Q¹. 172 *Plate sin* clothe sin with armour (THEOBALD; F¹: "Place sinnes"). 175 *able 'em* warrant them, vouch for them. 176 *Take that of me* Lear imagines that Gloucester is a criminal, and makes a gesture as if he were handing him a pardon signed and sealed [K]. 178 *scurvy* vile. 181 *matter and impertinency* good sense and incoherent talk [K].

We wawl and cry. I will preach to thee. Mark.

GLOU. Alack, alack the day!

LEAR. When we are born, we cry that we are come
    To this great stage of fools. This' a good block.   190
    It were a delicate stratagem to shoe
    A troop of horse with felt. I'll put't in proof,
    And when I have stol'n upon these son-in-laws,
    Then kill, kill, kill, kill, kill, kill!

Enter a GENTLEMAN [*with* ATTENDANTS].

GENT. O, here he is! Lay hand upon him.—Sir,   195
    Your most dear daughter—

LEAR. No rescue? What, a prisoner? I am even
    The natural fool of fortune. Use me well;
    You shall have ransom. Let me have a surgeon;
    I am cut to th' brains.   200

GENT.   You shall have anything.

LEAR. No seconds? All myself?
    Why, this would make a man a man of salt,
    To use his eyes for garden waterpots,
    Ay, and laying autumn's dust.   205

GENT.   Good sir—

LEAR. I will die bravely, like a smug bridegroom. What!
    I will be jovial. Come, come, I am a king;
    My masters, know you that?

GENT. You are a royal one, and we obey you.   210

LEAR. Then there's life in't. Come, an you get it, you shall get it by
    running. Sa, sa, sa, sa!

Exit running. [ATTENDANTS *follow.*]

GENT. A sight most pitiful in the meanest wretch,
    Past speaking of in a king! Thou hast one daughter
    Who redeems nature from the general curse   215
    Which twain have brought her to.

EDG. Hail, gentle sir.

GENT.   Sir, speed you. What's your will?

EDG. Do you hear aught, sir, of a battle toward?

---

187 *wawl and cry* Synonymous (F¹; Q¹: "wayl and cry"). 190 *a good block* a hat of good fashion. Whether Lear is wearing a hat or not in the scene has been much debated. He probably pretends to be removing his hat as one about to deliver a sermon. 191 *delicate stratagem* neat trick. 192 *in proof* to the test. 193 *son-in-laws* F¹, Q¹; K: "sons-in-law." 198 *natural fool of fortune* one born to be the plaything or dupe of fortune. There may be a quibble on "natural" in the sense of "idiot." 200 *cut to th' brains* wounded in the head. Lear uses the term literally (thinking that he has a head wound) and figuratively (since he is mad). 203 *a man of salt* That tears are salt is a fact which Shakespeare never forgets [K]. 205 *Ay . . . dust* Q¹; not in F¹. 207 *bravely* in fine attire. "Smug" repeats the idea; it means "spick and span." Lear is thinking of his floral adornments [K]. 211 *life in't* hope in the situation. *Come* F¹; Q¹, K: "Nay." 212 *Sa, sa, sa, sa* an old hunting cry to call a hound or to urge the dogs forward in chase of the hare. It was also in common use as a rallying cry, or as an interjection of challenge and defiance. Here the King challenges his pursuers: "Come on! come on! Catch me if you can!" And so he runs off the stage, waving his arm in a defiant gesture [K]. 214 *one* Q¹; F¹: "a." 215 *general* universal. 219 *toward* in preparation.

GENT. Most sure and vulgar. Every one hears that
  Which can distinguish sound.   220
EDG.   But, by your favour,
  How near's the other army?
GENT. Near and on speedy foot. The main descry
  Stands on the hourly thought.
EDG.   I thank you, sir. That's all.   225
GENT. Though that the Queen on special cause is here,
  Her army is mov'd on.
EDG.   I thank you, sir.
      Exit [GENTLEMAN].
GLOU. You ever-gentle gods, take my breath from me;
  Let not my worser spirit tempt me again   230
  To die before you please!
EDG.   Well pray you, father.
GLOU. Now, good sir, what are you?
EDG. A most poor man, made tame to fortune's blows,
  Who, by the art of known and feeling sorrows,   235
  Am pregnant to good pity. Give me your hand;
  I'll lead you to some biding.
GLOU.   Hearty thanks.
  The bounty and the benison of heaven
  To boot, and boot!   240
     Enter [OSWALD *the*] STEWARD.
OSW.   A proclaim'd prize! Most happy!
  That eyeless head of thine was first fram'd flesh
  To raise my fortunes. Thou old unhappy traitor,
  Briefly thyself remember. The sword is out
  That must destroy thee.   245
GLOU.   Now let thy friendly hand
  Put strength enough to't.
     [EDGAR *interposes*.]
OSW.   Wherefore, bold peasant,
  Dar'st thou support a publish'd traitor? Hence!
  Lest that th' infection of his fortune take   250
  Like hold on thee. Let go his arm.
EDG. Chill not let go, zir, without vurther 'cagion.
OSW. Let go, slave, or thou diest!

220 *vulgar* common knowledge. 224–5 *The main descry . . . thought* the main body of men is expected to be seen at any hour now. 231 *worser spirit* evil side of my nature. 233 *father* old man. 235 *tame* humbly submissive. 236 *by the art . . . sorrows* instructed by heart-felt sorrows I have known. 237 *pregnant to* readily susceptible to. 238 *biding* resting place, refuge. 240–1 *The bounty . . . and boot* besides giving you my thanks, I pray heaven to favour and bless you, and may that favour and blessing be your reward [K]. 242 *proclaim'd prize* fugitive with a price on his head. *happy* opportune. 245 *Briefly thyself remember* think of your sins quickly (so as to reconcile yourself to heaven before death). 247 *friendly* since I long for death [K]. 250 *publish'd* proclaimed. 253 *Chill . . . vurther 'cagion* Edgar assumes the lingo that, from Elizabethan time to the end of the eighteenth century, served as the stage dialect of rusticity. It accords well enough with the dialect of Somersetshire, but the dramatists were not finical [K]. *Chill* I will. *vurther 'cagion* further occasion.

EDG. Good gentleman, go your gait, and let poor voke pass. An chud   255
  ha' bin zwagger'd out of my life, 'twould not ha' bin zo long as 'tis
  by a vortnight. Nay, come not near th' old man. Keep out, che
  vore ye, or Ise try whether your costard or my ballow be the
  harder. Chill be plain with you.
OSW. Out, dunghill!   260
        They fight.
EDG. Chill pick your teeth, zir. Come! No matter vor your foins.
        [OSWALD *falls.*]
OSW. Slave, thou hast slain me. Villain, take my purse.
  If ever thou wilt thrive, bury my body,
  And give the letters which thou find'st about me
  To Edmund Earl of Gloucester. Seek him out   265
  Upon the British party. O, untimely death! Death!
        He dies.
EDG. I know thee well. A serviceable villain,
  As duteous to the vices of thy mistress
  As badness would desire.
GLOU.   What, is he dead?   270
EDG. Sit you down, father; rest you.
  Let's see his pockets; the letters that he speaks of
  May be my friends. He's dead. I am only sorry
  He had no other deathsman. Let us see.
  Leave, gentle wax; and, manners, blame us not.   275
  To know our enemies' minds, we rip their hearts;
  Their papers, is more lawful.
        Reads the letter.
  "Let our reciprocal vows be rememb'red. You have many oppor-
  tunities to cut him off. If your will want not, time and place will
  be fruitfully offer'd. There is nothing done, if he return the con-   280
  queror. Then am I the prisoner, and his bed my jail; from the
  loathed warmth whereof deliver me, and supply the place for
  your labour.
  "Your (wife, so I would say) affectionate servant,
                              "GONERIL."   285
  O indistinguish'd space of woman's will!
  A plot upon her virtuous husband's life,
  And the exchange my brother! Here in the sands
  Thee I'll rake up, the post unsanctified
  Of murderous lechers; and in the mature time   290

---

255 *gait* way. *voke* folk. *chud* I would. 257–8 *che vore ye* I warn you.
258 *Ise* I shall. *costard* head. *ballow* cudgel. 261 *foins* sword thrusts. 262
Villain serf. 264 *letters* Oswald was carrying a letter to Edmund from Goneril
(IV.2.20–21; IV.58.25). "Letters" is common in the sense of "letter" (Latin
"litterae" [K]. 266 *British* Q¹; F¹: "English." *party* side. 272 *the letters* F¹;
Q¹, K: "these letters." 274 *deathsman* executioner. 276 *we rip* F¹; Q¹: "wee'd
rip"; K: "we'ld rip." 286 *indistinguish'd space* limitless range. *will* lust. 289
rake up bury hastily and without ceremony [K]. *post* messenger. 290 *in the
mature time* when time is ripe.

With this ungracious paper strike the sight
Of the death-practis'd Duke. For him 'tis well
That of thy death and business I can tell.
GLOU. The King is mad. How stiff is my vile sense,   295
That I stand up, and have ingenious feeling
Of my huge sorrows! Better I were distract.
So should my thoughts be sever'd from my griefs,
And woes by wrong imaginations lose
The knowledge of themselves.
    A drum afar off.
                           Give me your hand.   300
EDG.
    Far off methinks I hear the beaten drum.
    Come, father, I'll bestow you with a friend.
    Exeunt.

291 *ungracious* abominable. 292 *death-practis'd Duke* Duke whose death is plotted. 295 *ingenious feeling* acute mental consciousness [K]. 296 *distract* insane. 298 *wrong imaginations* illusions. 302 *bestow you* provide a refuge for you.

SCENE 7

    [*A tent in the French camp.*]
    Enter CORDELIA, KENT, DOCTOR, *and* GENTLEMAN.
COR. O thou good Kent, how shall I live and work
    To match thy goodness? My life will be too short
    And every measure fail me.
KENT. To be acknowledg'd, madam, is o'erpaid.   5
    All my reports go with the modest truth;
    Nor, more nor clipp'd, but so.
COR.   Be better suited.
    These weeds are memories of those worser hours.
    I prithee put them off.
KENT.   Pardon, dear madam.   10
    Yet to be known shortens my made intent.
    My boon I make it that you know me not
    Till time and I think meet.
COR. Then be't so, my good lord. [*To the* DOCTOR] How does the King?
DOCT. Madam, sleeps still.   15
COR. O you kind gods,
    Cure this great breach in his abused nature!
    Th' untun'd and jarring senses, O, wind up

IV.7. 3 *every measure fail me* since thy goodness is unmeasurable. 5 *All my reports . . . truth* everything that I have told you (about the King and his sufferings) corresponds exactly with a moderate expression of the facts [K]. 7 *suited* clothed. Kent is still disguised as a servingman [K]. 8 *weeds* clothes. *memories* reminders. 11 *shortens my made intent* interferes with (shortens) the plan I have made. 12 *My boon I make it* I ask it of you as a special favour [K]. 13 *meet* proper. 18 *wind up* put into proper tune—as the strings of a musical instrument are tightened.

Of this child-changed father!

DOCT.   So please your Majesty   20
That we may wake the King? He hath slept long.

COR. Be govern'd by your knowledge, and proceed
I' th' sway of your own will. Is he array'd?
    Enter LEAR *in a chair carried by* SERVANTS.

GENT. Ay, madam. In the heaviness of sleep
We put fresh garments on him.   25

DOCT. Be by, good madam, when we do awake him.
I doubt not of his temperance.

COR.   Very well.
    [*Music.*]

DOCT. Please you draw near. Louder the music there!

COR. O my dear father, restoration hang   30
Thy medicine on my lips, and let this kiss
Repair those violent harms that my two sisters
Have in thy reverence made!

KENT.   Kind and dear princess!

COR. Had you not been their father, these white flakes   35
Had challeng'd pity of them. Was this a face
To be oppos'd against the warring winds?
To stand against the deep dread-bolted thunder?
In the most terrible and nimble stroke
Of quick cross lightning? to watch—poor perdu!—   40
With this thin helm? Mine enemy's dog,
Though he had bit me, should have stood that night
Against my fire; and wast thou fain, poor father,
To hovel thee with swine and rogues forlorn,
In short and musty straw? Alack, alack!   45
'Tis wonder that thy life and wits at once
Had not concluded all.—He wakes. Speak to him.

DOCT. Madam, do you; 'tis fittest.

COR. How does my royal lord? How fares your Majesty?

LEAR. You do me wrong to take me out o' th' grave.   50
Thou art a soul in bliss; but I am bound
Upon a wheel of fire, that mine own tears
Do scald like molten lead.

19 *child-changed* The meaning may be deliberately ambiguous: (a) changed into a child (b) changed—made mad—by his children. 23 *I' th' sway of* governed by. *array'd* dressed (in his royal robes). 27 *doubt not* Q¹; F¹: "doubt." *temperance* normal self-control [K]. 28–9 *Very well . . . there* Q¹; not in F¹. 29 *the music* The beneficial effect of music in the treatment of madness is an ancient theory. [K]. 33 *in thy reverence* in thee, to whom all reverence is due [K]. 35 *white flakes* Lear's white hair hangs down in long straight strands [K]. 37 *warring* Q¹; F¹: "iarring." 38–41 *To stand . . . helm* Q¹; not in F¹. 38 *dread-bolted* with its terrible thunderbolts. 40 *cross* zigzag. *perdu* a solitary sentinel keeping watch far away from the main body and therefore in a very dangerous position [K]. 41 *this thin helm* his scanty locks [K]. 43 *fain* glad. 44 *rogues* vagabonds. 45 *short and musty straw* Long, clean straw would make a good bed. The straw in the hovel was damp and musty and had been broken up into short lengths by constant use as bedding [K]. 47 *concluded all* come to a complete end [K].

COR.   Sir, do you know me?
LEAR. You are a spirit, I know. When did you die?   55
COR. Still, still, far wide!
DOCT. He's scarce awake. Let him alone awhile.
LEAR. Where have I been? Where am I? Fair daylight?
  I am mightily abus'd. I should e'en die with pity,
  To see another thus. I know not what to say.   60
  I will not swear these are my hands. Let's see.
  I feel this pin prick. Would I were assur'd
  Of my condition!
COR.   O, look upon me, sir,
  And hold your hands in benediction o'er me.   65
  No, sir, you must not kneel.
LEAR.   Pray, do not mock me.
  I am a very foolish fond old man,
  Fourscore and upward, not an hour more nor less;
  And, to deal plainly,   70
  I fear I am not in my perfect mind.
  Methinks I should know you, and know this man;
  Yet I am doubtful; for I am mainly ignorant
  What place this is; and all the skill I have
  Remembers not these garments; nor I know not   75
  Where I did lodge last night. Do not laugh at me;
  For (as I am a man) I think this lady
  To be my child Cordelia.
COR.   And so I am! I am!
LEAR. Be your tears wet? Yes, faith. I pray weep not.   80
  If you have poison for me, I will drink it.
  I know you do not love me; for your sisters
  Have, as I do remember, done me wrong.
  You have some cause, they have not.
COR.   No cause, no cause.   85
LEAR. Am I in France?
KENT.   In your own kingdom, sir.
LEAR. Do not abuse me.
DOCT. Be comforted, good madam. The great rage
  You see is kill'd in him; and yet it is danger   90
  To make him even o'er the time he has lost.
  Desire him to go in. Trouble him no more

55 *When* Q²; F¹, Q¹: "Where." This reading has been much debated. 56 *wide*
wide of the mark, distracted [K].   57 *scarce awake* We should observe that Lear
is no longer delirious. He merely needs a few minutes to adjust himself to the
present situation, for he has no memory of what has happened in the interval.
His confusion is well understood by the Doctor [K]. 59 *abus'd* deceived, deluded.
Lear cannot trust the evidence of his senses [K].   66 *No, sir* Q¹; not in F¹.   68
fond doting. 69 *not . . . less* F¹; not in Q¹.   73 *mainly* very, absolutely.   74
skill power of mind [K].   80 *Be your tears wet* Lear still fears that he is suffering
from a delusion [K].   88 *abuse* deceive.   89 *great rage* violent delirium.   90-1
and yet . . . has lost Q¹; not in F¹.   91 *even o'er* fill up the gap in. The metaphor
may be drawn from the language of commercial bookkeeping. To "even over"
means to make accounts even.

Till further settling.

COR. Will't please your Highness walk?

LEAR.   You must bear with me.
  Pray you now, forget and forgive. I am old and foolish.   95
      Exeunt all but KENT *and* GENTLEMAN.

GENT. Holds it true, sir, that the Duke of Cornwall was so slain?

KENT. Most certain, sir.

GENT. Who is conductor of his people?

KENT. As 'tis said, the bastard son of Gloucester.

GENT. They say Edgar, his banish'd son, is with the Earl of Kent in   100
  Germany.

KENT. Report is changeable. 'Tis time to look about; the powers of
  the kingdom approach apace.

GENT. The arbitrement is like to be bloody. Fare you well, sir.
  [*Exit.*]   105

KENT. My point and period will be throughly wrought,
  Or well or ill, as this day's battle 's fought.
      Exit.

93 *Till further settling* until he was grown calmer. 94 *walk* withdraw. 97–107 *Holds . . . fought* Q¹; not in F¹. 99 *conductor* leader, general. 103 *powers* armies. 105 *arbitrement* decision. *like* likely. 106–7 *My point . . . fought* the completion of my lot in life will be worked out, for good or ill, according as this battle results in victory or defeat [K]. 106 *throughly* thoroughly, completely.

ACT FIVE

SCENE 1

[*The British camp near Dover.*]
Enter, with Drum and Colours, EDMUND, REGAN, GENTLEMEN,
and SOLDIERS.

EDM. Know of the Duke if his last purpose hold,
  Or whether since he is advis'd by aught
  To change the course. He's full of alteration
  And self-reproving. Bring his constant pleasure.
    [*Exit an* OFFICER.]

REG. Our sister's man is certainly miscarried.   5

EDM. 'Tis to be doubted, madam.

REG.   Now, sweet lord,
  You know the goodness I intend upon you.
  Tell me—but truly—but then speak the truth—
  Do you not love my sister?   10

V.1. 1 *his last purpose* i.e. to join us in the battle against Cordelia's forces [K]. 2 *advis'd by aught* instructed by (induced by consideration of) anything [K]. 3 *alteration* vacillation. 4 *self-reproving* self-reproach. *constant pleasure* firm decision. 5 *sister's man* i.e. Oswald. *miscarried* come to harm. 6 *doubted* feared. 8 *intend upon you* mean to bestow upon you.

EDM.   In honour'd love.

REG. But have you never found my brother's way
  To the forfended place?

EDM.   That thought abuses you.

REG. I am doubtful that you have been conjunct   15
  And bosom'd with her, as far as we call hers.

EDM. No, by mine honour, madam.

REG. I never shall endure her. Dear my lord,
  Be not familiar with her.

EDM.   Fear me not.   20
  She and the Duke her husband!
    Enter, with Drum and Colours, ALBANY, GONERIL, SOLDIERS.

GON. [*aside*] I had rather lose the battle than that sister
  Should loosen him and me.

ALB. Our very loving sister, well bemet.
  Sir, this I hear: the King is come to his daughter,   25
  With others whom the rigour of our state
  Forc'd to cry out. Where I could not be honest,
  I never yet was valiant. For this business,
  It touches us as France invades our land,
  Not bolds the King, with others whom, I fear,   30
  Most just and heavy causes make oppose.

EDM. Sir, you speak nobly.

REG.   Why is this reason'd?

GON. Combine together 'gainst the enemy;
  For these domestic and particular broils   35
  Are not the question here.

ALB.   Let's then determine
  With th' ancient of war on our proceeding.

EDM. I shall attend you presently at your tent.

REG. Sister, you'll go with us?   40

GON. No.

REG. 'Tis most convenient. Pray go with us.

GON. [*aside*] O, ho, I know the riddle.—I will go.
    [*As they are going out,*] *enter* EDGAR [*disguised*].

11 *honour'd* honourable. 13 *forfended* forbidden. 14–16 *That thought . . . call hers* Q¹; *not in* F¹. 14 *abuses* deceives. 15 *am doubtful* suspect. *conjunct* united. 16 *bosom'd* intimate (breast to breast). *as far . . . hers* in the fullest sense of the word; in respect to all that she has and is [K]. 20 *Fear me not* don't distrust me. 22–3 *I had . . . me* Q¹; not in F¹. 25 *hear* Q¹; F¹: "heard." 26 *state* government. 27 *cry out* protest. 27–32 *Where I . . . speak nobly* Q¹; not in F¹. 27 *be honest* be honourable; act with a good conscience [K]. 29 *touches* concerns (Q¹; Q², K: "toucheth"). 29–31 *as France . . . make oppose* insofar as the French king is invading Britain, but not insofar as he is supporting King Lear and others who (as I fear) have just cause to oppose us. Albany implies that the government of Britain has been tyrannical of late [K]. 33 *reason'd* being argued. 35 *domestic and particular* family and personal [K]. 38 *th' ancient of war* our veteran officers, who are men of experience [K]. 39 *I shall . . . tent* Q¹; not in F¹. *presently* immediately. 42 *convenient* proper. *Pray go* F¹; Q¹, K: "Pray you go." 43 *I know the riddle* I understand her hidden meaning; she is afraid to leave Edmund and me together [K].

EDG. If e'er your Grace had speech with man so poor,
   Hear me one word. 45
ALB.   I'll overtake you.—Speak.
     Exeunt [all but ALBANY *and* EDGAR*].*
EDG. Before you fight the battle, ope this letter.
   If you have victory, let the trumpet sound
   For him that brought it. Wretched though I seem,
   I can produce a champion that will prove 50
   What is avouched there. If you miscarry,
   Your business of the world that so an end,
   And machination ceases. Fortune love you!
ALB. Stay till I have read the letter.
EDG.   I was forbid it. 55
   When time shall serve, let but the herald cry,
   And I'll appear again.
ALB. Why, fare thee well. I will o'erlook thy paper.
     *Exit [*EDGAR*].*
     Enter EDMUND.
EDM. The enemy 's in view; draw up your powers.
   Here is the guess of their true strength and forces 60
   By diligent discovery; but your haste
   Is now urg'd on you.
ALB.   We will greet the time.
     Exit.
EDM. To both these sisters have I sworn my love;
   Each jealous of the other, as the stung 65
   Are of the adder. Which of them shall I take?
   Both? one? or neither? Neither can be enjoy'd,
   If both remain alive. To take the widow
   Exasperates, makes mad her sister Goneril;
   And hardly shall I carry out my side, 70
   Her husband being alive. Now then, we'll use
   His countenance for the battle, which being done,
   Let her who would be rid of him devise
   His speedy taking off. As for the mercy
   Which he intends to Lear and to Cordelia— 75
   The battle done, and they within our power,
   Shall never see his pardon; for my state
   Stands on me to defend, not to debate.
     Exit.

49 *For him to* summon him. 51 *avouched* asserted. *miscarry* are defeated in battle. 53 *And . . . ceases* F¹; not in Q¹. *machination* plotting (against your life). 58 *o'erlook* read over. 59 *powers* troops. 61 *diligent discovery* careful reconnoitering. 61–2 *your haste . . . on you* rapid action on your part is urgently necessary [K]. 63 *greet the time* meet the demands of the emergency promptly. 65 *jealous* suspicious. 70 *carry out my side* bring my plans to a successful issue. Edmund aspires to the kingship [K]. 72 *countenance* authority and support. 77–8 *my state . . . debate* the condition of my affairs is such that it is incumbent on me to protect myself by action; it leaves me no time to consider rights and wrongs [K].

SCENE 2

[*A field between the two camps.*]
Alarum within. Enter, with Drum and Colours, the POWERS OF
FRANCE *over the stage,* CORDELIA *with her* FATHER *in her hand,
and exeunt.*
Enter EDGAR *and* GLOUCESTER.

EDG. Here, father, take the shadow of this tree
　For your good host. Pray that the right may thrive.
　If ever I return to you again,
　I'll bring you comfort.
GLOU. 　　　　　　　Grace go with you, sir!　　　　5
　　Exit [EDGAR].
　Alarum and retreat within. Enter EDGAR.
EDG. Away, old man! give me thy hand! away!
　King Lear hath lost, he and his daughter ta'en.
　Give me thy hand! come on!
GLOU. No further, sir. A man may rot even here.
EDG. What, in ill thoughts again? Men must endure　　10
　Their going hence, even as their coming hither;
　Ripeness is all. Come on.
GLOU. 　　　　　　　And that's true too.
　　Exeunt.

V.2. 2 *good host* shelterer. 5 *Grace* the favour of the gods [K]. 10 *ill
thoughts* thoughts of suicide. *endure* suffer through. 11 *going hence* death.
coming hither birth. 12 *Ripeness is all* the only thing that is important in life
is to be ready for death when it comes [K]. 13 *And . . . too* F¹; not in Q¹.

SCENE 3

[*The British camp, near Dover.*]
Enter, in conquest, with Drum and Colours, EDMUND; LEAR *and*
CORDELIA *as prisoners;* SOLDIERS, CAPTAIN.

EDM. Some officers take them away. Good guard
　Until their greater pleasures first be known
　That are to censure them.
COR. 　　　　　　　We are not the first
　Who with best meaning have incurr'd the worst.　　5
　For thee, oppressed king, am I cast down;
　Myself could else outfrown false Fortune's frown.
　Shall we not see these daughters and these sisters?
LEAR. No, no, no, no! Come, let's away to prison.
　We two alone will sing like birds i' th' cage.　　10
　When thou dost ask me blessing, I'll kneel down
　And ask of thee forgiveness. So we'll live,
　And pray, and sing, and tell old tales, and laugh

V.3. 2 *their greater pleasures* the wishes of those persons of higher rank [K]. 3
censure pass judgment on. 5 *meaning* intentions.

At gilded butterflies, and hear poor rogues
Talk of court news; and we'll talk with them too—   15
Who loses and who wins; who's in, who's out—
And take upon 's the mystery of things,
As if we were God's spies; and we'll wear out,
In a wall'd prison, packs and sects of great ones
That ebb and flow by th' moon.   20
EDM.   Take them away.
LEAR. Upon such sacrifices, my Cordelia,
The gods themselves throw incense. Have I caught thee?
He that parts us shall bring a brand from heaven
And fire us hence like foxes. Wipe thine eyes.   25
The goodyears shall devour 'em, flesh and fell,
Ere they shall make us weep! We'll see 'em starv'd first.
Come.
     Exeunt [LEAR *and* CORDELIA, *guarded*].
EDM.   Come hither, Captain; hark.
Take thou this note [*gives a paper*]. Go follow them to prison.   30
One step I have advanc'd thee. If thou dost
As this instructs thee, thou dost make thy way
To noble fortunes. Know thou this, that men
Are as the time is. To be tender-minded
Does not become a sword. Thy great employment   35
Will not bear question. Either say thou'lt do't,
Or thrive by other means.
CAPT.   I'll do't, my lord.
EDM. About it! and write happy when th' hast done.
Mark—I say, instantly; and carry it so   40
As I have set it down.
CAPT. I cannot draw a cart, nor eat dried oats;
If it be man's work, I'll do't.
     Exit.
     Flourish. Enter ALBANY, GONERIL, REGAN, SOLDIERS.

14 *gilded butterflies* A common expression for gay, elaborately dressed courtiers.
17 *take upon 's the mystery of things* assume (in our talk) that we can explain
all the mysteries of human affairs [K].   18 *As if we were God's spies* as if we
had been commissioned by God, as his angels, to survey the doings of mankind.
19 *packs* conniving cliques. *sects* parties, sets.   20 *ebb and flow by th' moon*
gain and lose by the month, as the moon changes.   22–3 *Upon such . . . incense* upon such sacrifices as thou hast made for my sake the gods themselves
attend [K].   24 *He . . . heaven* no human shall ever part us again [K].   25 *fire
. . . foxes* as foxes are driven from their holes by fire and smoke [K].   26 *goodyears* evil forces, pestilence, or plague. The origin of the expression is uncertain,
but it seems generally to have been used in this sense. *fell* skin.   30 *this note*
This is Edmund's writ ordering the death of Lear and Cordelia. See lines 282–96.
He has special authority as Regan's commissioned substitute in the campaign
(lines 70–1) [K].   33–4 *men . . . time is* i.e., they may be merciful in time of
peace but must be savage in war [K].   35 *become* befit.   36 *bear question* admit
discussion.   39 *write happy* call yourself fortunate.   40 *carry it so* manage the
affair in such a way.   42–3 *I cannot . . . I'll do't* A bit of rough humour based
on the proverbial contrast between a man and a horse (thought of as a stupid
animal and a beast of burden) [K] (Q¹; not in F¹).

ALB. Sir, you have show'd to-day your valiant strain,
And fortune led you well. You have the captives   45
Who were the opposites of this day's strife.
I do require them of you, so to use them
As we shall find their merits and our safety
May equally determine.
EDM.   Sir, I thought it fit   50
To send the old and miserable King
To some retention and appointed guard;
Whose age had charms in it, whose title more,
To pluck the common bosom on his side
And turn our impress'd lances in our eyes   55
Which do command them. With him I sent the Queen,
My reason all the same; and they are ready
To-morrow, or at further space, t' appear
Where you shall hold your session. At this time
We sweat and bleed: the friend hath lost his friend;   60
And the best quarrels, in the heat, are curs'd
By those that feel their sharpness.
The question of Cordelia and her father
Requires a fitter place.
ALB.   Sir, by your patience,   65
I hold you but a subject of this war,
Not as a brother.
REG.   That's as we list to grace him.
Methinks our pleasure might have been demanded
Ere you had spoke so far. He led our powers,   70
Bore the commission of my place and person,
The which immediacy may well stand up
And call itself your brother.
GON.   Not so hot!
In his own grace he doth exalt himself   75
More than in your addition.
REG.   In my rights
By me invested, he compeers the best.
GON. That were the most if he should husband you.

44 *strain* lineage. Albany implies that Edmund has shown himself worthy of being
a legitimate son of Gloucester [K]. 46 *opposites* opponents, enemies. 47 *I do*
F¹; Q¹, K: "We do." 48 *merits* deserts. 52 *To some . . . guard* to a place
where they could be held in custody by guards designated for that purpose [K].
53 *had* F¹; Q¹, K: "has." 54 *To pluck . . . side* to attract strongly the feelings
of the rank and file of men to take his part [K]. 55 *impress'd* enlisted by con-
scription. 56 *Which* who. 59–64 *At this . . . place* Q¹; not in F¹. 61 *quarrels*
causes. 64 *Requires a fitter place* requires for its settlement a fitter place than
the camp [K]. 65 *by your patience* if you will not be offended by my frankness.
A phrase of courteous apology [K]. 68 *list* choose. *grace* honour 69 *pleasure*
wishes. *demanded* asked. 71 *Bore . . . and person* had the authority belonging to my rank and represented me personally [K]. 72 *The which immediacy* and
the fact that he was thus my immediate representative, clothed with all my
authority [K]. 75 *grace* merit and honour. 76 *addition* titles bestowed upon
him. 78 *compeers* equals. 79 *were the most* would be the fullest (investiture
in your rights).

REG. Jesters do oft prove prophets.   80
GON.   Holla, holla!
   That eye that told you so look'd but asquint.
REG. Lady, I am not well; else I should answer
   From a full-flowing stomach. General,
   Take thou my soldiers, prisoners, patrimony;   85
   Dispose of them, of me; the walls are thine.
   Witness the world that I create thee here
   My lord and master.
GON.   Mean you to enjoy him?
ALB. The let-alone lies not in your good will.   90
EDM. Nor in thine, lord.
ALB.   Half-blooded fellow, yes.
REG. [to EDMUND] Let the drum strike, and prove my title thine.
ALB. Stay yet; hear reason. Edmund, I arrest thee
   On capital treason; and, in thine attaint,   95
   This gilded serpent [points to GONERIL]. For your claim, fair sister,
   I bar it in the interest of my wife.
   'Tis she is subcontracted to this lord,
   And I, her husband, contradict your banes.
   If you will marry, make your loves to me;   100
   My lady is bespoke.
GON.   An interlude!
ALB. Thou art arm'd, Gloucester. Let the trumpet sound.
   If none appear to prove upon thy person
   Thy heinous, manifest, and many treasons,   105
   There is my pledge [throws down a glove]! I'll make it on thy heart,
   Ere I taste bread, thou art in nothing less
   Than I have here proclaim'd thee.
REG.   Sick, O, sick!
GON. [aside] If not, I'll ne'er trust medicine.   110

82 *look'd but asquint* did not see straight. 84 *full-flowing stomach* a full tide
of angry resentment. "Stomach" for "wrath" is common [K]. 86 *Dispose . . .*
thine F¹; not in Q¹. *are* F²; F¹ "is." *walls are thine* you have won the walls;
you have taken my defences by storm. The metaphor by which a woman or a
woman's heart is identified with a castle or walled town defending itself against
besiegers was common in the Middle Ages and had become conventional long
before Shakespeare's time [K]. 89 *enjoy* possess. 90 *let-alone* prohibition.
92 *Half-blooded fellow* bastard. 95 *in thine attaint* as a sharer in the treason of
which you are guilty. Treason was a crime that "corrupted the blood" of the
traitor –i.e. deprived his kindred of their civil rights [K] (Q¹; F¹: "in thy arrest").
97 *bar* ROWE; F¹, Q¹: "bare." 98 *subcontracted* bound by a contract which
depends for its validity on the fulfillment or abrogation of a previous contract
[K]. Albany, of course, is being sarcastic. 99 *banes* banns, announcements of
intention to marry. 100 *loves* courtship. 101 *bespoke* betrothed. 102 *interlude*
farce. An "interlude" was a brief play, usually comical—so called from its
coming in an interval of festivities. Goneril's contempt for her husband's irony
seems well deserved [K]. 103 *Thou art arm'd* Edmund still wears the armour
he wore in the battle [K]. *Let . . . sound* Albany is acting in accordance with
the instructions that he has received from Edgar in the letter mentioned in
V.1.47 [K]. 106 *make it* demonstrate it to be true (F¹; Q¹, K: "proue it"). 107
in nothing in no one detail. 110 *medicine* Goneril has poisoned her sister [K].

EDM. There's my exchange [*throws down a glove*]. What in the world
    he is
  That names me traitor, villain-like he lies.
  Call by thy trumpet. He that dares approach,
  On him, on you, who not? I will maintain   115
  My truth and honour firmly.
ALB. A herald, ho!
EDM.   A herald, ho, a herald!
ALB. Trust to thy single virtue; for thy soldiers,
  All levied in my name, have in my name   120
  Took their discharge.
REG.   My sickness grows upon me.
ALB. She is not well. Convey her to my tent.
    [*Exit* REGAN, *led.*]
    Enter a HERALD.
  Come hither, herald. Let the trumpet sound,
  And read out this.   125
CAPT. Sound, trumpet!
    A trumpet sounds.
HER. [*reads*] "If any man of quality or degree within the lists of the
  army will maintain upon Edmund, supposed Earl of Gloucester,
  that he is a manifold traitor, let him appear by the third sound of
  the trumpet. He is bold in his defence."   130
EDM. Sound!
    First trumpet.
HER. Again!
    Second trumpet.
HER. Again!
    Third trumpet.
    Trumpet answers within.
    Enter EDGAR, *armed, at the third sound, a* TRUMPET *before him.*
ALB. Ask him his purposes, why he appears
  Upon this call o' th' trumpet.   135
HER.   What are you?
  Your name, your quality? and why you answer
  This present summons?
EDG.   Know my name is lost;
  By treason's tooth bare-gnawn and canker-bit.   140
  Yet am I noble as the adversary
  I come to cope.
ALB.   Which is that adversary?
EDG. What's he that speaks for Edmund Earl of Gloucester?
EDM. Himself. What say'st thou to him?   145

---

111 *What* whoever and of whatever rank. 117 *A herald, ho, a herald* Q¹; not in
F¹. 119 *single virtue* unaided ability. 122 *grows upon* begins to overpower.
126 *Sound, trumpet* Q¹; not in F¹. 127 *quality or degree* rank or high position.
lists limits. 140 *canker-bit* eaten away by the canker—a caterpillar that feeds
on rosebuds, destroying them before they open. 142 *cope* cope with, meet in
combat.

EDG.   Draw thy sword,
    That, if my speech offend a noble heart,
    Thy arm may do thee justice. Here is mine.
    Behold, it is the privilege of mine honours,
    My oath, and my profession. I protest—   150
    Maugre thy strength, youth, place, and eminence,
    Despite thy victor sword and fire-new fortune,
    Thy valour and thy heart—thou art a traitor;
    False to thy gods, thy brother, and thy father;
    Conspirant 'gainst this high illustrious prince;   155
    And from th' extremest upward of thy head
    To the descent and dust below thy foot,
    A most toad-spotted traitor. Say thou "no,"
    This sword, this arm, and my best spirits are bent
    To prove upon thy heart, whereto I speak,   160
    Thou liest.
EDM.   In wisdom I should ask thy name;
    But since thy outside looks so fair and warlike,
    And that thy tongue some say of breeding breathes,
    What safe and nicely I might well delay   165
    By rule of knighthood, I disdain and spurn.
    Back do I toss those treasons to thy head;
    With the hell-hated lie o'erwhelm thy heart;
    Which—for they yet glance by and scarcely bruise—
    This sword of mine shall give them instant way   170
    Where they shall rest for ever. Trumpets, speak!
        Alarums. Fight. [EDMUND *falls.*]
ALB. Save him, save him!

---

148 *arm* sword.   149 *the privilege of mine honours* Edgar means that, being a
knight, he has the privilege of his knighthood—namely, to challenge to single
combat anyone whom he has reason to accuse of an offence against knightly
honour. Treason is the most flagrant of such offences [K] (POPE; F¹: "my
priuiledge. The priuiledge of mine Honours"; Q¹: "the priuiledge of my tongue").
150 *My oath* the oath I swore when I was dubbed knight [K]. *profession* function—as knight.   151 *Maugre* in spite of.   152 *victor* victorious (in the recent
battle).   *fire-new* brand-new—just finished on the smith's forge. Edgar refers to
Edmund's recent elevation to the rank of Earl of Gloucester [K].   153 *heart*
courage.   155 *Conspirant* engaged in a conspiracy.   157 *To the descent . . .
foot* to the sole of thy foot and the dust beneath it [K].   *below* F¹; Q¹, K:
"beneath."   158 *toad-spotted* spotted with treason as the toad is marked with
spots that exude venom [K].   159 *bent* directed.   160 *whereto I speak* Edgar's
accusation comes from the heart and is addressed to the heart and conscience of
Edmund [K].   162 *wisdom* prudence. He is not bound by his knighthood to fight
with a man of lower social rank.   164 *some say of breeding breathes* shows some
touch (say) of a gentleman's education [K].   165 *What safe . . . delay* F¹; not in
Q¹.   165–6 *What safe . . . spurn* I scorn to delay the combat, as I might delay it,
in accordance with the code of chivalry, if I cared to insist on the strict rules of
the code [K].   165 *safe* without infringing upon the rules.   *nicely* punctiliously.   168
hell-hated hateful as hell.   169 *Which* i.e., the treasons.   171 *Where . . . ever* if
he succeeds in the battle the treason will remain forever with the defeated Edgar.
172 *Save him* Apparently Albany does not wish Edmund to die until he has had
a chance to expose him by means of the letter.

GON.   This is practice, Gloucester.
  By th' law of arms thou wast not bound to answer
  An unknown opposite. Thou art not vanquish'd,   175
  But cozen'd and beguil'd.
ALB.   Shut your mouth, dame,
  Or with this paper shall I stop it. [*Shows her her letter to* ED-
    MUND.]—[*To* EDMUND.] Hold, sir.
    [*To* GONERIL] Thou worse than any name, read thine own evil.   180
  No tearing, lady! I perceive you know it.
GON. Say if I do—the laws are mine, not thine.
  Who can arraign me for't?
ALB.   Most monstrous! O!
  Know'st thou this paper?   185
GON.   Ask me not what I know.
    Exit.
ALB. Go after her. She's desperate; govern her.
    [*Exit an* OFFICER.]
EDM. What you have charg'd me with, that have I done,
  And more, much more. The time will bring it out.
  'Tis past, and so am I.—But what art thou   190
  That hast this fortune on me? If thou'rt noble,
  I do forgive thee.
EDG.   Let's exchange charity.
  I am no less in blood than thou art, Edmund;
  If more, the more th' hast wrong'd me.   195
  My name is Edgar and thy father's son.
  The gods are just, and of our pleasant vices
  Make instruments to plague us.
  The dark and vicious place where thee he got
  Cost him his eyes.   200
EDM.   Th' hast spoken right; 'tis true.
  The wheel is come full circle; I am here.
ALB. Methought thy very gait did prophesy
  A royal nobleness. I must embrace thee.
  Let sorrow split my heart if ever I   205
  Did hate thee, or thy father!
EDG.   Worthy prince, I know't.
ALB. Where have you hid yourself?
  How have you known the miseries of your father?

173 *practice* trickery (F¹; Q¹, K: "mere practice"). 174 *arms* Q¹; F¹: "Warre."
176 *cozen'd* cheated. 184 *O* F¹; not in Q¹, K. 187 *govern* restrain. 193 *exchange charity* forgive one another. 195 *If more* if greater (since he is legitimate
and Edmund is not). 198 *plague* F¹; Q¹, K: "scourge." 199 *place* the adulterous
bed. *got* begot. 202 *The wheel . . . here* I began life at the very lowest point
on Fortune's wheel. As the wheel revolved, I rose to the summit. Now its
revolution is completed, and here I am—at the very bottom, where I was at the
beginning. Fortune sits by her wheel and turns in constantly (cf. II.2.168). On
this wheel are mortals, who are therefore sometimes rising, sometimes at the
summit, and sometimes descending or at the very bottom of their fate [K].
203 *prophesy* promise.

EDG. By nursing them, my lord. List a brief tale;   210
  And when 'tis told, O that my heart would burst!
  The bloody proclamation to escape
  That follow'd me so near (O, our lives' sweetness!
  That we the pain of death would hourly die
  Rather than die at once!) taught me to shift   215
  Into a madman's rags, t' assume a semblance
  That very dogs disdain'd; and in this habit
  Met I my father with his bleeding rings,
  Their precious stones new lost; became his guide,
  Led him, begg'd for him, sav'd him from despair;   220
  Never (O fault!) reveal'd myself unto him
  Until some half hour past, when I was arm'd,
  Not sure, though hoping of this good success,
  I ask'd his blessing, and from first to last
  Told him our pilgrimage. But his flaw'd heart   225
  (Alack, too weak the conflict to support!)
  'Twixt two extremes of passion, joy and grief,
  Burst smilingly.
EDM.   This speech of yours hath mov'd me,
  And shall perchance do good; but speak you on;   230
  You look as you had something more to say.
ALB. If there be more, more woeful, hold it in;
  For I am almost ready to dissolve,
  Hearing of this.
EDG.   This would have seem'd a period   235
  To such as love not sorrow; but another,
  To amplify too much, would make much more,
  And top extremity.
  Whilst I was big in clamour, came there a man,
  Who, having seen me in my worst estate,   240
  Shunn'd my abhorr'd society; but then, finding
  Who 'twas that so endur'd, with his strong arms
  He fastened on my neck, and bellowed out
  As he'd burst heaven; threw him on my father;
  Told the most piteous tale of Lear and him   245
  That ever ear receiv'd; which in recounting
  His grief grew puissant, and the strings of life
  Began to crack. Twice then the trumpets sounded,
  And there I left him tranc'd.

210 *List* listen to. 214–15 *That we . . . at once* that we prefer to continually
suffer the pain of death rather than die at once. 214 *That we* F¹, Q¹, K: "That
with." 218 *rings* eye sockets. 221 *fault* error in judgment. 225 *our* F¹; Q¹, K: "my."
pilgrimage journey, wanderings about together. *flaw'd* i.e. on account of what
it had already suffered [K]. 233 *dissolve* melt into tears. 235–53 *This would
. . . a slave* Q¹; not in F¹. 235 *This would . . . period* it would have seemed
that sorrow had run its course [K]. 239 *big in clamour* loud in my lamenta-
tions [K]. 240 *estate* condition. 244 *threw him on my father* threw himself on
the body of my father [K]: *him on* THEOBALD; Q¹: "me on." 247 *puissant*
powerful, overmastering. *strings of life* heartstrings.

ALB.   But who was this?   250

EDG. Kent, sir, the banish'd Kent; who in disguise
  Followed his enemy king and did him service
  Improper for a slave.
    Enter a GENTLEMAN *with a bloody knife.*
GENT. Help, help! O, help!
EDG.   What kind of help?   255
ALB.   Speak, man.
EDG. What means that bloody knife?
GENT.   'Tis hot, it smokes.
  It came even from the heart of—O, she's dead!
ALB. Who dead? Speak, man.   260
GENT. Your lady, sir, your lady! and her sister
  By her is poisoned; she hath confess'd it.
EDM. I was contracted to them both. All three
  Now marry in an instant.
    Enter KENT.
EDG.   Here comes Kent.   265
ALB. Produce the bodies, be they alive or dead.
  [*Exit* GENTLEMAN.]
  This judgment of the heavens, that makes us tremble,
  Touches us not with pity. O, is this he?
  The time will not allow the compliment
  That very manners urges.   270
KENT.   I am come
  To bid my king and master aye good night.
  Is he not here?
ALB.   Great thing of us forgot!
  Speak, Edmund, where's the King? and where's Cordelia?   275
    The bodies of GONERIL *and* REGAN *are brought in.*
  Seest thou this object, Kent?
KENT. Alack, why thus?
EDM.   Yet Edmund was belov'd.
  The one the other poisoned for my sake,
  And after slew herself.   280
ALB. Even so. Cover their faces.
EDM. I pant for life. Some good I mean to do,
  Despite of mine own nature. Quickly send
  (Be brief in't) to the castle; for my writ
  Is on the life of Lear and on Cordelia.   285
  Nay, send in time.
ALB.   Run, run, O, run!

---

253 *Improper for a slave* unfitting even for a slave [K].   258 *smokes* steams.
264 *marry* are united (by death)   266 *the* F¹; Q¹, K: "their."   269 *compliment*
ceremony.   272 *aye* for ever.   274 *Great thing . . . forgot* This amnesia on
everybody's part is necessary for the climax that follows, but—though the audience thinks little of it—the reader always feels a shock [K].   276 *this object*
this sight. In Elizabethan English "object" often means all that one sees at the
moment [K].   278 *Yet* after all, in spite of everything.   280 *after* afterwards.

EDG. To who, my lord? Who has the office? Send
   Thy token of reprieve.
EDM. Well thought on. Take my sword;   290
   Give it the Captain.
ALB.   Haste thee for thy life.
   [*Exit* EDGAR.]
EDM. He hath commission from thy wife and me
   To hang Cordelia in the prison and
   To lay the blame upon her own despair,   295
   That she fordid herself.
ALB. The gods defend her! Bear him hence awhile.
   [EDMUND *is borne off*.]
   Enter LEAR, *with* CORDELIA [*dead*] *in his arms,* [EDGAR, CAPTAIN,
   and others following].
LEAR. Howl, howl, howl! O, you are men of stones.
   Had I your tongues and eyes, I'ld use them so
   That heaven's vault should crack. She's gone for ever!   300
   I know when one is dead, and when one lives.
   She's dead as earth. Lend me a looking glass.
   If that her breath will mist or stain the stone,
   Why, then she lives.
KENT.   Is this the promis'd end?   305
EDG. Or image of that horror?
ALB.   Fall and cease!
LEAR. This feather stirs; she lives! If it be so,
   It is a chance which does redeem all sorrows
   That ever I have felt.   310
KENT.   O my good master!
LEAR. Prithee away!
EDG.   'Tis noble Kent, your friend.
LEAR. A plague upon you, murderers, traitors all!
   I might have sav'd her; now she's gone for ever!   315
   Cordelia, Cordelia! stay a little. Ha!
   What is't thou say'st? Her voice was ever soft,
   Gentle, and low—an excellent thing in woman.
   I kill'd the slave that was a-hanging thee.
CAPT. 'Tis true, my lords, he did.   320
LEAR.   Did I not, fellow?
   I have seen the day, with my good biting falchion
   I would have made them skip. I am old now,

288 *office* commission.   290 *my sword* as proof that you are the bearer of orders
from me [K].   292 *Haste . . . life* Q¹; F¹ gives the speech to Edgar.   296 *forbid
herself* committed suicide.   298 *Howl . . . howl* F¹; the word is repeated four
times in Q¹, K.   *stones* F¹, Q¹; POPE, K: "stone."   303 *stone* surface of the mirror.
305 *the promis'd end* the Day of Doom that the prophets foretell [K].   306 *image*
exact likeness. *Fall and cease* Addressed to the universe: "Let the end of all
things come" [K].   309 *redeem* repay in full; atone for [K].   315 *I might have
sav'd her.* We are not to suppose that Cordelia was alive when Lear brought
her in. He was deluded by his desperate hope [K].   322 *falchion* a small light
sword with the point bent inward.   323 *them* Q¹; F¹: "him."

And these same crosses spoil me. Who are you?
Mine eyes are not o' th' best. I'll tell you straight.   325
KENT. If fortune brag of two she lov'd and hated,
   One of them we behold.
LEAR. This' a dull sight. Are you not Kent?
KENT.   The same—
   Your servant Kent. Where is your servant Caius?   330
LEAR. He's a good fellow, I can tell you that.
   He'll strike, and quickly too. He's dead and rotten.
KENT. No, my good lord; I am the very man—
LEAR. I'll see that straight.
KENT. That from your first of difference and decay   335
   Have followed your sad steps.
LEAR.   You're welcome hither.
KENT. Nor no man else! All's cheerless, dark, and deadly.
   Your eldest daughters have fordone themselves,
   And desperately are dead.   340
LEAR.   Ay, so I think.
ALB. He knows not what he says; and vain is it
   That we present us to him.
EDG.   Very bootless.
    Enter a CAPTAIN.
CAPT. Edmund is dead, my lord.   345
ALB.   That's but a trifle here.
   You lords and noble friends, know our intent.
   What comfort to this great decay may come
   Shall be applied. For us, we will resign,
   During the life of this old Majesty,   350
   To him our absolute power; [*to* EDGAR *and* KENT] you to your rights;
   With boot, and such addition as your honours
   Have more than merited.—All friends shall taste
   The wages of their virtue, and all foes
   The cup of their deservings.—O, see, see!   355
LEAR. And my poor fool is hang'd! No, no, no life!

324 *these same crosses* these troubles of mine. A "cross" is anything that vexes
or thwarts one [K]. 325 *straight* in a moment. 326–7 *If fortune . . . behold*
in the whole course of human history we cannot find a stranger example of
Fortune's inconstancy than Lear's life affords [K]. 328 *dull sight* Either (a)
melancholy spectacle, the body of Cordelia, or (b) his own failing eyesight.
Critics have been divided. 330 *Caius* the name Kent had assumed in disguise.
334 *see* attend to. *straight* immediately. 335 *from your . . . decay* from the
very beginning of your decline in fortunes. Decay is synonymous with "difference"
[K]. 338 *Nor no man else* nor is any one else welcome. Kent implies that this is
a time when no one can be greeted as a guest—this is no occasion for the courtesies of normal life [K]. 339 *fordone* destroyed. 340 *desperately* in despair.
344 *bootless* useless, in vain. 348 *comfort* help and support. *this great decay*
this great man, thus fallen into weakness. Such use of an abstract noun to describe a person was common in Elizabethan English [K]. 349 *resign* The play
ends as it had begun, with a resignation of kingship; Lear dies restored to the
kingship he had surrendered. 352 *boot* addition. 353 *taste* experience. 356 *my
poor fool* i.e. Cordelia. "Fool" was often used as a term of affection [K].

Why should a dog, a horse, a rat, have life,
And thou no breath at all? Thou'lt come no more,
Never, never, never, never, never!
Pray you undo this button. Thank you, sir.   360
Do you see this? Look on her! look! her lips!
Look there, look there!
    He dies.

EDG.   He faints! My lord, my lord!
KENT. Break, heart; I prithee break!
EDG.   Look up, my lord.   365
KENT. Vex not his ghost. O, let him pass! He hates him
    That would upon the rack of this tough world
    Stretch him out longer.
EDG.   He is gone indeed.
KENT. The wonder is, he hath endur'd so long.   370
    He but usurp'd his life.
ALB. Bear them from hence. Our present business
    Is general woe. [*To* KENT *and* EDGAR] Friends of my soul, you twain
    Rule in this realm, and the gor'd state sustain.
KENT. I have a journey, sir, shortly to go.   375
    My master calls me; I must not say no.
ALB. The weight of this sad time we must obey,
    Speak what we feel, not what we ought to say.
    The oldest hath borne most; we that are young
    Shall never see so much, nor live so long.   380
    Exeunt with a dead march.

If, as has been suggested, Cordelia and the Fool were played by the same boy actor, both characters may be here indicated. Some critics have held that Lear, his mind wandering, is no longer capable of distinguishing between the two people he has most fully loved. 360 *this button* The button is at Lear's throat—for he feels suffocation—not one of Cordelia's buttons, as has been sometimes suggested. *Do you . . . there* F[1]; not in Q[1]. 362 *look there* It has been suggested by some critics—most notably A. C. Bradley and R. W. Chambers—that Lear dies in a final burst of joy, thinking that Cordelia lives. If so, his death would parallel closely that of Gloucester, both being influenced by Sidney's account in THE ARCADIA of the death of the blind King of Paphlagonia. The matter has been one of great critical controversy. 366 *his ghost* his departing spirit [K]. 367 *the rack* A common torture in Shakespeare's time. The victim was extended and bound upon a frame and levers were applied to stretch his joints even to dislocation [K]. 371 *usurp'd* possessed wrongfully—he has lived longer than any man naturally should. 377–80 *The weight . . . so long* Q[1]; F[1] gives the speech to Edgar. The Quartos are correct, for such a concluding speech (serving as an epilogue) would, in a tragedy, regularly be assigned to the person of highest rank who survives [K]. 379 *hath* F[1]; Q[1], K: "haue."

THE BODY OF AN AMERICAN

John Dos Passos

WHEREAStheCongressoftheunitedstates
byaconcurrentresolutionadoptedon
the4thdayofmarchlastauthorizedtheSecretary
ofwartocausetobebroughttotheunitedstates
thebodyofanAmericanwhowasamemberofthe
americanexpeditionaryforcesineuropewho
losthislifeduringtheworldwarandwhose
identityhasnotbeenestablishedforburialinthe
memorialamphitheatreofthenationalcemetery
atarlingtonvirginia

In the tarpaper morgue at Charlons-
sur-Marne in the reek of chloride of lime
and the dead, they picked out the pine
box that held all that was left of

enie menie minie moe plenty other pine
boxes stacked up there containing what
they'd scraped up of Richard Roe

and other person or persons unknown.
Only one can go. How did they pick John
Doe?

Make sure he aint a dinge, boys,

make sure he aint a guinea or a kike,

how can you tell a guy's a hunredper-
cent when all you've got's a gunnysack
full of bones, bronze buttons stamped
with the screaming eagle and a pair of
roll puttees?

. . . and the gagging chloride and the
puky dirtstench of the yearold dead . . .

The day withal was too meaningful and
tragic for applause. Silence, tears, songs and
prayer, muffled drums and soft music were
the instrumentalities today of national appro-
bation.

John Doe was born (thudding din of
blood in love into the shuddering soar of
a man and a woman alone indeed together lurching into

and ninemonths sick drowse waking
into scared agony and the pain and blood
and mess of birth). John Doe was born
and raised in Brooklyn, in Memphis,
near the lakefront in Cleveland, Ohio, in
the stench of the stockyards in Chi, on
Beacon Hill, in an old brick house in Alexandria Virginia, on Telegraph Hill, in a
halftimbered Tudor cottage in Portland
the city of roses,

in the Lying-In Hospital old Morgan
endowed on Stuyvesant Square, across the
railroad tracks, out near the country
club, in a shack cabin tenement apart-
menthouse exclusive residential suburb;

scion of one of the best families in the
social register, won first prize in the baby
parade at Coronado Beach, was marbles
champion of the Little Rock grammar-
schools, crack basketballplayer at the
Booneville High, quarterback at the State
Reformatory, having saved the sheriff's
kid from drowning in the Little Missouri
River was invited to Washington to be
photographed shaking hands with the
President on the White Housesteps;—

though this was a time of mourning, such
an assemblage necessarily has about it a
touch of color. In the boxes are seen the
court uniforms of foreign diplomats, the gold
braid of our own and foreign fleets and
armies, the black of the conventional morning dress of American statesmen, the vari-
colored furs and outdoor wrapping garments
of mothers and sisters come to mourn, the
drab and blue of soldiers and sailors, the
glitter of musical instruments and the white
and black of a vested choir

—busboy harvestiff hogcaller boyscout
champeen cornshucker of Western Kansas bellhop at the United States Hotel at
Saratoga Springs office boy callboy fruiter

telephone lineman longshoreman lumberjack plumber's helper,

worked for an exterminating company in Union City, filled pipes in an opium joint in Trenton, N. J.

Y.M.C.A. secretary, express agent, truckdriver, fordmechanic, sold books in Denver Colorado: Madam would you be willing to help a young man work his way through college?

President Harding, with a reverence seemingly more significant because of his high temporal station, concluded his speech:

We are met today to pay the impersonal tribute; the name of him whose body lies before us took flight with his imperishable soul . . .

as a typical soldier of this representative democracy he fought and died believing in the indisputable justice of his country's cause . . .

by raising his right hand and asking the thousands within the sound of his voice to join in the prayer:

Our Father which art in heaven hallowed be thy name . . .

Naked he went into the army;

they weighed you, measured you, looked for flat feet, squeezed your penis to see if you had clap, looked up your anus to see if you had piles, counted your teeth, made you cough, listened to your heart and lungs, made you read the letters on the card, charted your urine and your intelligence,

gave you a service record for a future (imperishable soul)

and an identification tag stamped with your serial number to hang around your neck, issued OD regulation equipment, a condiment can and a copy of the articles of war.

Atten'SHUN suck in your gut you c——r wipe that smile off your face eyes

right wattja tink dis is a choirch-social? For-war-D'ARCH.

John Doe

and Richard Roe and other person or persons unknown

drilled hiked, manual of arms, ate slum, learned to salute, to soldier, to loaf in the latrines, forbidden to smoke on deck, overseas guard duty, forty men and eight horses, shortarm inspection and the ping of shrapnel and the shrill bullets combing the air and the sorehead woodpeckers the machineguns mud cooties gasmasks and the itch.

Say feller tell me how I can get back to my outfit.

John Doe had a head

for twentyodd years intensely the nerves of the eyes the ears the palate the tongue the fingers the toes the armpits, the nerves warm-feeling under the skin charged the coiled brain with hurt sweet warm cold mine must dont sayings print headlines:

Thou shalt not the multiplication table long division, Now is the time for all good men knocks but once at a young man's door, It's a great life if Ish gebibbel, The first five years'll be the Safety First, Suppose a hun tried to rape your my country right or wrong, Catch 'em young, What he dont know wont treat 'em rough, Tell 'em nothin, He got what was coming to him he got his, This is a white man's country, Kick the bucket, Gone west, If you dont like it you can croaked him

Say buddy cant you tell me how I can get back to my outfit?

Cant help jumpin when them things go off, give me the trots them things do. I lost my identification tag swimmin in the Marne, roughhousing with a guy while we was waitin to be deloused, in bed with a girl named Jeanne (Love moving picture wet French postcard dream began with saltpeter in the coffee and ended at the propho station);—

Say soldier for chrissake cant you tell me how I can get back to my outfit?

John Doe's
heart pumped blood:
alive thudding silence of blood in your ears
down in the clearing in the Oregon forest where the punkins were punkincolor pouring into the blood through the eyes and the fallcolored trees and the bronze hoopers were hopping through the dry grass, where tiny striped snails hung on the underside of the blades and the flies hummed, wasps droned, bumblebees buzzed, and the woods smelt of wine and mushrooms and apples, homey smell of fall pouring into the blood,
and I dropped the tin hat and the sweaty pack and lay flat with the dogday sun licking my throat and adamsapple and the tight skin over the breastbone.

The shell had his number on it.

The blood ran into the ground.

The service record dropped out of the filing cabinet when the quartermaster sergeant got blotto that time they had to pack up and leave the billets in a hurry.

The identification tag was in the bottom of the Marne.

The blood ran into the ground, the brains oozed out of the cracked skull and were licked up by the trenchrats, the belly swelled and raised a generation of bluebottle flies,

and the incorruptible skeleton,
and the scraps of dried viscera and skin bundled in khaki

they took to Chalons-sur-Marne
and laid it out neat in a pine coffin
and took it home to God's Country on a battleship
and buried it in a sarcophagus in the Memorial Amphitheatre in the Arlington National Cemetery
and draped the Old Glory over it
and the bugler played taps
and Mr. Harding prayed to God and the diplomats and the generals and the admirals and the brass-hats and the politicians and the handsomely dressed ladies out of the society column of the *Washington Post* stood up solemn
and thought how beautiful sad Old Glory God's Country it was to have the bugler play taps and the three volleys made their ears ring.

Where his chest ought to have been they pinned
the Congressional Medal, the D.S.C., the Medaille Militaire, the Belgian Croix de Guerre, the Italian gold medal, the Vitutea Militara sent by Queen Marie of Rumania, the Czechoslovak war cross, the Virtuti Militari of the Poles, a wreath sent by Hamilton Fish, Jr., of New York, and a little wampum presented by a deputation of Arizona redskins in warpaint and feathers. All the Washingtonians brought flowers.

Woodrow Wilson brought a bouquet of poppies.

THAT EVENING SUN

William Faulkner

MONDAY is no different from any other weekday in Jefferson now. The streets are paved now, and the telephone and electric companies are cutting down more and more of the shade trees—the water oaks, the maples and locusts and elms—to make room for iron poles bearing clusters of bloated and ghostly and bloodless grapes, and we have a city laundry which makes the rounds on Monday morning, gathering the bundles of clothes into bright-colored, specially-made motor cars: the soiled wearing of a whole week now flees apparitionlike behind alert and irritable electric horns, with a long diminishing noise of rubber and asphalt like tearing silk, and even the Negro women who still take in white people's washing after the old custom, fetch and deliver it in automobiles.

But fifteen years ago, on Monday morning the quiet, dusty, shady streets would be full of Negro women with, balanced on their steady, turbaned heads, bundles of clothes tied up in sheets, almost as large as cotton bales, carried so without touch of hand between the kitchen door of the white house and the blackened washpot beside a cabin door in Negro Hollow.

Nancy would set her bundle on the top of her head, then upon the bundle in turn she would set the black straw sailor hat which she wore winter and summer. She was tall, with a high, sad face sunken a little where her teeth were missing. Sometimes we would go a part of the way down the lane and across the pasture with her, to watch the balanced bundle and the hat that never bobbed nor wavered, even when she walked down into the ditch and up the other side and stooped through the fence. She would go down on her hands and knees and crawl through the gap, her head rigid, uptilted, the bundle steady as a rock or a balloon, and rise to her feet again and go on.

Sometimes the husbands of the washing women would fetch and deliver the clothes, but Jesus never did that for Nancy, even before father told him to stay away from our house, even when Dilsey was sick and Nancy would come to cook for us.

And then about half the time we'd have to go down the lane to Nancy's cabin and tell her to come on and cook breakfast. We would stop at the ditch, because father told us to not have anything to do with Jesus—he was a short black man, with a razor scar down his face—and we would throw rocks at Nancy's house until she came to the door, leaning her head around it without any clothes on.

"What yawl mean, chunking my house?" Nancy said. "What you little devils mean?"

"Father says for you to come on and get breakfast," Caddy said. "Father says it's over a half an hour now, and you've got to come this minute."

"I aint studying no breakfast," Nancy said. "I going to get my sleep out."

"I bet you're drunk," Jason said. "Father says you're drunk. Are you drunk, Nancy?"

"Who says I is?" Nancy said. "I got to get my sleep out. I aint studying no breakfast."

So after a while we quit chunking the cabin and went back home. When she finally came, it was too late for me to go to school. So we thought it was whisky until that day they arrested her again and they were taking her to jail and they passed Mr Stovall. He was the cashier in the bank and a deacon in the Baptist church, and Nancy began to say:

"When you going to pay me, white man? When you going to pay me, white man? It's been three times now since you paid me a cent—" Mr Stovall knocked her down, but she kept on saying, "When you going to pay me, white man? It's been three times now since—" until Mr Stovall kicked her in the mouth with his heel and the marshal caught Mr Stovall back, and Nancy lying in the street, laughing. She turned her head and spat out some blood and teeth and said, "It's been three times now since he paid me a cent."

That was how she lost her teeth, and all that day they told about Nancy and Mr Stovall, and all that night the ones that passed the jail could hear Nancy singing and yelling. They could see her hands holding to the window bars, and a lot of them stopped along the fence, listening to her and to the jailer trying to make her stop. She didn't shut up until almost daylight, when the jailer began to hear a bumping and a scraping upstairs and he went up there and found Nancy hanging from the window bar. He said that it was cocaine and not whisky, because no nigger would try to commit suicide unless he was full of cocaine, because a nigger full of cocaine wasn't a nigger any longer.

The jailer cut her down and revived her; then he beat her, whipped her. She had hung herself with her dress. She had fixed it all right, but when they arrested her she didn't have on anything except a dress and so she didn't have anything to tie her hands with and she couldn't make her hands let go of the window ledge. So the jailer heard the noise and ran up there and found Nancy hanging from the window, stark naked, her belly already swelling out a little, like a little balloon.

When Dilsey was sick in her cabin and Nancy was cooking for us, we could see her apron swelling out; that was before father told Jesus to stay away from the house. Jesus was in the kitchen, sitting behind the stove, with his razor scar on his black face like a piece of dirty string. He said it was a watermelon that Nancy had under her dress.

"It never come off your vine, though," Nancy said.

"Off of what vine?" Caddy said.

"I can cut down the vine it did come off of," Jesus said.

"What makes you want to talk like that before these chillen?" Nancy said. "Whyn't you go on to work? You done et. You want Mr Jason to catch you hanging around his kitchen, talking that way before these chillen?"

"Talking what way?" Caddy said. "What vine?"

"I cant hang around white man's kitchen," Jesus said. "But white man can hang around mine. White man can come in my house, but I cant stop him. When white man want to come in my house, I aint got no house. I cant stop him, but he cant kick me outen it. He cant do that."

Dilsey was still sick in her cabin. Father told Jesus to stay off our place. Dilsey was still sick. It was a long time. We were in the library after supper.

"Isn't Nancy through in the kitchen yet?" mother said. "It seems to me that she has had plenty of time to have finished the dishes."

"Let Quentin go and see," father said. "Go and see if Nancy is through, Quentin. Tell her she can go on home."

I went to the kitchen. Nancy was through. The dishes were put away and the fire was out. Nancy was sitting in a chair, close to the cold stove. She looked at me.

"Mother wants to know if you are through," I said.

"Yes," Nancy said. She looked at me. "I done finished." She looked at me.

"What is it?" I said. "What is it?"

"I aint nothing but a nigger," Nancy said. "It aint none of my fault."

She looked at me, sitting in the chair before the cold stove, the sailor hat on her head. I went back to the library. It was the cold stove and all, when you think of a kitchen being warm and busy and cheerful. And with a cold stove and the dishes all put away, and nobody wanting to eat at that hour.

"Is she through?" mother said.

"Yessum," I said.

"What is she doing?" mother said.

"She's not doing anything. She's through."

"I'll go and see," father said.

"Maybe she's waiting for Jesus to come and take her home," Caddy said.

"Jesus is gone," I said. Nancy told us how one morning she woke up and Jesus was gone.

"He quit me," Nancy said. "Done gone to Memphis, I reckon. Dodging them city *po*-lice for a while, I reckon."

"And a good riddance," father said. "I hope he stays there."

"Nancy's scaired of the dark," Jason said.

"So are you," Caddy said.

"I'm not," Jason said.

"Scairy cat," Caddy said.

"I'm not," Jason said.

"You, Candace!" mother said. Father came back.

"I am going to walk down the lane with Nancy," he said. "She says that Jesus is back."

"Has she seen him?" mother said.

"No. Some Negro sent her word that he was back in town. I wont be long."

"You'll leave me alone, to take Nancy home?" mother said. "Is her safety more precious to you than mine?"

"I wont be long," father said.

"You'll leave these children unprotected, with that Negro about?"

"I'm going too," Caddy said. "Let me go, Father."

"What would he do with them, if he were unfortunate enough to have them?" father said.

"I want to go, too," Jason said.

"Jason!" mother said. She was speaking to father. You could tell that by the way she said the name. Like she believed that all day father had been trying to think of doing the thing she wouldn't like the most, and that she knew all the time that after a while he would think of it. I stayed quiet, because father and I both knew that mother would want him to make me stay with her if she just thought of it in time. So father didn't look at me. I was the oldest. I was nine and Caddy was seven and Jason was five.

"Nonsense," father said. "We wont be long."

Nancy had her hat on. We came to the lane. "Jesus always been good to me," Nancy said. "Whenever he had two dollars, one of them was mine." We walked in the lane. "If I can just get through the lane," Nancy said, "I be all right then."

The lane was always dark. "This is where Jason got scared on Hallowe'en," Caddy said.

"I didn't," Jason said.

"Cant Aunt Rachel do anything with him?" father said. Aunt Rachel was old. She lived in a cabin beyond Nancy's, by herself. She had white hair and she smoked a pipe in the door, all day long; she didn't work any more. They said she was Jesus' mother. Sometimes she said she was and sometimes she said she wasn't any kin to Jesus.

"Yes, you did," Caddy said. "You were scairder than Frony. You were scairder than T.P. even. Scairder than niggers."

"Cant nobody do nothing with him," Nancy said. "He say I done woke up the devil in him and aint but one thing going to lay it down again."

"Well, he's gone now," father said. "There's nothing for you to be afraid of now. And if you'd just let white men alone."

"Let what white men alone?" Caddy said. "How let them alone?"

"He aint gone nowhere," Nancy said. "I can feel him. I can feel him now, in this lane. He hearing us talk, every word, hid somewhere, waiting. I aint seen him, and I aint going to see him again but once more, with that razor in his mouth. That razor on that string down his back, inside his shirt. And then I aint going to be even surprised."

"I wasn't scaired," Jason said.

"If you'd behave yourself, you'd have kept out of this," father said. "But it's all right now. He's probably in St. Louis now. Probably got another wife by now and forgot all about you."

"If he has, I better not find out about it," Nancy said. "I'd stand there right over them, and every time he wropped her, I'd cut that arm off. I'd cut his head off and I'd slit her belly and I'd shove—"

"Hush," father said.

"Slit whose belly, Nancy?" Caddy said.

"I wasn't scaired," Jason said. "I'd walk right down this lane by myself."

"Yah," Caddy said. "You wouldn't dare to put your foot down in it if we were not here too."

II

Dilsey was still sick, so we took Nancy home every night until mother said, "How much longer is this going on? I to be left alone in this big house while you take home a frightened Negro?"

We fixed a pallet in the kitchen for Nancy. One night we waked up, hearing the sound. It was not singing and it was not crying, coming up the dark stairs. There was a light in mother's room and we heard father going down the hall, down the back stairs, and Caddy and I went into the hall. The floor was cold. Our toes curled away from it while we listened to the sound. It was like singing and it wasn't like singing, like the sounds that Negroes make.

Then it stopped and we heard father going down the back stairs, and we went to the head of the stairs. Then the sound began again, in the stairway, not loud, and we could see Nancy's eyes halfway up the stairs, against the wall. They looked like cat's eyes do, like a big cat against the wall, watching us. When we came down the steps to where she was, she quit making the sound again, and we stood there until father came back up from the kitchen, with his pistol in his hand. He went back down with Nancy and they came back with Nancy's pallet.

We spread the pallet in our room. After the light in mother's room went off, we could see Nancy's eyes again. "Nancy," Caddy whispered, "are you asleep, Nancy?"

Nancy whispered something. It was oh or no, I dont know which. Like nobody had made it, like it came from nowhere and went nowhere, until it was like Nancy was not there at all; that I had looked so hard at her eyes on the stairs that they had got printed on my eyeballs, like the sun does when you have closed your eyes and there is no sun. "Jesus," Nancy whispered. "Jesus."

"Was it Jesus?" Caddy said. "Did he try to come into the kitchen?"

"Jesus," Nancy said. Like this: Jeeeeee-eeeeeeeeeesus, until the sound went out, like a match or a candle does.

"It's the other Jesus she means," I said.

"Can you see us, Nancy?" Caddy whispered. "Can you see our eyes too?"

"I aint nothing but a nigger," Nancy said. "God knows. God knows."

"What did you see down there in the kitchen?" Caddy whispered. "What tried to get in?"

"God knows," Nancy said. We could see her eyes. "God knows."

Dilsey got well. She cooked dinner. "You'd better stay in bed a day or two longer," father said.

"What for?" Dilsey said. "If I had been a day later, this place would be to rack and ruin. Get on out of here now, and let me get my kitchen straight again."

Dilsey cooked supper too. And that night, just before dark, Nancy came into the kitchen.

"How do you know he's back?" Dilsey said. "You aint seen him."

"Jesus is a nigger," Jason said.

"I can feel him," Nancy said. "I can feel him laying yonder in the ditch."

"Tonight?" Dilsey said. "Is he there tonight?"

"Dilsey's a nigger too," Jason said.

"You try to eat something," Dilsey said.

"I dont want nothing," Nancy said.

"I aint a nigger," Jason said.

"Drink some coffee," Dilsey said. She poured a cup of coffee for Nancy. "Do you know he's out there tonight? How come you know it's tonight?"

"I know," Nancy said. "He's there, waiting. I know. I done lived with him too long. I know what he is fixing to do fore he know it himself."

"Drink some coffee," Dilsey said. Nancy held the cup to her mouth and blew into the cup. Her mouth pursed out like a spreading adder's, like a rubber mouth, like she had blown all the color out of her lips with blowing the coffee.

"I aint a nigger," Jason said. "Are you a nigger, Nancy?"

"I hellborn, child," Nancy said. "I wont be nothing soon. I going back where I come from soon."

III

She began to drink the coffee. While she was drinking, holding the cup in both hands, she began to make the sound again. She made the sound into the cup and the coffee sploshed out onto her hands and her dress. Her eyes looked at us and she sat there, her elbows on her knees, holding the cup in both hands, looking at us across the wet cup, making the sound. "Look at Nancy," Jason said. "Nancy cant cook for us now. Dilsey's got well now."

"You hush up," Dilsey said. Nancy held the cup in both hands, looking at us, making the sound, like there were two of them: one looking at us and the other making the sound. "Whyn't you let Mr Jason telefoam the marshal?" Dilsey said. Nancy stopped then, holding the cup in her long brown hands. She tried to drink some coffee again, but it sploshed out of the cup, onto her hands and her dress, and she put the cup down. Jason watched her.

"I cant swallow it," Nancy said. "I swallows but it wont go down me."

"You go down to the cabin," Dilsey said. "Frony will fix you a pallet and I'll be there soon."

"Wont no nigger stop him," Nancy said.

"I aint a nigger," Jason said. "Am I, Dilsey?"

"I reckon not," Dilsey said. She looked at Nancy. "I dont reckon so. What you going to do, then?"

Nancy looked at us. Her eyes went fast, like she was afraid there wasn't time to look, without hardly moving at all. She looked at us, at all three of us at one time. "You member that night I stayed in yawls' room?" she said. She told about how we waked up early the next morning, and played. We had to play quiet, on her pallet, until father woke up and it was time to get breakfast. "Go and ask your maw to let me stay here tonight," Nancy said. "I wont need no pallet. We can play some more."

Caddy asked mother. Jason went too. "I cant have Negroes sleeping in the bedrooms," mother said. Jason cried. He cried until mother said he couldn't have any dessert for three days if he didn't stop. Then Jason said he would stop if Dilsey would make a chocolate cake. Father was there.

"Why dont you do something about it?" mother said. "What do we have officers for?"

"Why is Nancy afraid of Jesus?" Caddy said. "Are you afraid of father, mother?"

"What could the officers do?" father said. "If Nancy hasn't seen him, how could the officers find him?"

"Then why is she afraid?" mother said.

"She says he is there. She says she knows he is there tonight."

"Yet we pay taxes," mother said. "I must wait here alone in this big house while you take a Negro woman home."

"You know that I am not lying outside with a razor," father said.

"I'll stop if Dilsey will make a chocolate cake," Jason said. Mother told us to go out and father said he didn't know if Jason would get a chocolate cake or not, but he knew what Jason was going to get in about a minute. We went back to the kitchen and told Nancy.

"Father said for you to go home and lock the door, and you'll be all right," Caddy said. "All right from what, Nancy? Is Jesus mad at you?" Nancy was holding the coffee cup in her hands again, her elbows on her knees and her hands holding the cup between her knees. She was looking into the cup. "What have you done that made Jesus mad?" Caddy said. Nancy let the cup go. It didn't break on the floor, but the coffee spilled out, and Nancy sat there with her hands still making the shape of the cup. She began to make the sound again, not loud. Not singing and not unsinging. We watched her.

"Here," Dilsey said. "You quit that, now. You get aholt of yourself. You wait here. I going to get Versh to walk home with you." Dilsey went out.

We looked at Nancy. Her shoulders kept shaking, but she quit making the sound. We watched her. "What's Jesus going to do to you?" Caddy said. "He went away."

Nancy looked at us. "We had fun that night I stayed in yawls' room, didn't we?"

"I didn't," Jason said. "I didn't have any fun."

"You were asleep in mother's room," Caddy said. "You were not there."

"Let's go down to my house and have some more fun," Nancy said.

"Mother wont let us," I said. "It's too late now."

"Don't bother her," Nancy said. "We can tell her in the morning. She wont mind."

"She wouldn't let us," I said.

"Don't ask her now," Nancy said. "Don't bother her now."

"She didn't say we couldn't go," Caddy said.

"We didn't ask," I said.

"If you go, I'll tell," Jason said.

"We'll have fun," Nancy said. "They wont mind, just to my house. I been working for yawl a long time. They wont mind."

"I'm not afraid to go," Caddy said. "Jason is the one that's afraid. He'll tell."

"I'm not," Jason said.

"Yes, you are," Caddy said. "You'll tell."

"I wont tell," Jason said. "I'm not afraid."

"Jason aint afraid to go with me," Nancy said. "Is you, Jason?"

"Jason is going to tell," Caddy said. The lane was dark. We passed the pasture gate. "I bet if something was to jump out from behind that gate, Jason would holler."

"I wouldn't," Jason said. We walked down the lane. Nancy was talking loud.

"What are you talking so loud for, Nancy?" Caddy said.

"Who; me?" Nancy said. "Listen at Quentin and Caddy and Jason saying I'm talking loud."

"You talk like there was five of us here," Caddy said. "You talk like father was here too."

"Who; me talking loud, Mr Jason?" Nancy said.

"Nancy called Jason 'Mister,' " Caddy said.

"Listen how Caddy and Quentin and Jason talk," Nancy said.

"We're not talking loud," Caddy said.

"You're the one that's talking like father—"

"Hush," Nancy said; "hush, Mr Jason."

"Nancy called Jason 'Mister' aguh—"

"Hush," Nancy said. She was talking loud when we crossed the ditch and stooped through the fence where she used to stoop through with the clothes on her head. Then we came to her house. We were going fast then. She opened the door. The smell of the house was like the lamp and the smell of Nancy was like the wick, like they were waiting for one another to begin to smell. She lit the lamp and closed the door and put the bar up. Then she quit talking loud, looking at us.

"What're we going to do?" Caddy said.

"What do yawl want to do?" Nancy said.

"You said we would have some fun," Caddy said.

There was something about Nancy's house; something you could smell besides Nancy and the house. Jason smelled it, even. "I don't want to stay here," he said. "I want to go home."

"Go home, then," Caddy said.

"I don't want to go by myself," Jason said.

"We're going to have some fun," Nancy said.

"How?" Caddy said.

Nancy stood by the door. She was looking at us, only it was like she had emptied her eyes, like she had quit using them. "What do you want to do?" she said.

"Tell us a story," Caddy said. "Can you tell a story?"

"Yes," Nancy said.

"Tell it," Caddy said. We looked at Nancy. "You don't know any stories."

"Yes," Nancy said. "Yes, I do."

She came and sat in a chair before the hearth. There was a little fire there. Nancy built it up, when it was already hot inside. She built a good blaze. She told a story. She talked like her eyes looked, like her eyes watching us and her voice talking to us did not belong to her. Like she was living somewhere else, waiting somewhere else. She was outside the cabin. Her voice was inside and the shape of her, the Nancy that could stoop under a barbed wire fence with a bundle of clothes balanced on her head as though without weight, like a balloon, was there. But that was all. "And so this here queen come walking up to the ditch, where that bad man was hiding. She was walking up to the ditch, and she say, 'If I can just get past this here ditch,' was what she say. . . ."

"What ditch?" Caddy said. "A ditch like that one out there? Why did a queen want to go into a ditch?"

"To get to her house," Nancy said. She looked at us. "She had to cross the ditch to get into her house quick and bar the door."

"Why did she want to go home and bar the door?" Caddy said.

IV

Nancy looked at us. She quit talking. She looked at us. Jason's legs stuck straight out of his pants where he sat on Nancy's lap. "I don't think that's a good story," he said. "I want to go home."

"Maybe we had better," Caddy said. She got up from the floor. "I bet they are looking for us right now." She went toward the door.

"No," Nancy said. "Don't open it." She got up quick and passed Caddy. She didn't touch the door, the wooden bar.

"Why not?" Caddy said.

"Come back to the lamp," Nancy said. "We'll have fun. You don't have to go."

"We ought to go," Caddy said. "Unless we have a lot of fun." She and Nancy came back to the fire, the lamp.

"I want to go home," Jason said. "I'm going to tell."

"I know another story," Nancy said. She stood close to the lamp. She looked at Caddy, like when your eyes look up at a stick balanced on your nose. She had to look down to see Caddy, but her eyes looked like that, like when you are balancing a stick.

"I wont listen to it," Jason said. "I'll bang on the floor."

"It's a good one," Nancy said. "It's better than the other one."

"What's it about?" Caddy said. Nancy was standing by the lamp. Her hand was on the lamp, against the light, long and brown.

"Your hand is on that hot globe," Caddy said. "Don't it feel hot to your hand?"

Nancy looked at her hand on the lamp chimney. She took her hand away, slow. She stood there, looking at Caddy, wringing her long hand as though it were tied to her wrist with a string.

"Let's do something else," Caddy said.

"I want to go home," Jason said.

"I got some popcorn," Nancy said. She looked at Caddy and then at Jason and then at me and then at Caddy again. "I got some popcorn."

"I don't like popcorn," Jason said. "I'd rather have candy."

Nancy looked at Jason. "You can hold the popper." She was still wringing her hand; it was long and limp and brown.

"All right," Jason said. "I'll stay a while if I can do that. Caddy can't hold it. I'll want to go home again if Caddy holds the popper."

Nancy built up the fire. "Look at Nancy putting her hands in the fire," Caddy said. "What's the matter with you, Nancy?"

"I got popcorn," Nancy said. "I got some." She took the popper from under the bed. It was broken. Jason began to cry.

"Now we can't have any popcorn," he said.

"We ought to go home, anyway," Caddy said. "Come on, Quentin."

"Wait," Nancy said; "wait. I can fix it. Don't you want to help me fix it?"

"I don't think I want any," Caddy said. "It's too late now."

"You help me, Jason," Nancy said. "Don't you want to help me?"

"No," Jason said. "I want to go home."

"Hush," Nancy said; "hush. Watch. Watch me. I can fix it so Jason can hold it and pop the corn." She got a piece of wire and fixed the popper.

"It wont hold good," Caddy said.

"Yes, it will," Nancy said. "Yawl watch. Yawl help me shell some corn."

The popcorn was under the bed too. We shelled it into the popper and Nancy helped Jason hold the popper over the fire.

"It's not popping," Jason said. "I want to go home."

"You wait," Nancy said. "It'll begin to pop. We'll have fun then." She was sitting close to the fire. The lamp was turned up so high it was beginning to smoke.

"Why don't you turn it down some?" I said.

"It's all right," Nancy said. "I'll clean it. Yawl wait. The popcorn will start in a minute."

"I don't believe it's going to start," Caddy said. "We ought to start home, anyway. They'll be worried."

"No," Nancy said. "It's going to pop. Dilsey will tell um yawl with me. I been working for yawl long time. They wont mind if yawl at my house. You wait, now. It'll start popping any minute now."

Then Jason got some smoke in his eyes and he began to cry. He dropped the popper into the fire. Nancy got a wet rag and wiped Jason's face, but he didn't stop crying.

"Hush," she said. "Hush." But he didn't hush. Caddy took the popper out of the fire.

"It's burned up," she said. "You'll have to get some more popcorn, Nancy."

"Did you put all of it in?" Nancy said.

"Yes," Caddy said. Nancy looked at Caddy. Then she took the popper and opened it and poured the cinders into her apron and began to sort the grains, her hands long and brown, and we watching her.

"Haven't you got any more?" Caddy said.

"Yes," Nancy said; "yes. Look. This here aint burnt. All we need to do is—"

"I want to go home," Jason said. "I'm going to tell."

"Hush," Caddy said. We all listened. Nancy's head was already turned toward the barred door, her eyes filled with red lamplight. "Somebody is coming," Caddy said.

Then Nancy began to make that sound again, not loud, sitting there above the fire, her long hands dangling between her knees; all of a sudden water began to come out on her face in big drops, running down her face, carrying in each one a little turning ball of firelight like a spark until it dropped off her chin. "She's not crying," I said.

"I aint crying," Nancy said. Her eyes were closed. "I aint crying. Who is it?"

"I don't know," Caddy said. She went to the door and looked out. "We've got to go now," she said. "Here comes father."

"I'm going to tell," Jason said. "Yawl made me come."

The water still ran down Nancy's face. She turned in her chair. "Listen. Tell him. Tell him we going to have fun. Tell him I take good care of yawl until in the morning. Tell him to let me come home with yawl and sleep on the floor. Tell him I wont need no pallet. We'll have fun. You remember last time how we had so much fun?"

"I didn't have fun," Jason said. "You hurt me. You put smoke in my eyes. I'm going to tell."

V

Father came in. He looked at us. Nancy did not get up.

"Tell him," she said.

"Caddy made us come down here," Jason said. "I didn't want to."

Father came to the fire. Nancy looked up at him. "Can't you go to Aunt Rachel's and stay?" he said. Nancy looked up at father, her hands between her knees. "He's not here," father said. "I would have seen him. There's not a soul in sight."

"He in the ditch," Nancy said. "He waiting in the ditch yonder."

"Nonsense," father said. He looked at Nancy. "Do you know he's there?"

"I got the sign," Nancy said.

"What sign?"

"I got it. It was on the table when I come in. It was a hog-bone, with blood meat still on it, laying by the lamp. He's out there. When yawl walk out that door, I gone."

"Gone where, Nancy?" Caddy said.

"I'm not a tattletale," Jason said.

"Nonsense," father said.

"He out there," Nancy said. "He looking through that window this minute, waiting for yawl to go. Then I gone."

"Nonsense," father said. "Lock up your house and we'll take you on to Aunt Rachel's."

" 'Twont do no good," Nancy said. She didn't look at father now, but he looked down at her, at her long, limp, moving hands. "Putting it off wont do no good."

"Then what do you want to do?" father said.

"I don't know," Nancy said. "I can't do nothing. Just put it off. And that don't do no good. I reckon it belong to me. I reckon what I going to get aint no more than mine."

"Get what?" Caddy said. "What's yours?"

"Nothing," father said. "You all must get to bed."

"Caddy made me come," Jason said.

"Go on to Aunt Rachel's," father said.

"It wont do no good," Nancy said. She sat before the fire, her elbows on her knees, her long hands between her knees. "When even your own kitchen wouldn't do no good. When even if I was sleeping on the floor in the room with your chillen, and the next morning there I am, and blood—"

"Hush," father said. "Lock the door and put out the lamp and go to bed."

"I scared of the dark," Nancy said. "I scared for it to happen in the dark."

"You mean you're going to sit right here with the lamp lighted?" father said. Then Nancy began to make the sound again, sitting before the fire, her long hands between her knees. "Ah, damnation," father said. "Come along, chillen. It's past bedtime."

"When yawl go home, I gone," Nancy said. She talked quieter now, and her face looked quiet, like her hands. "Anyway, I got my coffin money saved up with Mr Lovelady." Mr Lovelady was a short, dirty man who collected the Negro insurance, coming around to the cabins or the kitchens every Saturday morning, to collect fifteen cents. He and his wife lived at the hotel. One morning his wife committed suicide. They had a child, a little girl. He and the child went away. After a week or two he came back alone. We would see him going along the lanes and the back streets on Saturday mornings.

"Nonsense," father said. "You'll be the first thing I'll see in the kitchen tomorrow morning."

"You'll see what you'll see, I reckon," Nancy said. "But it will take the Lord to say what that will be."

VI

We left her sitting before the fire.

"Come and put the bar up," father said. But she didn't move. She didn't look at us again, sitting quietly there between the lamp and the fire. From some distance down the lane we could look back and see her through the open door.

"What, Father?" Caddy said. "What's going to happen?"

"Nothing," father said. Jason was on father's back, so Jason was the tallest of all of us. We went down into the ditch. I looked at it, quiet. I couldn't see much where the moonlight and the shadows tangled.

"If Jesus is hid here, he can see us, can't he?" Caddy said.

"He's not there," father said. "He went away a long time ago."

"You made me come," Jason said, high; against the sky it looked like father had two heads, a little one and a big one. "I didn't want to."

We went up out of the ditch. We could still see Nancy's house and the open door, but we couldn't see Nancy now, sitting before the fire with the door open, because she was tired. "I just done got tired," she said. "I just a nigger. It aint no fault of mine."

But we could hear her, because she began just after we came up out of the ditch, the sound that was not singing and not unsinging. "Who will do our washing now, Father?" I said.

"I'm not a nigger," Jason said, high and close above father's head.

"You're worse," Caddy said, "you are a tattletale. If something was to jump out, you'd be scairder than a nigger."

"I wouldn't," Jason said.

"You'd cry," Caddy said.

"Caddy," father said.

"I wouldn't!" Jason said.

"Scairy cat," Caddy said.

"Candace!" father said.

THE KILLERS

Ernest Hemingway

THE door of Henry's lunchroom opened and the two men came in. They sat down at the counter.

"What's yours?" George asked them.

"I don't know," one of the men said. "What do you want to eat, Al?"

"I don't know," said Al. "I don't know what I want to eat."

Outside it was getting dark. The streetlight came on outside the window. The two men at the counter read the menu. From the other end of the counter Nick Adams watched them. He had been talking to George when they came in.

"I'll have a roast pork tenderloin with apple sauce and mashed potatoes," the first man said.

"It isn't ready yet."

"What the hell do you put it on the card for?"

"That's the dinner," George explained. "You can get that at six o'clock."

George looked at the clock on the wall behind the counter.

"It's five o'clock."

"The clock says twenty minutes past five," the second man said.

"It's twenty minutes fast."

"Oh, to hell with the clock," the first man said. "What have you got to eat?"

"I can give you any kind of sandwiches," George said. "You can have ham and eggs, bacon and eggs, liver and bacon, or a steak."

"Give me chicken croquettes with green peas and cream sauce and mashed potatoes."

"That's the dinner."

"Everything we want's the dinner, eh? That's the way you work it."

"I can give you ham and eggs, bacon and eggs, liver——"

"I'll take the ham and eggs," the man called Al said. He wore a derby hat and a black overcoat buttoned across the chest. His face was small and white and he had tight lips. He wore a silk muffler and gloves.

"Give me bacon and eggs," said the other man. He was about the same size as Al. Their faces were different, but they were dressed like twins. Both wore overcoats too tight for them. They sat leaning forward, their elbows on the counter.

"Got anything to drink?" Al asked.

"Silver beer, bevo, ginger-ale," George said.

"I mean you got anything to *drink?*"

"Just those I said."

"This is a hot town," said the other. "What do they call it?"

"Summit."

"Ever hear of it?" Al asked his friend.

"No," said the friend.

"What do you do here nights?" Al asked.

"They eat the dinner," his friend said. "They all come here and eat the big dinner."

"That's right," George said.

"So you think that's right?" Al asked George.

"Sure."

"You're a pretty bright boy, aren't you?"

"Sure," said George.

"Well, you're not," said the other little man. "Is he, Al?"

"He's dumb," said Al. He turned to Nick. "What's your name?"

"Adams."

"Another bright boy," Al said. "Ain't he a bright boy, Max?"

"The town's full of bright boys," Max said.

George put the two platters, one of ham and eggs, the other of bacon and eggs, on the counter. He set down two side-dishes of fried potatoes and closed the wicket into the kitchen.

"Which is yours?" he asked Al.

"Don't you remember?"

"Ham and eggs."

"Just a bright boy," Max said. He leaned forward and took the ham and eggs. Both men ate with their gloves on. George watched them eat.

"What are *you* looking at?" Max looked at George.

"Nothing."

"The hell you were. You were looking at me."

"Maybe the boy meant it for a joke, Max," Al said.

George laughed.

"*You* don't have to laugh," Max said to him. "*You* don't have to laugh at all, see?"

"All right," said George.

"So he thinks it's all right." Max turned to Al. "He thinks it's all right. That's a good one."

"Oh, he's a thinker," Al said. They went on eating.

"What's the bright boy's name down the counter?" Al asked Max.

"Hey, bright boy," Max said to Nick. "You go around on the other side of the counter with your boy friend."

"What's the idea?" Nick asked.

"There isn't any idea."

"You better go around, bright boy," Al said. Nick went around behind the counter.

"What's the idea?" George asked.

"None of your damn business," Al said. "Who's out in the kitchen?"

"The nigger."

"What do you mean the nigger?"

"The nigger that cooks."

"Tell him to come in."

"What's the idea?"

"Tell him to come in."

"Where do you think you are?"

"We know damn well where we are," the man called Max said. "Do we look silly?"

"You talk silly," Al said to him. "What the hell do you argue with this kid for? Listen," he said to George, "tell the nigger to come out here."

"What are you going to do to him?"

"Nothing. Use your head, bright boy. What would we do to a nigger?"

George opened the slit that opened back into the kitchen. "Sam," he called. "Come in here a minute."

The door to the kitchen opened and the nigger came in. "What was it?" he asked. The two men at the counter took a look at him.

"All right, nigger. You stand right there," Al said.

Sam, the nigger, standing in his apron, looked at the two men sitting at the counter. "Yes, sir," he said. Al got down from his stool.

"I'm going back to the kitchen with the nigger and bright boy," he said. "Go on back to the kitchen, nigger. You go with him, bright boy." The little man walked after Nick and Sam, the cook, back into the kitchen. The door shut after them. The man called Max sat at the counter opposite George. He didn't look at George but looked in the mirror that ran along back of the counter. Henry's had been made over from a saloon into a lunch-counter.

"Well, bright boy," Max said, looking into the mirror, "why don't you say something?"

"What's it all about?"

"Hey, Al," Max called, "bright boy wants to know what it's all about."

"Why don't you tell him?" Al's voice came from the kitchen.

"What do you think it's all about?"

"I don't know."

"What do you think?"

Max looked into the mirror all the time he was talking.

"I wouldn't say."

"Hey, Al, bright boy says he wouldn't say what he thinks it's all about."

"I can hear you, all right," Al said from the kitchen. He had propped open the slit that dishes passed through into the kitchen with a catsup bottle. "Listen, bright boy," he said from the kitchen to George. "Stand a little further along the bar. You move a little to the left, Max." He was like a photographer arranging for a group picture.

"Talk to me, bright boy," Max said. "What do you think's going to happen?"

George did not say anything.

"I'll tell you," Max said. "We're going to kill a Swede. Do you know a big Swede named Ole Andreson?"

"Yes."

"He comes here to eat every night, don't he?"

"Sometimes he comes here."

"He comes here at six o'clock, don't he?"

"If he comes."

"We know all that, bright boy," Max said. "Talk about something else. Ever go to the movies?"

"Once in a while."

"You ought to go to the movies more. The movies are fine for a bright boy like you."

"What are you going to kill Ole Andreson for? What did he ever do to you?"

"He never had a chance to do anything to us. He never even seen us."

"And he's only going to see us once," Al said from the kitchen.

"What are you going to kill him for, then?" George asked.

"We're killing him for a friend. Just to oblige a friend, bright boy."

"Shut up," said Al from the kitchen. "You talk too goddam much."

"Well, I got to keep bright boy amused. Don't I, bright boy?"

"You talk too damn much," Al said. "The nigger and my bright boy are amused by themselves. I got them tied up like a couple of girl friends in the convent."

"I suppose you were in a convent."

"You never know."

"You were in a kosher convent. That's where you were."

George looked up at the clock.

"If anybody comes in you tell them the cook is off, and if they keep after it, you tell them you'll go back and cook yourself. Do you get that, bright boy?"

"All right," George said. "What you going to do with us afterward?"

"That'll depend," Max said. "That's one of those things you never know at the time."

George looked up at the clock. It was a quarter past six. The door from the street opened. A street-car motorman came in.

"Hello, George," he said. "Can I get supper?"

"Sam's gone out," George said. "He'll be back in about half an hour."

"I'd better go up the street," the motorman said. George looked at the clock. It was twenty minutes past six.

"That was nice, bright boy," Max said. "You're a regular little gentleman."

"He knew I'd blow his head off," Al said from the kitchen.

"No," said Max. "It ain't that. Bright boy is nice. He's a nice boy. I like him."

At six-fifty-five George said: "He's not coming."

Two other people had been in the lunch-room. Once George had gone out to the kitchen and made a ham-and-egg sandwich "to go" that a man wanted to take with him. Inside the kitchen he saw Al, his derby hat tipped back, sitting on a stool beside the wicket with the muzzle of a sawed-off shotgun resting on the ledge. Nick and the cook were back to back in the corner, a towel tied in each of their mouths. George had cooked the sandwich, wrapped it up in oiled paper, put it in a bag, brought it in, and the man had paid for it and gone out.

"Bright boy can do everything," Max said. "He can cook and everything. You'd make some girl a nice wife, bright boy."

"Yes?" George said. "Your friend, Ole Andreson, isn't going to come."

"We'll give him ten minutes," Max said.

Max watched the mirror and the clock. The hands of the clock marked seven o'clock, and then five minutes past seven.

"Come on, Al," said Max. "We better go. He's not coming."

"Better give him five minutes," Al said from the kitchen.

In the five minutes a man came in, and George explained that the cook was sick.

"Why the hell don't you get another cook?" the man asked. "Aren't you running a lunch-counter?" He went out.

"Come on, Al," Max said.

"What about the two bright boys and the nigger?"

"They're all right."

"You think so?"

"Sure. We're through with it."

"I don't like it," said Al. "It's sloppy. You talk too much."

"Oh, what the hell," said Max. "We got to keep amused, haven't we?"

"You talk too much, all the same," Al said. He came out from the kitchen. The cut-off barrels of the shotgun made a slight bulge under the waist of his too tight-fitting overcoat. He straightened his coat with his gloved hands.

"So long, bright boy," he said to George. "You got a lot of luck."

"That's the truth," Max said. "You ought to play the races, bright boy."

The two of them went out the door. George watched them, through the window, pass under the arc-light and across the street. In their tight overcoats and derby hats they looked like a vaudeville team. George went back through the swinging-door into the kitchen and untied Nick and the cook.

"I don't want any more of that," said Sam, the cook. "I don't want any more of that."

Nick stood up. He had never had a towel in his mouth before.

"Say," he said. "What the hell?" He was trying to swagger it off.

"They were going to kill Ole Andreson," George said. "They were going to shoot him when he came in to eat."

"Ole Andreson?"

"Sure."

The cook felt the corners of his mouth with his thumbs.

"They all gone?" he asked.

"Yeah," said George. "They're gone now."

"I don't like it," said the cook. "I don't like any of it at all."

"Listen," George said to Nick. "You better go see Ole Andreson."

"All right."

"You better not have anything to do with it at all," Sam, the cook, said. "You better stay way out of it."

"Don't go if you don't want to," George said.

"Mixing up in this ain't going to get you anywhere," the cook said. "You stay out of it."

"I'll go see him," Nick said to George. "Where does he live?"

The cook turned away.

"Little boys always know what they want to do," he said.

"He lives up at Hirsch's rooming-house," George said to Nick.

"I'll go up there."

Outside the arc-light shone through the bare branches of a tree. Nick walked up the street beside the car-tracks and turned at the next arc-light down a side-street. Three houses up the street was Hirsch's rooming house. Nick walked up the two steps and pushed the bell. A woman came to the door.

"Is Ole Andreson here?"

"Do you want to see him?"

"Yes, if he's in."

Nick followed the woman up a flight

of stairs and back to the end of a corridor. She knocked on the door.

"Who is it?"

"It's somebody to see you, Mr. Andreson," the woman said.

"It's Nick Adams."

"Come in."

Nick opened the door and went into the room. Ole Andreson was lying on the bed with all his clothes on. He had been a heavyweight prizefighter and he was too long for the bed. He lay with his head on two pillows. He did not look at Nick.

"What was it?" he asked.

"I was up at Henry's," Nick said, "and two fellows came in and tied up me and the cook, and they said they were going to kill you."

It sounded silly when he said it. Ole Andreson said nothing.

"They put us out in the kitchen," Nick went on. "They were going to shoot you when you came in to supper."

Ole Andreson looked at the wall and did not say anything.

"George thought I better come and tell you about it."

"There isn't anything I can do about it," Ole Andreson said.

"I'll tell you what they were like."

"I don't want to know what they were like," Ole Andreson said. He looked at the wall. "Thanks for coming to tell me about it."

"That's all right."

Nick looked at the big man lying on the bed.

"Don't you want me to go and see the police?"

"No," Ole Andreson said. "That wouldn't do any good."

"Isn't there something I could do?"

"No. There ain't anything to do."

"Maybe it was just a bluff."

"No. It ain't just a bluff."

Ole Andreson rolled over toward the wall.

"The only thing is," he said, talking toward the wall, "I just can't make up my mind to go out. I been in here all day."

"Couldn't you get out of town?"

"No," Ole Andreson said. "I'm through with all that running around."

He looked at the wall.

"There ain't anything to do now."

"Couldn't you fix it up some way?"

"No. I got in wrong." He talked in the same flat voice. "There ain't anything to do. After a while I'll make up my mind to go out."

"I better go back and see George," Nick said.

"So long," said Ole Andreson. He did not look toward Nick. "Thanks for coming around."

Nick went out. As he shut the door he saw Ole Andreson with all his clothes on, lying on the bed looking at the wall.

"He's been in his room all day," the landlady said downstairs. "I guess he don't feel well. I said to him: 'Mr. Andreson, you ought to go out and take a walk on a nice fall day like this,' but he didn't feel like it."

"He doesn't want to go out."

"I'm sorry he don't feel well," the woman said. "He's an awfully nice man. He was in the ring, you know."

"I know it."

"You'd never know it except from the way his face is," the woman said. They stood talking just inside the street door. "He's just as gentle."

"Well, good night, Mrs. Hirsch," Nick said.

"I'm not Mrs. Hirsch," the woman said. "She owns the place, I just look after it for her. I'm Mrs. Bell."

"Well, good night, Mrs. Bell," Nick said.

"Good night," the woman said.

Nick walked up the dark street to the corner under the arc-light, and then along the car-tracks to Henry's eating-house. George was inside, back of the counter.

"Did you see Ole?"

"Yes," said Nick. "He's in his room and he won't go out."

The cook opened the door from the kitchen when he heard Nick's voice.

"I don't even listen to it," he said and shut the door.

"Did you tell him about it?" George asked.

"Sure. I told him but he knows what it's all about."

"What's he going to do?"

"Nothing."

"They'll kill him."

"I guess they will."

"He must have got mixed up in something in Chicago."

"I guess so," said Nick.

"It's a hell of a thing."

"It's an awful thing," Nick said.

They did not say anything. George reached down for a towel and wiped the counter.

"I wonder what he did?" Nick said.

"Double-crossed somebody. That's what they kill them for."

"I'm going to get out of this town," Nick said.

"Yes," said George. "That's a good thing to do."

"I can't stand to think about him waiting in the room and knowing he's going to get it. It's too damned awful."

"Well," said George, "you better not think about it."

THE TUNNEL

Valdemar Karklins

THE Arlberg train was approaching the most picturesque stretch of scenery between Bregenz and the Arl Pass. It was a fine day; the passengers, even those who had grown up in these valleys and had seen the mountains innumerable times, craned their necks to gaze out of the window to the right where view upon view of a travel-poster beauty unfolded before their eyes. Some time went by before they noticed the man who sat silently in the corner by the window, sunk into himself and paying no attention to the mountain scenery.

The compartment was narrow and so crowded that a young man in Tyrolese costume and with bare knees stood with his back against the window on the left where nothing could be seen but naked rock, and a fat little girl squatted on her mother's basket on the floor. People sat so tightly packed shoulder to shoulder and hip to hip on the hard, straight wooden benches that they could scarcely move or raise their arms. A farmer and his wife sat there, both middle-aged, and two youngish women—the fat girl's mother, tall and bony, and a smaller woman, rather plump, with dark eyes and hair; there was a very stout man, dressed in rough grey homespun: he was reading a newspaper and his face was hidden from view. At the end of the row, by the window where nothing but a wall of brown rock was to be seen, there sat an elderly, rosy-faced couple, keeping a little apart from the others. They had a rather dignified air and their clothes were new and well-made, probably they were townspeople travelling to Innsbruck or Salzburg. Yes, and across the narrow passage, on a seat apart, by the door which served also as a

window, there sat the silent, dark-complexioned man, the prisoner-of-war whom nobody noticed because he differed in no way from the other prisoners-of-war whom people had got used to seeing in trains. Perhaps there was a difference, though, a certain look in his eyes. But it was only later that the passengers became aware of it.

The electric train rushed along the curving rails, rumbling and clattering as if the axles and wheels had not been oiled all through the war. But people forgot the noise as they looked out of the window, and the peace of sun-lit mountains streamed into the compartment. Sometimes, the valley formed a narrow ravine, and the mountains cast a blue shadow down into its depth; in other places it opened out to a width of a few miles, and there were hamlets and houses nestling in its warm, green lap. The walls of rock on the opposite side were clear and distinct; but lightly coloured air played across the bottom of the valley, gently shimmering in the sun, and the houses, the fields, men and beasts seemed to sway a little—like pebbles and shells beneath clear, swift water. As they gazed out of the window, the townspeople felt a light, airy sensation in their breast, and it seemed to them that one might easily fly across the valley even without wings. But the farmers looked at the tiny, dwarfed figures, dotted about the green meadows down below, and at the toy-like barns which were scattered across the slopes, and they thought of the weather and of hay-making.

"Ah, beautiful fatherland," said the bony woman, the girl's mother, and her thick, solid features relaxed into gentle wistfulness. "What happiness it must be to see it again after years away from home!" With a moist look, she regarded the prisoner-of-war by the window.

"Yes. . . . There's no place like one's own country," the plump, dark-haired woman remarked in the same tone. Her black eyes rested for a moment on the prisoner-of-war's expressionless face, and she sighed. "They are lucky, those who are still alive and can come back. How many have been left behind, dead, lying in foreign soil!"

Both women had the rather deep but melodious voices of mountain-dwellers; every word was clearly audible in spite of the noisy train. Now the other people in the compartment glanced at the soldier by the window, and at that moment they noticed the look in his eyes.

A few months ago this home-coming had still been something new, the first happy experience after the grim years of the war. People had been hoping for it desperately, longing for it to happen, and then it came: the French Government released the Austrian prisoners-of-war, and groups of them began to return. Their names were announced over the radio and in the newspapers a day or at least a few hours before their arrival. At every station people gathered to meet them, there was an enthusiastic welcome, relatives embraced, sisters and wives in tears, neighbours waited to shake hands, there were gifts and surprises: the happy ending of a long drama, enacted upon a hundred small stages against the majestic backcloth of mountains bathed in the golden summer light. Gradually the excitement subsided. The relatives of the local mountain-dwellers had either returned or they had been expected in vain. Those who still kept arriving were mostly strangers; in order not to be sent back to what was now the Russian Zone, they had lied and said they had relatives in the Tyrol. These men chose some station at random, alighted from the train and wandered aimlessly about, taking care to avoid the offices of the French occupation forces, trying to find work, begging for food, and occasionally stealing. The local people felt pity for them but regarded them with suspicion as they went by: they were dirty, their clothes tattered and soaked with sweat, their footwear falling to pieces, and they were exhausted, starving, sick. Many people would have liked to help them, but nobody had any food to spare; and, anyway, how could one be sure that their clothes were not crawling with typhus-carrying lice. They dragged themselves along, seeking, hoping; after all, they were young and, if they were lucky, a war widow tired of loneliness might take a fancy to one of them and let him stay with her.

All the people in the compartment looked at the prisoner-of-war who sat by the window. Nobody spoke; the stout man lowered his newspaper and peered across it, regarding him through a pair of cheap glasses with metal frames. Then they dropped their eyes or turned aside, feeling a litle uncomfortable; the stout man returned to the perusal of his newspaper. Yes, he was one of those. He sat slumped forward as though his shoulders were weighed down by unforgettable misfortunes; his faded, shabby uniform was crumpled and filthy as if he had only the day before been lying in a muddy trench; he was dirty, he had not shaved for three or four days—yes, he was like the rest of them. His face was brown, tanned by sweat and sun, a youngish face, almost handsome if the jaw had been less prominent and the upper lip not quite so narrow and drawn in—features which gave the Tyrolese their characteristic goat-like expression. Perhaps he was also from the mountains, though of a different locality. But there was a peculiar look in his eyes, dark and yet burning with a strange fire, and when people met his gaze they had to lower their eyes. He gave the impression of a wild creature glaring out of a cave; although the carriage was flooded with light it seemed as if the soldier's unblinking eyes were glimmering in the dark.

Once more, the passengers looked out of the window. Perhaps they knew it by the position of the sun or perhaps they saw smoke rising from chimneys in the valley; suddenly they realized that it was time for lunch, and they all felt hungry. There was still a certain awkwardness about such a situation, people still remembered the war years when it was uncomfortable to eat in trains because of the hungry looks of one's fellow-passengers. In those days one used to nibble secretly at sandwiches wrapped in paper, holding them in such a way that no one could see what they were made of: some people did not even have dry bread. But, now it was no longer a crime if one could afford a few things.

The farmer and his wife were the first to eat. The stoutish, sun-burnt husband climbed on the bench and took his rucksack from the rack above; his small, thin wife extracted from it a knife, a home-baked loaf of bread and a lump of butter. She buttered a slice, handed it to her husband, and cut another one for herself. They ate, bent forward, their heads lowered, never looking about them, as if to show that it was nobody's business what they were doing. The plump, dark-haired woman took a box of cakes out of her large handbag and ate slowly, with evident relish, now and then licking her lips or her fingers. The townspeople unwrapped thinly cut sandwiches of white bread, and a strong smell of good cheese immediately pervaded the compartment. They did not touch the sandwiches with their hands but held them between crackling grease-proof paper. When they had finished eating they wiped their fingers in a napkin. The husband pulled a flask, encased in fine brown leather, out of his coat pocket and slowly, as though performing a solemn ceremony, un-

screwed first the shiny top and then the dainty little silver cup underneath, filled it carefully and drank from it; then he filled it for his wife. They sipped with the pleasure of connoisseurs, closing their eyes and slightly pursing their lips with contentment or the strength of the liquid. The whole compartment filled with the heady fragrance of good brandy, and the men knew at once that it was genuine French cognac. Yes, nowadays one again encountered people who knew how to live, who got on well in the world; it was no longer necessary to hide one's wealth as one did during the lean years, though there still were many people who barely eked out an existence. The young man in the Tyrolese jacket, standing close-by at the window, stepped from one foot to the other, looking out although there was nothing to be seen; finally he pulled an apple out of his trouser-pocket and bit into it with strong, white teeth, his mouth watering.

The tall, broad-shouldered woman made the girl get up from the basket, took out some brown honey-cake, crisp pretzels and a bottle of milk; they both began to eat. The girl stood before her mother, now and then doing a little hop and skip with her straight, fat legs, munching the salty pretzels and drinking milk from the bottle. The train gave a lurch, and milk spilled down her chin.

"Pour it into your mouth, silly, don't pour it on your chest," the mother told her off in an undertone and wiped the girl's chest with a checked handkerchief. The damp patch on the light-coloured dress attracted the attention of the other passengers, and they involuntarily noticed that the little girl had breasts. She was young, only ten or twelve years old, with a round face, narrow eyes and a wide mouth; her hips and her straight, fat legs were still those of a child, but, strange, she already had breasts, not fully developed, rather like little mounds of fat, yet plainly visible. The young Tyrolese with the bare knees stared for a while at the damp spot which the mother was rubbing with her handkerchief; then he turned away.

It would be difficult to say who noticed it first, but suddenly it seemed to all the passengers that the food they ate was turning dry in their mouths and sticking in their throats: there are looks which one can feel even without raising one's eyes. Simultaneously, they all remembered something, and an uncomfortable silence spread through the compartment. The prisoner-of-war's hungry eyes seemed to be counting every morsel they ate.

The plump, dark-haired woman made the beginning. She took a fresh sandwich from her bag, got up and offered it to the prisoner-of-war with a few polite words. He gave a start, as if frightened, and raised his head; murmuring something that sounded like gratitude, he began to eat. Instantly, all the other passengers in the compartment burst into activity, the ice was broken, they hurriedly rummaged in their bundles, bags and pockets and gave him whatever they each had: cakes, slices of cheese, eggs, sandwiches. The elderly lady produced an orange from her elegant leather case. The buxom, dark-haired woman, her red lips smiling, stood for a while beside the prisoner-of-war and watched him eat; when she turned to go back to her seat she put her hand on his shoulder, as if by accident. The man ate with an air of indifference, he did not hurry himself, but everything he was given disappeared quickly in his mouth. The expression in his eyes, though, never changed; something like hunger went on smouldering in them. Perhaps it was hunger, but of a kind that could not be appeased with bread; or perhaps it was no longer possible to appease it at all.

Suddenly they all felt a desire to speak. A bond had sprung up between them; they experienced a warm rush of exhilaration. Giving bread to the hungry made them feel nobler and better, and this moved them to such an extent that the women were on the verge of tears. Only one passenger had given nothing to the prisoner-of-war: the stout man who was eating bread while he read the newspaper he had spread across his knees. One of the women asked him whether he was not going to give the soldier anything, but he said indifferently: "I? Why should I? He hasn't asked me," and continued reading his paper. It was impossible to tell from his expressionless face and slow, imperturbable voice whether he was a miserly egoist or some odd character who had his own way of looking at things. Nobody bothered about him; such a small discordant note could not impair the general feeling of sympathy and pity which flooded the compartment with greater warmth even than the afternoon sun shining in through the window. The women leaned closer towards the prisoner-of-war and tried to enter into conversation with him; they felt that they already had a certain share in his life or at least the right to know something more about him. They asked where he was going and where his relatives lived. But the prisoner-of-war merely mumbled something from under his nose, and even those sitting closest to him could not make out what he said; he continued eating, stuffing his mouth full of food, until he had eaten everything they had given him. Then he again sat silent and motionless, with drooping shoulders, his dark, hollow face empty of expression, and stared like a wild creature out of a cave. His behaviour seemed strange, but after a while it dawned upon the woman that there was an obvious explanation for it.

"Yes, the things they had to go through," the broad-shouldered, bony woman sighed, holding the fat girl between her knees. Having eaten well, the girl looked tired and drowsy. "My husband . . . he also came home from France recently. Oh, the terrible things he keeps telling about!"

The plump, dark-haired woman sitting next to her said thoughtfully: "Yes. . . . But they are lucky, all the same. My husband will never came back. He fell in Italy, at Monte Cassino."

"Lucky?" The tall woman raised her head. "Don't say that. One dies only once, and then one has peace, one doesn't suffer any more. But there are sufferings that are worse than death, ten times worse. My husband tells me . . ."

"I can't understand how it is possible," the small, stocky farmer chimed in. "It is said that the French are a civilised nation. But the way they treated their prisoners, well, savages wouldn't do things like that. Really, I can't understand it."

"Hatred," said the young man in the Tyrolese jacket. "Blind, animal hatred. The French hate us."

"My husband says they were taken prisoners in the Ardennes, in the last big attack, and they were marched off to a camp somewhere in Brittany, I don't remember the name of the place. Sometimes they went by rail, but mostly they had to march, hundreds of kilometres. Through countless villages, and it was the same everywhere. They were so exhausted that they could scarcely drag their feet along, and in every village they had to run the gauntlet. The narrow streets full of people, and all like wild beasts. Curses and stones fell on them like hail, and chamber-pots were emptied over them from the windows. They held with their hands over their heads, but many were hit by bricks, and they fell down and were left lying there. And the guards did not do anything, they only grinned. And so it went on, from village to village, for hundreds of kilometres."

For a moment all the passengers in the compartment were silent, conjuring up this picture of utter horror. Then somebody looked out of the window where bluish mountains gleamed in the sunlight, and exclaimed: "A waterfall!"

"A waterfall," cried the girl and ran to the window, stumbling over the stout man's outstretched legs. "Where is it? I want to see the waterfall!"

The tall, broad-shouldered woman continued: "And in the transit camp almost half of them died from starvation and diseases. They were cooped up behind barbed-wire fences, several thousands of them. And while they were waiting to be distributed among different camps they got nothing to eat for a whole week. They ate grass. Something had gone wrong with the supplies, or there were too many of them, and nobody bothered their heads about them. Perhaps it was done out of revenge, how can one tell. But they got nothing to eat, for a whole week or more. They ate grass. My husband was there himself. Many of them died from starvation and diseases, and others went mad."

Nobody spoke. The wheels of the train clattered and rumbled.

"I can't understand it," the farmer said again. "Surely the French are a civilised nation."

The stout man remarked behind his newspaper: "Perhaps our side did the same. Such is war."

"We'd never do such things," exclaimed the young Tyrolese. It was evident from his indignant tone that he had been a soldier himself. "War can be humane, too." He glared in the direction of the stout man, his angry glance merely came up against the newspaper.

After a while, when the conversation had already been forgotten and nobody any longer expected him to answer, the stout man, preoccupied with his own thoughts, said: "Humane!" And after a few moments, with a short laugh, he exclaimed: "Humane war!" But nobody paid any attention to him, and he did not speak again.

The train entered a short tunnel, the carriage seemed to plunge down a well, darkness roared outside the windows; then the noise ceased and daylight poured into the compartment, so brilliant and sudden that it dazzled people's eyes.

The passengers were still turning over in their minds what the woman with the large hands and feet had told them about the prisoners running the gauntlet, the men eating grass. Now they regarded the prisoner-of-war with different eyes; he was no longer a stranger; caught up in the warm flood of sympathy, pity, and kindness, they felt he had become one of them, closely related and dear. In a way, this was one of life's rare moments of perfect beauty: the hearts of these people—strangers thrown together by accident—were as pure, bright and at peace as the valleys, brimming over with light and the tranquillity of the heavens, which lay along the road they all pursued together. One after the other, they again rose from their seats and gave whatever each still had left to give. The women opened their handbags and produced sweets and chocolate they had saved up for the children; the young Tyrolese pulled out a box with a few cigarettes and put it into the prisoner-of-war's pocket; and the townspeople exchanged glances, consulted in whispers and gave him a few marks. The buxom, dark-haired woman gazed at him for a long time and said in a slightly choked voice: "What he must have been through! Poor soul. Who knows whether he still has a home; many of them have lost all their relatives." But the prisoner-of-war kept silent, his deep-set eyes burning, his dark brow lowered, as if he did not understand anything that was being said. He remained alone, cut off from the rest who all felt purer and nobler because this day they had given more than they had ever done, and their faces showed how moved they were— except the stout man who stolidly perused his newspaper, turned it over and began to read another page.

"Two waterfalls," cried the girl, flattening her nose against the window-pane. "A big one and a little one!" She was cramped for space where she stood, the fat, clumsy child; she fidgeted and fussed and pushed against the prisoner-of-war's legs, and when the train suddenly gave a lurch she accidentally sat down on his knee.

"Come here at once," her mother called, but the girl pouted and whined: "I want to see! Can't I stay here? I want to see the waterfalls!"

"All right, stay there, but sit quietly, don't prance about." And the prisoner-of-war, without glancing at her or raising his head, put his arm round the girl to steady her.

The train had to pass through two tunnels in quick succession. The railroad was a technical masterpiece: the train ran along a narrow ledge which hugged the mountainside, a bluish-green precipice falling steeply away to the right and a greyish-brown wall of rock rising into the clouds to the left. At times the train scurried into a black opening which went straight through the centre of a hill. The electric bulbs were either burnt out or had been removed because of the blackout in the war years, and the passengers had to sit in darkness when the train made its way through the tunnels; but they were used to it.

The engine gave a long-drawn whistle as it approached the tunnels; the sound, thrown against the wall of rock, echoed and re-echoed dully as though caught within a huge empty barrel. When the train once more emerged into daylight the sun on the mountains seemed so bright that it momentarily blinded the passengers. Blinking, they suddenly noticed that the look in the prisoner-of-war's eyes had lost its strange fixedness; his gaze was keen, animated, and his face perceptibly flushed. He sat close to the window where the sun shone upon him with full force; his eyes devoured the plump, flabby girl sitting on his lap; he held her round the waist, and thick, whitish veins stood out on the back of his hand which looked moist and hot. The stout man lowered his newspaper; he looked in the direction of the prisoner-of-war and the girl, and his brow slowly furrowed with suspicion and mounting anger. The darkness of the tunnel had interrupted his reading; perhaps he was thinking of something unpleasant he had seen in the paper. He did not say anything.

Again the engine gave a whistle; there was a signpost by the roadside—"Arlberg Tunnel, 10,126m"—and this time the carriage passed into prolonged darkness.

The passengers waited, silent, with growing impatience. Their feeling of fellowship died away; oppressed and suffocated by the dark, they each were alone once more and beset by vague fears. It seemed as if this time the tunnel would never end. Then the train slackened its speed, soon it barely crawled, and finally stopped altogether.

Far ahead in the distance the outline of the engine could be seen against a faint glimmer of light, and there was the sound of quick, hurried voices. Perhaps workmen were repairing the line, and the train had been stopped by their red signal lamp, or perhaps freight was being unloaded. The passengers sat and waited in the dark compartment, desultorily talking in undertones. For a moment, which seemed interminable, nothing at all could be seen or heard; there was only the darkness. The summer day with its white sun and blue mountains, the sky with its lightly drifting clouds, the valley and its verdant meadows—all had vanished as suddenly and completely as if they had never existed. Silence and darkness bore down upon the passengers with the massive weight of the ten-mile stretch of mountain above them. Someone with a lantern ran along the train towards the engine. The lantern rocked to and fro, and faint yellowish light flickered across the brown and grey rock which looked like the wall of a cellar. Heavy, resounding footsteps hurried past. Far ahead, a

whistle blew, and the train began to move. All noises, however familiar, sounded strange and hollow, doors of compartments shut with the finality of heavy lids being slammed down; the shrill sound of iron and the droning of the rails were like a child's screams, a sick man's groans. Very slowly, light began to dawn outside the windows; then, faster and faster, the train approached the white, radiant day. As the compartment blazed into light the large, broad-shouldered woman screamed: "Hannerl! Where are you? Hannerl!" All eyes turned to the corner where the prisoner-of-war had been sitting with the girl.

The seat by the window was empty.

They all started to their feet; getting in each other's way, they ran up and down the carriage—all, except the stout man who remained sitting with outstretched legs. But they already knew that they would find neither the girl nor the prisoner-of-war. In a flash they guessed what had happened and, however incredible and frightful it was, they somehow felt they had foreseen it all. While the mother was still lamenting and wringing her hands and the others were searching the carriage, the young man in the Tyrolese jacket had already leaped across the stout man's legs and pulled the alarm signal. The train had not yet gathered speed, and it stopped a short distance from the tunnel.

They jumped out, and ran. At first the tall woman was ahead of them all; she took long strides, screaming, flinging her arms about, her clothes and hair streaming in the wind. But when she entered the tunnel she was already tired out, and the young Tyrolese overtook her. The farmers, the stocky, sun-burnt man and his thin wife, followed close upon his heels; they were no longer young, and their movements were heavy, but they were good runners. Behind them came the plump, dark-haired woman, clutching her handbag—she had not forgotten it, not even in the hurry and excitement, she had obviously learnt to look after it in the war years. The townspeople brought up the rear. They did not run, they followed at a distance and placed their feet carefully for the ground was uneven and full of stones; there was no path there, people ran along the bank of rubble at the side of the tunnel or jumped from sleeper to sleeper.

After a few hundred yards it became almost completely dark in the tunnel. When they looked back they saw a circle of light far behind them—as though they were glancing down the long barrel of a gun; when they looked ahead they saw the rails faintly glimmering in a mysterious rosy light somewhere far away. They ran through the darkness, stumbled, fell, rose again, and ran on. They could not see anything where they were, but they all had the same picture imprinted upon their minds: framed in the dazzling mountain sun, the prisoner-of-war sitting by the window, his burning eyes devouring the girl, holding her with a trembling hand.

"Hannerl!" the mother shouted at intervals, her voice shrill, almost metallic. "Hannerrrrl!" Her cry beat against the stone walls of the narrow tunnel and died away in the dark.

"Quicker," panted the young Tyrolese, "quicker!"

When they had forgotten the daylight, and when their eyes got used to the night which lay beneath the mountain, the tunnel was no longer completely dark: there was a suffused, reddish twilight ahead of them, something like the reflection from a dying fire. The young man was the first to reach the spot where workmen had been repairing the line; a lantern burned dimly on the ground, and another on the wall. He snatched up the nearest one and ran deeper into the tunnel. It could not be far now.

The yellow light of the grimy lantern flitted across the blocks of brown and grey rock which lined the tunnel on both sides and hung so low overhead that it looked as if the ceiling might collapse at any moment. The tunnel was damp and chilly; winter seemed still to lie in hiding here. The brown rock was patchy with greyish rime, and some of the grey stones seemed bedewed with perspiration. Moisture had gathered in the crevices between the stone slabs; it was black and shiny like tar and, in other places, thick and brown like blood. Water kept dripping from the ceiling, and cool drops occasionally fell on the hot brows of the people who ran on and on.

"Hannerrrrl!" the mother screamed, breathless, half suffocated with fear. And at long last there was a faint answer, barely audible. It was impossible to tell from which direction it came, whether from above, behind, or in front. They stopped, listened, and ran on.

Then they caught sight of something light-coloured, perhaps a discarded piece of clothing, or a newspaper thrown out of a passing train. But the mother recognized it from far off, and she flung herself forward and overtook the Tyrolese.

The girl was half lying, half sitting, her back against the wall of rock; she was crying. Her fat, round face was pale and dirty, she had been rubbing it with muddy hands, and her hair fell over her eyes. Her white woolen stockings had slipped down her calves, and one leg was bleeding. Choking with tears, the mother threw herself down beside her and stretched out her big hands to clasp the girl to her.

Both men stopped, panting and gasping; their breath condensed into grey clouds in the cold, damp air. The light of the lantern fell upon the girl, and they looked at her, their mouths open, their fists clenched.

"What a brute," the stocky farmer said softly. "What a swine!"

"Where is he?" asked the young Tyrolese, bending over the girl. "Where's he gone?" He was hot and out of breath, but his face looked almost white, and the muscles in his jaw twitched. The girl could not tell him anything; it was dark, she had not been able to see.

"I can't understand how a man can be such a scoundrel," said the farmer, shaking his head. "And we shared our food with him. What a villain."

The young man raised the lantern above his head and looked around him, but the weak yellowish light did not reach far. They went backwards and forwards, held their breath, and listened. They breathed, and clouds of steam stood in the cold air, filling the space of light around the lantern. The girl sobbed and pressed her face into her mother's wide skirts.

Suddenly the earth and the walls of the tunnel began to vibrate, and drops of water were shaken off the ceiling. The tremor increased, and the stone foundation on which they all stood seemed to heave like a horse beneath its rider. A train was approaching; clanging and thundering, it shook the narrow tunnel and filled it with a hideous din. It was going in the opposite direction, from Salzburg to Bregenz. For a short moment, as the train bore down upon them, they thought they would all be run over— there seemed to be no room to stand out of its way. The headlights of the engine plunged the tunnel into glaring white light. They clung to the damp walls of rocks and let the train pass.

At that moment they saw him. He jumped out of the shadows, a bare fifteen or twenty paces from where they stood, and tried to leap onto the running train. He was plainly visible, outlined against the lights of the engine and the sheaves of white sparks which tumbled against the angular walls of rock. He ran out of the dark, crouched like a cat, and jumped.

The train had slightly lowered its speed as it entered the tunnel, but even so it was still going fast. This was a bold leap.

For an instant it seemed that he had succeeded: he had caught hold of a door-handle and was trying to gain a foothold. But he was violently swung against the side of the carriage, the weight of his body wrenched his fingers from the door-handle, and he fell to the ground. Rarely would anyone have found courage for such a leap; the prisoner-of-war had the courage, and he might have succeeded if the train had been going less fast. But he did not succeed; he fell to the ground, rolled over, and lay motionless.

And now at last they had got him. Still running, the young Tyrolese bent down, picked up a stone and threw it. The stone caught the man's leg; he groaned with pain and doubled up, clasping his knee in both hands. He tried to get up and run away, but he could not; perhaps he had injured himself as he fell. Another stone hit him in the chest, and he sank back, his head against the wall of the tunnel. But the girl's mother was already upon him.

Spitting and hissing, she clawed his face and hair. She would have scratched his eyes out if he had not quickly covered his face with his hands. She had flung herself upon the prisoner-of-war, her knees on his chest, her long arms twitching and shaking; she was beside herself, she scarcely knew what she was doing. The two men looked on and waited until she had tired herself out. The prisoner-of-war turned over, his face to the ground, and writhed like a large grey caterpillar; every time he tried to get up he fell back.

Then the stoutish farmer started to belabour him. He stood up beside him, bent forward and kicked his sides and back with his strong hobnailed boots, and when the prisoner-of-war rolled over the farmer kicked him in the chest and shoulders and wherever he happened to get at him; when the man raised his head he hit him with his fists. His movements were slow and unhurried, he hit and kicked methodically, grunting a little, much as if he were chopping wood or hoeing weeds in his garden.

The prisoner-of-war did not scream, but after each kick he groaned and rolled slightly sideways. The young Tyrolese had placed the lantern on the ground; he stood close by, bent forward as if ready to spring, and waited. When the farmer stopped the Tyrolese looked round for a weapon, a piece of wood or metal; but there were only the stones on which they stood, sharp-edged limestone and pieces of rock, materials used for railway embankments. As there was nothing else at hand they picked up stones and threw them, one after the other, aiming at the man's head and chest. The prisoner-of-war rolled and twisted on the ground, protecting his face and skull with his hands, and twitched convulsively every time he was hit. Whenever the men paused for a moment he hesitantly withdrew his hands from his face and stole a glance at them. In spite of the pain, his face was strangely expressionless; he seemed to accept the stones with the same indifference and docility as he had accepted bread from those very hands not long ago. Only his eyes glittered like a wild creature's.

To the chance observer it would have seemed that these people were participating in some weird ritual. The sooty lantern spread only a narrow circle of light, and nothing was visible but their faces and hands: white, trembling with hatred and cold fury. Their bent figures threw large shadows across the ceiling and the walls of the tunnel, and the dark, restless shadows spread out and contracted, rose and fell with the same hatred, the same intensity of fury, uniting the men who moved in the dank twilight as if caught up in a nightmarish dance around a fire in a cave.

The townspeople had by now also come up. They stood a little apart from the others as if to show that they had no share in what was happening, but they stood close enough to have a good view. There was no anger, no hostility in their faces; they looked surprised and rather disgusted —as a chauffeur might look when he steps out of his car and glances at some animal he has run over, a rabbit or a dog.

The girl had calmed down and was no longer crying. The men were bobbing up and down in front of the lantern, and the girl's face was indistinct in the shadows. The mother bent over her; they talked quietly.

"What did he do to you?"

"He . . . pressed his chin against my cheek," said the girl. "He has such bristles!"

"What else did he do to you?" the mother demanded. "Answer me!"

The girl put her finger into her mouth and thought for a bit. "He carried me. And then he fell, and I ran away. I ran and I ran. And I hurt my knee on the stones."

The mother was silent for a moment. Then she asked: "Why did you cry?"

"I was afraid of the darkness." She pulled her finger out of her mouth and began to sob. "And my knee hurts."

The men stood by the prisoner-of-war, straightening their backs. They breathed lightly and quickly, and their breath enveloped their heads in small grey clouds of steam. They were still angry, but they no longer raised their hands against him: they did not want to kill the prisoner-of-war and get into trouble over it. They stood and looked at him, not sure what to do next.

"What shall we do with him?" asked the farmer. "Shall we hand him over to the police?"

The mother quickly interposed: "No, better not. I don't want it to get into the newspapers, everybody would talk about it. She says he hadn't yet done anything to her. She ran away from him."

There was a short silence. The men were plunged into thought and scratched their heads.

"What a brute," the young Tyrolese

muttered through his teeth, picking up the lantern. "I'd beat him, until—"

"Well, he's had his lesson. He'll remember it next time. Only, I can't understand how a man . . ."

The farmer's wife said: "It's the effect of the war. The whole place is overrun with criminals these days." She turned and glanced at the prisoner-of-war. "We must go back to the train. Are you going to . . . leave him here?"

"Let him rot," said the young Tyrolese with a contemptuous gesture. "I'm damned if I carry him."

They walked rapidly through the tunnel towards the exit, never once looking back, almost like running away, like trying to forget something. None of them noticed that a woman, the plump, dark-haired, black-eyed woman, had stayed behind with the prisoner-of-war. The light of the lantern gradually faded away in the distance. Now and then, as it lit up the stone walls, the tunnel seemed to expand and the grimy rock and the glistening drops of water on the ceiling were plainly visible; and then it contracted into a narrow space and sank into thick, shapeless darkness. As long as it was still possible to see by the light of the lantern the dark-haired woman wiped the prisoner-of-war's brow and temples with her handkerchief.

It had taken the conductor a long time to go from carriage to carriage. He found the stout man sitting alone in the compartment.

"Why did you stop the train? You'll have to pay a fine."

The stout man raised his eyes from the newspaper. "I didn't stop the train."

"But the alarm signal was pulled in this compartment. What has happened here?"

"I think a child fell from the train in the tunnel, and a prisoner-of-war seems to have jumped after her." The stout man reflected for a moment. "At least, that's what I think. But I'm not sure; one couldn't see anything."

"Did somebody go to find the child?"

The stout man nodded. "Yes, all of them."

The conductor opened the door, leaned out and shouted to the engine-driver. A whistle sounded, the train returned to the entrance of the tunnel, and stopped. They waited and waited; time dragged slowly on. Some of the passengers got out and walked impatiently up and down beside the train. The conductor stood leaning against the window; he wrote something in his note-book. At last voices were heard, and six, seven people climbed into the compartment—the townspeople, the farmer and his wife, the young Tyrolese, the mother and the girl. The stout man was still sitting in the same attitude, with outstretched legs. He did not look up; apparently he was not interested to know what had happened, he merely seemed to be annoyed because of the delay. They glanced coldly at him and climbed over his legs to get back to their seats; but none of them spoke. The train began to move; it gave a vigorous jerk, in a hurry to make up for lost time. The conductor spoke to the little girl's mother and again wrote down a few things in his note-book. As the train drew near a station the stout man folded up his newspaper and put it into his pocket.

"Conductor," he said, "give me my crutches. They are under the seat."

The conductor bent down and pulled out two long, thin, tubular metal crutches of the kind supplied by the army to war cripples. Slowly, with great effort, pushing first the one and then the other crutch under his armpits, the stout man rose. His broad face with its solid features turned crimson, and he breathed heavily. His massive body swung like a sack between the crutches; his long, lifeless legs hung down, his feet dragging on the floor. Without looking about him, he approached the door.

"Can I do anything to help you?" asked the conductor.

"No, you can do nothing to help me," said the stout man, slowly, cautiously climbing out of the carriage.

The people in the compartment gazed after him while the train stood at the station. Nobody spoke.

Some time went by until at last some railwaymen came along the tunnel, carrying a lantern and various tools, and they found the prisoner-of-war lying by the rails. The dark-haired woman was sitting beside him. Dressed in a thin summer frock, she shivered a little in the cold, damp air. The prisoner-of-war was breathing unevenly. The woman touched his shoulder.

"Can you get up?" she asked gently.

The prisoner-of-war opened his eyes and gave a start as he saw the lights about him.

"I . . . " he muttered, "I . . . "

"Has he hurt himself?" asked one of the workmen.

The woman nodded.

They grasped him under the arms and helped him to his feet; the plump, dark-haired woman held him firmly, her arm around his waist. Her hand was warm and steady. One of the workmen supported him on the other side, and another man walked ahead of them with the lantern. The prisoner-of-war staggered and limped, reeling dizzily; now and then he groaned and almost sank to the ground. The woman took his arm and put it around her shoulder; now she could support him better, and it was easier to walk. But, even so, it took them almost half an hour until they reached the end of the tunnel. The workmen turned back, and the prisoner-of-war and the dark-haired woman went on alone.

"You'll come with me," she said, holding him closer; maybe she could support him better by holding him tightly, or maybe she was becoming bolder. Her voice was warm and full of sympathy, and it was already tinged with the joy of ownership, of organizing and managing. Her soft flank pressed against him as though she wanted to give him some of her warmth. "It isn't far to St. Anton, it's just ahead of us. There we'll wait for the next train. And then you'll come home with me. Or perhaps you'd like to rest a little?"

The prisoner-of-war started to speak, but his words were indistinct as though he were half asleep, on the point of waking from a nightmare. "I . . . I'm thirsty . . . water."

The woman glanced about her, but there was no house anywhere near, and they went on. They walked out of step, their arms about each other, and soon grew tired. The midday sun burned like fire, and there was no breath of air on the slope of the mountain. Beads of perspiration stood on their foreheads, and they could feel the damp flesh through their clothes.

The day was very different from what it had seemed when looked at through the train window. All nature was so saturated with sun and silence that it seemed there was no room left for feelings or thoughts. Reaching out towards Innsbruck, the wide expanse of the valley lay before them like a green bowl filled to the brim with blue and golden light. There were chimneys smoking far down below, and cars and horse-drawn vehicles rolled swiftly along the roads, but they were as tiny as ants, and no sound reached up to the shoulder of the hill. A large hawk floated in the light and the silence, casting an almost motionless shadow on the parched earth. Sweltering heat lay heavily on the slopes, and the snow on the mountain-peaks seemed to be melting in the hot blue day like silver in a huge blue oven. The silence was so great and lofty that human sorrow and anger, suffering and hatred seemed petty, dispensable, incredibly trivial; it was sufficient merely to be silent and to exist— like the mountains, the trees, the pellucid air.

"Tell me, dear, what you wanted with that girl," the woman said after a while, "with that child."

The prisoner-of-war hesitated and glanced about him as if afraid that he might be overheard; then he answered in a half-whisper: "They wouldn't have given her to me. She has already been stolen from me once. I know everything." There was a gleam in his eyes. "But I shall find her again."

The dark-haired woman did not stop, but she slowed down and looked in his face. It was streaming with sweat, and the furrows along his cheeks were encrusted with thin, dark streaks of blood. His eyes glittered.

"You are talking wildly," she said. "You'll have to rest for a long time. Perhaps you are in a fever."

He shook his head, and with an air of secrecy he leaned closer towards her and whispered in her ear: "They have stolen everything from me, Lottie and the girl, and the house, too. The house has also been stolen, there is only a hole left in the ground. But I shall find her, I have already been in Bregenz, and now I'm going to Innsbruck." He increased his pace, impatiently straining forward.

"Don't you think that they took her away to Innsbruck?"

The dark-haired woman walked for a long while looking straight ahead; suddenly all pliancy and softness had left her, her legs moved stiffly. She slowly withdrew her arm and let him go; he had recovered his strength and was able to walk by himself.

"You have long black hair," he said amiably, looking at her. "Good that it wasn't burnt."

"Don't speak now," she said in a strange voice. "Come, I'll take you to the station and show you the way." She glanced back across her shoulder to where the railwaymen had parted from them, and then she gazed ahead, trying to judge how far they still had to go until they reached the station. She began to hurry.

They walked in silence, the woman a few paces ahead, the prisoner-of-war following. The sun burned more and more fiercely, and the railway lines ahead of them shimmered as though they were melting. It was no longer far to the station.

*[Translated from the
Latvian by Ruth Speirs]*

THE WALL

Jean-Paul Sartre

THEY pushed us into a large white room and my eyes began to blink because the light hurt them. Then I saw a table and four fellows seated at the table, civilians, looking at some papers. The other prisoners were herded together at one end and we were obliged to cross the entire room to join them. There were several I knew, and others who must have been foreigners. The two in front of me were blond with round heads. They looked alike. I imagine they were French. The smaller one kept pulling at his trousers, out of nervousness.

This lasted about three hours. I was dog-tired and my head was empty. But the room was well-heated, which struck me as rather agreeable; we had not stopped shivering for twenty-four hours. The guards led the prisoners in one after the other in front of the table. Then the four fellows asked them their names and what they did. Most of the time that was all—or perhaps from time to time they would ask such questions as: "Did you help sabotage the munitions?" or, "Where were you on the morning of the ninth and what were you doing?" They didn"t even listen to the replies, or at least they didn't seem to. They just remained silent for a moment and looked straight ahead, then they began to write. They asked Tom if it was true he had served in the International Brigade. Tom couldn't say he hadn't because of the papers they had found in his jacket. They didn't ask Juan anything, but after he told them his name, they wrote for a long while.

"It's my brother José who's the anarchist," Juan said. "You know perfectly well he's not here now. I don't belong to any party. I never did take part in politics." They didn't answer.

Then Juan said, "I didn't do anything. And I'm not going to pay for what the others did."

His lips were trembling. A guard told him to stop talking and led him away. It was my turn.

"Your name is Pablo Ibbieta?"

I said yes.

The fellow looked at his papers and said, "Where is Ramon Gris?"

"I don't know."

"You hid him in your house from the sixth to the nineteenth."

"I did not."

They continued to write for a moment and the guards led me away. In the hall, Tom and Juan were waiting between two guards. We started walking. Tom asked one of the guards, "Was that just the preliminary questioning, or was that the trial?" "That was the trial," the guard said. "So now what? What are they going to do with us?" The guard answered drily, "The verdict will be told you in your cell."

In reality, our cell was one of the cellars of the hospital. It was terribly cold there because it was very drafty. We had been shivering all night long and it had hardly been any better during the day. I had spent the preceding five days in a cellar in the archbishop's palace, a sort of dungeon that must have dated back to the Middle Ages. There were lots of prisoners and not much room, so they housed them just anywhere. But I was not homesick for my dungeon. I hadn't been cold there, but I had been alone, and that gets to be irritating. In the cellar I had company. Juan didn't say a word; he was afraid, and besides, he was too young to have anything to say. But Tom was a good talker and knew Spanish well.

In the cellar there were a bench and four straw mattresses. When they led us back we sat down and waited in silence. After a while Tom said, "Our goose is cooked."

"I think so too," I said. "But I don't believe they'll do anything to the kid."

Tom said, "They haven't got anything on him. He's the brother of a fellow who's fighting, and that's all."

I looked at Juan. He didn't seem to have heard.

Tom continued, "You know what they do in Saragossa? They lay the guys across the road and then they drive over them with trucks. It was a Moroccan deserter who told us that. They say it's just to save ammunition."

I said, "Well, it doesn't save gasoline."

I was irritated with Tom; he shouldn't have said that.

He went on, "There are officers walking up and down the roads with their hands in their pockets, smoking, and they see that it's done right. Do you think they'd put 'em out of their misery? Like hell they do. They just let 'em holler. Sometimes as long as an hour. The Moroccan said the first time he almost puked."

"I don't believe they do that here," I said, "unless they really are short of ammunition."

The daylight came in through four air vents and a round opening that had been cut in the ceiling, to the left, and which opened directly onto the sky. It was through this hole, which was ordinarily closed by means of a trapdoor, that they unloaded coal into the cellar. Directly under the hole, there was a big pile of coal dust; it had been intended for heating the hospital, but at the beginning of the war they had evacuated the patients and the coal had stayed there unused; it even got rained on from time to time, when they forgot to close the trapdoor.

Tom started to shiver. "God damn it," he said, "I'm shivering. There, it is starting again."

He rose and began to do gymnastic exercises. At each movement, his shirt opened and showed his white, hairy chest. He lay down on his back, lifted his legs in the air and began to do the scissors movement. I watched his big buttocks tremble. Tom was tough, but he had too much fat on him. I kept thinking that soon bullets and bayonet points would sink into that mass of tender flesh as though it were a pat of butter.

I wasn't exactly cold, but I couldn't feel my shoulders or my arms. From time to time, I had the impression that something was missing and I began to look around for my jacket. Then I would suddenly remember they hadn't given me a jacket. It was rather awkward. They had taken our clothes to give them to their own soldiers and had left us only our shirts and these cotton trousers the hospital patients wore in mid-summer. After a moment, Tom got up and sat down beside me, breathless.

"Did you get warmed up?"

"Damn it, no. But I'm all out of breath."

Around eight o'clock in the evening, a Major came in with two falangists.

"What are the names of those three over there?" he asked the guard.

"Steinbock, Ibbieta and Mirbal," said the guard.

The Major put on his glasses and examined his list.

"Steinbock—Steinbock. . . . Here it is. You are condemned to death. You'll be shot tomorrow morning."

He looked at his list again.

"The other two, also," he said.

"That's not possible," said Juan. "Not me."

The Major looked at him with surprise.

"What's your name?"

"Juan Mirbal."

"Well, your name is here," said the Major, "and you're condemned to death."

"I didn't do anything," said Juan.

The Major shrugged his shoulders and turned toward Tom and me.

"You are both Basque?"

"No, nobody's Basque."

He appeared exasperated.

"I was told there were three Basques. I'm not going to waste my time running after them. I suppose you don't want a priest?"

We didn't even answer.

Then he said, "A Belgian doctor will be around in a little while. He has permission to stay with you all night."

He gave a military salute and left.

"What did I tell you?" Tom said. "We're in for something swell."

"Yes," I said. "It's a damned shame for the kid."

I said that to be fair, but I really didn't like the kid. His face was too refined and it was disfigured by fear and suffering, which had twisted all his features. Three days ago, he was just a kid with a kind of affected manner some people like. But now he looked like an aging fairy, and I thought to myself he would never be young again, even if they let him go. It wouldn't have been a bad thing to show him a little pity, but pity makes me sick, and besides, I couldn't stand him. He hadn't said anything more, but he had turned gray. His face and hands were gray. He sat down again and stared, round-eyed, at the ground. Tom was good-hearted and tried to take him by the arm, but the kid drew himself away violently and made an ugly face. "Leave him alone," I said quietly. "Can't you see he's going to start to bawl?" Tom obeyed regretfully. He would have liked to console the kid; that would have kept him occupied and he wouldn't have been tempted to think about himself. But it got on my nerves. I had never

thought about death, for the reason that the question had never come up. But now it had come up, and there was nothing else to do but think about it.

Tom started talking. "Say, did you ever bump anybody off?" he asked me. I didn't answer. He started to explain to me that he had bumped off six fellows since August. He hadn't yet realized what we were in for, and I saw clearly he didn't *want* to realize it. I myself hadn't quite taken it in. I wondered if it hurt very much. I thought about the bullets; I imagined their fiery hail going through my body. All that was beside the real question; but I was calm, we had all night in which to realize it. After a while Tom stopped talking and I looked at him out of the corner of my eye. I saw that he, too, had turned gray and that he looked pretty miserable. I said to myself, "It's starting." It was almost dark, a dull light filtered through the air vents across the coal pile and made a big spot under the sky. Through the hole in the ceiling I could already see a star. The night was going to be clear and cold.

The door opened and two guards entered. They were followed by a blond man in a tan uniform. He greeted us.

"I'm the doctor," he said. "I've been authorized to give you any assistance you may require in these painful circumstances."

He had an agreeable, cultivated voice.

I said to him, "What are you going to do here?"

"Whatever you want to do. I shall do everything in my power to lighten these few hours."

"Why did you come to us? There are lots of others: the hospital's full of them."

"I was sent here," he answered vaguely. "You'd probably like to smoke, wouldn't you?" he added suddenly. "I've got some cigarettes and even some cigars."

He passed around some English cigarettes and some *puros,* but we refused them. I looked him straight in the eye and he appeared uncomfortable.

"You didn't come here out of compassion," I said to him. "In fact, I know who you are. I saw you with some fascists in the barracks yard the day I was arrested."

I was about to continue, when all at once something happened to me which surprised me: the presence of this doctor had suddenly ceased to interest me. Usually, when I've got hold of a man I don't let go. But somehow the desire to speak had left me. I shrugged my shoulders and turned away. A little later, I looked up and saw he was watching me with an air of curiosity. The guards had sat down on one of the mattresses. Pedro, the tall thin one, was twiddling his thumbs, while the other one shook his head occasionally to keep from falling asleep.

"Do you want some light?" Pedro suddenly asked the doctor. The other fellow nodded, "Yes." I think he was not over-intelligent, but doubtless he was not malicious. As I looked at his big, cold, blue eyes, it seemed to me the worst thing about him was his lack of imagination. Pedro went out and came back with an oil lamp which he set on the corner of the bench. It gave a poor light, but it was better than nothing; the night before we had been left in the dark. For a long while I stared at the circle of light the lamp threw on the ceiling. I was fascinated. Then, suddenly, I came to, the light circle paled, and I felt as if I were being crushed under an enormous weight. It wasn't the thought of death, and it wasn't fear; it was something anonymous. My cheeks were burning hot and my head ached.

I roused myself and looked at my two companions. Tom had his head in his hands and only the fat, white nape of his neck was visible. Juan was by far the worst off; his mouth was wide open and his nostrils were trembling. The doctor came over to him and touched him on the shoulder, as though to comfort him; but his eyes remained cold. Then I saw the Belgian slide his hand furtively down Juan's arm to his wrist. Indifferent, Juan let himself be handled. Then, as though absent-mindedly, the Belgian laid three fingers over his wrist; at the same time, he drew away somewhat and managed to turn his back to me. But I leaned over backward and saw him take out his watch and look at it a moment before relinquishing the boy's wrist. After a moment, he let the inert hand fall and went and leaned against the wall. Then, as if he had suddenly remembered something very important that had to be noted down immediately, he took a notebook from his pocket and wrote a few lines in it. "The son-of-a-bitch," I thought angrily. "He better not come and feel my pulse; I'll give him a punch in his dirty jaw."

He didn't come near me, but I felt he was looking at me. I raised my head and looked back at him. In an impersonal voice, he said, "Don't you think it's frightfully cold here?"

He looked purple with cold.

"I'm not cold," I answered him.

He kept looking at me with a hard expression. Suddenly I understood, and I lifted my hands to my face. I was covered with sweat. Here, in this cellar, in midwinter, right in a draft, I was sweating. I ran my fingers through my hair, which was stiff with sweat; at the same time, I realized my shirt was damp and sticking to my skin. I had been streaming with perspiration for an hour, at least, and had felt nothing. But this fact hadn't escaped that Belgian swine. He had seen the drops rolling down my face and had said to himself that it showed an almost pathological terror; and he himself had felt normal and proud of it because he was cold. I wanted to get up and go punch his face in, but I had hardly started to make a move before my shame and anger had disappeared. I dropped back onto the bench with indifference.

I was content to rub my neck with my handkerchief because now I felt the sweat dripping from my hair onto the nape of my neck and that was disagreeable. I soon gave up rubbing myself, however, for it didn't do any good; my handkerchief was already wringing wet and I was still sweating. My buttocks, too, were sweating, and my damp trousers stuck to the bench.

Suddenly, Juan said, "You're a doctor, aren't you?"

"Yes," said the Belgian.

"Do people suffer—very long?"

"Oh! When . . . ? No, no," said the Belgian, in a paternal voice, "it's quickly over."

His manner was as reassuring as if he had been answering a paying patient.

"But I . . . Somebody told me—they often have to fire two volleys."

"Sometimes," said the Belgian, raising his head, "it just happens that the first volley doesn't hit any of the vital organs."

"So then they have to reload their guns and aim all over again?" Juan thought for a moment, then added hoarsely, "But that takes time!"

He was terribly afraid of suffering. He couldn't think about anything else, but that went with his age. As for me, I hardly thought about it any more and it certainly was not fear of suffering that made me perspire.

I rose and walked toward the pile of coal dust. Tom gave a start and looked at me with a look of hate. I irritated him because my shoes squeaked. I wondered if my face was as putty-colored as his. Then I noticed that he, too, was sweating. The sky was magnificent; no light at all came into our dark corner and I had only to lift my head to see the Big Bear. But it didn't look the way it had looked before. Two days ago, from my cell in the archbishop's palace, I could see a big patch of sky and each time of day brought back a different memory. In the morning, when the sky was a deep blue, and light, I thought of beaches along the Atlantic; at

noon, I could see the sun, and I remembered a bar in Seville where I used to drink manzanilla and eat anchovies and olives; in the afternoon, I was in the shade, and I thought of the deep shadow which covers half of the arena while the other half gleams in the sunlight: it really gave me a pang to see the whole earth reflected in the sky like that. Now, however, no matter how much I looked up in the air, the sky no longer recalled anything. I liked it better that way. I came back and sat down next to Tom. There was a long silence.

Then Tom began to talk in a low voice. He had to keep talking, otherwise he lost his way in his own thoughts. I believe he was talking to me, but he didn't look at me. No doubt he was afraid to look at me, because I was gray and sweating. We were both alike and worse than mirrors for each other. He looked at the Belgian, the only one who was alive.

"Say, do you understand? I don't."

Then I, too, began to talk in a low voice. I was watching the Belgian.

"Understand what? What's the matter?"

"Something's going to happen to us that I don't understand."

There was a strange odor about Tom. It seemed to me that I was more sensitive to odors than ordinarily. With a sneer, I said, "You'll understand, later."

"That's not so sure," he said stubbornly. "I'm willing to be courageous, but at least I ought to know. . . . Listen, they're going to take us out into the courtyard. All right. The fellows will be standing in line in front of us. How many of them will there be?"

"Oh, I don't know. Five, or eight. Not more."

"That's enough. Let's say there'll be eight of them. Somebody will shout 'Shoulder arms!' and I'll see all eight rifles aimed at me. I'm sure I'm going to feel like going through the wall. I'll push against the wall as hard as I can with my back, and the wall won't give in.

The way it is in a nightmare. . . . I can imagine all that. Ah, if you only knew how well I can imagine it!"

"Skip it!" I said. "I can imagine it too."

"It must hurt like the devil. You know they aim at your eyes and mouth so as to disfigure you," he added maliciously. "I can feel the wounds already. For the last hour I've been having pains in my head and neck. Not real pains—it's worse still. They're the pains I'll feel tomorrow morning. And after that, then what?"

I understood perfectly well what he meant, but I didn't want to seem to understand. As for the pains, I, too, felt them all through my body, like a lot of little gashes. I couldn't get used to them, but I was like him, I didn't think they were very important.

"After that," I said roughly, "you'll be eating daisies."

He started talking to himself, not taking his eyes off the Belgian, who didn't seem to be listening to him. I knew what he had come for, and that what we were thinking didn't interest him. He had come to look at our bodies, our bodies which were dying alive.

"It's like in a nightmare," said Tom. "You want to think of something, you keep having the impression you've got it, that you're going to understand, and then it slips away from you, it eludes you and it's gone again. I say to myself, afterwards, there won't be anything. But I don't really understand what that means. There are moments when I almost do—and then it's gone again. I start to think of the pains, the bullets, the noise of the shooting. I am a materialist, I swear it; and I'm not going crazy, either. But there's something wrong. I see my own corpse. That's not hard, but it's *I* who see it, with *my* eyes. I'll have to get to the point where I think—where I think I won't see anything more. I won't hear anything more, and the world will go on for the others. We're not made to think that way, Pablo. Believe me, I've already stayed awake all night waiting for something. But this is not the same thing. This will grab us from behind, Pablo, and we won't be ready for it."

"Shut up," I said. "Do you want me to call a father confessor?"

He didn't answer. I had already noticed that he had a tendency to prophesy and call me "Pablo" in a kind of pale voice. I didn't like that very much, but it seems all the Irish are like that. I had a vague impression that he smelled of urine. Actually, I didn't like Tom very much, and I didn't see why, just because we were going to die together, I should like him any better. There are certain fellows with whom it would be different—with Ramon Gris, for instance. But between Tom and Juan, I felt alone. In fact, I liked it better that way. With Ramon I might have grown soft. But I felt terribly hard at that moment, and I wanted to stay hard.

Tom kept on muttering, in a kind of absent-minded way. He was certainly talking to keep from thinking. Naturally, I agreed with him, and I could have said everything he was saying. It's not *natural* to die. And since I was going to die, nothing seemed natural any more: neither the coal pile, nor the bench, nor Pedro's dirty old face. Only it was disagreeable for me to think the same things Tom thought. And I knew perfectly well that all night long, within five minutes of each other, we would keep on thinking things at the same time, sweating or shivering at the same time. I looked at him sideways and, for the first time, he seemed strange to me. He had death written on his face. My pride was wounded. For twenty-four hours I had lived side by side with Tom, I had listened to him, I had talked to him, and I knew we had nothing in common. And now we were as alike as twin brothers, simply because we were going to die together. Tom took my hand without looking at me.

"Pablo, I wonder . . . I wonder if it's true that we just cease to exist."

I drew my hand away.

"Look between your feet, you dirty dog."

There was a puddle between his feet and water was dripping from his trousers.

"What's the matter?" he said frightened.

"You're wetting your pants," I said to him.

"It's not true," he said furiously. "I can't be . . . I don't feel anything."

The Belgian had come closer to him. With an air of false concern, he asked, "Aren't you feeling well?"

Tom didn't answer. The Belgian looked at the puddle without comment.

"I don't know what that is," Tom said savagely, "but I'm not afraid. I swear to you, I'm not afraid."

The Belgian made no answer. Tom rose and went to the corner. He came back, buttoning his fly, and sat down, without a word. The Belgian was taking notes.

We were watching the doctor. Juan was watching him too. All three of us were watching him because he was alive. He had the gestures of a living person, the interests of a living person; he was shivering in this cellar the way living people shiver; he had an obedient, well-fed body. We, on the other hand, didn't feel our bodies any more—not the same way, in any case. I felt like touching my trousers, but I didn't dare to. I looked at the Belgian, well-planted on his two legs, master of his muscles—and able to plan for tomorrow. We were like three shadows deprived of blood; we were watching him and sucking his life like vampires.

Finally he came over to Juan. Was he going to lay his hand on the nape of Juan's neck for some professional reason, or had he obeyed a charitable impulse? If he had acted out of charity, it was the one and only time during the whole night. He fondled Juan's head and the nape of his neck. The kid let him do it, without taking his eyes off him. Then, suddenly, he took hold of the doctor's hand and looked at it in a funny way. He held the Belgian's hand between his own two hands and there was nothing pleasing about them, those two gray paws squeezing that fat red hand. I sensed what was going to happen and Tom must have sensed it, too. But all the Belgian saw was emotion, and he smiled paternally. After a moment, the kid lifted the big red paw to his mouth and started to bite it. The Belgian drew back quickly and stumbled toward the wall. For a second, he looked at us with horror. He must have suddenly understood that we were not men like himself. I began to laugh, and one of the guards started up. The other had fallen asleep with his eyes wide open, showing only the whites.

I felt tired and over-excited at the same time. I didn't want to think any more about what was going to happen at dawn —about death. It didn't make sense, and I never got beyond just words, or emptiness. But whenever I tried to think about something else I saw the barrels of rifles aimed at me. I must have lived through my execution twenty times in succession; one time I thought it was the real thing; I must have dozed off for a moment. They were dragging me toward the wall and I was resisting; I was imploring their pardon. I woke with a start and looked at the Belgian. I was afraid I had cried out in my sleep. But he was smoothing his mustache; he hadn't noticed anything. If I had wanted to, I believe I could have slept for a while. I had been awake for the last forty-eight hours, and I was worn out. But I didn't want to lose two hours of life. They would have had to come and wake me at dawn. I would have followed them, drunk with sleep, and I would have gone off without so much as "Gosh!" I didn't want it that way, I didn't want to die like an animal. I wanted to understand. Besides, I was afraid of having nightmares. I got up and began to walk up and down and, so as to think about something else, I began to think about my past life. Memories crowded in on me, helter-skelter.

Some were good and some were bad—at least that was how I had thought of them *before*. There were faces and happenings. I saw the face of a little *novilero* who had gotten himself horned during the *Feria,* in Valencia. I saw the face of one of my uncles, of Ramon Gris. I remembered all kinds of things that had happened: how I had been on strike for thre months in 1926, and had almost died of hunger. I recalled a night I had spent on a bench in Granada; I hadn't eaten for three days, I was nearly wild, I didn't want to give up the sponge. I had to smile. With what eagerness I had run after happiness, and women, and liberty! And to what end? I had wanted to liberate Spain, I admired Py Margall, I had belonged to the anarchist movement. I had spoken at public meetings. I took everything as seriously as if I had been immortal.

At that time I had the impression that I had my whole life before me, and I thought to myself, "It's all a god-damned lie." Now it wasn't worth anything because it was finished. I wondered how I had ever been able to go out and have a good time with girls. I wouldn't have lifted my little finger if I had ever imagined that I would die like this. I saw my life before me, finished, closed, like a bag, and yet what was inside was not finished. For a moment I tried to appraise it. I would have liked to say to myself, "It's been a good life." But it couldn't be appraised, it was only an outline. I had spent my time writing checks on eternity, and had understood nothing. Now, I didn't miss anything. There were a lot of things I might have missed: the taste of manzanilla, for instance, or the swims I used to take in summer in a little creek near Cadiz. But death had taken the charm out of everything.

Suddenly the Belgian had a wonderful idea.

"My friends," he said to us, "if you want me to—and providing the military authorities give their consent—I could undertake to deliver a word or some token from you to your loved ones. . . ."

Tom growled, "I haven't got anybody."

I didn't answer. Tom waited for a moment, then he looked at me with curiosity. "Aren't you going to send any message to Concha?"

"No."

I hated that sort of sentimental conspiracy. Of course, it was my fault, since I had mentioned Concha the night before, and I should have kept my mouth shut. I had been with her for a year. Even as late as last night, I would have cut my arm off with a hatchet just to see her again for five minutes. That was why I had mentioned her. I couldn't help it. Now I didn't care any more about seeing her. I hadn't anything more to say to her. I didn't even want to hold her in my arms. I loathed my body because it had turned gray and was sweating—and I wasn't even sure that I didn't loathe hers too. Concha would cry when she heard about my death; for months she would have no more interest in life. But still it was I who was going to die. I thought of her beautiful, loving eyes. When she looked at me something went from her to me. But I thought to myself that it was all over; if she looked at me *now* her gaze would not leave her eyes, it would not reach out to me. I was alone.

Tom too, was alone, but not the same way. He was seated astride his chair and had begun to look at the bench with a sort of smile, with surprise, even. He reached out his hand and touched the wood cautiously, as though he were afraid of breaking something, then he drew his hand back hurriedly, and shivered. I wouldn't have amused myself touching that bench, if I had been Tom, that was just some more Irish play-acting. But somehow it seemed to me too that the different objects had something funny about them. They seemed to have grown paler, less massive than before. I had only to look at the bench, the lamp or the pile of coal dust to feel I was going to die. Naturally, I couldn't think clearly about my death, but I saw it everywhere, even on the different objects, the way they had withdrawn and kept their distance, tactfully, like people talking at the bedside of a dying person. It was *his own death* Tom had just touched on the bench.

In the state I was in, if they had come and told me I could go home quietly, that my life would be saved, it would have left me cold. A few hours, or a few years of waiting are all the same, when you've lost the illusion of being eternal. Nothing mattered to me any more. In a way, I was calm. But it was a horrible kind of calm—because of my body. My body—I saw with its eyes and I heard with its ears, but it was no longer I. It sweat and trembled independently, and I didn't recognize it any longer. I was obliged to touch it and look at it to know what was happening to it, just as if it had been someone else's body. At times I still felt it. I felt a slipping, a sort of headlong plunging, as in a falling airplane, or else I heard my heart beating. But this didn't give me confidence. In fact, everything that came from my body had something damned dubious about it. Most of the time it was silent, it stayed put and I didn't feel anything other than a sort of heaviness, a loathsome presence against me. I had the impression of being bound to an enormous vermin.

The Belgian took out his watch and looked at it.

"It's half-past three," he said.

The son-of-a-bitch! He must have done it on purpose. Tom jumped up. We hadn't yet realized the time was passing. The night surrounded us like a formless, dark mass; I didn't even remember it had started.

Juan started to shout. Wringing his hands, he implored, "I don't want to die! I don't want to die!"

He ran the whole length of the cellar with his arms in the air, then he dropped down onto one of the mattresses, sobbing.

Tom looked at him with dismal eyes and didn't even try to console him any more. The fact was, it was no use; the kid made more noise than we did, but he was less affected, really. He was like a sick person who defends himself against his malady with a high fever. When there's not even any fever left, it's much more serious.

He was crying. I could tell he felt sorry for himself; he was thinking about death. For one second, one single second, I too felt like crying, crying out of pity for myself. But just the contrary happened. I took one look at the kid, saw his thin, sobbing shoulders, and I felt I was inhuman. I couldn't feel pity either for these others or for myself. I said to myself, "I want to die decently."

Tom had gotten up and was standing just under the round opening looking out for the first signs of daylight. I was determined, I wanted to die decently, and I only thought about that. But underneath, ever since the doctor had told us the time, I felt time slipping, flowing by, one drop at a time.

It was still dark when I heard Tom's voice.

"Do you hear them?"

"Yes."

People were walking in the courtyard.

"What the hell are they doing? After all, they can't shoot in the dark."

After a moment, we didn't hear anything more. I said to Tom, "There's the daylight."

Pedro got up yawning, and came and blew out the lamp. He turned to the man beside him. "It's hellish cold."

The cellar had grown gray. We could hear shots at a distance.

"It's about to start," I said to Tom. "That must be in the back courtyard."

Tom asked the doctor to give him a cigarette. I didn't want any; I didn't want either cigarettes or alcohol. From that moment on, the shooting didn't stop.

"Can you take it in?" Tom said.

He started to add something, then he

stopped and began to watch the door. The door opened and a lieutenant came in with four soldiers. Tom dropped his cigarette.

"Steinbock?"

Tom didn't answer. Pedro pointed him out.

"Juan Mirbal?"

"He's the one on the mattress."

"Stand up," said the Lieutenant.

Juan didn't move. Two soldiers took hold of him by the armpits and stood him up on his feet. But as soon as they let go of him he fell down.

The soldiers hesitated a moment.

"He's not the first one to get sick," said the Lieutenant. "You'll have to carry him, the two of you. We'll arrange things when we get there." He turned to Tom. "All right, come along."

Tom left between two soldiers. Two other soldiers followed, carrying the kid by his arms and legs. He was not unconscious; his eyes were wide open and tears were rolling down his cheeks. When I started to go out, the Lieutenant stopped me.

"Are you Ibbieta?"

"Yes."

"You wait here. They'll come and get you later on."

They left. The Belgian and the two jailers left too, and I was alone. I didn't understand what had happened to me, but I would have liked it better if they had ended it all right away. I heard the volleys at almost regular intervals; at each one, I shuddered. I felt like howling and tearing my hair. But instead, I gritted my teeth and pushed by hands deep into my pockets, because I wanted to stay decent.

An hour later, they came to fetch me and took me up to the first floor in a little room which smelt of cigar smoke and was so hot it seemed to me suffocating. Here there were two officers sitting in comfortable chairs, smoking, with papers spread out on their knees.

"Your name is Ibbieta?"

"Yes."

"Where is Ramon Gris?"

"I don't know."

The man who questioned me was small and stocky. He had hard eyes behind his glasses.

"Come nearer," he said to me.

I went nearer. He rose and took me by the arms, looking at me in a way calculated to make me go through the floor. At the same time he pinched my arms with all his might. He didn't mean to hurt me; it was quite a game; he wanted to dominate me. He also seemed to think it was necessary to blow his fetid breath right into my face. We stood like that for a moment, only I felt more like laughing than anything else. It takes a lot more than that to intimidate a man who's about to die: it didn't work. He pushed me away violently and sat down again.

"It's your life or his," he said. "You'll be allowed to go free if you tell us where he is."

After all, these two bedizened fellows with their riding crops and boots were just men who were going to die one day. A little later than I, perhaps, but not a great deal. And there they were, looking for names among their papers, running after other men in order to put them in prison or do away with them entirely. They had their opinions on the future of Spain and on other subjects. Their petty activities seemed to me to be offensive and ludicrous. I could no longer put myself in their place. I had the impression they were crazy.

The little fat fellow kept looking at me, tapping his boots with his riding crop. All his gestures were calculated to make him appear like a spirited, ferocious animal.

"Well? Do you understand?"

"I don't know where Gris is," I said. "I thought he was in Madrid."

The other officer lifted his pale hand indolently. This indolence was also calculated. I saw through all their little tricks, and I was dumbfounded that men should still exist who took pleasure in that kind of thing.

"You have fifteen minutes to think it over," he said slowly. "Take him to the linen-room, and bring him back here in fifteen minutes. If he continues to refuse, he'll be executed at once."

They knew what they were doing. I had spent the night waiting. After that, they had made me wait another hour in the cellar, while they shot Tom and Juan, and now they locked me in the linen-room. They must have arranged the whole thing the night before. They figured that sooner or later people's nerves wear out and they hoped to get me that way.

They made a big mistake. In the linen-room I sat down on a ladder because I felt very weak, and I began to think things over. Not their proposition, however. Naturally I knew where Gris was. He was hiding in his cousins' house, about two miles outside of the city. I knew, too, that I would not reveal his hiding place, unless they tortured me (but they didn't seem to be considering that). All that was definitely settled and didn't interest me in the least. Only I would have liked to understand the reasons for my own conduct. I would rather die than betray Gris. Why? I no longer liked Ramon Gris. My friendship for him had died shortly before dawn along with my love for Concha, along with my own desire to live. Of course I still admired him—he was hard. But it was not for that reason that I was willing to die in his place; his life was no more valuable than mine. No life was of any value. A man was going to be stood up against a wall and fired at till he dropped dead. It didn't make any difference whether it was I or Gris or somebody else. I knew perfectly well he was more useful to the Spanish cause than I was, but I didn't give a God damn about Spain or anarchy, either; nothing had any importance now. And yet, there I was. I could save my skin by betraying Gris and I re-fused to do it. It seemed more ludicrous to me than anything else; it was stubbornness.

I thought to myself, "Am I hardheaded!" And I was seized with a strange sort of cheerfulness.

They came to fetch me and took me back to the two officers. A rat darted out under our feet and that amused me. I turned to one of the falangists and said to him, "Did you see that rat?"

He made no reply. He was gloomy, and took himself very seriously. As for me, I felt like laughing, but I restrained myself because I was afraid that if I started, I wouldn't be able to stop. The falangist wore mustaches. I kept after him, "You ought to cut off those mustaches, you fool."

I was amused by the fact that he let hair grow all over his face while he was still alive. He gave me a kind of half-hearted kick, and I shut up.

"Well," said the fat officer, "have you thought things over?"

I looked at them with curiosity, like insects of a very rare species.

"I know where he is," I said. "He's hiding in the cemetery. Either in one of the vaults, or in the gravediggers' shack."

I said that just to make fools of them. I wanted to see them get up and fasten their belts and bustle about giving orders.

They jumped to their feet.

"Fine. Moles, go ask Lieutenant Lopez for fifteen men. And as for you," the little fat fellow said to me, "if you've told the truth, I don't go back on my word. But you'll pay for this, if you're pulling our leg."

They left noisily and I waited in peace, still guarded by the falangists. From time to time I smiled at the thought of the face they were going to make. I felt dull and malicious. I could see them lifting up the gravestones, or opening the doors of the vaults one by one. I saw the whole situation as though I were another person: the prisoner determined to play the hero, the solemn falangists with their mustaches and the men in uniform running around among the graves. It was irresistibly funny.

After half an hour, the little fat fellow came back alone. I thought he had come to give the order to execute me. The others must have stayed in the cemetery.

The officer looked at me. He didn't look at all foolish.

"Take him out in the big courtyard with the others," he said. "When military operations are over, a regular tribunal will decide his case."

I thought I must have misunderstood.

"So they're not—they're not going to shoot me?" I asked.

"Not now, in any case. Afterwards, that doesn't concern me."

I still didn't understand.

"But why?" I said to him.

He shrugged his shoulders without replying, and the soldiers led me away. In the big courtyard there were a hundred or so prisoners, women, children and a few old men. I started to walk around the grass plot in the middle. I felt absolutely idiotic. At noon we were fed in the dining hall. Two or three fellows spoke to me. I must have known them, but I didn't answer. I didn't even know where I was.

Toward evening, about ten new prisoners were pushed into the courtyard. I recognized Garcia, the baker.

He said to me, "Lucky dog! I didn't expect to find you alive."

"They condemned me to death," I said, "and then they changed their minds. I don't know why."

"I was arrested at two o'clock," Garcia said.

"What for?"

Garcia took no part in politics.

"I don't know," he said. "They arrest everybody who doesn't think the way they do."

He lowered his voice.

"They got Gris."

I began to tremble.

"When?"

"This morning. He acted like a damned fool. He left his cousins' house Tuesday because of a disagreement. There were any number of fellows who would have hidden him, but he didn't want to be indebted to anybody any more. He said, 'I would have hidden at Ibbieta's, but since they've got him, I'll go hide in the cemetery.'"

"In the cemetery?"

"Yes. It was the god-damnedest thing. Naturally they passed by there this morning; that had to happen. They found him in the gravediggers' shack. They opened fire at him and they finished him off."

"In the cemetery!"

Everything went around in circles, and when I came to I was sitting on the ground. I laughed so hard the tears came to my eyes.

A PRIMER OF EXISTENTIALISM

Gordon E. Bigelow

For some years I fought the word by irritably looking the other way whenever I stumbled across it, hoping that like dadaism and some of the other "isms" of the French *avant garde* it would go away if I ignored it. But existentialism was apparently more than the picture it evoked of uncombed beards, smoky basement cafes, and French beatniks regaling one another between sips of absinthe with brilliant variations on the theme of despair. It turned out to be of major importance to literature and the arts, to philosophy and theology, and of increasing importance to the social sciences. To learn more about it, I read several of the self-styled introductions to the subject, with the baffled sensation of a man who reads a critical introduction to a novel only to find that he must read the novel before he can understand the introduction. Therefore, I should like to provide here something most discussions of existentialism take for granted, a simple statement of its basic characteristics. This is a reckless thing to do because there are several kinds of existentialism and what one says of one kind may not be true of another, but there is an area of agreement, and it is this common ground that I should like to set forth here. We should not run into trouble so long as we understand from the outset that the six major themes outlined below will apply in varying degrees to particular existentialists. A reader should be able to go from here to the existentialists themselves, to the more specialized critiques of them, or be able to recognize an existentialist theme or coloration in literature when he sees it.

A word first about the kinds of existentialism. Like transcendentalism of the last century, there are almost as many varieties of this *ism* as there are individual writers to whom the word is applied (not all of them claim it). But without being facetious we might group them into two main kinds, the *ungodly* and the *godly*. To take the ungodly or atheistic first, we would list as the chief spokesmen among many others Jean-Paul Sartre, Albert Camus, and Simone de Beauvoir. Several of this important group of French writers had rigorous and significant experience in the Resistance during the Nazi occupation of France in World War II. Out of the despair which came with the collapse of their nation during those terrible years they found unexpected strength in the single indomitable human spirit, which even under severe torture could maintain the spirit of resistance, the unextinguishable ability to say "No." From this irreducible core in the human spirit, they erected after the war a philosophy which was a twentieth-century variation of the philosophy of Descartes. But instead of saying "I think, therefore I am," they said "I can say No, therefore I exist." As we shall presently see, the use of the word "exist" is one of prime significance. This group is chiefly responsible for giving existentialism its status in the popular mind as a literary-philosophical cult.

Of the godly or theistic existentialists we should mention first a mid-nineteenth-century Danish writer, Søren Kierkegaard; two contemporary French Roman Catholics, Gabriel Marcel and Jacques Maritain; two Protestant theologians, Paul Tillich and Nicholas Berdyaev; and Martin Buber, an important contemporary Jewish theologian. Taken to-

[363]

gether, their writings constitute one of the most significant developments in modern theology. Behind both groups of existentialists stand other important figures, chiefly philosophers, who exert powerful influence upon the movement— Blaise Pascal, Friedrich Nietzsche, Henri Bergson, Martin Heidegger, Karl Jaspers, among others. Several literary figures, notably Tolstoy and Dostoievsky, are frequently cited because existentialist attitudes and themes are prominent in their writings. The eclectic nature of this movement should already be sufficiently clear and the danger of applying too rigidly to any particular figure the general characteristics of the movement which I now make bold to describe:

1. EXISTENCE BEFORE ESSENCE. Existentialism gets its name from an insistence that human life is understandable only in terms of an individual man's existence, his particular experience of life. It says that a man *lives* (has existence) rather than *is* (has being or essence), and that every man's experience of life is unique, radically different from everyone else's and can be understood truly only in terms of his involvement in life or commitment to it. It strenuously shuns that view which assumes an ideal of Man or Mankind, a universal of human nature of which each man is only one example. It eschews the question of Greek philosophy, *"What is mankind?"* which suggests that man can be defined if he is ranged in his proper place in the order of nature; it asks instead the question of Job in St. Augustine, *"Who am I?"* with its suggestion of the uniqueness and mystery of each human life and its emphasis upon the subjective or personal rather than the objective or impersonal. From the outside a man appears to be just another natural creature; from the inside he is an entire universe, the center of infinity. The existentialist insists upon this latter radically subjective view, and from this grows much of the rest of existentialism.

2. REASON IS IMPOTENT TO DEAL WITH THE DEPTHS OF HUMAN LIFE. There are two parts to this proposition—first, that human reason is relatively weak and imperfect, and second, that there are dark places in human life which are "nonreason" and to which reason scarcely penetrates. Since Plato, Western civilization has usually assumed a separation of reason from the rest of the human psyche, and has glorified reason as suited to command the nonrational part. The classic statement of this separation appears in the *Phaedrus,* where Plato describes the psyche in the myth of the chariot which is drawn by the white steeds of the emotions and the black unruly steeds of the appetites. The driver of the chariot is Reason who holds the reins which control the horses and the whip to subdue the surging black steeds of passion. Only the driver, the rational nature, is given human form; the rest of the psyche, the nonrational part, is given a lower, animal form. This separation and exaltation of reason is carried further in the allegory of the cave in the *Republic.* You recall the sombre picture of human life with which the story begins: men are chained in the dark in a cave, with their backs to a flickering firelight, able to see only uncertain shadows moving on the wall before them, able to hear only confused echoes of sounds. One of the men, breaking free from his chains, is able to turn and look upon the objects themselves and the light which casts the shadows; even, at last, he is able to work his way entirely out of the cave into the sunlight beyond. All this he is able to do through his reason; he escapes from the bondage of error, from time and change, from death itself, into the realm of changeless eternal ideas or Truth, and the lower nature which had chained him in darkness is left behind.

Existentialism in our time, and this is one of its most important characteristics, insists upon reuniting the "lower" or irrational parts of the psyche with the "higher." It insists that man must be taken in his wholeness and not in some divided state, that whole man contains not only intellect but also anxiety, guilt, and the will to power—which modify and sometimes overwhelm the reason. A man seen in this light is fundamentally ambiguous, if not mysterious, full of contradictions and tensions which cannot be dissolved simply by taking thought. "Human life," said Berdyaev, "is permeated by underground streams." One is reminded of D. H. Lawrence's outburst against Franklin and his rational attempt to achieve moral perfection: "The Perfectability of Man! . . . The perfectability of which man? I am many men. Which of them are you going to perfect? I am not a mechanical contrivance. . . . It's a queer thing is a man's soul. It is the whole of him. Which means it is the unknown as well as the known. . . . The soul of man is a dark vast forest, with wild life in it." The emphasis in existentialism is not on idea but upon the thinker who has the idea. It accepts not only his power of thought, but his contingency and fallibility, his frailty, his body, blood, and bones, and above all his death. Kierkegaard emphasized the distinction between *subjective* truth (what a person *is*) and *objective* truth (what a person *knows*), and said that we encounter the true self not in the detachment of thought but in the involvement and agony of choice and in the pathos of commitment to our choice. This distrust of rational systems helps to explain why many existential writers in their own expression are paradoxical or prophetic or gnomic, why their works often belong more to literature than to philosophy.

3. ALIENATION OR ESTRANGEMENT. One major result of the dissociation of reason from the rest of the psyche has been the growth of science, which has become one of the hallmarks of Western civiliza-tion, and an ever-increasing rational ordering of men in society. As the existentialists view them, the main forces of history since the Renaissance have progressively separated man from concrete earthy existence, have forced him to live at ever higher levels of abstraction, have collectivized individual man out of existence, have driven God from the heavens, or what is the same thing, from the hearts of men. They are convinced that modern man lives in a fourfold condition of alienation: from God, from nature, from other men, from his own true self.

The estrangement of God is most shockingly expressed by Nietzsche's anguished cry, "God is dead," a cry which has continuously echoed through the writings of the existentialists, particularly the French. This theme of spiritual barrenness is a commonplace in literature of this century, from Eliot's "Hollow Man" to the novels of Dos Passos, Hemingway, and Faulkner. It often appears in writers not commonly associated with the existentialists as in this remarkable passage from *A Story-Teller's Story,* where Sherwood Anderson describes his own awakening to his spiritual emptiness. He tells of walking alone late at night along a moonlit road when,

I had suddenly an odd, and to my own seeming, a ridiculous desire to abase myself before something not human and so stepping into the moonlit road, I knelt in the dust. Having no God, the gods having been taken from me by the life about me, as a personal God has been taken from all modern men by a force within that man himself does not understand but that is called the intellect, I kept smiling at the figure I cut in my own eyes as I knelt in the road. . . .

There was no God in the sky, no God in myself, no conviction in myself that I had the power to believe in a God, and so I merely knelt in the dust in silence and no words came to my lips.

In another passage Anderson wondered if the giving of itself by an entire generation to mechanical things was not really making all men impotent, if the desire for a greater navy, a greater army, taller public buildings, was not a sign of growing impotence. He felt that Puritanism and the industrialism which was its offspring had sterilized modern life, and proposed that men return to a healthful animal vigor by renewed contact with simple things of the earth, among them untrammeled sexual expression. One is reminded of the unkempt and delectable raffishness of Steinbeck's *Cannery Row* or of D. H. Lawrence's quasi-religious doctrine of sex, "blood-consciousness" and the "divine otherness" of animal existence.

Man's estrangement from nature has been a major theme in literature at least since Rousseau and the Romantic movement, and can hardly be said to be the property of existentialists. But this group nevertheless adds its own insistence that one of modern man's most urgent dangers is that he builds ever higher the brick and steel walls of technology which shut him away from a health-giving life according to "nature." Their treatment of this theme is most commonly expressed as part of a broader insistence that modern man needs to shun abstraction and return to "concreteness" or "wholeness."

A third estrangement has occurred at the social level and its sign is a growing dismay at man's helplessness before the great machine-like colossus of industrialized society. This is another major theme of Western literature, and here again, though they hardly discovered the danger or began the protest, the existentialists in our time renew the protest against any pattern or force which would stifle the unique and spontaneous in individual life. The crowding of men into cities, the subdivision of labor which submerges the man in his economic function, the burgeoning of centralized government, the growth of advertising, propaganda, and mass media of entertainment and communication—all the things which force men into Riesman's "Lonely Crowd"—these same things drive men asunder by destroying their individuality and making them live on the surface of life, content to deal with things rather than people. "Exteriorization," says Berdyaev, "is the source of slavery, whereas freedom is interiorization. Slavery always indicates alienation, the ejection of human nature into the external." This kind of alienation is exemplified by Zero, in Elmer Rice's play "The Adding Machine." Zero's twenty-five years as a bookkeeper in a department store have dried up his humanity, making him incapable of love, of friendship, of any deeply felt, freely expressed emotion. Such estrangement is often given as the reason for man's inhumanity to man, the explanation for injustice in modern society. In Camus' short novel, aptly called *The Stranger,* a young man is convicted by a court of murder. This is a homicide which he has actually committed under extenuating circumstances. But the court never listens to any of the relevant evidence, seems never to hear anything that pertains to the crime itself; it convicts the young man on wholly irrelevant grounds —because he had behaved in an unconventional way at his mother's funeral the day before the homicide. In this book one feels the same dream-like distortion of reality as in the trial scene in *Alice in Wonderland,* a suffocating sense of being enclosed by events which are irrational or absurd but also inexorable. Most disturbing of all is the young man's aloneness, the impermeable membrane of estrangement which surrounds him and prevents anyone else from penetrating to his experience of life or sympathizing with it.

The fourth kind of alienation, man's estrangement from his own true self, especially as his nature is distorted by an exaltation of reason, is another theme having an extensive history as a major part of the Romantic revolt. Of the many writers who treat the theme, Hawthorne comes particularly close to the emphasis of contemporary existentialists. His Ethan Brand, Dr. Rappaccini, and Roger Chillingworth are a recurrent figure who represents the dislocation in human nature which results when an overdeveloped or misapplied intellect severs "the magnetic chain of human sympathy." Hawthorne is thoroughly existential in his concern for the sanctity of the individual human soul, as well as his preoccupation with sin and the dark side of human nature, which must be seen in part as his attempt to build back some fullness to the flattened image of man bequeathed to him by the Enlightenment. Whitman was trying to do this when he added flesh and bone and a sexual nature to the spiritualized image of man he inherited from Emerson, though his image remains diffused and attenuated by the same cosmic optimism. Many of the nineteenth-century depictions of man represent him as a figure of power or of potential power, sometimes as daimonic, like Melville's Ahab, but after World War I the power is gone; man is not merely distorted or truncated, he is hollow, powerless, faceless. At the time when his command over natural forces seems to be unlimited, man is pictured as weak, ridden with nameless dread. And this brings us to another of the major themes of existentialism.

4. "FEAR AND TREMBLING," ANXIETY. At Stockholm when he accepted the Nobel Prize, William Faulkner said that "Our tragedy today is a general and universal physical fear so long sustained by now that we can even bear it. There are no longer problems of the spirit. There is only one question: When will I be blown up?" The optimistic vision of the Enlightenment which saw man, through reason and its extensions in science, conquering all nature and solving all social and political problems in a continuous upward spiral of Progress, cracked open like a melon on the rock of World War I. The theories which held such high hopes died in that sickening and unimaginable butchery. Here was a concrete fact of human nature and society which the theories could not contain. The Great Depression and World War II deepened the sense of dismay which the loss of these ideals brought, but only with the atomic bomb did this become an unbearable terror, a threat of instant annihilation which confronted all men, even those most insulated by the thick crust of material goods and services. Now the most unthinking person could sense that each advance in mechanical technique carried not only a chromium and plush promise of comfort but a threat as well.

Sartre, following Kierkegaard, speaks of another kind of anxiety which oppresses modern man—"the anguish of Abraham"—the necessity which is laid upon him to make moral choices on his own responsibility. A military officer in wartime knows the agony of choice which forces him to sacrifice part of his army to preserve the rest, as does a man in high political office, who must make decisions affecting the lives of millions. The existentialists claim that each of us must make moral decisions in our own lives which involve the same anguish. Kierkegaard finds that this necessity is one thing which makes each life unique, which makes it impossible to speculate or generalize about human life, because each man's case is irretrievably his own, something in which he is personally and passionately involved. His book *Fear and ·Trembling* is an elaborate and fascinating commentary on the Old Testament story of Abraham, who was commanded by God to sacrifice his beloved son Isaac. Abraham thus becomes the emblem of man who must make a harrowing choice, in this case between love for his son and love for God, between the universal moral law which says categorically, "thou shalt not kill," and the unique inner demand of his religious faith. Abraham's decision, which is to violate the abstract and collective moral law, has to be made not in arrogance but in fear and trembling, one of the inferences being that sometimes one must make an exception to the general law because he is (existentially) an exception, a concrete being whose existence can never be completely subsumed under any universal.

5. THE ENCOUNTER WITH NOTHING-NESS. For the man alienated from God, from nature, from his fellow man and from himself, what is left at last but Nothingness? The testimony of the existentialists is that this is where modern man now finds himself, not on the highway of upward Progress toward a radiant Utopia but on the brink of a catastrophic precipice, below which yawns the absolute void, an uncompromised black Nothingness. In one sense this is Eliot's Wasteland inhabited by his Hollow Man, who is

Shape without form, shade without color
Paralyzed force, gesture without motion.

This is what moves E. A. Robinson's Richard Cory, the man who is everything that might make us wish that we were in his place, to go home one calm summer night and put a bullet through his head.

One of the most convincing statements of the encounter with Nothingness is made by Leo Tolstoy in "My Confession." He tells how in good health, in the prime of life, when he had everything that a man could desire—wealth, fame, aristocratic social position, a beautiful wife and children, a brilliant mind and great artistic talent in the height of their powers, he nevertheless was seized with a growing uneasiness, a nameless discontent which he could not shake or alleviate. His experience was like that of a man who falls sick, with symptoms which he disregards as insignificant; but the symptoms return again and again until they merge into a continuous suffering. And the patient suddenly is confronted with the overwhelming fact that what he took for mere indisposition is more important to him than anything else on earth, that it is death! "I felt the ground on which I stood was crumbling, that there was nothing for me to stand on, that what I had been living for was nothing, that I had no reason for living. . . . To stop was impossible, to go back was impossible; and it was impossible to shut my eyes so as to see that there was nothing before me but suffering and actual death, absolute annihilation." This is the "Sickness Unto Death" of Kierkegaard, the despair in which one wishes to die but cannot. Hemingway's short story, "A Clean, Well-Lighted Place," gives an unforgettable expression of this theme. At the end of the story, the old waiter climbs into bed late at night saying to himself, "What did he fear? It was not fear or dread. It was a nothing which he knew too well. It was all a nothing and a man was nothing too. . . . Nada y pues nada, y nada y pues nada." And then because he has experienced the death of God he goes on to recite the Lord's Prayer in blasphemous despair: "Our Nothing who art in Nothing, nothing be thy nothing. . . ." And then the Ave Maria, "Hail nothing, full of nothing. . . ." This is stark, even for Hemingway, but the old waiter does no more than name the void felt by most people in the early Hemingway novels, a hunger they seek to assuage with alcohol, sex, and violence in an aimless progress from bar to bed to bull-ring. It goes without saying that much of the despair and pessimism in other contemporary authors springs from a similar sense of the void in modern life.

6. FREEDOM. Sooner or later, as a theme that includes all the others, the

[ABOVE] PETER BRUEGHEL, detail from "Landscape with the Fall of Icarus" [Musée Royaux des Beaux-Arts, Brussels].

[BELOW] BEN SHAHN, "The Red Stairway" [City Art Museum of St. Louis].

existentialist writings bear upon freedom. The themes we have outlined above describe either some loss of man's freedom or some threat to it, and all existentialists of whatever sort are concerned to enlarge the range of human freedom.

For the avowed atheists like Sartre freedom means human autonomy. In a purposeless universe man is *condemned* to freedom because he is the only creature who is "self-surpassing," who can become something other than he is. Precisely because there is no God to give purpose to the universe, each man must accept individual responsibility for his own becoming, a burden made heavier by the fact that in choosing for himself he chooses for all men "the image of man as he ought to be." A man *is* the sum total of the acts that make up his life— no more, no less—and though the coward has made himself cowardly, it is always possible for him to change and make himself heroic. In Sartre's novel, *The Age of Reason,* one of the least likable of the characters, almost overwhelmed by despair and self-disgust at his homosexual tendencies, is on the point of solving his problem by mutilating himself with a razor, when in an effort of will he throws the instrument down, and we are given to understand that from this moment he will have mastery over his aberrant drive. Thus in the daily course of ordinary life must men shape their becoming in Sartre's world.

The religious existentialists interpret man's freedom differently. They use much the same language as Sartre, develop the same themes concerning the predicament of man, but always include God as a radical factor. They stress the man of faith rather than the man of will. They interpret man's existential condition as a state of alienation from his essential nature which is God-like, the problem of his life being to heal the chasm between the two, that is, to find salvation. The mystery and ambiguity of man's existence they attribute to his being the intersection of two realms. "Man bears within himself," writes Berdyaev, "the image which is both the image of man and the image of God, and is the image of man as far as the image of God is actualized." Tillich describes salvation as "the act in which the cleavage between the essential being and the existential situation is overcome." Freedom here, as for Sartre, involves an acceptance of responsibility for choice and a *commitment* to one's choice. This is the meaning of faith, a faith like Abraham's, the commitment which is an agonizing sacrifice of one's own desire and will and dearest treasure to God's will.

A final word. Just as one should not expect to find in a particular writer all of the characteristics of existentialism as we have described them, he should also be aware that some of the most striking expressions of existentialism in literature and the arts come to us by indirection, often through symbols or through innovations in conventional form. Take the preoccupation of contemporary writers with time. In *The Sound and the Fury,* Faulkner both collapses and expands normal clock time, or by juxtapositions of past and present blurs time into a single amorphous pool. He does this by using various forms of "stream of consciousness" or other techniques which see life in terms of unique, subjective experience— that is, existentially. The conventional view of externalized life, a rational orderly progression cut into uniform segments by the hands of a clock, he rejects in favor of a view which sees life as opaque, ambiguous, and irrational—that is, as the existentialist sees it. Graham Greene does something like this in *The Power and the Glory.* He creates a scene isolated in time and cut off from the rest of the world, steamy and suffocating as if a bell jar had been placed over it. Through this atmosphere fetid with impending death and human suffering, stumbles the whiskey priest, lonely and confused, pursued by a police lieutenant who has experienced the void and the death of God.

Such expressions in literature do not mean necessarily that the authors are conscious existentialist theorizers, or even that they know the writings of such theorizers. Faulkner may never have read Heidegger—or St. Augustine—both of whom attempt to demonstrate that time is more within a man and subject to his unique experience of it than it is outside him. But it is legitimate to call Faulkner's views of time and life "existential" in this novel because in recent years existentialist theorizers have given such views a local habitation and a name. One of the attractions, and one of the dangers, of existential themes is that they become like Sir Thomas Browne's quincunx: once one begins to look for them, he sees them everywhere. But if one applies restraint and discrimination, he will find that they illuminate much of contemporary literature and sometimes the literature of the past as well.

KING LEAR or ENDGAME

Jan Kott

KING LEAR
Dost thou call me fool, boy?
FOOL
All thy other titles thou hast given away; that thou wast
born with.

(King Lear, I, 4)

We are all born mad. Some remain so.

(Waiting for Godot, II)

I

THE attitude of modern criticism to *King Lear* is ambiguous and somehow embarrassed. Doubtless *King Lear* is still recognized as a masterpiece, besides which even *Macbeth* and *Hamlet* seem tame and pedestrian. *King Lear* is compared to Bach's *Mass in B Minor,* to Beethoven's *Fifth* and *Ninth* Symphonies, to Wagner's *Parsifal,* Michelangelo's *Last Judgement,* or Dante's *Purgatory* and *Inferno.* But at the same time *King Lear* gives one the impression of a high mountain that everyone admires, yet no one particularly wishes to climb. It is as if the play had lost its power to excite on the stage and in reading; as if it were out of place in our time, or, at any rate, had no place in the modern theatre. But the question is: what is modern theatre?

The apogee of *King Lear's* theatrical history was reached no doubt in the romantic era. *King Lear* fit the romantic theatre perfectly; but only conceived as a melodrama, full of horrors, dealing with a tragic king, deprived of his crown, conspired against by heaven and earth, nature and men. Charles Lamb might well laugh at early nineteenth-century performances in which a miserable old man wandered about the stage bare-headed, stick in hand, in an artificial storm and rain. But the theatre was soon to attain the full power of illusion. Diorama, scene changes effected by means of new stage machinery without bringing the curtain down, made it possible suddenly, almost miraculously to transform a Gothic castle into a mountainous region, or a blood-red sunset into a stormy night. Lightning and thunder, rain and wind, seemed like the real thing. It was easy for the romantic imagination to find its favourite landscape: gloomy castles, hovels, deserted spots, mysterious and awe-inspiring places, towering rocks gleaming white in the moonlight. *King Lear* was also in keeping with the romantic style of acting, since it offered scope for the sweeping gestures, terrifying scenes, and violent soliloquies, loudly delivered, so popular with Kean and his school. The actor's task was to demonstrate the blackest depths of the human soul. Lear's and Gloucester's unhappy fate was to arouse pity and terror, to shock the audience. And so it did. Suffering purified Lear and restored his tragic greatness. Shakespeare's *King Lear* was the "black theatre" of romanticism.

Then came the turn of historical, antiquarian and realistic Shakespeare. Stage designers were sent to Rome to copy features of the Forum for sets to *Julius Caesar.* Crowds of extras were dressed in period costume. Copies were made of medieval dress, Renaissance jewelry,

Elizabethan furniture. Sets became more and more solid and imposing. The stage was turned into a large exhibition of historical props. A balcony had to be a real balcony; a palace, a real palace; a street, a real street. Real trees were substituted for the old painted landscape.

At the time attempts were made to set *King Lear* also in a definite historical period. With the help of archeologists Celtic burial places were reconstructed on the stage. Lear became an old druid. Theatrical machinery was more and more perfect, so that storm, wind and rain could drown the actors' voices more and more effectively. As a result of the odd marriage between new and perfected theatre techniques and archeological reconstruction of a Celtic tomb, only the plot remained of Shakespeare's play. In such a theatre Shakespeare was indeed out of place: he was untheatrical.

The turn of the century brought a revolution in Shakespearean studies. For the first time his plays began to be interpreted through the theatre of his time. A generation of scholars was busy patiently recreating the Elizabethan stage, style of acting and theatrical traditions. Granville-Barker in his famous *Prefaces to Shakespeare* showed, or at least tried to show, how *Lear* must have been played at the Globe. The return to the so-called "authentic" Shakespeare began. From now on the storm was to rage in Lear's and Gloucester's breasts rather than on the stage. The trouble was, however, that the demented old man, tearing his long white beard, suddenly became ridiculous. He should have been tragic, but he no longer was.

Nearly all Shakespeare's expositions have an amazing speed and directness in the way conflicts are shown and put into action and the whole tone of the play is set. The exposition of *King Lear* seems preposterous if one is to look for psychological verisimilitude in it. A great and powerful king holds a competition of rhetoric among his daughters, as to which one of them will best express her love for him, and makes the division of his kingdom depend on its outcome. He does not see or understand anything: Regan's and Goneril's hypocrisy is all too evident. Regarded as a person, a character, Lear is ridiculous, naive and stupid. When he goes mad, he can arouse only compassion, never pity and terror.

Gloucester, too, is naive and ridiculous. In the early scenes he seems a stock character from a comedy of manners. Robert Speaight compares him to a gentleman of somewhat old-fashioned views who strolls on a Sunday along St. James's Street complete with bowler hat and umbrella.[1] Nothing about him hints at the tragic old man whose eyes will be gouged out. It is true that Polonius in *Hamlet* is also a comic figure, who later is stabbed to death. But his death is grotesque, too, while Lear and Gloucester are to go through immense sufferings.

Producers have found it virtually impossible to cope with the plot of *King Lear*. When realistically treated, Lear and Gloucester were too ridiculous to appear tragic heroes. If the exposition was treated as a fairy tale or legend, the cruelty of Shakespeare's world, too, became unreal. Yet the cruelty of *Lear* was to the Elizabethans a contemporary reality, and has remained real since. But it is a philosophical cruelty. Neither the romantic, nor the naturalistic theatre was able to show that sort of cruelty; only the new theatre can. In this new theatre there are no characters, and the tragic element has been superseded by grotesque. Grotesque is more cruel than tragedy.

The exposition of *King Lear* is as absurd, and as necessary as the arrival at Güllen of multi-millionairess Claire

[1] See R. Speaight, *Nature in Shakespearian Tragedy,* London, 1955.

Zachanassian and her entourage, including a new husband, a couple of eunuchs, a large coffin, and a tiger in a cage in Dürrenmatt's *Visit*. The exposition of *King Lear* shows a world that is to be destroyed.

Since the end of the eighteenth century no dramatist has had a greater impact on European drama than Shakespeare. But the theatres in which Shakespeare's plays have been produced were in turn influenced by contemporary plays. Shakespeare has been a living influence in so far as contemporary plays, through which his dramas were interpreted, were a living force themselves. When Shakespeare is dull and dead on the stage, it means that not only the theatre but also the plays written in that particular period are dead. This is one of the reasons why Shakespeare's universality has never dated.

The book devoted to "Shakespeare and the new drama" has not yet been written. Perhaps it is too early for such a book to appear. But it is odd how often the word "Shakespearean" is uttered when one speaks about Brecht, Dürrenmatt, or Beckett. These three names stand, of course, for three different kinds of theatrical vision, and the word "Shakespearean" means something different in relation to each of them. It may be invoked to compare with Dürrenmatt's full-bloodedness, sharpness, lack of cohesion, and stylistic confusion; with Brecht's epic quality; or with Beckett's new *Theatrum mundi*.[2] But every one of these three kinds of drama and theatre has more similarities to Shakespeare and medieval morality plays than to nineteenth-century drama, whether romantic, or naturalistic. Only in this sense can the new theatre be called anti-theatre.

A striking feature of the new theatre is its grotesque quality. Despite appearances

[2] "Universal Theatre" (literally, "theatre of the world").

to the contrary, this new grotesque has not replaced the old drama and the comedy of manners. It deals with problems, conflicts and themes of tragedy such as: human fate, the meaning of existence, freedom and inevitability, the discrepancy between the absolute and the fragile human order. Grotesque means tragedy re-written in different terms. Maurice Regnault's statement: "the absence of tragedy in a tragic world gives birth to comedy" is only seemingly paradoxical. Grotesque exists in a tragic world. Both the tragic and the grotesque vision of the world are composed as it were of the same elements. In a tragic and grotesque world, situations are imposed, compulsory and inescapable. Freedom of choice and decision are part of this compulsory situation, in which both the tragic hero and the grotesque actor must always lose their struggle against the absolute. The downfall of the tragic hero is a confirmation and recognition of the absolute; whereas the downfall of the grotesque actor means mockery of the absolute and its desecration. The absolute is transformed into a blind mechanism, a kind of automaton. Mockery is directed not only at the tormentor, but also at the victim who believed in the tormentor's justice, raising him to the level of the absolute. The victim has consecrated his tormentor by recognizing himself as victim.

In the final instance tragedy is an appraisal of human fate, a measure of the absolute. The grotesque is a criticism of the absolute in the name of frail human experience. That is why tragedy brings catharsis, while grotesque offers no consolation whatsoever. "Tragedy," wrote Gorgias of Leontium, "is a swindle in which the swindler is more just than the swindled, and the swindled wiser than the swindler." One may travesty this aphorism by saying that grotesque is a swindle in which the swindled is more just than the swindler, and the swindler wiser than the swindled. Claire Zachanassian in Dürrenmatt's *Visit* is wiser than Anton Schill, but he is more just than she is. Schill's death, like Polonius's death in *Hamlet,* is grotesque. Neither Schill, nor the inhabitants of Güllen are tragic heroes. The old lady with her artificial breasts, teeth and limbs is not a goddess; she hardly even exists, she might almost have been invented. Schill and the people of Güllen find themselves in a situation in which there is no room for tragedy, but only for grotesque. "Comedy," writes Ionesco in his *Expérience du théâtre,* "is a feeling of absurdity, and seems more hopeless than tragedy; comedy allows no way out of a given situation." [3]

The tragic and the grotesque worlds are closed, and there is no escape from them. In the tragic world this compulsory situation has been imposed in turn by the Gods, Fate, the Christian God, Nature, and History that has been endowed with reason and inevitability.

On the other side, opposed to this arrangement, there was always man. If Nature was the absolute, man was unnatural. If man was natural, the absolute was represented by Grace, without which there was no salvation. In the world of the grotesque, downfall cannot be justified by, or blamed on, the absolute. The absolute is not endowed with any ultimate reasons; it is stronger, and that is all. The absolute is absurd. Maybe that is why the grotesque often makes use of the concept of a mechanism which has been put in motion and cannot be stopped. Various kinds of impersonal and hostile mechanisms have taken the place of God, Nature and History, found in the old tragedy. The notion of absurd mechanism is probably the last metaphysical concept remaining in modern grotesque. But this absurd mechanism is not transcendental

[3] E. Ionesco, *"Expérience du théâtre,"* Nouvelle Revue Française, February 1958.

any more in relation to man, or at any rate to mankind. It is a trap set by man himself into which he has fallen.

The scene of tragedy has mostly been a natural landscape. Raging nature witnessed man's downfall, or—as in *King Lear*—played an active part in the action. Modern grotesque usually takes place in the midst of civilization. Nature has evaporated from it almost completely. Man is confined to a room and surrounded by inanimate objects. But objects have now been raised to the status of symbols of human fate, or situation, and perform a similar function to that played in Shakespeare by forest, storm, or eclipse of the sun. Even Sartre's hell is just a vast hotel consisting of rooms and corridors, beyond which there are more rooms and more corridors. This hell "behind closed doors" does not need any metaphysical aids.

Ionesco's hell is arranged on similar lines. A new tenant moves into an empty flat. Furniture is brought in. There is more and more furniture. Furniture surrounds the tenant on all sides. He is surrounded already by four wardrobes but more are brought in. He has been closed in by furniture. He can no longer be seen. He has been brought down to the level of inanimate objects and has become an object himself.

In Beckett's *Endgame* there is a room with a wheel-chair and two dustbins. A picture hangs face to the wall. There is also a staircase, a telescope and a whistle. All that remains of nature is sand in the dustbins, a flea, and the part of man that belongs to nature: his body.

HAMM
Nature has forgotten us.
CLOV
There's no more nature.
HAMM
No more nature! You exaggerate.
CLOV
In the vicinity.

HAMM

But we breathe, we change! We lose our hair, our teeth! Our bloom! Our ideals!

CLOV

Then she hasn't forgotten us.

(p. 16) [4]

It can easily be shown how, in the new theatre, tragic situations become grotesque. Such a classic situation of tragedy is the necessity of making a choice between opposing values. Antigone is doomed to choose between human and divine order; between Creon's demands, and those of the absolute. The tragedy lies in the very principle of choice by which one of the values must be annihilated. The cruelty of the absolute lies in demanding such a choice and in imposing a situation which excludes the possibility of a compromise, and where one of the alternatives is death. The absolute is greedy and demands everything; the hero's death is its confirmation.

The tragic situation becomes grotesque when both alternatives of the choice imposed are absurd, irrelevant or compromising. The hero has to play, even if there is no game. Every move is bad, but he cannot throw down his cards. To throw down the cards would also be a bad move.

It is this situation that Dürrenmatt's Romulus finds himself in. He is the last emperor of a crumbling empire. He will not alter the course of history. History has made a fool of him. He can either die in a spectacular fashion, or lie on his bed and wait to be butchered. He can surrender, compose speeches, or commit suicide. In his position as the last Roman emperor, every one of these solutions is compromising and ridiculous. History has turned Romulus into a clown, and yet demands that he treat her seriously.

[4] All quotations from Beckett are given in the author's own translation. Page references in quotations from *Endgame* and *Act Without Words* apply to the Faber & Faber edition of 1958.

Romulus has only one good move to make: consciously to accept the part of a clown and play it to the end. He can breed chickens. In this way the historical inevitability will have been made a fool of. The absolute will have been flouted.

Antigone is a tragedy of choice, *Oedipus* a tragedy of "unmerited guilt" and destiny. The gods loyally warn the protagonist that fate has destined him to be a patricide and his own mother's husband. The hero has full freedom of decision and action. The gods do not interfere; they just watch and wait until he makes a mistake. Then they punish him. The gods are just, and punish the hero for a crime he has indeed committed, and only after he has committed it. But the protagonist had to commit a crime. Oedipus wanted to cheat fate, but did not and could not escape it. He fell into a trap, made his mistake, killed his father and married his mother. What is to happen will happen.

The tragedy of Oedipus may, perhaps, be posed as a problem belonging to the theory of game. The game is just, i.e. at the outset both partners must have the same chances of losing or winning, and both must play according to the same rules. In its game with Oedipus fate does not invoke the help of the gods, does not change the laws of nature. Fate wins its game without recourse to miracles.

The game must be just, but at the same time must be so arranged that the same party always wins; so that Oedipus always loses.

Let us imagine an electronic computer, which plays chess and calculates any number of moves in advance. A man must play chess with an electronic computer, cannot leave or break the game, and has to lose the game. His defeat is just, because it is effected according to the rules of the game; he loses because he has made a mistake. But he could not have won.

A man losing the chess game with an electronic computer, whom he himself has fed with combinatorial analysis and rules, whom he himself has "taught" to play, is not a tragic hero any more. If he plays that chess game from the moment he was born until he dies, and if he has to lose, he will at most be the hero of a tragi-grotesque. All that is left of tragedy, is the concept of "unmerited guilt", the inevitable defeat, and unavoidable mistake. But the absolute has ceased to exist. It has been replaced by the absurdity of the human situation.

The absurdity does not consist in the fact that man-made mechanisms are in certain conditions stronger, and even wiser, than he. The absurdity consists in the fact that they create a compulsory situation by forcing him to a game in which the probability of his total defeat constantly increases. The Christian view of the end of the world, with the Last Judgement and its segregation of the just and the unjust, is pathetic. The end of the world caused by the big bomb is spectacular, but grotesque just the same. Such an end of the world is intellectually unacceptable, whether to Christians or to Marxists. It would be a silly ending.

The comparison between fate's game with Oedipus, and a game of chess with an electronic computer, is not precise enough. An automatic device to play chess, even if it could compute any number of moves, need not win all the time. It would simply more often win than lose. But among automatic devices that really exist one could find a much better example. There is a machine for a game similar to tossing coins for "heads or tails". I put a coin on the table the way I like, with "heads" or "tails" on top. The machine does not see the coin, but it is to make out how I have put it. If it gives the right answer, it wins. I inform the machine whether it has given the right answer. I put the coin again, and so on. After a time the machine begins to win

by giving the right answers more and more often. It has memorized and learned my system; it has deciphered me as it were. It foresees that after three "heads" I will put two "tails". I change the system, and play using a different method. The blind machine learns this one too, and begins to win again. I am endowed with free will and have the freedom of choice. I can put "heads" or "tails". But in the end, like Oedipus, I must lose the game.

There is a move by which I do not lose. I do not put the coin on the table, I do not choose. I simply toss it. I have given up the system, and left matters to chance. Now the machine and I have even chances. The possibility of win and loss, of "heads" or "tails" is the same. It amounts to fifty-fifty. The machine wanted me to treat it seriously, to play rationally with it, using a system, a method. But I do not want to. It is I who have now seen through the machine's method.

The machine stands for fate, which acts on the principle of the law of averages. In order to have even chances with fate I must become fate myself; I must chance my luck; act with a fifty-fifty chance. A man who, when playing with the machine, gives up his free will and freedom of choice, adopts an attitude to fate similar to that which Dürrenmatt's Romulus adopted with regard to historical necessity. Instead of putting the coin with "heads" on top a hundred times in succession, or "heads" and "tails" in turn, or two "tails" after ten "heads", he would just toss the coin up. That kind of man most certainly is not a tragic hero. He has adopted a clownish attitude to fate. Romulus is such a man.

In modern tragedy fate, gods and nature have been replaced by history. History is the only frame of reference, the final authority to accept or reject the validity of human actions. It is unavoidable and realizes its ultimate aims; it is objective "reason", as well as objective "progress". In this scheme of things history is a theatre with actors, but without an audience. No one watches the performance, for everybody is taking part. The script of this grand spectacle has been composed in advance and includes a necessary epilogue, which will explain everything. But, as in the *commedia dell'arte,* the text has not been written down. The actors improvise and only some of them foresee correctly what will happen in the following acts. In this particular theatre the scene changes with the actors; they are constantly setting it up and pulling it down again.

Actors are often wrong, but their mistakes have been foreseen by the scenario. One might even say that mistakes are the basis of the script, and that it is thanks to them that the action unfolds. History contains both the past and the future. Actors from previous scenes keep coming back, repeating old conflicts, and want to play parts that are long since over. They needlessly prolong the performance and have to be removed from the stage. They arrived too late. Other actors have arrived too early and start performing a scene from the next act, without noticing that the stage is not yet ready for them. They want to speed up the performance, but this cannot be done: every act has to be performed in its proper order. Those who arrive too early are also removed from the stage.

It is these parts that nineteenth-century philosophy and literature considered tragic. For Hegel the tragic heroes of history were those who came too late. Their reasons were noble but one-sided. They had been correct in the previous era, in the preceding act. If they continue to insist on them, they must be crushed by history. La Vendée was for Hegel an example of historical tragedy. Count Henry in Krasiński's *Undivine Comedy* is a Hegelian tragic hero.

Those who came too early, striving in vain to speed up the course of history, are also history's tragic heroes. Their reasons, too, are one-sided; they will become valid only at the next historical phase, in the succeeding act. They failed to understand that freedom is only the conscious recognition of necessity. Consequently they were annihilated by historical necessity, which solves only those problems that are capable of solution. The Paris Commune is an example of this kind of historical tragedy. Pancrace in *Undivine Comedy* is a tragic hero of history thus conceived.

The grotesque mocks the historical absolute, as it has mocked the absolutes of gods, nature and destiny. It does so by means of the so-called "barrel of laughs", a popular feature of any fun-fair: a score or more of people try to keep their balance while the upturned barrel revolves round its axis. One can only keep one's balance by moving on the bottom of the barrel in the opposite direction to, and with the same speed as, its movement. This is not at all easy. Those who move too fast or too slow in relation to the barrel's movement are bound to fall. The barrel brings them up, then they roll downwards trying desperately to cling to the moving floor. The more violent their gestures and their grip on the walls, the more difficult it is for them to get up, and the funnier they look.

The barrel is put in motion by a motor, which is transcendental in relation to it. However, one may easily imagine a barrel that is set in motion by the people inside it: by those who manage to preserve their balance and those who fall over. A barrel like this would be immanent. Its movements would, of course, be variable: sometimes it would revolve in one direction, sometimes in the other. It would be even more difficult to preserve one's balance in a barrel like this: one would have to change step all the time, move forward and backward, faster or slower. In such an immanent barrel many more people would fall over. But neither those who fall because they move too fast, nor those who fall because they move too slow, are tragic heroes. They are just grotesque. They will be grotesque even if there is no way out of this immanent barrel. The social mechanism shown in most of Adamov's plays is very much like the barrel of laughs.

The world of tragedy and the world of grotesque have a similar structure. Grotesque takes over the themes of tragedy and poses the same fundamental questions. Only its answers are different. This dispute about the tragic and grotesque interpretations of human fate reflects the everlasting conflict of two philosophies and two ways of thinking; of two opposing attitudes defined by the Polish philosopher Leszek Kolakowski as the irreconcilable antagonism between the priest and the clown. Between tragedy and grotesque there is the same conflict for or against such notions as eschatology, belief in the absolute, hope for the ultimate solution of the contradiction between the moral order and every-day practice. Tragedy is the theatre of priests, grotesque is the theatre of clowns.

This conflict between two philosophies and two types of theatre becomes particularly acute in times of great upheavals. When established values have been overthrown, and there is no appeal, to God, Nature, or History, from the tortures inflicted by the cruel world, the clown becomes the central figure in the theatre. He accompanies the exiled trio—the king, the nobleman and his son—on their cruel wanderings through the cold endless night which has fallen on the world; through the "cold night" which, as in Shakespeare's *King Lear,* "will turn us all to fools and madmen."

II

After his eyes have been gouged out, Gloucester wants to throw himself over the cliffs of Dover into the sea. He is led by his own son, who feigns madness. Both have reached the depths of human suffering; the top of "the pyramid of suffering", as Juliusz Slowacki has described *King Lear.* But on the stage there are just two actors, one playing a blind man, the other playing a man who plays a madman. They walk together.

GLOUCESTER
When shall I come to th' top of that same hill?
EDGAR
You do climb up it now. Look how we labour.
GLOUCESTER
Methinks the ground is even.
EDGAR
                    Horrible steep.
Hark, do you hear the sea?
GLOUCESTER
                    No, truly.
                    (IV, 6)

It is easy to imagine this scene. The text itself provides stage directions. Edgar is supporting Gloucester; he lifts his feet high pretending to walk uphill. Gloucester, too, lifts his feet, as if expecting the ground to rise, but underneath his foot there is only air. This entire scene is written for a very definite type of theatre, namely pantomime.

This pantomime only makes sense if enacted on a flat and level stage.

Edgar feigns madness, but in doing so he must adopt the right gestures. In its theatrical expression this is a scene in which a madman leads a blind man and talks him into believing in a non-existing mountain. In another moment a landscape will be sketched in. Shakespeare often creates a landscape on an empty stage. A few words, and the diffused, soft afternoon light at the Globe changes into night, evening, or morning. But no other Shakespearean landscape is so exact, precise and clear as this one. It is like a Breughel painting thick with people, objects and events. A little human figure hanging halfway down the cliff is gathering samphire. Fishermen walking on the beach are like mice. A ship seems a little boat, a boat is floating like a buoy.

It is this abyss of Shakespeare's imagination that Slowacki makes the hero of his *Kordian* look into:

Come! Here, on the top stand still. Your
  head will whirl,
When you cast your eyes on the abyss below
  your feet.
Crows flying there half-way no bigger are
  than beetles.
And there, too, someone is toiling, gathering weed.
He looks no bigger than a human head.
And there on the beach the fishermen seem
  like ants . . .

This veristic and perspective landscape created on an empty stage is not meant to serve as part of the decor, or to replace the non-existent settings. Slowacki understood perfectly the dramatic purpose of this scene:

Oh, Shakespeare! Spirit! You have built a
  mountain
Higher than that created by God.
For you have talked of an abyss to a man
  blind . . .

The landscape is now just a score for the pantomime. Gloucester and Edgar have reached the top of the cliff. The landscape is now below them.

Give me your hand. You are now within a
  foot
Of th' extreme verge. For all beneath the
  moon
Would I not leap upright.
                    (*King Lear,* IV, 6)

In Shakespeare's time the actors probably put their feet forward through a small balustrade above the apron-stage, immediately over the heads of the "groundlings". But we are not concerned here with an historical reconstruction of the Elizabethan stage. It is the presence and importance of the mime that is significant. Shakespeare is stubborn. Gloucester has already jumped over the precipice. Both actors are at the foot of a non-existent cliff. The same landscape is now above them. The mime continues.

GLOUCESTER
But have I fall'n, or no?
            EDGAR
From the dread summit of this chalky bourn.
Look up a-height. The shrill-gorg'd lark so
  far
Cannot be seen or heard. Do but look up.
                              (IV, 6)

The mime creates a scenic area: the top and bottom of the cliff, the precipice. Shakespeare makes use of all the means of anti-illusionist theatre in order to create a most realistic and concrete landscape. A landscape which is only a blind man's illusion. There is perspective in it, light, men and things, even sounds. From the height of the cliff the sea cannot be heard, but there is mention of its roar. From the foot of the cliff the lark cannot be heard, but there is mention of its song. In this landscape sounds are present by their very absence: the silence is filled with them, just as the empty stage is filled with the mountain.

The scene of the suicidal leap is also a mime. Gloucester kneels in a last prayer and then, in accordance with tradition of the play's English performances, falls over. He is now at the bottom of the cliff. But there was no height; it was an illusion. Gloucester knelt down on an empty stage, fell over and got up. At this point disillusion follows.[5]

The non-existent cliff is not meant just to deceive the blind man. For a short while we, too, believed in this landscape and in the mime. The meaning of this parable is not easy to define. But one thing is clear: this type of parable is not to be thought of outside the theatre, or

[5] Compare the analysis of this scene in G. Wilson Knight's most original study of the grotesque elements in *King Lear* (treated somewhat differently from in my essay): " 'King Lear' and the Comedy of the Grotesque," in *The Wheel of Fire,* London, 1957.

rather outside a certain kind of theatre. In narrative prose Edgar could, of course, lead the blind Gloucester to the cliffs of Dover, let him jump down from a stone and make him believe that he was jumping from the top of a cliff. But he might just as well lead him a day's journey away from the castle and make him jump from a stone on any heap of sand. In film and in prose there is only the choice between a real stone lying in the sand and an equally real jump from the top of a chalk cliff into the sea. One cannot transpose Gloucester's suicide attempt to the screen, unless one were to film a stage performance. But in the naturalistic, or even stylized theatre, with the precipice painted or projected onto a screen, Shakespeare's parable would be completely oblierated.

The stage must be empty. On it a suicide, or rather its symbol, has been performed. Mime is the performance of symbols. In Ionesco's *Le tueur sans gages* [6] the Architect, who is at the same time the commissioner of police, shows Berenger round the *Cité Radieuse*.[7] On an empty stage Berenger sniffs at non-existent flowers and taps non-existent walls. The Radiant City exists and does not exist, or rather it has existed always and everywhere. And that is why it is so terrifying. Similarly, the Shakespearean precipice at Dover exists and does not exist. It is the abyss, waiting all the time. The abyss, into which one can jump, is everywhere.

By a few words of dialogue Shakespeare often turned the platform stage, the inner stage, or the gallery into a London street, a forest, a palace, a ship, or a castle battlement. But these were always real places of action. Townspeople gathered outside the Tower, lovers wandered through the forest, Brutus murdered Caesar in the Forum. The white precipice at Dover performs a different

6 "The Assassin Without Pay."
7 "The Radiant City."

function. Gloucester does not jump from the top of the cliff, or from a stone. For once, in *King Lear,* Shakespeare shows the paradox of pure theatre. It is the same theatrical paradox that Ionesco uses in his *Le tueur sans gages.*

In the naturalistic theatre one can perform a murder scene, or a scene of terror. The shot may be fired from a revolver or a toy pistol. But in the mime there is no difference between a revolver and a toy pistol: in fact neither exists. Like death, the shot is only a performance, a parable, a symbol.

Gloucester, falling over on flat, even boards, plays a scene from a great morality play. He is no longer a court dignitary whose eyes have been gouged out because he showed mercy to the banished king. The action is no longer confined to Elizabethan or Celtic England. Gloucester is Everyman, and the stage becomes the medieval *Theatrum Mundi.* A Biblical parable is now enacted; the one about the rich man who became a beggar, and the blind man who recovered his inner sight when he lost his eyes. Everyman begins his wanderings through the world. In medieval mystery plays also the stage was empty, but in the background there were four mansions, four gates representing Earth, Purgatory, Heaven and Hell. In *King Lear* the stage is empty throughout: there is nothing, except the cruel earth, where man goes on his journey from the cradle to the grave. The theme of *King Lear* is an enquiry into the meaning of this journey, into the existence or non-existence of Heaven and Hell.

From the middle of Act II to the end of Act IV, Shakespeare takes up a Biblical theme. But this new *Book of Job* or a new Dantean *Inferno* was written towards the close of the Renaissance. In Shakespeare's play there is neither Christian Heaven, nor the heaven predicted and believed in by humanists. *King Lear* makes a tragic mockery of all eschatologies: of the heaven promised on earth, and the Heaven promised after death; in fact—of both Christian and secular theodicies; of cosmogony and of the rational view of history; of the gods and the good nature, of man made in "image and likeness." In *King Lear* both the medieval and the Renaissance orders of established values disintegrate. All that remains at the end of this gigantic pantomime, is the earth—empty and bleeding. On this earth, through which tempest has passed leaving only stones, the King, the Fool, the Blind Man and the Madman carry on their distracted dialogue.

The blind Gloucester falls over on the empty stage. His suicidal leap is tragic. Gloucester has reached the depths of human misery; so has Edgar, who pretends to be mad Tom in order to save his father. But the pantomime performed by actors on the stage is grotesque, and has something of a circus about it. The blind Gloucester who has climbed a nonexistent height and fallen over on flat boards, is a clown. A philosophical buffoonery of the sort found in modern theatre has been performed.

> Whistle from left wing.
> He (the man) does not move.
> He looks at his hands, looks round for scissors, sees them, goes and picks them up, starts to trim his nails, stops, runs his finger along blade of scissors, goes and lays them on small cube, turns aside, opens his collar, frees his neck and fingers it.
> The small cube is pulled up and disappears in flies, carrying away rope and scissors.
> He turns to take scissors, sees what has happened.
> He turns aside, reflects.
> He goes and sits down on big cube.
> The big cube is pulled from under him. He falls. The big cube is pulled up and disappears in flies.
> He remains lying on his side, his face towards auditorium, staring before him.
> (*Act Without Words*, pp. 59–60)

The *Act Without Words* closes Beckett's *Endgame*, providing as it were its final interpretation. Remaining vestiges of characters, action and situation have been further reduced here. All that remains is one situation acting as a parable of universal human fate. A total situation. Man has been thrown onto the empty stage. He tries to escape into the wings, but is kicked back. From above a tree with some leaves, a jug of water, tailoring scissors, and some cubes are pulled down on ropes. The man tries to hide in the shade of the leaves, but the tree is pulled up. He tries to catch hold of the jug, but it rises into the air. He attempts suicide, but this, too, proves impossible. "The bough folds down against trunk." (p. 59) The man sits down and thinks. The jug and the tree appear again. The man does not move.

In this ending to *Endgame* the forces external to man—gods, fate, world—are not indifferent, but sneering and malicious. They tempt him all the time. These forces are stronger than he. Man must be defeated and cannot escape from the situation that has been imposed on him. All he can do is to give up; refuse to play blindman's buff. Only by the possibility of refusal can he surmount the external forces.

It is easy to see how close to the Bible this parable is, even in its metaphors: palm, its shadow, water. The force above and beyond man is strongly reminiscent of the Old Testament God. This is also a *Book of Job,* but without an optimistic ending.

This new *Book of Job* is shown in buffo, as a circus pantomime. *Act Without Words* is performed by a clown. The philosophical parable may be interpreted as tragedy or grotesque, but its artistic expression is grotesque only. Gloucester's suicide attempt, too, is merely a circus somersault on an empty stage. Gloucester's and Edgar's situation is tragic, but it has been shown in pantomime, the classic expression of buffoonery. In Shakespeare clowns often ape the gestures of kings and heroes, but only in *King Lear* are great tragic scenes shown through clowning.

It is not only the suicide mime that is grotesque. The accompanying dialogue is also cruel and mocking. The blind Gloucester kneels and prays:

O you mighty gods!
This world I do renounce, and, in your
sights
Shake patiently my great affliction off.
If I could bear it longer, and not fall
To quarrel with your great opposeless wills,
My snuff and loathed part of nature should
Burn itself out. If Edgar live, O, bless him!
(IV, 6)

Gloucester's suicide has a meaning only if the gods exist. It is a protest against undeserved suffering and the world's injustice. This protest is made in a definite direction. It refers to eschatology. Even if the gods are cruel, they must take this suicide into consideration. It will count in the final reckoning between gods and man. Its sole value lies in its reference to the absolute.

But if the gods, and their moral order in the world, do not exist, Gloucester's suicide does not solve or alter anything. It is only a somersault on an empty stage. It is deceptive and unsuccessful on the factual, as well as on the metaphysical plane. Not only the pantomime, but the whole situation is then grotesque. From the beginning to the end. It is waiting for a Godot who does not come.

ESTRAGON
Why don't we hang ourselves?
VLADIMIR
With what?
ESTRAGON
You haven't got a bit of rope?
VLADIMIR
No.
ESTRAGON
Then we can't.
VLADIMIR
Let's go.
ESTRAGON
Wait, there's my belt.

VLADIMIR
It's too short.
ESTRAGON
You could hang on to my legs.
VLADIMIR
And who'd hang on to mine?
ESTRAGON
True.
VLADIMIR
Show all the same. (*Estragon loosens the cord that holds up his trousers which, much too big for him, fall about his ankles. They look at the cord.*) It might do at a pinch. But is it strong enough?
ESTRAGON
We'll soon see. Here.
(*They each take an end of the cord and pull. It breaks. They almost fall.*)
VLADIMIR
Not worth a curse.
(*Waiting for Godot,* II)

Gloucester did fall, and he got up again. He made his suicide attempt, but he failed to shake the world. Nothing has changed. Edgar's comment is ironical:

. . . Had he been where he thought,
By this had thought been past.
(IV, 6)

If there are no gods, suicide makes no sense. Death exists in any case. Suicide cannot alter human fate, but only accelerate it. It ceases to be a protest. It is a surrender. It becomes the acceptance of world's greatest cruelty—death. Gloucester has finally realized:

. . . Henceforth I'll bear
Affliction till it do cry out itself
'Enough, enough,' and die.
(IV, 6)

And once again, in the last act:

No further, sir. A man may rot even here.
(V, 2)

After his grotesque suicide the blind Gloucester talks to the deranged Lear. Estragon and Vladimir carry on a very similar conversation, interrupted by the despairing cries of the blind Pozzo, who has fallen down and cannot get up. Pozzo would find it easiest to understand Gloucester:

. . . one day I went blind, one day we'll go deaf, one day we were born, one day we shall die . . . They give birth astride of a grave, the light gleams an instant, then it's night once more.

(*Waiting for Godot,* II)

Shakespeare had said as much, in fewer words:

. . . Men must endure
Their going hence, even as their coming
  hither;
Ripeness is all.

(V, 2)

But it was Ionesco who put it most briefly of all, in his *Tueur sans gages:* "We shall all die, this is the only serious alienation."

III

The theme of *King Lear* is the decay and fall of the world. The play opens like the Histories, with the division of the realm and the king's abdication. It also ends like the Histories, with the proclamation of a new king. Between the prologue and the epilogue there is a civil war. But unlike the Histories and Trage- dies, in *King Lear* the world is not healed again. In *King Lear* there is no young and resolute Fortinbras to ascend the throne of Denmark; no cool-headed Octavius to become Augustus Caesar; no noble Malcolm to "give to our tables, meat, sleep to our nights." In the epi- logues to the Histories and Tragedies the new monarch invites those present to his coronation. In *King Lear* there will be no coronation. There is no one whom Edgar can invite to it. Everybody has died or been murdered. Gloucester was right when he said: "This great world / Shall so wear out to naught." Those who have survived—Edgar, Albany and Kent—are,

as Lear has been, just "ruin'd piece[s] of nature".

Of the twelve major characters half are just and good, the other half, unjust and bad. It is a division as consistent and abstract as in a morality play. But this is a morality play in which every one will be destroyed: noble characters along with base ones, the persecutors with the persecuted, the torturers with the tor- tured. Vivisection will go on until the stage is empty. The decay and fall of the world will be shown on two levels, on two different kinds of stage, as it were. One of these may be called Macbeth's stage, the other, Job's stage.

Macbeth's stage is the scene of crime. At the beginning there is a nursery tale of two bad daughters and one good daughter. The good daughter will die hanged in prison. The bad daughters will also die, but not until they have become adulterers, and one of them also a poisoner and murderess of her husband. All bonds, all laws, whether divine, natural or human, are broken. Social or- der, from the kingdom to the family, will crumble into dust. There are no longer kings and subjects, fathers and children, husbands and wives. There are only huge Renaissance monsters, devouring one another like beasts of prey. Every- thing has been condensed, drawn in broad outlines, characters are hardly marked. The history of the world can do without psychology and without rhetoric. It is just action. These violent sequences are merely an illustration and an example, and perform the function of a black, real- istic counterpart to "Job's stage".

For it is Job's stage that constitutes the main scene. On it the ironic, clownish morality play on human fate will be per- formed. But before that happens, all the characters must be uprooted from their social positions and pulled down, to final degradation. They must reach rock-bot- tom. The downfall is not merely a philo- sophical parable, as Gloucester's leap over the supposed precipice is. The theme of downfall is carried through by Shakespeare stubbornly, consistently and is repeated at least four times. The fall is at the same time physical and spiritual, bodily and social.

At the beginning there was a king with his court and ministers. Later, there are just four beggars wandering about in a wilderness, exposed to raging winds and rain. The fall may be slow, or sudden. Lear has at first a retinue of a hundred men, then fifty, then only one. Kent is banished by one angry gesture of the king. But the process of degradation is always the same. Everything that distinguishes a man—his titles, social position, even name—is lost. Names are not needed any more. Every one is just a shadow of himself; just a man.

KING LEAR
Doth any here know me? This is not Lear.
Doth Lear walk thus? speak thus?
. . . .
Who is it that can tell me who I am?
FOOL
Lear's shadow.
(I, 4)

And once more the same question, and the same answer. The banished Kent returns in disguise to his king.

KING LEAR
How now? What art thou?
KENT
A man, sir.
(I, 4)

A naked man has no name. Before the morality commences, every one must be naked. Naked like a worm.

Then Job arose, and rent his mantle, and shaved his head, and fell down upon the ground, and worshipped.
And said, Naked came I out of my mother's womb, and naked shall return thither.
(*Book of Job,* I, 20–21)

Biblical imagery in this new *Book of*

Job is no mere chance. Edgar says that he will with his "nakedness outface / The winds and persecutions of the sky." (II, 3) This theme returns obstinately, and with an equal consistency:

I' th' last night's storm I such a fellow saw,
Which made me think a man a worm.
(IV, 1)

A downfall means suffering and torment. It may be a physical or spiritual torment, or both. Lear will lose his wits; Kent will be put in the stocks; Gloucester will have his eyes gouged out and will attempt suicide. For a man to become naked, or rather to become nothing but man, it is not enough to deprive him of his name, social position and character. One must also maim and massacre him both morally and physically. Turn him—like King Lear—into a "ruin'd piece of nature", and only then ask him who he is. For it is the new Renaissance Job who is to judge the events on "Macbeth's stage".

A Polish critic, Andrzej Falkiewicz, has observed this process of maiming and mutilating man, not in Shakespeare, but in modern literature and drama.[8] He compares it to the peeling of an onion. One takes off the husk, and then peels the layers of onion one by one. Where does an onion end and what is in its core? The blind man is a man, the madman is a man, the doting old man is a man. Man and nothing but man. A nobody, who suffers, tries to give his suffering a meaning or nobility, who revolts or accepts his suffering, and who must die.

O gods! Who is't can say 'I am at the worst'?
I am worse than e'er I was.
. . . .
And worse I may be yet. The worst is not
So long as we can say 'This is the worst.'
(IV, 1)

Vladimir and Estragon talk to each other in a very similar fashion. They

[8] A. Falkiewicz, "Theatrical Experiment of the Fifties," *Dialog,* No. 9, 1959 (in Polish).

gibber, but in that gibber there are remnants of the same eschatology:

VLADIMIR

We're in no danger of ever thinking any
  more.

ESTRAGON

Then what are we complaining about?

VLADIMIR

Thinking is not the worst.

ESTRAGON

Perhaps not. But at least there's that.

VLADIMIR

That what?

ESTRAGON

That's the idea, let's ask each other questions.

VLADIMIR

What do you mean, at least there's that?

ESTRAGON

That much less misery.

VLADIMIR

True.

ESTRAGON

Well? If we gave thanks for our mercies?

VLADIMIR

What is terrible is to *have* thought.

(*Waiting for Godot,* II)

Pozzo is proud and pompous when in the first part of *Waiting for Godot* he leads on a rope the starving Lucky. Their relation is still that of master and servant, the exploiter and the exploited. When they appear for the second time Pozzo is blind and Lucky is dumb. They are still joined by the same rope. But now they are just two men.

'Tis the time's plague when madmen lead the
  blind.

(IV, 1)

Almost like in Breughel's famous picture, Edgar is leading the blind Gloucester to the precipice at Dover. This is just the theme of *Endgame;* Beckett was the first to see it in *King Lear;* he eliminated all action, everything external, and repeated it in its skeleton form.

Clov cannot sit down, the blind Hamm cannot get up, moves only in his wheelchair, and passes water only by means of a catheter. Nell and Nagg have "lost their shanks" and are almost breathing their last in dustbins. But Hamm continues to be the master, and his wheel-chair brings to mind a throne. In the London production he was dressed in a faded purple gown and wiped his face with a blood-red handkerchief. He was, like King Lear, a degraded and powerless tyrant, a "ruin'd piece of nature". He was a King Lear in the scene in Act IV, where Lear meets the blind Gloucester and after a great frantic monologue gives the order that one of his shoes be taken off, as it pinches him. It is the same pinching shoe that one of the clowns in *Waiting for Godot* will take off at the beginning of the scene.

This is the cruel and mocking "peeling of an onion", Shakespearean and modern alike. The onion is peeled to the very last, to the suffering "nothing". This is the theme of the fall. The concept of man has been reduced and all situations have shrunk to the one ultimate, total and concentrated human fate. To Vladimir's question "What is in this bag?", the blind Pozzo replies: "Sand". Clov in *Endgame* lifts the lid of the dustbin to find out what is happening to Nagg. "He's crying," he reports. To this Hamm replies: "Then he's living."

He's crying, then he's living. English critics have regarded it as Beckett's reply to the Cartesian formula of man, which was in itself a reduction of the theological formula. But in fact Beckett simply repeats after Shakespeare:

. . . We came crying hither; . . .

.   .   .   .

When we are born, we cry that we are come
To this great stage of fools.

(IV, 6)

The world is real, and the shoe really pinches. Suffering is also real. But the gesture with which the ruin of a man demands that his pinching shoe be taken off is ridiculous. Just as ridiculous as blind Gloucester's somersault on the flat empty stage.

The Biblical Job, too, is the ruin of a man. But this ruin constantly talks to God. He curses, imprecates, blasphemes. Ultimately he admits that God is right. He has justified his sufferings and ennobled them. He included them in the metaphysical and absolute order. The *Book of Job* is a theatre of the priests. Whereas in both Shakespearean and Beckettian *Endgames* the *Book of Job* is performed by clowns. But here, too, the gods are invoked throughout by all the characters; by Lear, Gloucester, Kent, even Albany:

KING LEAR
By Jupiter, I swear no!
KENT
By Juno, I swear ay!
(II, 4)

At first gods have Greek names. Then they are only gods, great and terrifying judges high above, who are supposed to intervene sooner or later. But the gods do not intervene. They are silent. Gradually the tone becomes more and more ironical. The ruin of a man invoking God is ever more ridiculous. The action becomes more and more cruel, but at the same time assumes a more and more clownish character:

By the kind gods, 'tis most ignobly done
To pluck me by the beard.
(III, 7)

Defeat, suffering, cruelty have a meaning even when gods are cruel. Even then. It is the last theological chance to justify suffering. The Biblical Job knew about it well when he called on God:

If the scourge slay suddenly, he will laugh at the trial of the innocent.
(*Book of Job,* IX, 23)

From the just God, one can still appeal to the unjust God. Says Gloucester after his eyes have been gouged out:

As flies to wanton boys are we to th' gods.
They kill us for their sport.
(IV, 1)

But as long as gods exist, all can yet be saved:

Hearken unto this, O Job: stand still, and consider the wondrous works of God.
(*Book of Job,* XXXVII, 14)

The Bible is Beckett's favourite reading. After all, the passage sounds like the dialogue in *Endgame:*

CLOV
They said to me, Here's the place, raise your head and look at all that beauty. That order! They said to me, Come now you're not a brute beast, think upon these things and you'll see how all becomes clear. And simple! They said to me, What skilled attention they get, all these dying of their wounds.

HAMM
Enough!

CLOV
I say to myself—sometimes, Clov, you must learn to suffer better than that if you want them to weary of punishing you. I say to myself—sometimes, Clov, you must be their better than if you want them to let you go—one day.
(pp. 50–51)

Clov is a clown, but he is more unhappy than Hamm. Clov's gabble is still eschatological, just as Lucky's in *Waiting for Godot.* In this dialogue of "human ruins" Hamm alone has realized the folly of all suffering. He has one reply to make to eschatology: "Take it easy . . . Peace to our . . . arses". Both couples: Pozzo who has been made blind, and Lucky who has been made dumb, on the one hand, Hamm who cannot get up, and Clov who cannot sit down, on the other, have been taken from the Endgame of *King Lear:*

KING LEAR
Read.

GLOUCESTER
What, with the case of eyes?

. . . .

KING LEAR
What, art mad? A man may see how the world goes with no eyes. Look with thine ears.

(IV, 6)

These are Biblical parables. The blind see clearly, madmen tell the truth. After all, they are all mad. "There are four of them"—writes Camus—"one by profession, one by choice, two by the suffering they have been through. They are four torn bodies, four unfathomable faces of the same fate." [9] The Fool accompanies Lear on the cold night of madness; Edgar takes the blind Gloucester through a grotesque suicide. Lear's invocations on the gods are countered by the Fool's scatological jokes; Gloucester's prayers by Edgar's clownish demonology:

Frateretto calls me, and tells me Nero is an angler in the lake of darkness. Pray, innocent, and beware the foul fiend. . . . The foul fiend bites my back. . . . Purr! the cat is gray.

(III, 6)

But Edgar's demonology is no more than a parody, a travesty of contemporary Egyptian dream books and books on witchcraft; a great and brutal gibe, in fact. He gibes at himself, at Job, conversing with God. For above "Job's stage", there is in *King Lear* only "Macbeth's stage". On it people murder, butcher and torture one another, commit adultery and fornication, divide kingdoms. From the point of view of a Job who has ceased to talk to God, they are clowns. Clowns who do not yet know they are clowns.

KING LEAR
. . . Come, come, I am a king;
My masters, know you that?

[9] A. Camus, *Le Mythe de Sisyphe*, Paris, 1942.

GENTLEMEN
You are a royal one, and we obey you.
KING LEAR
Then there's life in't. Nay, an you get it, you shall get it by running. Sa, sa, sa, sa!

(IV, 6)

The zero hour has come. Lear has come to understand it at last. Just as blind Hamm came to understand everything, although he was bound to his wheel-throne. And Pozzo, when he turned blind and fell over his sand-filled bags:

POZZO
I woke up one fine day as blind as Fortune . . .
VLADIMIR
And when was that?
POZZO
I don't know . . . Don't question me! The blind have no notion of time. The things of time are hidden from them too.

(*Waiting for Godot*, II)

And this is how King Lear ends his final frantic tirade:

No rescue? What, a prisoner? I am even
The natural fool of fortune.

(IV, 6)

In a moment he will run off the stage. Before that happens he will ask for his pinching shoe to be taken off. He is clown now, so he can afford to do this. On "Job's stage" four clowns have performed the old medieval *sotie* about the decay and fall of the world. But in both Shakespearean and Beckettian *Endgames* it is the modern world that fell; the Renaissance world, and ours. Accounts have been settled in a very similar way.

IV

The original clown was Harlequin. There is something in him of an animal, a faun and a devil. That is why he wears a black mask. He rushes about and seems to transform himself into different shapes.

The laws of space and time do not seem to apply to him. He changes his guises in a flash and can be in several places at once. He is a demon of movement. In Goldoni's play *The Servant of Two Masters,* as produced by the Piccolo Teatro of Milan, Harlequin, sitting on the brim of a wooden platform, plucked a hair from his head, lengthened or shortened it, pulled it through his ears, or put it on his nose and kept it rigid in the air. Harlequin is a prestidigitator. He is servant who really does not serve anybody and jockeys everybody away. He sneers at merchants and lovers, at marquesses and soldiers. He makes fun of love and ambition, of power and money. He is wiser than his masters, although he seems only to be more clever. He is independent, because he has realized that the world is simply folly.

Puck from *A Midsummer Night's Dream* is a popular goblin of English folklore, a Robin Goodfellow. But he is also the Harlequin of the Renaissance *commedia dell'arte.* He, too, is a quick-change artist, a prestidigitator and producer of the comedy of errors. He confuses the couples of lovers and causes Titania to caress an ass's head. In fact, he makes them all ridiculous, Titania and Oberon no less than Hermia and Lysander, Helena and Demetrius. He exposes the folly of love. He is accident, fate, chance. Chance happens to be ironical, though it does not know about it itself. Puck plays practical jokes. He does not know what he has done. That is why he can turn somersaults on the stage, just as Harlequin does.

Buffoonery is a philosophy and a profession at the same time. Touchstone and Feste are professional clowns. They wear jesters' attire, and are in service of the prince. They have not ceased to be Harlequins and are not above pantomime. But they do not produce the performance any more; they do not even take part in it, but merely comment on it. That is why

they are jeering and bitter. The position of a jester is ambiguous and abounds in internal contradictions, arising from the discrepancy between profession and philosophy. The profession of a jester, like that of an intellectual, consists in providing entertainment. His philosophy demands of him that he tell the truth and abolish myths. The Fool in *King Lear* does not even have a name, he is just a Fool, pure Fool. But he is the first fool to be aware of the fool's position:

FOOL
Prithee, nuncle, keep a schoolmaster that can teach thy fool to lie. I would fain learn to lie.
KING LEAR
An you lie, sirrah, we'll have you whipp'd.
FOOL
I marvel what kin thou and thy daughters are. They'll have me whipp'd for speaking true; thou'lt have me whipp'd for lying; and sometimes I am whipp'd for holding my peace. I had rather be any kind o'thing than a fool! And yet I would not be thee, nuncle. Thou hast pared thy wit o' both sides and left nothing i'th' middle.

(I, 4)

A fool who has recognized himself for a fool, who has accepted the fact that he is only a jester in the service of the prince, ceases to be a clown. But the clown's philosophy is based on the assumption that every one is a fool; and the greatest fool is he who does not know he is a fool: the prince himself. That is why the clown has to make fools of others; otherwise he would not be a clown. The clown is subject to alienations because he is a clown, but at the same time he cannot accept the alienation; he rejects it when he becomes aware of it. The clown has the social position of the bastard, as described many times by Sartre. The bastard is a bastard for as long as he accepts his bastard's position and regards it as inevitable. The bastard ceases to be a bastard when he does not consider himself a bastard any more. But at this point the bastard must abolish the division into bastards and legitimate offspring. He then enters into opposition against the foundations of social order, or at least exposes them. Social pressures want to limit the Clown to his part of a clown, to pin the label "clown" on him. But he does not accept this part. On the contrary: he constantly pins that label on others:

KING LEAR
Dost thou call me fool, boy?
FOOL
All thy other titles thou hast given away; that thou wast born with.
KENT
This is not altogether fool, my lord.
FOOL
No, faith; lords and great men will not let me. If I had a monopoly out, they would have part on't. And ladies too, they will not let me have all the fool to myself; they'll be snatching.

(I, 4)

This is the opening of the "clowns' play", performed on "Job's stage". In his very first scene, the Fool offers Lear his fool's cap. For buffoonery is not only a philosophy, it is also a kind of theatre. To us it is the most contemporary aspect of *King Lear*. Only it has to be seen and interpreted properly. For this reason one must reject all the romantic and natural-istic accessories; the opera and melo-drama about the old man who, driven out by his daughters, wanders about bare-headed in a storm and goes mad as a re-sult of his misfortunes. But, as in the case of Hamlet, there is method in this mad-ness. Madness in *King Lear* is a philos-ophy, a conscious cross-over to the posi-tion of the Clown. Leszek Kolakowski writes:

The Clown is he who, although moving in high society, is not part of it, and tells un-pleasant things to everybody in it; who dis-putes everything regarded as evident. He would not be able to do all this, if he were part of that society himself; then he could at most be a drawing-room scandalizer. The Clown must stand aside and observe the good society from outside, in order to dis-cover the non-evidence of evidence, and non-finality of its finality. At the same time he must move in good society in order to get to know its sacred cows, and have occasion to tell the unpleasant things. . . . The philosophy of Clowns is the philosophy that in every epoch shows up as doubtful what has been regarded as most certain; it reveals contradictions inherent in what seems to have been proven by visual experi-ence; it holds up to ridicule what seems ob-vious common sense, and discovers truth in the absurd.[10]

Let us now turn to *King Lear:*

FOOL
Give me an egg, nuncle, and I'll give thee two crowns.
KING LEAR
What two crowns shall they be?
FOOL
Why, after I have cut the egg i' th' middle and eat up the meat, the two crowns of the egg. When thou clovest thy crown i' th' middle and gav'st away both parts, thou bor'st thine ass on thy back o'er the dirt. . . . Now thou art an O without a figure. I am better than thou art now: I am a fool, thou art nothing.

(I, 4)

After the crown had been torn off his head, Richard II asked for a mirror. He cast a look, and broke the mirror. He saw in the mirror his own unchanged face; the same that had belonged to a king. This amazed him. In *King Lear* the degrada-tion occurs gradually, step by step. Lear divided his kingdom and gave away his power, but wanted to remain a king. He believed that a king could not cease to be a king, just as the sun could not cease to shine. He believed in pure majesty, in the pure idea of kingship. In historical dramas royal majesty is deprived of its sacred character by a stab of the dagger,

[10] L. Kolakowski, "The Priest and the Clown —Reflections on Theological Heritage in Modern Thinking" (in Polish), *Twórczość,* No. 10, 1959, pp. 82–83.

or by the brutal tearing off of the crown from a living king's head. In *King Lear* it is the Fool who deprives majesty of its sacredness.

Lear and Gloucester are adherents of eschatology; they desperately believe in the existence of absolutes. They invoke the gods, believe in justice, appeal to laws of nature. They have fallen off "Macbeth's stage", but remain its prisoners. Only the Fool stands outside "Macbeth's stage", just as he has stood outside "Job's stage". He is looking from the outside and does not follow any ideology. He rejects all appearances, of law, justice, moral order. He sees brute force, cruelty and lust. He has no illusions and does not seek consolation in the existence of natural or supernatural order, which provides for the punishment of evil and reward of good. Lear, insisting on his fictitious majesty, seems ridiculous to him. All the more ridiculous because he does not see how ridiculous he is. But the Fool does not desert his ridiculous, degraded king, and accompanies him on his way to madness. The Fool knows that the only true madness is to regard this world as rational. The feudal order is absurd and can be described only in terms of the absurd. The world stands upside down:

When usurers tell their gold i' th' field,
And bawds and whores do churches build:
Then shall the realm of Albion
Come to great confusion.
Then comes the time, who lives to see't,
That going shall be us'd with feet.

(III, 2)

Hamlet escaped into madness not only to confuse informers and deceive Claudius. Madness to him was also a philosophy, a criticism of pure reason, a great, ironic clearing of accounts with the world, which has left its orbit. The Fool adopts the language Hamlet used in the scenes in which he feigned madness. There is nothing left in it now of Greek and Roman rhetoric, so popular in the Renaissance; nothing left of the cold and noble Senecan indifference to the inevitable destiny. Lear, Gloucester, Kent, Albany, even Edmund still use rhetoric. The Fool's language is different. It abounds in Biblical travesties and inverted medieval parables. One can find in it splendid baroque surrealist expressions, sudden leaps of imagination, condensations and epitomes, brutal, vulgar and scatological comparisons. His rhymes are like limericks. The Fool uses dialectics, paradox and the absurd kind of humour. His language is that of our modern grotesque. The same grotesque that exposes the absurdity of apparent reality and of the absolute by means of a great and universal *reductio ad absurdum*.

KING LEAR
O me, my heart, my rising heart! But down!
FOOL
Cry to it, nuncle, as the cockney did to the eels when she put 'em i' th' paste alive. She knapp'd 'em o' th' coxcombs with a stick and cried 'Down, wantons, down!' 'Twas her brother that, in pure kindness to his horse, buttered his hay.

(II, 4)

The Fool appears on the stage when Lear's fall is only beginning. He disappears by the end of Act III. His last words are: "And I'll go to bed at noon." He will not be seen or heard again. A clown is not needed any more. King Lear has gone through the school of clown's philosophy. When he meets Gloucester for the last time, he will speak the Fool's language and look at "Macbeth's stage" the way the Fool has looked at it: "They told me I was everything. 'Tis a lie—I am not ague-proof." (IV, 6)

INSTITUTIONALIZED LYNCH

G. Legman

> Art fell on its knees. Pressure was put on the publishers
> . . . English fiction became pure . . . But at this point
> human nature intervened; poor human nature! when you
> pinch it in one place it bulges out in another, after the
> fashion of a lady's figure.
> —George Moore *Confessions of a Young Man* (1886)

THE censor's unequivocal 'You must not!' is seldom answered with an equally uncompromising 'I will!' Ashamed to oppose the censor's morality, and afraid to contravene his authority, the writer's first reaction is to evade the censorship, to see what can be sneaked through, what can be gotten away with, what can be disguised just enough to pass the censor but not so much as to escape the audience.

Hypocrisy, equivoque, misdirection: these are the subterfuges to which censors are blind, upon which audiences smile. The bawdy word, the rebel thought, the concept still taboo: these the author backs in upon the stage, masked and muffled, with arrows tangled in their hair pointing all in fraudulent directions. Words, thoughts, ideas—all are punned upon, hinted at, symbolized, turned upside-down and acrosticked, acted out in idiotic mummery, and finally, for the benefit of the dullest, are lettered out in kindergarten style. Thus Shakespeare's 'Her very *C*'s, her *U*'s, '*n*' her *T*'s' (*Twelfth Night*, II.v.88), the meaning of which puzzles professors so much, audiences so little. When genius must stoop to the nursery subterfuge of spelling its tabooed word out, nothing is to be expected of lesser craftsmen in resisting the censorship of sex.

The author pauses before truth, one eye furtively upon the censor, the other leering at his audience. He gibbers, he capers, he thumbs his nose and fires off popguns, but the truth is not in him. Now, as in Isaiah's time, truth is fallen in the street, dragged back & forth in mud lest the censor see it. His integrity forfeit— pawned, gone & forgotten—the author juggles nonsense before the censor's face, the sense of nonsense behind his back. He tips his audience the broad wink of the elliptical dash——batters them clownishly on the head with a bladderful of asterisks, pokes them in the ribs with a knowing blank to represent *coitus inconsummatus;* takes up his castrated tale again with 'Later. . . .'

He is a writer. He is Prometheus. His is the guardianship of light. But fear infects him. And from leader—light bearer —he has fallen away to jester and dishonorable jape. Truth is falsified, falseness made more false, darkness dissipated not at all by his flameless fire.

What can be said for men of letters whose vindication of the basic human right to freedom of speech can rise no higher than piddling and surreptitious naughtiness, cocked snooks when the censor's back is turned? Only that this sort of humor is not undertaken by grown men strictly as humor, but rather as their resistance to an oppressive censorship, for the sheer éclat of twitting and outwitting it. That, as resistance, it is ineffective, is due primarily to its being scaled so very small. For pranks and paraphrase and token resistance have their limits, and these are quickly reached. Having buffooned it to the end of the censorship tether—and it is short—the only recourse for both artist and audience is transvaluation, displacement, the siphoning off of the suppressible urge for expression elsewhere.

What is the 'elsewhere' of sex? Religion suggests prayer. Psychiatry proposes sublimation. The man & woman in the street are interested in neither. Tranvaluation requires a fully equivalent satisfaction substituted for that suppressed. A sanctity that would equivalue a lifetime of sex, in depth and intensity, is beyond reach of all but saints. Sublimation to this same degree is impossible in our culture to all save an enfranchised élite: the bridge-builders, war-makers, movie-actresses. A thousand men must die to write one general's name in history, ten thousand women be damned to neurosis to pay one actress' wage; a million lives sink in the mud of the Nile to build one pyramid, found one concert series, immortalize one ironmonger's name in philanthropy. Sublimation is not for the million—unless through self-sacrifice—seldom for the few.

Professional moral elements, busying themselves with censorship, prefer to believe that sex can be replaced by physical and emotional exertions measurably less violent than itself, such as calisthenics, cold baths, and bingo. The sinister absurdity of this pious hope is everywhere obvious. The one thing, and the only thing short of total sublimation, that can replace sex has become increasingly familiar decade by decade since the general introduction of Puritan censorship about 1740, and has reached so gargantuan a stage of formal development all around us that reflection upon the possible next step is plainly terrifying.

There is *no* mundane substitute for sex except sadism. You may search the in-dexes to Krafft-Ebing, Ellis, Hirschfeld, Guyon, or any dozen sex scientists, but you will find no other human activity that can replace sex completely—*spurlos versenkt*.[1] Narcissism, homosexuality, zoöphily: these are clearly misdirections of ordinary sexual acts toward biologically unsuitable recipients. Fetichisms in all their number seldom supersede sexuality, generally do no more than to excite to it by a deviant concentration upon one attractive feature—breast, hair, foot, buttock, or whatever—an interest usually spread over all. But sadism does substitute. It is complete in itself. It can dispense with all earthly relation to sex—can dispense even with orgasm—thus allowing its adherents publicly to preen themselves on the 'purity' of their ruthless delights.

Geoffrey Gorer, the foremost student of the Marquis de Sade, makes the literary connection very plain in his *Bali & Angkor,* 1936:

In English literature we can trace a series of secular mythologies, or accepted beliefs . . . to-day in the ecstasies of sexual love and violence, or (to use a single word for both manifestations) in *thrills*. The various uses of this word in current speech are sufficiently indicative. People talk of the thrill of love, the aesthetic thrill, the religious thrill, the thrill of danger, the thrill of murder, of robbery, and sudden death. Unfortunately we believe in our mythologies instead of using them, a disastrous and most dangerous situation . . . especially as the law does everything possible to prevent people enjoying the heaven which is in their art so endlessly preached at them, so that most people are in a chronic state of unsatisfied sexual desire . . . What is particularly dangerous is that despite all the prohibitions of convention and law people do acquire sexual experience, and for the greater part, find out that they have been stuffed with lies, that though pleasant, it is no such lasting ecstasy and final solution as art

[1] sunken (gone) without a trace.

would leave us to suppose; and then they are ready for the other half of our myth, violence.

It is no accident that the end of Restoration bawdry coincided precisely with the fullest flowering of literary sadism in England. The Elizabethans had wrung blood in plenty out of sex—in *Romeo & Juliet,* a 'love'-play, seven of the characters are carted off dead—but there was no dearth of lust. Times change. The elegant eighteenth-century littérateurs, Johnson and Pope, are famous equally for the sexual purity of their writing, the sadistic cruelty of their speech. Sex being forbidden, violence took its place.

First had come the martyrologies and revenger-dramas, more than a century before, then the pirate almanacs and highwaymen lives; but these gave way quickly to the more refined brutality of Richardson's *Pamela* and Walpole's 'Gothic' novel. The whipped, stripped, and humiliated heroine-victim died a thousand deaths before the public grew bored with her writhings, applauded her lampooning in *Northanger Abbey* and the *Ingoldsby Legends*. While in France the Marquis de Sade added sex to the Gothic pattern—and gained thereby a century of mixed obloquy and praise for the British 'sadism' he had merely borrowed—the Anglo-American public, still eschewing sex, turned to fiercer pleasures in the murder-mystery, adapted by Edgar Allan Poe from the pirate & highwaymen memoirs.

Examine the journalistic detail of the first murder-mystery, published in Philadelphia, 1841, in *Graham's Lady's & Gentleman's Magazine:*

On a chair lay a razor, besmeared with blood. On the hearth were two or three long and thick tresses of grey human hair, also dabbled in blood, and seeming to have been pulled out by the roots . . .
Of Madame L'Espanaye no traces were

here seen; but, an unusual quantity of soot being observed in the fire-place, a search was made in the chimney, and (horrible to relate!) the corpse of the daughter, head downward, was dragged therefrom; it having been thus forced up the narrow aperture for a considerable distance [. . . Dr. Freud, please note]. The body was quite warm. Upon examining it, many excoriations were perceived, no doubt occasioned by the violence with which it had been thrust up and disengaged. Upon the face were many severe scratches, and upon the throat dark bruises, and deep indentations of finger nails, as if the deceased had been throttled to death.

After a thorough investigation of every portion of the house, without further discovery, the party made its way into a small paved yard in the rear of the building, where lay the corpse of the old lady, with her throat so entirely cut that, upon an attempt to raise her, the head fell off, and rolled to some distance. The body, as well as the head, was fearfully mutilated—the former so much so as scarcely to retain any semblance of humanity.

To this horrible mystery there is not as yet, we believe, the slightest clew.

This is legal. This is printable. This is classic. But would it be legal, would it be printable, would it be classic if, instead of the details of murder and death, Poe had substituted with equal artistic precision the details of that act out of which life emerges? Apparently not. His second murder-mystery involved a girl (pardon the expression) no better than she should be; but Gaboriau, Wilkie Collins, Dickens, and Doyle cleaned all that out. By the time the murder-mystery was reimported to America, about thirty years ago, it was entirely sexless. Only sadism and pleasure in death had stood the crossing.

Poe's great contribution had been the enheroing of the avenger instead of the criminal, and with this one significant sop to moral pose, literary murder became respectable. The reading public went on a century-long debauch of printed sadism to replace the sex notoriously absent in Victorian literature. (For weaker stomachs, with a religious turn, the ghost story simultaneously served up masochist terrors.)

This is not the place to study the nineteenth century's love of death: the delight in funereal pomp, the clerical and poetical gloatings over the death of little children —nothing to compare with our own daily newsphotos of dying babies and squashed dogs—the special Christmas numbers of household magazines, specially chock full of murder; the reprint after expurgated reprint (in eight volumes each) of Foxe's Book of Martyrs, the endless purified editions of the State Trials in twenty-guinea sets and penny chapbooks, with now & again a poetic *procès-verbal,* as in the twelve-fold necrophily of Browning's laundered 'masterpiece,' *The Ring and the Book:* 'telling the story of a hideous murder twelve times over,' the *Encyclopaedia Britannica* marvels, '. . . insisting upon every detail with the minuteness of a law report.'

Nowhere, so much as in contemporary fiction, has this movement to substitute sadism for sex progressed so far and become so blatant. Yet so pervasive and so disguised is this perversion—in the exact sense of the word—that, when attacked at all, literature is attacked today not as sadism and sex-hatred but as overstressed normality: as 'obscenity.'

Two masks serve to cover our transvaluation of censored sexuality into sadism and literary lynch—the murder-mystery and the 'spirited' heroine. (More violent than either, the comic-book is reserved as yet for children.) The murder-mystery is still the more popular, and for that reason perhaps the more dangerous, but the two are not different in any integral respect. The 'spirited' heroine merely enacts openly the sadistic pursuit and ultimate flagellation and destruction that the murder-mystery generally expresses only in symbols: in an appeal that passes through the censorship of the conscious mind disguised as justice, disguised as an exercise in mental agility, disguised as light, 'relaxing' entertainment.

For the real victim in the murder-mystery of our much consumption—as George Jean Nathan has pointed out—is not the murder*ee* but the murder*er*. The murdered individual is seldom pictured as an object of sympathy. More likely he (or she) is described as a 'swine' who should have been killed off years before, and whose murderer should really be given the Nobel prize. This is done partly to pose a large number of enemies—in the jargon, 'suspects'—but to a greater degree in order not to excite any impulses of sympathy or tenderness in the reader, even for the victim; since the entire purpose of the murder book is to excite and satisfy quite different impulses.

By casting one living individual into the character of a murderer, he is thrown automatically outside the pale of humanity, and neither justice nor mercy need be shown him. He can be tracked down callously and with superhuman intelligence by the much-mannered detective with whom the reader is clearly expected to identify himself—except, perhaps, in the first few chapters, where he savors the details of the kill in the character of the killer. The inane mannerisms and exotic eruditions—more recently the mock-virile 'toughness'—of the detective-superman are solely intended (if their easing the writer's task be omitted from the consideration) to pose a high degree of superior individuality for him, and thus to increase the gratification and certainty with which the reader will project himself into the detective personality. Naturally, this projectibility-/-coefficient is the measure of the length and financial success of the series in which the particular detective appears.

The reader *is,* then, the detective—the

supra-legal avenger. The police, who might snatch his prey from his private vengeance to public justice, are endlessly depicted as flat-footed bunglers, utterly incapable of bringing a routine murder to solution. And merely through committing this single murder—seldom more, unless forced into them to cover his tracks —the detective's prey (that is to say, the reader's prey) is degraded from the right to mercy, and is hounded without a qualm to his public humiliation before the assembled characters in the last chapter and to his eventual and inevitable suicide on the last page. This final humiliation and/ or life-for-a-life suicide has, of course, become standard in murder-mysteries as being easier to write, less anti-climactic, and more titillatingly violent than courtroom justice—such as it might be—might be.

This pattern degradation of the murderer-victim from the right to mercy, to justice, due process of law, or even a lousy cot in the county jail is the hallmark and, in fact, the definition of lynching—whether armchair or hilltop. It works on the important but seldom stated principle by which, for instance, we arrange to have lambs slaughtered for food: They are very pretty little animals, and their bleating is quite piteous, but they simply are not human and they simply do not count.

In the same way Germans were given to understand that Jews are not human and, as such, can properly be gassed, electrocuted, and incinerated wholesale. In precisely the same way we are thrilled by a newsreel of the burning to death of a Japanese before our eyes. It is merely necessary to propagandize us first into an acceptance of the non-human status of the Japanese. This done, our previously conditioned sympathy with the underdog or with the inhumanly treated human can be shoved beneath the surface, and we are then properly able to enjoy photographs of a Japanese lynched with a flammen-

werfer or his skull denuded of flesh, fitted with a brass top, and used as a tobacco humidor. Naturally, similar photographs of the body of an American burned to death or so desecrated by a Japanese would still strike us as bestial and inhuman.

Through ignorance of the principle here involved, Northerners tend to assume a very superior attitude of deploring when confronted with the fact of the lynching of Negroes in the South. They tend to think of Southerners as a gang of barbarians and murderers, of their well-publicized gallantry as a mere archaic pose. Yet there are thousands—perhaps millions—of Southerners who, for the plain protection of their economic interest, prefer to think of the Negro as non-human, and of his lynching as no more culpable, really, than the squashing of a cockroach in a sink; and who would feel no more outrage to their gallant impulses in castrating, branding, or killing a Negro than a friendly Westerner feels in castrating, branding, or killing a bull.

We Northerners, in precisely the same way, can accept with vapid equanimity the instantaneous obliteration of a hundred thousand Japanese, Germans, Russians, Martians, or any other group designated as enemy non-humans (reserving, of course, the right to execute enemy generals for slapping or underfeeding our prisoners of war), Englishmen deal in precisely the same way with Hindus and Jews, and—to revert—the reading public deals in precisely the same fashion with the synthetic murderer in its murder-fantasies. There is no difference, unless it be that all but the murder-mystery reader have some excuse. He alone lynches in cold blood.

Observe his specific requirements, his calmness, tabulated by Mr. Stephen Leacock in the *Saturday Review of Literature* for July 8th, 1939. The world only a matter of months from the total conflagration of war, the Canadian humorist placidly congratulates himself thus:

I am one of those who like each night, after the fret and worry of the day, to enjoy about twenty cents' worth of murder before turning off the light and going to sleep. Twenty cents a night is about the cost of this, for first class murder by our best writers. Ten-cent murder is apt to be either stale or too suggestive of crime.

Did you say 'relaxing'? Soporific! Murder-lullabies for grown-ups, like the Gebrüder Grimm's blood-thirsty folk-tales, their sex watered down and their blood-thirstiness jazzed up from Giambattista Basile's originals. Mr. Leacock's concluding bit of advice is also worthy of any compleat lyncher's consideration:

Don't be afraid to hang the criminal at the end; better lay the story, if you can, in a jurisdiction where they hang them, because to us, the readers, the electric chair sounds too uncomfortable. But hanging is old and respectable . . . I mean we want him *hanged* [Mr. Leacock's italics]; don't let him fall into the sea out of his aeroplane. It's not good enough. Hold him tight by the pants till you get him to the gallows.

Mr. Leacock is presumably kidding, but his bare-naked, unexpurgated accents of bloodlust would be printable even if—as one may suspect—he was entirely serious. The murder-mystery reader feels no shame, cannot see himself for the super-murderer that he patently is. His murder-victim kills just once. He, the reader, kills three hundred times a year—daily except Sunday—generally just before going to sleep. 'First class murder by our best writers.'

One understands that the murder-mystery is a sort of intellectual puzzle, 'mental exercise' for mentalities too dim or too jaded for the symbolic combats of cross-word puzzles and chess. But why, then, this persistent pathological paddling in guts & blood? Why this intense, in-variable I-am-the-man insistence upon personal vengeance in a culture where revenge is disgraceful, the taking of the law into one's own hands a crime? Why must it be murder, murder, murder, murder?

Are there no other mental exercises than the contemplation of death? Not for the mystery-reader. In 1926, the year that the 'detective' mystery mushroomed into prominence in America, E. M. Wrong, its first serious apologist, found it necessary to record that:

Time has . . . exalted murder, which used to be only one of several offences, to a position of natural supremacy.

There are good reasons for this. What we want in our detective fiction is not a semblance of real life, where murder is infrequent and petty larceny common . . . Hatred that is strong enough to bring murder is familiar enough to be intelligible to nearly every one, yet far enough from our normal experience to let us watch as detached observers [!] for we do not feel that it is our own crimes that are unmasked. So for many reasons murder is advisable, though not necessary. The author, if he withholds its appeal, must give us compensation in some other way.

(The Oxford University Press, that publishes Mr. Wrong's little anthology of murder—in its 'World's Classics' series—simultaneously offers for sale an expurgated Herrick and a bowdlerized Shakespeare. What is the 'compensation in some other way' that readers of Oxford's desexualized Herrick and Shakespeare are supposed to seek?)

Twenty years ago—despite Mr. Wrong's manifesto—the 'mental exercise' whitewash might still have held some drops of water. Today the Who-Stole-the-Necklace-or-The-Mystery-of-the-Butler's-Past sort of milk & mush is a drug on the market, and even the most apologetic of the British enthusiasts do not absorb it in any number. The international *Cumulative Book Index* tries to distinguish only between 'detective' murders and murders merely mysterious, attempting no category for mysteries based on crimes other than murder. For that matter, murder is generally less gruesome than the 'compensation in some other way'—impending death, plague, or unspecified doom threatening all of humanity or even London—that writers of the non-lethal mystery see fit to bring in. It is, in any case, a vanishing form, and any possible *bona fide* in the 'mental exercise' defense has vanished with it.

Even fifteen years ago, when Harry Stephen Keeler (and 'Ellery Queen') created murders with the solution sealed, announcing that all the clues had been given and that the reader should be able to logic out the murderer's identity, no one wanted to bother and this feature was quickly dropped. That readers commonly abort the whole 'mental exercise' angle, and sneak a glimpse at the solution beforehand, is so well known that writers are hard put to it to think up tricks to forfend them—like making the narrator the murderer, and having the denouncement narrated by someone else. The reader-pack yelps. "Who Cares Who Killed Roger Ackroyd?" They care. They want to know *who* they are hunting down. Though the murder-mystery is ostensibly a glorification of law & order ('Crime does not pay' and so forth) the reader wants to cheat while reading it. How now, mental exercise?

Make no mistake about it: the murder-mystery reader is a lyncher. A solid citizen by day, by night he rides hooded to watch human beings die. He may, certainly does, think of himself as a mere, harmless literary escapist. He may actually believe that his nightly passion to murder the murderer of his own creating adds up to nothing more than pleasant, law-abiding, purely meaningless recreation—light entertainment, and all that. He may imagine that the mental torture, the anxiety, the pounding heart and ter-

ror (*jargonicè,* 'suspense'), the desperate twistings & turnings, and the final, ingeniously contrived humiliation and death of the murderer—three hundred violent and excited pages of it—all these, he may imagine, are no part of his interest.

Yet remove from the murder-mystery this element of sadism—of manhunt and lynch—and what is left? A flabby mush of greed, mistaken identity, or vernacular chit-chat. Wholly without attraction for nine in every ten readers, the non-lethal mystery does not sell, is not read, and is now therefore seldom encountered. *The* 'mystery' is the murder-mystery. And the murder-mystery reader wants blood, death, and lynching. But not the blood of the 'victim,' whose unwept death—presumably the whole justification for the protracted lynch that follows—is lackadaisically presented on page one as a *fait accompli,* an utterly routine knock-down-&-drag-out bit of ritual. The murder-mystery reader wants the murderer's blood.

And again, where is the difference? The murderer may have killed from the noblest of motives. His 'victim' may have been a blackmailer, a drug-peddler (of anything but alcohol), a sadist (*sic*), a human ghoul. It may all even have been a mistake. But what are the reader's motives? He has none. He is quite calm. His interest in law & order is infinitesimal—so much so, that he enthroned the murder-book as our prime literary fare (one third of all fiction printed) in the midst of the illegal, nation-wide whiskey-jag of the 1920's. The murders that he avenges are written to order for him. Wholly synthetic, they would not exist at all but for his endless thirst for blood. He picks up his nightly 'mystery,' prepared to lynch down whatever miserable murderer his author chooses to present. He is unprejudiced. He has no personal grudge. He will kill *any*body. He kills for pleasure.

It may be pointed out that, in this, murder-mystery *aficionados* differ in no way from the readers of newspaper accounts—voyeurism at second hand—of courtroom trials and executions. This is certainly true. William Bolitho's definition of the murder trial (in *Murder for Profit,* 1926, page 3) might with equal propriety be applied to the murder-mystery, for both, equally, are

the celebration of a human sacrifice by suffocation, to which modern men are excited in a crowd by the recital of some bloody deed whose details awaken hate and fear to which the coming execution is the fore-shadowed, fore-tasted complementary. Everything there . . . is devised to create that hoarse atmosphere in which alone modern men, in a state of peace, can work themselves up to a corporate killing.

It may even be pointed out that the human sacrifice of, and to, the murderer in books—three hundred of them a year, every year (not counting reprints) with an audience in millions—appeals to the same socially accepted bloodlust as that thought desirable at prize- & bull fights. This, also, is true. It might be questioned, however, whether the lulling along of these death-pleasure emotionalisms through symbolic satisfaction in books and arenas does more than to keep them ever-fresh in the race, waiting only for the stress of economic struggle, religious factionalism, and war to free them from the limitations of symbolism and scapegoatry, and allow them brutal and delighted play.

There is a sort of Gresham's Law by which bad art drives out good. Murder having replaced sex in the popular arts, the glorification of one requires the degradation of the other. Death calls down anathema on love. Pronouncing judgment on March 29th, 1948, in the Winters case, the Supreme Court of the United States of America all but declared, as its studied decision—re-argued three times in as many years—that so far as art and literature are concerned, sex is worse than murder.

This stupefying pronouncement is now the law of the land, and will remain so probably for decades. For all practical purposes it has always been the law. The New York Penal Law § 1141(2)—now struck down by the Supreme Court— which made literary 'bloodshed' at least as bad as sex, has been a dead letter for over half a century, nullified and ignored ever since it was passed in 1884 in New York and in twenty-three other states since.

Meanwhile, the anti-obscenity subsection (1) of the same law is still very much alive. Thousands of persons have been prosecuted, and most of them fined or imprisoned, under this subsection and the Postal Law similar—which triples the penalty for obscenity, but neglects to mention 'bloodshed' at all. But it would be difficult to find more than three solitary cases in these last sixty-five years— *Strohm,* 160 Illinois 582; *McKee,* 73 Connecticut 18; and now *Winters,* 294 N.Y. 545—prosecuted anywhere in the country for the publication of 'pictures, or stories of deeds of bloodshed, lust or crime.' In the face of disinterest such as this, the Supreme Court's decision is merely the catching up of the law with the national temper.

The error in the inferior court, that brought the Winters case to the Supreme Court in the first place, had been the gratuitous interpretation of the law as requiring the stories or pictures of bloodshed &c. to be 'so massed as to become vehicles for inciting' to crime—the purpose being to ban murder-magazines without banning books. Nevertheless, so great (according to the Supreme Court) are the legislative powers of the judiciary, that this mere statement by an inferior court 'puts these words in the statute as definitely as if it had been so amended by the legislature.' And, on the principal ground that the New York Penal Law § 1141(2) had been thus 'amended' into ambiguity, the original laws of twenty-three other states were declared unconstitutional. *Fiat justicia.*

This retroactive hanky-panky is not, however, half so significant as the fact that, and the illogic with which, simultaneously, the prohibition against obscenity was affirmed:

The impossibility [says the Supreme Court] of defining the precise line between permissible uncertainty in statutes, caused by describing crimes by words well understood through long use in the criminal law—obscene, lewd, lascivious, filthy, indecent or disgusting—and the unconstitutional vagueness that leaves a person uncertain as to the kind of prohibited conduct—massing stories to incite crime—has resulted in three arguments of this case in this court. (333 U.S. 518.)

This is, of course, clear warning—twice repeated—that the Supreme Court majority fully intends to find the obscenity law (1) constitutional when it comes finally to be argued before it, though it has found the 'bloodshed' law (2) unconstitutional. It does not matter. The prejudice clearly apparent behind the foreground technicalities of the Winters decision is, after all, the national opinion as well: that sex in literature is worse than murder. In life, however, the situation is the reverse. So that we are faced in our culture by the insurmountable schizophrenic contradiction that sex, which is legal in fact, is a crime on paper, while murder—a crime in fact—is, on paper, the best seller of all time.

It therefore does not matter in the least what the Supreme Court decides concerning sex. It is not law that keeps the censorship going. The Comstocks, the Sumners, the virgin sex-experts of the Catholic Church (and the postal inspectors they control)—even the liberal lawyers who expurgate books beforehand for our pusillanimous publishers—these are not the censor. The American censorship of sex is internalized. The men & women in the street carry it around with them in their heads. *They* are the censor, and to the degree that the law mirrors their wonted censorship, the law can be enforced and will be obeyed. Where the law diverges from the *mores* of the times—in our time, the substitution of an allowable sadism for a censored sexuality—the law is worthless and unenforceable.

The proof of this will be in the sequel to the *Hecate County* fiasco, in which—the first obscenity case since Winters' to reach the Supreme Court (October 25th, 1948)—the law was silently upheld in a tie vote. No one imagines that if sex should be exonerated by the Supreme Court, in a moment of headlong consistency, obscenity would for a moment become legal. No one is so foolish as to think that if the obscenity laws of the states, Post Office, Federal Communications Commission, and Customs combined should be declared unconstitutional, pornography could be openly published in the United States, as bloodshed, bloodlust, and crime are published.

Hardly. New laws would be passed overnight, avoiding whatever technical errors might cause the present obscenity laws to fall. The legislative courage might even be found to abandon the multiple and 'permissible' uncertainty of meaningless adjectives like 'obscene, lewd, lascivious, filthy, indecent or disgusting' —saying nothing, in their overlapping terror, but that they are afraid—and to set up frank and objective criteria of guilt: that (with, of course, the usual exceptions for technical treatises, 'detective stories . . . reports of battle carnage, &c.'—*verbum sat sapienti*) [2] the description of sexual relations of any kind, or of the genital organs of either sex, in text or in pictures, is a crime; or—if safety is still to be sought in subjectivity—that any passage of text, or any picture, that gives seven of twelve good men & true an erection is, by that test, criminal.

[2] a word to the wise is sufficient.

On the other hand, let new laws against the exploitation of literary bloodshed now be passed—even under the subterfuge of protecting children, and in all the wordings and with all the preambles that Justice Felix Frankfurter's minority opinion carefully indicates such laws must have if they are not to fall before the Supreme Court as § 1141(2) has fallen—and what, precisely, will be achieved? A new dead letter, a new unenforced and unenforceable law, will have been written on the books of half, or perhaps this time all, the states. The Postal Law, which punishes obscenity as a crime where the states find it only a misdemeanor, might even see its way clear to banning literary bloodshed too—something it has never yet thought to do. Three cases might possibly be prosecuted in the next sixty-five years, during which prosecutions the professional liberals of the American Civil Liberties Union and the Authors' League can be expected to pop up, *amicus curiae*,[3] to assail this unbearable restraint of free speech. Meanwhile, the staggering amount of sadism in all our pulp- & pocket-literature will rise from its present thousands of tons yearly to millions, from its present fifty percent or more to the intended saturation point of one hundred and one—Aldus' incunabular dream of popular classics come true as a nightmare.

With the exception of C. Day-Lewis ('Nicholas Blake') and Donat O'Donnell, who know what a murder-mystery is— and why—Mr. Howard Haycraft and his assembled experts in *The Art of the Mystery Story* (1946)—likewise Miss Barbara Howes and hers, in *Chimera,* Summer 1947—confess themselves frankly puzzled as to why, except for the money in it, they write about murder, and why anybody wants to read about it. Their provisional solution, and apology, seems to be that human beings naturally lust

[3] friend of the court.

after blood, and that the murder-writer is a sort of literary pimp, who serves the socially useful purpose of giving vicarious satisfaction on paper to this natural urge, thus keeping it from finding expression in lethal fact.

That 'mystery' writers are murder-pimps would be hard to gainsay. But the presumption that we, all of us, have some 'natural' component of bloodlust is presumption indeed. We have nothing of the sort. No animal kills for pleasure alone. But—we do have our frustrations. We do have our fears. We all have our inadequacies: sexual, economic, and personal. And it is for these that the prizefight, the fox hunt, the sports page, tabloid, comic-book, and murder-mystery supply a safe, cheap, socially water-tight solution: institutionalized amok.

Are you impotent, frigid? Does your wife insult you in bed, your husband dominate you? Why get a divorce? Divorce is expensive—for Catholics, impossible. A murder-book is only ten cents to borrow, twenty-five cents to own—free, gratis & for nothing to write. Strangle your spouse nightly on paper. (The murder-mystery is the foundation of the family: it prevents divorce.) Does your boss tyrannize and exploit you? Don't shoot him—you'll hang for it. Kill him nightly on paper—you the detective, he the hounded-down murderer. (The murder-mystery is the mainstay of usury: it prevents revolution.) Are you weak, stupid, namby-pamby, ineffective? Don't improve yourself. Don't turn against your constricting, recalcitrant environment. Dissipate the aggression you feel, siphon off your endocrine resources, be a killer, nightly—three hundred nights a year— for a dollar a week. Absurdly simple, cheaper than a hunting license, and you hunt human beings. (The murder-mystery is the backbone of civilization: it dispenses utterly with intelligence.)

Human blood in the gladiatorial arena kept Roman slave hordes satisfied with their dole of bread. *Panem et circenses.*[4] Not by bread alone does man live. He needs blood spilled before his eyes, too, or he may want butter on that bread. Next after fire, the murder-mystery is society's most valuable servant. Without it, there might be some changes made.

Optimistically, perhaps, the Right Reverend Monsignor Ronald Knox finds the murder-mystery 'in danger of getting played out.' (*The Tablet,* London, Xmas 1946, vol. 188: page 355.) And modestly, as becomes the author of *The Viaduct Murder, The Body in the Silo,* &c. &c— and, between murders, Bible translator and domestic prelate to His Holiness the Pope—Monsignor Knox adds:

Nobody can have failed to notice that while the public demand remains unshaken . . . the means of writing [a 'detective mystery'] with any symptom of originality about it, becomes rarer with each succeeding year. The game is getting played out . . . the stories get cleverer and cleverer, but the readers are getting cleverer . . . too.

Perhaps. But Monsignor Knox is misled. The literary quality of the murder-mystery has nothing to do with its sales. The murder-reading public is not hungry for style; it is thirsty for blood. The puzzle element, the cleverness of writers or audience, the word 'mystery' itself—all are simply frauds: pretty lamb-chop panties of paper with which genteelly to grab hold of the raw meat of sadism. The problem, however, is not one of wilful pathology. The literate population of Great Britain and America is not largely composed of fantasy-sadists out of malice prepense. They cannot help themselves.

Nor are they comfortable in their uncontrollable letch for death. A gnawing guilt disturbs them. And they must dither and blather, refer nervously to 'the search for certainty in an uncertain world,' to 'puzzles,' to 'pattern,' and plain 'addiction.' They must write yearly de-

[4] Bread and circuses.

fenses—with no attack ever yet published. They must point with anxious pride to kings and lesser fry (the frustrated do-gooders: Lincoln, Wilson, Roosevelt) sharing their lethal 'relaxation,' to an *arbiter homicidiarum* hustling a murder-library into the White House, to a Catholic priest with five murder-mysteries 'to his credit' and a Marxist critic ('Caudwell'-Sprigg) with six, to the titubating comedy of a titled English philosopher carving up a Christmas pudden of self-congratulation for himself and the other 'mystery'-fanciers of Great Britain with the nincumpoop suggestion that reading about murder will 'realise . . . the unification of mankind' and 'abolish war.' (Lord Bertrand Russell, in *The Listener,* Xmas 1948, vol. 40: page 1010.)

Least innocent, because they are most aware, are the amateurs of murder— the writers especially—the feuilletonist clergymen, the pansy intellectuals, the homicidal housewives and pseudonymous college-professors, all swilling happily through paper straws at their hot cathartic toddy of blood. Least guilty, because stupidest, are the professionals—the word-mongers: publishers and their hacks —hip-deep in murder strictly for the dollar, the merest puppets of their *Zeitgeist.*[5] And they will tell you that only the public is responsible, only the reader-mass is culpable. And yet, are even these to blame?

The frustrations implicit in twentieth-century life, that make necessary our diet of murder, have not been resolved and cannot be resolved within the framework of our profit-economy and anti-sexual morality. Love being unwholesome, and revolution unhealthy, only one petcock of release is left us: we may dream of violence, of death; watch it in arenas, quiver over it on paper, run amok in fantasy, identifying ourselves always with the killer, the killer of killers—the superman. Our need is acute. The demand is

[5] The spirit of the time.

paramount. And blood and death and violence will therefore continue to be supplied.

Like the Talmudic pig, holding up its cloven forefeet from the dung-wallow where it lies, grunting 'Clean! I'm clean!' murder-writers and readers are anxious to demonstrate that at least their feet are kosher: there is no sex anywhere to be seen. (The exceptions, and what they actually prove, will be considered later.) Absorbed in their obedience to the Sixth Commandment—the one against killing —reminding themselves nightly of its sinfulness, they would view with consternation the proposal that, simultaneously and by similar means (let us say three hundred juicily titled pornographic novels yearly, all ending with horrible punishment in the venereal ward), society might show its reverence for the Seventh. No. This goose and this gander require different sauces. Literary murder is respectable, 'relaxing,' anything you please. Literary sex—it doesn't even have to be adultery—is 'obscene.'

Mr. Rex Stout, who opines (in Howard Haycraft's cynically-titled centenary, *Murder for Pleasure: The Life & Times of the Detective Story*, 1941, page vii) that 'people who don't like mystery stories are anarchists,' warily announces over the radio that if 'by romance . . . you mean love . . . I'm out of it. I'm a writer of murder-mysteries and I'm not supposed to know anything about it.' (The Author Meets the Critics, December 5th, 1946.) Naturally, Mr. Stout, naturally. When 'our best writers' are profitably peddling murder, and our best critic, Edmund Wilson, is barely escaping jail for 'obscenity,' who wants to bother with love?

In the midst of death, love is no part of our dream. Our imaginations stuffed with murder, we are too moral for sex. Drugged on blood and death, murder upon murder, two abreast, three hundred deep, year after bloody year; killing for the pure lust of killing—for the lack of courage to rebel; usurping, in the name of justice, the prerogatives of all justice, human & divine; our multi-millions of 'mystery' readers *prefer* their transvalued pattern—empty of sex, reeking with sadism—within the boundaries of which, as it would seem, no one dares to attack them.

DOVER BEACH

The sea is calm to-night.
The tide is full, the moon lies fair
Upon the straits;—on the French coast, the light
Gleams, and is gone; the cliffs of England stand,
Glimmering and vast, out in the tranquil bay.   5
Come to the window, sweet is the night air!
Only, from the lone line of spray
Where the sea meets the moon-blanch'd land,
Listen! you hear the grating roar
Of pebbles which the waves draw back, and fling,   10
At their return, up the high strand,
Begin, and cease, and then again begin,
With tremulous cadence slow, and bring
The eternal note of sadness in.

Sophocles [1] long ago   15
Heard it on the Ægæan, and it brought
Into his mind the turbid ebb and flow
Of human misery; we
Find also in the sound a thought,
Hearing it by this distant northern sea.   20

The Sea of Faith
Was once, too, at the full, and round earth's shore
Lay like the folds of a bright girdle furl'd.
But now I only hear
Its melancholy, long, withdrawing roar,   25
Retreating, to the breath
Of the night-wind down the vast edges drear
And naked shingles of the world.

Ah, love, let us be true
To one another! for the world, which seems   30
To lie before us like a land of dreams,
So various, so beautiful, so new,
Hath really neither joy, nor love, nor light,
Nor certitude, nor peace, nor help for pain;
And we are here as on a darkling plain   35
Swept with confused alarms of struggle and flight,
Where ignorant armies clash by night.

MATTHEW ARNOLD

[1] *Sophocles:* Greek dramatist.

LONDON

I wander thro' each charter'd street,
Near where the charter'd Thames does flow,
And mark in every face I meet
Marks of weakness, marks of woe.

In every cry of every Man,   5
In every Infant's cry of fear,
In every voice, in every ban,
The mind-forg'd manacles I hear.

How the Chimney-sweeper's cry
Every black'ning Church appalls;   10
And the hapless Soldier's sigh
Runs in blood down Palace walls.

But most thro' midnight streets I hear
How the youthful Harlot's curse
Blasts the new born Infant's tear,   15
and Blights with plagues the Marriage hearse.

WILLIAM BLAKE

A POISON TREE

I was angry with my friend:
I told my wrath, my wrath did end.
I was angry with my foe:
I told it not, my wrath did grow.

And I watered it in fears   5
Night and morning with my tears;
And I sunned it with smiles,
And with soft deceitful wiles.

And it grew both day and night,
Till it bore an apple bright;   10
And my foe beheld it shine,
And he knew that it was mine,

And into my garden stole
When the night had veiled the pole:
In the morning, glad, I see   15
My foe outstretched beneath the tree.

WILLIAM BLAKE

THE TIGER

Tiger! Tiger! burning bright
In the forests of the night,
What immortal hand or eye
Could frame thy fearful symmetry?

In what distant deeps or skies   5
Burnt the fire of thine eyes?
On what wings dare he aspire?
What the hand dare seize the fire?

And what shoulder, and what art,
Could twist the sinews of thy heart?   10
And, when thy heart began to beat,
What dread hand? and what dread feet?

What the hammer? what the chain?
In what furnace was thy brain?
What the anvil? what dread grasp   15
Dare its deadly terrors clasp?

When the stars threw down their spears,
And watered heaven with their tears,
Did he smile his work to see?
Did he who made the Lamb make thee?

Tiger! Tiger! burning bright   21
In the forests of the night,
What immortal hand or eye
Dare frame thy fearful symmetry?

WILLIAM BLAKE

UCCELLO [1]

   They will never die on that battlefield
nor the shade of wolves recruit their hoard like brides of
wheat on all horizons waiting there to consume battle's end
   There will be no dead to tighten their loose bellies
no heap of starched horses to redsmash their bright eyes   5
   or advance their eat of dead
   They would rather hungersulk with mad tongues
than believe that on that field no man dies

   They will never die who fight so embraced
breath to breath   eye knowing eye   impossible to die   10
or move   no light seeping through   no maced arm
nothing but horse outpanting horse   shield brilliant upon
shield   all made starry by the dot ray of a helmeted eye
ah   how difficult to fall between those knitted lances
And those banners! angry as to flush insignia across its   15
   erasure of sky
   You'd think he'd paint his armies by the coldest rivers
have rows of iron skulls flashing in the dark
   You'd think it impossible for any man to die
each combatant's mouth is a castle of song   20
each iron fist a dreamy gong   flail resounding flail
      like cries of gold
how I dream to join such battle!
a silver man on a black horse with red standard and striped
   lance   never to die but to be endless   25
   a golden prince of pictorial war

GREGORY CORSO

[1] Paolo Uccello, Italian painter 1396–1475.

[COME, GAZE WITH ME UPON THIS DOME]

come, gaze with me upon this dome
of many coloured glass, and see
his mother's pride, his father's joy,
unto whom duty whispers low

"thou must!" and who replies "I can!"   5
—yon clean upstanding well dressed boy
that with his peers full oft hath quaffed
the wine of life and found it sweet—

a tear within his stern blue eye,
upon his firm white lips a smile,   10
one thought alone: to do or die
for God for country and for Yale

above his blond determined head
the sacred flag of truth unfurled,
in the bright heyday of his youth   15
the upper class American

unsullied stands, before the world:
with manly heart and conscience free,
upon the front steps of her home
by the high minded pure young girl   20

much kissed, by loving relatives
well fed, and fully photographed
the son of man goes forth to war
with trumpets clap and syphilis

E. E. CUMMINGS

[I SING OF OLAF GLAD AND BIG]

i sing of Olaf glad and big
whose warmest heart recoiled at war:
a conscientious object-or

his wellbelovéd colonel(trig
westpointer most succinctly bred)   5
took erring Olaf soon in hand;
but—though an host of overjoyed
noncoms(first knocking on the head
him)do through icy waters roll

that helplessness which others stroke   10
with brushes recently employed
anent this muddy toiletbowl,
while kindred intellects evoke
allegiance per blunt instruments—
Olaf(being to all intents   15
a corpse and wanting any rag
upon what God unto him gave)
responds, without getting annoyed
"I will not kiss your f.ing flag"

straightway the silver bird looked grave   20
(departing hurriedly to shave)
but—though all kinds of officers
(a yearning nation's blueeyed pride)
their passive prey did kick and curse
until for wear their clarion   25
voices and boots were much the worse,
and egged the firstclassprivates on
his rectum wickedly to tease
by means of skilfully applied
bayonets roasted hot with heat—   30
Olaf(upon what were once knees)
does almost ceaselessly repeat
"there is some s. I will not eat"

our president,being of which
assertions duly notified   35
threw the yellowsonofabitch
into a dungeon,where he died
Christ(of His mercy infinite)
i pray to see;and Olaf,too

preponderatingly because   40
unless statistics lie he was
more brave than me:more blond than you.

E. E. CUMMINGS

[MY SWEET OLD ETCETERA]

my sweet old etcetera
aunt lucy during the recent

war could and what
is more did tell you just
what everybody was fighting   5

for,
my sister
isabel created hundreds
(and
hundreds) of socks not to   10
mention shirts fleaproof earwarmers

etcetera wristers etcetera, my
mother hoped that

i would die etcetera
bravely of course my father used   15
to become hoarse talking about how it was
a privilege and if only he
could meanwhile my

self etcetera lay quietly
in the deep mud et   20
cetera
(dreaming,
et
  cetera, of
Your smile   25
eyes knees and of your Etcetera)

E. E. CUMMINGS

WINTER FOR AN UNTENABLE SITUATION

Outside it is cold. Inside,
although the fire has gone out
and all the furniture is burnt,
it is much warmer. Oh let
the white refrigerator car   5
of day go by in glacial thunder:
when it gets dark, and when
the branches of the tree outside
look wet because it is so dark,
oh we will burn the house itself   10
for warmth, the wet tree too,
you will burn me, I will burn you,
and when the last brick of the fireplace
has been cracked for its nut of warmth
and the last bone cracked for its coal   15
and the andirons themselves sucked cold,
we will move on!, remembering
the burning house, the burning tree,

the burning you, the burning me,
the ashes, the brick-dust, the bitter iron,   20
and the time when we were warm,
and say, "Those were the good old days."

ALAN DUGAN

THE FURY OF AERIAL BOMBARDMENT

You would think the fury of aerial bombardment
Would rouse God to relent; the infinite spaces
Are still silent. He looks on shock-pried faces.
History, even, does not know what is meant.

You would feel that after so many centuries   5
God would give man to repent; yet he can kill
As Cain [1] could, but with multitudinous will,
No farther advanced than in his ancient furies.

Was man made stupid to see his own stupidity?
Is God by definition indifferent, beyond us all?   10
Is the eternal truth man's fighting soul
Wherein the Beast ravens in its own avidity?

Of Van Wettering I speak, and Averill,
Names on a list, whose faces I do not recall
But they are gone to early death, who late in school   15
Distinguished the belt feed lever from the belt holding pawl.

RICHARD EBERHART

THE HOLLOW MEN

A penny for the Old Guy [2]

I

We are the hollow men
We are the stuffed men
Leaning together
Headpiece filled with straw Alas!
Our dried voices, when   5
We whisper together

---

[1] The first murderer. Cain killed his brother Abel. See Genesis iv.
[2] Guy Fawkes, English conspirator in Gunpowder Plot 1570–1606.

Are quiet and meaningless
As wind in dry grass
Or rats' feet over broken glass
In our dry cellar   10

   Shape without form, shade without colour,
Paralysed force, gesture without motion;

   Those who have crossed
With direct eyes, to death's other Kingdom
Remember us—if at all—not as lost   15
Violent souls, but only
As the hollow men
The stuffed men.

II

Eyes I dare not meet in dreams
In death's dream kingdom   20
These do not appear:
There, the eyes are
Sunlight on a broken column
There, is a tree swinging
And voices are   25
In the wind's singing
More distant and more solemn
Than a fading star.

   Let me be no nearer
In death's dream kingdom   30
Let me also wear
Such deliberate disguises
Rat's coat, crowskin, crossed staves
In a field
Behaving as the wind behaves   35
No nearer—

   Not that final meeting
In the twilight kingdom

III

This is the dead land
This is cactus land   40
Here the stone images
Are raised, here they receive
The supplication of a dead man's hand
Under the twinkle of a fading star.

   Is it like this   45
In death's other kingdom

Waking alone
At the hour when we are
Trembling with tenderness
Lips that would kiss   50
Form prayers to broken stone.

IV

The eyes are not here
There are no eyes here
In this valley of dying stars
In this hollow valley   55
This broken jaw of our lost kingdoms

   In this last of meeting places
We grope together
And avoid speech
Gathered on this beach of the tumid river   60

   Sightless, unless
The eyes reappear
As the perpetual star
Multifoliate rose
Of death's twilight kingdom   65
The hope only
Of empty men.

V

Here we go round the prickly pear
Prickly pear prickly pear
Here we go round the prickly pear   70
At five o'clock in the morning.

   Between the idea
And the reality
Between the motion
And the act   75
Falls the Shadow
                                   For Thine is the Kingdom

   Between the conception
And the creation
Between the emotion   80
And the response
Falls the Shadow
                                   Life is very long

   Between the desire
And the spasm   85
Between the potency

And the existence
Between the essence
And the descent
Falls the Shadow   90
                                                    For Thine is the Kingdom

    For Thine is
Life is
For Thine is the

    This is the way the world ends   95
This is the way the world ends
This is the way the world ends
Not with a bang but a whimper.

                              T. S. ELIOT

JOURNEY OF THE MAGI

'A cold coming we had of it,
Just the worst time of the year
For a journey, and such a long journey:
The ways deep and the weather sharp,
The very dead of winter.'   5
And the camels galled, sore-footed, refractory,
Lying down in the melting snow.
There were times we regretted
The summer palaces on slopes, the terraces,
And the silken girls bringing sherbet.   10
Then the camel men cursing and grumbling
And running away, and wanting their liquor and women,
And the night-fires going out, and the lack of shelters,
And the cities hostile and the towns unfriendly
And the villages dirty and charging high prices: 15
A hard time we had of it.
At the end we preferred to travel all night,
Sleeping in snatches,
With the voices singing in our ears, saying
That this was all folly.   20

    Then at dawn we came down to a temperate valley,
Wet, below the snow line, smelling of vegetation;
With a running stream and a water-mill beating the darkness,
And three trees on the low sky,
And an old white horse galloped away in the meadow.   25

Then we came to a tavern with vine-leaves over the lintel,
Six hands at an open door dicing for pieces of silver,
And feet kicking the empty wine-skins.
But there was no information, and so we continued
And arrived at evening, not a moment too soon 30
Finding the place; it was (you may say) satisfactory.

    All this was a long time ago, I remember,
And I would do it again, but set down
This set down
This: were we led all that way for 35
Birth or Death? There was a Birth, certainly,
We had evidence and no doubt. I had seen birth and death,
But had thought they were different; this Birth was
Hard and bitter agony for us, like Death, our death.
We returned to our places, these Kingdoms, 40
But no longer at ease here, in the old dispensation,
With an alien people clutching their gods.
I should be glad of another death.

T. S. ELIOT

SWEENEY AMONG THE NIGHTINGALES

ὤμοι, πέπληγμαι καιρίαν πληγὴν ἔσω.[1]

Apeneck Sweeney spreads his knees
Letting his arms hang down to laugh,
The zebra stripes along his jaw
Swelling to maculate giraffe.

    The circles of the stormy moon 5
Slide westward toward the River Plate,
Death and the Raven drift above
And Sweeney guards the hornèd gate.

    Gloomy Orion and the Dog
Are veiled; and hushed the shrunken seas; 10
The person in the Spanish cape
Tries to sit on Sweeney's knees

    Slips and pulls the table cloth
Overturns a coffee-cup,
Reorganized upon the floor 15
She yawns and draws a stocking up;

[1] "Ah me, I have been struck a mortal blow within," from the play *Agamemnon* by Aeschylus.

The silent man in mocha brown
Sprawls at the window-sill and gapes;
The waiter brings in oranges
Bananas figs and hothouse grapes;   20

The silent vertebrate in brown
Contracts and concentrates, withdraws;
Rachel *née* Rabinovitch
Tears at the grapes with murderous paws;

She and the lady in the cape   25
Are suspect, thought to be in league;
Therefore the man with heavy eyes
Declines the gambit, shows fatigue,

Leaves the room and reappears
Outside the window, leaning in,   30
Branches of wistaria
Circumscribe a golden grin;

The host with someone indistinct
Converses at the door apart,
The nightingales are singing near   35
The Convent of the Sacred Heart,

And sang within the bloody wood
When Agamemnon cried aloud,
And let their liquid siftings fall
To stain the stiff dishonoured shroud.   40

T. S. ELIOT

WHISPERS OF IMMORTALITY

Webster was much possessed by death
And saw the skull beneath the skin;
And breastless creatures under ground
Leaned backward with a lipless grin.

Daffodil bulbs instead of balls   5
Stared from the sockets of the eyes!
He knew that thought clings round dead limbs
Tightening its lusts and luxuries.

Donne, I suppose, was such another
Who found no substitute for sense,   10
To seize and clutch and penetrate;
Expert beyond experience,

He knew the anguish of the marrow
The ague of the skeleton;
No contact possible to flesh   15
Allayed the fever of the bone.

.   .   .   .   .

Grishkin is nice: her Russian eye
Is underlined for emphasis;
Uncorseted, her friendly bust
Gives promise of pneumatic bliss.   20

The couched Brazilian jaguar
Compels the scampering marmoset
With subtle effluence of cat;
Grishkin has a maisonette;

The sleek Brazilian jaguar   25
Does not in its arboreal gloom
Distil so rank a feline smell
As Grishkin in a drawing-room.

And even the Abstract Entities
Circumambulate her charm;   30
But our lot crawls between dry ribs
To keep our metaphysics warm.

T. S. ELIOT

THE SUBVERTED FLOWER

She drew back; he was calm:
"It is this that had the power."
And he lashed his open palm
With the tender-headed flower.
He smiled for her to smile,   5
But she was either blind
Or willfully unkind.
He eyed her for a while
For a woman and a puzzle.
He flicked and flung the flower,   10
And another sort of smile
Caught up like finger tips
The corners of his lips
And cracked his ragged muzzle.
She was standing to the waist   15
In goldenrod and brake,
Her shining hair displaced.

He stretched her either arm
As if she made it ache
To clasp her—not to harm;   20
As if he could not spare
To touch her neck and hair.
"If this has come to us
And not to me alone—"
So she thought she heard him say;   25
Though with every word he spoke
His lips were sucked and blown
And the effort made him choke
Like a tiger at a bone.
She had to lean away.   30
She dared not stir a foot,
Lest movement should provoke
The demon of pursuit
That slumbers in a brute.
It was then her mother's call   35
From inside the garden wall
Made her steal a look of fear
To see if he could hear
And would pounce to end it all
Before her mother came.   40
She looked and saw the shame:
A hand hung like a paw,
An arm worked like a saw
As if to be persuasive,
An ingratiating laugh   45
That cut the snout in half,
An eye become evasive.
A girl could only see
That a flower had marred a man,
But what she could not see   50
Was that the flower might be
Other than base and fetid:
That the flower had done but part,
And what the flower began
Her own too meager heart   55
Had terribly completed.
She looked and saw the worst.
And the dog or what it was,
Obeying bestial laws,
A coward save at night,   60
Turned from the place and ran.
She heard him stumble first
And use his hands in flight.
She heard him bark outright.
And oh, for one so young   65
The bitter words she spit

Like some tenacious bit
That will not leave the tongue.
She plucked her lips for it,
And still the horror clung.   70
Her mother wiped the foam
From her chin, picked up her comb
And drew her backward home.

R O B E R T   F R O S T

HOWL, PARTS I AND II

for Carl Solomon

I

I saw the best minds of my generation destroyed by madness, starving hysterical naked,
dragging themselves through the negro streets at dawn looking for an angry fix,
angelheaded hipsters burning for the ancient heavenly connection to the starry dynamo
     in the machinery of night,
who poverty and tatters and hollow-eyed and high sat up smoking in the supernatural
     darkness of cold-water flats floating across the tops of cities contemplating jazz,
who bared their brains to Heaven under the El and saw Mohammedan angels staggering
     on tenement roofs illuminated,
who passed through universities with radiant cool eyes hallucinating Arkansas and
     Blake-light tragedy among the scholars of war,
who were expelled from the academies for crazy & publishing obscene odes on the
     windows of the skull,
who cowered in unshaven rooms in underwear, burning their money in wastebaskets
     and listening to the Terror through the wall,
who got busted in their pubic beards returning through Laredo with a belt of marijuana
     for New York,
who ate fire in paint hotels or drank turpentine in Paradise Alley, death, or purgatoried
     their torsos night after night
with dreams, with drugs, with waking nightmares, alcohol and cock and endless balls,
incomparable blind streets of shuddering cloud and lightning in the mind leaping toward
     poles of Canada & Paterson, illuminating all the motionless world of Time between,
Peyote solidities of halls, backyard green tree cemetery dawns, wine drunkenness over
     the rooftops, storefront boroughs of teahead joyride neon blinking traffic light, sun
     and moon and tree vibrations in the roaring winter dusks of Brooklyn, ashcan rant-
     ings and kind king light of mind,
who chained themselves to subways for the endless ride from Battery to holy Bronx on
     benzedrine until the noise of wheels and children brought them down shuddering
     mouth-wracked and battered bleak of brain all drained of brilliance in the drear
     light of Zoo,
who sank all night in submarine light of Bickford's floated out and sat through the stale
     beer afternoon in desolate Fugazzi's listening to the crack of doom on the hydrogen
     jukebox,

who talked continuously seventy hours from park to pad to bar to Bellevue to museum to the Brooklyn Bridge,

a lost battalion of platonic conversationalists jumping down the stoops off fire escapes off windowsills off Empire State out of the moon,

yacketayakking screaming vomiting whispering facts and memories and anecdotes and eyeball kicks and shocks of hospitals and jails and wars,

whole intellects disgorged in total recall for seven days and nights with brilliant eyes, meat for the Synagogue cast on the pavement,

who vanished into nowhere Zen New Jersey leaving a trail of ambiguous picture postcards of Atlantic City Hall,

suffering Eastern sweats and Tangerian bone-grindings and migraines of China under junk-withdrawal in Newark's bleak furnished room,

who wandered around and around at midnight in the railroad yard wondering where to go, and went, leaving no broken hearts,

who lit cigarettes in boxcars boxcars boxcars racketing through snow toward lonesome farms in grandfather night,

who studied Plotinus Poe St. John of the Cross telepathy and bop kaballa because the cosmos instinctively vibrated at their feet in Kansas,

who loned it through the streets of Idaho seeking visionary indian angels who were visionary indian angels,

who thought they were only mad when Baltimore gleamed in supernatural ecstasy,

who jumped in limousines with the Chinaman of Oklahoma on the impulse of winter midnight streetlight smalltown rain,

who lounged hungry and lonesome through Houston seeking jazz or sex or soup, and followed the brilliant Spaniard to converse about America and Eternity, a hopeless task, and so took ship to Africa,

who disappeared into the volcanoes of Mexico leaving behind nothing but the shadow of dungarees and the lava and ash of poetry scattered in fireplace Chicago,

who reappeared on the West Coast investigating the F.B.I. in beards and shorts with big pacifist eyes sexy in their dark skin passing out incomprehensible leaflets,

who burned cigarette holes in their arms protesting the narcotic tobacco haze of Capitalism,

who distributed Supercommunist pamphlets in Union Square weeping and undressing while the sirens of Los Alamos wailed them down, and wailed down Wall, and the Staten Island ferry also wailed,

who broke down crying in white gymnasiums naked and trembling before the machinery of other skeletons,

who bit detectives in the neck and shrieked with delight in policecars for committing no crime but their own wild cooking pederasty and intoxication,

who howled on their knees in the subway and were dragged off the roof waving genitals and manuscripts,

who let themselves be fucked in the ass by saintly motorcyclists, and screamed with joy,

who blew and were blown by those human seraphim, the sailors, caresses of Atlantic and Caribbean love,

who balled in the morning in the evenings in rosegardens and the grass of public parks and cemeteries scattering their semen freely to whomever come who may,

who hiccupped endlessly trying to giggle but wound up with a sob behind a partition in a Turkish Bath when the blonde & naked angel came to pierce them with a sword,

who lost their loveboys to the three old shrews of fate the one eyed shrew of the heterosexual dollar the one eyed shrew that winks out of the womb and the one eyed shrew that does nothing but sit on her ass and snip the intellectual golden threads of the craftsman's loom,

who copulated ecstatic and insatiate with a bottle of beer a sweetheart a package of cigarettes a candle and fell off the bed, and continued along the floor and down the hall and ended fainting on the wall with a vision of ultimate cunt and come eluding the last gyzym of consciousness.

who sweetened the snatches of a million girls trembling in the sunset, and were red eyed in the morning but prepared to sweeten the snatch of the sunrise, flashing buttocks under barns and naked in the lake,

who went out whoring through Colorado in myriad stolen nightcars, N.C., secret hero of these poems, cocksman and Adonis of Denver—joy to the memory of his innumerable lays of girls in empty lots & diner backyards, moviehouses' rickety rows, on mountain tops in caves or with gaunt waitresses in familiar roadside lonely petticoat upliftings & especially secret gas-station solipsisms of johns, & hometown alleys too,

who faded out in vast sordid movies, were shifted in dreams, woke on a sudden Manhattan, and picked themselves up out of basements hungover with heartless Tokay and horrors of Third Avenue iron dreams & stumbled to unemployment offices,

who walked all night with their shoes full of blood on the snowbank docks waiting for a door in the East River to open to a room full of steamheat and opium,

who created great suicidal dramas on the apartment cliff-banks of the Hudson under the wartime blue floodlight of the moon & their heads shall be crowned with laurel in oblivion,

who ate the lamb stew of the imagination or digested the crab at the muddy bottom of the rivers of Bowery,

who wept at the romance of the streets with their pushcarts full of onions and bad music,

who sat in boxes breathing in the darkness under the bridge, and rose up to build harpsichords in their lofts,

who coughed on the sixth floor of Harlem crowned with flame under the tubercular sky surrounded by orange crates of theology,

who scribbled all night rocking and rolling over lofty incantations which in the yellow morning where stanzas of gibberish,

who cooked rotten animals lung heart feet borsht & tortillas dreaming of the pure vegetable kingdom,

who plunged themselves under meat trucks looking for an egg,

who threw their watches off the roof to cast their ballot for Eternity outside of Time, & alarm clocks fell on their heads every day for the next decade,

who cut their wrists three times successively unsuccessfully, gave up and were forced to open antique stores where they thought they were growing old and cried,

who were burned alive in their innocent flannel suits on Madison Avenue amid blasts of leaden verse & the tanked-up clatter of the iron regiments of fashion & the nitro-glycerine shrieks of the fairies of advertising & the mustard gas of sinister intelligent editors, or were run down by the drunken taxicabs of Absolute Reality,

who jumped off the Brooklyn Bridge this actually happened and walked away unknown and forgotten into the ghostly daze of Chinatown soup alleyways & firetrucks, not even one free beer,

who sang out of their windows in despair, fell out of the subway window, jumped in the filthy Passaic, leaped on negroes, cried all over the street, danced on broken wineglasses barefoot smashed phonograph records of nostalgic European 1930's German jazz finished the whiskey and threw up groaning into the bloody toilet, moans in their ears and the blast of colossal steamwhistles,

who barreled down the highways of the past journeying to each other's hotrod-Golgotha jail-solitude watch or Birmingham jazz incarnation,

who drove crosscountry seventytwo hours to find out if I had a vision or you had a vision or he had a vision to find out Eternity,

who journeyed to Denver, who died in Denver, who came back to Denver & waited in vain, who watched over Denver & brooded & loned in Denver and finally went away to find out the Time, & now Denver is lonesome for her heroes,

who fell on their knees in hopeless cathedrals praying for each other's salvation and light and breasts, until the soul illuminated its hair for a second,

who crashed through their minds in jail waiting for impossible criminals with golden heads and the charm of reality in their hearts who sang sweet blues to Alcatraz,

who retired to Mexico to cultivate a habit, or Rocky Mount to tender Buddha or Tangiers to boys or Southern Pacific to the black locomotive or Harvard to Narcissus to Woodlawn to the daisychain or grave,

who demanded sanity trials accusing the radio of hypnotism & were left with their insanity & their hands & a hung jury,

who threw potato salad at CCNY lecturers on Dadaism and subsequently presented themselves on the granite steps of the madhouse with shaven heads and harlequin speech of suicide, demanding instantaneous lobotomy,

and who were given instead the concrete void of insulin metrasol electricity hydrotherapy psychotherapy occupational therapy pingpong & amnesia,

who in humorless protest overturned only one symbolic pingpong table, resting briefly in catatonia,

returning years later truly bald except for a wig of blood, and tears and fingers, to the visible madman doom of the wards of the madtowns of the East,

Pilgrim State's Rockland's and Greystone's foetid halls, bickering with the echoes of the soul, rocking and rolling in the midnight solitude-bench dolmen-realms of love, dream of life a nightmare, bodies turned to stone as heavy as the moon,

with mother finally ******, and the last fantastic book flung out of the tenement window, and the last door closed at 4 AM and the last telephone slammed at the wall in reply and the last furnished room emptied down to the last piece of mental furniture, a yellow paper rose twisted on a wire hanger in the closet, and even that imaginary, nothing but a hopeful little bit of hallucination—

ah, Carl, while you are not safe I am not safe, and now you're really in the total animal soup of time—

and who therefore ran through the icy streets obscssed with a sudden flash of the alchemy of the use of the ellipse the catalog the meter & the vibrating plane,

who dreamt and made incarnate gaps in Time & Space through images juxtaposed, and trapped the archangel of the soul between 2 visual images and joined the elemental verbs and set the noun and dash of consciousness together jumping with sensation of Pater Omnipotens Aeterna Deus [1]

to recreate the syntax and measure of poor human prose and stand before you speechless and intelligent and shaking with shame, rejected yet confessing out the soul to conform to the rhythm of thought in his naked and endless head,

[1] All-powerful Father eternal God.

the madmen bum and angel beat in Time, unknown, yet putting down here what might
be left to say in time come after death,

and rose reincarnate in the ghostly clothes of jazz in the goldhorn shadow of the band
and blew the suffering of America's naked mind for love into an eli eli lamma
lamma sabacthani [2] saxophone cry that shivered the cities down to the last radio

with the absolute heart of the poem of life butchered out of their own bodies good to
eat a thousand years.

II

What sphinx of cement and aluminum bashed open their skulls and ate up their brains
and imagination?

Moloch! [3] Solitude! Filth! Ugliness! Ashcans and unobtainable dollars! Children screaming under the stairways! Boys sobbing in armies! Old men weeping in the parks!

Moloch! Moloch! Nightmare of Moloch! Moloch the loveless! Mental Moloch! Moloch
the heavy judger of men!

Moloch the incomprehensible prison! Moloch the crossbone soulless jailhouse and Congress of sorrows! Moloch whose buildings are judgement! Moloch the vast stone of
war! Moloch the stunned governments!

Moloch whose mind is pure machinery! Moloch whose blood is running money! Moloch
whose fingers are ten armies! Moloch whose breast is a cannibal dynamo! Moloch
whose ear is a smoking tomb!

Moloch whose eyes are a thousand blind windows! Moloch whose skyscrapers stand in
the long streets like endless Jehovahs! Moloch whose factories dream and croak in
the fog! Moloch whose smokestacks and antennae crown the cities!

Moloch whose love is endless oil and stone! Moloch whose soul is electricity and banks!
Moloch whose poverty is the specter of genius! Moloch whose fate is a cloud of
sexless hydrogen! Moloch whose name is the Mind!

Moloch in whom I sit lonely! Moloch in whom I dream Angels! Crazy in Moloch!
Cocksucker in Moloch! Lacklove and manless in Moloch!

Moloch who entered my soul early! Moloch in whom I am a consciousness without a
body! Moloch who frightened me out of my natural ecstasy! Moloch whom I
abandon! Wake up in Moloch! Light streaming out of the sky!

Moloch! Moloch! Robot apartments! invisible suburbs! skeleton treasuries! blind capi-
tals! demonic industries! spectral nations! invincible madhouses! granite cocks!
monstrous bombs!

They broke their backs lifting Moloch to Heaven! Pavements, trees, radios, tons! lifting
the city to Heaven which exists and is everywhere about us!

Visions! omens! hallucinations! miracles! ecstasies! gone down the American river!

Dreams! adorations! illuminations! religions! the whole boatload of sensitive bullshit!

Breakthroughs! over the river! flips and crucifixions! gone down the flood! Highs!
Epiphanies! Despairs! Ten years' animal screams and suicides! Minds! New loves!
Mad generation! down on the rocks of Time!

Real holy laughter in the river! They saw it all! the wild eyes! the holy yells! They bade
farewell! They jumped off the roof! to solitude! waving! carrying flowers! Down
to the river! into the street!

ALLEN GINSBERG

[2] O God, O God, why hast thou forsaken me? (St. Matthew xxvii. 46).

[3] Moloch: an ancient god who demanded human sacrifice.

CHANNEL FIRING

That night your great guns, unawares,
Shook all our coffins as we lay,
And broke the chancel window-squares,
We thought it was the Judgment-day

And sat upright. While drearisome   5
Arose the howl of wakened hounds:
The mouse let fall the altar-crumb,
The worms drew back into the mounds,

The glebe cow drooled. Till God called, "No;
It's gunnery practice out at sea   10
Just as before you went below;
The world is as it used to be:

"All nations striving strong to make
Red war yet redder. Mad as hatters
They do no more for Christés sake   15
Than you who are helpless in such matters.

"That this is not the judgment hour
For some of them's a blessed thing,
For if it were they'd have to scour
Hell's floor for so much threatening . . .   20

"Ha, ha. It will be warmer when
I blow the trumpet (if indeed
I ever do; for you are men,
And rest eternal sorely need)."

So down we lay again. "I wonder,   25
Will the world ever saner be,"
Said one, "than when He sent us under
In our indifferent century!"

And many a skeleton shook his head.
"Instead of preaching forty year,"   30
My neighbor Parson Thirdly said,
"I wish I had stuck to pipes and beer."

Again the guns disturbed the hour,
Roaring their readiness to avenge.
As far inland as Stourton Tower,[1]   35
And Camelot,[2] and starlit Stonehenge.[3]

THOMAS HARDY

[1] King Alfred's Tower in Stourton, England.
[2] The location of King Arthur's palace.
[3] Upright stones near Salisbury, England, that may date from as early as the bronze age.

THE MAN HE KILLED

"Had he and I but met
By some old ancient inn,
We should have sat us down to wet
Right many a nipperkin!

"But ranged as infantry,   5
And staring face to face,
I shot at him as he at me,
And killed him in his place.

"I shot him dead because—
Because he was my foe,   10
Just so: my foe of course he was;
That's clear enough; although

"He thought he'd 'list, perhaps,
Offhand like—just as I—
Was out of work—had sold his traps—   15
No other reason why.

"Yes; quaint and curious war is!
You shoot a fellow down
You'd treat if met where any bar is,
Or help to half-a-crown."   20

THOMAS HARDY

[NO WORST, THERE IS NONE]

No worst, there is none. Pitched past pitch of grief,
More pangs will, schooled at forepangs, wilder wring.
Comforter, where, where is your comforting?
Mary, mother of us, where is your relief?

My cries heave, herds-long, huddle in a main, a chief   5
Woe, world-sorrow; on an age-old anvil wince and sing—
Then lull, then leave off. Fury had shrieked "No ling—
ering! Let me be fell: force I must be brief."

  O the mind, mind has mountains; cliffs of fall
Frightful, sheer, no-man-fathomed. Hold them cheap   10
May who ne'er hung there. Nor does long our small
Durance deal with that steep or deep. Here! creep,

Wretch, under a comfort serves in a whirlwind: all
Life death does end and each day dies with sleep.

GERARD MANLEY HOPKINS

PIKE

Pike, three inches long, perfect
Pike in all parts, green tigering the gold.
Killers from the egg: the malevolent aged grin.
They dance on the surface among the flies.

Or move, stunned by their own grandeur,   5
Over a bed of emerald, silhouette
Of submarine delicacy and horror.
A hundred feet long in their world.

In ponds, under the heat-struck lily pads—
Gloom of their stillness: 10
Logged on last year's black leaves, watching upwards.
Or hung in amber cavern of weeds.

The jaws' hooked clamp and fangs
Not to be changed at this date;
A life subdued to its instrument;   15
The gills kneading quietly, and the pectorals.

Three we kept behind glass,
Jungled in weed: three inches, four,
And four and a half: fed dry to them—
Suddenly there were two. Finally one   20

With a sag belly and the grin it was born with.
And indeed they spare nobody.
Two, six pounds each, over two feet long,
High and dry and dead in the willow-herb—

One jammed past its gills down the other's gullet: 25
The outside eye stared: as a vice locks—
The same iron in this eye
Though its film shrank in death.

A pond I fished, fifty yards across,
Whose lilies and muscular tench   30
Had outlasted every visible stone
Of the monastery that planted them—

Stilled legendary depth:
It was deep as England. It held
Pike too immense to stir, so immense and old   35
That past nightfall I dared not cast

But silently cast and fished
With the hair frozen on my head
For what might move, for what eye might move,
The still splashes on the dark pond,   40

Owls hushing the floating woods
Frail on my ear against the dream
Darkness beneath night's darkness had freed,
That rose slowly towards me, watching.

TED HUGHES

THE DEATH OF THE BALL TURRET GUNNER

From my mother's sleep I fell into the State,
And I hunched in its belly till my wet fur froze.
Six miles from earth, loosed from its dream of life,
I woke to black flak and the nightmare fighters.
When I died they washed me out of the turret with a hose.   5

RANDALL JARRELL

8TH AIR FORCE

If, in an odd angle of the hutment,
A puppy laps the water from a can
Of flowers, and the drunk sergeant shaving
Whistles *O Paradiso!* [1]—shall I say that man
Is not as men have said: a wolf to man?   5

The other murderers troop in yawning;
Three of them play Pitch, one sleeps, and one
Lies counting missions, lies there sweating
Till even his heart beats: One; One; One.
O murderers! . . . Still, this is how it's done: 10

This is a war. . . . But since these play, before they die,
Like puppies with their puppy; since, a man,

[1] From *L'Africaine* by Meyerbeer.

I did as these have done, but did not die—
I will content the people as I can
And give up these to them: Behold the man!   15

I have suffered, in a dream, because of him,
Many things; for this last saviour, man,
I have lied as I lie now. But what is lying?
Men wash their hands, in blood, as best they can:
I find no fault in this just man.   20

RANDALL JARRELL

90 NORTH

At home, in my flannel gown, like a bear to its floe,
I clambered to bed; up the globe's impossible sides
I sailed all night—till at last, with my black beard,
My furs and my dogs, I stood at the northern pole.

There in the childish night my companions lay frozen,   5
The stiff furs knocked at my starveling throat,
And I gave my great sigh—the flakes came huddling;
Were they really my end? In the darkness I turned to my rest

Here, the flag snaps in the glare and silence
Of the unbroken ice. And I stand here,   10
The dogs bark, my beard is black, and I stare
At the North Pole. And now what? Why, go back.

Turn as I please, my step is to the south.
The world—my world spins on this final point
Of cold and wretchedness: all lines, all winds   15
End in this whirlpool I at last discover.

And it is meaningless. In the child's bed
After the night's voyage, in that warm world
Where people work and suffer till the death
That crowns the pain—in that Cloud-Cuckoo-Land [1]   20

I reached my North and it had meaning.
Here at the actual pole of my existence,
Where all that I have done is meaningless,
Where I die or live by accident alone—

Where, living or dying, I am still alone;   25

[1] The kingdom of the birds in Aristophanes' comedy *The Birds*.

HIERONYMUS BOSCH, "The Garden of Delights" [Museo del Prado, Madrid].

Here where North, the night, the berg of death
Crowd to me out of the ignorant darkness
I see at last that all the knowledge

I wrung from the darkness—that the darkness flung me—   30
Is worthless as ignorance: nothing comes from nothing,
The darkness from the darkness. Pain comes from the darkness,
And we call it wisdom. It is pain.

RANDALL JARRELL

NEWSREEL

Enter the dream-house, brothers and sisters, leaving
Your debts asleep, your history at the door:
This is the home for heroes, and this loving
Darkness a fur you can afford.

Fish in their tank electrically heated   5
Nose without envy the glass wall: for them
Clerk, spy, nurse, killer, prince, the great and the defeated,
Move in a mute day-dream.

Bathed in this common source, you gape incurious
At what your active hours have willed—   10
Sleep-walking on that silver wall, the furious
Sick shapes and pregnant fancies of your world.

There is the mayor opening the oyster season:
A society wedding: the autumn hats look swell:
An old crocks' race, and a politician   15
In fishing-waders to prove that all is well.

Oh, look at the warplanes! Screaming hysteric treble
In that long power-dive, like gannets they fall steep.
But what are they to trouble—
These silver shadows to trouble your watery, womb-deep sleep?   20

See the big guns, rising, groping, erected
To plant death in your world's soft womb.
Fire-bud, smoke-blossom, iron seed projected—
Are these exotics? They will grow nearer home:

Grow nearer home—and out of the dream-house stumbling   25
One night into a strangling air and the flung

Rags of children and thunder of stone niagaras tumbling.
You'll know you slept too long.

C. DAY LEWIS

TO HIS COY MISTRESS

Had we but world enough, and time,
This coyness, lady, were no crime.
We would sit down, and think which way
To walk, and pass our long love's day.
Thou by the Indian Ganges' side   5
Shouldst rubies find; I by the tide
Of Humber would complain. I would
Love you ten years before the flood:
And you should if you please refuse
Till the conversion of the Jews.   10
My vegetable love should grow
Vaster than empires and more slow;
An hundred years should go to praise
Thine eyes, and on thy forehead gaze;
Two hundred to adore each breast,   15
But thirty thousand to the rest;
An age at least to every part,
And the last age should show your heart.
For, lady, you deserve this state,
Nor would I love at lower rate.   20
   But at my back I always hear
Time's wingéd chariot hurrying near;
And yonder all before us lie
Deserts of vast eternity.
Thy beauty shall no more be found,   25
Nor, in thy marble vault, shall sound
My echoing song; then worms shall try
That long-preserved virginity,
And your quaint honour turn to dust,
And into ashes all my lust: 30
The grave's a fine and private place,
But none, I think, do there embrace.
   Now therefore, while the youthful hue
Sits on thy skin like morning dew,
And while thy willing soul transpires   35
At every pore with instant fires,
Now let us sport us while we may,
And now, like am'rous birds of prey,
Rather at once our time devour

Than languish in his slow-chapped pow'r.   40
Let us roll all our strength and all
Our sweetness up into one ball:
And tear our pleasures with rough strife,
Through the iron gates of life:
Thus, though we cannot make our sun   45
Stand still, yet we will make him run.

ANDREW MARVELL

ANTHEM FOR DOOMED YOUTH

What passing-bells for these who die as cattle?
Only the monstrous anger of the guns.
Only the stuttering rifle's rapid rattle
Can patter out their hasty orisions.
No mockeries for them; no prayers nor bells,   5
Nor any voice of mourning save the choirs,—
The shrill, demented choirs of wailing shells;
And bugles calling for them from sad shires.

What candles may be held to speed them all?
Not in the hands of boys, but in their eyes   10
Shall shine the holy glimmers of good-byes.
The pallor of girls' brows shall be their pall;
Their flowers the tenderness of patient minds,
And each slow dusk a drawing-down of blinds.

WILFRED OWEN

DULCE ET DECORUM EST

Bent double, like old beggars under sacks,
Knock-kneed, coughing like hags, we cursed through sludge,
Till on the haunting flares we turned our backs,
And towards our distant rest began to trudge.
Men marched asleep. Many had lost their boots,   5
But limped on, blood-shod. All went lame, all blind;
Drunk with fatigue; deaf even to the hoots
of gas-shells dropping softly behind.

Gas! Gas! Quick, boys!—An ecstasy of fumbling,
Fitting the clumsy helmets just in time,   10
But someone still was yelling out and stumbling

And flound'ring like a man in fire or lime.—
Dim through the misty panes and thick green light,
As under a green sea, I saw him drowning.

In all my dreams before my helpless sight   15
He plunges at me, guttering, choking, drowning.

If in some smothering dreams, you too could pace
Behind the wagon that we flung him in,
And watch the white eyes wilting in his face,
His hanging face, like a devil's sick of sin,   20
If you could hear, at every jolt, the blood
Come gargling from the froth-corrupted lungs,
Bitten as the cud
Of vile, incurable sores on innocent tongues,—
My friend, you would not tell with such high zest   25
To children ardent for some desperate glory,
The old lie: *Dulce et decorum est*
Pro patria mori.[1]

WILFRED OWEN

GREATER LOVE

Red lips are not so red
   As the stained stones kissed by the English dead.
Kindness of wooed and wooer
Seems shame to their love pure.
O Love, your eyes lose lure   5
   When I behold eyes blinded in my stead!

Your slender attitude
   Trembles not exquisite like limbs knife-skewed,
Rolling and rolling there
Where God seems not to care;   10
Till the fierce love they bear
   Cramps them in death's extreme decrepitude.

Your voice sings not so soft,—
   Though even as wind murmuring through raftered loft,—
Your dear voice is not dear,   15
Gentle, and evening clear,
As theirs whom none now hear
   Now earth has stopped their piteous mouths that coughed.

[1] From Horace: "It is sweet and proper to die for one's country."

Heart, you were never hot,
   Nor large, nor full like hearts made great with shot;   20
And though your hand be pale,
Paler are all which trail
Your cross through flame and hail:
   Weep, you may weep, for you may touch them not.

WILFRED OWEN

INSENSIBILITY

Happy are men who yet before they are killed
Can let their veins run cold.
Whom no compassion fleers
Or makes their feet
Sore on the alleys cobbled with their brothers.   5
The front line withers,
But they are troops who fade, not flowers,
For poets' tearful fooling:
Men, gaps for filling:
Losses who might have fought   10
Longer; but no one bothers.

And some cease feeling
Even themselves or for themselves.
Dullness best solves
The tease and doubt of shelling,   15
And Chance's strange arithmetic
Comes simpler than the reckoning of their shilling.
They keep no check on armies' decimation.

Happy are these who lose imagination:
They have enough to carry with ammunition.   20
Their spirit drags no pack,
Their old wounds save with cold can not more ache.
Having seen all things red,
Their eyes are rid
Of the hurt of the colour of blood for ever.   25
And terror's first constriction over,
Their hearts remain small-drawn.
Their senses in some scorching cautery of battle
Now long since ironed,
Can laugh among the dying, unconcerned.   30

Happy the soldier home, with not a notion
How somewhere, every dawn, some men attack,

And many sighs are drained.
Happy the lad whose mind was never trained:
His days are worth forgetting more than not. 35
He sings along the march
Which we march taciturn, because of dusk,
The long, forlorn, relentless trend
From larger day to huger night.

We wise, who with a thought besmirch 40
Blood over all our soul,
How should we see our task
But through his blunt and lashless eyes?
Alive, he is not vital overmuch;
Dying, not mortal overmuch; 45
Nor sad, nor proud,
Nor curious at all.
He cannot tell
Old men's placidity from his.

But cursed are dullards whom no cannon stuns, 50
That they should be as stones;
Wretched are they, and mean
With paucity that never was simplicity.
By choice they made themselves immune
To pity and whatever moans in man 55
Before the last sea and the hapless stars;
Whatever mourns when many leave these shores;
Whatever shares
The eternal reciprocity of tears.

WILFRED OWEN

LESSONS OF THE WAR: NAMING OF PARTS

(to Alan Michell)

*Vixi duellis nuper idoneus
Et militavi non sine gloria* [1]

Today we have naming of parts. Yesterday,
We had daily cleaning. And tomorrow morning,
We shall have what to do after firing. But today,
Today we have naming of parts. Japonica
Glistens like coral in all of the neighbouring gardens, 5
    And today we have naming of parts.

[1] I have lived of late in a manner suitable to wars, and have followed the military life not without glory.

This is the lower sling swivel. And this
Is the upper sling swivel, whose use you will see,
When you are given your slings. And this is the piling swivel,
Which in your case you have not got. The branches 10
Hold in the gardens their silent, eloquent gestures,
    Which in our case we have not got.

This is the safety-catch, which is always released
With an easy flick of the thumb. And please do not let me
See anyone using his finger. You can do it quite easy 15
If you have any strength in your thumb. The blossoms
Are fragile and motionless, never letting anyone see
    Any of them using their finger.

And this you can see is the bolt. The purpose of this
Is to open the breech, as you see. We can slide it 20
Rapidly backwards and forwards: we call this
Easing the spring. And rapidly backwards and forwards
The early bees are assaulting and fumbling the flowers:
    They call it easing the Spring.

They call it easing the Spring: it is perfectly easy 25
If you have any strength in your thumb: like the bolt,
And the breech, and the cocking-piece, and the point of balance,
Which in our case we have not got; and the almond-blossom
Silent in all of the gardens and the bees going backwards and forwards,
    For today we have naming of parts. 30

HENRY REED

MR. FLOOD'S PARTY

Old Eben Flood, climbing alone one night
Over the hill between the town below
And the forsaken upland hermitage
That held as much as he should ever know
On earth again of home, paused warily. 5
The road was his with not a native near;
And Eben, having leisure, said aloud,
For no man else in Tilbury Town to hear:

"Well, Mr. Flood, we have the harvest moon
Again, and we may not have many more; 10
The bird is on the wing, the poet says,
And you and I have said it here before.
Drink to the bird." He raised up to the light

The jug that he had gone so far to fill,
And answered huskily: "Well, Mr. Flood,   15
Since you propose it, I believe I will."

Alone, as if enduring to the end
A valiant armor of scarred hopes outworn,
He stood there in the middle of the road
Like Roland's [1] ghost winding a silent horn.   20
Below him, in the town among the trees,
Where friends of other days had honored him,
A phantom salutation of the dead
Rang thinly till old Eben's eyes were dim.

Then, as a mother lays her sleeping child   25
Down tenderly, fearing it may awake,
He set the jug down slowly at his feet
With trembling care, knowing that most things break;
And only when assured that on firm earth
It stood, as the uncertain lives of men   30
Assuredly did not, he paced away,
And with his hand extended paused again:

"Well, Mr. Flood, we have not met like this
In a long time; and many a change has come
To both of us, I fear, since last it was   35
We had a drop together. Welcome home!"
Convivially returning with himself,
Again he raised the jug up to the light;
And with an acquiescent quaver said:
"Well, Mr. Flood, if you insist, I might.   40

"Only a very little, Mr. Flood—
For auld lang syne. No more, sir; that will do."
So, for the time, apparently it did,
And Eben evidently thought so too;
For soon amid the silver loneliness   45
Of night he lifted up his voice and sang,
Secure, with only two moons listening,
Until the whole harmonious landscape rang—

"For auld lang syne." The weary throat gave out,
The last word wavered; and the song being done,   50
He raised again the jug regretfully
And shook his head, and was again alone.
There was not much that was ahead of him,
And there was nothing in the town below—

[1] French medieval warrior.

Where strangers would have shut the many doors   55
That many friends had opened long ago.

EDWIN ARLINGTON ROBINSON

[IN A DARK TIME]

In a dark time, the eye begins to see,
I meet my shadow in the deepening shade;
I hear my echo in the echoing wood—
A lord of nature weeping to a tree.
I live between the heron and the wren,   5
Beasts of the hill and serpents of the den.

What's madness but nobility of soul
At odds with circumstance? The day's on fire!
I know the purity of pure despair,
My shadow pinned against a sweating wall.   10
That place among the rocks—is it a cave,
Or winding path? The edge is what I have.

A steady storm of correspondences!
A night flowing with birds, a ragged moon,
And in broad day the midnight come again!   15
A man goes far to find out what he is—
Death of the self in a long, tearless night,
All natural shapes blazing unnatural light.

Dark, dark my light, and darker my desire.
My soul, like some heat-maddened summer fly,   20
Keeps buzzing at the sill. Which I is *I?*
A fallen man, I climb out of my fear.
The mind enters itself, and God the mind,
And one is One, free in the tearing wind.

THEODORE ROETHKE

SONNETS

29

When, in disgrace with Fortune and men's eyes,
I all alone beweep my outcast state,
And trouble deaf heaven with my bootless cries,

And look upon myself and curse my fate,
Wishing me like to one more rich in hope,   5
Featur'd like him, like him with friends possess'd,
Desiring this man's art, and that man's scope,
With what I most enjoy contented least;
Yet in these thoughts myself almost despising,
Haply I think on thee, and then my state,   10
Like to the lark at break of day arising
From sullen earth, sings hymns at heaven's gate;
    For thy sweet love remember'd such wealth brings,
    That then I scorn to change my state with kings.

30

When to the sessions of sweet silent thought
I summon up remembrance of things past,
I sigh the lack of many a thing I sought,
And with old woes new wail my dear time's waste.
Then can I drown an eye, unus'd to flow,   5
For precious friends hid in death's dateless night,
And weep afresh love's long since cancell'd woe,
And moan th' expense of many a vanish'd sight.
Then can I grieve at grievances foregone,
And heavily from woe to woe tell o'er   10
The sad account of fore-bemoaned moan,
Which I new pay as if not paid before.
    But if the while I think on thee, dear friend,
    All losses are restor'd, and sorrows end.

66

Tired with all these, for restful death I cry,
As to behold desert a beggar born,
And needy nothing trimm'd in jollity,
And purest faith unhappily forsworn,
And gilded honour shamefully misplac'd,   5
And maiden virtue rudely strumpeted,
And right perfection wrongfully disgrac'd,
And strength by limping sway disabled,
And art made tongue-tied by authority,
And folly, doctor-like controlling skill,   10
And simple truth miscall'd simplicity,
And captive good attending captain ill.
    Tired with all these, from these would I be gone,
    Save that to die, I leave my love alone.

73

That time of year thou mayst in me behold,
When yellow leaves, or none, or few, do hang
Upon those boughs which shake against the cold,
Bare ruin'd choirs, where late the sweet birds sang.

In me thou seest the twilight of such day,   5
As after sunset fadeth in the west,
Which by and by black night doth take away,
Death's second self, that seals up all in rest.
In me thou seest the glowing of such fire,
That on the ashes of his youth doth lie,   10
As the death-bed whereon it must expire,
Consum'd with that which it was nourish'd by.
  This thou perceiv'st, which makes thy love more strong,
  To love that well which thou must leave ere long.

129

Th' expense of spirit in a waste of shame
Is lust in action, and till action lust
Is perjur'd, murd'rous, bloody, full of blame,
Savage, extreme, rude, cruel, not to trust,
Enjoy'd no sooner but despised straight,   5
Past reason hunted, and no sooner had,
Past reason hated, as a swallowed bait,
On purpose laid to make the taker mad;
Mad in pursuit, and in possession so,
Had, having, and in quest to have, extreme,   10
A bliss in proof, and prov'd, a very woe,
Before, a joy propos'd; behind, a dream.
  All this the world well knows, yet none knows well
  To shun the heaven that leads men to this hell.

WILLIAM SHAKESPEARE

AUTO WRECK

Its quick soft silver bell beating, beating,
And down the dark one ruby flare
Pulsing out red light like an artery,
The ambulance at top speed floating down
Past beacons and illuminated clocks   5
Wings in a heavy curve, dips down,
And brakes speed, entering the crowd.
The doors leap open, emptying light;
Stretchers are laid out, the mangled lifted
And stowed into the little hospital,   10
Then the bell, breaking the hush, tolls once,
And the ambulance with its terrible cargo
Rocking, slightly rocking, moves away,
As the doors, an afterthought, are closed.

We are deranged, walking among the cops   15
Who sweep glass and are large and composed.
One is still making notes under the light.
One with a bucket douches ponds of blood
Into the street and gutter.
One hangs lanterns on the wrecks that cling, 20
Empty husks of locusts, to iron poles.

Our throats were tight as tourniquets,
Our feet were bound with splints, but now,
Like convalescents intimate and gauche,
We speak through sickly smiles and warn   25
With the stubborn saw of common sense,
The grim joke and the banal resolution.
The traffic moves around with care,
But we remain, touching a wound
That opens to our richest horror.   30
Already old, the question Who shall die?
Becomes unspoken Who is innocent?

For death in war is done by hands;
Suicide has cause and stillbirth, logic;
And cancer, simple as a flower, blooms.   35
But this invites the occult mind,
Cancels our physics with a sneer,
And spatters all we knew of denouement
Across the expedient and wicked stones.

KARL SHAPIRO

DOMINATION OF BLACK

At night, by the fire,
The colors of the bushes
And of the fallen leaves,
Repeating themselves,
Turned in the room,   5
Like the leaves themselves
Turning in the wind.
Yes: but the color of the heavy hemlocks
Came striding.
And I remembered the cry of the peacocks. 10

The colors of their tails
Were like the leaves themselves
Turning in the wind,

In the twilight wind.
They swept over the room,   15
Just as they flew from the boughs of the hemlocks
Down to the ground.
I heard them cry—the peacocks.
Was it a cry against the twilight
Or against the leaves themselves   20
Turning in the wind,
Turning as the flames
Turned in the fire,
Turning as the tails of the peacocks
Turned in the loud fire,   25
Loud as the hemlocks
Full of the cry of the peacocks?
Or was it a cry against the hemlocks?

Out of the window,
I saw how the planets gathered   30
Like the leaves themselves
Turning in the wind.
I saw how the night came,
Came striding like the color of the heavy hemlocks.
I felt afraid.   35
And I remembered the cry of the peacocks.

WALLACE STEVENS

ODE TO THE CONFEDERATE DEAD

Row after row with strict impunity
The headstones yield their names to the element,
The wind whirrs without recollection;
In the riven troughs the splayed leaves
Pile up, of nature the casual sacrament   5
To the seasonal eternity of death,
Then driven by the fierce scrutiny
Of heaven to their election in the vast breath,
They sough the rumor of mortality.

Autumn is desolation in the plot   10
Of a thousand acres, where these memories grow
From the inexhaustible bodies that are not
Dead, but feed the grass row after rich row:
Think of the autumns that have come and gone!—
Ambitious November with the humors of the year,   15
With a particular zeal for every slab,

Staining the uncomfortable angels that rot
On the slabs, a wing chipped here, an arm there:
The brute curiosity of an angel's stare
Turns you, like them, to stone,   20
Transforms the heaving air
Till plunged to a heavier world below
You shift your sea-space blindly
Heaving, turning like the blind crab.

   Dazed by the wind, only the wind   25
   The leaves flying, plunge

You know who have waited by the wall
The twilight certainty of an animal,
Those midnight restitutions of the blood
You know—the immitigable pines, the smoky frieze   30
Of the sky, the sudden call: you know the rage,
The cold pool left by the mounting flood,
Of muted Zeno and Parmenides.
You who have waited for the angry resolution
Of those desires that should be yours tomorrow,   35
You know the unimportant shrift of death
And praise the vision
And praise the arrogant circumstance
Of those who fall
Rank upon rank, hurried beyond decision—   40
Here by the sagging gate, stopped by the wall.

   Seeing, seeing only the leaves
   Flying, plunge and expire

Turn your eyes to the immoderate past,
Turn to the inscrutable infantry rising   45
Demons out of the earth—they will not last.
Stonewall, Stonewall, and the sunken fields of hemp,
Shiloh, Antietam, Malvern Hill, Bull Run.
Lost in that orient of the thick and fast
You will curse the setting sun.   50

   Cursing only the leaves crying
   Like an old man in a storm

You hear the shout, the crazy hemlocks point
With troubled fingers to the silence which
Smothers you, a mummy, in time.   55

                The hound bitch
Toothless and dying, in a musty cellar
Hears the wind only.
          Now that the salt of their blood

Stiffens the saltier oblivion of the sea,   60
Seals the malignant purity of the flood,
What shall we who count our days and bow
Our heads with a commemorial woe
In the ribboned coats of grim felicity,
What shall we say of the bones, unclean,   65
Whose verdurous anonymity will grow?

The ragged arms, the ragged heads and eyes
Lost in these acres of the insane green?
The gray lean spiders come, they come and go;
In a tangle of willows without light   70
The singular screech-owl's tight
Invisible lyric seeds the mind
With the furious murmur of their chivalry.

   We shall say only the leaves
    Flying, plunge and expire   75

We shall say only the leaves whispering
In the improbable mist of nightfall
That flies on multiple wing:
Night is the beginning and the end
And in between the ends of distraction   80
Waits mute speculation, the patient curse
That stones the eyes, or like the jaguar leaps
For his own image in a jungle pool, his victim.

What shall we say who have knowledge
Carried to the heart? Shall we take the act   85
To the grave? Shall we, more hopeful, set up the grave
In the house? The ravenous grave?
                   Leave now
The shut gate and the decomposing wall:
The gentle serpent, green in the mulberry bush,   90
Riots with his tongue through the hush—
Sentinel of the grave who counts us all!

ALLEN TATE

AN IRISH AIRMAN FORESEES HIS DEATH

I KNOW that I shall meet my fate
Somewhere among the clouds above;
Those that I fight I do not hate,
Those that I guard I do not love;
My country is Kiltartan Cross,   5

My countrymen Kiltartan's poor,
No likely end could bring them loss
Or leave them happier than before.
Nor law, nor duty bade me fight,
Nor public men, nor cheering crowds,   10
A lonely impulse of delight
Drove to this tumult in the clouds;
I balanced all, brought all to mind,
The years to come seemed waste of breath,
A waste of breath the years behind   15
In balance with this life, this death.

W. B. YEATS

THE SECOND COMING

Turning and turning in the widening gyre
The falcon cannot hear the falconer;
Things fall apart; the centre cannot hold;
Mere anarchy is loosed upon the world,
The blood-dimmed tide is loosed, and everywhere   5
The ceremony of innocence is drowned;
The best lack all conviction, while the worst
Are full of passionate intensity.

Surely some revelation is at hand;
Surely the Second Coming is at hand.   10
The Second Coming! Hardly are those words out
When a vast image out of *Spiritus Mundi* [1]
Troubles my sight: somewhere in sands of the desert
A shape with lion body and the head of a man,
A gaze blank and pitiless as the sun,   15
Is moving its slow thighs, while all about it
Reel shadows of the indignant desert birds.
The darkness drops again; but now I know
That twenty centuries of stony sleep
Were vexed to nightmare by a rocking cradle,   20
And what rough beast, its hour come round at last,
Slouches towards Bethlehem to be born?

W. B. YEATS

[1] The vital or natural force of the world.

BABII YAR [1]

No monument stands over Babii Yar.
A drop sheer as a crude gravestone.
I am afraid.
        Today I am as old in years
as all the Jewish people.   5
Now I seem to be
        a Jew.
Here I plod through ancient Egypt.
Here I perish crucified, on the cross,
and to this day I bear the scars of nails.   10
I seem to be
        Dreyfus.
The Philistine
            is both informer and judge.
I am behind bars.   15
            Beset on every side.
Hounded,
      spat on,
            slandered.
Squealing, dainty ladies in flounced Brussels lace   20
stick their parasols into my face.
I seem to be then
            a young boy in Byelostok.
Blood runs, spilling over the floors.
The bar-room rabble-rousers   25
give off a stench of vodka and onion.
A boot kicks me aside, helpless.
In vain I plead with these pogrom bullies.
While they jeer and shout,
            "Beat the Yids. Save Russia!"   30
some grain-marketeer beats up my mother.
O my Russian people!
         I know
           you
are international to the core.   35
But those with unclean hands
have often made a jingle of your purest name.
I know the goodness of my land.
How vile these antisemites—
            without a qualm   40
they pompously called themselves
"The Union of the Russian People"!
I seem to be

[1] A ravine outside Kiev.

Anne Frank [2]
transparent   45
          as a branch in April.
And I love.
          And have no need of phrases.
My need
          is that we gaze into each other.   50
How little we can see
                    or smell!
We are denied the leaves,
                         we are denied the sky.
Yet we can do so much—   55
                    tenderly
embrace each other in a darkened room.
They're coming here?
                    Be not afraid. Those are the booming
sounds of spring: 60
               spring is coming here.
Come then to me.
               Quick, give me your lips.
Are they smashing down the door?
                              No, it's the ice cracking . . .   65
The wild grasses rustle over Babii Yar.
The trees look ominous,
                    like judges.
Here all things scream silently,
                         and, baring my head,   70
I slowly feel myself
                    turning gray.
And I myself
               am one massive, soundless scream
above the thousand thousand buried here.   75
I am
          each old man
                    here shot dead.
I am
          every child   80
               here shot dead.
Nothing in me
               shall ever forget!
The "Internationale," [3] let it
                         thunder   85
when the last antisemite on earth
is buried forever.

---

[2] A young Jewish girl who, along with most of the members of her family, died in a German concentration camp in World War II.
[3] A rallying song of communism.

In my blood there is no Jewish blood.
In their callous rage, all antisemites
must hate me now as a Jew.   90
For that reason
        I am a true Russian!

YEVGENY YEVTUSHENKO

THE GARDEN OF
DELIGHTS

T HE triptych "The Garden of Delights," painted by the artist Hieronymus Bosch about sixty years before Brueghel's "Fall of Icarus,"
seems at variance with Brueghel's painting. Brueghel's peaceful
countryside in which round, solid, healthy man is centrally located vastly
differs in feeling from the garden Bosch presents. Bosch's central panel
shows a garden in which the art historian H. W. Janson says the delights
are those of carnal desire. Should the viewer feel repugnance, horror or
pleasure at the scene? The panel on the left depicts the Garden of Eden.
Grotesque tortures make up the panel on the right. Why are the scenes of
carnal desire in the important position? If Eden represents God's Garden
of Delights and if the torture scene represents Satan's Garden of Delights,
does the central panel depict man's? Going about their lives in a landscape
that is neither Eden nor Hell, Brueghel's figures seem to care only for
their immediate interests. In this third section many selections stress the
meaning to be found in an acceptance of life.

According to John Ruskin, art critic and historian, Robert Browning's
"The Bishop Orders His Tomb at Saint Praxed's Church" captures the
Renaissance spirit better than any other contemporary English writing he

[447]

knew. Brueghel's painting is also an example of Renaissance art. But the world of the painting and the world of the bishop have little in common. The bishop loved the classical world inordinately, as he loved the world itself inordinately. Although Brueghel visited Italy, the Italian Renaissance did not influence him as heavily as the world he saw around him. Those bare legs disappearing in the green water may imply Brueghel's attitude toward an undue love of the past, of Greek and Roman art, of ancient language, of brown Greek manuscripts and of ancient mythology. He celebrated contemporary Flemish life. The corpse in the bushes perhaps is a reminder of the impermanence of life, but neither the corpse nor Icarus is of importance to the farmer, the shepherd, the fisherman or the sailors.

In the first section of *Icarus,* the selections hopefully raised some questions about the responsibility of art and of society to themselves and to one another. The section is entitled "The Road Not Taken," and Icarus, synonymous with the artist, took one path and society another. In the second section, the selections depict the time as dark regardless of the paths taken. Weeds and flowers are not to be definitely distinguished. The Bosch triptych was undoubtedly arranged chronologically—beginning, middle, and end—from left to right, so that in one sense it is an allegory of man's place between Eden and Hell. But the three gardens can be seen as one garden, seen at different times. Yeats' wise Chinese old men perceive oneness despite the great disparities in the scene below their ancient, glittering, gay eyes. Crazy Jane told the moralist bishop that ". . . nothing can be sole or whole/That has not been rent." Molly Bloom eulogizes life by her affirmation of love. As editors of *Icarus: An Anthology of Literature,* we questioned whether to place "In a Dark Time" second or last. We decided to place it second and "The Garden of Delights" last, as a suggestion that darkness may hopefully fade to delights.

A final word to the student: if anthologists and professors of literature exist only because there are artists, the student is well advised to pay more heed to art than to the text and the teacher.

A PHOENIX TOO FREQUENT

Christopher Fry

CHARACTERS

Doto, the maid
Tegeus, a soldier

Dynamene, a young Roman widow

[*An underground tomb, in darkness except for the very low light of an oil-lamp. Above ground the starlight shows a line of trees on which hang the bodies of several men. It also penetrates a gate and falls on to the first of the steps which descend into the darkness of the tomb.* DOTO *talks to herself in the dark.*]

DOTO. Nothing but the harmless day gone into black
Is all the dark is. And so what's my trouble?
Demons is so much wind. Are so much wind.
I've plenty to fill my thoughts. All that I ask
Is don't keep turning men over in my mind,
Venerable Aphrodite. I've had my last one
And thank you. I thank thee. He smelt of sour grass
And was likeable. He collected ebony quoits.
  [*An owl hoots near at hand.*]
O Zeus! O some god or other, where is the oil?
Fire's from Prometheus. I thank thee. If I   10
Mean to die I'd better see what I'm doing.
  [*She fills the lamp with oil. The flame burns up brightly and
  shows* DYNAMENE, *beautiful and young, leaning asleep beside a
  bier.*]
Honestly, I would rather have to sleep
With a bald bee-keeper who was wearing his boots
Than spend more days fasting and thirsting and crying
In a tomb. I shouldn't have said that. Pretend
I didn't hear myself. But life and death
Is cat and dog in this double-bed of a world.
My master, my poor master, was a man
Whose nose was as straight as a little buttress,
And now he has taken it into Elysium   20
Where it won't be noticed among all the other straightness.
  [*The owl cries again and wakens* DYNAMENE.]
Oh, them owls. Those owls. It's woken her.

---

6 *Aphrodite* The goddess of love. 10 *Prometheus* A Titan who stole fire from
the gods to give to man. Regarded as the founder of civilization.

DYNAMENE. Ah! I'm breathless. I caught up with the ship
But it spread its wings, creaking a cry of *Dew,*
Dew! and flew figurehead foremost into the sun.
DOTO. How crazy, madam.
DYN.   Doto, draw back the curtains.
I'll take my barley-water.
DOTO.   We're not at home
Now, madam. It's the master's tomb.
DYN.   Of course!
Oh, I'm wretched. Already I have disfigured
My vigil. My cynical eyelids have soon dropped me   30
In a dream.
DOTO.   But then it's possible, madam, you might
Find yourself in bed with him again
In a dream, madam. Was he on the ship?
DYN. He was the ship.
DOTO.   Oh. That makes it different.
DYN. He was the ship. He had such a deck, Doto,
Such a white, scrubbed deck. Such a stern prow,
Such a proud stern, so slim from port to starboard.
If ever you meet a man with such fine masts
Give your life to him, Doto. The figurehead
Bore his own features, so serene in the brow   40
And hung with a little seaweed. O Virilius,
My husband, you have left a wake in my soul.
You cut the glassy water with a diamond keel.
I must cry again.
DOTO.   What, when you mean to join him?
Don't you believe he will be glad to see you, madam?
Thankful to see you, I should imagine, among
Them shapes and shades; all shapes of shapes and all
Shades of shades, from what I've heard. I know
I shall feel odd at first with Cerberus,
Sop or no sop. Still, I know how you feel, madam.   50
You think he may find a temptation in Hades
I shouldn't worry. It would help him to settle down.
        [DYNAMENE *weeps.*]
It would only be *fun,* madam. He couldn't go far
With a shade.
DYN.   He was one of the coming men.
He was certain to have become the most well-organized provost
The town has known, once they had made him provost.
He was so punctual, you could regulate
The sun by him. He made the world succumb
To his daily revolution of habit. But who,
In the world he has gone to, will appreciate that?   60
O poor Virilius! To be a coming man

49 *Cerberus* A many-headed dog that guards the entrance to the infernal regions.

Already gone—it must be distraction.
Why did you leave me walking about our ambitions
Like a cat in the ruins of a house? Promising husband,
Why did you insult me by dying? Virilius,
Now I keep no flower, except in the vase
Of the tomb.

DOTO.　　　　　O poor madam! O poor master!
I presume so far as to cry somewhat for myself
As well. I know you won't mind, madam. It's two
Days not eating makes me think of my uncle's　　　　　70
Shop in the country, where he has a hardware business,
Basins, pots, ewers, and alabaster birds.
He makes you die of laughing. O madam,
Isn't it sad?
　　[*They both weep.*]

DYN.　　　　How could I have allowed you
To come and die of my grief? Doto, it puts
A terrible responsibility on me. Have you
No grief of your own you could die of?

DOTO.　　　　　　　　　　　　Not really, madam.

DYN. Nothing?

DOTO.　　　　Not really. They was all one to me.
Well, all but two was all one to me. And they,
Strange enough, was two who kept recurring.　　　　　80
I could never be sure if they had gone for good
Or not; and so that kept things cheerful, madam.
One always gave a wink before he deserted me,
The other slapped me as it were behind, madam;
Then they would be away for some months.

DYN.　　　　　　　　　　　　Oh Doto,
What an unhappy life you were having to lead.

DOTO. Yes, I'm sure. But never mind, madam,
It seemed quite lively then. And now I know
It's what you say; life is more big than a bed
And full of miracles and mysteries like　　　　　90
One man made for one woman, etcetera, etcetera.
Lovely. I feel sung, madam, by a baritone
In mixed company with everyone pleased.
And so I had to come with you here, madam,
For the last sad chorus of me. It's all
Fresh to me. Death's a new interest in life,
If it doesn't disturb you, madam, to have me crying.
It's because of us not having breakfast again.
And the master, of course. And the beautiful world.
And you crying too, madam. Oh—Oh!　　　　　100

DYN. I can't forbid your crying; but you must cry
On the other side of the tomb. I'm becoming confused.
This is my personal grief and my sacrifice
Of self, solus. Right over there, darling girl.

DOTO. What here?

DYN.   Now, if you wish, you may cry, Doto.
   But our tears are very different. For me
   The world is all with Charon, all, all,
   Even the metal and plume of the rose garden,
   And the forest where the sea fumes overhead
   In vegetable tides, and particularly   110
   The entrance to the warm baths in Arcite Street
   Where we first met;—all!—the sun itself
   Trails an evening hand in the sultry river
   Far away down by Acheron. I am lonely,
   Virilius. Where is the punctual eye
   And where is the cautious voice which made
   Balance-sheets sound like Homer and Homer sound
   Like balance-sheets? The precision of limbs, the amiable
   Laugh, the exact festivity? Gone from the world.
   You were the peroration of nature, Virilius.   120
   You explained everything to me, even the extremely
   Complicated gods. You wrote them down
   In seventy columns. Dear curling calligraphy!
   Gone from the world, once and for all. And I taught you
   In your perceptive moments to appreciate me.
   You said I was harmonious, Virilius,
   Moulded and harmonious, little matronal
   Ox-eye, your package. And then I would walk
   Up and down largely, as it were making my own
   Sunlight. What a mad blacksmith creation is   130
   Who blows his furnaces until the stars fly upward
   And iron Time is hot and politicians glow
   And bulbs and roots sizzle into hyacinth
   And orchis, and the sand puts out the lion,
   Roaring yellow, and oceans bud with porpoises,
   Blenny, tunny and the almost unexisting
   Blindfish; throats are cut, the masterpiece
   Looms out of labour; nations and rebellions
   Are spat out to hang on the wind—and all is gone
   In one Virilius, wearing his office tunic,   140
   Checking the pence column as he went.
   Where's animation now? What is there that stays
   To dance? The eye of the one-eyed world is out.
    [*She weeps*]

DOTO. I shall try to grieve a little, too.
   I would take lessons, I imagine, to do it out loud
   For long. If I could only remember
   Any one of those fellows without wanting to laugh.
   Hopeless, I am. Now those good pair of shoes
   I gave away without thinking, that's a different—

114 *Acheron* One of the rivers of Hades.

Well, I've cried enough about *them,* I suppose   150
Poor madam, poor master.
    [TEGEUS *comes through the gate to the top of the steps.*]
TEGEUS.   What's your trouble?
DOTO.   Oh!
   Oh! Oh, a man. I thought for a moment it was something
With harm in it. Trust a man to be where it's dark.
What is it? Can't you sleep?
TEG.   Now, listen—
DOTO.   Hush!
   Remember you're in the grave. You must go away.
Madam is occupied.
TEG.   What, here?
DOTO.   Becoming
   Dead. We both are.
TEG.   What's going on here?
DOTO.   Grief.
   Are you satisfied now?
TEG.   Less and less. Do you know
   What the time is?
DOTO.   I'm not interested.
   We've done with all that. Go away. Be a gentleman.   160
If we can't be free of men in a grave
Death's a dead loss.
TEG.   It's two in the morning. All
   I ask is what are women doing down here
At two in the morning?
DOTO.   Can't you see she's crying?
   Or is she sleeping again? Either way
She's making arrangements to join her husband.
TEG.   Where?
DOTO. Good god, in the Underworld, dear man. Haven't you learnt
   About life and death?
TEG.   In a manner, yes; in a manner;
   The rudiments. So the lady means to die?
DOTO. For love; beautiful, curious madam.
TEG.   Not curious;   170
   I've had thoughts like it. Death is a kind of love.
Not anything I can explain.
DOTO.   You'd better come in
   And sit down.
TEG.   I'd be grateful.
DOTO.   Do. It will be my last
   Chance to have company in the flesh.
TEG.   Do you mean
   You're going too?
DOTO.   Oh, certainly I am.
   Not anything I can explain.
It all started with madam saying a man

Was two men really, and I'd only noticed one,
One each, I mean. It seems he has a soul
As well as his other troubles. And I like to know   180
What I'm getting with a man. I'm inquisitive,
I suppose you'd call me.

TEG.   It takes some courage.

DOTO.   Well, yes
And no. I'm fond of change.

TEG.   Would you object
To have me eating my supper here?

DOTO.   Be careful
Of the crumbs. We don't want a lot of squeaking mice
Just when we're dying.

TEG.   What a sigh she gave then.
Down the air like a slow comet.
And now she's all dark again. Mother of me.
How long has this been going on?

DOTO.   Two days.
It should have been three by now, but at first   190
Madam had difficulty with the Town Council. They said
They couldn't have a tomb used as a private residence.
But madam told them she wouldn't be eating here,
Only suffering, and they thought that would be all right.

TEG. Two of you. Marvellous. Who would have said
I should ever have stumbled on anything like this?
Do you have to cry? Yes, I suppose so. It's all
Quite reasonable.

DOTO.   Your supper and your knees.
That's what's making me cry. I can't bear sympathy
And they're sympathetic.

TEG.   Please eat a bit of something.   200
I've no appetite left.

DOTO.   And see her go ahead of me?
Wrap it up; put it away. You sex of wicked beards!
It's no wonder you have to shave off your black souls
Every day as they push through your chins.
I'll turn my back on you. It means utter
Contempt. Eat? Utter contempt. Oh, little new rolls!

TEG. Forget it, forget it; please forget it. Remember
I've had no experience of this kind of thing before.
Indeed I'm as sorry as I know how to be. Ssh,
We'll disturb her. She sighed again. O Zeus,   210
It's terrible! Asleep, and still sighing.
Mourning has made a warren in her spirit,
All that way below. Ponos! the heart
Is the devil of a medicine.

DOTO.   And I don't intend
To turn round.

TEG.   I understand how you must feel.

Would it be—have you any objection
To my having a drink? I have a little wine here.
And, you probably see how it is: grief's in order,
And death's in order, and women—I can usually
Manage that too; but not all three together   220
At this hour of the morning. So you'll excuse me.
How about you? It would make me more comfortable
If you'd take a smell of it.
DOTO.   One for the road?
TEG. One for the road.
DOTO.   It's the dust in my throat. The tomb
Is so dusty. Thanks, I will. There's no point in dying
Of everything, simultaneous.
TEG.   It's lucky.
I brought two bowls. I was expecting to keep
A drain for my relief when he comes in the morning.
DOTO. Are you on duty?
TEG.   Yes.
DOTO.   It looks like it.
TEG.   Well,
Here's your good health.
DOTO.   What good is that going to do me?   230
Here's to an easy crossing and not too much waiting
About on the bank. Do you have to tremble like that?
TEG. The idea—I can't get used to it.
DOTO.   For a member
Of the forces, you're peculiarly queasy. I wish
Those owls were in Hades—oh no; let them stay where they are.
Have you never had nothing to do with corpses before?
TEG. I've got six of them outside.
DOTO.   Morpheus, that's plenty.
What are they doing there?
TEG.   Hanging.
DOTO.   Hanging?
TEG.   On trees.
Five plane trees and a holly. The holly-berries
Are just reddening. Another drink?
DOTO.   Why not?
TEG. It's from Samos. Here's—
DOTO.   All right. Let's just drink it.   240
—How did they get in that predicament?
TEG. The sandy-haired fellow said we should collaborate
With everybody; the little man said he wouldn't
Collaborate with anybody; the old one
Said that the Pleiades weren't sisters but cousins
And anyway were manufactured in Lacedaemon.
The fourth said that we hanged men for nothing.

240 *Samos* An island off the west coast of Asia Minor. 245 *Pleiades* Seven
daughters of Atlas who were turned into a group of seven stars.

The other two said nothing. Now they hang
About at the corner of the night, they're present
And absent, horribly obsequious to every   250
Move in the air, and yet they keep me standing
For five hours at a stretch.
DOTO.   The wine has gone
Down to my knees.
TEG.   And up to your cheeks. You're looking
Fresher. If only—
DOTO.   Madam? She never would.
Shall I ask her?
TEG.   No; no, don't dare, don't breathe it.
This is privilege, to come so near
To what is undeceiving and uncorrupt
And undivided; this is the clear fashion
For all souls, a ribbon to bind the unruly
Curls of living, a faith, a hope, Zeus   260
Yes, a fine thing. I am human, and this
Is human fidelity, and we can be proud
And unphilosophical.
DOTO.   I need to dance
But I haven't the use of my legs.
TEG.   No, no, don't dance,
Or, at least, only inwards; don't dance; cry
Again. We'll put a moat of tears
Round her bastion of love, and save
The world. It's something, it's more than something,
It's regeneration, to see how a human cheek
Can become as pale as a pool.
DOTO.   Do you love me, handsome?   270
TEG. To have found life, after all, unambiguous!
DOTO. Did you say Yes?
TEG.   Certainly; just now I love all men.
DOTO. So do I.
TEG.   And the world is a good creature again.
I'd begun to see it as mildew, verdigris,
Rust, woodrot, or as though the sky had uttered
An oval twirling blasphemy with occasional vistas
In country districts. I was within an ace
Of volunteering for overseas service. Despair
Abroad can always nurse pleasant thoughts of home.
Integrity, by god!   280
DOTO.   I love all the world
And the movement of the apple in your throat.
So shall you kiss me? It would be better, I should think,
To go moistly to Hades.
TEG.   Her's is the way,
Luminous with sorrow.
DOTO.   Then I'll take

Another little swiggy. I love all men,
Everybody, even you, and I'll pick you
Some outrageous honeysuckle for your helmet,
If only it lived here. Pardon.
DYN.   Doto. Who is it?
DOTO. Honeysuckle, madam. Because of the bees.
  Go back to sleep, madam.
DYN.   What person is it?   290
DOTO. Yes, I see what you mean, madam. It's a kind of
  Corporal talking to his soul, on a five-hour shift,
  Madam, with six bodies. He's been having his supper.
TEG. I'm going. It's terrible that we should have disturbed her.
DOTO. He was delighted to see you so sad, madam.
  It has stopped him going abroad.
DYN.   One with six bodies?
  A messenger, a guide to where we go.
  It is possible he has come to show us the way
  Out of these squalid suburbs of life, a shade,
  A gorgon, who has come swimming up, against   300
  The falls of my tears (for which in truth he would need
  Many limbs) to guide me to Virilius.
  I shall go quietly.
TEG.   I do assure you—
  Such clumsiness, such a vile and unforgivable
  Intrusion. I shall obliterate myself
  Immediately.
DOTO.   Oblit—oh, what a pity
  To oblit. Pardon. Don't let him, the nice fellow.
DYN. Sir: your other five bodies: where are they?
TEG.   Madam—
  Outside; I have them outside. On trees.
DYN.   Quack!
TEG. What do I reply?
DYN.   Quack, charlatan!   310
  You've never known the gods. You came to mock me.
  Doto, this never was a gorgon, never.
  Nor a gentleman either. He's completely spurious.
  Admit it, you creature. Have you even a feather
  Of the supernatural in your system? Have you?
TEG. Some of my relations—
DYN.   Well?
TEG.   Are dead, I think;
  That is to say I have connexions—
DYN.   Connexions
  With pickpockets. It's a shameless imposition.
  Does the army provide you with no amusements?
  If I were still of the world, and not cloistered   320
  In a colourless landscape of winter thought
  Where the approaching Spring is desired oblivion,

I should write sharply to your commanding officer.
It should be done, it should be done. If my fingers
Weren't so cold I would do it now. But they are,
Horribly cold. And why should insolence matter
When my colour of life is unreal, a blush on death,
A partial mere diaphane? I don't know
Why it should matter. Oafish, non-commissioned
Young man! The boots of your conscience will pinch for ever 330
If life's dignity has any self-protection.
Oh, I have to sit down. The tomb's going round.

DOTO. Oh, madam, don't give over. I can't remember
When things were so lively. He looks marvellously
Marvellously uncomfortable. Go on, madam.
Can't you, madam? Oh, madam, don't you feel up to it?
There, do you see her, you acorn-chewing infantryman?
You've made her cry, you square-bashing barbarian.

TEG. O history, my private history, why
Was I led here? What stigmatism has got   340
Into my stars? Why wasn't it my brother?
He has a tacit misunderstanding with everybody
And washes in it. Why wasn't it my mother?
She makes a collection of other people's tears
And dries them all. Let them forget I came;
And lie in the terrible black crystal of grief
Which held them, before I broke it. Outside, Tegeus.

DOTO. Hey, I don't think so, I shouldn't say so. Come
Down again, uniform. Do you think you're going
To half kill an unprotected lady and then   350
Back out upwards? Do you think you can leave her like this?

TEG. Yes, yes, I'll leave her. O directorate of gods,
How can I? Beauty's bit is between my teeth.
She has added another torture to me. Bottom
Of Hades' bottom.

DOTO.   Madam. Madam, the corporal
Has some wine here. It will revive you, madam.
And then you can go at him again, madam.

TEG. It's the opposite of everything you've said,
I swear. I swear by Horkos and the Styx,
I swear by the nine acres of Tityos,   360
I swear the Hypnotic oath, by all the Titans—
By Koeos, Krios, Iapetos, Kronos, and so on—
By the three Hekatoncheires, by the insomnia
Of Tisiphone, by Jove, by jove, and the dew
On the feet of my boyhood, I am innocent
Of mocking you. Am I a Salmoneus
That, seeing such a flame of sorrow—

DYN.   You needn't

---

366 *Salmoneus* Son of Aeolus. Killed for deeming himself an equal to Zeus.

Labour to prove your secondary education.
Perhaps I jumped to a wrong conclusion, perhaps
I was hasty.
DOTO.   How easy to swear if you're properly educated.   370
Wasn't it pretty, madam? Pardon.
DYN.   If I misjudged you
I apologize, I apologize. Will you please leave us?
You were wrong to come here. In a place of mourning
Light itself is a trespasser; nothing can have
The right of entrance except those natural symbols
Of morality, the jabbing, funeral, sleek-
With-omen raven, the death-watch beetle which mocks
Time: particularly, I'm afraid, the spider
Weaving his home with swift self-generated
Threads of slaughter; and, of course, the worm.   380
I wish it could be otherwise. Oh dear,
They aren't easy to live with.
DOTO.   Not even a *little* wine, madam?
DYN. Here, Doto?
DOTO.   Well, on the steps perhaps,
Except it's so draughty.
DYN.   Doto! Here?
DOTO.   No, madam;
I quite see.
DYN.   I might be wise to strengthen myself
In order to fast again; it would make me abler
For grief. I will breathe a little of it, Doto.
DOTO. Thank god. Where's the bottle?
DYN.   What an exquisite bowl.
TEG. Now that it's peacetime we have pottery classes.
DYN. You made it yourself?
TEG.   Yes. Do you see the design?   390
The corded god, tied also by the rays
Of the sun, and the astonished ship erupting
Into vines and vine-leaves, inverted pyramids
Of grapes, the uplifted hands of the men (the raiders),
And here the headlong sea, itself almost
Venturing into leaves and tendrils, and Proteus
With his beard braiding the wind, and this
Held by other hands is a drowned sailor—
DYN. Always, always.
DOTO.   Hold the bowl steady, madam.
Pardon.   400
DYN. Doto, have you been drinking?
DOTO.   Here, madam?
I coaxed some a little way towards my mouth, madam,
But I scarcely swallowed except because I had to. The hiccup

396 *Proteus* God of the sea.

Is from no breakfast, madam, and not meant to be funny.

DYN. You may drink this too. Oh, how the inveterate body,
Even when cut from the heart, insists on leaf,
Puts out, with a separate meaningless will,
Fronds to intercept the thankless sun.
How it does, oh, how it does. And how it confuses
The nature of the mind.

TEG.   Yes, yes, the confusion;   410
That's something I understand better than anything.

DYN. When the thoughts would die, the instincts will set sail
For life. And when the thoughts are alert for life
The instincts will rage to be destroyed on the rocks.
To Virilius it was not so; his brain was an ironing-board
For all crumpled indecision: and I follow him,
The hawser of my world. You don't belong here,
You see; you don't belong here at all.

TEG.   If only
I did. If only you knew the effort it costs me
To mount those steps again into an untrustworthy,   420
Unpredictable, unenlightened night,
And turn my back on—on a state of affairs,
I can only call it a vision, a hope, a promise,
A—By that I mean loyalty, enduring passsion,
Unrecking bravery and beauty all in one.

DOTO. He means you, or you and me; or me, madam.

TEG. It only remains for me to thank you, and to say
That whatever awaits me and for however long
I may be played by this poor musician, existence,
Your person and sacrifice will leave their trace   430
As clear upon me as the shape of the hills
Around my birthplace. Now I must leave you to your husband.

DOTO. Oh! You, madam.

DYN.   I'll tell you what I will do.
I will drink with you to the memory of my husband,
Because I have been curt, because you are kind,
And because I'm extremely thirsty. And then we will say
Good-bye and part to go to our opposite corruptions,
The world and the grave.

TEG.   The climax to the vision.

DYN. [*Drinking.*] My husband, and all he stood for.

TEG.   Stands for.

DYN.   Stands for.

TEG. Your husband.

DOTO.   The master.

DYN.   How good it is,   440
How it sings to the throat, purling with summer.

TEG. It has a twin nature, winter and warmth in one,
Moon and meadow. Do you agree?

DYN.   Perfectly;

A cold bell sounding in a golden month.

TEG. Crystal in harvest.

DYN.   Perhaps a nightingale
Sobbing among the pears.

TEG.   In an old autumnal midnight.

DOTO. Grapes.—Pardon. There's some more here.

TEG.   Plenty.
I drink to the memory of your husband.

DYN.   My husband.

DOTO.   The master.

DYN. He was careless in his choice of wines.

TEG.   And yet
Rendering to living its rightful poise is not   450
Unimportant.

DYN.   A mystery's in the world
Where a little liquid, with flavour, quality, and fume
Can be as no other, can hint and flute our senses
As though a music played in harvest hollows
And a movement was in the swathes of our memory.
Why should scent, why should flavour come
With such wings upon us? Parsley, for instance.

TEG. Seaweed.

DYN.   Lime trees.

DOTO.   Horses.

TEG.   Fruit in the fire.

DYN. Do I know your name?

TEG.   Tegeus.

DYN.   That's very thin for you,
It hardly covers your bones. Something quite different,   460
Altogether other. I shall think of it presently.

TEG. Darker vowels, perhaps.

DYN.   Yes, certainly darker vowels.
And your consonants should have a slight angle,
And a certain temperature. Do you know what I mean?
It will come to me.

TEG.   Now *your* name—

DYN.   It is nothing
To any purpose. I'll be to you the She
In the tomb. You have the air of a natural-historian
As though you were accustomed to handling birds' eggs,
Or tadpoles, or putting labels on moths. You see?
The genius of dumb things, that they are nameless.   470
Have I found the seat of the weevil in human brains?
Our names. They make us broody; we sit and sit
To hatch them into reputation and dignity.
And then they set upon us and become despair,
Guilt and remorse. We go where they lead. We dance
Attendance on something wished upon us by the wife
Of our mother's physician. But insects meet and part

And put the woods about them, fill the dusk
And freckle the light and go and come without
A name among them, without the wish of a name   480
And very pleasant too. Did I interrupt you?
TEG. I forget. We'll have no names then.
DYN.   I should like
You to have a name, I don't know why; a small one
To fill out the conversation.
TEG.   I should like
You to have a name too, if only for something
To remember. Have you still some wine in your bowl?
DYN. Not altogether.
TEG.   We haven't come to the end
By several inches. Did I splash you?
DYN.   It doesn't matter.
Well, here's to my husband's name.
TEG.   Your husband's name.
DOTO. The master.
DYN.   It was kind of you to come.   490
TEG. It was more than coming. I followed my future here,
As we all do if we're sufficiently inattentive
And don't vex ourselves with questions; or do I mean
Attentive? If so, attentive to what? Do I sound
Incoherent?
DYN.   You're wrong. There isn't a future here,
Not here, not for you.
TEG.   Your name's Dynamene.
DYN. Who—Have I been utterly irreverent? Are you—
Who made you say that? Forgive me the question,
But are you dark or light? I mean which shade
Of the supernatural? Or if neither, what prompted you?   500
TEG. Dynamene——
DYN.   No, but I'm sure you're the friend of nature,
It must be so, I think I see little Phoebuses
Rising and setting in your eyes.
DOTO.   They're not little Phoebuses,
They're hoodwinks, madam. Your name is on your brooch.
No little Phoebuses to-night.
DYN.   That's twice
You've played me a trick. Oh, I know practical jokes
Are common on Olympus, but haven't we at all
Developed since the gods were born? Are gods
And men both to remain immortal adolescents?
How tiresome it all is.
TEG.   It was you, each time,   510
Who said I was supernatural. When did I say so?
You're making me into whatever you imagine

502 *Phoebus* (Apollo) the sun god.

And then you blame me because I can't live up to it.

DYN. I shall call you Chromis. It has a breadlike sound.
 I think of you as a crisp loaf.

TEG.   And now
 You'll insult me because I'm not sliceable.

DYN. I think drinking is harmful to our tempers.

TEG. If I seem to be frowning, that is only because
 I'm looking directly into your light: I must look
 Angrily, or shut my eyes.

DYN.   Shut them.—Oh,   520
 You have eyelashes! A new perspective of you.
 Is that how you look when you sleep?

TEG.   My jaw drops down.

DYN. Show me how.

TEG.   Like this.

DYN.   It makes an irresistible
 Moron of you. Will you waken now?
 It's morning; I see a thin dust of daylight
 Blowing on to the steps.

TEG.   Already? Dynamene,
 You're tricked again. This time by the moon.

DYN.   Oh, well,
 Moon's daylight, then. Doto is asleep.

TEG.   Doto
 Is asleep . . .

DYN.   Chromis, what made you walk about
 In the night? What, I wonder, made you not stay 530
 Sleeping wherever you slept? Was it the friction
 Of the world on your mind? Those two are difficult
 To make agree. Chromis—now try to learn
 To answer your name. I won't say Tegeus.

TEG.   And I
 Won't say Dynamene.

DYN.   Not?

TEG.   It makes you real.
 Forgive me, a terrible thing has happened. Shall I
 Say it and perhaps destroy myself for you?
 Forgive me first, or, more than that, forgive
 Nature who winds her furtive stream all through
 Our reason. Do you forgive me?

DYN.   I'll forgive   540
 Anything, if it's the only way I can know
 What you have to tell me.

TEG.   I felt us to be alone;
 Here in a grave, separate from any life,
 I and the only one of beauty, the only
 Persuasive key to all my senses,
 In spite of my having lain day after day
 And pored upon the sepals, corolla, stamen, and bracts

Of the yellow bog-iris. Then my body ventured
A step towards interrupting your perfection of purpose
And my own renewed faith in human nature.   550
Would you have believed that possible?
DYN.   I have never
Been greatly moved by the yellow bog-iris. Alas,
It's as I said. This place is for none but the spider,
Raven and worms, not for a living man.
TEG. It has been a place of blessing to me. It will always
Play in me, a fountain of confidence
When the world is arid. But I know it is true
I have to leave it, and though it withers my soul
I must let you make your journey.
DYN.   No.
TEG.   Not true?
DYN. We can talk of something quite different.
TEG.   Yes, we can!   560
Oh yes, we will! Is it your opinion
That no one believes who hasn't learned to doubt?
Or, another thing, if we persuade ourselves
To one particular Persuasion, become Sophist,
Stoic, Platonist, anything whatever,
Would you say that there must be areas of soul
Lying unproductive therefore, or dishonoured
Or blind?
DYN.   No, I don't know.
TEG.   No. It's impossible
To tell. Dynamene, if only I had
Two cakes of pearl-barley and hydromel   570
I could see you to Hades, leave you with your husband
And come back to the world.
DYN.   Ambition, I suppose,
Is an appetite particular to man.
What is your definition?
TEG.   The desire to find
A reason for living.
DYN.   But then, suppose it leads,
As often, one way or another, it does, to death.
TEG. Then that may be life's reason. Oh, but how
Could I bear to return, Dynamene? The earth's
Daylight would be my grave if I had left you
In that unearthly night.
DYN.   O Chromis——
TEG.   Tell me.   580
What is your opinion of Progress? Does it, for example,
Exist? Is there ever progression without retrogression?
Therefore is it not true that mankind

564–565 *Sophist, Stoic, Platonist* Philosophers.

Can more justly be said increasingly to Gress?
As the material improves, the craftsmanship deteriorates
And honour and virtue remain the same. I love you,
Dynamene.

DYN. Would you consider we go round and round?

TEG. We concertina, I think; taking each time 590
A larger breath, so that the farther we go out
The farther we have to go in.

DYN.   There'll come a time
When it will be unbearable to continue.

TEG. Unbearable.

DYN.   Perhaps we had better have something
To eat. The wine has made your eyes so quick
I am breathless beside them. It *is*
Your eyes, I think; or your intelligence
Holding my intelligence up above you
Between its hands. Or the cut of your uniform.

TEG. Here's a new roll with honey. In the gods' names
Let's sober ourselves.

DYN.   As soon as possible.

TEG.   Have you 600
Any notion of algebra?

DYN.   We'll discuss you, Chromis.
We will discuss you, till you're nothing but words.

TEG. I? There is nothing, of course, I would rather discuss,
Except—if it would be no intrusion—you, Dynamene.

DYN. No, you couldn't want to. But your birthplace, Chromis,
With the hills that placed themselves in you for ever
As you say, where was it?

TEG.   My father's farm at Pyxa.

DYN. There? Could it be there?

TEG.   I was born in the hills
Between showers, a quarter of an hour before milking time.
Do you know Pyxa? It stretches to the crossing of two 610
Troublesome roads, and buries its back in beechwood,
From which come the white owls of our nights
And the mulling and cradling of doves in the day.
I attribute my character to those shadows
And heavy roots; and my interest in music
To the sudden melodious escape of the young river
Where it breaks from nosing through the cresses and kingcups.
That's honestly so.

DYN.   You used to climb about
Among the windfallen tower of Phrasidemus
Looking for bees' nests.

TEG.   What? When have I 620
Said so?

DYN.   Why, all the children did.

TEG. Yes: but in the name of light, how do you *know* that?

DYN. I played there once, on holiday.

TEG.   O Klotho,
  Lachesis and Atropos!

DYN.   It's the strangest chance:
  I may have seen, for a moment, your boyhood.

TEG.   I may
  Have seen something like an early flower
  Something like a girl. If I only could remember how I must
  Have seen you. Were you after the short white violets?
  Maybe I blundered past you, taking your look,
  And scarcely acknowledged how a star   630
  Ran through me, to live in the brooks of my blood for ever.
  Or I saw you playing at hiding in the cave
  Where the ferns are and the water drips.

DYN. I was quite plain and fat and I was usually
  Hitting someone. I wish I could remember you.
  I'm envious of the days and children who saw you
  Then. It is curiously a little painful
  Not to share your past.

TEG.   How did it come
  Our stars could mingle for an afternoon
  So long ago, and then forget us or tease us   640
  Or helplessly look on the dark high seas
  Of our separation, while time drank
  The golden hours? What hesitant fate is that?

DYN. Time? Time? Why—how old are we?

TEG.   Young,
  Thank both our mothers, but still we're older than to-night
  And so older than we should be. Wasn't I born
  In love with what, only now, I have grown to meet?
  I'll tell you something else. I was born entirely
  For this reason. I was born to fill a gap
  In the world's experience, which had never known   650
  Chromis loving Dynamene.

DYN.   You are so
  Excited, poor Chromis. What is it? Here you sit
  With a woman who has wept away all claims
  To appearance, unbecoming in her oldest clothes,
  With not a trace of liveliness, a drab
  Of melancholy, entirely shadow without
  A smear of sun. Forgive me if I tell you
  That you fall easily into superlatives.

TEG. Very well. I'll say nothing, then. I'll fume
  With feeling.

DYN.   Now you go to the extreme. Certainly   660
  You must speak. You may have more to say. Besides
  You might let your silence run away with you

623–4 *Klotho, Lachesis, Atropos* The three goddesses of fate.

And not say something that you should. And how
Should I answer you then? Chromis, you boy,
I can't look away from you. You use
The lamplight and the moon so skilfully,
So arrestingly, in and around your furrows.
A humorous ploughman goes whistling to a team
Of sad sorrow, to and fro in your brow
And over your arable cheek. Laugh for me. Have you   670
Cried for women, ever?
TEG.   In looking about for you.
But I have recognized them for what they were.
DYN. What were they?
TEG.   Never you: never, although
They could walk with bright distinction into all men's
Longest memories, never you, by a hint
Or a faint quality, or at least not more
Than reflectively, stars lost and uncertain
In the sea, compared with the shining salt, the shiners,
The galaxies, the clusters, the bright grain whirling
Over the black threshing-floor of space.   680
Will you make some effort to believe that?
DYN.   No, no effort.
It lifts me and carries me. It may be wild
But it comes to me with a charm, like trust indeed,
And eats out of my heart, dear Chromis,
Absurd, disconcerting Chromis. You make me
Feel I wish I could look my best for you.
I wish, at least, that I could believe myself
To be showing some beauty for you, to put in the scales
Between us. But they dip to you, they sink
With masculine victory.
TEG.   Eros, no! No!   690
If this is less than your best, then never, in my presence,
Be more than your less: never! If you should bring
More to your mouth or to your eyes, a moisture
Or a flake of light, anything, anything fatally
More, perfection would fetch her unsparing rod
Out of pickle to flay me, and what would have been love
Will be the end of me. O Dynamene,
Let me unload something of my lips' longing
On to yours receiving. Oh, when I cross
Like this the hurt of the little space between us   700
I come a journey from the wrenching ice
To walk in the sun. That is the feeling.
DYN.   Chromis,
Where am I going? No, don't answer. It's death
I desire, not you.
TEG.   Where is the difference? Call me
Death instead of Chromis. I'll answer to anything.

It's desire all the same, of death in me, or me
In death, but Chromis either way. Is it so?
Do you not love me, Dynamene?

DYN.   How could it happen?
I'm going to my husband. I'm too far on the way
To admit myself to life again. Love's in Hades.   710

TEG. Also here. And here are we, not there
In Hades. Is your husband expecting you?

DYN. Surely, surely?

TEG.   Not necessarily. I,
If I had been your husband, would never dream
Of expecting you. I should remember your body
Descending stairs in the floating light, but not
Descending in Hades. I should say "I have left
My wealth warm on the earth, and, hell, earth needs it."
"Was all I taught her of love," I should say, "so poor
That she will leave her flesh and become shadow?"   720
"Wasn't our love for each other" (I should continue)
"Infused with life, and life infused with our love?
Very well; repeat me in love, repeat me in life,
And let me sing in your blood for ever."

DYN. Stop, stop, I shall be dragged apart!
Why should the fates do everything to keep me
From dying honourably? They must have got
Tired of honour in Elysium. Chromis, it's terrible
To be susceptible to two conflicting norths.
I have the constitution of a whirlpool.   730
Am I actually twirling, or is it just sensation?

TEG. You're still; still as darkness.

DYN.   What appears
Is so unlike what is. And what is madness
To those who only observe, is often wisdom
To those to whom it happens.

TEG.   Are we compelled
To go into all this?

DYN.   Why, how could I return
To my friends? Am I to be an entertainment?

TEG. That's for to-morrow. To-night I need to kiss you,
Dynamene. Let's see what the whirlpool does
Between my arms; let it whirl on my breast. O love,   740
Come in.

DYN.   I am there before I reach you; my body
Only follows to join my longing which
Is holding you already.—Now I am
All one again.

TEG.   I feel as the gods feel:
This is their sensation of life, not a man's:

728 *Elysium* Paradise.

Their suspension of immortality, to enrich
Themselves with time. O life, O death, O body,
O spirit, O Dynamene.

DYN.   O all
In myself; it so covets all in you,
My care, my Chromis. Then I shall be   750
Creation.

TEG.   You have the skies already;
Out of them you are buffeting me with your gales
Of beauty. Can we be made of dust, as they tell us?
What! dust with dust releasing such a light
And such an apparition of the world
Within one body? A thread of your hair has stung me.
Why do you push me away?

DYN.   There's so much metal
About you. Do I have to be imprisoned
In an armoury?

TEG.   Give your hand to the buckles and then
To me.   760

DYN. Don't help; I'll do them all myself.

TEG. O time and patience! I want you back again.

DYN. We have a lifetime. O Chromis, think, think
Of that. And even unfastening a buckle
Is loving. And not easy. Very well,
You can help me. Chromis, what zone of miracle
Did you step into to direct you in the dark
To where I waited, not knowing I waited?

TEG.   I saw
The lamplight. That was only the appearance
Of some great gesture in the bed of fortune.   770
I saw the lamplight.

DYN.   But here? So far from life?
What brought you near enough to see lamplight?

TEG.   Zeus,
That reminds me.

DYN.   What is it, Chromis?

TEG.   I'm on duty.

DYN. Is it warm enough to do without your greaves?

TEG. Darling loom of magic, I must go back
To take a look at those boys. The whole business
Of guard had gone out of my mind.

DYN.   What boys, my heart?

TEG. My six bodies.

DYN.   Chromis, not that joke
Again.

TEG. No joke, sweet. To-day our city   780
Held a sextuple hanging. I'm minding the bodies
Until five o'clock. Already I've been away
For half an hour.

DYN.   What can they do, poor bodies,
    In half an hour, or half a century?
    You don't really mean to go?
TEG.   Only to make
    My conscience easy. Then, Dynamene,
    No cloud can rise on love, no hovering thought
    Fidget, and the night will be only to *us*.
DYN. But if every half-hour——
TEG.   Hush, smile of my soul,
    My sprig, my sovereign: this is to hold your eyes,   790
    I sign my lips on them both: this is to keep
    Your forehead—do you feel the claim of my kiss
    Falling into your thought? And now your throat
    Is a white branch and my lips two singing birds—
    They are coming to rest. Throat, remember me
    Until I come back in five minutes. Over all
    Here is my parole: I give it to your mouth
    To give me again before it's dry. I promise:
    Before it's dry, or not long after.
DYN.   Run,
    Run all the way. You needn't be afraid of stumbling.   800
    There's plenty of moon. The fields are blue. Oh, wait,
    Wait! My darling. No, not now: it will keep
    Until I see you; I'll have it here at my lips.
    Hurry.
TEG. So long, my haven.
DYN.   Hurry, hurry!
    [*Exit* TEGEUS.]
DOTO. Yes, madam, hurry; of course. Are we there
    Already? How nice. Death doesn't take
    Any doing at all. We were gulped into Hades
    An easy as an oyster.
DYN.   Doto!
DOTO.   Hurry, hurry,
    Yes, madam.—But they've taken out all my bones.   810
    I haven't a bone left. I'm a Shadow: wonderfully shady
    In the legs. We shall have to sit out eternity, madam,
    If they've done the same to you.
DYN.   You'd better wake up.
    If you can't go to sleep again, you'd better wake up.
    Oh dear.—We're still alive, Doto, do you hear me?
DOTO. You must speak for yourself, madam. I'm quite dead.
    I'll tell you how I know. I feel
    Invisible. I'm a wraith, madam; I'm only
    Waiting to be wafted.
DYN.   If only you *would* be.
    Do you see where you are? Look. Do you see?   820
DOTO. Yes. You're right, madam. We're still alive.
    Isn't it enough to make you swear?

Here we are, dying to be dead,
And where does it get us?

DYN.   Perhaps you should try to die
In some other place. Yes! Perhaps the air here
Suits you too well. You were sleeping very heavily.

DOTO. And all the time you alone and dying.
I shouldn't have. Has the corporal been long gone,
Madam?

DYN.   He came and went, came and went,
You know the way.

DOTO.   Very well I do. And went   830
He should have, come he should never. Oh dear, he must
Have disturbed you, madam.

DYN.   He could be said
To've disturbed me. Listen; I have something to say to you.

DOTO. I expect so, madam. Maybe I *could* have kept him out
But men are in before I wish they wasn't.
I think quickly enough, but I get behindhand
With what I ought to be saying. It's a kind of stammer
In my way of life, madam.

DYN.   I have been unkind,
I have sinfully wronged you, Doto.

DOTO.   Never, madam.

DYN. Oh yes. I was letting you die with me, Doto, without   840
Any fair reason. I was drowning you
In grief that wasn't yours. That was wrong. Doto.

DOTO. But I haven't got anything against dying, madam.
I may *like* the situation, as far as I like
Any situation, madam. Now if you'd said mangling.
A lot of mangling, I might have thought twice about staying,
We all have our dislikes, madam.

DYN.   I'm asking you
To leave me, Doto, at once, as quickly as possible,
Now, before—now, Doto, and let me forget
My bad mind which confidently expected you   850
To companion me to Hades. Now good-bye,
Good-bye.

DOTO.   No, it's not good-bye at all.
I shouldn't know another night of sleep, wondering
How you got on, or what I was missing, come to that.
I should be anxious about you, too. When you belong
To an upper class, the netherworld might come strange.
Now I was born nether, madam, though not
As nether as some. No, it's not good-bye, madam.

DYN. Oh Doto, go; you must, you must! And if I seem
Without gratitude, forgive me. It isn't so,   860
It is far, far from so. But I can only
Regain my peace of mind if I know you're gone.

DOTO. Besides, look at the time, madam. Where should I go

At three in the morning? Even if I was to think
Of going; and think of it I never shall.
DYN. Think of the unmatchable world, Doto.
DOTO.   I do
Think of it, madam. And when I think of it, what
Have I thought? Well, it depends, madam.
DYN.   I insist,
Obey me! At once! Doto!
DOTO.   Here I sit.
DYN. What shall I do with you?
DOTO.   Ignore me, madam.   870
I know my place. I shall die quite unobtrusive.
Oh look, the corporal's forgotten to take his equipment.
DYN. Could he be so careless?
DOTO.   I shouldn't hardly have thought so.
Poor fellow. They'll go and deduct it off his credits.
I suppose, madam, I suppose he couldn't be thinking
Of coming back?
DYN.   He'll think of these. He will notice
He isn't wearing them. He'll come; he is sure to come.
DOTO. Oh.
DYN.   I know he will.
DOTO.   Oh, oh.
Is that all for to-night, madam? May I go now, madam?
DYN. Doto! Will you?
DOTO.   Just you try to stop me, madam.   880
Sometimes going is a kind of instinct with me.
I'll leave death to some other occasion.
DYN.   Do,
Doto. Any other time. Now you must hurry.
I won't delay you from life another moment.
Oh, Doto, good-bye.
DOTO.   Good-bye. Life is unusual,
Isn't it, madam? Remember me to Cerberus.
      [*Re-enter* TEGEUS. DOTO *passes him on the steps.*]
DOTO. [*As she goes.*] You left something behind. Ye gods, what a
      moon!
DYN. Chromis, it's true; my lips are hardly dry.
Time runs again; the void is space again;
Space has life again; Dynamene has Chromis.   890
TEG. It's over.
DYN.   Chromis, you're sick. As white as wool.
Come, you covered the distance too quickly.
Rest in my arms; get your breath again.
TEG. I've breathed one night too many. Why did I see you,
Why in the name of life did I see you?
DYN.   Why?
Weren't we gifted with each other? O heart,
What do you mean?
TEG.   I mean that joy is nothing

But the parent of doom. Why should I have found
Your constancy such balm to the world and yet
Find, by the same vision, its destruction   900
A necessity? We're set upon by love
To make us incompetent to steer ourselves,
To make us docile to fate. I should have known:
Indulgences, not fulfilment, is what the world
Permits us.

DYN.   Chromis, is this intelligible?
Help me to follow you. What did you meet in the fields
·To bring about all this talk? Do you still love me?

TEG. What good will it do us? I've lost a body.

DYN.   A body?
One of the six? Well, it isn't with them you propose
To love me; and you couldn't keep it for ever.   910
Are we going to allow a body that isn't there
To come between us?

TEG.   But I'm responsible for it.
I have to account for it in the morning. Surely
You see, Dynamene, the horror we're faced with?
The relatives have had time to cut him down
And take him away for burial. It means
A court martial. No doubt about the sentence.
I shall take the place of the missing man.
To be hanged, Dynamene! Hanged, Dynamene!

DYN. No; it's monstrous! Your life is yours, Chromis.   920

TEG. Anything but. That's why I have to take it.
At the best we live our lives on loan,
At the worst in chains. And I was never born
To have life. Then for what? To be had by it,
And so are we all. But I'll make it what it is,
By making it nothing.

DYN.   Chromis, you're frightening.
What are you meaning to do?

TEG.   I have to die,
Dance of my heart, I have to die, to die,
To part us, to go to my sword and let it part us.
I'll have my free will even if I'm compelled to it.   930
I'll kill myself.

DYN.   Oh, no! No, Chromis!
It's all unreasonable—no such horror
Can come of a pure accident. Have you hanged?
How can they hang you for simply not being somewhere?
How can they hang you for losing a dead man?
They must have wanted to lose him, or they wouldn't
Have hanged him No, you're scaring yourself for nothing
And making me frantic.

TEG.   It's section six, paragraph
Three in the Regulations. That's my doom.
I've read it for myself. And, by my doom,   940

Since I have to die, let me die here, in love,
Promoted by your kiss to tower, in dying,
High above my birth. For god's sake let me die
On a wave of life, Dynamane, with an action
I can take some pride in. How could I settle to death
Knowing that you last saw me stripped and strangled
On a holly tree? Demoted first and then hanged!

DYN. Am I supposed to love the corporal
Or you? It's you I love, from head to foot
And out to the ends of your spirit. What shall I do   950
If you die? How could I follow you? I should find you
Discussing me with my husband, comparing your feelings,
Exchanging reactions. Where should I put myself?
Or am I to live on alone, or find in life
Another source of love, in memory
Of Virilius and of you?

TEG.   Dynamene,
Not that! Since everything in the lives of men
Is brief to indifference, let our love at least
Echo and perpetuate itself uniquely
As long as time allows you. Though you go   960
To the limit of age, it won't be far to contain me.

DYN. It will seem like eternity ground into days and days.

TEG. Can I be certain of you, for ever?

DYN.   But, Chromis,
Surely you said——

TEG.   Surely we have sensed
Our passion to be greater than mortal? Must I
Die believing it is dying with me?

DYN.   Chromis,
You must never die, never! It would be
An offence against truth.

TEG.   I cannot live to be hanged.
It would be an offence against life. Give me my sword,
Dynamene. O Hades, when you look pale   970
You take the heart out of me. I could die
Without a sword by seeing you suffer. Quickly!
Give me my heart back again with your lips
And I'll live the rest of my ambitions
In a last kiss.

DYN.   Oh, no, no, no!
Give my blessing to your desertion of me?
Never, Chromis, never. Kiss you and then
Let you go? Love you, for death to have you?
Am I to be made the fool of courts martial?
Who are they who think they can discipline souls   980
Right off the earth? What discipline is that?
Chromis, love is the only discipline
And we're the disciples of love. I hold you to that:
Hold you, hold you.

TEG.   We have no chance. It's determined
  In section six, paragraph three, of the Regulations.
  That has more power than love. It can snuff the great
  Candles of creation. It makes me able
  To do the impossible, to leave you, to go from the light
  That keeps you.
DYN.   No!
TEG.   O dark, it does. Good-bye,
  My memory of earth, my dear most dear   990
  Beyond every expectation. I was wrong
  To want you to keep our vows existent
  In the vacuum that's coming. It would make you
  A heaviness to the world, when you should be,
  As you are, a form of light. Dynamene, turn
  Your head away. I'm going to let my sword
  Solve all the riddles.
DYN.   Chromis, I have it! I know!
  Virilius will help you.
TEG.   Virilius?
DYN. My husband. He can be the other body.
TEG. Your husband can?
DYN.   He has no further use   1000
  For what he left of himself to lie with us here.
  Is there any reason why he shouldn't hang
  On your holly tree? Better, far better, he,
  Than you who are still alive, and surely better
  Than *idling* into corruption?
TEG.   Hang your husband?
  Dynamene, it's terrible, horrible.
DYN. How little you can understand. I loved
  His life not his death. And now we can give his death
  The power of life. Not horrible: wonderful!
  Isn't it so? That I should be able to feel   1010
  He moves again in the world, accomplishing
  Our welfare? It's more than my grief could do.
TEG. What can I say?
DYN.   That you love me; as I love him
  And you. Let's celebrate your safety then.
  Where's the bottle? There's some wine unfinished in this bowl.
  I'll share it with you. Now forget the fear
  We were in; look at me, Chromis. Come away
  From the pit you nearly dropped us in. My darling,
  I give you Virilius.
TEG.   Virilius.
  And all that follows.
DOTO. [*On the steps, with the bottle.*]
                    The master. Both the masters.   1020

CURTAIN

ULYSSES

THE MOLLY BLOOM SOLILOQUY

James Joyce

Molly Bloom, lying awake alongside her sleeping husband Leopold
Bloom, remembers their courtship on Gibraltar, and as she recalls
the smells, sights and tastes of that time, as well as some from her
immediate Dublin surroundings, she brings us in touch with one of
her life's most vivid moments.

. . . whatll I wear shall I wear a white rose or those fairy cakes in Liptons I love the smell of a rich big shop at 7½ d. a lb or the other ones with the cherries in them and the pinky sugar 11d a couple of lbs of course a nice plant for the middle of the table Id get that cheaper in wait wheres this I saw them not long ago I love flowers Id love to have the whole place swimming in roses God of heaven theres nothing like nature the wild mountains then the sea and the waves rushing then the beautiful country with fields of oats and wheat and all kinds of things and all the fine cattle going about that would do your heart good to see rivers and lakes and flowers all sorts of shapes and smells and colours springing up even out of the ditches primroses and violets nature it is as for them saying theres no God I wouldnt give a snap of my two fingers for all their learning why dont they go and create something I often asked him athcists or whatever they call themselves go and wash the cobbles off themselves first then they go howling for the priest and they dying and why why because theyre afraid of hell on account of their bad conscience ah yes I know them well who was the first person in the universe before there was anybody that made it all who ah that they dont know neither do I so there you are they might

as well try to stop the sun from rising tomorrow the sun shines for you he said the day we were lying among the rhododendrons on Howth head in the grey tweed suit and his straw hat the day I got him to propose to me yes first I gave him the bit of seedcake out of my mouth and it was leapyear like now yes 16 years ago my God after that long kiss I near lost my breath yes he said I was a flower of the mountain yes so we are flowers all a womans body yes that was one true thing he said in his life and the sun shines for you today yes that was why I liked him because I saw he understood or felt what a woman is and I knew I could always get round him and I gave him all the pleasure I could leading him on till he asked me to say yes and I wouldnt answer first only looked out over the sea and the sky I was thinking of so many things he didnt know of Mulvey and Mr. Stanhope and Hester and father and old captain Groves and the sailors playing all birds fly and I say stoop and washing up dishes they called it on the pier and the sentry in front of the governors house with the thing round his white helmet poor devil half roasted and the Spanish girls laughing in their shawls and their tall combs and the auctions in the morning the Greeks and the jews and the Arabs and the devil knows who else from all the ends of Europe and Duke street and the fowl market all clucking outside Larby Sharons and the poor donkeys slipping half asleep and the vague fellows in the cloaks asleep in the shade on the steps and the big wheels of the carts of the bulls and the old castle thousands of years old yes and those handsome Moors all in white and turbans like kings asking you to sit down in their little bit of a shop and Ronda with the old windows of the posadas glancing eyes a lattice hid for her lover to kiss the iron and the wineshops half open at night and the castanets and the night we missed the boat at Algeciras the watchman going about serene with his lamp and O that awful deepdown torrent O and the sea the sea crimson sometimes like fire and the glori-ous sunsets and the figtrees in the Alameda gardens yes and all the queer little streets and pink and blue and yellow houses and the rosegardens and the jessamine and geraniums and cactuses and Gibraltar as a girl where I was a Flower of the mountain yes when I put the rose in my hair like the Andalusian girls used or shall I wear a red yes and how he kissed me under the Moorish wall and I thought well as well him as another and then I asked him with my eyes to ask again yes and then he asked me would I yes to say yes my mountain flower and first I put my arms around him yes and drew him down to me so he could feel my breasts all perfume yes and his heart was going like mad and yes I said yes I will Yes.

A STORY

Dylan Thomas

IF you can call it a story. There's no real beginning or end and there's very little in the middle. It is all about a day's outing, by charabanc, to Porthcawl, which, of course, the charabanc never reached, and it happened when I was so high and much nicer.

I was staying at the time with my uncle and his wife. Although she was my aunt, I never thought of her as anything but the wife of my uncle, partly because he was so big and trumpeting and red-hairy and used to fill every inch of the hot little house like an old buffalo squeezed into an airing cupboard, and partly because she was so small and silk and quick and made no noise at all as she whisked about on padded paws, dusting the china dogs, feeding the buffalo, setting the mouse-traps that never caught her; and once she sleaked out of the room, to squeak in a nook or nibble in the hayloft, you forgot she had ever been there.

But there he was, always, a steaming hulk of an uncle, his braces straining like hawsers, crammed behind the counter of the tiny shop at the front of the house, and breathing like a brass band; or guzzling and blustery in the kitchen over his gutsy supper, too big for everything except the great black boats of his boots. As he ate, the house grew smaller; he billowed out over the furniture, the loud check meadow of his waistcoat littered, as though after a picnic, with cigarette ends, peelings, cabbage stalks, birds' bones, gravy; and the forest fire of his hair crackled among the hooked hams from the ceiling. She was so small she could hit him only if she stood on a chair; and every Saturday night at half-past ten he would lift her up, under his arm, onto a chair, in the kitchen so that she could hit him on the head with whatever was handy, which was always a china dog. On Sundays, and when pickled, he sang high tenor, and had won many cups.

The first I heard of the annual outing was when I was sitting one evening on a bag of rice behind the counter, under one of my uncle's stomachs, reading an advertisement for sheepdip, which was all there was to read. The shop was full of my uncle, and when Mr. Benjamin Franklyn, Mr. Weazley, Noah Bowen, and Will Sentry came in, I thought it would burst. It was like all being together in a drawer that smelled of cheese and turps, and twist tobacco and sweet biscuits and snuff and waistcoat. Mr. Benjamin Franklyn said that he had collected enough money for the charabanc and twenty cases of pale ale and a pound apiece over that he would distribute among the members of the outing when they first stopped for refreshment, and he was about sick and tired, he said, of being followed by Will Sentry.

"All day long, wherever I go," he said, "he's after me like a collie with one eye. I got a shadow of my own *and* a dog. I don't need no Tom, Dick or Harry pursuing me with his dirty muffler on."

Will Sentry blushed, and said, "It's only oily. I got a bicycle."

"A man has no privacy at all," Mr. Franklyn went on. "I tell you he sticks so close I'm afraid to go out the back in case I sit in his lap. It's a wonder to me," he said, "he don't follow me into bed at night."

"Wife won't let," Will Sentry said.

And that started Mr. Franklyn off again, and they tried to soothe him down by saying, "Don't you mind Will Sentry." "No harm in old Will." "He's only keeping an eye on the money, Benjie."

"Aren't I honest?" asked Mr. Franklyn in surprise. There was no answer for some time; then Noah Bowen said, "You know what the committee is. Ever since Bob the Fiddle they don't feel safe with a new treasurer."

"Do you think *I'm* going to drink the outing funds, like Bob the Fiddle did?" said Mr. Franklyn.

"You *might*," said my uncle, slowly.

"I resign," said Mr. Franklyn.

"Not with our money you won't," Will Sentry said.

"Who put the dynamite in the salmon pool?" said Mr. Weazley, but nobody took any notice of him. And, after a time, they all began to play cards in the thickening dusk of the hot, cheesy shop, and my uncle blew and bugled whenever he won, and Mr. Weazley grumbled like a dredger, and I fell to sleep on the gravy-scented mountain meadow of uncle's waistcoat.

On Sunday evening, after Bethesda, Mr. Franklyn walked into the kitchen where my uncle and I were eating sardines from the tin with spoons because it was Sunday and his wife would not let us play draughts. She was somewhere in the kitchen, too. Perhaps she was inside the grandmother clock, hanging from the weights and breathing. Then, a second later, the door opened again and Will Sentry edged into the room, twiddling his hard, round hat. He and Mr. Franklyn sat down on the settee, stiff and moth-balled and black in their chapel and funeral suits.

"I brought the list," said Mr. Franklyn. "Every member fully paid. You ask Will Sentry."

My uncle put on his spectacles, wiped his whiskery mouth with a handkerchief big as a Union Jack, laid down his spoon of sardines, took Mr. Franklyn's list of names, removed the spectacles so that he could read, and then ticked the names off one by one.

"Enoch Davies. Aye. He's good with his fists. You never know. Little Gerwain. Very melodious bass. Mr. Cadwalladwr. That's right. He can tell opening time better than my watch. Mr. Weazley. Of course. He's been to Paris. Pity he suffers so much in the charabanc. Stopped us nine times last year between the Beehive and the Red Dragon. Noah Bowen. Ah, very peaceable. He's got a tongue like a turtledove. Never a argument with Noah Bowen. Jenkins Loughor. Keep him off economics. It cost us a plateglass window. And ten pints for the Sergeant. Mr. Jervis. Very tidy."

"He tried to put a pig in the charra," Will Sentry said.

"Live and let live," said my uncle.

Will Sentry blushed.

"Sinbad the Sailor's Arms. Got to keep in with him. Old O. Jones."

"Why old O. Jones?" said Will Sentry.

"Old O. Jones always goes," said my uncle.

I looked down at the kitchen table. The tin of sardines was gone. By Gee, I said to myself, Uncle's wife is quick as a flash.

"Cuthbert Johnny Fortnight. Now there's a card," said my uncle.

"He whistles after women," Will Sentry said.

"So do you," said Mr. Benjamin Franklyn, "in your mind."

My uncle at last approved the whole list, pausing only to say, when he came across one name, "If we weren't a Christian community, we'd chuck that Bob the Fiddle in the sea."

"We can do that in Porthcawl," said Mr. Franklyn, and soon after that he went, Will Sentry no more than an inch behind him, their Sunday-bright boots squeaking on the kitchen cobbles.

And then, suddenly, there was my uncle's wife standing in front of the dresser, with a china dog in one hand. By

Gee, I said to myself again, did you ever see such a woman, if that's what she is. The lamps were not lit yet in the kitchen and she stood in a wood of shadows, with the plates on the dresser behind her shining—like pink and white eyes.

"If you go on that outing on Saturday, Mr. Thomas," she said to my uncle in her small, silk voice, "I'm going home to my mother's."

Holy Mo, I thought, she's got a mother. Now that's one old bald mouse of a hundred and five I won't be wanting to meet in a dark lane.

"It's me or the outing, Mr. Thomas."

I would have made my choice at once, but it was almost half a minute before my uncle said, "Well, then, Sarah, it's the outing, my love." He lifted her up, under his arm, onto a chair in the kitchen, and she hit him on the head with the china dog. Then he lifted her down again, and then I said good night.

For the rest of the week my uncle's wife whisked quiet and quick round the house with her darting duster, my uncle blew and bugled and swole, and I kept myself busy all the time being up to no good. And then at breakfast time on Saturday morning, the morning of the outing, I found a note on the kitchen table. It said, "There's some eggs in the pantry. Take your boots off before you go to bed." My uncle's wife had gone, as quick as a flash.

When my uncle saw the note, he tugged out the flag of his handkerchief and blew such a hubbub of trumpets that the plates on the dresser shook. "It's the same every year," he said. And then he looked at me. "But this year it's different. *You'll* have to come on the outing, too, and what the members will say I dare not think."

The charabanc drew up outside, and when the members of the outing saw my uncle and me squeeze out of the shop together, both of us cat-licked and brushed in our Sunday best, they snarled like a zoo.

"Are you bringing a *boy?*" asked Mr. Benjamin Franklyn as we climbed into the charabanc. He looked at me with horror.

"Boys is nasty," said Mr. Weazley.

"He hasn't paid his contributions," Will Sentry said.

"No room for boys. Boys get sick in charabancs."

"So do you, Enoch Davies," said my uncle.

"Might as well bring *women.*"

The way they said it, women were worse than boys.

"Better than bringing grandfathers."

"Grandfathers is nasty, too," said Mr. Weazley.

"What can we do with him when we stop for refreshments?"

"I'm a grandfather," said Mr. Weazley.

"Twenty-six minutes to opening time," shouted an old man in a panama hat, not looking at a watch. They forgot me at once.

"Good old Mr. Cadwalladwr," they cried, and the charabanc started off down the village street.

A few cold women stood at their doorways, grimly watching us go. A very small boy waved goodbye, and his mother boxed his ears. It was a beautiful August morning.

We were out of the village, and over the bridge, and up the hill toward Steeplehat Wood when Mr. Franklyn, with his list of names in his hand, called out loud, "Where's old O. Jones?"

"Where's old O.?"

"We've left old O. behind."

"Can't go without old O."

And though Mr. Weazley hissed all the way, we turned and drove back to the village, where, outside the Prince of Wales, old O. Jones was waiting patiently and alone with a canvas bag.

"I didn't want to come at all," old O.

Jones said as they hoisted him into the charabanc and clapped him on the back and pushed him on a seat and stuck a bottle in his hand, "but I always go." And over the bridge and up the hill and under the deep green wood and along the dusty road we wove, slow cows and ducks flying by, until "Stop the bus!" Mr. Weazley cried, "I left my teeth on the mantelpiece."

"Never you mind," they said, "you're not going to bite nobody," and they gave him a bottle with a straw.

"I might want to smile," he said.

"Not you," they said.

"What's the time, Mr. Cadwalladwr?"

"Twelve minutes to go," shouted back the old man in the panama, and they all began to curse him.

The charabanc pulled up outside the Mountain Sheep, a small, unhappy public house with a thatched roof like a wig with ringworm. From a flagpole by the Gents fluttered the flag of Siam. I knew it was the flag of Siam because of cigarette cards. The landlord stood at the door to welcome us, simpering like a wolf. He was a long, lean, black-fanged man with a greased love-curl and pouncing eyes. "What a beautiful August day!" he said, and touched his love-curl with a claw. That was the way he must have welcomed the Mountain Sheep before he ate it, I said to myself. The members rushed out, bleating, and into the bar.

"You keep an eye on the charra," my uncle said, "see nobody steals it now."

"There's nobody to steal it," I said, "except some cows," but my uncle was gustily blowing his bugle in the bar. I looked at the cows opposite, and they looked at me. There was nothing else for us to do. Forty-five minutes passed, like a very slow cloud. The sun shone down on the lonely road, the lost, unwanted boy, and the lake-eyed cows. In the dark bar they were so happy they were breaking glasses. A Shoni-Onion Breton man, with

a beret and a necklace of onions, bicycled down the road and stopped at the door. *"Quelle un grand matin, monsieur,"* [1] I said.

"There's French, boy bach!" he said.

I followed him down the passage, and peered into the bar. I could hardly recognize the members of the outing. They had all changed color. Beetroot, rhubarb and puce, they hollered and rollicked in that dark, damp hole like enormous ancient bad boys, and my uncle surged in the middle, all red whiskers and bellies. On the floor was broken glass and Mr. Weazley.

"Drinks all round," cried Bob the Fiddle, a small, absconding man with bright blue eyes and a plump smile.

"Who's been robbing the orphans?"

"Who sold his little babby to the gyppoes?"

"Trust old Bob, he'll let you down."

"You will have your little joke," said Bob the Fiddle, smiling like a razor, "but I forgive you, boys."

Out of the fug and babel I heard: "Where's old O. Jones?" "Where are you, old O.?" "He's in the kitchen cooking his dinner." "He never forgets his dinner time." "Good old O. Jones." "Come out and fight." "No, not now, later." "No, now when I'm in a temper." "Look at Will Sentry, he's proper snobbled." "Look at his willful feet." "Look at Mr. Weazley lording it on the floor."

Mr. Weazley got up, hissing like a gander. "That boy pushed me down deliberate," he said, pointing to me at the door, and I slunk away down the passage and out to the mild, good cows.

Time clouded over, the cows wondered, I threw a stone at them and they wandered, wondering, away. Then out blew my uncle, ballooning, and one by one the members lumbered after him in a grizzle. They had drunk the Mountain Sheep dry. Mr. Weazley had won a string of onions

[1] What a fine morning, sir.

that the Shoni-Onion man had raffled in the bar.

"What's the good of onions if you left your teeth on the mantelpiece?" he said. And when I looked through the back window of the thundering charabanc, I saw the pub grow smaller in the distance. And the flag of Siam, from the flagpole by the Gents, fluttered now at half mast.

The Blue Bull, the Dragon, the Star of Wales, the Twll in the Wall, the Sour Grapes, the Shepherd's Arms, the Bells of Aberdovey: I had nothing to do in the whole wild August world but remember the names where the outing stopped and keep an eye on the charabanc. And whenever it passed a public house, Mr. Weazley would cough like a billy goat and cry, "Stop the bus, I'm dying of breath." And back we would all have to go.

Closing time meant nothing to the members of that outing. Behind locked doors, they hymned and rumpused all the beautiful afternoon. And, when a policeman entered the Druid's Tap by the back door, and found them all choral with beer, "Sssh!" said Noah Bowen, "the pub is shut."

"Where do you come from?" he said in his buttoned, blue voice.

They told him.

"I got a auntie there," the policeman said. And very soon he was singing "Asleep in the Deep."

Off we drove again at last, the charabanc bouncing with tenors and flagons, and came to a river that rushed along among willows.

"Water!" they shouted.

"Porthcawl!" sang my uncle.

"Where's the donkeys?" said Mr. Weazley.

And out they lurched, to paddle and whoop in the cool, white, winding water. Mr. Franklyn, trying to polka on the slippery stones, fell in twice. "Nothing is simple," he said with dignity as he oozed up the bank.

"It's cold!" they cried.

"It's lovely!"

"It's smooth as a moth's nose!"

"It's *better* than Porthcawl!"

And dusk came down warm and gentle on thirty wild, wet, pickled, splashing men without a care in the world at the end of the world in the west of Wales. And, "Who goes there?" called Will Sentry to a wild duck flying.

They stopped at the Hermit's Nest for a rum to keep out the cold. "I played for Aberavon in 1898," said a stranger to Enoch Davies.

"Liar," said Enoch Davies.

"I can show the photos," said the stranger.

"Forged," said Enoch Davies.

"And I'll show you my cap at home."

"Stolen."

"I got friends to prove it," the stranger said in a fury.

"Bribed," said Enoch Davies.

On the way home, through the simmering moonsplashed dark, old O. Jones began to cook his supper on a primus stove in the middle of the charabanc. Mr. Weazley coughed himself blue in the smoke. "Stop the bus!" he cried, "I'm dying of breath." We all climbed down into the moonlight. There was not a public house in sight. So they carried out the remaining cases, and the primus stove, and old O. Jones himself, and took them into a field, and sat down in a circle in the field and drank and sang while old O. Jones cooked sausage and mash and the moon flew above us. And there I drifted to sleep against my uncle's mountainous waistcoat, and, as I slept, "Who goes there?" called out Will Sentry to the flying moon.

THE GRANGERFORDS TAKE ME IN

Mark Twain

Seeking to escape a restrictive and sterile society, Huck and the Negro
slave Jim voyage down the Mississippi on a raft. Separated for a time,
they make their way alone. Huck is befriended by the Grangerfords,
who are destroying themselves in a feud with another southern family.
Huck visits the room of the late Emmeline Grangerford, a room that
the family maintains as a shrine. The story is told in the words of the
young Huck.

THEY had pictures hung on the walls
—mainly Washingtons and Lafa-
yettes, and battles, and Highland Marys,
and one called "Signing the Declaration."
There was some that they called crayons,
which one of the daughters which was
dead made her own self when she was
only fifteen years old. They was different
from any pictures I ever see before—
blacker, mostly, than is common. One
was a woman in a slim black dress, belted
small under the armpits, with bulges
like a cabbage in the middle of the
sleeves, and a large black scoop-shovel
bonnet with a black veil, and white slim
ankles crossed about with black tape and
very wee black slippers, like a chisel, and
she was leaning pensive on a tombstone
on her right elbow under a weeping willow, and her other hand hanging down
her side holding a white handkerchief
and a reticule, and underneath the picture
it said "Shall I Never See Thee More
Alas." Another one was a young lady with
her hair all combed up straight to the
top of her head and knotted there in
front of a comb like a chair-back, and
she was crying into a handkerchief and
had a dead bird laying on its back in her
other hand with its heels up, and underneath the picture it said "I Shall Never
Hear Thy Sweet Chirrup More Alas."
There was one where a young lady was at
a window looking up at the moon, and

tears running down her cheeks; and she
had an open letter in one hand with black
sealing wax showing on one edge of it,
and she was mashing a locket with a
chain to it against her mouth and underneath the picture it said "And Art Thou
Gone Yes Thou Art Gone Alas." These
was all nice pictures, I reckon, but I
didn't somehow seem to take to them, because if ever I was down a little they always give me the fantods. Everybody was
sorry she died, because she had laid out
a lot more of these pictures to do and a
body could see by what she had done
what they had lost. But I reckoned that
with her disposition she was having a
better time in the graveyard. She was at
work on what they said was her greatest
picture when she took sick, and every day
and every night it was her prayer to be allowed to live till she got it done, but she
never got the chance. It was a picture of
a young woman in a long white gown,
standing on the rail of a bridge all ready
to jump off, with her hair all down her
back, and looking up to the moon with
the tears running down her face, and she
had two arms folded across her breast
and two arms stretched out in front and
two more reaching up towards the moon
—and the idea was to see which pair
would look best and then scratch out all
the other arms; but, as I was saying,
she died before she got her mind made

up and now they kept this picture over the head of the bed in her room, and every time her birthday come they hung flowers on it. Other times it was hid with a little curtain. The young woman in the picture had a kind of a nice sweet face but there was so many arms it made her look too spidery, seemed to me.

This young girl kept a scrap-book when she was alive, and used to paste obituaries and accidents and cases of patient suffering in it out of the *Presbyterian Observer,* and write poetry after them out of her own head. It was very good poetry. This is what she wrote about a boy by the name of Stephen Dowling Bots that fell down a well and was drownded:

ODE TO STEPHEN DOWLING BOTS, DEC'D

And did young Stephen sicken,
    And did young Stephen die?
And did the sad hearts thicken
    And did the mourners cry?

No; such was not the fate of
    Young Stephen Dowling Bots;
Though sad hearts round him thickened,
    'Twas not from sickness' shots.

No whooping-cough did rack his frame,
    Nor measles drear with spots;
Not these impaired the sacred name
    Of Stephen Dowling Bots.

Despised love struck not with woe
    That head of curly knots,
Nor stomach troubles laid him low,
    Young Stephen Dowling Bots.

O no. Then list with tearful eye,
    Whilst I his fate do tell.
His soul did from this cold world fly
    By falling down a well.

They got him out and emptied him;
    Alas it was too late;
His spirit was gone for to sport aloft
    In the realms of the good and great.

If Emmeline Grangerford could make

poetry like that before she was fourteen, there ain't no telling what she could 'a' done by and by. Buck said she could rattle off poetry like nothing. She didn't ever have to stop to think. He said she would slap down a line, and if she couldn't find anything to rhyme with it she would just scratch it out and slap down another one and go ahead. She warn't particular; she could write about anything you choose to give her to write about just so it was sadful. Every time a man died or a woman died or a child died, she would be on hand with her "tribute" before he was cold. She called them tributes. The neighbors said it was the doctor first, then Emmeline, then the undertaker—the undertaker never got in ahead of Emmeline but once, and then she hung fire on a rhyme for the dead person's name, which was Whistler. She warn't ever the same after that; she never complained but she kind of pined away and did not live long. Poor thing, many's the time I made myself go up to the little room that used to be hers and get out her poor old scrap-book and read in it when her pictures had been aggravating me and I had soured on her a little. I liked all that family, dead ones and all, and warn't going to let anything come between us. Poor Emmeline made poetry about all the dead people when she was alive, and it didn't seem right that there warn't nobody to make some about her now she was gone; so I tried to sweat out a verse or two myself but I couldn't seem to make it go somehow. They kept Emmeline's room trim and nice, and all the things fixed in it just the way she liked to have them when she was live, and nobody ever slept there. The old lady took care of the room herself, though there was plenty of niggers, and she sewed there a good deal and read her Bible there mostly.

Well, as I was saying about the parlor, there was beautiful curtains on the windows: white, with pictures painted on them of castles with vines all down the walls and cattle coming down to drink. There was a little old piano, too, that had tin pans in it, I reckon, and nothing was ever so lovely as to hear the young ladies sing "The Last Link Is Broken" and play "The Battle of Prague" on it. The walls of all the rooms was plastered and most had carpets on the floors, and the whole house was whitewashed on the outside.

It was a double house and the big open place betwixt them was roofed and floored, and sometimes the table was set there in the middle of the day, and it was a cool, comfortable place. Nothing couldn't be better. And warn't the cooking good, and just bushels of it too!

THE DIARY OF ADAM AND EVE

Mark Twain

PART I—EXTRACTS FROM ADAM'S DIARY

Monday This new creature with the long hair is a good deal in the way. It is always hanging around and following me about. I don't like this; I am not used to company. I wish it would stay with the other animals. . . . Cloudy today, wind in the east; think we shall have rain. . . . *We?* Where did I get that word?—I remember now—the new creature uses it.

Tuesday Been examining the great waterfall. It is the finest thing on the estate, I think. The new creature calls it Niagara Falls—why, I am sure I do not know. Says it *looks* like Niagara Falls. That is not a reason, it is a mere waywardness and imbecility. I get no chance to name anything myself. The new creature names everything that comes along, before I can get in a protest. And always that same pretext is offered—it *looks* like the thing. There is the dodo, for instance. She says the moment one looks at it one sees at a glance that it "looks like a dodo." It will have to keep that name, no doubt. It wearies me to fret about it, and it does no good, anyway. Dodo! It looks no more like a dodo than I do.

Wednesday Built me a shelter against the rain, but could not have it to myself in peace. The new creature intruded. When I tried to put it out it shed water out of the holes it looks with, and wiped it away with the back of its paws, and made a noise such as some of the other animals make when they are in distress. I wish it would not talk; it is always talking. That sounds like a cheap fling at the poor creature, a slur; but I do not mean it so.

I have never heard the human voice before, and any new and strange sound intruding itself here upon the solemn hush of these dreaming solitudes offends my ear and seems a false note. And this new sound is so close to me; it is right at my shoulder, right at my ear, first on one side and then on the other, and I am used only to sounds that are more or less distant from me.

Friday The naming goes recklessly on, in spite of anything I can do. I had a very good name for the estate, and it was musical and pretty—Garden of Eden. Privately, I continue to call it that, but not any longer publicly. The new creature says it is all woods and rocks and scenery, and therefore has no resemblance to a garden. Says it *looks* like a park, and does not look like anything *but* a park. Consequently, without consulting me, it has been new-named—Niagara Falls Park. This is sufficiently highhanded, it seems to me. And already there is a sign up:

KEEP OFF
THE GRASS

My life is not as happy as it was.

Saturday The new creature eats too much fruit. We are going to run short, most likely. "We" again—that is *its* word; mine, too, now, from hearing it so much. Good deal of fog this morning. I do not go out in the fog myself. The new creature does. It goes out in all weathers, and stumps right in with its muddy feet. And talks. It used to be so pleasant and quiet here.

Sunday Pulled through. This day is getting to be more and more trying. It was selected and set apart last November

[486]

as a day of rest. I had already six of them per week before. This morning found the new creature trying to clod apples out of that forbidden tree.

Monday The new creature says its name is Eve. That is all right, I have no objections. Says it is to call it by, when I want it to come. I said it was superfluous, then. The word evidently raised me in its respect; and indeed it is a large, good word and will bear repetition. It says it is not an It, it is a She. This is probably doubtful; yet it is all one to me; what she is were nothing to me if she would but go by herself and not talk.

Tuesday She has littered the whole estate with execrable names and offensive signs:

THIS WAY TO THE WHIRLPOOL
THIS WAY TO GOAT ISLAND
CAVE OF THE WINDS THIS WAY

She says this park would make a tidy summer resort if there was any custom for it. Summer resort—another invention of hers—just words, without any meaning. What is a summer resort? But it is best not to ask her, she has such a rage for explaining.

Friday She has taken to beseeching me to stop going over the Falls. What harm does it do? Says it makes her shudder. I wonder why; I have always done it—always liked the plunge, and coolness. I supposed it was what the Falls were for. They have no other use that I can see, and they must have been made for something. She says they were only made for scenery—like the rhinoceros and the mastodon.

I went over the Falls in a barrel—not satisfactory to her. Went over in a tub—still not satisfactory. Swam the Whirlpool and the Rapids in a fig-leaf suit. It got much damaged. Hence, tedious complaints about my extravagance. I am too much hampered here. What I need is change of scene.

Saturday I escaped last Tuesday night, and traveled two days, and built me another shelter in a secluded place, and obliterated my tracks as well as I could, but she hunted me out by means of a beast which she has tamed and calls a wolf, and came making that pitiful noise again, and shedding that water out of the places she looks with. I was obliged to return with her, but will presently emigrate again when occasion offers. She engages herself in many foolish things; among others, to study out why the animals called lions and tigers live on grass and flowers, when, as she says, the sort of teeth they wear would indicate that they were intended to eat each other. This is foolish, because to do that would be to kill each other, and that would introduce what, as I understand it, is called "death"; and death, as I have been told, has not yet entered the Park. Which is a pity, on some accounts.

Sunday Pulled through.

Monday I believe I see what the week is for: it is to give time to rest up from the weariness of Sunday. It seems a good idea. . . . She has been climbing that tree again. Clodded her out of it. She said nobody was looking. Seems to consider that a sufficient justification for chancing any dangerous thing. Told her that. The word justification moved her admiration—and envy, too, I thought. It is a good word.

Tuesday She told me she was made out of a rib taken from my body. This is at least doubtful, if not more than that. I have not missed any rib. . . . She is in much trouble about the buzzard; says grass does not agree with it; is afraid she can't raise it; thinks it was intended to live on decayed flesh. The buzzard must get along the best it can with what it is provided. We cannot overturn the whole scheme to accommodate the buzzard.

Saturday She fell in the pond yesterday when she was looking at herself in it, which she is always doing. She nearly strangled, and said it was most uncomfortable. This made her sorry for the creatures which live in there, which she calls fish, for she continues to fasten names on to things that don't need them and don't come when they are called by them, which is a matter of no consequence to her, she is such a numskull, anyway; so she got a lot of them out and brought them in last night and put them in my bed to keep warm, but I have noticed them now and then all day and I don't see that they are any happier there than they were before, only quieter. When night comes I shall throw them outdoors. I will not sleep with them again, for I find them clammy and unpleasant to lie among when a person hasn't anything on.

Sunday Pulled through.

Tuesday She has taken up with a snake now. The other animals are glad, for she was always experimenting with them and bothering them; and I am glad because the snake talks, and this enables me to get a rest.

Friday She says the snake advises her to try the fruit of that tree, and says the result will be a great and fine and noble education. I told her there would be another result, too—it would introduce death into the world. That was a mistake —it had been better to keep the remark to myself; it only gave her an idea—she could save the sick buzzard, and furnish fresh meat to the despondent lions and tigers. I advised her to keep away from the tree. She said she wouldn't. I foresee trouble. Will emigrate.

Wednesday I have had a variegated time. I escaped last night, and rode a horse all night as fast as he could go, hoping to get clear out of the Park and hide in some other country before the trouble should begin; but it was not to be. About an hour after sun-up, as I was riding through a flowery plain where thousands of animals were grazing, slumbering, or playing with each other, according to their wont, all of a sudden they broke into a tempest of frightful noises, and in one moment the plain was a frantic commotion and every beast was destroying its neighbor. I knew what it meant—Eve had eaten that fruit, and death was come into the world. . . . The tigers ate my horse, paying no attention when I ordered them to desist, and they would have eaten me if I had stayed—which I didn't, but went away in much haste. . . . I found this place, outside the Park, and was fairly comfortable for a few days, but she has found me out. Found me out, and has named the place Tonawanda—says it *looks* like that. In fact I was not sorry she came, for there are but meager pickings here, and she brought some of those apples. I was obliged to eat them, I was so hungry. It was against my principles, but I find that principles have no real force except when one is well fed. . . . She came curtained in boughs and bunches of leaves, and when I asked her what she meant by such nonsense, and snatched them away and threw them down, she tittered and blushed. I had never seen a person titter and blush before, and to me it seemed unbecoming and idiotic. She said I would soon know how it was myself. This was correct. Hungry as I was, I laid down the apple half-eaten—certainly the best one I ever saw, considering the lateness of the season—and arrayed myself in the discarded boughs and branches, and then spoke to her with some severity and ordered her to go and get some more and not make such a spectacle of herself. She did it, and after this we crept down to where the wild-beast battle had been, and collected some skins, and I made her patch together a couple of suits proper for public occasions. They are uncomfortable, it is true, but stylish, and that is the main point about clothes. . . . I find she is a good deal of a companion. I see I should be lonesome and depressed without her, now that I have lost my property. Another thing, she says it is ordered that we work for our living hereafter. She will be useful. I will superintend.

Ten Days Later She accuses *me* of being the cause of our disaster! She says, with apparent sincerity and truth, that the Serpent assured her that the forbidden fruit was not apples, it was chestnuts. I said I was innocent, then, for I had not eaten any chestnuts. She said the Serpent informed her that "chestnut" was a figurative term meaning an aged and moldy joke. I turned pale at that, for I have made many jokes to pass the weary time, and some of them could have been of that sort, though I had honestly supposed that they were new when I made them. She asked me if I had made one just at the time of the catastrophe. I was obliged to admit that I had made one to myself, though not aloud. It was this. I was thinking about the Falls, and I said to myself, "How wonderful it is to see that vast body of water tumble down there!" Then in an instant a bright thought flashed into my head, and I let it fly, saying, "It would be a deal more wonderful to see it tumble *up* there!"—and I was just about to kill myself with laughing at it when all nature broke loose in war and death and I had to flee for my life. "There," she said, with triumph, "that is just it; the Serpent mentioned that very jest, and called it the First Chestnut, and said it was coeval with the creation." Alas, I am indeed to blame. Would that I were not witty; oh, that I had never had that radiant thought!

Next Year We have named it Cain. She caught it while I was up country trapping on the North Shore of the Erie; caught it in the timber a couple of miles from our dug-out—or it might have been four, she isn't certain which. It resembles us in some ways, and may be a relation. That is what she thinks, but this is an error, in my judgment. The difference in size warrants the conclusion that it is a different and new kind of animal—a fish, perhaps, though when I put it in the water to see, it sank, and she plunged in and snatched it out before there was opportunity for the experiment to determine the matter. I still think it is a fish, but she is indifferent about what it is, and will not let me have it to try. I do not understand this. The coming of the creature seems to have changed her whole nature and made her unreasonable about experiments. She thinks more of it than she does of any of the other animals, but is not able to explain why. Her mind is disordered—everything shows it. Sometimes she carries the fish in her arms half the night when it complains and wants to get to the water. At such times the water comes out of the places in her face that she looks out of, and she pats the fish on the back and makes soft sounds with her mouth to soothe it, and betrays sorrow and solicitude in a hundred ways. I have never seen her do like this with any other fish, and it troubles me greatly. She used to carry the young tigers around so, and play with them, before we lost our property, but it was only play; she never took on about them like this when their dinner diagreed with them.

Sunday She doesn't work, Sundays, but lies around all tired out, and likes to have the fish wallow over her; and she makes fool noises to amuse it, and pretends to chew its paws, and that makes it laugh. I have not seen a fish before that could laugh. This makes me doubt. . . . I have come to like Sunday myself. Superintending all the week tires a body so. There ought to be more Sundays. In the old days they were tough, but now they come handy.

Wednesday It isn't a fish. I cannot quite make out what it is. It makes curious devilish noises when not satisfied, and says "goo-goo" when it is. It is not one of us, for it doesn't walk; it is not a bird, for it doesn't fly; it is not a frog, for it doesn't hop; it is not a snake, for it doesn't crawl, I feel sure it is not a fish, though I cannot get a chance to find out whether it can swim or not. It merely lies around, and mostly on its back, with its feet up. I have not seen any other animal do that before. I said I believed it was an enigma; but she only admired the word without understanding it. In my judgment it is either an enigma or some kind of a bug. If it dies, I will take it apart and see what its arrangements are. I never had a thing perplex me so.

Three Months Later The perplexity augments instead of diminishing. I sleep but little. It has ceased from lying around, and goes about on its four legs now. Yet it differs from the other four-legged animals, in that its front legs are unusually short, consequently this causes the main part of its person to stick up uncomfortably high in the air, and this is not attractive. It is built much as we are, but its method of traveling shows that it is not of our breed. The short front legs and long hind ones indicate that it is of the kangaroo family, but it is a marked variation of the species, since the true kangaroo hops, whereas this one never does. Still it is a curious and interesting variety, and has not been catalogued before. As I discovered it, I have felt justified in securing the credit of the discovery by attaching my name to it, and hence have called it *Kangaroorum Adamiensis*. . . . It must have been a young one when it came, for it has grown exceedingly since. It must be five times as big, now, as it was then, and when discontented it is able to make from twenty-two to thirty-eight times the noise it made at first. Coercion does not modify this, but has the contrary effect. For this reason I discontinued the system. She reconciles it by persuasion, and by giving it things which she had previously told me she wouldn't give it. As already observed, I was not at home when it first came, and she told me she found it in the woods. It seems odd that it should be the only one, yet it must be so, for I have worn myself out these many weeks trying to find another-one to add to my collection, and for this one to play

with; for surely then it would be quieter and we could tame it more easily. But I find none, nor any vestige of any; and strangest of all, no tracks. It has to live on the ground, it cannot help itself; therefore, how does it get about without leaving a track? I have set a dozen traps, but they do no good. I catch all small animals except that one; animals that merely go into the trap out of curiosity, I think, to see what the milk is there for. They never drink it.

Three Months Later The Kangaroo still continues to grow, which is very strange and perplexing. I never knew one to be so long getting its growth. It has fur on its head now; not like kangaroo fur, but exactly like our hair except that it is much finer and softer, and instead of being black is red. I am like to lose my mind over the capricious and harassing developments of this unclassifiable zoological freak. If I could catch another one —but that is hopeless; it is a new variety, and the only sample; this is plain. But I caught a true kangaroo and brought it in, thinking that this one, being lonesome, would rather have that for company than have no kin at all, or any animal it could feel a nearness to or get sympathy from in its forlorn condition here among strangers who do not know its ways or habits, or what to do to make it feel that it is among friends; but it was a mistake—it went into such fits at the sight of the kangaroo that I was convinced it had never seen one before. I pity the poor noisy little animal, but there is nothing I can do to make it happy. If I could tame it—but that is out of the question; the more I try the worse I seem to make it. It grieves me to the heart to see it in its little storms of sorrow and passion. I wanted to let it go, but she wouldn't hear of it. That seemed cruel and not like her; and yet she may be right. It might be lonelier than ever; for since I cannot find another one, how could *it*?

Five Months Later It is not a kangaroo. No, for it supports itself by holding to her finger, and thus goes a few steps on its hind legs, and then falls down. It is probably some kind of a bear; and yet it has no tail—as yet—and no fur, except on its head. It still keeps on growing—that is a curious circumstance, for bears get their growth earlier than this. Bears are dangerous—since our catastrophe—and I shall not be satisfied to have this one prowling about the place much longer without a muzzle on. I have offered to get her a kangaroo if she would let this one go, but it did no good—she is determined to run us into all sorts of foolish risks, I think. She was not like this before she lost her mind.

A Fortnight Later I examined its mouth. There is no danger yet: it has only one tooth. It has no tail yet. It makes more noise now than it ever did before —and mainly at night. I have moved out. But I shall go over, mornings, to breakfast, and see if it has more teeth. If it gets a mouthful of teeth it will be time for it to go, tail or no tail, for a bear does not need a tail in order to be dangerous.

Four Months Later I have been off hunting and fishing a month, up in the region that she calls Buffalo; I don't know why, unless it is because there are not any buffaloes there. Meantime the bear has learned to paddle around all by itself on its hind legs, and says "poppa" and "momma." It is certainly a new species. This resemblance to words may be purely accidental, of course, and may have no purpose or meaning; but even in that case it is still extraordinary, and is a thing which no other bear can do. This imitation of speech, taken together with general absence of fur and entire absence of tail, sufficiently indicates that this is a new kind of bear. The further study of it will be exceedingly interesting. Meantime I will go off on a far expedition among the forests of the north and make an exhaustive search. There must certainly be another one somewhere, and this one will be less dangerous when it has company of its own species. I will go straightway; but I will muzzle this one first.

Three Months Later It has been a weary, weary hunt, yet I have had no success. In the mean time, without stirring from the home estate, she has caught another one! I never saw such luck. I might have hunted these woods a hundred years, I never would have run across that thing.

Next Day I have been comparing the new one with the old one, and it is perfectly plain that they are the same breed. I was going to stuff one of them for my collection, but she is prejudiced against it for some reason or other; so I have relinquished the idea, though I think it is a mistake. It would be an irreparable loss to science if they should get away. The old one is tamer than it was and can laugh and talk like the parrot, having learned this, no doubt, from being with the parrot so much, and having the imitative faculty in a highly developed degree. I shall be astonished if it turns out to be a new kind of parrot; and yet I ought not to be astonished, for it has already been everything else it could think of since those first days when it was a fish. The new one is as ugly now as the old one was at first; has the same sulphur-and-raw-meat complexion and the same singular head without any fur on it. She calls it Abel.

Ten Years Later They are *boys;* we found it out long ago. It was their coming in that small, immature shape that puzzled us; we were not used to it. There are some girls now. Abel is a good boy, but if Cain had stayed a bear it would have improved him. After all these years, I see that I was mistaken about Eve in the beginning; it is better to live outside the Garden with her than inside it without her. At first I thought she talked too much; but now I should be sorry to have that voice fall silent and pass out of my life. Blessed be the chestnut that brought us near together and taught me to know the goodness of her heart and the sweetness of her spirit!

PART II—EVE'S DIARY
(*Translated from the original*)

Saturday I am almost a whole day old, now. I arrived yesterday. That is as it seems to me. And it must be so, for if there was a day-before-yesterday I was not there when it happened, or I should remember it. It could be, of course, that it did happen, and that I was not noticing. Very well; I will be very watchful now, and if any day-before-yesterdays happen I will make a note of it. It will be best to start right and not let the record get confused, for some instinct tells me that these details are going to be important to the historian some day. For I feel like an experiment, I feel exactly like an experiment; it would be impossible for a person to feel more like an experiment than I do, and so I am coming to feel convinced that that is what I *am*—an experiment; just an experiment, and nothing more.

Then if I am an experiment, am I the whole of it? No, I think not; I think the rest of it is part of it. I am the main part of it, but I think the rest of it has its share in the matter. Is my position assured, or do I have to watch it and take care of it? The latter, perhaps. Some instinct tells me that eternal vigilance is the price of supremacy. [That is a good phrase, I think, for one so young.]

Everything looks better to-day than it did yesterday. In the rush of finishing up yesterday, the mountains were left in a ragged condition, and some of the plains were so cluttered with rubbish and remnants that the aspects were quite distressing. Noble and beautiful works of art should not be subjected to haste; and this majestic new world is indeed a most noble and beautiful work. And certainly marvelously near to being perfect, notwithstanding the shortness of the time. There are too many stars in some places and not enough in others, but that can be remedied presently, no doubt. The moon got loose last night, and slid down and fell out of the scheme—a very great loss; it breaks my heart to think of it. There isn't another thing among the ornaments and decorations that is comparable to it for beauty and finish. It should have been fastened better. If we can only get it back again—

But of course there is no telling where it went to. And besides, whoever gets it will hide it; I know it because I would do it myself. I believe I can be honest in all other matters, but I already begin to realize that the core and center of my nature is love of the beautiful, a passion for the beautiful, and that it would not be safe to trust me with a moon that belonged to another person and that person didn't know I had it. I could give up a moon that I found in the daytime, because I should be afraid some one was looking; but if I found it in the dark, I am sure I should find some kind of an excuse for not saying anything about it. For I do love moons, they are so pretty and so romantic. I wish we had five or six; I would never go to bed; I should never get tired lying on the moss-bank and looking up at them.

Stars are good, too. I wish I could get some to put in my hair. But I suppose I never can. You would be surprised to find how far off they are, for they do not look it. When they first showed, last night, I tried to knock some down with a pole, but it didn't reach, which astonished me; then I tried clods till I was all tired out, but I never got one. It was because I am left-handed and cannot throw good. Even when I aimed at the one I wasn't after I couldn't hit the other one, though I did make some close shots, for I saw the black blot of the clod sail right into the midst of the golden clusters forty or fifty times, just barely missing them, and if I could have held out a little longer maybe I could have got one.

So I cried a little, which was natural, I suppose, for one of my age, and after I was rested I got a basket and started for a place on the extreme rim of the circle, where the stars were close to the ground and I could get them with my hands, which would be better, anyway, because I could gather them tenderly then, and not break them. But it was farther than I thought, and at last I had to give it up; I was so tired I couldn't drag my feet another step; and besides, they were sore and hurt me very much.

I couldn't get back home; it was too far and turning cold; but I found some tigers and nestled in among them and was most adorably comfortable, and their breath was sweet and pleasant, because they live on strawberries. I had never seen a tiger before, but I knew them in a minute by the stripes. If I could have one of those skins, it would make a lovely gown.

To-day I am getting better ideas about distances. I was so eager to get hold of every pretty thing that I giddily grabbed for it, sometimes when it was too far off, and sometimes when it was but six inches away but seemed a foot—alas, with thorns between! I learned a lesson; also I made an axiom, all out of my own head —my very first one: *The scratched Experiment shuns the thorn.* I think it is a very good one for one so young.

I followed the other Experiment around, yesterday afternoon, at a distance, to see what it might be for, if I could. But I was not able to make out. I think it is a man. I had never seen a man, but it looked like one, and I feel sure that that is what it is. I realize that I feel more curiosity about it than about any of the other reptiles. If it is a reptile, and I suppose it is; for it has frowsy hair and blue eyes, and looks like a reptile. It has no hips; it tapers like a carrot; when it stands, it spreads itself apart like a derrick; so I think it is a reptile, though it may be architecture.

I was afraid of it at first, and started to run every time it turned around, for I thought it was going to chase me; but by and by I found it was only trying to get away, so after that I was not timid any more, but tracked it along, several hours, about twenty yards behind, which made it nervous and unhappy. At last it was a good deal worried, and climbed a tree. I waited a good while, then gave it up and went home.

To-day the same thing over. I've got it up the tree again.

Sunday It is up there yet. Resting, apparently. But that is a subterfuge: Sunday isn't the day of rest; Saturday is appointed for that. It looks to me like a creature that is more interested in resting than in anything else. It would tire me to rest so much. It tires me just to sit around and watch the tree. I do wonder what it is for; I never see it do anything.

They returned the moon last night, and I was *so* happy! I think it is very honest of them. It slid down and fell off again, but I was not distressed; there is no need to worry when one has that kind of neighbors; they will fetch it back. I wish I could do something to show my appreciation. I would like to send them some stars, for we have more than we can use. I mean I, not we, for I can see that the reptile cares nothing for such things.

It has low tastes, and is not kind. When I went there yesterday evening in the gloaming it had crept down and was trying to catch the little speckled fishes that play in the pool, and I had to clod it to make it go up the tree again and let them alone. I wonder if *that* is what it is for? Hasn't it any heart? Hasn't it any compassion for those little creatures? Can it be that it was designed and manufactured for such ungentle work? It has the look of it. One of the clods took it back of the ear, and it used language. It gave me a thrill, for it was the first time I had ever heard speech, except my own. I did not understand the words, but they seemed expressive.

When I found it could talk I felt a new interest in it, for I love to talk; I talk, all day, and in my sleep, too, and I am very interesting, but if I had another to talk to I could be twice as interesting, and would never stop, if desired.

If this reptile is a man, it isn't an *it,* is it? That wouldn't be grammatical, would it? I think it would be *he.* I think so. In that case one would parse it thus: nominative, *he;* dative, *him;* possessive, *his'n.* Well, I will consider it a man and call it he until it turns out to be something else. This will be handier than having so many uncertainties.

Next week Sunday All the week I tagged around after him and tried to get acquainted. I had to do the talking, because he was shy, but I didn't mind it. He seemed pleased to have me around, and I used the sociable "we" a good deal, because it seemed to flatter him to be included.

Wednesday We are getting along very well indeed, now, and getting better and better acquainted. He does not try to avoid me any more, which is a good sign, and shows that he likes to have me with him. That pleases me, and I study to be useful to him in every way I can, so as to increase his regard. During the last day or two I have taken all the work of naming things off his hands, and this has been a great relief to him, for he has not gift in that line, and is evidently very grateful. He can't think of a rational name to save him, but I do not let him see that I am aware of his defect. Whenever a new creature comes along I name it before he has time to expose himself by an awkward silence. In this way I have saved him many embarrassments. I have no defect like his. The minute I set eyes on an animal I know what it is. I don't have to reflect a moment; the right name comes out instantly, just as if it were an inspiration, as no doubt it is, for I am sure it wasn't in me half a minute before. I seem to know just by the shape of the creature and the way it acts what animal it is.

When the dodo came along he thought it was a wildcat—I saw it in his eye. But I saved him. And I was careful not to do it in a way that could hurt his pride. I just spoke up in a quite natural way of pleased surprise, and not as if I was dreaming of conveying information, and said, "Well, I do declare, if there isn't the dodo!" I explained—without seeming to be explaining—how I knew it for a dodo, and although I thought maybe he was a little piqued that I knew the creature when he didn't, it was quite evident that he admired me. That was very agreeable, and I thought of it more than once with gratification before I slept. How little a thing can make us happy when we feel that we have earned it!

Thursday My first sorrow. Yesterday he avoided me and seemed to wish I would not talk to him. I could not believe it, and thought there was some mistake, for I loved to be with him, and loved to hear him talk, and so how could it be that he could feel unkind toward me when I had not done anything? But at last it seemed true, so I went away and sat lonely in the place where I first saw him the morning that we were made and I did not know what he was and was indifferent about him; but now it was a mournful place, and every little thing spoke of him, and my heart was very sore. I did not know why very clearly, for it was a new feeling; I had not experienced it before, and it was all a mystery, and I could not make it out.

But when night came I could not bear the lonesomeness, and went to the new shelter which he has built, to ask him what I had done that was wrong and how I could mend it and get back his kindness again; but he put me out in the rain, and it was my first sorrow.

Sunday It is pleasant again, now, and I am happy; but those were heavy days;

I do not think of them when I can help it.

I tried to get him some of those apples, but I cannot learn to throw straight. I failed, but I think the good intention pleased him. They are forbidden, and he says I shall come to harm; but so I come to harm through pleasing him, why shall I care for that harm?

Monday This morning I told him my name, hoping it would interest him. But he did not care for it. It is strange. If he should tell me his name, I would care. I think it would be pleasanter in my ears than any other sound.

He talks very little. Perhaps it is because he is not bright, and is sensitive about it and wishes to conceal it. It is such a pity that he should feel so, for brightness is nothing; it is in the heart that the values lie. I wish I could make him understand that a loving good heart is riches, and riches enough, and that without it intellect is poverty.

Although he talks so little, he has quite a considerable vocabulary. This morning he used a surprisingly good word. He evidently recognized, himself, that it was a good one, for he worked it in twice afterward, casually. It was not good casual art, still it showed that he possesses a certain quality of perception. Without a doubt that seed can be made to grow, if cultivated.

Where did he get that word? I do not think I have ever used it.

No, he took no interest in my name. I tried to hide my disappointment, but I suppose I did not succeed. I went away and sat on the moss-bank with my feet in the water. It is where I go when I hunger for companionship, some one to look at, some one to talk to. It is not enough—that lovely white body painted there in the pool—but it is something, and something is better than utter loneliness. It talks when I talk; it is sad when I am sad; it comforts me with its sympathy; it says, "Do not be downhearted, you poor friendless girl; I will be your friend." It *is* a good friend to me, and my only one; it is my sister.

That first time that she forsook me! ah, I shall never forget that—never, never. My heart was lead in my body! I said, "She was all I had, and now she is gone!" In my despair I said, "Break, my heart; I cannot bear my life any more!" and hid my face in my hands, and there was no solace for me. And when I took them away, after a little, there she was again, white and shining and beautiful, and I sprang into her arms!

That was perfect happiness; I had known happiness before, but it was not like this, which was ecstasy. I never doubted her afterward. Sometimes she stayed away—maybe an hour, maybe almost the whole day, but I waited and did not doubt; I said, "She is busy, or she is gone a journey, but she will come." And it was so: she always did. At night she would not come if it was dark, for she was a timid little thing; but if there was a moon she would come. I am not afraid of the dark, but she is younger than I am; she was born after I was. Many and many are the visits I have paid her; she is my comfort and my refuge when my life is hard—and it is mainly that.

Tuesday All the morning I was at work improving the estate; and I purposely kept away from him in the hope that he would get lonely and come. But he did not.

At noon I stopped for the day and took my recreation by flitting all about with the bees and the butterflies and reveling in the flowers, those beautiful creatures that catch the smile of God out of the sky and preserve it! I gathered them, and made them into wreaths and garlands and clothed myself in them while I ate my luncheon—apples, of course; then I sat in the shade and wished and waited. But he did not come.

But no matter. Nothing would have

come of it, for he does not care for flowers. He calls them rubbish, and cannot tell one from another, and thinks it is superior to feel like that. He does not care for me, he does not care for flowers, he does not care for the painted sky at eventide—is there anything he does care for, except building shacks to coop himself up in from the good clean rain, and thumping the melons, and sampling the grapes, and fingering the fruit on the trees, to see how those properties are coming along?

I laid a dry stick on the ground and tried to bore a hole in it with another one, in order to carry out a scheme that I had, and soon I got an awful fright. A thin, transparent bluish film rose out of the hole, and I dropped everything and ran! I thought it was a spirit, and I *was* so frightened! But I looked back, and it was not coming; so I leaned against a rock and rested and panted, and let my limbs go on trembling until they got steady again; then I crept warily back, alert, watching, and ready to fly if there was occasion; and when I was come near, I parted the branches of a rose-bush and peeped through—wishing the man was about, I was looking so cunning and pretty—but the sprite was gone. I went there, and there was a pinch of delicate pink dust in the hole. I put my finger in, to feel it, and said *ouch!* and took it out again. It was a cruel pain. I put my finger in my mouth; and by standing first on one foot and then the other, and grunting, I presently eased my misery; then I was full of interest, and began to examine.

I was curious to know what the pink dust was. Suddenly the name of it occurred to me, though I had never heard of it before. It was *fire!* I was as certain of it as a person could be of anything in the world. So without hesitation I named it that—fire.

I had created something that didn't exist before; I had added a new thing to the world's uncountable properties; I

realized this, and was proud of my achievement, and was going to run and find him and tell him about it, thinking to raise myself in his esteem—but I reflected, and did not do it. No—he would not care for it. He would ask what it was good for, and what could I answer? for if it was not *good* for something, but only beautiful, merely beautiful—

So I sighed, and did not go. For it wasn't good for anything; it could not build a shack, it could not improve melons, it could not hurry a fruit crop; it was useless, it was a foolishness and a vanity; he would despise it and say cutting words. But to me it was not despicable; I said, "Oh, you fire, I love you, you dainty pink creature, for you are *beautiful*—and that is enough!" and was going to gather it to my breast. But refrained. Then I made another maxim out of my own head, though it was so nearly like the first one that I was afraid it was only a plagiarism: *"The burnt Experiment shuns the fire."*

I wrought again; and when I had made a good deal of fire-dust I emptied it into a handful of dry brown grass, intending to carry it home and keep it always and play with it; but the wind struck it and it sprayed up and spat out at me fiercely, and I dropped it and ran. When I looked back the blue spirit was towering up and stretching and rolling away like a cloud, and instantly I thought of the name of it—*smoke!*—though, upon my word, I had never heard of smoke before.

Soon, brilliant yellow and red flares shot up through the smoke, and I named them in an instant—*flames*—and I was right, too, though these were the very first flames that had ever been in the world. They climbed the trees, they flashed splendidly in and out of the vast and increasing volume of tumbling smoke, and I had to clap my hands and laugh and dance in my rapture, it was so new and strange and so wonderful and so beautiful!

He came running, and stopped and gazed, and said not a word for many minutes. Then he asked what it was. Ah, it was too bad that he should ask such a direct question. I had to answer it, of course, and I did. I said it was fire. If it annoyed him that I should know and he must ask, that was not my fault; I had no desire to annoy him. After a pause he asked:

"How did it come?"

Another direct question, and it also had to have a direct answer.

"I made it."

The fire was traveling farther and farther off. He went to the edge of the burned place and stood looking down, and said:

"What are these?"

"Fire-coals."

He picked up one to examine it, but changed his mind and put it down again. Then he went away. *Nothing* interests him.

But I was interested. There were ashes, gray and soft and delicate and pretty—I knew what they were at once. And the embers; I knew the embers, too. I found my apples, and raked them out, and was glad; for I am very young and my appetite is active. But I was disappointed; they were all burst open and spoiled. Spoiled apparently; but it was not so; they were better than raw ones. Fire is beautiful; some day it will be useful. I think.

Friday I saw him again, for a moment, last Monday at nightfall, but only for a moment. I was hoping he would praise me for trying to improve the estate, for I had meant well and had worked hard. But he was not pleased, and turned away and left me. He was also displeased on another account: I tried once more to persuade him to stop going over the Falls. That was because the fire had revealed to me a new passion—quite new, and distinctly different from love, grief, and those others which I had already discovered—*fear*. And it is horrible!—I wish I had never discovered it; it gives me dark moments, it spoils my happiness, it makes me shiver and tremble and shudder. But I could not persuade him, for he has not discovered fear yet, and so he could not understand me.

Extract from Adam's Diary

Perhaps I ought to remember that she is very young, a mere girl, and make allowances. She is all interest, eagerness, vivacity, the world is to her a charm, a wonder, a mystery, a joy; she can't speak for delight when she finds a new flower, she must pet it and caress it and smell it and talk to it, and pour out endearing names upon it. And she is color-mad: brown rocks, yellow sand, gray moss, green foliage, blue sky; the pearl of the dawn, the purple shadows on the mountains, the golden islands floating in crimson seas at sunset, the pallid moon sailing through the shredded cloud-rack, the star-jewels glittering in the wastes of space —none of them is of any practical value, so far as I can see, but because they have color and majesty, that is enough for her, and she loses her mind over them. If she could quiet down and keep still a couple of minutes at a time, it would be a reposeful spectacle. In that case I think I could enjoy looking at her; indeed I am sure I could, for I am coming to realize that she is a quite remarkably comely creature—lithe, slender, trim, rounded, shapely, nimble, graceful; and once when she was standing marble-white and sun-drenched on a boulder, with her young head tilted back and her hand shading her eyes, watching the flight of a bird in the sky, I recognized that she was beautiful.

Monday noon If there is anything on the planet that she is not interested in it is not in my list. There are animals that I am indifferent to, but it is not so with her. She has no discrimination, she takes to all of them, she thinks they are all treasures, every new one is welcome.

When the mighty brontosaurus came striding into camp, she regarded it as an acquisition, I considered it a calamity; that is a good sample of the lack of harmony that prevails in our views of things. She wanted to domesticate it, I wanted to make it a present of the homestead and move out. She believed it could be tamed by kind treatment and would be a good pet; I said a pet twenty-one feet high and eighty-four feet long would be no proper thing to have about the place, because, even with the best intentions and without meaning any harm, it could sit down on the house and mash it, for any one could see by the look of its eye that it was absentminded.

Still, her heart was set upon having that monster, and she couldn't give it up. She thought we could start a dairy with it, and wanted me to help her milk it; but I wouldn't; it was too risky. The sex wasn't right, and we hadn't any ladder anyway. Then she wanted to ride it, and look at the scenery. Thirty or forty feet of its tail was lying on the ground, like a fallen tree, and she thought she could climb it, but she was mistaken; when she got to the steep place it was too slick and down she came, and would have hurt herself but for me.

Was she satisfied now? No. Nothing ever satisfies her but demonstration; untested theories are not in her line, and she won't have them. It is the right spirit, I concede it; it attracts me; I feel the influence of it; if I were with her more I think I should take it up myself. Well, she had one theory remaining about this colossus: she thought that if we could tame him and make him friendly we could stand him in the river and use him for a bridge. It turned out that he was already plenty tame enough—at least as far as she was concerned—so she tried her theory, but it failed: every time she got him properly placed in the river and went ashore to cross over on him, he came out and followed her around like a pet mountain. Like the other animals. They all do that.

Friday Tuesday—Wednesday—Thursday—and to-day: all without seeing him. It is a long time to be alone; still, it is better to be alone than unwelcome.

I *had* to have company—I was made for it, I think—so I made friends with the animals. They are just charming, and they have the kindest disposition and the politest ways; they never look sour, they never let you feel that you are intruding, they smile at you and wag their tail, if they've got one, and they are always ready

for a romp or an excursion or anything you want to propose. I think they are perfect gentlemen. All these days we have had such good times, and it hasn't been lonesome for me, ever. Lonesome! No, I should say not. Why, there's always a swarm of them around—sometimes as much as four or five acres—you can't count them; and when you stand on a rock in the midst and look out over the furry expanse it is so mottled and splashed and gay with color and frisking sheen and sun-flash, and so rippled with stripes, that you might think it was a lake, only you know it isn't; and there's storms of sociable birds, and hurricanes of whirring wings; and when the sun strikes all that feathery commotion, you have a blazing up of all the colors you can think of, enough to put your eyes out.

We have made long excursions, and I have seen a great deal of the world; almost all of it, I think; and so I am the first traveler, and the only one. When we are on the march, it is an imposing sight—there's nothing like it anywhere. For comfort I ride a tiger or a leopard, because it is soft and has a round back that fits me, and because they are such pretty animals; but for long distance or for scenery I ride the elephant. He hoists me up with his trunk, but I can get off myself; when we are ready to camp, he sits and I slide down the back way.

The birds and animals are all friendly to each other, and there are no disputes about anything. They all talk, and they all talk to me, but it must be a foreign language, for I cannot make out a word they say; yet they often understand me when I talk back, particularly the dog and the elephant. It makes me ashamed. It shows that they are brighter than I am, and are therefore my superiors. It annoys me, for I want to be the principal Experiment myself—and I intend to be, too.

I have learned a number of things, and am educated, now, but I wasn't at first. I was ignorant at first. At first it used to vex me because, with all my watching, I was never smart enough to be around when the water was running uphill; but now I do not mind it. I have experimented and experimented until now I know it never does run uphill, except in the dark. I know it does in the dark, because the pool never goes dry, which it would, of course, if the water didn't come back in the night. It is best to prove things by actual experiment; then you *know;* whereas if you depend on guessing and supposing and conjecturing, you will never get educated.

Some things you *can't* find out; but you will never know you can't by guessing and supposing: no, you have to be patient and go on experimenting until you find out that you can't find out. And it is delightful to have it that way, it makes the world so interesting. If there wasn't anything to find out, it would be dull. Even trying to find out and not finding out is just as interesting as trying to find out and finding out, and I don't know but more so. The secret of the water was a treasure until I *got* it; then the excitement all went away, and I recognized a sense of loss.

By experiment I know that wood swims, and dry leaves, and feathers, and plenty of other things; therefore by all that cumulative evidence you know that a rock will swim; but you have to put up with simply knowing it, for there isn't any way to prove it—up to now. But I shall find a way—then *that* excitement will go. Such things make me sad; because by and by when I have found out everything there won't be any more excitements, and I do love excitements so! The other night I couldn't sleep for thinking about it.

At first I couldn't make out what I was made for, but now I think it was to search out the secrets of this wonderful world and be happy and thank the Giver of it all for devising it. I think there are many things to learn yet—I hope so; and by economizing and not hurrying too fast I think they will last weeks and weeks. I hope so. When you cast up a feather it sails away on the air and goes out of sight; then you throw up a clod and it doesn't. It comes down, every time. I have tried it and tried it, and it is always so. I wonder why it is? Of course it *doesn't* come down, but why should it *seem* to? I suppose it is an optical illusion. I mean, one of them is. I don't know which one. It may be the feather, it may be the clod; I can't prove which it is, I can only demonstrate that one or the other is a fake, and let a person take his choice.

By watching, I know that the stars are not going to last. I have seen some of the best ones melt and run down the sky. Since one can melt, they can all melt; since they can all melt, they can all melt the same night. That sorrow will come—I know it. I mean to sit up every night and look at them as long as I can keep awake; and I will impress those sparkling fields on my memory, so that by and by when they are taken away I can by my fancy restore those lovely myriads to the black sky and make them sparkle again, and double them by the blur of my tears.

AFTER THE FALL

When I look back, the Garden is a dream to me. It was beautiful, surpassingly beautiful, enchantingly beautiful; and now it is lost, and I shall not see it any more.

The Garden is lost, but I have found *him,* and am content. He loves me as well as he can; I love him with all the strength of my passionate nature, and this, I think, is proper to my youth and sex. If I ask myself why I love him, I find I do not know, and do not really much care to know; so I suppose that this kind of love is not a product of reasoning and statistics, like one's love for other reptiles and animals. I think that this must be so. I love certain birds because of their song; but I do not love Adam on account of his singing—no, it is not that; the more he sings the more I do not get reconciled to it. Yet I ask him to sing, because I wish to learn to like everything he is interested in. I am sure I can learn, because at first I could not stand it, but now I can. It sours the milk, but it doesn't matter; I can get used to that kind of milk.

It is not on account of his brightness that I love him—no, it is not that. He is not to blame for his brightness, such as it is, for he did not make it himself; he is as God made him, and that is sufficient. There was a wise purpose in it, *that* I know. In time it will develop, though I think it will not be sudden; and besides, there is no hurry; he is well enough just as he is.

It is not on account of his gracious and considerate ways and his delicacy that I love him. No, he has lacks in these regards, but he is well enough just so, and is improving.

It is not on account of his industry that I love him—no, it is not that. I think he has it in him, and I do not know why he conceals it from me. It is my only pain. Otherwise he is frank and open with me, now. I am sure he keeps nothing from me but this. It grieves me that he should have a secret from me, and sometimes it spoils my sleep, thinking of it, but I will put it out of my mind; it shall not trouble my happiness, which is otherwise full to overflowing.

It is not on account of his education that I love him—no, it is not that. He is self-educated, and does really know a multitude of things, but they are not so.

It is not on account of his chivalry that I love him—no, it is not that. He told on me, but I do not blame him; it is a peculiarity of sex, I think, and he did not make his sex. Of course I would not have told on him, I would have perished first; but that is a peculiarity of sex, too, and I do not take credit for it, for I did not make my sex.

Then why is it that I love him? *Merely because he is masculine,* I think.

At bottom he is good, and I love him for that, but I could love him without it. If he should beat me and abuse me, I should go on loving him. I know it. It is a matter of sex, I think.

He is strong and handsome, and I love him for that, and I admire him and am proud of him, but I could love him without those qualities. If he were plain, I should love him; if he were a wreck, I should love him; and I would work for him, and slave over him, and pray for him, and watch by his bedside until I died.

Yes, I think I love him merely because he is *mine* and is *masculine.* There is no other reason, I suppose. And so I think it is as I first said: that this kind of love is not a product of reasonings and statistics. It just *comes*—none knows whence—and cannot explain itself. And doesn't need to. It is what I think. But I am only a girl, and the first that has examined this matter, and it may turn out that in my ignorance and inexperience I have not got it right.

Forty Years Later

It is my prayer, it is my longing, that we may pass from this life together—a longing which shall never perish from the earth, but shall have place in the heart of every wife that loves, until the end of time; and it shall be called by my name.

But if one of us must go first, it is my prayer that it shall be I; for he is strong, I am weak, I am not so necessary to him as he is to me—life without him would not be life; how could I endure it? This prayer is also immortal, and will not cease from being offered up while my race continues. I am the first wife; and in the last wife I shall be repeated.

At Eve's Grave

ADAM: Wheresoever she was, *there* was Eden.

MRS. CONFEDRINGTON

Mary Walker

In the narrow street behind the church was a cafe with lace curtains and glass-topped tables where Mrs. Confedrington drank coffee on market days between her shopping.

It was Friday morning and she stood at the counter waiting for the girl to finish her row of knitting and take the fourpence. An impressive row of bottled fruits filled the shelf high on the wall behind the counter. The jars were arranged in careful order, the tallest at the ends and the shortest in the middle, like a platoon drawn up for inspection. Mrs. Confedrington inspected them. The last loop of wool slipped over the points and joined the other stitches, leaving one long green needle bare.

"Yes?" said the girl. She had curly blond hair ("The Bleach That Hollywood Prefers") and wide green eyes and a soft little mouth for draping round chocolates and popular songs about love.

Mrs. Confedrington caught a refreshing glimpse of her own face in the mirror under the gooseberry jars.

"Ha!" she said. "One coffee, miss." She swept four pennies across the counter with a thin, rather dirty hand, and noted with further refreshment the interesting length of her nicotine-soaked fingers.

The vicar overtook her at the door. "Your umbrella, Mrs. Confedrington."

It was an old, a sensible umbrella, with a yellow handle like a rigid banana. But there was no longer an old, sensible vicar; only this young man with his heavy horn-rimmed glasses and a smell of incense about him. Not that it mattered a toss to Mrs. Confedrington.

"Thank you." She saw his eyes lingering over her and wondered what were his conclusions.

She strode into the street, though it was not her custom to stride, for she thought it the duty of women to be beautiful.

"What a hat!" said the young vicar cautiously, under his breath, as he returned to his coffee, and pianissimo, "What a face!"

As she turned the corner into the main street a child tugging on her mother's hand paused in mid-blow at her celluloid windmill. "Mummy!" said her awed, clear voice, "Look!"

Mrs. Confedrington passed superbly on to the butcher's. " 'Ere comes 'Elen of Troy," said the young assistant to Mr. Flaxman. Flaxman grunted, moving his hands, themselves like lumps of frozen meat, among the bloody carvings of the slab.

Protective coloration, Mrs. Confedrington thought, remembering botany lessons of thirty years ago. Not so protective, though. Suppose he should suddenly hack one of them off in mistake for a chop?

If he had sold it to her she woud certainly have cooked it and she and Leopold would have eaten it unaware. It was no great matter what dish appeared at that table where Leopold sat hunched over the composition of his daily crossword puzzle with a dictionary of quotations at his elbow and his spectacles pushed up on his forehead, while his wife, lost to the world, tipped her chair forward and peered at the *Collected Poems of T. S. Eliot* propped on the vinegar and mustard half of an old-fashioned cruet.

Four glass cherries and a long marguerite flourished on her black straw hat.

[501]

" 'Ighly unsuitable," said Mr. Flaxman, shaking his head between two hanging strings of sausage, as he watched her approach. No need to make people look when she had a nose that size to start with and a mouth going all ways at one time and eyes like a fish that has been dead a long time.

"Well, mum, what will it be?"

She knew what he was thinking and it still amused her, after all the years he had been thinking it. Poor Flaxman! Year in, year out at his grisly trade, what would he know of beauty?

Her turn for liver. He wrapped it roughly and finished the parcel with an outer sheet of newspaper.

She remembered Leopold, peevish at the breakfast table. "I do like a paper with some guts in it," he'd said. She gave a shout of laughter, and the cherries battered on the daisy petals.

"Is she cracked as well, Mr. Flaxman?" asked the assistant in a hushed voice when she had left the shop.

"Absolutely dotty, 'Erbert."

"I'd not like to be 'er old man," said Herbert, sniggering.

Mr. Flaxman took up a long knife and wiped the blade across his white apron. "Don't matter to 'im. 'E's as cracked as she is."

Swinging her basket, Mrs. Confedrington passed serenely down High Street. Serenely conscious she was of the impact of her surrealist beauty that withered the passers by.

They're not ready for me, she told herself. Any more than they were ready for the great artists—the nearsighted, conventional minds. She likened herself to a picture by Picasso, a masterpiece that had beauty only for the initiated few. And then, of course, she began to think of Leopold.

At that moment Leopold was on his way to the spare room to look at his silkworms. He had finished the puzzle early and was prowling about the house disconsolately in his black velvet smoking jacket, waiting for Mrs. Confedrington to come home.

The silkworms were in a large shoe box with a pattern of holes pierced in the lid. "Black Gents Shoes, Size 9," the label said. He chuckled as he raised the lid. "Odd. I don't know any black gents." He let a little extra light into the box and peered under the raised lid at the soft yellow cocoons inside. "Nearly had your sleep out now," he told them. "You'll be glad to wake up—'catching your heart up at the feel of June'," he added. Leopold's solvers were literary types who thrived on quotation and allusion, so that he should hardly open his mouth any more without someone else's words coming out of it. "They'll have caught their hearts up long before June, anyway," he muttered irritably, and closed the lid and wandered into the front bedroom. He stared out the window, wishing for her to come home.

Suddenly she was there, inside the gate, under the monkey puzzle tree. He waved and she brandished her basket at him.

" 'She walks in beauty, like the night'," he whispered as he ran downstairs to meet her. "I missed you," he said.

"That was nice of you. Let's sit down for a minute."

They sat side by side on the stairs and stretched their legs out comfortably. She pointed to the parcel of liver. "A paper with some guts in it," she said, and he laughed delightedly.

"Do you know my silkworms are in a box that says, 'black gents shoes'? And the joke of it is I don't know a single Negro."

She gave her habitual shout of appreciation. "Leopold," she said a moment later, "there is no one else like us in the world; we are the same one. I walk in your sleep and you talk in my dreams. Leopold, do you think we have invented each other?"

"If we have, you are most talented— and I am a genius."

"I can't remember any life before you."

" 'I wonder, by my troth, what thou and I did till we loved'," Leopold mused, trying to think far back, then he looked up at her quickly. "That's a fine hat. A completely esoteric hat. Other women never wear hats like that."

"No," she said, "No." And she took off the hat she had held in her lap, cuddling the glass fruit with her interesting fingers.

Leopold sprang up briskly. "Beans on toast and coffee for lunch. I'll make it."

When he had gone she rose slowly and went up the stairs, smiling, queening it, a collector's piece. The collector, meanwhile, hacked away in the kitchen, opening a tin of beans.

Mrs. Confedrington took the esoteric hat into her bedroom and laid it carefully on the bed. She went to the mirror and began to comb her hair. She could see out of the tail of her eye the window cleaner outside on his ladder, polishing the panes with a wash leather. It was best to ignore him. She went on calmly with her combing.

With a single exception of Leopold, Mrs. Confedrington had always avoided encounter. There was, alas, so little appreciation in the world. But sometimes she misjudged. As in the case of Sammy Cohen out there on the ladder, for instance.

Sammy gave up all pretense of polishing when he saw her and leaned one elbow on the top rung and gazed in, watching the vigorous movement of the comb through her thick hair.

Lunch with Leopold, Mrs. Confedrington was saying to herself. He was burning the toast, she realized, but what did it matter? What mattered was the oneness, the aloneness, the savoring of beauty that was only for the two of them.

But Leopold, stirring the coffee, had a sudden glimpse of catastrophe and rushed to the bottom of the stairs. Supposing their alone-togetherness should end, supposing people should begin to know better and popular taste, and should crowd him out? "Rachel!" he cried.

She smiled a little at the panic in his voice. What should he fear? None but he would ever have an eye for her secrets.

And yet the encroaching waves were already lapping around their walls. Sammy Cohen, outside on the ladder, was nobody's fool. He went to W. E. A. classes and could read novels in Esperanto.

As Mrs. Confedrington ran out of the room and down the stairs to the unique Leopold, "Ah!" said Sammy Cohen. "What a beautiful woman!"

THE ARTIST LOOKS AT THE STARS
AND OTHER THINGS

Henry Miller

Henry Miller's *The Colossus of Maroussi* is a book about Greece and Miller's travels there in the late 1930s in the company of the English novelist and poet, Lawrence Durrell.

BETWEEN the time of my return and my departure for Crete three or four little incidents occurred which I feel impelled to make brief mention of. The first was "Juarez," the American film which ran for several weeks at one of the leading theatres. Despite the fact that Greece is under a dictatorship this film, which was only slightly modified after the first few showings, was shown night and day to an increasingly packed house. The atmosphere was tense, the applause distinctly Republican. For many reasons the film had acute significance for the Greek people. One felt that the spirit of Venizelos was still alive. In that blunt and magnificent speech which Juarez makes to the assembled plenipotentiaries of the foreign powers one felt that the tragic plight of Mexico under Maximilian had curious and throbbing analogies with the present perilous position of Greece. The only true friend which Greece has at this moment, the only relatively disinterested one, is America. Of that I shall have more to say when I come to Crete, the birthplace of Venizelos as well as of El Greco. But to witness the showing of a film in which all forms of dictatorship is dramatically denounced, to witness it in the midst of an audience whose hands are tied, except to applaud, is an impressive event. It was one of those rare moments when I felt that, in a world which is almost entirely gagged, shackled and manacled, to be an American is almost a luxury.

The second event was a visit to the astronomical observatory in Athens, arranged for Durrell and myself by Theodore Stephanides who, as an amateur astronomer, has made admittedly important astronomical discoveries. The officials received us very cordially, thanks to the generous aid given them by American fellow-workers in this field. I had never looked through the telescope of a bona fide observatory before. Nor had Durrell, I presume. The experience was sensational, though probably not altogether in accord with the expectations of our hosts. Our remarks, which were juvenile and ecstatic, seemed to bewilder them. We certainly did not display the orthodox reactions to the wonders that were unfolded. I shall never forget their utter amazement when Durrell, who was gazing at the Pleiades, suddenly exclaimed— *"Rosicrucian!"* What did he mean by that? they wanted to know. I mounted the ladder and took a look for myself. I doubt if I can describe the effect of that first breathless vision of a splintered star world. The image I shall always retain is that of Chartres, an effulgent rose window shattered by a hand grenade. I mean it in a double or triple sense—of awesome, indestructible beauty, of cosmic violation, of world ruin suspended in the sky like a fatal omen, of the eternality of beauty even when blasted and desecrated. "As above so below," runs the famous saying of Hermes Trismegistus. To see the Pleiades through a powerful telescope is to sense the sublime and awesome truth of these words. In his highest flights, musical and architectural above all, for they are one, man gives the illusion of rivalling the order, the majesty and the splendor of the heavens; in his fits of destruction the evil and the desolation which he spreads seems incomparable until we reflect on the great stellar shake-ups brought on by the mental aberrations of the unknown Wizard. Our hosts seemed impervious to such reflections; they spoke knowingly of weights, distances, substances, etc. They were removed from the normal activities of their fellow-men in a quite different way from ourselves. For them beauty was incidental, for us everything. For them the physicomathematical world palped, calibred, weighed and transmitted by their instruments was reality itself, the stars and planets mere proof of their excellent and infallible reasoning. For Durrell and myself reality lay wholly beyond the reach of their puny instruments which in themselves were nothing more than clumsy reflections of their circumscribed imagination locked forever in the hypothetical prison of logic. Their astronomical figures and calculations, intended to impress and overawe us, only caused us to smile indulgently or to very impolitely laugh outright at them. Speaking for myself, facts and figures have always left me unimpressed. A light year is no more impressive to me than a second, or a split second. This is a game for the feeble-minded which can go on ad nauseam backwards and forwards without taking us anywhere. Similarly I am not more convinced of the reality of a star when I see it through the telescope. It may be more brilliant, more wondrous, it may be a thousand times or a million times bigger than when seen with the naked eye, but it is not a whit more real. To say that this is what a thing *really* looks like, just because one sees it larger and grander, seems to me quite fatuous. It is just as real to me if I don't see it at all but merely imagine it to be there. And

finally, even when to my own eye and the eye of the astronomer it possesses the same dimensions, the same brilliance, it definitely does not look the same to us both—Durrell's very exclamation is sufficient to prove that.

But let us pass on—to Saturn. Saturn, and our moon likewise, when seen through a magnifying lens, are impressive to the layman in a way which the scientist must instinctively deplore and deprecate. No facts or figures about Saturn, no magnification, can explain the unreasonably disquieting sensation which the sight of this planet produces upon the mind of the spectator. Saturn is a living symbol of gloom, morbidity, disaster, fatality. Its milk-white hue inevitably arouses associations with tripe, dead gray matter, vulnerable organs hidden from sight, loathsome diseases, test-tubes, laboratory specimens, catarrh, rheum, ectoplasm, melancholy shades, morbid phenomena, incuba and succuba, war, sterility, anaemia, indecision, defeatism, constipation, anti-toxins, feeble novels, hernia, meningitis, dead-letter laws, red tape, working class conditions, sweat shops, Y. M. C. A's, Christian Endeavor meetings, spiritist seances, poets like T. S. Eliot, zealots like Alexander Dowie, healers like Mary Baker Eddy, statesmen like Chamberlain, trivial fatalities like slipping on a banana peel and cracking one's skull, dreaming of better days and getting wedged between two motor trucks, drowning in one's own bathtub, killing one's best friend accidentally, dying of hiccoughs instead of on the battle field, and so on ad infinitum. Saturn is malefic through force of inertia. Its ring, which is only paperweight in thickness, according to the savants, is the wedding ring which signifies death or misfortune devoid of all significance. Saturn, whatever it may be to the astronomer, is the sign of senseless fatality to the man in the street. He carries it in his heart because his whole life, devoid of significance as it is, is wrapped up in this ultimate symbol which, if all else fails to do him in, this he can count upon to finish him off. Saturn is life in suspense, not dead so much as deathless, i.e. incabale of dying. Saturn is like dead bone in the ear—double mastoid for the soul. Saturn is like a roll of wall-paper wrong side out and smeared with that catarrhal paste which wall-paperers find so indispensable in their metier. Saturn is a vast agglomeration of those evil looking shreds which one hawks up the morning after he has smoked several packs of crisp, toasted, coughless, inspiring cigarettes. Saturn is postponement manifesting itself as an accomplishment in itself. Saturn is doubt, perplexity, scepticism, facts for fact's sake and no hokum, no mysticism, understand? Saturn is the diabolical sweat of learning for its own sake, the congealed fog of the monomaniac's ceaseless pursuit of what is always just beyond his nose. Saturn is deliciously melancholic because it knows and recognizes nothing beyond melancholy; it swims in its own fat. Saturn is the symbol of all omens and superstitions, the phony proof of divine entropy, phony because if it were true that the universe is running down Saturn would have melted away long ago. Saturn is as eternal as fear and irresolution, growing more milky, more cloudy, with each compromise, each capitulation. Timid souls cry for Saturn just as children are reputed to cry for Castoria. Saturn gives us only what we ask for, never an ounce extra. Saturn is the white hope of the white race which prattles endlessly about the wonders of nature and spends its time killing off the greatest wonder of all—MAN. Saturn is the stellar impostor setting itself up as the grand cosmocrator of Fate, Monsieur le Paris, the automatic pole-axer of a world smitten with ataraxy. Let the heavens sing its glory—this lymphatic globe of doubt and ennui will never cease to cast its milk-white rays of lifeless gloom.

This is the emotional photograph of a planet whose unorthodox influence still weighs heavily upon the almost extinct consciousness of man. It is the most cheerless spectacle in the heavens. It corresponds to every craven image conceived in the heart of man; it is the single repository of all the despair and defeat to which the human race from time immemorial has succumbed. It will become invisible only when man has purged it from his consciousness.

The third event was of a wholy different order—a jazz seance at the austere bachelor chambers of Seferiades in the Rue Kydathenaion, one of the streets I was instinctively attracted to on my first exploration of Athens. Seferiades, who is a cross between bull and panther by nature, has strong Virgo traits, speaking astrologically. That is to say, he has a passion for collecting, as did Goethe who was one of the best Virgo types the world has ever known. The first shock I had on entering his placc on this particular occasion was that of meeting his most gracious and most lovely sister, Jeanne. She impressed me immediately as being of royal descent, perhaps of the Egyptian line—in any case, distinctly trans-Pontine. As I was gazing at her ecstatically I was suddenly startled by the sound of Cab Calloway's baboon-like voice. Seferiades looked at me with that warm Asiatic smile which always spread over his face like nectar and ambrosia. "Do you know that piece?" he said, beaming with pleasure. "I have some others, if you'd care to hear them," and he pointed to a file of albums about a yard long. "What about Louis Armstrong, do you like him?" he continued. "Here's a Fats Waller record. Wait a minute, have you ever heard Count Basie—or Peewee Russell?" He knew every virtuoso of any account; he was a subscriber to "Le Jazz Hot" I soon discovered. In a few moments we were talking about the Café Boudon in Montmartre where the great Negro performers of the night clubs repair before and after work. He wanted to hear about the American Negro, about life behind the scene. What influence did the Negro have upon American life, what did the American people think of Negro literature? Was it true that there was a Negro aristocracy, a cultural aristocracy which was superior to the white American cultural groups? Could a man like Duke Ellington register at the Savoy-Plaza without embarrassment? What about Caldwell and Faulkner—was it a true picture of the South which they gave? And so on. As I've remarked before, Seferiades is an indefatigable questioner. No detail is too trivial for him to overlook. His curiosity is insatiable, his knowledge vast and varied. After entertaining me with a selection of the most up to date jazz numbers he wanted to know if I should like to hear some exotic music of which he had an interesting variety. While searching for a record he would ply me with questions about some recondite English poet or about the circumstances surrounding Ambrose Bierce's disappearance or what did I know about the Greenberg manuscripts which Hart Crane had made use of. Or, having found the record he was looking for he would suddenly switch to a little anecdote about his life in Albania which, in some curiously dissociated way, had to do with a poem by T. S. Eliot or St. Jean Perse. I speak of these divagations of his because they were a refreshing antidote to the sort of obsessive, single-tracked and wholly mirthless order of conversation indulged in by the English literati in Athens. An evening with these buttery-mouthed jakes always left me in a suicidal mood. A Greek is alive to the finger-tips; he oozes vitality, he's effervescent, he's ubiquitous in spirit. The Englishman is lymphatic, made for the arm-chair, the fireside, the dingy tavern, the didactic tread-mill. Durrell used to take a perverse delight in observing my discomfiture in the presence of his countrymen: they were one and all like animated cartoons from his "Black Book," that devastating

chronicle of the English death. In the presence of an Englishman Katsimbalis would positively dry up. Nobody really hated them—they were simply insufferable.

Later that evening I had the privilege of meeting some Greek women, friends of Seferiades' sister. Here again I was impressed by the absence of those glaring defects which make even the most beautiful American or English woman seem positively ugly. The Greek woman, even when she is cultured, is first and foremost a woman. She sheds a distinct fragrance; she warms and thrills you. Due to the absorption of Greeks from Asia Minor the new generation of Athenian womanhood has improved in beauty and vigor. The ordinary Greek girl whom one sees on the street is superior in every way to her American counterpart; above all she has character and race, a combination which makes for deathless beauty and which forever distinguishes the descendants of ancient peoples from the bastard off-shoots of the New World. How can I ever forget the young girl whom we passed one day at the foot of the Acropolis? Perhaps she was ten, perhaps she was fourteen years of age; her hair was reddish gold, her features as noble, as grave and austere as those of the caryatids on the Erectheum. She was playing with some comrades in a little clearing before a clump of ramshackle shanties which had somehow escaped the general demolition. Any one who has read "Death in Venice" will appreciate my sincerity when I say that no woman, not even the loveliest woman I have ever seen, is or was capable of arousing in me such a feeling of adoration as this young girl elicited. If Fate were to put her in my path again I know not what folly I might commit. She was child, virgin, angel, seductress, priestess, harlot, prophetess all in one. She was neither ancient Greek nor modern Greek; she was of no race or time or class, but unique, fabulously unique. In that slow, sustained smile which she gave us as we paused a moment to gaze at her there was that enigmatic quality which da Vinci has immortalized, which one finds everywhere in Buddhistic art, which one finds in the great caves of India and on the facades of her temples, which one finds in the dancers of Java and of Bali and in primitive races, especialy in Africa; which indeed seems to be the culminating expression of the spiritual achievement of the human race, but which to-day is totally absent in the countenance of the Western woman. Let me add a strange reflection—that the nearest approximation to this enigmatic quality which I ever noted was in the smile of a peasant woman at Corfu, a woman with six toes, decidedly ugly, and considered by every one as something of a monster. She used to come to the well, as is the custom of the peasant women, to fill her jug, to do her washing, and to gossip. The well was situated at the foot of a steep declivity around which there wandered a goat-like path. In every direction there were thick shady olive groves broken here and there by ravines which formed the beds of mountain streams which in Summer were completely dried up. The well had an extraordinary fascination for me; it was a place reserved for the female beast of burden, for the strong, buxom virgin who could carry her jug of water strapped to her back with grace and ease, for the old toothless hag whose curved back was still capable of sustaining a staggering load of firewood, for the widow with her straggling flock of children, for the servant girls who laughed too easily, for wives who took over the work of their lazy husbands, for every species of female, in short, except the grand mistress or the idle English women of the vicinity. When I first saw the women staggering up the steep slopes, like the women of old in the Bible, I felt a pang of distress. The very manner of strapping the heavy jug to the back gave me a feeling of humiliation. The more so

because the men who might have performed this humble task were more than likely sitting in the cool of a tavern or lying prone under an olive tree. My first thought was to relieve the young maid at our house of a minor task; I wanted to feel one of those jugs on my own back, to know with my own muscular aches what that repeated journey to the well meant. When I communicated my desire to Durrell he threw up his hands in horror. It wasn't done, he exclaimed, laughing at my ignorance. I told him it didn't matter to me in the least whether it was done or not done, that he was robbing me of a joy which I had never tasted. He begged me not to do it, for *his* sake—he said he would lose caste, that the Greeks would laugh at us. In short, he made such a point of it that I was obliged to abandon the idea. But on my rambles through the hills I usually made a point of stopping at the well to slake my thirst. There one day I espied the monster with six toes. She was standing in her bare feet, ankle deep in mud, washing a bundle of clothes. That she was ugly I could not deny, but there are all kinds of ugliness and hers was the sort which instead of repelling attracts. To begin with she was strong, sinewy, vital, an animal endowed with a human soul and with indisputable sexual powers. When she bent over to wring out a pair of pants the vitality in her limbs rippled and flashed through the tattered and bedraggled skirt which clung to her swarthy flesh. Her eyes glowed like coals, like the eyes of a Bedouin woman. Her lips were blood red and her strong even teeth as white as chalk. The thick black hair hung over her shoulders in rich, oily strands, as though saturated with olive oil. Renoir would have found her beautiful; he would not have noticed the six toes or the coarseness of her features. He would have followed the rippling flesh, the full globes of her teats, the easy, swaying stance, the superabundant strength of her arms, her legs, her torso; he would have been ravished by the full, generous slit of the mouth, by the dark and burning glance of the eye, by the massive contours of the head and the gleaming black waves which fell in cascades down her sturdy, columnar neck. He would have caught the animal lust, the ardor unquenchable, the fire in the guts, the tenacity of the tigress, the hunger, the rapacity, the all-devouring appetite of the oversexed female who is not wanted because she has an extra toe.

Anyhow, Renoir apart, there was something in this woman's smile which the sight of the young girl at the base of the Acropolis revived. I said it was the nearest approximation to that enigmatic quality engraved in the countenance of the girl with the reddish gold hair. By that, paradoxical though it may sound, I mean that it was wholly antipodal. The monster might well have been the one to give birth to that startling figure of beauty; she might because in her starved dream of love her embrace had spanned a void beyond the imagination of the most desperately love-lorn woman. All her powers of seduction had been driven back into the coffin of sex where, in the darkness of her loins, passion and desire burned to a thick smoke. Disclaiming all hope of seducing man her lust had turned towards forbidden objects of desire—towards the animals of the field, towards inanimate things, towards objects of veneration, towards mythological deities. Her smile had in it something of the intoxication of parched earth after a sudden and furious downpour; it was the smile of the insatiable one to whom a thousand burning kisses are only the incentive to renewed assaults. In some strange and inexplicable fashion she has remained in my memory as the symbol of that hunger for unbounded love which I sensed in a lesser degree in all Greek women. It is almost the symbol of Greece itself, this unappeasable lust for beauty, passion, love.

LOVE WINGED MY HOPES

Love winged my hopes and taught me how to fly
Far from base earth, but not to mount too high:
    For true pleasure
    Lives in measure,
    Which if men forsake,   5
Blinded, they into folly run, and grief for pleasure take.

But my vain hopes, proud of their new-taught flight,
Enamored, sought to woo the sun's fair light,
    Whose rich brightnes
    Moved their lightness   10
    To aspire so high
That, all scorched and consumed with fire, now drowned in woe they lie.

And none but Love their woeful hap did rue,
For Love did not know that their desires were true;
    Though Fate frownèd,   15
    And now drownèd
    They in sorrow dwell;
It was the purest light of heaven for whose fair love they fell.

ANONYMOUS

IN WESTMINSTER ABBEY

Let me take this other glove off
    As the *vox humana* [1] swells,
And the beauteous fields of Eden
    Bask beneath the Abbey bells.
Here, where England's statesmen lie,   5
Listen to a lady's cry.

Gracious Lord, oh bomb the Germans.
    Spare their women for Thy Sake,
And if that is not too easy
    We will pardon Thy Mistake.   10
But, gracious Lord, whate'er shall be,
Don't let anyone bomb me.

Keep our Empire undismembered
    Guide our Forces by Thy Hand,
Gallant blacks from far Jamaica,   15
    Honduras and Togoland;

[1] An organ reed stop made to give a sound imitative of the human voice.

Protect them Lord in all their fights,
And, even more, protect the whites.

Think of what our Nation stands for,
   Books from Boots' and country lanes,   20
Free speech, free passes, class distinction,
   Democracy and proper drains.
Lord, put beneath Thy special care
One-eighty-nine Cadogan Square.

Although dear Lord I am a sinner,   25
   I have done no major crime;
Now I'll come to Evening Service
   Whensoever I have time.
So, Lord, reserve for me a crown,
And do not let my shares go down.   30

I will labour for Thy Kingdom,
   Help our lads to win the war,
Send white feathers to the cowards,
   Join the Women's Army Corps,
Then wash the Steps around Thy Throne   35
In the Eternal Safety Zone.

Now I feel a little better,
   What a treat to hear Thy Word,
Where the bones of leading statesmen,
   Have so often been interred.   40
And now, dear Lord, I cannot wait
Because I have a luncheon date.

JOHN BETJEMAN

AUGURIES OF INNOCENCE

To see a world in a grain of sand,
   And a heaven in a wild flower;
Hold infinity in the palm of your hand,
   And eternity in an hour.

A robin redbreast in a cage   5
Puts all heaven in a rage;
A dove-house filled with doves and pigeons
Shudders hell through all its regions.
A dog starved at his master's gate
Predicts the ruin of the state.   10

A game-cock clipped and armed for fight
Doth the rising sun affright;
A horse misused upon the road
Calls to heaven for human blood.
Every wolf's and lion's howl   15
Raises from hell a human soul;
Each outcry of the hunted hare
A fibre from the brain does tear;
A skylark wounded on the wing
Doth make a cherub cease to sing.   20
He who shall hurt the little wren
Shall never be beloved by men;
He who the ox to wrath has moved
Shall never be by woman loved;
He who shall train the horse to war   25
Shall never pass the polar bar.
The wanton boy that kills the fly
Shall feel the spider's enmity;
He who torments the chafer's sprite
Weaves a bower in endless night.   30
The caterpillar on the leaf
Repeats to thee thy mother's grief;
The wild deer wandering here and there
Keep the human soul from care;
The lamb misused breeds public strife,   35
And yet forgives the butcher's knife.
Kill not the moth nor butterfly,
For the last judgment draweth nigh;
The beggar's dog and widow's cat,
Feed them and thou shalt grow fat.   40
Every tear from every eye
Becomes a babe in eternity;
The bleat, the bark, bellow, and roar,
Are waves that beat on heaven's shore.

The bat, that flits at close of eve,   45
Has left the brain that won't believe;
The owl, that calls upon the night,
Speaks the unbeliever's fright;
The gnat, that sings his summer's song,
Poison gets from Slander's tongue;   50
The poison of the snake and newt
Is the sweat of Envy's foot;
The poison of the honey-bee
Is the artist's jealousy;
The strongest poison ever known   55
Came from Caesar's laurel crown.
Nought can deform the human race
Like to the armorer's iron brace;

The soldier armed with sword and gun
Palsied strikes the summer's sun.   60
When gold and gems adorn the plough,
To peaceful arts shall Envy bow.
The beggar's rags fluttering in air
Do to rags the heavens tear;
The prince's robes and beggar's rags   65
Are toadstools on the miser's bags.

One mite wrung from the laborer's hands
Shall buy and sell the miser's lands,
Or, if protected from on high,
Shall that whole nation sell and buy;   70
The poor man's farthing is worth more
Than all the gold on Afric's shore.
The whore and gambler, by the state
Licensed, built that nation's fate;
The harlot's cry from street to street   75
Shall weave Old England's winding sheet;
The winner's shout, the loser's curse,
Shall dance before dead England's hearse.

He who mocks the infant's faith
Shall be mocked in age and death;   80
He who shall teach the child to doubt
The rotting grave shall ne'er get out;
He who respects the infant's faith
Triumphs over hell and death.
The babe is more than swaddling-bands   85
Throughout all these human lands;
Tools were made, and born were hands,
Every farmer understands.

The questioner who sits so sly
Shall never know how to reply;   90
He who replies to words of doubt
Doth put the light of knowledge out;
A riddle, or the cricket's cry,
Is to doubt a fit reply.
The child's toys and the old man's reasons   95
Are the fruits of the two seasons.
The emmet's inch and eagle's mile
Make lame philosophy to smile.
A truth that's told with bad intent
Beats all the lies you can invent.   100
He who doubts from what he sees
Will ne'er believe, do what you please;
If the sun and moon should doubt,
They'd immediately go out.

Every night and every morn 105
Some to misery are born;
Every morn and every night
Some are born to sweet delight;
Some are born to sweet delight,
Some are born to endless night. 110
Joy and woe are woven fine,
A clothing for the soul divine;
Under every grief and pine
Runs a joy with silken twine.
It is right it should be so; 115
Man was made for joy and woe;
And, when this we rightly know,
Safely through the world we go.

We are led to believe a lie
When we see *with* not *through* the eye, 120
Which was born in a night to perish in a night
When the soul slept in beams of light.
God appears, and God is light
To those poor souls who dwell in night,
But doth a human form display 125
To those who dwell in realms of day.

WILLIAM BLAKE

THE CLOD AND THE PEBBLE

"Love seeketh not Itself to please,
Nor for itself hath any care,
But for another gives its ease,
And builds a Heaven in Hell's despair."

So sung a little Clod of Clay 5
Trodden with the cattle's feet,
But a Pebble of the brook
Warbled out these metres meet:

"Love seeketh only Self to please,
To bind another to Its delight, 10
Joys in another's loss of ease,
And builds a Hell in Heaven's despite."

WILLIAM BLAKE

FOR THE SEXES, THE GATES OF PARADISE

PROLOGUE

Mutual Forgivenes of each Vice,
Such are the Gates of Paradise.
Against the Accuser's chief desire,
Who walk'd among the Stones of Fire,
Jehovah's Finger Wrote the Law: 5
Then Wept! then rose in Zeal & Awe,
And the Dead Corpse from Sinai's heat
Buried beneath his Mercy Seat.
O Christians, Christians! tell me Why
You rear it on your Altars high.   10

THE KEYS

The Catterpiller on the Leaf
Reminds thee of thy Mother's Grief.

OF THE GATES

My Eternal Man set in Repose,
The Female from his darknes rose
And she found me beneath a Tree,   15
A Mandrake, & in her Veil hid me.
Serpent Reasonings us entice
Of Good & Evil, Virtue & Vice.
Doubt Self Jealous, Wat'ry folly,
Struggling thro' Earth's Melancholy.   20
Naked in Air, in Shame & Fear,
Blind in Fire with shield & spear,
Two Horn'd Reasoning, Cloven Fiction,
In Doubt, which is Self contradiction,
A dark Hermaphodite We stood,   25
Rational Truth, Root of Evil & Good.
Round me flew the Flaming Sword;
Round her snowy Whirlwinds roar'd,
Freezing her Veil, the Mundane Shell.
I rent the Veil where the Dead dwell: 30
When weary Man enters his Cave
He meets his Saviour in the Grave.
Some find a Female Garment there,
And some a Male, Woven with care,
Lest the Sexual Garments sweet   35
Should grow a devouring Winding sheet.
One Dies! Alas! the Living & Dead,
One is slain & One is fled.
In Vain-glory hatcht & nurst,
By double Spectres Self Accurst,   40

My Son! my Son! thou treatest me
But as I have instructed thee.
On the shadows of the Moon
Climbing thro' Night's highest noon.
In Time's Ocean falling drown'd.   45
In Aged Ignorance profound,
Holy & cold, I clip'd the Wings
Of all Sublunary Things,
And in depths of my Dungeons
Closed the Father & the Sons.   50
But when once I did descry
The Immortal Man that cannot Die,
Thro' evening shades I haste away
To close the Labours of my Day.
The Door of Death I open found   55
And the Worm Weaving in the Ground:
Thou'rt my Mother from the Womb,
Wife, Sister, Daughter, to the Tomb,
Weaving to Dreams the Sexual strife
And weeping over the Web of Life.   60

EPILOGUE

To The Accuser who is
The God of This World

TRULY, My Satan, thou art but a Dunce,
And dost not know the Garment from the Man.
Every Harlot was a Virgin once,
Nor can'st thou ever change Kate into Nan.

Tho' thou art Worship'd by the Names Divine.   65
Of Jesus & Jehovah, thou art still
The Son of Morn in weary Night's decline,
The lost Traveller's Dream under the Hill.

WILLIAM BLAKE

THE GARDEN OF LOVE

I went to the Garden of Love,
And saw what I never had seen:
A Chapel was built in the midst,
Where I used to play on the green.

And the gates of this Chapel were shut,   5
And "Thou shalt not" writ over the door;

So I turned to the Garden of Love
That so many sweet flowers bore.

And I saw it was filled with graves,
And tombstones where flowers should be;   10
    And priests in black gowns were walking their rounds,
And binding with briars my joys and desires.

WILLIAM BLAKE

[I SAW A CHAPEL ALL OF GOLD]

I saw a chapel all of gold
That none did dare to enter in,
And many weeping stood without,
Weeping, mourning, worshipping.

I saw a serpent rise between   5
The white pillars of the door,
And he forc'd & forc'd & forc'd,
Down the golden hinges tore.

And along the pavement sweet,
Set with pearls & rubies bright,   10
All his slimy length he drew,
Till upon the altar white

Vomiting his poison out
On the bread & on the wine.
So I turn'd into a sty   15
And laid me down among the swine.

WILLIAM BLAKE

MARRIAGE

for Mr. and Mrs. Mike Goldberg

Should I get married? Should I be good?
Astound the girl next door
with my velvet suit and faustus hood?
Don't take her to movies but to cemeteries
tell about werewolf bathtubs and forked clarinets   5
then desire her and kiss her and all the preliminaries
and she going just so far and I understanding why
not getting angry saying You must feel! It's beautiful to feel!
Instead take her in my arms
lean against an old crooked tombstone   10
and woo her the entire night the constellations in the sky—

When she introduces me to her parents
back straightened, hair finally combed, strangled by a tie,
should I sit knees together on their 3rd-degree sofa
and not ask Where's the bathroom?   15
How else to feel other than I am,

a young man who often thinks Flash Gordon soap—
O how terrible it must be for a young man
seated before a family and the family thinking
We never saw him before! He wants our Mary Lou!   20
After tea and homemade cookies they ask What do you do?
Should I tell them: Would they like me then?
Say All right get married, we're losing a daughter
but we're gaining a son—
And should I then ask Where's the bathroom?   25
O God, and the wedding! All her family and her friends
and only a handful of mine all scroungy and bearded
just waiting to get at the drinks and food—
And the priest! he looking at me as if I masturbated
asking me Do you take this woman   30
for your lawful wedded wife?
And I, trembling what to say, say Pie Glue!
I kiss the bride all those corny men slapping me on the back:
She's all yours, boy! Ha-ha-ha!
And in their eyes you could see   35
some obscene honeymoon going on—
Then all that absurd rice and clanky cans and shoes
Niagara Falls! Hordes of us! Husbands! Wives! Flowers!
All streaming into cozy hotels
All going to do the same thing tonight   40
The indifferent clerk he knowing what was going to happen
The lobby zombies they knowing what
The whistling elevator man he knowing
The winking bellboy knowing
Everybody knows! I'd be almost inclined not to do anything!   45
Stay up all night! Stare that hotel clerk in the eye!
Screaming: I deny honeymoon! I deny honeymoon!
running rampant into those almost climactic suites
yelling Radio belly! Cat shovel!
O I'd live in Niagara forever! in a dark cave beneath the Falls   50
I'd sit there the Mad Honeymooner
devising ways to break marriages; a scourge of bigamy
a saint of divorce—
But I should get married I should be good
How nice it'd be to come home to her   55
and sit by the fireplace and she in the kitchen
aproned young and lovely wanting my baby
and so happy about me she burns the roast beef
and comes crying to me and I get up from my big papa chair
saying Christmas teeth! Radiant brains! Apple deaf!   60
God what a husband I'd make! Yes, I should get married!
So much to do! like sneaking into Mr. Jones' house late at night
and cover his golf clubs with 1920 Norwegian books
Like hanging a picture of Rimbaud on the lawnmower
Like pasting Tannu Tuva postage stamps   65

all over the picket fence
Like when Mrs. Kindhead comes to collect
for the Community Chest
grab her and tell her There are unfavorable omens in the sky!
And when the mayor comes to get my vote tell him   70
When are you going to stop people killing whales!
And when the milkman comes leave him a note in the bottle
Penguin dust, bring me penguin dust, I want penguin dust—

Yet if I should get married and it's Connecticut and snow
and she gives birth to a child and I am sleepless, worn,   75
up for nights, head bowed against a quiet window,
the past behind me,
finding myself in the most common of situations
a trembling man
knowledged with responsibility not twig-smear   80
nor Roman coin soup—
O what would that be like!
Surely I'd give it for a nipple a rubber Tacitus
For a rattle a bag of broken Bach records
Tack Della Francesca all over its crib   85
Sew the Greek alphabet on its bib
And build for its playpen a roofless Parthenon—

No, I doubt I'd be that kind of father
not rural not snow no quiet window
but hot smelly tight New York City   90
seven flights up, roaches and rats in the walls
a fat Reichian wife screeching over potatoes Get a job!
And five nose-running brats in love with Batman
And the neighbors all toothless and dry haired
like those hag masses of the 18th century   95
all wanting to come in and watch TV
The landlord wants his rent
Grocery store Blue Cross Gas & Electric Knights of Columbus
Impossible to lie back and dream Telephone snow,
ghost parking—   100
No! I should not get married I should never get married!

But—imagine if I were married to a beautiful
sophisticated woman
tall and pale wearing an elegant black dress
and long black gloves   105
holding a cigarette holder in one hand
and a highball in the other
and we lived high up in a penthouse with a huge window
from which we could see all of New York
and even farther on clearer days   110
No, can't imagine myself married to that pleasant prison dream—

O but what about love? I forget love
not that I am incapable of love
it's just that I see love as odd as wearing shoes—
I never wanted to marry a girl who was like my mother   115
And Ingrid Bergman was always impossible
And there's maybe a girl now but she's already married
And I don't like men and—
but there's got to be somebody!
Because what if I'm 60 years old and not married,   120
all alone in a furnished room with pee stains on my underwear
and everybody else is married! All the universe married but me!

Ah, yet well I know that were a woman possible
as I am possible
then marriage would be possible—   125
Like SHE in her lonely alien gaud waiting her Egyptian lover
so I wait—bereft of 2,000 years and the bath of life.

GREGORY CORSO

[HOW MANY PALTRY, FOOLISH, PAINTED THINGS]

How many paltry, foolish, painted things
That now in coaches trouble every street
Shall be forgotten, whom no poet sings,
Ere they be well wrapped in their winding sheet?
Where I to thee eternity shall give   5
When nothing else remaineth of these days,
And queens hereafter shall be glad to live
Upon the alms of thy superfluous praise.
Virgins and matrons reading these my rhymes
Shall be so much delighted with thy story   10
That they shall grieve they lived not in these times
To have seen thee, their sex's only glory.
   So shalt thou fly above the vulgar throng,
   Still to survive in my immortal song.

MICHAEL DRAYTON

[SINCE THERE'S NO HELP]

Since there's no help, come let us kiss and part;
Nay, I have done, you get no more of me,

And I am glad, yea glad with all my heart
That thus so cleanly I myself can free;
Shake hands forever, cancel all our vows,   5
And when we meet at any time again,
Be it not seen in either of our brows
That we one jot of former love retain.
Now at the last gasp of Love's latest breath,
When, his pulse failing, Passion speechless lies,   10
When Faith is kneeling by his bed of death,
And Innocence is closing up his eyes,
   Now, if thou wouldst, when all have given him over,
   From death to life thou mightst him yet recover.

MICHAEL DRAYTON

[DEATH BE NOT PROUD]

X

Death be not proud, though some have called thee
Mighty and dreadfull, for, thou art not soe,
For, those, whom thou think'st, thou dost overthrow,
Die not, poore death, nor yet canst thou kill mee.
From rest and sleepe, which but thy pictures bee,   5
Much pleasure, then from thee, much more must flow,
And soonest our best men with thee doe goe,
Rest of their bones, and soules deliverie.
Thou art slave to Fate, Chance, kings, and desperate men,
And dost with poyson, warre, and sicknesse dwell,   10
And poppie, or charmes can make us sleepe as well,
And better than thy stroake; why swell'st thou then?
One short sleepe past, wee wake eternally,
And death shall be no more; death, thou shalt die.

JOHN DONNE

THE EXTASIE

Where, like a pillow on a bed,
   A Pregnant banke swel'd up, to rest
The violets reclining head,
   Sat we two, one anothers best.
Our hands were firmely cimented   5
   With a fast balme, which thence did spring,
Our eye-beames twisted, and did thred
   Our eyes, upon one double string;

So to'entergraft our hands, as yet
    Was all the meanes to make us one,   10
And pictures in our eyes to get
    Was all our propagation.
As 'twixt two equall Armies, Fate
    Suspends uncertaine victorie,
Our soules, (which to advance their state,   15
    Were gone out,) hung 'twixt her, and mee.
And whil'st our soules negotiate there,
    Wee like sepulchrall statues lay;
All day, the same our postures were,
    And wee said nothing, all the day.   20
If any, so by love refin'd,
    That he soules language understood,
And by good love were growen all minde,
    Within convenient distance stood,
He (though he knew not which soul spake,   25
    Because both meant, both spake the same)
Might thence a new concoction take,
    And part farre purer than he came.
This Extasie doth unperplex
    (We said) and tell us what we love,   30
Wee see by this, it was not sexe,
    Wee see, we saw not what did move:
But as all severall soules containe
    Mixture of things, they know not what,
Love, these mixt soules, doth mixe againe,   35
    And makes both one, each this and that.
A single violet transplant,
    The strength, the colour, and the size,
(All which before was poore, and scant,)
    Redoubles still, and multiplies.   40
When love, with one another so
    Interinanimates two soules,
That abler soule, which thence doth flow,
    Defects of lonelinesses controules.
Wee then, who are this new soule, know,   45
    Of what we are compos'd, and made,
For, th'Atomies of which we grow,
    Are soules, whom no change can invade.
But O alas, so long, so farre
    Our bodies why doe wee forbeare?   50
They are ours, though they are not wee, Wee are
    The intelligences, they the spheares.
We owe them thankes, because they thus,
    Did us, to us, at first convay,
Yeelded their forces, sense, to us,   55
    Nor are drosse to us, but allay.

On man heavens influence workes not so,
 But that it first imprints the ayre,
Soe soule into the soule may flow,
 Though it to body first repaire.   60
As our blood labours to beget
 Spirits, as like soules as it can,
Because such fingers need to knit
 That subtile knot, which makes us man:
So must pure lovers soules descend   65
 T'affections, and to faculties,
Which sense may reach and apprehend,
 Else a great Prince in prison lies.
To'our bodies turne wee then, that so
 Weake men on love reveal'd may looke;   70
Loves mysteries in soules doe grow,
 But yet the body is his booke.
And if some lover, such as wee,
 Have heard this dialogue of one,
Let him still marke us, he shall see   75
 Small change, when we'are to bodies gone.

JOHN DONNE

THE FLEA

Marke but this flea, and marke in this,
How little that which thou deny'st me is;
It suck'd me first, and now sucks thee,
And in this flea, our two bloods mingled bee;
Thou know'st that this cannot be said   5
A sinne, nor shame, nor losse of maidenhead,
 Yet this enjoyes before it wooe,
 And pamper'd swells with one blood made of two,
 And this, alas, is more than wee would doe.

Oh stay, three lives in one flea spare,   10
Where wee almost, yea more than maryed are.
This flea is you and I, and this
Our mariage bed, and mariage temple is;
Though parents grudge, and you, w'are met,
And cloysterd in these living walls of Jet.   15
 Though use make you apt to kill mee,
 Let not to that, selfe murder added bee,
 And sacrilege, three sinnes in killing three.

Cruell and sodaine, hast thou since
Purpled thy naile, in blood of innocence?   20
Wherein could this flea guilty bee,
Except in that drop which it suckt from thee?
Yet thou triumph'st, and saist that thou
Find'st not thy selfe, nor mee the weaker now;
   'Tis true, then learne how false, feares bee;   25
   Just so much honor, when thou yeeld'st to mee,
   Will wast, as this flea's death tooke life from thee.

JOHN DONNE

[GOE, AND CATCHE A FALLING STARRE]

Goe, and catche a falling starre,
   Get with child a mandrake roote,
Tell me, where all past yeares are,
   Or who cleft the Divels foot,
Teach me to heare Mermaides singing,   5
Or to keep off envies stinging,
        And finde
        What winde
Serves to advance an honest minde.

If thou beest borne to strange sights,   10
   Things invisible to see,
Ride ten thousand daies and nights,
   Till age snow white haires on thee,
Thou, when thou retorn'st, wilt tell mee
All strange wonders that befell thee,   15
        And sweare
        No where
Lives a woman true, and faire.

If thou findst one, let mee know,
   Such a Pilgrimage were sweet;   20
Yet doe not, I would not goe,
   Though at next doore wee might meet,
Though shee were true, when you met her,
And last, till you write your letter,
        Yet shee   25
        Will bee
False, ere I come, to two, or three.

JOHN DONNE

THE GOOD-MORROW

I wonder by my troth, what thou, and I
Did, till we lov'd? were we not wean'd till then?
But suck'd on countrey pleasures, childishly?
Or snorted we in the seaven sleepers den?
T'was so; But this, all pleasures fancies bee.   5
If ever any beauty I did see,
Which I desir'd, and got, t'was but a dreame of thee.

And now good morrow to our waking soules,
Which watch not one another out of feare;
For love, all love of other sights controules,   10
And makes one little roome, and every where.
Let sea-discoverers to new worlds have gone,
Let Maps to other, worlds on worlds have showne,
Let us possesse one world, each hath one, and is one.

My face is thine eye, thine in mine appeares,   15
And true plaine hearts doe in the faces rest,
Where can we finde two better hemispheares
Without sharpe North, without declining West?
What ever dyes, was not mixt equally;
If our two loves be one, or, thou and I   20
Love so alike, that none doe slacken, none can die.

JOHN DONNE

THE INDIFFERENT

I can love both faire and browne,
Her whom abundance melts, and her whom want betraies,
Her who loves lonenesse best, and her who maskes and plaies,
Her whom the country form'd, and whom the town,
Her who beleeves, and her who tries,   5
Her who still weepes with spungie eyes,
And her who is dry corke, and never cries;
I can love her, and her, and you and you,
I can love any, so she be not true.

Will no other vice content you?   10
Will it not serve your turn to do, as did your mothers?
Or have you all old vices spent, and now would finde out others?
Or doth a feare, that men are true, torment you?
Oh we are not, be not you so,
Let mee, and doe you, twenty know.   15

Rob mee, but binde me not, and let me goe.
Must I, who came to travaile thorow you,
Grow your fixt subject, because you are true?

Venus heard me sigh this song,
And by Loves sweetest Part, Variety, she swore,   20
She heard not this till now; and that it should be so no more.
She went, examin'd, and return'd ere long,
And said, alas, Some two or three
Poore Heretiques in love there bee,
Which thinke to stablish dangerous constancie.   25
But I have told them, since you will be true,
You shall be true to them, who're false to you.

JOHN DONNE

THE CANONIZATION

For Godsake hold your tongue, and let me love,
   Or chide my palsie, or my gout,
My five gray haires, or ruin'd fortune flout,
      With wealth your state, your minde with Arts improve,
         Take you a course, get you a place,   5
         Observe his honour, or his grace,
Or the Kings reall, or his stamped face
   Contemplate, what you will, approve,
   So you will let me love.

Alas, alas, who's injur'd by my love?   10
   What merchants ships have my sighs drown'd?
Who saies my teares have overflow'd his ground?
      When did my colds a forward spring remove?
         When did the heats which my veines fill
         Adde one more to the plaguie Bill?   15
Soldiers finde warres, and Lawyers finde out still
   Litigious men, which quarrels move,
   Though she and I do love.

Call us what you will, wee are made such by love;
   Call her one, mee another flye,   20
We'are Tapers too, and at our owne cost die,
      And wee in us finde th'Eagle and the Dove.
         The Phoenix ridle hath more wit
         By us, we two being one, are it.
So to one neutrall thing both sexes fit,   25
   Wee dye and rise the same, and prove
   Mysterious by this love.

Wee can dye by it, if not live by love,
    And if unfit for tombes and hearse
Our legend bee, it will be fit for verse;   30
    And if no peece of Chronicle wee prove,
      We'll build in sonnets pretty roomes;
      As well a well wrought urne becomes
The greatest ashes, as halfe-acre tombes,
    And by these hymnes, all shall approve   35
    Us *Canoniz'd* for Love:

And thus invoke us; You whom reverend love
    Made one anothers hermitage;
You, to whom love was peace, that now is rage;
    Who did the whole worlds soule contract, and drove   40
      Into the glasses of your eyes
      (So made such mirrors, and such spies,
That they did all to you epitomize,)
    Countries, Townes, Courts: Beg from above
    A patterne of your love!   45

JOHN DONNE

LOVERS INFINITENESSE

If yet I have not all thy love,
Deare, I shall never have it all,
I cannot breath one other sigh, to move,
Nor can intreat one other tear to fall,
And all my treasure, which should purchase thee,   5
Sighs, teares, and oathes, and letters I have spent.
Yet no more can be due to mee,
Than at the bargaine made was ment,
If then thy gift of love were partiall,
That some to mee, some should to others fall,   10
    Deare, I shall never have Thee All.

Or if then thou gavest mee all,
All was but All, which thou hadst then;
But if in thy heart, since, there be or shall,
New love created bee, by other men,   15
Which have their stocks intire, and can in teares,
In sighs, in oathes, and letters outbid mee,
This new love may beget new feares,
For, this love was not vowed by thee.
And yet it was, thy gift being generall,   20
The ground, thy heart is mine, what ever shall
    Grow there, deare, I should have it all.

Yet I would not have all yet,
Hee that hath all can have no more,
And since my love doth every day admit   25
New growth, thou shouldst have new rewards in store;
Thou canst not every day give me thy heart,
If thou canst give it, then thou never gavest it:
Loves riddles are, that though thy heart depart,
It stayes at home, and thou with losing savest it: 30
But wee will have a way more liberall,
Than changing hearts, to joyne them, so wee shall
   Be one, and one anothers All.

JOHN DONNE

[SWEETEST LOVE, I DO NOT GOE]

Sweetest love, I do not goe,
   For wearinesse of thee,
Nor in hope the world can show
   A fitter Love for mee;
     But since that I   5
Must dye at last, 'tis best,
To use my selfe in jest
   Thus by fain'd deaths to dye;

Yesternight the Sunne went hence,
   And yet is here today,   10
He hath no desire nor sense,
   Nor halfe so short a way:
     Then feare not mee,
But beleeve that I shall make
Speedier journeyes, since I take   15
   More wings and spurres than hee.

O how feeble is mans power,
   That if good fortune fall,
Cannot adde another houre,
   Nor a lost houre recall!   20
     But come bad chance,
And wee joyne to'it our strength,
And wee teach it art and length,
   It selfe o'r us to'advance.

When thou sigh'st, thou sigh's not winde,   25
   But sigh'st my soule away,

When thou weep'st, unkindly kinde,
　My life's blood doth decay.
　　It cannot bee
That thou lov'st mee, as thou say'st,　　　　　　　　30
If in thine my life thou waste,
　That art the best of mee.

Let not thy divining heart
　Forethinke me any ill,
Destiny may take thy part,　　　　　　　　　　　35
　And may thy feares fulfill;
　　But thinke that wee
Are but turn'd aside to sleepe;
They who one another keepe
　Alive, ne'r parted bee.　　　　　　　　　　　40

JOHN DONNE

A VALEDICTION: FORBIDDING MOURNING

As virtuous men passe mildly away,
　And whisper to their soules, to goe,
Whilst some of their sad friends doe say,
　The breath goes now, and some say, no:

So let us melt, and make no noise,　　　　　　　　5
　No teare-floods, nor sigh-tempests move,
T'were prophanation of our joyes
　To tell the layetie our love.

Moving of th'earth brings harmes and feares,
　Men reckon what it did and meant,　　　　　　　　10
But trepidation of the spheares,
　Though greater farre, is innocent.

Dull sublunary lovers love
　(Whose soule is sense) cannot admit
Absence, because it doth remove　　　　　　　　15
　Those things which elemented it.

But we by a love, so much refin'd,
　That our selves know not what it is,
Inter-assured of the mind,
　Care lesse, eyes, lips, and hands to misse.　　　　　　　20

Our two soules therefore, which are one,
   Though I must goe, endure not yet
A breach, but an expansion,
   Like gold to ayery thinnesse beate.

If they be two, they are two so   25
   As stiffe twin compasses are two,
Thy soule the fixt foot, makes no show
   To move, but doth, if th'other doe.

And though it in the center sit,
   Yet when the other far doth rome,   30
It leanes, and hearkens after it,
   And growes erect, as that comes home.

 Such wilt thou be to mee, who must
   Like th'other foot, obliquely runne;
Thy firmnes drawes my circle just,   35
   And makes me end, where I begunne.

JOHN DONNE

ELEGY

I know but will not tell
you, Aunt Irene, why there
are soap-suds in the whiskey:
Uncle Robert had to have
a drink while shaving. May   5
there be no bloodshed in your house
this morning of my father's death
and no unkept appearance
in the living, since he has
to wear the rouge and lipstick   10
of your ceremony, mother,
for the first and last time:
father, hello and goodbye.

ALAN DUGAN

MACAVITY: THE MYSTERY CAT

Macavity's a Mystery Cat: he's called the Hidden Paw—
For he's the master criminal who can defy the Law.
He's the bafflement of Scotland Yard, the Flying Squad's despair:
For when they reach the scene of crime—*Macavity's not there!*

   Macavity, Macavity, there's no one like Macavity,   5
He's broken every human law, he breaks the law of gravity.
His powers of levitation would make a fakir stare,
And when you reach the scene of crime—*Macavity's not there!*

You may seek him in the basement, you may look up in the air—
But I tell you once and once again, *Macavity's not there!* 10

    Macavity's a ginger cat, he's very tall and thin;
You would know him if you saw him, for his eyes are sunken in.
His brow is deeply lined with thought, his head is highly domed;
His coat is dusty from neglect, his whiskers are uncombed.
He sways his head from side to side, with movements like a snake; 15
And when you think he's half asleep, he's always wide awake.

    Macavity, Macavity, there's no one like Macavity,
For he's a fiend in feline shape, a monster of depravity.
You may meet him in a by-street, you may see him in the square—
But when a crime's discovered, then *Macavity's not there!* 20

    He's outwardly respectable. (They say he cheats at cards.)
And his footprints are not found in any file of Scotland Yard's.
And when the larder's looted, or the jewel-case is rifled,
Or when the milk is missing, or another Peke's been stifled,
Or the greenhouse glass is broken, and the trellis past repair— 25
Ay, there's the wonder of the thing! *Macavity's not there!*

    And when the Foreign Office find a Treaty's gone astray,
Or the Admiralty lose some plans and drawings by the way,
There may be a scrap of paper in the hall or on the stair—
But it's useless to investigate—*Macavity's not there!* 30
And when the loss has been disclosed, the Secret Service say:
"It *must* have been Macavity!"—but he's a mile away.
You'll be sure to find him resting, or a-licking of his thumbs,
Or engaged in doing complicated long division sums.

    Macavity, Macavity, there's no one like Macavity, 35
There never was a Cat of such deceitfulness and suavity.
He always has an alibi, and one or two to spare:
At whatever time the deed took place—MACAVITY WASN'T THERE!
And they say that all the Cats whose wicked deeds are widely known
(I might mention Mungojerrie, I might mention Griddlebone) 40
Are nothing more than agents for the Cat who all the time
Just controls their operations: the Napoleon of Crime!

T. S. ELIOT

TWO TRAMPS IN MUD-TIME

    Out of the mud two strangers came
    And caught me splitting wood in the yard.
    And one of them put me off my aim

By hailing cheerily "Hit them hard!"
I knew pretty well why he dropped behind   5
And let the other go on a way.
I knew pretty well what he had in mind:
He wanted to take my job for pay.

Good blocks of beech it was I split,
As large around as the chopping-block;   10
And every piece I squarely hit
Fell splinterless as a cloven rock.
The blows that a life of self-control
Spares to strike for the common good
That day, giving a loose to my soul,   15
I spent on the unimportant wood.

The sun was warm but the wind was chill.
You know how it is with an April day:
When the sun is out and the wind is still,
You're one month on in the middle of May.   20
But if you so much as dare to speak,
A cloud comes over the sunlit arch,
A wind comes off a frozen peak,
And you're two months back in the middle of March.

A bluebird comes tenderly up to alight   25
And fronts the wind to unruffle a plume,
His song so pitched as not to excite
A single flower as yet to bloom.
It is snowing a flake: and he half knew
Winter was only playing possum.   30
Except in color he isn't blue,
But he wouldn't advise a thing to blossom.

The water for which we may have to look
In summertime with a witching-wand,
In every wheelrut's now a brook,   35
In every print of a hoof a pond.
Be glad of water, but don't forget
The lurking frost in the earth beneath
That will steal forth after the sun is set
And show on the water its crystal teeth.   40

The time when most I loved my task
These two must make me love it more
By coming with what they came to ask.
You'd think I never had felt before
The weight of an ax-head poised aloft,   45
The grip on earth of outspread feet.

The life of muscles rocking soft
And smooth and moist in vernal heat.

Out of the woods two hulking tramps
(From sleeping God knows where last night,   50
But not long since in the lumber camps).
They thought all chopping was theirs of right.
Men of the woods and lumberjacks,
They judged me by their appropriate tool.
Except as a fellow handled an ax,   55
They had no way of knowing a fool.

Nothing on either side was said.
They knew they had but to stay their stay
And all their logic would fill my head:
As that I had no right to play   60
With what was another man's work for gain.
My right might be love but theirs was need.
And where the two exist in twain
Theirs was the better right—agreed.

But yield who will to their separation,   65
My object in life is to unite
My avocation and my vocation
As my two eyes make one in sight.
Only where love and need are one,
And the work is play for mortal stakes,   70
Is the deed ever really done
For Heaven and the future's sakes.

ROBERT FROST

DOWN, WANTON, DOWN!

Down, wanton, down! Have you no shame
That at the whisper of Love's name,
Or Beauty's, presto! up you raise
Your angry head and stand at gaze?

Poor bombard-captain, sworn to reach   5
The ravelin and effect a breach—
Indifferent what you storm or why,
So be that in the breach you die!

Love may be blind, but Love at least
Knows what is man and what mere beast;   10

Or Beauty wayward, but requires
More delicacy from her squires.

Tell me, my witless, whose one boast
Could be your staunchness at the post,
When were you made a man of parts   15
To think fine and profess the arts?

Will many-gifted Beauty come
Bowing to your bald rule of thumb,
Or Love swear loyalty to your crown?
Be gone, have done! Down, wanton, down!   20

ROBERT GRAVES

THE COLLAR

I struck the board and cried, "No more;
    I will abroad!
What? shall I ever sigh and pine?
My lines and life are free, free as the road,
    Loose as the wind, as large as store.   5
        Shall I be still in suit?
Have I no harvest but a thorn
    To let me blood, and not restore
What I have lost with cordial fruit?
    Sure there was wine   10
Before my sighs did dry it; there was corn
    Before my tears did drown it.
    Is the year only lost to me?
        Have I no bays to crown it,
No flowers, no garlands gay? all blasted?   15
        All wasted?
    Not so, my heart; but there is fruit,
        And thou hast hands.
    Recover all thy sigh-blown age
On double pleasures: leave thy cold dispute   20
Of what is fit, and not. Forsake thy cage,
        Thy rope of sands,
Which petty thoughts have made, and made to thee
    Good cable, to enforce and draw,
        And be thy law,   25
    While thou didst wink and wouldst not see.
        Away; take heed;
        I will abroad.

Call in thy death's head there; tie up thy fears.
  He that forbears   30
   To suit and serve his need,
    Deserves his load."
But as I raved and grew more fierce and wild
  At every word,
   Methought I heard one calling, *Child!*   35
    And I replied, *My Lord.*

GEORGE HERBERT

NOT MARBLE NOR THE GILDED MONUMENTS

The praisers of women in their proud and beautiful poems,
Naming the grave mouth and the hair and the eyes,
Boasted those they loved should be forever remembered:
These were lies.

The words sound but the face in the Istrian sun is forgotten. 5
The poet speaks but to her dead ears no more.
The sleek throat is gone—and the breast that was troubled
 to listen:
Shadow from door.

Therefore I will not praise your knees nor your fine walking
Telling you men shall remember your name as long 10
As lips move or breath is spent or the iron of English
Rings from a tongue.

I shall say you were young, and your arms straight, and
 your mouth scarlet:
I shall say you will die and none will remember you:
Your arms change, and none remember the swish of your
 garments, 15
Nor the click of your shoe.

Not with my hand's strength, not with difficult labor
Springing the obstinate words to the bones of your breast
And the stubborn line to your young stride and the breath
 to your breathing
And the beat to your haste 20

Shall I prevail on the hearts of unborn men to remember.
(What is a dead girl but a shadowy ghost
Or a dead man's voice but a distant and vain affirmation
Like dream words most)

Therefore I will not speak of the undying glory of women. 25
I will say you were young and straight and your skin fair
And you stood in the door and the sun was a shadow of
    leaves on your shoulders
And a leaf on your hair—

I will not speak of the famous beauty of dead women:
I will say the shape of a leaf lay once on your hair. 30
Till the world ends and the eyes are out and the mouths
    broken
Look! It is there!

ARCHIBALD MACLEISH

THE RIVER-MERCHANT'S WIFE: A LETTER

While my hair was still cut straight across my forehead
I played about the front gate, pulling flowers.
You came by on bamboo stilts, playing horse,
You walked about my seat, playing with blue plums.
And we went on living in the village of Chokan: 5
Two small people, without dislike or suspicion.

At fourteen I married My Lord you.
I never laughed, being bashful.
Lowering my head, I looked at the wall.
Called to, a thousand times, I never looked back. 10

At fifteen I stopped scowling,
I desired my dust to be mingled with yours
Forever and forever and forever.
Why should I climb the look out?

At sixteen you departed, 15
You went into far Ku-to-yen, by the river of swirling eddies,
And you have been gone five months.
The monkeys make sorrowful noise overhead.

You dragged your feet when you went out.
By the gate now, the moss is grown, the different mosses, 20
Too deep to clear them away!
The leaves fall early this autumn, in wind.
The paired butterflies are already yellow with August
Over the grass in the West garden;
They hurt me. I grow older. 25
If you are coming down through the narrows of the river Kiang,

Please let me know beforehand,
And I will come out to meet you
> As far as Cho-fu-Sa.

> *By Rihaku*

EZRA POUND

SALUTATION

O generation of the thoroughly smug
   and thoroughly uncomfortable,
I have seen fishermen picnicking in the sun,
I have seen them with untidy families,
I have seen their smiles full of teeth
   and heard ungainly laughter.
And I am happier than you are,   5
And they were happier than I am;
And the fish swim in the lake
   and do not even own clothing.

EZRA POUND

SONG OF THE BOWMEN OF SHU

Here we are, picking the first fern-shoots
And saying: When shall we get back to our country?
Here we are because we have the Ken-nin for our foemen,
We have no comfort because of these Mongols.
We grub the soft fern-shoots,   5
When anyone says "Return," the others are full of sorrow.
Sorrowful minds, sorrow is strong, we are hungry and thirsty.
Our defence is not yet made sure, no one can let his friend return.
We grub the old fern-stalks.
We say: Will we be let to go back in October?   10
There is no ease in royal affairs, we have no comfort.
Our sorrow is bitter, but we would not return to our country.
What flower has come into blossom?
Whose chariot? The General's.
Horses, his horses even, are tired. They were strong.   15
We have no rest, three battles a month.
By heaven, his horses are tired.
The generals are on them, the soldiers are by them.
The horses are well trained, the generals have ivory arrows
   and quivers ornamented with fish-skin.

The enemy is swift, we must be careful.   20
When we set out, the willows were drooping with spring,
We come back in the snow,
We go slowly, we are hungry and thirsty,
Our mind is full of sorrow, who will know of our grief?
                              By Bunno
                              Reputedly 1100 B.C.

EZRA POUND

BEN JONSON ENTERTAINS A MAN
FROM STRATFORD

You are a friend then, as I make it out,
Of our man Shakespeare, who alone of us
Will put an ass's head in Fairyland
As he would add a shilling to more shillings,
All most harmonious—and out of his   5
Miraculous inviolable increase
Fills Ilion, Rome, or any town you like
Of olden time with timeless Englishmen;
And I must wonder what you think of him—
All you down there where your small Avon flows   10
By Stratford, and where you're an Alderman.
Some, for a guess, would have him riding back
To be a farrier there, or say a dyer;
Or maybe one of your adept surveyors;
Or like enough the wizard of all tanners.   15
Not you—no fear of that; for I discern
In you a kindling of the flame that saves—
The nimble element, the true caloric;
I see it, and was told of it, moreover,
By our discriminate friend himself, no other.   20
Had you been one of the sad average,
As he would have it—meaning, as I take it,
The sinew and the solvent of our Island,
You'd not be buying beer for this Terpander's
Approved and estimated friend Ben Jonson;   25
He'd never foist it as a part of his
Contingent entertainment of a townsman
While he goes off rehearsing, as he must,
If he shall ever be the Duke of Stratford.
And my words are no shadow on your town—   30
Far from it; for one town's as like another
As all are unlike London. Oh, he knows it—

And there's the Stratford in him; he denies it,
And there's the Shakespeare in him. So, God help him!

I tell him he needs Greek; but neither God   35
Nor Greek will help him. Nothing will help that man.
You see the fates have given him so much,
He must have all or perish—or look out
Of London, where he sees too many lords.
They're part of half what ails him: I suppose   40
There's nothing fouler down among the demons
Than what it is he feels when he remembers
The dust and sweat and ointment of his calling
With his lords looking on and laughing at him.
King as he is, he can't be king *de facto*,   45
And that's as well, because he wouldn't like it;
He'd frame a lower rating of men then
Than he has now; and after that would come
An abdication or an apoplexy.
He can't be king, not even king of Stratford—   50
Though half the world, if not the whole of it,
May crown him with a crown that fits no king
Save Lord Apollo's homesick emissary:
Not there on Avon, or on any stream
Where Naiads and their white arms are no more   55
Shall he find home again. It's all too bad.
But there's a comfort, for he'll have that House—
The best you ever saw; and he'll be there
Anon, as you're an Alderman. Good God!
He makes me lie awake o'nights and laugh.   60

And you have known him from his origin,
You tell me; and a most uncommon urchin
He must have been to the few seeing ones—
A trifle terrifying, I dare say,
Discovering a world with his man's eyes,   65
Quite as another lad might see some finches,
If he looked hard and had an eye for Nature.
But this one had his eyes and their fortelling,
And he had you to fare with, and what else?
He must have had a father and a mother—   70
In fact I've heard him say so—and a dog,
As a boy should, I venture; and the dog,
Most likely, was the only man who knew him.
A dog, for all I know, is what he needs
As much as anything right here today,   75
To counsel him about his disillusions,
Old aches, and parturitions of what's coming—
A dog of orders, an emeritus,

To wag his tail at him when he comes home,
And then to put his paws up on his knees   80
And say, "For God's sake, what's it all about?"

I don't know whether he needs a dog or not—
Or what he needs. I tell him he needs Greek;
I'll talk of rules and Aristotle with him,
And if his tongue's at home he'll say to that,   85
"I have your word that Aristotle knows,
And you mine that I don't know Aristotle."
He's all at odds with all the unities,
And what's yet worse, it doesn't seem to matter;
He treads along through Time's old wilderness   90
As if the tramp of all the centuries
Had left no roads—and there are none, for him;
He doesn't see them, even with those eyes—
And that's a pity, or I say it is.
Accordingly we have him as we have him—   95
Going his way, the way that he goes best,
A pleasant animal with no great noise
Or nonsense anywhere to set him off—
Save only divers and inclement devils
Have made of late his heart their dwelling-place.   100
A flame half ready to fly out sometimes
At some annoyance may be fanned up in him,
But soon it falls, and when it falls goes out;
He knows how little room there is in there
For crude and futile animosities,   105
And how much for the joy of being whole,
And how much for long sorrow and old pain.
On our side there arc some who may be given
To grow old wondering what he thinks of us
And some above us, who are, in his eyes,   110
Above himself—and that's quite right and English.
Yet here we smile, or disappoint the gods
Who made it so; the gods have always eyes
To see men scratch; and they see one down here
Who itches, manor-bitten, to the bone,   115
Albeit he knows himself—yes, yes, he knows—
The lord of more than England and of more
Than all the seas of England in all time
Shall ever wash. D'ye wonder that I laugh?
He sees me, and he doesn't seem to care;   120
And why the devil should he? I can't tell you.
I'll meet him out alone of a bright Sunday,
Trim, rather spruce, and quite the gentleman.
"What, ho, my lord!" say I. He doesn't hear me;
Wherefore I have to pause and look at him.   125
He's not enormous, but one looks at him.

A little on the round if you insist,
For now, God save the mark, he's growing old;
He's five and forty, and to hear him talk
These days you'd call him eighty; then you'd add   130
More years to that. He's old enough to be
The father of a world, and so he is.
"Ben, you're a scholar, what's the time of day?"
Says he; and there shines out of him again
An aged light that has no age or station—   135
The mystery that's his—a mischievous
Half-mad serenity that laughs at fame
For being won so easy, and at friends
Who laugh at him for what he wants the most,
And for his dukedom down in Warwickshire;—   140
By which you see we're all a little jealous. . . .
Poor Greene! I fear the color of his name
Was even as that of his ascending soul;
And he was one where there are many others—
Some scrivening to the end against their fate,   145
Their puppets all in ink and all to die there;
And some with hands that once would shade an eye
That scanned Euripides and Aeschylus
Will reach by this time for a pot-house mop
To slush their fist and last of royalties.   150
Poor devils! and they all play to his hand;
For so it was in Athens and old Rome.
But that's not here or there; I've wandered off.
Greene does it, or I'm careful. Where's that boy?

Yes, he'll go back to Stratford. And we'll miss him?   155
Dear sir, there'll be no London here without him.
We'll all be riding, one of these fine days,
Down there to see him   and his wife won't like us;
And then we'll think of what he never said
Of women—which, if taken all in all   160
With what he did say, would buy many horses.
Though nowadays he's not so much for women.
"So few of them," he says, "are worth the guessing."
But there's a worm at work when he says that,
And while he says it one feels in the air   165
A deal of circumambient hocus-pocus.
They've had him dancing till his toes were tender,
And he can feel 'em now, come chilly rains.
There's no long cry for going into it,
However, and we don't know much about it.   170
But you in Stratford, like most here in London,
Have more now in the *Sonnets* than you paid for;
He's put one there with all her poison on,
To make a singing fiction of a shadow

That's in his life a fact, and always will be.   175
But she's no care of ours, though Time, I fear,
Will have a more reverberant ado
About her than about another one
Who seems to have decoyed him, married him,
And sent him scuttling on his way to London—   180
With much already learned, and more to learn,
And more to follow. Lord! how I see him now,
Pretending, maybe trying, to be like us.
Whatever he may have meant, we never had him;
He failed us, or escaped, or what you will—   185
And there was that about him (God knows what—
We'd flayed another had he tried it on us)
That made as many of us as had wits
More fond of all his easy distances
Than one another's noise and clap-your-shoulder   190
But think you not, my friend, he'd never talk!
Talk? He was eldritch at it; and we listened—
Thereby acquiring much we knew before
About ourselves, and hitherto had held
Irrelevant, or not prime to the purpose.   195
And there were some, of course, and there be now,
Disordered and reduced amazedly
To resignation by the mystic seal
Of young finality the gods had laid
On everything that made him a young demon;   200
And one or two shot looks at him already
As he had been their executioner;
And once or twice he was, not knowing it—
Or knowing, being sorry for poor clay
And saying nothing. . . Yet, for all his engines,   205
You'll meet a thousand of an afternoon
Who strut and sun themselves and see around 'em
A world made out of more that has a reason
Than his, I swear, that he sees here to-day;
Though he may scarcely give a Fool an exit   210
But we mark how he sees in everything
A law that, given that we flout it once too often,
Brings fire and iron down on our naked heads.
To me it looks as if the power that made him,
For fear of giving all things to one creature,   215
Left out the first—faith, innocence, illusion,
Whatever 'tis that keep us out o'Bedlam—
And thereby, for his too consuming vision,
Empowered him out of nature; though to see him,
You'd never guess what's going on inside him.   220
He'll break out some day like a keg of ale
With too much independent frenzy in it;
And all for cellaring what he knows won't keep,

And what he'd best forget—but that he can't.
You'll have it, and have more than I'm foretelling; 225
And there'll be such a roaring at the Globe
As never stunned the bleeding gladiators.
He'll have to change the color of its hair
A bit, for now he calls it Cleopatra.
Black hair would never do for Cleopatra. 230
But you and I are not yet two old women,
And you're a man of office. What he does
Is more to you than how it is he does it—
And that's what the Lord God has never told him.
They work together, and the Devil helps 'em; 235
They do it of a morning, or if not,
They do it of a night; in which event
He's peevish of a morning. He seems old;
He's not the proper stomach or the sleep—
And they're two sovran agents to conserve him 240
Against the fiery art that has no mercy
But what's in that prodigious grand new House.
I gather something happening in his boyhood
Fulfilled him with a boy's determination
To make all Stratford 'ware of him. Well, well, 245
I hope at last he'll have his joy of it,
And all his pigs and sheep and bellowing beeves,
And frogs and owls and unicorns, moreover,
Be less than hell to his attendant ears.
Oh, past a doubt we'll all go down to see him. 250

He may be wise. With London two days off,
Down there some wind of heaven may yet revive him,
But there's no quickening breath from anywhere
Shall make of him again the poised young faun
From Warwickshire, who'd made, it seems, already 255
A legend of himself before I came
To blink before the last of his first lightning.
Whatever there be, there'll be no more of that;
The coming on of his old monster Time
Has made him a still man; and he has dreams 260
Were fair to think on once, and all found hollow.
He knows how much of what men paint themselves
Would blister in the light of what they are;
He sees how much of what was great now shares
An eminence transformed and ordinary; 265
He knows too much of what the world has hushed
In others, to be loud now for himself;
He knows now at what height low enemies
May reach his heart, and high friends let him fall;
But what not even such as he may know 270
Bedevils him the worst: his lark may sing

At heaven's gate how he will, and for as long
As joy may listen, but *he* sees no gate,
Save one whereat the spent clay waits a little
Before the churchyard has it, and the worm.   275

Not long ago, late in an afternoon,
I came on him unseen down Lambeth way,
And on my life I was afear'd of him:
He gloomed and mumbled like a soul from Tophet,
His hands behind him and his head bent solemn.   280
"What is it now," said I, "another woman?"
That made him sorry for me, and he smiled.
"No, Ben," he mused; "it's Nothing. It's all Nothing.
We come, we go; and when we're done, we're done;
Spiders and flies—we're mostly one or t'other—   285
We come, we go; and when we're done, we're done."
"By God, you sing that song as if you knew it!"
Said I, by way of cheering him; "what ails ye?"
"I think I must have come down here to think,"
Says he to that, and pulls his little beard;   290
"Your fly will serve as well as anybody,
And what's his hour? He flies, and flies, and flies,
And in his fly's mind has a brave appearance;
And then your spider gets him in her net,
And eats him out, and hangs him up to dry.   295
That's Nature, the kind mother of us all.
And then your slattern housemaid swings her broom,
And where's your spider? And that's Nature, also.
It's Nature and it's Nothing. It's all Nothing.
It's all a world where bugs and emperors   300
Go singularly back to the same dust,
Each in his time; and the old, ordered stars
That sang together, Ben, will sing the same
Old stave tomorrow."

            When he talks like that,   305
There's nothing for a human man to do
But lead him to some grateful nook like this
Where we be now, and there to make him drink.
He'll drink, for love of me, and then be sick;
A sad sign always in a man of parts,   310
And always very ominous. The great
Should be as large in liquor as in love—
And our great friend is not so large in either:
One disaffects him, and the other fails him;
Whatso he drinks that has an antic in it,   315
He's wondering what's to pay in his insides;
And while his eyes are on the Cyprian
He's fribbling all the time with that damned House.

We laugh here at his thrift, but after all
It may be thrift that saves him from the devil; 320
God gave it, anyhow—and we'll suppose
He knew the compound of his handiwork.
Today the clouds are with him, but anon
He'll out of 'em enough to shake the tree
Of life itself and bring down fruit unheard-of— 325
And, throwing in the bruised and whole together,
Prepare a wine to make us drunk with wonder;
And if he live, there'll be a sunset spell
Thrown over him as over a glassed lake
That yesterday was all a black wild water. 330

God send he live to give us, if no more,
What now's a-rampage in him, and exhibit,
With a decent half-allegiance to the ages
An earnest of at least a casual eye
Turned once on what he owes to Gutenberg, 335
And to the fealty of more centuries
Than are as yet a picture in our vision.
"There's time enough—I'll do it when I'm old,
And we're immortal men," he says to that;
And then he says to me, "Ben, what's 'immortal'? 340
Think you by any force of ordination
It may be nothing of a sort more noisy
Than a small oblivion of component ashes
That of a dream-addicted world was once
A moving atomy much like your friend here?" 345
Nothing will help that man. To make him laugh
I said then he was a mad mountebank—
And by the Lord I nearer made him cry.
I could have eat an eft then, on my knees,
Tails, claws, and all of him; for I had stung 350
The king of men, who had no sting for me,
And I had hurt him in his memories;
And I say now, as I shall say again,
I love the man this side idolatry.
He'll do it when he's old, he says. I wonder. 355
He may not be so ancient as all that.
For such as he, the thing that is to do
Will do itself—but there's a reckoning;
The sessions that are now too much his own,
The rolling inward of a still outside, 360
The churning out of all those blood-fed lines,
The nights of many schemes and little sleep,
The full brain hammered hot with too much thinking,
The vexed heart over-worn with too much aching—
This weary jangling of conjoined affairs 365
Made out of elements that have no end,

And all confused at once, I understand,
Is not what makes a man to live forever.
O, no, not now! He'll not be going now:
There'll be time yet for God knows what explosions   370
Before he goes. He'll stay awhile. Just wait:
Just wait a year or two for Cleopatra,
For she's to be a balsam and a comfort;
And that's not all a jape of mine now, either.
For granted once the old way of Apollo   375
Sings in a man, he may then, if he's able,
Strike unafraid whatever strings he will
Upon the last and wildest of new lyres;
Nor out of his new magic, though it hymn
The shrieks of dungeoned hell, shall he create   380
A madness or a gloom to shut quite out
A cleaving daylight, and a last great calm
Triumphant over shipwreck and all storms.
He might have given Aristotle creeps,
But surely would have given him his *katharsis*.   385
He'll not be going yet. There's too much yet
Unsung within the man. But when he goes,
I'd stake ye coin o' the realm his only care
For a phantom world he sounded and found wanting
Will be a portion here, a portion there,   390
Of this or that thing or some other thing
That has a patent and intrinsical
Equivalence in those egregious shillings.
And yet he knows, God help him! Tell me, now,
If ever there was anything let loose   395
On earth by gods or devils heretofore
Like this mad, careful, proud, indifferent Shakespeare!
Where was it, if it ever was? By heaven,
'Twas never yet in Rhodes or Pergamon—
In Thebes or Nineveh, a thing like this!   400
No thing like this was ever out of England;
And that he knows. I wonder if he cares.
Perhaps he does. . . . O Lord, that House in Stratford!

EDWIN ARLINGTON ROBINSON

FLAMMONDE

The man Flammonde, from God knows where,
With firm address and foreign air,
With news of nations in his talk
And something royal in his walk,

With glint of iron in his eyes,   5
But never doubt, nor yet surprise,
Appeared, and stayed, and held his head
As one by kings accredited.

Erect, with his alert repose
About him, and about his clothes,   10
He pictured all tradition hears
Of what we owe to fifty years.
His cleansing heritage of taste
Paraded neither want nor waste;
And what he needed for his fee   15
To live, he borrowed graciously.

He never told us what he was,
Or what mischance, or other cause,
Had banished him from better days
To play the Prince of Castaways.   20
Meanwhile he played surpassing well
A part, for most, unplayable;
In fine, one pauses, half afraid
To say for certain that he played.

For that, one may as well forego   25
Conviction as to yes or no;
Nor can I say just how intense
Would then have been the difference
To several, who, having striven
In vain to get what he was given,   30
Would see the stranger taken on
By friends not easy to be won.

Morever, many a malcontent
He soothed and found munificent;
His courtesy beguiled and foiled   35
Suspicion that his years were soiled;
His men distinguished any crowd,
His credit strengthened when he bowed;
And women, young and old, were fond
Of looking at the man Flammonde.   40

There was a woman in our town
On whom the fashion was to frown;
But while our talk renewed the tinge
Of a long-faded scarlet fringe,
The man Flammonde saw none of that,   45
And what he saw we wondered at—
That none of us, in her distress,
Could hide or find our littleness.

There was a boy that all agreed
Had shut within him the rare seed   50
Of learning. We could understand,
But none of us could lift a hand.
The man Flammonde appraised the youth,
And told a few of us the truth;
And thereby, for a little gold,   55
A flowered future was unrolled.

There were two citizens who fought
For years and years, and over nought;
They made life awkward for their friends,
And shortened their own dividends.   60
The man Flammonde said what was wrong
Should be made right; nor was it long
Before they were again in line,
And had each other in to dine.

And these I mention are but four   65
Of many out of many more.
So much for them. But what of him—
So firm in every look and limb?
What small satanic sort of kink
Was in his brain? What broken link   70
Withheld him from the destinies
That came so near to being his?

What was he, when we came to sift
His meaning, and to note the drift
Of incommunicable ways   75
That make us ponder while we praise?
Why was it that his charm revealed
Somehow the surface of a shield?
What was it that we never caught?
What was he, and what was he not?   80

How much it was of him we met
We cannot ever know; nor yet
Shall all he gave us quite atone
For what was his, and his alone;
Nor need we now, since he knew best,   85
Nourish an ethical unrest:
Rarely at once will nature give
The power to be Flammonde and live.

We cannot know how much we learn
From those who never will return,   90
Until a flash of unforeseen
Remembrance falls on what has been.

We've each a darkening hill to climb;
And this is why, from time to time
In Tilbury Town, we look beyond   95
Horizons for the man Flammonde.

EDWIN ARLINGTON ROBINSON

[I KNEW A WOMAN]

I knew a woman, lovely in her bones,
When small birds sighed, she would sigh back at them;
Ah, when she moved, she moved more ways than one:
The shapes a bright container can contain!
Of her choice virtues only gods should speak,   5
Or English poets who grew up on Greek
(I'd have them sing in chorus, cheek to cheek).

How well her wishes went! She stroked my chin,
She taught me Turn, and Counter-turn, and Stand;
She taught me Touch, that undulant white skin;   10
I nibbled meekly from her proffered hand;
She was the sickle; I, poor I, the rake,
Coming behind her for her pretty sake
(But what prodigious mowing we did make).

Love likes a gander, and adores a goose: 15
Her full lips pursed, the errant note to seize;
She played it quick, she played it light and loose;
My eyes, they dazzled at her flowing knees;
Her several parts could keep a pure repose,
Or one hip quiver with a mobile nose   20
(She moved in circles, and those circles moved).

Let seed be grass, and grass turn into hay:
I'm martyr to a motion not my own;
What's freedom for? To know eternity.
I swear she cast a shadow white as stone.   25
But who would count eternity in days?
These old bones live to learn her wanton ways:
(I measure time by how a body sways).

THEODORE ROETHKE

SONNETS

18

Shall I compare thee to a summer's day?
Thou art more lovely and more temperate.
Rough winds do shake the darling buds of May,
And summer's lease hath all too short a date.
Sometime too hot the eye of heaven shines,   5
And often is his gold complexion dimm'd;
And every fair from fair sometime declines,
By chance, or nature's changing course, untrimm'd;
But thy eternal summer shall not fade,
Nor lose possession of that fair thou ow'st,   10
Nor shall Death brag thou wander'st in his shade,
When in eternal lines to time thou grow'st,
   So long as men can breathe or eyes can see,
   So long lives this, and this gives life to thee.

53

What is your substance, whereof are you made,
That millions of strange shadows on you tend?
Since every one hath, every one, one shade,
And you, but one, can every shadow lend.
Describe Adonis, and the counterfeit   5
Is poorly imitated after you;
On Helen's cheek all art of beauty set,
And you in Grecian tires are painted new.
Speak of the spring, and foison of the year;
The one doth shadow of your beauty show,   10
The other as your bounty doth appear,
And you in every blessed shape we know.
   In all external grace you have some part,
   But you like none, none you, for constant heart.

55

Not marble, nor the gilded monuments
Of princes, shall outlive this powerful rhyme;
But you shall shine more bright in these contents
Than unswept stone, besmear'd with sluttish time.
When wasteful war shall statues overturn,   5
And broils root out the work of masonry,
Nor Mars his sword nor war's quick fire shall burn
The living record of your memory.
'Gainst death and all-oblivious enmity
Shall you pace forth; your praise shall still find room,   10
Even in the eyes of all posterity
That wears this world out to the ending doom.

So, till the judgement that yourself arise,
You live in this, and dwell in lovers' eyes.

60

Like as the waves make towards the pebbled shore,
So do our minutes hasten to their end;
Each changing place with that which goes before,
In sequent toil all forwards do contend.
Nativity, once in the main of light,   5
Crawls to maturity, wherewith being crown'd,
Crooked eclipses 'gainst his glory fight,
And Time that gave doth now his gift confound.
Time doth transfix the flourish set on youth,
And delves the parallels in beauty's brow,   10
Feeds on the rarities of nature's truth,
And nothing stands but for his scythe to mow.
    And yet to times in hope my verse shall stand,
    Praising thy worth, despite his cruel hand.

71

No longer mourn for me when I am dead
Than you shall hear the surly sullen bell
Give warning to the world that I am fled
From this vile world with vilest worms to dwell.
Nay, if you read this line, remember not   5
The hand that writ it, for I love you so,
That I in your sweet thought would be forgot,
If thinking on me then should make you woe.
O if, I say, you look upon this verse,
When I, perhaps, compounded am with clay,   10
Do not so much as my poor name rehearse,
But let your love even with my life decay,
    Lest the wise world should look into your moan,
    And mock you with me after I am gone.

116

Let me not to the marriage of true minds
Admit impediments. Love is not love
Which alters when it alteration finds,
Or bends with the remover to remove.
O no, it is an ever-fixed mark   5
That looks on tempests and is never shaken;
It is the star to every wand'ring bark,
Whose worth's unknown, although his height be taken.
Love's not Time's fool, though rosy lips and cheeks
Within his bending sickle's compass come.   10
Love alters not with his brief hours and weeks,
But bears it out even to the edge of doom.

If this be error and upon me proved,
I never writ, nor no man ever loved.

130

My mistress' eyes are nothing like the sun;
Coral is far more red than her lips' red;
If snow be white, why then her breasts are dun;
If hairs be wires, black wires grow on her head.
I have seen roses damask'd, red and white,   5
But no such roses see I in her cheeks,
And in some perfumes is there more delight
Than in the breath that from my mistress reeks.
I love to hear her speak, yet well I know,
That music hath a far more pleasing sound.   10
I grant I never saw a goddess go;
My mistress when she walks treads on the ground.
   And yet by heaven I think my love as rare
   As any she belied with false compare.

WILLIAM SHAKESPEARE

[LEAVE ME, O LOVE]

Leave me, O Love, which reachest but to dust;
And thou, my mind, aspire to higher things;
Grow rich in that which never taketh rust.
Whatever fades but fading pleasure brings.
Draw in thy beams, and humble all thy might   5
To that sweet yoke where lasting freedoms be;
Which breaks the clouds and opens forth the light
That doth both shine and give us sight to see.
O take fast hold; let that light be thy guide
In this small course which birth draws out to death,   10
And think how evil becometh him to slide
Who seeketh heaven, and comes of heavenly breath.
Then farewell, world; thy uttermost I see;
Eternal Love, maintain thy life in me.

SIR PHILIP SIDNEY

[WITH HOW SAD STEPS, O MOON]

With how sad steps, O Moon, thou climb'st the skies!
How silently, and with how wan a face!
What, may it be that even in heavenly place

That busy archer his sharp arrows tries?
Sure, if that long-with-love-acquainted eyes   5
Can judge of love, thou feel'st a lover's case.
I read it in thy looks; thy languished grace,
To me that feel the like, thy state descries.
Then, even of fellowship, O Moon, tell me,
Is constant love deemed there but want of wit?   10
Are beauties there as proud as here they be?
Do they above love to be loved, and yet
Those lovers scorn whom that love doth possess?
Do they call virtue there ungratefulness?

SIR PHILIP SIDNEY

STELLA'S[1] BIRTHDAY, 1720

All travellers at first incline
Where-e'er they see the fairest sign;
And, if they find the chambers neat,
And like the liquor and the meat,
Will call again, and recommend   5
The Angel-inn to ev'ry friend.
That though the painting grows decay'd?
The house will never lose its trade:
Nay, though the treach'rous tapster Thomas
Hangs a new angel two doors from us,   10
As fine as dauber's hands can make it,
In hopes that strangers may mistake it,
We think it both a shame and sin
To quit the true old Angel-inn.
    Now this is Stella's case, in fact: 15
An *angel's* face, a little crack'd;
(Could poets, or could painters fix
How *angels* look at thirty-six:)
This drew us in at first to find
In such a form an *angel's* mind;   20
And ev'ry virtue now supplies
The fainting rays of Stella's eyes.
See at her levee crowding swains,
Whom Stella freely entertains
With breeding, humour, wit, and sense;   25
And puts them but to small expence;
Their mind so plentifully fills,
And makes such reasonable bills,
So little gets for what she gives,

[1] Esther Johnson (1681–1728) was pupil, friend, and companion of Jonathan Swift.

We really wonder how she lives!   30
And, had her stock been less, no doubt
She must have long ago run out.
    Then who can think we'll quit the place,
When Doll hangs out a newer face;
Or stop and light at Cloe's head,   35
With scraps and leavings to be fed?
    Then, Cloe, still go on to prate
Of thirty-six, and thirty-eight;
Pursue your trade of scandal-picking,
Your hints, that Stella is no chicken;   40
Your innuendos, when you tell us
That Stella loves to talk with fellows:
And let me warn you to believe
A truth, for which your soul should grieve;
That, should you live to see the day   45
When Stella's locks must all be gray,
When age must print a furrow'd trace
On ev'ry feature of her face;
Though you, and all your senseless tribe,
Could art, or time, or nature bribe,   50
To make you look like beauty's queen,
And hold for ever at fifteen;
No bloom of youth can ever blind
The cracks and wrinkles of your mind;
All men of sense will pass your door,   55
And crowd to Stella's fourscore.

JONATHAN SWIFT

FERN HILL

Now as I was young and easy under the apple boughs
About the lilting house and happy as the grass was green,
   The night above the dingle starry,
     Time let me hail and climb
   Golden in the heydays of his eyes,   5
And honoured among wagons I was prince of the apple towns
And once below a time I lordly had the trees and leaves
    Trail with daisies and barley
   Down the rivers of the windfall light.

And as I was green and carefree, famous among the barns   10
About the happy yard and singing as the farm was home,
   In the sun that is young once only,
     Time let me play and be
   Golden in the mercy of his means,

And green and golden I was huntsman and herdsman, the calves   15
Sang to my horn, the foxes on the hills barked clear and cold,
    And the sabbath rang slowly
  In the pebbles of the holy streams.

All the sun long it was running, it was lovely, the hay
Fields high as the house, the tunes from the chimneys, it was air   20
    And playing, lovely and watery
      And fire green as grass.
    And nightly under the simple stars
As I rode to sleep the owls were bearing the farm away,
All the moon long I heard, blessed among stables, the nightjars   25
    Flying with the ricks, and the horses
      Flashing into the dark.

And then to awake, and the farm, like a wanderer white
With the dew, come back, the cock on his shoulder: it was all
    Shining, it was Adam and maiden,   30
      The sky gathered again
    And the sun grew round that very day.
So it must have been after the birth of the simple light
In the first, spinning place, the spellbound horses walking warm
    Out of the whinnying green stable   35
      On to the fields of praise.

And honoured among foxes and pheasants by the gay house
Under the new made clouds and happy as the heart was long,
    In the sun born over and over,
      I ran my heedless ways,   40
    My wishes raced through the house high hay
And nothing I cared, at my sky blue trades, that time allows
In all his tuneful turning so few and such morning songs
    Before the children green and golden
      Follow him out of grace.   45

Nothing I cared, in the lamb white days, that time would take me
Up to the swallow thronged loft by the shadow of my hand,
    In the moon that is always rising,
      Nor that riding to sleep
    I should hear him fly with the high fields   50
And wake to the farm forever fled from the childless land.
Oh as I was young and easy in the mercy of his means,
    Time held me green and dying
  Though I sang in my chains like the sea.

DYLAN THOMAS

[IF I WERE TICKLED BY THE RUB OF LOVE]

If I were tickled by the rub of love,
A rooking girl who stole me for her side,
Broke through her straws, breaking my bandaged string,
If the red tickle as the cattle calve
Still set to scratch a laughter from my lung,   5
I would not fear the apple nor the flood
Nor the bad blood of spring.

Shall it be male or female? say the cells,
And drop the plum like fire from the flesh.
If I were tickled by the hatching hair,   10
The winging bone that sprouted in the heels,
The itch of man upon the baby's thigh,
I would not fear the gallows nor the axe
Nor the crossed sticks of war.

Shall it be male or female? say the fingers   15
That chalk the walls with green girls and their men.
I would not fear the muscling-in of love
If I were tickled by the urchin hungers
Rehearsing heat upon a raw-edged nerve.
I would not fear the devil in the loin   20
Nor the outspoken grave.

DYLAN THOMAS

SONG OF THE QUEEN BEE

When the air is wine and the wind is free
And the morning sits on the lovely lea
And sunlight ripples on every tree,
Then love-in-air is the thing for me—
   I'm a bee,   5
   I'm a ravishing, rollicking, young queen bee,
   That's me.

I wish to state that I think it's great,
Oh, it's simply rare in the upper air,
   It's the place to pair   10
   With a bee.
Let old geneticists plot and plan,
They're stuffy people, to a man;

Let gossips whisper behind their fan.
  (Oh, she *does?*   15
  Buzz, buzz, buzz!)

My nuptial flight is sheer delight;
I'm a giddy girl who likes to swirl,
  To fly and soar
  And fly some more,   20
    I'm a bee.
And I wish to state that I'll always mate
  With whatever drone I encounter.

There's a kind of a wild and glad elation   25
In the natural way of insemination;
Who thinks that love is a handicap
Is a fuddydud and a common sap,
For I am a queen and I am a bee,
I'm devil-may-care and I'm fancy-free,
The test tube doesn't appeal to me,   30
  Not me,
  I'm a bee.
And I'm here to state that I'll *always* mate
  With whatever drone I encounter.

Let mares and cows, by calculating,   35
Improve themselves with loveless mating,
Let groundlings breed in the modern fashion,
I'll stick to the air and the grand old passion;
I may be small and I'm just a bee
But I *won't* have Science improving *me,*   40
  Not me,
  I'm a bee.
On a day that's fair with a wind that's free,
Any old drone is the lad for me.

I have no flair for love *moderne,*   45
It's far too studied, far too stern,
I'm just a bee—I'm wild, I'm free,
  That's me.
I can't afford to be too choosy;
In every queen there's a touch of floozy,   50
  And it's simply rare
  In the upper air
  And I wish to state
  That I'll *always* mate
With whatever drone I encounter.   55

Man is a fool for the latest movement,
He broods and broods on race improvement;

What boots it to improve a bee
If it means the end of ecstasy?
  (He ought to be there   60
  On a day that's fair,
  Oh, it's simply rare
    For a bee.)
Man's so wise he is growing foolish,
Some of his schemes are downright ghoulish;   65
He owns a bomb that'll end creation
And he wants to change the sex relation,
He thinks that love is a handicap,
He's a fuddydud, he's a simple sap;
Man is a meddler, man's a boob,   70
He looks for love in the depths of a tube,
His restless mind is forever ranging,
He thinks he's advancing as long as he's changing,
He cracks the atom, he racks his skull,
Man is meddlesome, man is dull,   75
Man is busy instead of idle,
Man is alarmingly suicidal,
  Me, I'm a bee.

I am a bee and I simply love it,
I am a bee and I'm darned glad of it   80
I am a bee, I know about love:
You go upstairs, you go above,
You do not pause to dine or sup,
The sky won't wait—it's a long trip up;
You rise, you soar, you take the blue,   85
It's you and me, kid, me and you,
It's everything, it's the nearest drone,
It's never a thing that you find alone.
  I'm a bee,
  I'm free.   90

If any old farmer can keep and hive me,
Then any old drone may catch and wive me;
I'm sorry for creatures who cannot pair
On a gorgeous day in the upper air,
I'm sorry for cows who have to boast   95
Of affairs they've had by parcel post,
I'm sorry for man with his plots and guile,
His test-tube manner, his test-tube smile;
I'll multiply and I'll increase
As I always have—by mere caprice;   100
For I am a queen and I am a bee,
I'm devil-may-care and I'm fancy-free,
Love-in-air is the thing for me,
  Oh, it's simply *rare*

In the beautiful air,
   And I wish to state
   That I'll *always* mate
With whatever drone I encounter.

E. B. WHITE

SONG OF MYSELF

1

I celebrate myself, and sing myself,
And what I assume you shall assume,
For every atom belonging to me as good belongs to you.

I loafe and invite my soul,
I lean and loafe at my ease observing a spear of summer grass.   5

My tongue, every atom of my blood, form'd from this soil, this air,
Born here of parents born here from parents the same, and their parents the
   same,
I, now thirty-seven years old in perfect health begin,
Hoping to cease not till death.   10
Creeds and schools in abeyance,
Retiring back a while sufficed at what they are, but never forgotten,
I harbor for good or bad, I permit to speak at every hazard,
Nature without check with original energy.

2

Houses and rooms are full of perfumes, the shelves are crowded with perfumes,
I breathe the fragrance myself and know it and like it,
The distillation would intoxicate me also, but I shall not let it.

The atmosphere is not a perfume, it has no taste of the distillation, it is odorless,
It is for my mouth forever, I am in love with it.   5
I will go to the bank by the wood and become undisguised and naked,
I am mad for it to be in contact with me.

The smoke of my own breath,
Echoes, ripples, buzz'd whispers, love-root, silk-thread, crotch and vine,
My respiration and inspiration, the beating of my heart, the passing of blood and   10
   air through my lungs,
The sniff of green leaves and dry leaves, and of the shore and dark-color'd sea-
   rocks, and of hay in the barn,
The sound of the belch'd words of my voice loss'd to the eddies of the wind,
A few light kisses, a few embraces, a reaching around of arms,   15
The play of shine and shade on the trees as the supple boughs wag,

The delight alone or in the rush of the streets, or along the fields and hill-sides,
The feeling of health, the full-moon trill, the song of me rising from bed and
    meeting the sun.
Have you reckon'd a thousand acres much? have you reckon'd the earth much?   20
Have you practis'd so long to learn to read?
Have you felt so proud to get at the meaning of poems?

Stop this day and night with me and you shall possess the origin of all poems,
You shall possess the good of the earth and sun, (there are millions of suns
    left,)   25
You shall no longer take things at second or third hand, nor look through the
    eyes of the dead, nor feed on the spectres in books,
You shall not look through my eyes either, nor take things from me,
You shall listen to all sides and filter them from your self.

3

I have heard what the talkers were talking, the talk of the beginning and the
    end,
But I do not talk of the beginning or the end.

There was never any more inception than there is now,
Nor any more youth or age than there is now,   5
And will never be any more perfection than there is now,
Nor any more heaven or hell than there is now.

Urge and urge and urge,
Always the procreant urge of the world.
Out of the dimness opposite equals advance, always substance and increase,   10
    always sex,
Always a knit of identity, always distinction, always a breed of life.
To elaborate is no avail, learn'd and unlearn'd feel that it is so.
Sure as the most certain sure, plumb in the uprights, well entretied, braced in the
    beams,   15
Stout as a horse, affectionate, haughty, electrical,
I and this mystery here we stand.

Clear and sweet is my soul, and clear and sweet is all that is not my soul.
Lack one lacks both, and the unseen is proved by the seen,
Till that becomes unseen and receives proof in its turn.   20
Showing the best and dividing it from the worst age vexes age,
Knowing the perfect fitness and equanimity of things, while they discuss
    I am silent, and go bathe and admire myself.
Welcome is every organ and attribute of me, and of any man hearty and clean,
Not an inch nor a particle of an inch is vile, and none shall be less familiar than 25
    the rest.
I am satisfied—I see, dance, laugh, sing;
As the hugging and loving bed-fellow sleeps at my side through the night,
    and withdraws at the peep of the day with stealthy tread,
Leaving me baskets cover'd with white towels swelling the house with their plenty, 30

Shall I postpone my acceptation and realization and scream at my eyes,
That they turn from gazing after and down the road,
And forthwith cipher and show me to a cent,
Exactly the value of one and exactly the value of two, and which is ahead?

4

Trippers and askers surround me,
People I meet, the effect upon me of my early life or the ward and city I live in,
    or the nation,
The latest dates, discoveries, inventions, societies, authors old and new,
My dinner, dress, associates, looks, compliments, dues,   5
The real or fancied indifference of some man or woman I love,
The sickness of one of my folks or of myself, or ill-doing or loss or lack of money,
    or depressions or exaltations,
Battles, the horrors of fratricidal war, the fever of doubtful news, the fitful events;
These come to me days and nights and go from me again,   10
But they are not the Me myself.

Apart from the pulling and hauling stands what I am,
Stands amused, complacent, compassionating, idle, unitary,
Looks down, is erect, or bends an arm on an impalpable certain rest,
Looking with side-curved head curious what will come next,   15
Both in and out of the game and watching and wondering at it.

Backward I see in my own days where I sweated through fog with linguists and
    contenders,
I have no mockings or arguments, I witness and wait.

31

I believe a leaf of grass is no less than the journey-work of the stars,
And the pismire is equally perfect, and a grain of sand, and the egg of the wren,
And the tree-toad is a chef-d'œuvre for the highest,
And the running blackberry would adorn the parlors of heaven,
And the narrowest hinge in my hand puts to scorn all machinery,   5
And the cow crunching with depress'd head surpasses any statue,
And a mouse is miracle enough to stagger sextillions of infidels.

I find I incorporate gneiss, coal, long-threaded moss, fruits, grains, esculent roots,
And am stucco'd with quadrupeds and birds all over,
And have distanced what is behind me for good reasons,   10
But call any thing back again when I desire it.

In vain the speeding or shyness,
In vain the plutonic rocks send their old heat against my approach,
In vain the mastodon retreats beneath its own powder'd bones,
In vain objects stand leagues off and assume manifold shapes,   15
In vain the ocean settling in hollows and the great monsters lying low,
In vain the buzzard houses herself with the sky,
In vain the snake slides through the creepers and logs,

In vain the elk takes to the inner passes of the woods,
In vain the razor-bill'd auk sails far north to Labrador,
I follow quickly, I ascend to the nest in the fissure of the cliff.   20

32

I think I could turn and live with animals, they are so placid and self-contain'd,
I stand and look at them long and long.

They do not sweat and whine about their condition,
They do not lie awake in the dark and weep for their sins,

They do not make me sick discussing their duty to God,   5
Not one is dissatisfied, not one is demented with the mania of owning things,
Not one kneels to another, nor to his kind that lived thousands of years ago,
Not one is respectable or unhappy over the whole earth.

So they show their relations to me and I accept them,
They bring me tokens of myself, they evince them plainly in their possession.   10

I wonder where they get those tokens,
Did I pass that way huge times ago and negligently drop them?

Myself moving forward then and now and forever,
Gathering and showing more always and with velocity,
Infinite and omnigenous, and the like of these among them,   15
Not too exclusive toward the reachers of my remembrancers,
Picking out here one that I love, and now go with him on brotherly terms.

A gigantic beauty of a stallion, fresh and responsive to my caresses,
Head high in the forehead, wide between the ears,
Limbs glossy and supple, tail dusting the ground,   20
Eyes full of sparkling wickedness, ears finely cut, flexibly moving.
His nostrils dilate as my heels embrace him,
His well-built limbs tremble with pleasure as we race around and return.

I but use you a minute, then I resign you, stallion,
Why do I need your paces when I myself out-gallop them?   25
Even as I stand or sit passing faster than you.

48

I have said that the soul is not more than the body,
And I have said that the body is not more than the soul,
And nothing, not God, is greater to one than one's self is,
And whoever walks a furlong without sympathy walks to his own funeral drest
    in his shroud,   5
And I or you pocketless of a dime may purchase the pick of the earth,
And to glance with an eye or show a bean in its pod confounds the learning of all
    times,

And there is no trade or employment but the young man following it may become
    a hero,   10
And there is no object so soft but it makes a hub for the wheel'd universe,
And I say to any man or woman, Let your soul stand cool and composed before a
    million universes.

And I say to mankind, Be not curious about God,
For I who am curious about each am not curious about God,   15
(No array of terms can say how much I am at peace about God and about death.)

I hear and behold God in every object, yet understand God not in the least,
Nor do I understand who there can be more wonderful than myself.

Why should I wish to see God better than this day?
I see something of God each hour of the twenty-four, and each moment then,   20
In the faces of men and women I see God, and in my own face in the glass,
I find letters from God dropt in the street, and every one is sign'd by God's name,
And I leave them where they are, for I know that wheresoe'er I go,
Others will punctually come for ever and ever.

49

And as to you Death, and you bitter hug of mortality, it is idle to try to alarm me.

To his work without flinching the accoucheur comes,
I see the elder-hand pressing receiving supporting,
I recline by the sills of the exquisite flexible doors,
And mark the outlet, and mark the relief and escape.   5
And as to you Corpse I think you are good manure, but that does not offend me,
I smell the white roses sweet-scented and growing,
I reach to the leafy lips, I reach to the polish'd breasts of melons.

And as to you Life I reckon you are the leavings of many deaths,
(No doubt I have died myself ten thousand times before.)   10

I hear you whispering there O stars of heaven,
O suns—O grass of graves—O perpetual transfers and promotions,
If you do not say any thing how can I say any thing?
Of the turbid pool that lies in the autumn forest,
Of the moon that descends the steeps of the soughing twilight,   15
Toss, sparkles of day and dusk—toss on the black stems that decay in the muck,
Toss to the moaning gibberish of the dry limbs.

I ascend from the moon, I ascend from the night,
I perceive that the ghastly glimmer is noonday sunbeams reflected,
And debouch to the steady and central from the offspring great or small.   20

WALT WHITMAN

[THEY FLEE FROM ME]

They flee from me, that sometime did me seek,
With naked foot stalking in my chamber.
I have seen them gentle, tame, and meek,
That now are wild, and do not remember
That sometime they put themselves in danger   5
To take bread at my hand; and now they range,
Busily seeking with a continual change.

Thanked be fortune, it hath been otherwise
Twenty times better; but once, in special,
In thin array, after a pleasant guise,   10
When her loose gown from her shoulders did fall,
And she me caught in her arms long and small,
And therewith all sweetly did me kiss
And softly said, "Dear heart, how like you this?"

It was no dream; I lay broad waking.   15
But all is turned, thorough my gentleness,
Into a strange fashion of foresaking;
And I have leave to go, of her goodness,
And she also to use new fangleness.
But since that I so kindely am served,   20
I fain would know what she hath deserved.

SIR THOMAS WYATT

BYZANTIUM [1]

The unpurged images of day recede;
The Emperor's drunken soldiery are abed;
Night resonance recedes, night-walkers' song
After great cathedral gong;
A starlit or a moonlit dome disdains   5
All that man is,
All mere complexities,
The fury and the mire of human veins.

Before me floats an image, man or shade,
Shade more than man, more image than a shade;   10
For Hades' bobbin bound in mummy-cloth
May unwind the winding path;
A mouth that has no moisture and no breath
Breathless mouths may summon;

[1] Ancient name for Istanbul.

I hail the superhuman; 15
I call it death-in-life and life-in-death.

Miracle, bird or golden handiwork,
More miracle than bird or handiwork,
Planted on the star-lit golden bough,
Can like the cocks of Hades crow, 20
Or, by the moon embittered, scorn aloud
In glory of changeless metal
Common bird or petal
And all complexities of mire or blood.

At midnight on the Emperor's pavement flit 25
Flames that no faggot feeds, nor steel has lit,
Nor storm disturbs, flames begotten of flame,
Where blood-begotten spirits come
And all complexities of fury leave,
Dying into a dance, 30
An agony of trance,
An agony of flame that cannot singe a sleeve.

Astraddle on the dolphin's mire and blood,
Spirit after spirit! The smithies break the flood,
The golden smithies of the Emperor! 35
Marbles of the dancing floor
Break bitter furies of complexity,
Those images that yet
Fresh images beget,
That dolphin-torn, that gong-tomented sea. 40

W. B. YEATS

CRAZY JANE TALKS WITH THE BISHOP

I met the Bishop on the road
And much said he and I.
'Those breasts are flat and fallen now,
Those veins must soon be dry;
Live in a heavenly mansion, 5
Not in some foul sty.'

'Fair and foul are near of kin,
And fair needs foul,' I cried.
'My friends are gone, but that's a truth
Nor grave nor bed denied, 10
Learned in bodily lowliness
And in the heart's pride.

'A woman can be proud and stiff
When on love intent;
But Love has pitched his mansion in   15
The place of excrement;
For nothing can be sole or whole
That has not been rent.'

W. B. YEATS

LAPIS LAZULI

I have heard that hysterical women say
They are sick of the palette and fiddle-bow,
Of poets that are always gay,
For everybody knows or else should know
That if nothing drastic is done   5
Aeroplane and Zeppelin will come out,
Pitch like King Billy bomb-balls in
Until the town lie beaten flat.

All perform their tragic play,
There struts Hamlet, there is Lear,   10
That's Ophelia, that Cordelia;
Yet they, should the last scene be there,
The great stage curtain about to drop,
If worthy their prominent part in the play,
Do not break up their lines to weep.   15
They know that Hamlet and Lear are gay;
Gaiety transfiguring all that dread.
All men have aimed at, found and lost;
Black out; Heaven blazing into the head:
Tragedy wrought to its uttermost.   20
Though Hamlet rambles and Lear rages,
And all the drop-scenes drop at once
Upon a hundred thousand stages,
It cannot grow by an inch or an ounce.

On their own feet they came, or on shipboard,   25
Camel-back, horse-back, ass-back, mule-back,
Old civilizations put to the sword.
Then they and their wisdom went to rack:
No handiwork of Callimachus,
Who handled marble as if it were bronze,   30
Made draperies that seemed to rise
When sea-wind swept the corner, stands;
His long lamp-chimney shaped like the stem
Of a slender palm, stood but a day;

All things fall and are built again,   35
And those that build them again are gay.

Two Chinamen, behind them a third,
Are carved in lapis lazuli,
Over them flies a long-legged bird,
A symbol of longevity;   40
The third, doubtless a serving-man,
Carries a musical instrument.

Every discoloration of the stone,
Every accidental crack or dent,
Seems a water-course or an avalanche,   45
Or lofty slope where it still snows
Though doubtless plum or cherry-branch
Sweetens the little half-way house
Those Chinamen climb towards, and I
Delight to imagine them seated there;   50
There, on the mountain and the sky,
On all the tragic scene they stare.
One asks for mournful melodies;
Accomplished fingers begin to play.
Their eyes mid many wrinkles, their eyes,   55
Their ancient, glittering eyes, are gay.

W. B. YEATS

THE LOVER TELLS OF THE ROSE IN HIS HEART

All things uncomely and broken, all things worn out and old,
The cry of a child by the roadway, the creak of a lumbering cart,
The heavy steps of the ploughman, splashing the wintry mould,
Are wronging your image that blossoms a rose in the deeps of my heart.

The wrong of unshapely things is a wrong too great to be told;   5
I hunger to build them anew and sit on a green knoll apart,
With the earth and the sky and the water, remade, like a casket of gold
For my dreams of your image that blossoms a rose in the deeps of my heart.

W. B. YEATS

NO SECOND TROY

Why should I blame her that she filled my days
With misery, or that she would of late

Have taught to ignorant men most violent ways,
Or hurled the little streets upon the great,
Had they but courage equal to desire?   5
What could have made her peaceful with a mind
That nobleness made simple as a fire,
With beauty like a tightened bow, a kind
That is not natural in an age like this,
Being high and solitary and most stern?   10
Why, what could she have done, being what she is?
Was there another Troy for her to burn?

W. B. YEATS

SAILING TO BYZANTIUM

I

That is no country for old men. The young
In one another's arms, birds in the trees
—Those dying generations—at their song,
The salmon-falls, the mackerel-crowded seas,
Fish, flesh, or fowl, commend all summer long   5
Whatever is begotten, born, and dies.
Caught in that sensual music all neglect
Monuments of unageing intellect.

II

An aged man is but a paltry thing,
A tattered coat upon a stick, unless   10
Soul clap its hands and sing, and louder sing
For every tatter in its mortal dress,
Nor is there singing school but studying
Monuments of its own magnificence;
And therefore I have sailed the seas and come   15
To the holy city of Byzantium.

III

O sages standing in God's holy fire
As in the gold mosaic of a wall,
Come from the holy fire, perne in a gyre,
And be the singing-masters of my soul.   20
Consume my heart away; sick with desire
And fastened to a dying animal
It knows not what it is; and gather me
Into the artifice of eternity.

IV

Once out of nature I shall never take   25
My bodily form from any natural thing,
But such a form as Grecian goldsmiths make
Of hammered gold and gold enamelling
To keep a drowsy Emperor awake;
Or set upon a golden bough to sing   30
To lords and ladies of Byzantium
Of what is past, or passing, or to come.

W. B. YEATS

ATGET, "NASTURTIUMS" [FROM *The World of Atget* BY BERENICE ABBOTT, BY PERMISSION OF HORIZON PRESS].

INDEXES

INDEX OF AUTHORS

INDEX OF FIRST LINES

INDEX OF TITLES

[579]